ConsumerGuide®

2002 EDITION

USED CAR & TRUCK BOOK

Publications International, Ltd.

CONTENTS

BE A SMART SHOPPER

Informed shoppers have an edge when negotiating price. To get the best deal, plan your moves and take your time.

• Know what you want, but be flexible. Narrow your list to two or three models that best suit your needs.

• Research your present vehicle's fair-market trade-in value ahead of time by checking published guides or consulting a local lending institution. A vehicle's trade-in value is expressed as its "wholesale" value (as opposed to the "retail" value, which would be a dealer's asking price if the car were placed on a lot).

• You might want to "shop" your car or truck to a few dealerships' used-car departments. Ask each manager what the dealer will pay for your vehicle in an outright sale, and get the bids in writing. Keep in mind, however, that you can usually get more money for your car if you sell it yourself to a private party.

• Shop competing sellers to compare prices on the same vehicle with the same or similar features. You're not likely to get the seller's "best" price for a vehicle just by asking (you'll usually have to dicker to obtain it), but this can give you an idea of how willing the seller is to negotiate. Never put a deposit on a car just to get a price quote.

• Don't allow a dealerships' salesperson to "steer" you toward a costlier vehicle or a version that comes with features you don't want.

• Don't give the impression that you're "in love" with a particular vehicle, though; a well-trained seller can use your emotions to gain the upper hand in price negotiations.

• Size up supply and demand for the car you want. A good deal on a slow-selling model might be below wholesale, while a popular, late-model car can still command close to the original selling price.

• If you have a trade-in, don't acknowledge this fact until you've secured a firm selling price from a salesperson. This way, he or she won't be able to "inflate" the trade-in value by manipulating the selling price of the vehicle (though this can work to your advantage if you need a larger down payment to qualify for financing). Never give your trade-in's keys to the salesperson—they may be held hostage while he or she pressures you to sign a sales contract on the spot.

• Test drive the exact car you've decided upon—before you buy. Think you want manual shift and a sport suspension? A 15-minute test drive might convince you to go with an automatic transmission and a softer suspension that produces a smoother ride.

WHICH CAR IS FOR YOU?

Like most purchases, buying a used car means weighing your wants against your needs. Both are important, but selecting the most logical vehicle for your family could save you thousands of dollars. Whether you base your decision strictly on practical considerations or you look for a certain car simply because you like it, planning ahead can save time, effort, and money.

We suggest that you base your decision on your specific needs. How old a car are you willing to consider? Do you demand luxury, or would more basic transportation do? Will an economical subcompact suffice, or do you require a big trunk and a spacious interior? If you're interested in a sporty or high-performance car, first check the Insurance Costs line under the Ratings head in each entry, or with your insurance agent. Some of these vehicles are subject to hefty insurance surcharges. If you're in the market for a minivan, truck, sport-utility vehicle, or larger car, make sure it will fit in your garage.

It's in your best interest to weigh all these considerations before you start shopping, but be flexible about the exact make, model, and year you'll settle for. Having an alternate choice in mind will give you a larger pool from which to choose. Naturally, the amount you can pay (or borrow) must be established first (see Finance Charges on page 10). Then the type of car you want should be determined, so let's take a look at some factors to consider.

Age: With rare exceptions, a car loses value in direct proportion to its age. But because cars last longer nowadays, age isn't as critical a factor as it used to be.

Size and/or Type: For many shoppers, vehicle size/type and passenger capacity can be the decisive factors.

• Subcompact: range from tiny commuter cars to adequate 4-passenger vehicles; nearly all 4-cylinder engines; a few 3-cylinder or V6 powered.

• Compact: mostly 4-door sedans; some wagons, hatchbacks, convertibles; typically 4-cylinder, perhaps a V6.

• Midsize: mostly 4-door notchbacks; some coupes, 4-door hatchbacks, and wagons; front-wheel drive is most common but rear-drive or 4-wheel drive possible; 6-cylinder engines are the rule, though a few have four cylinders and some a V8.

• Full-Size: mostly 4-door sedans; some wagons and 2-door coupes; some rear-drive with V8; others front-drive with V6.

• Minivan: Most minivans offer two front doors, a single sliding side door, and a rear hatch. A few have dual sliding doors (a recent trend), or four conventional doors and a rear hatch. Models may be front-, rear-, or all-wheel drive. Almost all minivans have available V6 power, but several still offer only 4-cylinder engines. Seating capacities range from five to eight passengers.

• Sport-Utility Vehicle: Wheelbase and overall length vary. All sport-utilities have at least two front doors, and many are available in 4-door configurations. Some have foldout cargo doors; others have hatch doors in back. Almost all sport-utility vehicles (SUVs) are available in either 2- or 4-wheel drive.

• Pickup Truck: Two sizes are available: compact and full-size. Most compacts come with 4- and 6-cylinder engines, while most full-size pickups have V8 engines.

Passenger Capacity: The EPA rates capacity by the number of seatbelts installed. Beware: Some cars with six belts realistically hold only five adults, or even four.

Cargo Volume: A sporty coupe with a fold-down back seat may be just as useful as a hatchback or wagon. Think about the cargo you carry. Compare floor area, depth, and how high a suitcase must be lifted in order to clear the opening.

Engines and Fuel Economy: As a general rule, a small engine is more economical than a larger one. But sometimes in heavier vehicles, a larger engine might actually consume less fuel. High-performance models nearly always guzzle more, and many of them demand premium gas. In fact, a surprising number of "ordinary" engines require premium—check before buying, or you'll be paying extra at every gas pump. Consider what type of driving you'll be doing. A larger engine may be just as efficient as a smaller one on the highway, but around town the smaller engine may return considerably better fuel economy.

Front-Wheel Drive (FWD) vs. Rear-Wheel Drive (RWD) vs. 4-Wheel Drive (4WD): Through the past decade, front-drive has almost become the norm, yet some rear-drive cars are still offered. FWD results in a lighter, more compact drivetrain and provides better winter traction. On the downside, the engine, transmission, differential, and driveshafts are all crammed under the hood, so service is more expensive.

Several cars and quite a few trucks offer either permanently engaged all-wheel drive or part-time 4WD. These systems are generally reliable—though more prone to problems than 2-wheel-drive systems. However, the added weight, complexity, and number of components will, over the long run, make the vehicle more expensive to repair and give it poorer fuel economy.

Base vs. Loaded Model: An ordinary, base-level car with few extras may be unexciting, but it generally costs less to buy and maintain. If you plan to resell the car later, choosing a higher trim level may be wiser.

Safety Features: An antilock braking system (ABS) prevents the wheels from locking up in a panic stop. That can give you the mobility to steer around an accident. We think it's well worth a higher price, and over the long run could more than pay for itself in avoided accidents.

Most recent models have a driver-side airbag, and frequently one for the front passenger, too. Remember that the airbags are a supplemental restraint system and only protect you in the case of a frontal collision; therefore, you should always wear your seatbelt.

In an effort to better protect occupants in side collisions, many manufacturers have begun installing side airbags in their cars. These work in similar fashion to front airbags, but vary widely in design. Some are fairly small and pop out from the side of the seat or from the door panel; occasionally they are only mounted on the driver's side, while a few luxury models may have them for all outboard front and rear passengers. "Curtain" and "tubular" side airbags that drop down from above the windows are also growing in popularity. These are intended to further protect occupants' heads in a side collision, and usually extend far enough to cover both the front and rear windows.

Cars to Avoid: Stay away from trouble-prone models, or cars that look like they have had some sort of body repair. Usually, cars of this sort will need extensive repairs to get things running right again.

Be careful when buying high-performance cars such as Camaros, Mustangs, and Corvettes; they may have been abused.

Unlisted Models: Some models have been omitted from this book for space reasons. This does not imply that a particular model is undesirable in any way. The reason for a model being omitted may be that is was only available for a short time or was produced in limited numbers.

WHERE TO LOOK

There are three primary sources of used cars: used-car departments of new- or used-car dealerships, independent used-car dealers, and private parties. Which is best? That depends on what you're looking for, how much time you have, and how much you're willing to pay.

Large new- and used-car dealers have traditionally been considered the best source of high-quality, late-model cars—many of them traded in on new models. On the downside, prices tend to be high.

Among new-car dealerships, your best bet may be a dealer who handles the make of car that interests you most. In addition to having a service department and large stock of parts for that make, this dealer is more likely to offer a warranty. Most manufacturers now offer "factory-certified" used cars through some (seldom all) of their deal-

USED CAR WORKSHEET

Use a copy of this blank worksheet to calculate costs for each car you're considering. Insist that the dealer explain any additional fees, and make sure the fees are legitimate before agreeing to pay them. Dealers and financing institutions must disclose complete interest-rate information and the total amount to be paid in interest.

Vehicle Make: _________________ Model: _____________________
Body Style: _________________ Year: _____________________

Selling price $_____________

+ State and/or local taxes $_____________

+ License fees $_____________

+ Additional fees $_____________

=Total purchase price $_____________

-Trade-in allowance $_____________

=Total amount due $_____________

- Down payment $_____________

=Amount to be financed $_____________

+Interest: $_____________

_______ months at _______ percent
annual percentage rate (APR)

=Total amount to be paid $_____________
(_______ monthly payments of $_________ each)

erships. Consumers appear to favor the idea. Even though certified cars tend to cost more, they bring a level of "peace of mind."

Superstores are the latest trend. Circuit City, the huge electronics retailer, started its first CarMax used-car store in 1993. Instead of dozens of used cars, such superstores might hold 500 or 1000 vehicles for sale. They promise a "customer-friendly," low-pressure atmosphere, typically with selling prices prominently posted, not subject to dickering. Many shoppers appear to like the concept. In a survey by *Advertising Age* and *Automotive Marketing* magazines, almost three-fourths of respondents who bought from a superstore said they were more pleased with the experience. No less interesting, more than half said they haggled over price.

Independent used-car dealers have long ranked high on the list of mistrusted business people. Many of their cars go to high-risk customers, who wouldn't otherwise be able to buy at all.

Always be wary. Even the best independents get most of their stock from wholesale auctions or larger dealers, so they know little or nothing about a vehicle's history. Most independents lack service facilities and are less likely to give arriving cars a thorough inspection. Their cars are typically older and scruffier than those on the franchised lot.

All these negatives may be offset by the independent's lower prices. If money is your main concern—or you like to gamble—an independent with a reputation for fairness may be a better choice than the new-car dealer down the street.

Private party sellers have no overhead, and usually offer shoppers a good price. Private sellers are also less likely to use high-pressure sales tactics. In some states, transactions between individuals are exempt from sales tax.

Still, even honest people tend not to disclose every little flaw in their vehicle. Nor does everyone know how to care for a car properly. The seller may truly believe his worn-out relic is in top shape. One easy way to verify information is to ask to see repair receipts. In addition, be very skeptical of undocumented oral statements.

Watch out for bandits. A few unscrupulous types continue to pose as private sellers, but are really pseudo-dealers without a business license or used car lot. These "curbstoners" purchase vehicles from private parties or at auctions, then try to pawn off their wares as pampered bargains.

Whether there's reason for suspicion or not, ALWAYS check the issue date on the car's title. If it's recent, the seller may be a "curbstoner"—or may have purchased a lemon that he or she is now trying to unload in a hurry. Walk away unless the owner has a reasonable explanation—and even then, think twice.

USED CAR PRICES

Because no two used cars are alike, it's impossible to calculate an absolute value for a specific vehicle. Appraisal is an art that even professionals don't always master—at least not without years of buy-and-sell experience. No book or computer program can give more than a rough guideline to valuations of a given model. This book gives average *retail* values. The following factors can either raise or lower those average values.

Depreciation With rare exception, every automobile loses value as it ages. How much and how quickly it depreciates depends on the make, model, equipment, mileage, and maintenance and driving history. How much depreciation is "normal?" The biggest drop occurs as it's driven off the lot. A few cars lose less than 10 percent of their value in a year. Most cars drop by 15 to 30 percent, or even more. Generally, the rate of depreciation slows dramatically after about the fifth year.

As a general rule, used cars with the highest resale value are those that sold strongly when new, whereas unpopular models lose value quickly. Such premium makes as BMW, Infiniti, and Volvo have generally retained their values better than most. So have Saturns, Hondas, and Toyotas. Economy cars and big cars both tend to fall faster than average. Imports tend to depreciate slower than domestics.

The astute used-car buyer can take advantage of these differences by selecting a model that depreciates rapidly at first, then levels off. The best time to buy, then, is when the vehicle reaches that leveling-off point.

Dealer Prices: Like all merchants, dealers set used-car prices so they deliver a margin of profit over the cost of buying the car at wholesale, plus overhead expense. Wholesale price is roughly the amount a dealer would pay for a car at auction. The gap between this and the dealer's retail (or asking) price equals the bargaining room you'll have.

All "book" prices are averages, so don't treat them as gospel. A dealer might whip out another book showing a figure more favorable to him. Some dealers will even post a "book" price right on the vehicle, accompanied by a lower selling price. Still, the price books—and the ranges in this book— serve as a starting point for negotiations.

Mileage: The average car travels about 10,000 miles a year. So a three-year-old compact with well under 30,000 miles is likely to cost more than average; past 40,000 miles, a bit less. Once the odometer hits 50,000 or so, a car rarely deserves a premium price for low mileage.

Condition: A vehicle in rough condition may be worth only a small fraction of the value of a "clean" example. Obviously, the risks of mechanical breakdown and major rusting increase with age. Expect to pay more if a car comes with documentation of regular maintenance. Such evidence of care is well worth a premium price.

Equipment: Generally, the greater the number of popular options a car has, the higher its price—unless those options don't work. Most buyers expect automatic transmission, air conditioning, and power steering and brakes, plus at least an AM/FM radio. Cars with high-performance or optional larger-displacement engines tend to command higher prices than base-engine models.

Market Conditions: Late-model prices generally drop in late summer and early autumn, when new models are introduced. After a short recovery, values bottom out in winter, then begin to rise as spring nears—and even more as summer approaches. Outside the snowbelt, however, the difference may be less dramatic.

Slack sales periods could be the best time to shop. Visit the dealership in deepest winter, or after a week of bad weather, and low demand might make them more amenable to a lower price. But not always.

Seasonal factors affect the value of certain models. In northern states, convertibles shoot up in value during spring and early summer, and drop drastically during fall and winter. Four-wheel-drive vehicles do just the opposite.

EQUIPMENT AND OPTIONS

Best advice: Keep it simple. A no-frills model might seem dull, but over the long haul it might save you hundreds of dollars in repairs compared to its "loaded" cousin. Here's what to expect from some popular options and features:

Adjustable suspension: adjusts car's ride and handling according to road conditions and/or performance needs; as a rule, offers plenty of potential trouble (and expense).

Airbag: safety feature on most late models; a major factor in reducing driver injury during frontal crashes; airbag-equipped cars should have an "SRS" (supplemental restraint system) notation on the steering wheel and/or an indicator light on the dashboard. Recent models may have an airbag for both the driver and front passenger; and several have side-impact airbags as well.

Air conditioning: may be essential in many climates for comfort, but needs periodic servicing and diminishes gas mileage. In the past few years, R-134a (CFC-free) refrigerant has been installed in all auto air conditioners; older cars have R-12 refrigerant. When recharging is needed, many technicians will be unable to supply that old refrigerant, and you may need to install a conversion kit to use the CFC-free substance.

Antilock brakes (ABS): computer-controlled unit helps prevent wheel lockup and skidding in hard stops; most useful in rain or snow, rising in popularity but likely to be found mainly on late-model used cars. Driving technique with antilock brakes is slightly different than with normal brakes.

Automatic transmission: typically delivers lower fuel mileage and less-responsive acceleration than manual shift, especially in subcompacts with small, low-powered engines; automatics are a lot more reliable than they used to be, but are still expensive to repair.

Cruise control: enhances long-distance comfort and may improve gas mileage; failure usually results in loss of cruise control use—expensive to repair, but at least you can usually continue driving while it's broken.

Four-wheel drive: helps wet-weather and slippery-road traction, but is more costly to repair; added weight cuts performance and mileage.

Overdrive transmission: usually an automatic transmission with four gear ratios, or a manual with five; boosts mileage without creating additional service problems; some overdrive automatics tend to shift too frequently between third and fourth gears. Nearly all late-model transmissions have an overdrive gear.

Power door locks/central locking: handy, particularly for families; locks should still work manually if system fails.

Power seats and windows: high probability of eventual trouble, and repairs are expensive; no manual override, so failures can be more than just inconvenient.

Rear-window defroster: electric type with wire elements embedded in glass is now almost universal; not a trouble spot.

Sunroof/moonroof: aids ventilation in mild weather; flip-up types may leak; sliding sunroofs, especially if power-operated, can also cause problems—particularly if they fail when open.

Tilt/telescope steering wheel: handy for driving comfort; not a major trouble spot.

Tinted glass: helps keep interior cool in hot weather and reduces glare; no maintenance needed. Beware of aftermarket installations as the film may peel or crack; may be illegal in certain areas.

Traction control: helpful on slippery roads, especially with rear-drive cars; rare on used cars, and some owners don't even know they have it.

Turbocharger/supercharger: both are potentially troublesome and costly to repair; they increase horsepower but reduce fuel mileage somewhat; most turbo engines are prone to annoying "throttle lag" that delays acceleration; may require more frequent oil changes and almost always require premium fuel.

Aftermarket equipment: as original-equipment stereos become better, fewer vehicles are being fitted with aftermarket units. However, radios aren't the only things an owner might change on his car. Some engines might have add-on performance gear or electrical system alterations.

Before buying, check a new-car buyer's guide to see what equipment was available on that car when it was new. Then, compare that list with what appears to be

---

BUYERS GUIDE

IMPORTANT: Spoken promises are difficult to enforce. Ask the dealer to put all promises in writing. Keep this form

VEHICLE MAKE   MODEL   YEAR   VIN NUMBER

DEALER STOCK NUMBER (Optional)

WARRANTIES FOR THIS VEHICLE:

☐ # AS IS - NO WARRANTY

YOU WILL PAY ALL COSTS FOR ANY REPAIRS. The dealer assumes no responsibility for any repairs regardless of any oral statements about the vehicle.

☐ # WARRANTY

☐ FULL   ☐ **LIMITED WARRANTY.** The dealer will pay _____% of the labor and _____% of the parts for the covered systems that fail during the warranty period. Ask the dealer for a copy of the warranty document for a full explanation of warranty coverage, exclusions, and the dealer's repair obligations. Under the law, "Implied warranties" may give you even more rights.

SYSTEMS COVERED: **DURATION:**

☐ **SERVICE CONTRACT.** A service contract is available at an extra charge on this vehicle. Ask for details as to coverage, deductable, price, and exclusions. If you buy a service contract within 90 days of the time of sale, state law "Implied warranties" may give you additional rights.

WARRANTIES FOR THIS VEHICLE:

☐ # IMPLIED WARRANTIES ONLY

This means that the dealer does not make any specific promises to fix things that need repair when you buy the vehicle or after the time of sale. But, state law "Implied warranties" may give you some rights to have the dealer take care of serious problems that were not apparent when you bought the vehicle.

installed. Many libraries carry older editions of Consumer Guide® buyer's guides and other helpful publications.

WARRANTIES AND SERVICE CONTRACTS

A fair number of dealers now offer a short-term or partial warranty on at least some of their used cars. "Certified" used cars have specific coverage. But most are sold "as is." Late models, however, might still be covered by a factory warranty that can be transferred to a second owner.

Unfortunately, it's not always easy to determine whether a given car might carry a transferable warranty, and if so, what it might cover. For one thing, some factory warranties can be difficult to interpret. While nearly all recent new-car warranties are transferable, some can only be transferred to a second owner. Also, some original purchasers may have bought extended warranties that are transferable to subsequent owners.

Every car sold in the U.S. is also required to carry a 5/50 emissions warranty (8/80 starting in 1995), which includes major items related to exhaust emissions, such as fuel injection components, engine computers, catalytic converters, and some ignition parts. Details should be spelled out in the car's warranty booklet.

Following are some general guidelines for popular makes, but be sure to check the car's owner's manual for specifics. Note: Warranties for earlier models, whose coverage would no longer be valid, have been omitted.

Buick/Cadillac/Chevrolet/GMC/Oldsmobile/Pontiac: Since 1992, GM has offered a 3-year/36,000-mile bumper-to bumper warranty (with 6/100 corrosion protection) with no deductible and no transfer fee. Recent Cadillacs and the Olds Aurora have 4-year/50,000-mile warranties.

Chrysler/Dodge/Plymouth/Jeep/Eagle: Starting in 1992, Chrysler offered a choice of 1-year/12,000-mile bumper-to-bumper warranty with 7/70 powertrain coverage, or a 3/36 bumper-to-bumper warranty, with no deductibles. In 1995, Chrysler products adopted a 3/36 bumper-to-bumper warranty across the board, with 7/100 corrosion protection. Corrosion coverage was later dropped to 5/100.

Ford/Lincoln/Mercury: Since 1992, Ford and Mercury vehicles have included a 3-year/36,000-mile bumper-to-bumper warranty with no deductible, plus a 6/100 corrosion warranty. In 1995, corrosion protec-

tion dropped to 5/unlimited. Recent Lincolns came with a 4-year/50,000-mile warranty.

Honda/Acura: Honda warranties since 1989 have been 3-year/36,000-mile bumper-to-bumper, plus 3/unlimited corrosion (later, 5/50,000then 5/unlimited) with no deductible. Acuras turned to 4/50 bumper-to-bumper (4/unlimited corrosion) for 1993, and later 5/50,000 corrosion.

Hyundai: A 3/36 bumper-to-bumper, 5/100 corrosion warranty was offered starting in 1991 with no deductible. For 1993, a 5/60 powertrain warranty was added; in 1999, Hyundai went to a 5/60 bumper-to-bumper, 10/100 powertrain.

Isuzu/Mazda: Each make has had a 3-year/50,000-mile bumper-to-bumper warranty, plus 5/unlimited corrosion coverage (6/100,000 for Isuzu). Isuzu also included 5/60 powertrain coverage, upped to 10/120 in 2000, save for the GM-built Hombre pickup.

Lexus: Started with 6-year/70,000-mile coverage, then changed to 4/50 bumper-to-bumper plus 6/70 powertrain, along with 6/unlimited corrosion.

Mitsubishi: Since 1992, all except Precis (see Hyundai listing) have carried a 3/36 bumper-to-bumper, 5/60 powertrain, and up to 7-year/100,000-mile corrosion protection, with no deductible.

Saab: Since 1991, bumper-to-bumper coverage has been 3-year/40,000-mile, powertrain warranty 6/80. In 1995, Saab's warranty changed to 4/50 bumper-to-bumper and 6/unlimited corrosion.

Toyota/Nissan/Subaru/Suzuki: Each of these Japanese-brand cars has come with a 3/36 bumper-to-bumper warranty and 5/unlimited corrosion coverage (3/unlimited for Suzuki and 12/unlimited for recent Toyotas), with no deductible. Toyota added 5/60 powertrain coverage for 1990; Nissan for '92; Subaru for '92.

Volkswagen: Since 1990, VW had offered a 2-year/ 24,000-mile bumper-to-bumper warranty, along with 5/50 powertrain coverage and 6/unlimited corrosion, with no deductible. In 1994, powertrain coverage was bumped to 10-year/100,000-mile for the initial owner only.

Volvo: For 1992, Volvo turned to 3/50 bumper-to-bumper coverage, accompanied by a corrosion warranty that covers the major structure for 8/unlimited and body rust for 5/unlimited. For 1994, bumper-to-bumper coverage was extended to 4/50.

Most warranty transfers can be handled through a dealer that sells that make of car. Or, there might be a form in the owner's manual that you can simply fill out and send

to the manufacturer. However, since the expiration date of a warranty is based on the car's date of sale, it may not be worthwhile to transfer (for instance) a 3/36 warranty on a '99 model. If the car was sold in April of that year, the warranty expires in April 2002, regardless of how many miles are on the odometer. On the other hand, if the car was sold in September 1998, it might be worth getting the warranty in your name, even if it's only for a few months.

A 1985 federal law, known as the Used Car Rule, requires all used cars and light-duty vans sold by dealers to display a window sticker that indicates whether the seller is offering a warranty; and if so, the kind of coverage the warranty provides. Some states have their own laws similar to the Used Car Rule, and cars sold in those states may not carry the federal sticker. Otherwise, every car offered for sale by a dealer must have a "FTC Buyers Guide" sticker posted in its window.

The sticker's objective is to ensure that consumers receive, prior to sale, written information telling them who must pay for repairs later. Although the Used Car Rule offers no incentive to dealers to offer a warranty, it does give buyers a better idea of their rights, and the questions they should ask. The sticker should also indicate if the car is covered by the remainder of a factory warranty. Read the details before buying.

The Buyers Guide sticker contains printed boxes marked "As Is—No Warranty" and "Warranty." A separate document is required if the dealer is offering the vehicle under the "Implied Warranty Only" provision. Here's a look at each warranty type:

As Is—No Warranty In checking this box, the dealer is saying, "What you see is what you get." The buyer is responsible for all repair costs after the sale, regardless of any oral promises.

Warranty Dealers checking this box guarantee to repair stated items for a specified period. The dealer must disclose whether he is offering a "full" or a "limited" warranty. A full warranty applies to anyone who owns the vehicle during a specified period. The dealer agrees to make the repair with no parts or labor charges, and to give a refund or replacement if a problem can't be fixed.

A limited warranty may cover only a stated percentage (often 50 percent) of the cost of repairs or parts, or it may contain other exclusions. Remember, a dealer who charges you 50 percent of the repair cost at an expensive shop (perhaps his own) may not be doing you a big favor. The charge levied for a repair is often high enough so half the

Similar Models

It is common for manufacturers to use the same automotive platform—a car's basic architecture—for more than one vehicle. These "similar models" share major mechanical components, including engines. However, they usually have individualized styling and are sold under different model names or even different brand names. Choosing the least-expensive member of the group might save you hundreds, even thousands, of dollars. .

DaimlerChrysler

Dodge	Chrysler	Plymouth	Other
Avenger	Sebring coupe	—	—
Caravan	Town & Country	Voyager	—
Intrepid	Concorde, LHS, 300M	—	Eagle Vision
Neon	—	Neon	—
Spirit	—	Acclaim	—
Stratus	Cirrus sedan and convertible	Breeze	—
—	—	Laser	Eagle Talon, Mitsubishi Eclipse
—	—	—	

Nissan North American, Inc.

Nissan	Infiniti	Other
Maxima	I30	—
Pathfinder	QX4	—
Quest	—	Mercury Villager

Ford Motor Company

Ford	Mercury	Lincoln	Other
Thunderbird	Cougar		
Taurus	Sable	—	—
Contour	Mystique		
Crown	Grand		
Victoria	Marquis	Town Car	
Escort	Tracer	—	—
Expedition	—	Navigator	
Explorer	Mountaineer	—	—
Probe	—	—	Mazda MX-6
Ranger	—	—	Mazda B-Series
Expedition	—	Navigator	
—	—	LS	Jaguar S-Type
—	Villager	—	NIssan Quest

American Honda Motor Company

Honda/Acura	Other
Acura SLX	Isuzu Trooper
Honda Odyssey	Isuzu Oasis
Honda Passport	Rodeo

Toyota Motor Sales, USA

Toyota	Lexus
Camry	ES 250, 300

Volkswagen of America

Volkswagen	Audi
Golf, Jetta, New Beetle	A4, TT
Passat	A6

General Motors

Chevrolet	Pontiac	Oldsmobile	Buick	Cadillac	GMC	Other Brand
Astro	—	—	—	—	Safari	—
Beretta, Corsica	—	—	—	—	—	—
Blazer	—	Bravada	—	—	Jimmy	—
Camaro	Firebird	—	—	—	—	—
Caprice/Impala SS	—	—	Roadmaster	Fleetwood	—	—
Cavalier	Sunfire, Sunbird	—	—	—	—	—
Impala,	Grand Prix	88, Intrigue	Century, Regal	—	—	—
Malibu	—	Cutlass	—	—	—	—
Monte Carlo	—	—	Regal	—	—	—
Prizm	—	—	—	—	—	Toyota Corolla
Venture, Lumina APV	Montana, Aztec, Trans Sport	Silhouette	—	—	—	—
S-10 Pickup	—	—	—	—	Sonoma	—
Silverado, C/K	—	—	—	—	Sierra	—
Suburban, Tahoe	—	—	—	—	Yukon/Denali Suburban	—
Tracker	—	—	—	—	—	Suzuki Vitara
—	—	98	Park Avenue	Seville, Eldorado	—	—
—	Bonneville	Aurora	LeSabre	—	—	—
—	Grand Am	Alero, Achieva	—	—	—	—
—	—	Cutlass Cierra	Century	—	—	—
—	—	Cutlass Supreme	Regal	—	—	—

total is enough for the dealer to break even. Your half may well be all profit.

Typical used-car warranties cover only the basic powertrain—engine and driveline components—for 30 days or 1000 miles. Some warranties are only good for one week.

Every warranty has limitations. Find out exactly which components and systems are covered, for how long, and for how many miles. Get in writing from the manager (not your salesman) precisely what portion of the repair costs you have to pay (the "deductible"). If the dealer agrees to make any repairs beyond those stated on the sticker, get his agreement in writing on the contract.

Implied Warranty Only In states where "As Is" sales are not allowed, the vehicle carries an implied warranty. By marking this box (on an alternate form), the dealer guarantees that the vehicle is fit for the purposes its designers intended. Implied warranties are usually good only for a limited period. Though the dealer makes no promises to repair the car, an implied warranty gives the buyer some legal leverage to get the seller to correct flaws that weren't evident when the vehicle was sold. Implied warranties vary by state, and may exist even if no written warranty is supplied.

FINANCE CHARGES

If you'll be financing your purchase, it's wise to establish how much you can afford to pay per month—before you start shopping. This will dictate the price range of the cars to consider.

Remember that most banks will require at least 20 to 25 percent down on a used-car loan—and will likely have a maximum amount (called Loan Value or Finance Value) that they'll let you borrow for a certain year and model of car. Finance Value is typically about 25 percent less than the normal retail value of the car, so this is a helpful way to tell if the seller is asking a reasonable price.

Negotiating a good price on a car is just the start. Shop for financing with the same dedication and you can save plenty. The best interest rates go to the customer with a steady job, permanent address, and good credit history. If your credit rating is poor, a used-car dealer who specializes in high-risk financing may be your only choice. But remember, the interest you pay will reflect the risk that dealer is taking.

"Buy Here-Pay Here" financing has been a growing trend, especially for lower-priced cars. It's a convenience for low-income shoppers, but likely to be accompanied by a high interest rate. For shoppers who must have transportation but lack a good credit record, it could be the only choice.

Avoid any lender that tacks processing fees or other extra charges onto the basic loan. Inspect all finance agreements carefully. Understand every figure, and make certain all calculations are correct. If figures don't come easily to you, bring along a friend to examine all documents. Here's what to look for on the form:

Sale Price The amount you've agreed to pay for the vehicle.

Down Payment The amount you've agreed to pay before taking delivery. The higher the down payment, the lower the loan amount and payments.

Trade-in Value The amount the dealer is giving you for your old car. This could cover most or all of the down payment. Trade-ins leave plenty of room for tricky maneuvers, so be sure you know exactly how much you're getting.

Annual Percentage Rate (APR) The percentage of the borrowed amount charged as interest each year. If the rate exceeds 15 percent or so, think twice before signing. Look in the newspaper to find out what rate banks are giving for used car loans. Usually, you can find charts in the sports or classified sections relating to new and used vehicle loans.

This amortization table can help you determine monthly payments on a given loan amount. If, for instance, you plan to borrow $5000 at 14 percent interest for three years, multiply $34.18 (the monthly payment for each $1000 of loan amount on a 3-year loan) by five ($5000). Your monthly payment on that $5000 loan would therefore be $170.90. Remember, you'd probably need to have at least $1250 (25 percent of the loan amount) as a down payment. The total of your down payment and your loan ($6250 in this example) will have to cover the cost of the car as well as any applicable sales tax and fees.

Loan Amount The number of dollars you're borrowing, sometimes known as the "bottom line."

Monthly payment The amount you'll have to come up with each month. Know exactly how and when each payment must be made.

Payment Period The number of months you'll be making those seemingly endless payments.

Total Vehicle Cost The sum of the monthly payments (including interest) and the down payment. This is how much the car will actually cost you, and it can be dramatically higher than the sale price alone.

VEHICLE AND PASSENGER SAFETY

Thanks to sophisticated engineering and extensive safety testing (combined

Monthly payment per $1000 of loan value

Interest Rate	1 Year	2 Years	3 Years	4 Years	5 Years
7%	86.53	44.77	30.88	23.95	19.80
8	86.99	45.23	31.34	24.41	20.28
9	87.45	45.68	31.80	24.89	20.76
10	87.92	46.15	32.27	25.37	21.25
11	88.39	46.61	32.74	25.85	21.75
12	88.85	47.08	33.22	26.34	22.25
13	89.32	47.55	33.70	26.83	22.76
14	89.79	48.02	34.18	27.33	23.27
15	90.26	48.49	34.67	27.84	23.79
16	90.74	48.97	35.16	28.35	24.32
18	91.68	49.93	36.16	29.38	25.40
20	92.63	50.90	37.16	30.43	26.49

with better roads, increased seat belt and infant car-seat use, reduced speed limits, and stricter drunk-driving laws), the number of auto-related fatalities has dropped dramatically in recent decades. An estimated 41,800 Americans perished in accidents during 2000, according to the National Highway Traffic Safety Administration (NHTSA). This translates into approximately 1.6 fatalities per 100 million miles traveled in cars or light-duty trucks. By comparison, 3.3 people died for every 100 million miles traveled in 1977. Still, motor-vehicle crashes continue to be the major cause of unintentional injuries for Americans of all ages, and are the leading cause of death for those age 6 to 33.

Thus, vehicular safety continues to be among new-car buyers' top concerns. All vehicles have become better engineered to protect occupants in a crash, and to help motorists avoid them in the first place. Engineers call these innovations passive and active safety features, respectively. More than 100 separate components in a typical vehicle contribute to its overall safety, and new-car purchasers seem more-than-willing to spend the extra money to help protect their loved ones. Fortunately, even the least-expensive vehicles today offer advanced safety features like antilock brakes and side-impact airbags that were only available on luxury cars a decade ago.

Today's cars and trucks are specifically designed and built to help passengers survive a wide range of types and severities of collisions. So-called "crumple zones" at the front and rear of a vehicle are engineered to absorb and redirect crash forces. Hoods are engineered to collapse so they won't be forced through the windshield. Doors are designed to remain intact and overlap upon impact so passengers will be able to exit the vehicle. Doors are also are equipped with more-secure hinges and latches so they won't spring open to eject passengers. Heavier firewalls and specially designed engine mounts help send components down and under the passenger area, so they won't come crashing into the front seat. Windshields are specially laminated to help prevent not only injuries from shattering glass, but ejection from the vehicle in a collision.

Stronger passenger compartments, reinforced by race-carlike "safety cage" structures offer cocoonlike protection to help keep the occupant area intact in an accident. Padded, energy-absorbing materials and other interior design elements further help reduce injuries. Head restraints, now being added to rear- as well as front seats, help prevent whiplash injuries. Some automakers, including Volvo, Saab, and General Motors, have introduced head restraints that move slightly under certain crash conditions to help further reduce neck injuries.

Still, all else being equal, the laws of physics dictate that a larger and heavier car will provide its passengers with better protection in a crash than would a smaller and lighter vehicle. That's because a larger car is able to absorb more of the crash energy in a collision. But it's not always practical, desirable, or financially possible to simply select the largest car or truck on a dealer's lot, purely for its physical mass. Plus, with engineers using increasingly lighter-weight construction and materials to help improve a vehicle's fuel economy, design elements such as these are particularly critical to passenger safety.sensors in side impacts, but rollover incidents as well

Within the confines of a vehicle, occupant restraints—primarily seat belts and supplementary airbags—are designed to protect against the effects of an accident's so-called "second collision." The "first collision" occurs when a vehicle crashes into an object. The second collision happens about one-fiftieth of a second later, when its otherwise unrestrained occupants, still moving forward at the vehicle's original speed, smash into the steering wheel, dashboard and/or windshield. Experts say buckling the three-point lap-and-shoulder harness is the most effective safeguard against the effects of the second collision. They are also a passenger's primary protection from being ejected from a vehicle. Seventy-five percent of those ejected from vehicles in collisions die from their injuries.

Fifty states and the District of Columbia mandate seat belt use. NHTSA reports that seat belt use is at an all-time high, with an estimated 73 percent of all motorists buckling up during 2000, compared to only 58 percent in 1994, the first year in which the agency began keeping statistics. Seat belts are credited with preventing more than 11,000 motor-vehicle deaths per year.

All vehicles come with 3-point lap/shoulder belts for the outboard seating positions. Most also have 2-point lap belts for the center seats, though a growing number of vehicles are using 3-point belts for the inboard seats.

It's vital that all vehicle occupants be buckled, not just those in the front seats. Unrestrained rear-seat passengers are tossed around like rag dolls during a collision or rollover, exposing themselves and front-seat occupants to injury.

Lap-and-shoulder belts must be worn somewhat snugly to be most effective. Experts say they'll not only offer greater protection in a collision, but will help keep you squarely in the seat during hard-cornering maneuvers. To that end, some vehicles include "pretensioners" that automatically pull the belts tight in a collision.

Belts can bother shorter people and children when they rest on the side of the neck or across the face (this is often an excuse for not wearing them). To help solve this problem, NHTSA requires all vehicles to include upper anchor positions for front-seat shoulder belts that are height-adjustable, allowing a more comfortable "fit" for passengers. Some vehicles also provide height adjustments for outboard rear shoulder-belts, and others include "comfort guides," that route a belt to a more comfortable position.

Airbags have been credited with saving an estimated 7,224 lives through mid 2001, according to NHTSA. Some luxury cars now have as many as 10 airbags spread around the front, rear, and side of their interiors. Though they add to a car's overall crashworthiness, both manufacturers and safety advocates are quick to point out that airbags are designed to augment, not replace, seat-belt use. According to NHTSA, the combination of seat belts and airbags is 75 percent effective in preventing serious head injuries and 66 percent effective in averting critical chest injuries.

Frontal airbags for the driver and passenger have been required by law in all new cars and trucks since 1999, though many vehicles offered one or both for at least a decade before the mandated deadline.

If sensors detect rapid deceleration, as in a frontal crash, a fabric cushion, installed in either the steering-wheel hub or the passenger's side of the dashboard inflates in about one-twentieth of a second. The cushion helps absorb the crash energy and prevent the occupant from hitting the dashboard and/or windshield. Contrary to how they're usually portrayed in movies and TV shows, deployed airbags deflate quickly to allow the driver to regain control of the car, if necessary.

Because of incidents in which early airbags caused fatal injuries in crashes, especially to shorter occupants, unbelted riders, and children (totaling 191 deaths in the U.S. through mid 2001), the latest generation of frontal airbags deploy with 20-to-35 percent less force than earlier versions. Still, as NHTSA-mandated warning stickers in all new vehicles point out, front-passenger airbags can cause fatal injuries in a crash to infants riding in rear-facing child seats.

While the obvious solution is to secure the child in the back seat, what if you don't have one? To that end, most pickup trucks and two-seat sport coupes now include an ignition-key activated shutoff switch for the passenger-side airbag.

In addition, so-called "smart" frontal airbags on some vehicles are able to deploy at different degrees of force, depending on the severity of the crash and the weight of the occupant. Some vehicles come with suppression systems that prevent airbags from deploying if sensors detect a child in the front passenger seat. Such airbags will be required in all vehicles by 2006. Also, to help make airbags safer, Ford has been offering adjustable accelerator and brake pedals in several of its vehicles that can be moved closer or farther away from the driver depending on his or her height. The adjustable pedals are particularly useful for shorter people, who must otherwise move the seat forward to reach the pedals, placing them close enough to the airbag for it to cause injuries in a collision.

Of course, not all crashes occur head-on into another vehicle or a fixed object—side-impact crashes account for 30 percent of all collisions, and are the second-leading cause of death and injury to vehicle occupants. As a result, the government mandates that all new cars come equipped with some form of side-impact protection. This is generally accomplished by adding a metal beam and extra foam padding inside the door, though an increasing number of models now offer side-impact airbags for front passengers. These are either mounted on the doors or located within the front-passenger seats. A few of the costliest luxury cars include them for rear-seat passengers as well.

NHTSA warns that children who ride in a seat that's protected by a side-impact airbag may be at risk of serious or fatal injuries if the child's head, neck, or chest is in close proximity to the airbag when it deploys.

Some vehicles now include head-protection airbags, either in addition to or instead of door- or seat-mounted side airbags. These are configured in either a curtain or tubular design, which generally extend from near the bottom of a car's windshield pillar, all the way to the roof just above the rear door on each side of the vehicle. The 2002 Ford Explorer and Mercury Mountaineer offer an optional airbag canopy system that not only protects passengers.

KEEPING CHILDREN SAFE

Children under the age of 13 belong in the back seat and need to be securely buckled. Most kids under the age of nine should ride in a child safety seat or booster seat.

Passenger-side airbags are hazardous to children 12 and younger who are riding in the front seat—even if they are belted. These children are too small and fragile to be so close to a deploying airbag, which inflates at up to 200 miles per hour.

The risks are greatest for infants. Safety officials warn that a rear-facing child seat should never be used in the front seat of a vehicle with a passenger-side airbag unless the bag can be disabled.

Of the 191 deaths attributed to airbags, 112 were children riding in the front passenger seat. Nineteen were in rear-facing child seats, and another 83 were unbelted or improperly belted.

Putting children under the age of 13 in the rear seat reduces the risk of injury in the most common type of accident—a frontal collision—because they will be further from the impact.

All 50 states and the District of Columbia require infants and toddlers to be in a child safety seat when riding in a car. However, many laws apply to children up to three or four years of age, and the cutoff ages vary widely. A few state laws apply specifically to children weighing 40 pounds or less.

The American Academy of Pediatrics says kids should not be restrained by a seat belt alone until they are about nine years old. Safety experts recommend that children under 20 pounds (or up to one year old) ride in a rear-facing safety seat, and children 20 to 40 pounds (about ages one to four) should ride in a forward-facing safety seat. Kids from 40 to about 80 pounds (roughly ages four to eight), should ride in a booster seat.

Bigger children can ride in back without a special seat if the shoulder belt fits. If the belt rubs their neck or face, then a booster seat is recommended.

NHTSA estimates that 68 percent of children under the age of five who die in crashes are not properly restrained. Child seats can reduce the death risk by 70 percent if correctly installed, yet NHTSA says as many as four out of five are improperly used.

A new universal child-seat attachment system required by NHTSA in all new vehicles makes it easier to install the seats properly. Previously, child seat manufacturers devised their own mounting systems, some of which proved problematic for users. Now, they have to use a simpler standard system for securing the seats to the vehicle. Additionally, forward-facing child seats must now come with a tether strap that secures the back of the seat to the vehicle for better head protection.

The new regulations are phasing in. All cars and light trucks must have them by September 1, 2002.

Most car manufacturers have, or aim to, beat the federal deadline. Many also offer free or low-cost installation of attachment points on older models.

Safety experts recommend consulting the instructions from both the child-seat maker and the vehicle manufacturer to make sure you're installing the seat correctly. The owner's manual for new vehicles usually has ample information on installing child seats. The first step is to secure the seat so that it won't move excessively in a collision. The next step is to properly secure the child with the belts attached to the seat.

Some car companies are helping parents determine if they have the right seat for their children and if it is properly installed. DaimlerChrysler's Fit for a Kid program (www.fitforakid.org or 877-Fit4Kid) offers free inspections and advice. General Motors works through the National Safe Kids Campaign to check and install seats (www.safekids.org or 800-441-1888; the Web site links to a child-seat buying guide from the American Academy of Pediatrics: www.aap.org). In addition, Ford Motor Company sponsors Boost America (www.boostamerica.org), which targets children age four to eight.

Built-in child safety seats are a factory option on some vehicles, mainly minivans, though some manufacturers have dropped them because of low demand. This handy feature is integrated into the seatback and folds out when needed. Some automakers also offer approved child seats as accessories.

In response to recent incidents of children inadvertently being locked in cargo areas, automakers are beginning to include inside trunk-release mechanisms in their cars to help them get out. Generally denoted by glow-in-the-dark markings, these mechanisms take little effort to engage. GM recently introduced a system for its midsize Chevrolet Impala and Monte Carlo. This system uses thermal detection to determine if someone is in the trunk; if so, it opens the trunk automatically.

INSURANCE

Insurance costs are influenced by numerous factors. Rates generally depend on the type of car you own and how high a risk you are to insure. States regulate most insurance laws, so the factors differ somewhat from one state to the next. Therefore, it's crucial to factor in insurance cost before you purchase any vehicle.

You and the drivers in your household are usually the primary factors in determining insurance costs. However, rates are also strongly influenced by your choice of vehicle and the way you use it. Any specific car will affect your insurance costs primarily in the area of comprehensive and collision coverage. Here are some of the types of insurance coverage for which you might have to pay premiums. Some states require that you carry at least minimum coverage in some of these areas.

Comprehensive provides physical damage protection to your vehicle arising from almost anything other than a "collision." Examples of items covered under comprehensive coverage are the following: vandalism, fire, theft, hail, and glass breakage. Comprehensive does not normally provide protection for mechanical breakdown.

Collision provides physical damage protection when your vehicle collides with (strikes) another vehicle or object. One noted exception is collision with an animal, which is usually covered under comprehensive.

Specialty vehicles—especially sports or performance cars—may require a premium surcharge. This will increase your entire policy cost regardless of your driving record. Some more exotic vehicles may represent unacceptable risks to insurance companies and will be much harder to insure, other

CG® Auto Check

Consumer Guide® offers Auto Check as a way of verifying the title of a used vehicle. For a reasonable fee, Auto Check allows you to check the title, emissions, and insurance history of a vehicle. To access a Consumer Guide® Auto Check report, you can log on to the internet and enter the following address: http://www.consumer-guide.com/vhr. You must have a major credit card and the vehicle identification number (VIN) of the vehicle you wish to check.

companies may not be willing to insure them at all.

Liability This protection is necessary to protect yourself should you injure people or damage property. Liability laws differ in each state. You should find out if your state is a "fault" or "no-fault" state. Then, discuss the specific amount of liability insurance needed with your insurance agent or broker.

Deductibles The dollar amount you have to pay, out of your own pocket, when you file an insurance claim. A higher deductible can be used to lower the comprehensive and collision portion of your insurance bill. The higher the deductible, the lower your premium. Deductibles are normally on a per-occurrence basis. This means three accidents will create three deductibles. The savings from higher deductibles must be weighed against your ability to pay that particular deductible amount yourself should a loss occur.

Once you have determined the vehicle or vehicles you are interested in, ask your insurance representative to advise you as to what impact that vehicle will have on your total premium. Review the claim handling procedures of the company you're with, and what you might expect should a loss occur. A particular insurance company may have low rates, but a confusing and difficult claim procedure. Is saving a few extra dollars worth the added time and trouble?
There are many companies that offer very low-cost auto insurance over the internet or via phone. Most of these agencies do not have claim offices. We suggest that ask for references before you consider one of these companies.

TYPES OF COVERAGE

Six types of coverage are included in most insurance policies:
• Bodily injury liability: Covers injury and/or death claims against you and legal costs if your car injures or kills someone.
• Property damage liability: Covers claims for property that your car damages in an accident. Because liability coverage protects the other party, it is required in most states.
• Medical payments: Pays for injuries to yourself and to occupants of your car. It is optional in some states. In "no-fault" states, personal injury protection replaces medical payments as part of the basic coverage.
• Uninsured motorist protection: Covers injuries caused to you or the occupants of your car by uninsured or hit-and-run drivers. "Under-insured" coverage is also available to cover claims you may make against a driver who has inadequate insurance.
• Collision coverage: Covers damage to your car up to its book value. Collision coverage carries a deductible, which is the amount per claim you have to pay before the insurance takes effect. The lower the deductible, the higher the premium. While it is legally optional, a lending institution or leasing company usually requires it.
• Comprehensive (physical damage): Covers damage to your car from theft, vandalism, fire, wind, flood, and other nonaccident causes. Comprehensive also carries a deductible.

WHY SOME CARS COST MORE

Insurance premiums are based partly on the price of the vehicle, which affects the replacement cost if it is stolen or "totaled" in an accident. How expensive the vehicle is to repair—including parts and labor—can also affect the cost. In addition, surcharges may apply to vehicles that are frequently stolen or involved in accidents.

Industrywide information on injury claims, collision repair costs, and theft rates by vehicle is available from the Highway Loss Data Institute (HLDI), 1005 North Glebe Road, Arlington, VA 22201 (www.carsafety.org). Also see the chart "Vehicles with Low and High Insurance Costs" in this section.

According to HLDI, the lowest injury claims are from large vehicles—cars, pickup trucks, and sport-utility vehicles. Small 2- and 4-door cars have the highest injury claims, and small cars are also among the highest in collision costs, along with sports cars. If you have your heart set on a sporty vehicle, you'll probably pay dearly; insuring a high-performance car can cost two or three times the amount for an ordinary model.

Sport-utility vehicles, the hottest market segment, tend to have higher insurance rates than mid- and full-size cars. SUVs are "hot" for other reasons: They are now among the most frequently stolen vehicles, and they are more expensive than most cars. SUVs can also cost more to fix after an accident if the 4-wheel-drive system is damaged.

However, insurance companies set rates based on their own experience. If Company A has more collision and theft claims for a particular vehicle than Company B, then A will charge more for the same coverage. It all boils down to a company's actual experience with a particular vehicle or category of drivers. That is why it pays to shop for insurance.

All-Wheel-Drive Versus Four-Wheel Drive

All sport-utility vehicles (SUVs) and pickup trucks are available with 4-wheel drive, and some cars and minivans are as well. But there are substantial differences in the types of 4WD systems offered. The most important determining factor is whether 4WD can be left engaged on dry pavement. Some 4WD systems must be "turned off" on dry pavement to avoid mechanical damage. Others can be left engaged, a convenience that relieves the driver of deciding when 4WD is needed. Here is a more detailed description of each system. In some cases, more than one system is available for a given vehicle. We describe 4WD systems based on the above criteria. What follows is a further explanation of how each functions:

4WD that must be disengaged on dry pavement. Also known as part-time 4WD, this is the most basic system. The transfer case provides a choice of settings, usually 2WD, 4WD High, and 4WD Low. It can usually be shifted from 2WD to 4WD High "on the fly," which means while driving down the road, but 4WD must be disengaged when running on dry pavement. This is because the transfer case provides a 50-50 power split, and there's no mechanical compensation for the differences in tire speeds that occur when rounding corners. Leaving 4WD engaged on dry pavement causes the transfer case to wear—and eventually fail. Repairing a 4WD transfer case is expensive. These systems are inconvenient in conditions of light rain or patchy snow because they must be switched back and forth while driving. To engage 4WD Low, which is typically used only in severe off-road driving, the vehicle must be brought to a complete stop.

4WD that can be left engaged on dry pavement. Also known as full-time 4WD, this system is more advanced—and more convenient. The transfer case has a choice of settings, usually 2WD, 4WD High, and 4WD Low, sometimes adding an Automatic 4WD or Full-time 4WD setting. These systems can be left engaged even when running on dry pavement. To engage 4WD Low, which is typically used only in severe off-road driving, the vehicle must be brought to a complete stop.

All-wheel-drive. This system locks both axles and distributes power in varying degrees to all four wheels automatically when it detects wheel slippage. The transfer case is always in 4WD, so the driver doesn't have to bother with a switch. Some truck and SUV systems offer a 4WD Low for serious off-road work.

It is important to note that while 4WD helps you "go in the snow," it does little to aid cornering ability and virtually nothing for braking. Many drivers, finding they can accelerate in snow as quickly as on dry roads, assume they can corner and brake as well. This is untrue, and often leads to over-confidence, which in turn leads to accidents.

Your age, gender, and driving record are key factors that affect your insurance premium. Single males under the age of 25 pay the highest rates. Statistics show they are involved in the most accidents, so insurance companies charge young men higher premiums than women of the same age. Married men, who statistically have fewer accidents, pay less than single men. A handful of states do not allow rates based on sex or age, but that prohibition has tended to result in higher rates for women, not lower rates for men.

If you are convicted of moving traffic violations or cause accidents, your premiums will likely go up, no matter what your age. Typically, Drivers with clean records—no tickets, no accidents—pay the lowest rates.

Where you live also plays a big role in how much you pay. Urban areas, with their greater population densities and heavier traffic, get higher rates than rural areas. Insurance premiums in mainly urban New Jersey—traditionally the most-expensive state—might run three times higher than those in North Dakota, a rural state with the lowest average premiums.

In most states, insurers set rates by zip codes. If you live in a major city like Chicago or Los Angeles, you will probably pay more than if you lived in a nearby suburb no matter what part of the city you might live in.

How Much Insurance Coverage Do You Need?

Without insurance, your property is put at risk in an accident that is your fault. The minimum amount of insurance required in your state is seldom enough.

State law may require as little liability coverage as $15,000 per person, $30,000 per accident, and $5000 property damage. If you can afford it, buy more than the minimum. After all, $10,000 for property damage may not be enough if you hit a $100,000 Mercedes-Benz.

The more assets and income you have, the more insurance you need. Most insurers recommend liability coverage of at least $100,000 per person, $300,000 per accident, and $50,000 property damage if you have assets to protect, such as a house.

Some insurers also recommend a $1 million "personal liability umbrella" policy issued in conjunction with homeowner's coverage that costs $200 to $300 a year. It can protect a family from financial ruin in a major lawsuit.

Checkout Time

So you've found a car you like, but before you buy you should thoroughly inspect it both on the inside and out. Used cars are always a gamble, but following these suggestions can help tip the odds in your favor:

1. Inspect the vehicle in daylight. Artificial lights (and rainy days) hide too many defects in body metal. Faded paint can look glossy when wet, and the rain may hide scratches. Also, engines actually run better in rain because wet air is denser.

2. Allow enough time to make a thorough inspection and to take a comprehensive test drive.

3. Bring a friend along. He or she may notice problems that escape your attention. Ask that friend to ride in the back seat. Some sounds are better heard from back there.

4. Concentrate. Take your time—you may even want to take notes. Ask plenty of questions. Try to ask questions that lead the seller to tell you more about the life of the vehicle.

5. Dress for the occasion. You should poke around the engine compartment—even if you know little about what makes a car go—and get down on the ground. Bring a flashlight. Check for parts that look new, they could be a sign of a recent repair.

6. Don't rule out a car because of minor problems that aren't difficult or costly to fix—or that you can live with. Concentrate on big defects.

7. Be thorough, but discreet. Neither dealers nor private sellers appreciate shoppers who spend hours probing every little detail.

8. Have your local mechanic give the car a thorough inspection before you buy. Most charge only about $50 for this service. The piece of mind it buys may be the best $50 you spend on your purchase.

Facts About the Car

A used car's former owner can be an invaluable source of information—provided that a dealer agrees to furnish that person's name and phone number. Some will balk; others will do it without even being asked. Check the glovebox for an owner's manual service schedule, or other documentation that could have the prior owner's name on it.

If you can reach the prior owner, be brief but to the point. You might want to ask:

• How long did you own the car? If the person was the owner for a brief time, ask why they sold the car.

• When did you buy the car? (the dealer's stated date should match the date on the title)

• Why did you sell it? Often, the seller might have found a problem with the vehicle and was trying to unload it on someone else.

• Has it been in an accident? Cars that were in major accidents sometimes never "feel" right again.

• Has the body been repaired or repainted? Is the car the same color as when the owner sold it? Maybe the dealer painted it quickly and cheaply to hide some flaws.

• Has it ever had any rust? Once a vehicle starts to rust, there is almost nothing you can do short of costly body work.

• How many miles were on it when they sold it? If there is a big difference from what the odometer shows, maybe the dealer has been using the vehicle for errands or driving it home at night. Service of this type can be especially hard on a vehicle as it is treated with little or no respect. Extra miles might even suggest that the vehicle was resold and then returned by a dissatisfied buyer.

• Where was it driven, for the most part? City or highway? Several thousand highway miles can equal only a few hundred city miles. Highway miles tend to be kinder to a vehicle's moving parts.

• Has the car had regular maintenance? Where?

All of this information is invaluable. It will give you insight into the car's past and help you to tell if the dealer is being straight with you.

Negotiating With the Seller

A surprising number of dealers have turned to single-price, no-bargaining used-car sales. Others have occasional one-price sale days. Sounds like paradise to some shoppers, but only if that no-haggle price isn't inflated. A dealer's claim that "You can't overpay" or "You get only the best price" doesn't prove the price is a reasonable one.

For most transactions, bargaining is still part of the process. Some buyers think haggling is great sport. Others dread the prospect.

Figure your top price ahead of time, but keep it to yourself. If you admit exactly how much you're able to spend, a seller will be glad to let you dispense that sum. If the seller rejects the opening offer, many shoppers immediately begin to point out all the car's shortcomings. Nitpicking every little defect isn't as effective as some folks think, and is more likely to make the seller defensive.

If the car you're considering is virtually faultless and priced fairly, be careful about trying to talk the seller down very much. Deals of that type don't come along every day, and the next person who looks at the car might snap it up.

On the other hand, do not be afraid to walk away. Odds are, the car will still be there tomorrow. Never put down a deposit on a car you do not definitely intend to buy. If a dealer or a private party wants a deposit, politely decline. If they insist, it's probably not a good idea to buy from that person. Though the dealer may show you what seems to be a contract for the deposit, the paper most likely binds you to buying the car, but not the dealer to selling you the car.

Seldom does a dealer's salesperson have full authority to close a deal. Normally, he or she takes your offer to a sales manager, who turns it down instantly. The rejection may take a few minutes to be relayed to you, however—a delay designed to make you think it was a tough decision. The salesperson will offer another figure, and you'll make a counteroffer that needs another approval. The goal is to wear you down—and keep you from leaving.

During all this haggling, it doesn't pay to be argumentative. If the final price is still too high, thank the seller for his or her time and walk away. The seller often will come back at the last second with a lower figure. If not, check back in a few days. If the car is still there, chances are you can knock the price down a bit more. And if time isn't important, check again after a few weeks.

Be realistic. Bargaining is acceptable, but don't expect to take away all the dealer's profit.

USED CAR CONTRACTS

When it's time to put your name on the dotted line, two rules could keep you from making a big mistake:

1. Sign nothing until you're completely ready to buy.

2. Get every detail of the agreement in writing.

Dealers work hard to wear you down. At traditional-type dealerships, you may be shuffled among several employees. Perhaps one will greet you, another shows the car, and a third tries to close the deal. Meanwhile, the sales manager waits to pass judgment.

Credit investigations and loan arrangements take time, so a few days may elapse between the time you decide to buy and the moment you drive away in your new chariot. Consider this delay a blessing: It gives you a final chance to reconsider.

You'll need cash or a checkbook to put down a deposit, which will reduce your risk of losing the car to another shopper. At some used-car dealership deposits may not automatically refundable, so try to avoid leaving one. Or if you must, give as little as possible. Don't offer a sum. Ask, 'What do you require?' or, 'What's the least they'll accept?'. Most of the time, $50 is sufficient. If you must leave a deposit, always get a receipt, plus a written agreement that your money will be refunded if a problem develops or you simply decide that you don't want the car. If a dealer is not wlling to hold the car for a day or two, be suspicious.

BILL OF SALE

I, __________________________________
(seller's name)

living at ____________________________
(address)

hereby sell to ________________________
(buyer's name)

of _______________________________
(buyer's address)

a ________________________________
(year, make)   (model)

automobile, Vehicle Identification Number ________________

As Is and As Shown, with clear title to same,

for the sum of \$ ______________________

Signed ____________________________
(buyer)

Signed ____________________________

(seller)
Date ____________________, __________

BILL OF SALE

A bill of sale, whether typed or handwritten, is essential when buying from a private party. Keep the wording simple; include only the essential details. Make two copies; the buyer and seller should sign both copies and each should keep one.

"Sign Right Here" Always read the contract carefully. Be certain it spells out every detail that's been discussed. Oral agreements mean nothing. Double-check all figures and calculations. Be especially careful if you're financing through the dealer: See that the loan amount, monthly payments, and other figures add up. Only when you know exactly what you're getting, and how much you're paying for the vehicle, are you ready to buy.

Take your time. Ask questions if you don't understand a clause or a figure. Don't feel foolish; it's foolish not to ask. Having a friend along not only offers moral support, but can keep you from leaping into a deal with pitfalls that you might overlook.

The contract should spell out precisely any repairs to be made before delivery. "Fix leak" isn't good enough. The words should describe exactly what is to be adjusted, replaced, or repaired. Never sign a contract with blank spaces or clauses you don't understand. Watch for charges a dealer might add to the contract after you've negotiated a purchase price. Unwarranted extra charges are common for new cars, but they also appear in used-car contracts. They gain the seller extra profit without appearing to jack up the car's sales price.

Check That Title This warning cannot be stressed enough. Too many used-car buyers wind up with stolen merchandise because they didn't examine the Certificate of Title closely.

The Vehicle Identification Number (VIN) is a long combination of numbers and letters stamped into a rectangular plate attached to the driver's side of the dashboard near the windshield. It can be read from outside the car. Some manufacturers also include the VIN on stickers in the trunk or on doorjambs—make sure these match the title.

You can also confirm the car's age by

checking the VIN, because its tenth symbol indicates the model year: L = 1990; M = 1991; N = 1992; P = 1993; R = 1994; S = 1995; T = 1996; V = 1997; W = 1998; X = 1999; Y = 2000. Many people have wound up with cars that were older than they thought, because they failed to check.

Examine the title for signs of alteration or erasure. Make certain there are no outstanding liens against the car (meaning that the seller owes someone else money on it). This will usually be noted on the title. If you're in doubt about anything, and unsatisfied with the explanations that are offered, walk away.

FREQUENTLY ASKED QUESTIONS

Why should I buy a used car? Even more than in the past, there are solid reasons for buying a secondhand vehicle: First, used cars have gained in stature, losing their stigma to a surprising degree. They're even bought by affluent folks nowadays. Second, cars are better than ever. They last longer, and—despite the horror stories that turn up—frequently lead relatively trouble-free lives. Third, modern warranties typically last long enough to cover at least a portion of a car's life after the first owner.

Every year, when the new-car prices are announced—and have risen again—a growing number of shoppers face disappointment. Now that the average new vehicle sells for more than $22,000, families with moderate incomes often have to dismiss their dreams of a brand-new model, and settle for secondhand.

Trouble is, even used cars aren't so cheap anymore. The average used vehicle in early 1997 sold at retail for $12,033, according to the National Automobile Dealers Association—just about half the cost of a typical new model. That's no small sum, considering that you face a greater risk of repairs and troubles whenever you buy a "pre-owned" vehicle.

What can I do for theft protection? Americans spend close to half a billion dollars yearly on security devices. Little can be done to stop a determined thief, but you can reduce the risk by choosing a car that thieves don't target.

Many recent models came equipped with factory-installed theft deterrent and alarms. Experts place little faith in aftermarket alarms, however, many of which go off without cause and annoy more than they protect. In fact, most insurance companies will not give discounts for some aftermarket alarms.

You may want to avoid an expensive radio in any kind of car, because it will invite break-ins. To combat radio theft, many radios feature antitheft circuitry. If the radio is removed from the car, it will not play until a secret code is punched in. That code is known only to the car's owner and to the dealer.

In most circumstances, a tough mechanical devise that grasps the car's steering wheel may provide greater protection than an antitheft alarm—especially a cheap one—but nothing is impregnable. A truly zealous thief can find a way to beat just about any type of gadget that's been devised.

The car I am looking at cost thousands more than you say. Certain models that attract collectors or enthusiasts may be worth more than the amounts shown in this book. Examples include: Chevrolet Camaro IROC-Z and comparable Pontiac Firebird Trans Am models; plus various anniversary and other special editions.

Just because a dealer asks a higher price for a car because it's a "special edition," doesn't mean it necessarily has greater value. Some of those specials were produced in substantial quantity, lacking dramatic features, and are worth little or nothing more than their non-special mates. Others were created for dealers in a particular area, mainly as promotional tools.

What about safety? All else being equal, a large car provides greater protection in a collision or crash. The laws of physics are hard to overrule: In a collision, the vehicle with the greater mass absorbs less of the impact energy. Large cars also have more sheetmetal and larger crumple-zones that help absorb some impact.

Insurance Institute for Highway Safety statistics have shown death rates directly proportional to size. The rate for the smallest cars (under 95-inch wheelbase) is more than 2½-times the rate for full-size cars. The National Highway Traffic Safety Administration learned that more fatalities result from car/light-truck collisions than car-to-car incidents.

On the other hand, many smaller cars nowadays are solidly built, even using roll-cage construction techniques. Factors beyond size and weight also contribute to safety, including the structural soundness of the vehicle and its safety equipment. In simulated tests, some smaller cars have rated better than larger ones. Besides, you might better avoid an accident in a smaller car than in a larger car.

Top performer among 1997 vehicles in the 35-mph tests performed by the National Highway Safety Administration was Ford's Windstar. Good scores also were earned by such vehicles as the Volvo 850, Nissan 200SX, and Ford Contour. Mitsubishi Galant, Toyota Tercel, Buick LeSabre, and Cadillac DeVille scored just a bit lower. In prior testing, the Audi A4 and A6, Honda Civic, Toyota Avalon, Ford Mustang convertible and Crown Victoria sedan, and Chevrolet C1500 and Ford F-150 pickup trucks scored well. So did Chrysler minivans, Mazda 626 and Millenia, Chevrolet Camaro and Lumina, Chrysler Sebring, Dodge Avenger, Honda Civic, and Pontiac Grand Am.

Should I trade in my old car or sell it myself? Most new- and used-car buyers trade in their old car. It's easy and usually covers all or most of the down payment on the new vehicle. However, dealers typically make more profit on used cars than on the sale of new ones, so they have a strong incentive to offer as little as possible for your old car.

Most importantly, avoid trading a car before it's paid for. If you do, the dealer will pay off your old loan, use any residual value as a down payment, then write another loan for the new car—with ample profit for himself.

One bonus to trading your old car in to a dealer is that you will lower the amount of sales tax on your new purchase. If your old car trades in for $1500, that money is subtracted from the retail price of the newer vehicle and will lower its sales tax base by $1500. So, if you are able to get $1500 from a dealer as trade, and your local sales tax is 7%, you would have to sell your old car to a private party for over $1605 before you were to make a profit.

Remember, a dealer will only give wholesale value—or less—for a used car. Sell it yourself and you might be able to get actual retail value. If the dealer is giving you more than fair value for your car, chances are they are making up the difference somewhere else in the deal.

Should I purchase an extended service contract? Even if a used car comes with a great warranty, you'll likely be encouraged to accept a service contract. Some salespeople will express wide-eyed amazement if you happen to decline. Why? Because it's typically a high-profit item, salespeople often are encouraged to push contracts.

Unlike a warranty, this is not included in the purchase price and will cost extra—a portion of which the dealer keeps. It's really an insurance policy, covering repair work for major mechanical breakdowns. Service contracts are issued by a third-party company, not by the manufacturer, and are underwritten by an insurer.

Service contracts typically cost at least $250 to $500—perhaps $1000 for a late-model car. Many people have paid far more. Service contracts normally cover major repairs only for a specified period of time. In most cases, you must pay a deductible—perhaps $100—on each covered repair. Some dealers offer a bewildering choice of contract terms and durations.

While the dealer might perform the actual work, you may have to negotiate payment with the insurer before anything is done. So, make certain you know who is issuing the contract, and who to contact for repairs.

Some service contracts cover only major components that are unlikely to fail during the coverage period.

Why are insurance rates so expensive? Ask

your insurance agent if other similar cars are rated the same, or if a change in engine size (e.g., 6-cylinder vs. V8), model (e.g., SE vs. SSE), or year of the car (e.g., 1991 vs. '92), would make a difference. Ask what impact driving record, deductibles, antitheft devices, future age changes, experience level, marital status, children, garaging, and/or location might have on your overall premium cost.

Should I lease or buy? Leasing a used car seemed to be a risky venture. As the practice grows more common, however, it might be worth considering—especially for vehicles that simply cost too much to buy.

Be wary, from start to finish. Leasing a new vehicle is risky enough, unless you know what you're doing. Doing it with a "previously owned" vehicle demands even more homework first.

When you lease a car, you effectively become its owner for the period of time specified in the lease. However, you do not get any of the benefits when it comes time to trade in your leased vehicle. Usually, anything that happens to a leased vehicle is the responsibility of the lessee, not the dealer. So, major repairs (which are more frequent on used cars) and any interior or exterior damage are your responsibility. As a lessee, you are also responsible for the insurance. If your car is totaled in an accident, and your insurance company gives you fair value for the car, that amount may not cover the actual value specified on the lease. You, as the lessee, are legally responsible for the remainder of that money.

The vehicle I am looking at has very low miles, what's up? Odometer "spinners" have never really gone out of business. In fact, after several years of decline, they've experienced a dramatic rebirth. Continued high demand for low-mileage, late-model vehicles evidently gives the criminally inclined too much temptation. If they don't have enough low-mileage cars on hand, they can always "create" a few by rolling back odometers. Lax vehicle-titling practices in certain states make the rollback problem even more serious.

Wholesale auctions keep close track of odometer readings, to help eradicate the problem. Several companies, including Consumer Guide's®, Auto Check maintain databases of vehicles, arranged by Vehicle Identification Number, complete with odometer-disclosure data—updated each time the vehicle was sold to another party. This information is available either to dealers or directly to consumers (for a fee). Ask the dealer about obtaining a report if there's any doubts.

The interior of the car I am buying smells musty? Hail, storms, and floods can wreak havoc upon a dealer's stock of vehicles. The National Automobile Dealers Association (NADA) issued a statement warning that

"problems due to flood damage may surface long after cleaning and restoration." The dealer group advised dealers and retail customers to follow these steps in checking for damage:

1. Carefully inspect the interior and engine, searching for water and grit that may suggest immersion.

2. Closely examine the area under the dashboard for signs of dried mud and residue.

3. Check upholstery, carpeting, and the trunk for any traces of mildew or mold, and for musty odors.

4. Inspect around the engine for residue left in crevices of the alternator, starter motor, power steering pump, and relays.

In addition to drying out a flood-damaged car thoroughly, components have to be "cleaned and relubricated to remove contamination to prevent rust and system failure." Even so, NADA warned, some problem areas are difficult, if not impossible, to dry and clean properly. Even long after the incident, a vehicle could develop intermittent electrical failures, as well as possible erosion in the brake system and other mechanical components.

Best bet for shoppers: Steer clear of any cars that display evidence of water damage, however slight.

HELPFUL ADDRESSES

Listed below are phone numbers and addresses for government agencies and consumer groups that may be able to help you resolve car-related problems. In addition, many state and local governments have consumer protection agencies that may be able to act faster than a federal agency.

Better Business Bureau
The Bureau provides reports on dealers and other consumer information, and operates Auto-Line arbitration service. There are offices in most major cities; check your local phone book for the nearest location, or call 1-800-955-5100 for general automotive complaints and to obtain information on initiating the arbitration process. BBB offices also offer helpful brochures for a small charge.

Center for Auto Safety
2001 S Street, NW
Washington, DC 20009
(202) 328-7700
www.autosafety.org
This non-profit organization lobbies on behalf of consumers in areas of vehicle safety and quality.

Environmental Protection Agency
401 M Street, SW
Washington, DC 20460
(202) 260-2090
www.epa.gov
Annual EPA Gas Mileage Guide, available free at dealerships, gives data on fuel economy; agency enforces emissions laws.

Federal Trade Commission
6th Street & Pennsylvania Avenues, NW
Washington, DC 20580
(202) 326-2222
www.ftc.gov
Regional offices are located in Atlanta, Boston, Chicago, Cleveland, Dallas, Denver, Los Angeles, New York, San Francisco, and Seattle. FTC has information on consumer complaints, deceptive practices, and arbitration. Write to Consumer Response Center for free fact sheets and brochures on "Buying a Used Car," "Vehicle Repossessions," "Warranties," "Advertising Consumer Leases," or "Service Contracts." Contact Division of Enforcement with complaints about window sticker violations; Division of Marketing Practices for warranty problems. Not all FTC publications are up-to-date.

Helm, Inc.
(800) 551-4123
www.helminc.com
Sells owner's manuals and servicing publications for Ford, GM, Acura, Honda, Hyundai, Isuzu, Kia, Subaru, and Suzuki vehicles. Call Monday-Friday from 8 A.M. to 6 P.M. (Eastern time).

Highway Loss Data Institute/Insurance Institute for Highway Safety
1005 N. Glebe Road
Arlington, VA 22201-4751
(703) 247-1500
www.highwaysafety.org
Insurance industry lobbying group compiles information on vehicle and highway safety. Inquire about brochures that are available free.

National Highway Traffic Safety Administration/Department of Transportation
400 Seventh Street, SW
Washington, DC 20590
www.nhtsa.dot.gov
NHTSA investigates safety defects and orders recalls. Consumer Hotline: (800) 424-9393 (in Washington, DC, (202) 366-0123). Hearing-impaired people may call (800) 424-9153 (in Washington, DC, (202) 366-7800). Brochures are available on odometer fraud, tire grades, safety belts and airbags, child safety seats, safety standards, new-car crash test results, safety recalls, and other information.

The *2002 Used Car & Truck Book* is packed with information to help you select a suitable vehicle and buy it for the right price. Inside you'll find reports on more than 270 different vehicles—from tiny subcompact cars to full-size pickup trucks.

Best Buys As might be expected, not all used vehicles are created equal—some are better buys than others. Throughout the body of this book you will see the ⬤ symbol. This indicates we feel that vehicle is a solid used car buy and one of the best values in its class. This is not to say that cars without the Best Buy symbol are bad choices, just that the Best Buys are better overall values. We base our Best Buy rating first and foremost on the vehicle itself and how well it does its job. We also consider factors like reliability, cost, and utility.

The Buying Guide The main Buying Guide section covers used cars, minivans, pickup trucks, and sport-utility vehicles from 1990 to 2001. Vehicles are listed alphabetically according to make (Buick, Ford, etc.), then by model (Accord, Cavalier, etc.), and finally in ascending year order. The years are grouped so that the entire generation of a vehicle is listed in one report. For example, the Dodge Caravan was redesigned in 1991 and then again in 1996. Hence, we get the Dodge Caravan 1991-95.

At the top of each listing is a photo of the covered vehicle. Though the picture may be of a 4-door body style, the report covers all models listed for those years. Keep in mind that some cars look completely different as 2- or 4-door models.

Following that, you will find the vehicle's *For* and *Against* points. These are not necessarily the only good or bad points of that particular vehicle; just the most pronounced.

Following the *For* and *Against* is the *Evaluation* section; providing performance, fuel economy, and passenger/cargo space information. Our auto editors discuss how the vehicle accelerates, rides, and handles, and may warn of major service problems. In short, the Evaluation section lets you

know what that vehicle would be like to live with on a daily basis.

In addition to an evaluation, we also provide a *Value* assessment for the speed reader. The *Value* paragraph gives you a quick overview of how the vehicle stacks up against others in the class and as a used car purchase.

The *Specifications* chart lists body styles and basic exterior measurements of each model, plus cargo capacity and fuel tank size. Dimensions often change slightly from year to year and vary among submodels, so an individual car may differ from figures shown.

The *Engines* chart lists all engines available in that particular vehicle: It lists the type (number of cylinders); displacement (size) in liters and cubic inches; horsepower (single figure or range for the period covered); and fuel economy estimates including EPA figures and actual mileage recorded in our tests of the car when new. The following key might help you understand the engine charts a little better:

> ohv = overhead valve; ohc = overhead camshaft; dohc = dual overhead camshafts; I = inline cylinders; V = cylinders in V configuration; flat = horizontally opposed cylinders; OD = overdrive transmission; NA = information not available.

Immediately following the *Engine charts* are the *Price charts*. These detail a range of average prices in year-by-year listings, for vehicles in three condition levels:

Good—a clean, low-mileage, solid-running vehicle that needs little or no repair. **Average**—a car with normal miles on the odometer, perhaps a few scrapes or dings; engine might need a minor repair or two, but runs acceptably well. **Poor**—might have potentially dangerous problems with the engine and/or body, or abnormally high mileage; definitely in need of mechanical attention. Valuations reflect wholesale prices paid by dealers at auction and retail prices on used-car lots. Each range covers all trim levels and engine types for a vehicle with a typical amount of equipment—usually an automatic transmission, air conditioning, stereo, etc. Fully loaded vehi-

cles may cost more. Keep in mind that these are guidelines only.

The *Average Replacement Costs* table lists the costs of likely repairs—things like air conditioning, brakes, and transmission repairs. The dollar amount listed includes the cost of the part(s) and labor for the average repair. Like the pricing information, replacement costs can vary widely depending on region.

No vehicle is perfect, so in our *Trouble Spots* section we list the most common problems for each vehicle. We also list the manufacturer's solutions for these problems. This section will help you determine whether that noise coming from the engine is a costly repair.

Finally, you get an abbreviated listing of major recalls for each vehicle in our *Recall History* table. Not all recalls issued by NHTSA may be listed. Since manufacturers are not required to fix recall defects free of charge after an eight-year period, minor defects or problems that would be apparent immediately, have been omitted. To obtain a complete list of recalls for the vehicle you intend to buy, call NHTSA at (800) 424-9393.

Thank you for choosing Consumer Guide® as your automotive information source. We welcome your comments. Feel free to write us at:

Used Car & Truck Book
Consumer Guide
7373 N. Cicero Avenue
Lincolnwood, IL 60712

You can also send an email to:
info@consumerguide.com
(Subject: Auto Editors)

1997-99 ACURA CL

1998 Acura 2.3CL

FOR Ride • Steering/handling • Acceleration (3.0CL)

AGAINST Automatic transmission performance • Acceleration (4-cylinder w/automatic)

EVALUATION Styling is unique; but inside, the CL coupe looks, feels, and behaves like a more robust, better-appointed Accord. Also like the Accord, handling is poised and sporty, while the ride is firm but comfortably absorbent. Because of its bigger tires, however, the CL does feel more athletic than an Accord. Both CL engines run smoothly, but the 4-cylinder version performs best with manual shift. With an automatic transmission, it loses energy. A 2.2CL with the 5-speed accelerated to 60 mph in 9.5 seconds—passable, but no powerhouse. Gas mileage was a bonus, however, averaging an impressive 22.2 mpg overall. The 2.3-liter engine installed in 1998 is about as quick and efficient as the initial 2.2-liter. With automatic, acceleration ranks only as adequate. In contrast, the 3.0-liter V6 delivers brisk acceleration. Unfortunately, with either engine the automatic transmission tends to shift with a bothersome jolt when pushing hard on the gas. In addition, the transmission sometimes seems almost confused about which gear to be in during stop-and-go driving. Four adults sit in reasonable comfort, which is a bonus for a sporty coupe. Of course, the interior is typical Acura/Honda, which means a comfortable driving position, unobstructed visibility, and simple, convenient instruments and controls. The power driver's seat in a 3.0CL automatically moves fore and aft to ease rear entry/exit, and it can sense obstructions and reverse direction as needed. Cargo space ranks as more than adequate, but there's only a pass-through opening to the trunk, not a folding rear seatback. Workmanship is top-notch, as expected from Honda's premium brand. This coupe feels robust even on rough roads and displays good detail finish.

VALUE All told, this is a competent, pleasant, and well-constructed coupe, marred only by unsatisfying operation of the automatic transmission. However, most of the CL's virtues are also available in the appealing but less costly Honda Accord. That's no surprise, since the cars share a number of components.

SPECIFICATIONS

	2-door coupe
Wheelbase, in.	106.5
Overall length, in.	190.0
Overall width, in.	70.1
Overall height, in.	54.7
Curb weight, lbs.	3009
Cargo volume, cu. ft.	12.0
Fuel capacity, gals.	17.1
Seating capacity	4
Front head room, in.	37.4
Max. front leg room, in.	42.9
Rear head room, in.	35.9
Min. rear leg room, in.	31.0

Powertrain layout: *transverse front-engine/front-wheel drive*

ENGINES

	ohc I4	ohc I4	ohc V6
Size, liters/cu. in.	2.2/132	2.3/137	3.0/183
Horsepower	145	150	200
Torque (lbs./ft.)	147	195	

EPA city/highway mpg

	ohc I4	ohc I4	ohc V6
5-speed OD manual	25/31	25/31	
4-speed OD automatic	23/29	23/29	20/28

City/highway mpg (as tested)	ohc I4	ohc I4	ohc V6
5-speed OD manual	22.2		
4-speed OD automatic			22.3

Built in USA

RETAIL PRICES

	GOOD	AVERAGE	POOR
1997 2.2CL	$10,500-11,500	$9,500-10,500	$6,700-7,400
1997 3.0CL	12,000-13,000	11,000-12,000	7,700-8,500
1998 2.3CL	13,000-14,200	12,000-13,100	8,500-9,400
1998 3.0CL	14,500-16,000	13,200-14,500	10,000-11,000
1999 2.3CL	16,000-17,000	14,500-15,500	11,000-11,800
1999 3.0CL	17,500-18,500	16,000-17,000	12,200-13,000

AVERAGE REPLACEMENT COSTS

A/C Compressor	$775	Clutch, Pressure Plate, Bearing	715
Alternator	365	Constant Velocity Joints	855
Automatic Transmission or Transaxle	950	Exhaust System	360
Brakes	190	Radiator	515
Timing Chain or Belt	235	Shocks and/or Struts	430

TROUBLE SPOTS

• **Mirrors.** Fluttering or whistling noises come from the outside mirrors due to a faulty run channel that must be replaced. (1997)

• **Seat.** The front passenger seat may not move forward when the access lever is pulled because the rear seat access cable comes loose. (1997)

• **Speedometer.** The indicated speed (on the speedometer) and true speed may not jibe. Speedometers were being replaced under extended warranty. (1997)

• **Sunroof/moonroof.** The moonroof seal may pop out when the roof is opened. (1997)

• **Seat.** The power seat may not move properly because the synchronizer cable comes loose from the seat. (1997)

• **Gauges.** The tachometer needle fluctuates, and the "D4" light blinks due to a problem with the transmission control module (TCM) that is, in most cases, replaced under goodwill. (1997)

• **Windows.** The windows rattle when partially open due to a problem with the guide pin and rear channel. (1997-98)

RECALL HISTORY

1997-98: Ball joints on certain cars could wear out prematurely and, in worst case, separate and cause front suspension to collapse. **1998:** Irregularity in transmission cover can limit movement of parking pawl actuation lever and prevent adequate engagement; car could roll down an incline while transmission is in "Park."

1990-93 ACURA INTEGRA

1990 Acura Integra GS 2-door hatchback

FOR Fuel economy • Acceleration (5-speed) • Handling/roadholding • Antilock brakes (GS, GS-R) • Reliability

AGAINST Acceleration (automatic transmission) • Rear-seat room (3-door)

EVALUATION Handling and roadholding are fine, if not quite as agile as the prior models. Integras hang on nicely around tight turns, suffering minimal body roll. Stopping power is especially impressive with the optional antilock braking. This car's personality varies according to its transmission. Acceleration from the basic twin-cam 4-cylinder engine is brisk and zesty with the 5-speed gearbox, but not nearly so lively with 4-speed automatic. The high-performance GS-R model demonstrated that it was subjectively faster than other Integras. But that smaller engine stays very busy, thanks to short gearing that keeps it spinning on the high side of 3000 rpm. On the plus side, both transmissions deliver attractive fuel mileage: 23-25 mpg around town and past 30 mpg on the highway. Even a GS-R managed 22.4 mpg in rigorous city/suburban driving. Abundant engine/road noise and vibration, on the other hand, remind occupants that Integras are not quite in the same refinement league as the larger Legends. Visibility is fine; controls are sensible and fall easily to hand. Analog gauges are well-marked and unobscured. A low driving position emphasizes the Integra's sporty nature. Seats are firm and supportive. The 4-door's longer wheelbase shows up in additional rear leg room. Sedans seat four adults without cramping, but the 3-door's rear seat is best for kids and cargo. Cargo space is better in the coupe, because of its fold-down rear seat.

VALUE Well-known for reliability and solid construction, these competent front-drivers offer plenty of refinement. Resale values have been strong, so even these older Integras aren't exactly inexpensive.

SPECIFICATIONS

	2-door hatchback	4-door sedan
Wheelbase, in.	100.4	102.4
Overall length, in.	172.9	176.5
Overall width, in.	67.4	67.4
Overall height, in.	52.2	52.8
Curb weight, lbs.	2560	2605
Cargo volume, cu. ft.	16.2	11.2
Fuel capacity, gals.	13.2	13.2
Seating capacity	4	5
Front head room, in.	38.5	38.7
Max. front leg room, in.	41.8	41.6
Rear head room, in.	34.7	36.8
Min. rear leg room, in.	28.6	31.7

Powertrain layout: transverse front-engine/front-wheel drive

ENGINES

	dohc I4	dohc I4
Size, liters/cu. in.	1.7/102	1.8/112
Horsepower	160	130-140
Torque (lbs./ft.)	117	121-126
EPA city/highway mpg		
5-speed OD manual	24/29	25/31
4-speed OD automatic		23/29
City/highway mpg (as tested)		
5-speed OD manual	22.4	25.7

Built in Japan

RETAIL PRICES

	GOOD	AVERAGE	POOR
1990 Integra	$1,400-2,500	$900-1,900	$200-600
1991 Integra	1,800-3,200	1,200-2,600	400-1,000
1992 Integra	2,500-4,000	1,800-3,300	600-1,400
1992 Integra GS-R	3,500-4,400	2,700-3,600	1,100-1,800
1993 Integra	3,200-4,800	2,500-4,000	1,000-2,000
1993 Integra GS-R	4,400-5,500	3,600-4,500	1,700-2,400

AVERAGE REPLACEMENT COSTS

A/C Compressor	$600	Constant Velocity Joints	720
Alternator	420	Exhaust System	505
Automatic Transmission or		Radiator	380
Transaxle	895	Shocks and/or Struts	620
Brakes	195	Timing Chain or Belt	225

TROUBLE SPOTS

- **Automatic transmission.** Cars with automatic transmissions may not upshift, shift erratically, or suffer from no kickdown. The problem is debris in the modulator valve that sticks open flooding the shift solenoids.

- **Clutch.** Cars with manual transmissions may suffer from short clutch life. Acura issued a revised clutch disc and pressure plate that wear longer.

- **Oil leak.** Oil behind power steering bracket is caused by a leaking camshaft seal. Chances are the timing belt is also contaminated by the oil and should be replaced.

- **Vehicle noise.** Squeaking noises may come from the rear of the car when going over bumps or speed bumps. The fix involves placing shims between the two rubber halves of the trailing arm bushings.

- **Brakes.** The antilock brake modulator solenoid was prone to leaks,

which sets an ABS trouble code number 1.

- **Hard starting.** The fuel pressure regulator may fail causing hard starting.

- **Alarm system.** The security system controller picks up stray interference, which can make it malfunction so that the car will not start. The ROM chip in the controller must be replaced.

RECALL HISTORY

1990-91: Front seatbelt release button can break and pieces can fall inside, causing improper operation.

1994-01 ACURA INTEGRA

1995 Acura Integra GS-R 4-door sedan

FOR Fuel economy • Acceleration (5-speed models) • Steering/handling • Roadholding • Antilock brakes (LS, GS-R)

AGAINST Acceleration (automatic transmission) • Rear-seat room • No antilock brakes (RS) • Tire noise

EVALUATION Integra engines rev like crazy, but lack enough low-end torque to perform with much zest with the automatic transmission. All Integras are swift with the 5-speed. When equipped with the automatic, progress slows considerably and the transmission constantly shifts between gears. Fuel economy is great. Our test LS averaged nearly 25 mpg in city/freeway driving, and a GS-R yielded an even more frugal 28.3 mpg. Both engines generate lots of noise at higher speeds, but cruise quietly. Tire hum is evident on all but mirror-smooth surfaces. Each Integra corners adeptly, with a bit less body lean than before and almost no front-drive "plowing," helped by sharp steering. The ride is slightly smoother than before, and the car's overall "feel" stouter. However, hatchbacks in particular still tend to bounce and jiggle on freeways, due in part to their shorter wheelbase. If you're fortunate enough to get your hands on a 1997 or '98 "Type-R" Integra, or the revived 2000 edition, you'll be in for the ride of your life. This limited-production model comes equipped with a highly modified 195-horsepower version of the 1.8-liter GS-R engine, sport-tuned suspension, and meaty 195/55VR/15 tires. Expect brisk acceleration, in the mid-6s. Built for performance, the Type-R omits some creature comforts (A/C for instance) and sound insulation to lose weight. Consequently, expect a noisier and bouncier ride than you get in other Integra models. Passenger space in the hatchback models isn't as good as in the Honda Civic hatchback. Medium-size people will fit fine up front, but only preteens are welcome in back. Because of its longer wheelbase, the sedan is roomier and more practical for buyers who often carry more than one passenger. Cargo room in the coupe is unexceptional. The glovebox offers scant space for anything other than the owner's manual. You can expect fine interior ergonomics and gauges in a typical Honda/Acura dashboard.

VALUE Any Integra should be reliable, but high resale value means they're not cheap secondhand. A Honda Civic actually offers many of the Integra's appealing features, at a considerably lower price.

SPECIFICATIONS

	2-door hatchback	4-door sedan
Wheelbase, in.	101.2	103.1
Overall length, in.	172.4	178.1
Overall width, in.	67.3	67.3
Overall height, in.	52.6	53.9
Curb weight, lbs.	2529	2628
Cargo volume, cu. ft.	13.0	11.0

	2-door hatchback	4-door sedan
Fuel capacity, gals.	13.2	13.2
Seating capacity	4	5
Front head room, in.	38.6	38.9
Max. front leg room, in.	42.7	42.2
Rear head room, in.	35.0	36.0
Min. rear leg room, in.	28.1	32.7

Powertrain layout: transverse front-engine/front-wheel drive

ENGINES

	dohc I4	dohc I4	dohc I4[1]
Size, liters/cu. in.	1.8/112	1.8/109	1.8/110
Horsepower	142	170	195
Torque (lbs./ft.)	127	128	130
EPA city/highway mpg			
5-speed OD manual	25/31	25/31	25/31
4-speed OD automatic	24/31		
City/highway mpg (as tested)			
5-speed OD manual	25.0	28.3	25.7

1. This highly modified Integra engine is only available on limited-production Type-R models, and comes mated to a 5-speed manual transmission. No Type-R models were available in 1999.

Built in Japan

RETAIL PRICES

	GOOD	AVERAGE	POOR
1994 Integra RS, LS	$4,500-5,700	$3,700-4,800	$1,600-2,400
1994 Integra GS-R	6,000-7,000	5,200-6,000	2,500-3,200
1995 Integra RS	5,700-6,500	4,800-5,600	2,200-2,800
1995 Integra LS, SE	6,200-8,000	5,300-7,000	2,500-3,600
1995 Integra GS-R	7,700-8,700	6,700-7,700	3,500-4,300
1996 Integra RS	7,200-8,000	6,200-7,000	3,000-3,800
1996 Integra LS, SE	8,200-9,800	7,200-8,800	3,800-5,000
1996 Integra GS-R	9,500-10,500	8,500-9,500	5,000-5,800
1997 Integra RS	8,700-9,700	7,700-8,700	4,200-5,000
1997 Integra LS, GS	10,000-11,200	9,000-10,200	5,500-6,500
1997 Integra GS-R	11,000-12,000	10,000-11,000	6,300-7,200
1997 Type-R Coupe	12,500-13,500	11,300-12,200	7,300-8,000
1998 Integra RS	10,000-11,000	9,000-10,000	5,500-6,400
1998 Integra LS, GS	11,300-12,700	10,300-11,500	6,500-7,500
1998 Integra GS-R	12,500-13,500	11,300-12,300	7,300-8,100
1998 Type-R Coupe	14,000-15,500	12,800-14,000	8,500-9,500
1999 Integra LS, GS	12,000-13,500	11,000-12,500	7,000-8,000
1999 Integra GS-R	13,500-15,000	12,200-13,500	8,000-9,000
2000 Integra LS, GS	14,000-15,500	13,000-14,300	8,500-9,500
2000 Integra GS-R	15,500-17,000	14,000-15,500	9,500-10,500
2000 Type-R Coupe	18,000-19,500	16,500-18,000	11,500-12,500
2001 Integra LS, GS	16,000-17,500	14,800-16,000	—
2001 Integra GS-R	17,500-19,000	16,000-17,500	—
2001 Type-R Coupe	19,500-21,000	18,000-19,500	—

AVERAGE REPLACEMENT COSTS

A/C Compressor	$530	Clutch, Pressure Plate, Bearing	580
Alternator	420	Constant Velocity Joints	480
Automatic Transmission or Transaxle	895	Exhaust System	505
Brakes	195	Radiator	380
Shocks and/or Struts	620	Timing Chain or Belt	255

TROUBLE SPOTS

• **Air conditioner.** The air conditioner may stop working because the drive belt has come off the pulley.

• **Trunk latch.** The rear hatch may be hard to close because the rubber stops are too tall. (1994-95)

RECALL HISTORY

1994: Retaining clip at automatic transmission can come off, so position of lever does not match actual transmission gear range.

1991-95 ACURA LEGEND

FOR Antilock brakes • Acceleration • Steering/handling • Instruments/controls • Passenger and cargo room

AGAINST Fuel economy • Rear-seat room (coupe) • Automatic transmission performance • Driver seating

1993 Acura Legend GS 4-door sedan

EVALUATION The higher-powered V6 engine in these Legends yields quick acceleration, but gas mileage is no bonus. Our tests ranged from 16-18 mpg in urban driving to the low 20s on the highway. Despite the momentary ignition-retard setup of the automatic transmission, midrange downshifts in earlier models still border on harsh and can get rough under hard acceleration. Performance also slips quite a bit with automatic. Ride quality is smoother and more absorbent than before. The taut ride is never harsh, but falls short of the suppleness displayed by some European rivals. Though stable, it can get harsh and abrupt over rough surfaces. Handling earns high marks, nearly like that of a sports car. Quick turns bring some body lean, but grip, balance, and control are laudable. Standard antilocking makes the brakes feel strong and secure. Though roomier in back than before, this is still essentially a spacious 4-seater. Front-seat occupants might lack head room with the sunroof, or find that the early nontilting, telescoping steering wheel crowds one's thighs. Leg room in the coupe's back seat is scant, and long doors hamper access. Trunks are hardly huge, but have a flat floor and handy bumper-height opening. Instruments and controls are logical, with a feather-touch feel.

VALUE Sporty manners, copious luxury (on LS), worthy workmanship, and stout construction help the Legend rival some more costly premium automobiles—including those from Infiniti and Lexus.

SPECIFICATIONS

	2-door coupe	4-door sedan
Wheelbase, in.	111.4	114.6
Overall length, in.	192.5	194.9
Overall width, in.	71.3	71.3
Overall height, in.	53.5	55.1
Curb weight, lbs.	3516	3516
Cargo volume, cu. ft.	14.1	14.8
Fuel capacity, gals.	18.0	18.0
Seating capacity	5	5
Front head room, in.	37.3	38.5
Max. front leg room, in.	42.9	42.7
Rear head room, in.	35.9	36.5
Min. rear leg room, in.	28.7	33.5

Powertrain layout: transverse front-engine/front-wheel drive

ENGINES

	ohc V6	ohc V6
Size, liters/cu. in.	3.2/196	3.2/196
Horsepower	200	230
Torque (lbs./ft.)	210	206
EPA city/highway mpg		
5-speed OD manual	18/25	
6-speed OD manual		18/26
4-speed OD automatic	19/24	18/23
City/highway mpg (as tested)		
4-speed OD automatic	19.2	20.2

Built in Japan

RETAIL PRICES

	GOOD	AVERAGE	POOR
1991 Legend coupe	$4,200-5,500	$3,400-4,600	$1,400-2,000
1991 Legend sedan	3,400-4,500	2,600-3,700	900-1,400
1992 Legend coupe	5,500-6,700	4,500-5,700	2,200-2,900
1992 Legend sedan	4,500-5,800	3,500-4,800	1,500-2,300
1993 Legend coupe	7,000-8,500	6,000-7,500	3,500-4,500
1993 Legend sedan	5,800-7,500	4,800-6,500	2,500-3,300
1994 Legend coupe	9,000-10,500	8,000-9,500	5,000-6,000
1994 Legend sedan	7,500-9,000	6,500-8,000	3,800-4,800
1995 Legend coupe	11,000-13,000	9,800-11,500	6,200-7,200
1995 Legend sedan	9,500-11,500	8,400-10,200	5,200-6,500

AVERAGE REPLACEMENT COSTS

A/C Compressor...........	$715	Clutch, Pressure Plate,	
Alternator.....................	360	Bearing	965
Automatic Transmission or		Constant Velocity Joints	555
Transaxle	1,005	Exhaust System	810
Brakes	200	Radiator.......................	530
Shocks and/or Struts....	895	Timing Chain or Belt.....	300

TROUBLE SPOTS

• **Engine noise.** Carbon buildup on the piston rings may cause piston slap. The fix is to clean the carbon using GM Top Engine Cleaner sucked in by way of a vacuum port on the throttle body.

• **Poor transmission shift.** Debris collects on the screen in the engine's air intake causing poor acceleration (all models) or lack of upshift (automatic transmission) at full throttle. (1991-94)

• **Audio system.** If the remote volume control doesn't work, or there is static when the remote is used, the volume control motor inside the radio is bad. (1991-92)

• **Steering problems.** Steering may be difficult during parking maneuvers due to a problem with the vehicle speed sensor in the power steering unit. (1991-94)

• **Steering noise.** Telescopic steering columns may groan when the wheel is turned because there is not enough lubrication on the column.

• **Cruise control.** The cruise control may not engage on 1994 models due to a faulty actuator.

• **Glove box.** The glove box light stays on because the switch plunger is too short, requiring an extension cap over the plunger to prevent a dead battery. (1991-92)

• **Security alarm.** The security alarm may not deactivate with the key in the driver's door, which sets off the alarm. Turning the key again may disarm it.

• **Steering problems.** The vehicle speed sensor (VSS) tends to fail, but a repair kit has been released so that the whole power steering assembly need not be replaced. (1991-94)

RECALL HISTORY

1991 sedan: Transmission shift cable bracket can be damaged and shift lever may not correctly indicate gear position. **1991-92 w/Bose audio:** A transistor in the speaker amplifier could overheat, resulting in smoke or the possibility of a fire. **1992:** Passenger-side airbag assembly in small number of cars was produced without igniter material, which would cause nondeployment or slow deployment in case of collision.

1996-01 ACURA RL

1998 Acura 3.5RL

FOR Acceleration • Handling • Ride • Quietness

AGAINST Rear head room • Steering feel

EVALUATION Despite the fact that the RL does not feel as snappy as the lighter-weight Legend, this sedan is much more luxurious. It also feels markedly stronger at low speeds, though overall acceleration ranks as good rather than great for a premium sedan. Our test RS accelerated to 60 mph in just over 8 seconds—swift for a relatively heavy sedan. The V6 engine is hushed at cruising speeds and emits a subdued, rich-sounding snarl during hard acceleration. Wind and tire noise also are modest. Gas mileage isn't bad, though the RL demands premium fuel. We averaged 19.8 mpg, with half of our driving on the highway. On-the-road performance is generally a pleasure. The RL simply sails over potholes, ruts, and other irregu-

larities with impressive solidity and no hint of shudder or rattle. Ride quality is firm yet supple and comfortable. The RL is agile for a large sedan. Despite its abundant exterior dimensions, the sedan handles like a smaller automobile. Steering is quick and precise, but it's too light and lacks feel around the center position of the wheel. Body lean is modest in tight corners. Brakes produce short, straight stops from high speeds. The driver gets a comfortable, easily tailored-to-suit position with a clear view all around. Controls are large, well positioned, and intuitive. Rear leg and knee room are greater than in the Legend. In the back seat, 6-footers will find their heads just brushing the roof, but front head space is ample. The interior offers plenty of spaces for odd items, and the flat-floored trunk is usefully shaped. Acura's optional on-board navigation system is accurate and easy to use, but fingerprints and certain light conditions can render its display almost unreadable at times.

VALUE All told, the 3.5RL is a pleasant luxury sedan, solid and well constructed, which does everything quite well. Few would ask for anything more on a lengthy journey. Though filled with luxury touches, too, the RL does not feel particularly ostentatious.

SPECIFICATIONS

	4-door sedan
Wheelbase, in.	114.6
Overall length, in.	195.1
Overall width, in.	71.3
Overall height, in.	56.6
Curb weight, lbs.	3660
Cargo volume, cu. ft.	14.0
Fuel capacity, gals.	18.0
Seating capacity	5
Front head room, in.	38.6
Max. front leg room, in.	42.2
Rear head room, in.	36.7
Min. rear leg room, in.	35.5

Powertrain layout: longitudinal front-engine/front-wheel drive

ENGINES

	ohc V6
Size, liters/cu. in.	3.5/212
Horsepower	210
Torque (lbs./ft.)	224

EPA city/highway mpg
4-speed OD automatic	19/25

City/highway mpg (as tested)
4-speed OD automatic	19.8

Built in Japan

RETAIL PRICES	GOOD	AVERAGE	POOR
1996 3.5 RL	$14,000-15,000	$12,800-13,800	$9,200-10,000
1996 3.5 RL Premium	15,000-16,000	13,800-14,800	9,900-10,800
1997 3.5 RL	17,000-18,000	15,500-16,500	11,500-12,400
1997 3.5 RL Premium	18,000-19,200	16,500-17,700	12,000-13,000
1998 3.5 RL	21,000-22,500	19,500-21,000	15,000-16,000
1998 3.5 RL Premium	22,000-23,500	20,500-22,000	16,000-17,000
1999 3.5 RL	25,000-26,500	23,500-25,000	19,000-20,000
1999 3.5 RL Premium	26,200-27,500	24,700-26,000	20,000-21,000
2000 3.5 RL	29,000-30,500	27,500-29,000	22,500-23,800
2000 3.5 RL Premium	30,200-31,700	28,700-30,200	24,500-25,500
2001 3.5 RL	33,000-34,500	31,500-33,000	—
2001 3.5 RL Premium	34,200-35,500	32,700-34,000	—

AVERAGE REPLACEMENT COSTS

A/C Compressor...........	$765	Clutch, Pressure Plate,	
Alternator.....................	490	Bearing	715
Automatic Transmission or		Constant Velocity Joints	1,010
Transaxle	1,020	Exhaust System	360
Brakes	180	Radiator.......................	610
Shocks and/or Struts....	460	Timing Chain or Belt.....	230

TROUBLE SPOTS

• **Seatbelts/safety.** The button that prevents the seatbelt tongue from sliding to the floor breaks. (1996-98)

• **Seat.** The driver's seat may rock because the bolts in the motor that controls the up/down movement come loose. (1996)

• **Speedometer.** The speedometer may read higher than actual speed. (1996)

RECALL HISTORY

1996-98: Ball joints on certain cars could wear out prematurely and, in worst case, separate and cause front suspension to collapse. **1996-99:** Bolt can loosen and fall out, allowing transmission to disengage from differential. Not only would the vehicle lose power to drive wheels without warning, but shifting into "Park" would not lock the wheels.

1996-99 ACURA SLX

1997 Acura SLX

FOR Passenger room • Cargo room

AGAINST Fuel economy • Ride • Entry/exit

EVALUATION An SLX offers plenty of room for people and cargo, though the tall step-up height makes entry/exit a chore. Acceleration in early models is more than adequate, and the engine is generally smooth and quiet. Fuel economy ranks as dismal. We averaged just 12.6 mpg in a mix of urban commuting and expressway cruising. An early Isuzu Trooper got 15.5 mpg with a lot of highway driving. The power boost of 1998-99 was immediately evident, and most welcome. A driver could now step away from a stop with swiftness that the prior 3.2-liter engine could not muster. Changing engines, the SLX also lost its slightly ponderous feeling during in-town driving. The infusion of torque coaxes prompter, more effective downshifting from the automatic transmission for highway passing. EPA gas-mileage estimates were unchanged with the new V6. An SLX suspension provides a stable highway ride, but does not soak up the big bumps all that well. Also, the ride feels harsh over rough pavement. Body roll is quite evident in tight turns. Power steering is slow and numb, too. Braking is good, but stopping distances are not exceptionally short. That's not exactly a surprise, considering the amount of weight that's being brought to a halt. Like Trooper, Acura's SLX is one of the roomiest SUVs around. You can expect plenty of head clearance, in both front and rear. The back seat is wide enough to fit three adults without squeezing.The tall build combines with large windows for fine visibility. Unfortunately, the steering wheel sits at a buslike angle that takes some getting used to. Some minor controls seem haphazardly placed.

VALUE All told, the SLX delivers a hefty, rugged feel. Excellent detail workmanship is evident throughout the vehicle. Abundant passenger and cargo room and solid construction are also definite "pluses." With the stronger 1998-99 engine, the SLX feels more competitive. Still, it doesn't rate as high in our estimation as a Chevrolet Tahoe or Ford Expedition. Many other alternatives might be considered, from the Ford Explorer to a Jeep Grand Cherokee or Land Rover Discovery.

SPECIFICATIONS

	4-door wagon
Wheelbase, in.	108.7
Overall length, in.	183.5
Overall width, in.	72.4
Overall height, in.	72.2
Curb weight, lbs.	4315
Cargo volume, cu. ft.	90.2
Fuel capacity, gals.	22.5
Seating capacity	5
Front head room, in.	39.8
Max. front leg room, in.	40.8
Rear head room, in.	39.8
Min. rear leg room, in.	39.1

Powertrain layout: longitudinal front-engine/4-wheel drive

ENGINES

	ohc V6	dohc V6
Size, liters/cu. in.	3.2/193	3.5/214
Horsepower	190	215
Torque (lbs./ft.)	188	230
EPA city/highway mpg		
4-speed OD automatic	14/18	14/18
City/highway mpg (as tested)		
4-speed OD automatic	12.6	14.5

Built in Japan

RETAIL PRICES

	GOOD	AVERAGE	POOR
1996 SLX	$9,000-10,000	$8,000-9,000	$5,200-6,000
1996 SLX Premium	10,000-11,200	9,000-10,200	6,000-6,800
1997 SLX	11,000-12,000	10,000-11,000	7,000-7,800
1997 SLX Premium	12,000-13,200	11,000-12,000	7,800-8,600
1998 SLX	13,500-14,800	12,300-13,500	8,500-9,500
1998 SLX Premium	14,500-16,000	13,000-14,500	9,000-10,000
1999 SLX	16,000-17,500	14,500-16,000	10,500-11,500
1999 SLX Premium	17,500-19,000	16,000-17,500	11,500-12,500

AVERAGE REPLACEMENT COSTS

A/C Compressor	$640	Clutch, Pressure Plate, Bearing	700
Alternator	445		
Automatic Transmission or Transaxle	1,020	Constant Velocity Joints	1,250
		Exhaust System	500
Brakes	575	Radiator	695
Shocks and/or Struts	1,180	Timing Chain or Belt	400

TROUBLE SPOTS

• **Vehicle noise.** A buzzing noise from the A-pillar (between the windshield and door) requires resealing with silicone sealant between the molding and pillar. (1996)

• **Vehicle noise.** If there is not enough limited slip additive in the rear differential, it chatters and vibrates when cornering. (1996-99)

• **Dashboard lights.** The 4WD indicator light may stay on due to problems with the vacuum solenoid valves that must be replaced. (1996-97)

• **Dashboard lights.** The four-wheel-drive indicator stays on when the vehicle is in two-wheel drive. (1996-97)

• **Doors.** The rubber molding between the doors and front pillar (A-pillar) comes loose and makes a buzzing noise. (1996)

• **Vehicle shake.** Vibration and chattering when cornering is usually due to lack of limited-slip differential (LSD) additive in the rear differential. (1996-99)

RECALL HISTORY

1996: Certain vehicles were built with incorrect rear center seatbelt buckle; tongue cannot be inserted. **1996-97:** Left front brake line can be damaged, resulting in fluid leakage, reduced brake effectiveness, and longer stopping distance. **1998:** Improperly-installed transfer gearbox nuts may loosen; propeller shaft can then separate, resulting in sudden loss of drive to wheels and possible damage to critical components.

1996-98 ACURA TL

1996 Acura 2.5TL

FOR Antilock brakes • Acceleration (3.2TL) • Steering/handling • Instruments/controls • Visibility

AGAINST Automatic transmission performance • Road noise (3.2TL) • Engine noise (2.5TL) • Rear-seat room

EVALUATION Superior in road behavior, both versions of the TL handle well and inspire confidence, helped by precise, neatly assisted steering with ample feedback, plus fine high-speed braking. Front-drive cornering is predictable, with modest body lean and good grip. With less weight up front, the 2.5TL tends to corner with a crisper feel and slightly less understeer. Each model rides well, the fully independent suspension delivering solid comfort and taut control while smoothing out the rough spots with ease. Road noise is most prominent in the 3.2TL.The automatic transmission is slow to kick down for passing. Also, its "Grade Logic" feature sometimes drops down a gear or two, whether you want it to or not. Though generally smooth, the 5-cylinder engine gets noisy when worked hard, emitting a coarse, throaty growl. Though not a slouch, it delivers only adequate pickup. Acceleration off-the-line is a bit lethargic, but the 2.5TL passes and merges quite quickly. Somewhat lumpy at idle, it's not as smooth as the silky, quiet V6 in the 3.2TL, which promises greater performance. Gas mileage is close to average for this league. In a mix of city, suburban, and highway driving, we managed 19.2 mpg with a 2.5TL and 18.3 mpg from the 3.2TL. Both engines demand premium gasoline, however. Interior space overall ranks as adequate rather than generous—unexceptional for the car's size, partly as a result of the typical Acura low profile. Head room is just adequate for 6-footers. The same is true of rear leg space, though it's five inches larger than in the prior Vigor. Not every driver and passenger might be delighted with seat comfort—especially the occupant of the center rear position, who must endure a hard seat and straddle a tall tunnel. Despite the low-slung styling, a glassy greenhouse with thin pillars produces easy viewing all around. Entry/exit is easy and the driving position is accommodating, facing fine instruments and controls.

VALUE Although these TL sedans are well-constructed, pleasant, and better than the previous Vigor in every way, they still fail to overshadow the competition in the midluxury league.

SPECIFICATIONS

	4-door sedan
Wheelbase, in.	111.8
Overall length, in.	191.5
Overall width, in.	70.3
Overall height, in.	55.3
Curb weight, lbs.	3252
Cargo volume, cu. ft.	14.1
Fuel capacity, gals.	17.2
Seating capacity	5
Front head room, in.	39.1
Max. front leg room, in.	43.7
Rear head room, in.	36.9
Min. rear leg room, in.	35.2

Powertrain layout: longitudinal front-engine/front-wheel drive

ENGINES

	ohc I5	ohc V6
Size, liters/cu. in.	2.5/152	3.2/196
Horsepower	176	200
Torque (lbs./ft.)	170	210
EPA city/highway mpg		
4-speed OD automatic	20/25	19/24
City/highway mpg (as tested)		
4-speed OD automatic	19.2	18.3

Built in Japan

RETAIL PRICES

	GOOD	AVERAGE	POOR
1996 2.5TL	$10,500-12,000	$9,500-11,000	$6,500-7,500
1996 3.2TL	12,200-13,700	11,200-12,700	8,000-9,000
1997 2.5TL	12,200-14,000	11,200-13,000	8,000-9,200
1997 3.2TL	14,200-16,000	13,200-15,000	9,500-10,800
1998 2.5TL	15,000-16,500	13,800-15,000	10,000-11,200
1998 3.2TL	17,000-18,500	15,800-17,000	11,800-12,800

AVERAGE REPLACEMENT COSTS

A/C Compressor	$725	Clutch, Pressure Plate, Bearing	1,010
Alternator	395	Constant Velocity Joints	810
Automatic Transmission or Transaxle	1,270	Exhaust System	610
Brakes	215	Radiator	445
Shocks and/or Struts	995	Timing Chain or Belt	230

TROUBLE SPOTS

- **Steering problems.** Power steering pump leaks because the pump shaft was not machined properly causing the seal to wear. (1996)
- **Audio system.** Radio interference is caused by the ignition coils. (1996-97)
- **Audio system.** The grille cloth pulls loose from the tweeter (speaker). (1995-96)
- **Vehicle noise.** Wind noise from the moonroof. (1996)

RECALL HISTORY

1996-98 3.2: Bolt can loosen and fall out, allowing transmission to disengage from differential. Not only would the vehicle lose power to drive wheels without warning, but shifting into "Park" would not lock the wheels. **1996-98:** Ball joints on certain cars could wear out prematurely and, in worst case, separate and cause front suspension to collapse.

1999-01 ACURA TL

2000 Acura 3.2TL

FOR Acceleration • Steering/handling • Build quality • Exterior finish • Interior materials

AGAINST Navigation system controls • Climate controls

EVALUATION Quick, quiet, and composed, the TL is a seriously polished performer with a smooth powertrain that takes an athletic approach to luxury. Acceleration is competitive, revealed by a 0-60 time of 8.2 seconds with an early model. Added sportiness stems from the exceptionally quick-shifting automatic/manual transmission. The five-speed automatic introduced for 2000 provides more relaxed cruising than many four-speed units, and also subtly improves acceleration. Impressive road manners include unerring high-speed stability, plus terrific grip and control in turns. The downside is a ride that's much firmer than such less-nimble competitors as the ES 300 and I30. Tire rumble and slap are more prominent than most rivals, but not objectionable. Engine and wind noise are low. Braking is swift and stable, but with more nosedive than expected. The driving position is low and sporty, but accommodating, in a cabin that feels roomier and more comfortable than before. Adults can stretch out in front. Back-seaters get good headroom and ample toe clearance, but only adequate leg space. Seat cushions offer unexceptional thigh support, but the driving position is set-and-forget comfortable. Gauges are large and legible, visibility unobstructed. Climate controls are far from the driver and, with the optional navigation system, inadequately sized and illuminated in an otherwise thoughtful layout. The navigation system is useful, but covers only selected U.S. population centers, and the touch screen is susceptible to fingerprints. Storage space is generous, though the trunklid hinges intrude into the cargo area.

VALUE Solidly built and impeccably finished, the TL equals or exceeds anything in its class for quality and utility. Its sporty nature should please the most demanding driver, though at risk of turning away entry-luxury buyers who expect Lexus-like isolation. With so many features for the price, the value-packed TL ranked as a Best Buy when new.

SPECIFICATIONS

	4-door sedan
Wheelbase, in.	108.1
Overall length, in.	192.9
Overall width, in.	70.3
Overall height, in.	55.7
Curb weight, lbs.	3447

	4-door sedan
Cargo volume, cu. ft.	14.3
Fuel capacity, gals.	17.2
Seating capacity	5
Front head room, in.	39.9
Max. front leg room, in.	42.4
Rear head room, in.	36.8
Min. rear leg room, in.	35.0

Powertrain layout: transverse front-engine/front-wheel drive

ENGINES

	ohc V6
Size, liters/cu. in.	3.2/196
Horsepower	225
Torque (lbs./ft.)	216

EPA city/highway mpg

4-speed OD automatic	19/27
5-speed OD automatic	19/29

City/highway mpg (as tested)

4-speed OD automatic	19.3

Built in USA

RETAIL PRICES

	GOOD	AVERAGE	POOR
1999 TL	$20,500-21,500	$19,500-20,500	$16,000-17,000
2000 TL	22,500-24,000	21,000-23,000	18,000-19,000
2001 TL	25,000-27,000	24,000-26,000	—

AVERAGE REPLACEMENT COSTS

A/C Compressor	$720	Constant Velocity Joints	820
Alternator	355	Exhaust System	950
Automatic Transmission or		Radiator	610
Transaxle	1,350	Shocks and/or Struts	1,495
Brakes	450	Timing Chain or Belt	400

TROUBLE SPOTS

• **Keyless entry.** Certain broadcast towers interfere with the keyless entry transmitter rendering it inoperative. (1999)

• **Fuel gauge.** Some higher-sulfer gasolines can damages the fuel gauge sending unit causing the gauge to display inaccurate readings. (1999)

• **Wipers.** The wipers streak/smear because washer fluid deteriorates the hoses. Replacement of the hoses and wiper blades is required. (1999-2001)

RECALL HISTORY

2000-01: Damaged vehicle may not have been repaired with the correct seatbelt buckles.

1992-94 ACURA VIGOR

1992 Acura Vigor GS

FOR Antilock brakes • Acceleration • Steering/handling • Cargo room

AGAINST Rear-seat room • Engine/road noise

EVALUATION Vigor's acceleration is strong, especially with the precise 5-speed manual shift. In fact, Vigor can push you back in your seat when tromping the gas toward the engine's 6800-rpm redline, but it's rather noisy in the process and suffers from vibration as well. In our tests of a model with the automatic, the Vigor reached 60 mph in just 8.8 seconds. Shifts with the early 4-speed automatic can get rough, sometimes lurching into a lower gear when stomping the gas pedal. Fuel mileage isn't bad, if unexceptional. We averaged 22.5 mpg with manual shift, but premium fuel is required. Agile handling and fine braking ability earn praise. So does the car's great outward view, plus satisfying detail finish. Body lean is moderate and the ride is satisfyingly flat, though the firm suspension delivers some jolts when going over poor pavement. Braking can be a tad touchy, but the antilock system works well. Tire noise could annoy, rumbling intrusively through most surfaces. The driver sits low, facing a dashboard with easy-to-read analog gauges. Interior controls are logical, smooth-working, and well within reach. Leg room is tight in back, and taller drivers may have trouble with head room in the front seat on models equipped with a sunroof. The Vigor's trunk is flat and roomy, extending far forward.

VALUE Vigors are not necessarily cheap, even today, but at least you get a load of Honda/Acura virtues. Therefore, Vigors are worth a look if you're searching for a moderately-posh, older midsize 4-door sedan that also promises a dash of sportiness.

SPECIFICATIONS

	4-door sedan
Wheelbase, in.	110.4
Overall length, in.	190.4
Overall width, in.	70.1
Overall height, in.	53.9
Curb weight, lbs.	3150
Cargo volume, cu. ft.	14.2
Fuel capacity, gals.	17.2
Seating capacity	5
Front head room, in.	38.8
Max. front leg room, in.	43.7
Rear head room, in.	36.2
Min. rear leg room, in.	30.3

Powertrain layout: longitudinal front-engine/front-wheel drive

ENGINES

	ohc I5
Size, liters/cu. in.	2.5/152
Horsepower	176
Torque (lbs./ft.)	170

EPA city/highway mpg

5-speed OD manual	20/27
4-speed OD automatic	20/26

City/highway mpg (as tested)

5-speed OD manual	22.5

Built in Japan

RETAIL PRICES

	GOOD	AVERAGE	POOR
1992 Vigor	$3,300-4,000	$2,600-3,200	$1,000-1,500
1993 Vigor	4,500-5,500	3,600-4,500	1,800-2,300
1994 Vigor	6,000-7,100	5,000-6,100	2,600-3,300

AVERAGE REPLACEMENT COSTS

A/C Compressor	$690	Clutch, Pressure Plate,	
Alternator	385	Bearing	675
Automatic Transmission or		Constant Velocity Joints	405
Transaxle	1,195	Exhaust System	610
Brakes	215	Radiator	525
Shocks and/or Struts	960	Timing Chain or Belt	215

TROUBLE SPOTS

• **Climate control.** A blower that operates only on high speed and makes a whistling sound probably has a blown power transistor caused by a bad commutator ring in the blower motor. (1992)

• **Steering problems.** If the car drifts to one side at highway speeds, the alignment may be incorrect and is corrected by loosening the transmission mount bolt and subframe bolts and shifting the subframe. (1992)

• **Hard starting.** If the engine is hard to start, the original owner may not have responded to the letter requesting that they have a redesigned distributor cap and engine harness cover installed. (1993)

• **Brakes.** If the parking brake doesn't release, a rivet on the handle must be loosened. (1993-94)

• **Doors.** Over time, the door lock actuator switch gets corroded which causes the alarm to go off when the door is unlocked and opened. (1992-93)

• **Doors.** The linkage separates inside the door if the rear door handle is pulled hard. (1992)

1993-98 AUDI 90/CABRIOLET

1993 Audi 90 S 4-door sedan

FOR Antilock brakes • Steering/handling • Wet-weather traction (Quattro) • Fuel economy

AGAINST Acceleration (automatic) • Road noise • Rear-seat room • Automatic transmission performance

EVALUATION Though a smooth runner, and a lot zippier than its predecessor when equipped with 5-speed manual shift, the V6 Audi lags in off-the-line acceleration with 4-speed automatic. Without a doubt, the engine runs smoothly and quietly, and power delivery is very linear. However, that automatic transmission drains the engine's ability to deliver quick bursts of speed in around-town driving. The automatic also shifts rather abruptly and tends to hold each gear too long. Audi's 5-speed gearbox, on the other hand, is smooth and precise. So is the car's clutch. The V6 engine demands premium fuel, though mileage is good. Expect plenty of tire and suspension noise on any imperfect surfaces, plus a ride that's a bit too firm on harsh urban pavements. Tar strips and small bumps do not go unnoticed, though bigger obstacles are taken in stride. Stable handling from the taut suspension imparts a secure feeling at highway speeds, with good grip in hard corners. The dashboard layout is businesslike, with clear audio and climate controls, plus a large round speedometer and tachometer. Interiors look a bit austere in the 90 S, but CS versions with their wood accents appear somewhat dressier. Either way, the materials that are used impart an impression of quality. Most drivers are likely to feel comfortable behind the wheel. Seats are firm and supportive, with height adjustments for the shoulder belt and lower cushion. Despite the longer wheelbase, interior dimensions are virtually identical to the previous model, but trunk space grew from 10.2 to 14.0 cubic feet, increasing its utility. Front-seat space is ample, but the rear lacks leg room, giving the interior a rather cramped ambience. Cabriolets look great but suffer from excessive body shake and flex on bumpy roads—out of character for the car's hefty price when new (and used, too). Performance is acceptable in day-to-day driving, but the lack of low-speed power and imperfect shift action makes it feel lethargic. Front seat space is adequate for average-size adults, and head room beats most convertibles. The rear seat is useful only for children. Controls are well-positioned, but the radio has too many small, poorly marked controls. Several competitors offer a glass rear window with electric defogger, in contrast to the Cabriolet's plastic pane. Recent models have been well-assembled. The "Audi Advantage" plan covered most routine maintenance for three years or 50,000 miles.

VALUE Audi's 90 had some attractive features, including a sporty manner (at least with the 5-speed), available 4-wheel drive, and solid feel. Nevertheless, it did not sell strongly in the "near-luxury" market, which was dominated by such Japanese-brand models as the Acura Vigor, Infiniti J30, Lexus ES 300, and Nissan Maxima SE. When these cars were new, dealers offered big discounts to spur sales, so expect to find lower-than-average used-car prices for all except convertibles and high-performance models.

SPECIFICATIONS

	2-door convertible	4-door sedan
Wheelbase, in.	100.6	102.8
Overall length, in.	176.0	180.3
Overall width, in.	67.6	66.7
Overall height, in.	54.3	54.3
Curb weight, lbs.	3494	3197
Cargo volume, cu. ft.	6.6	14.0
Fuel capacity, gals.	17.4	17.4
Seating capacity	4	5
Front head room, in.	38.3	37.8
Max. front leg room, in.	40.7	42.2
Rear head room, in.	36.4	37.2
Min. rear leg room, in.	26.5	32.5

Powertrain layout: longitudinal front-engine/front- or all-wheel drive

ENGINES

	ohc V6
Size, liters/cu. in.	2.8/169
Horsepower	172
Torque (lbs./ft.)	184
EPA city/highway mpg	
5-speed OD manual	20/26
4-speed OD automatic	18/26
City/highway mpg (as tested)	
4-speed OD automatic	18.7

Built in Germany

RETAIL PRICES

	GOOD	AVERAGE	POOR
1993 90 sedan	$3,800-4,600	$3,000-3,800	$1,300-1,900
1993 90 Quattro	5,000-60,00	4,200-5,100	2,200-2,700
1994 90 sedan	5,000-6,200	4,100-5,300	2,100-2,800
1994 90 Quattro	6,500-7,500	5,500-6,500	3,000-3,800
1994 Cabriolet	9,000-10,000	8,000-9,000	5,000-5,800
1995 90 sedan	6,300-7,300	5,300-6,300	2,900-3,600
1995 90 Quattro	7,800-8,800	6,800-7,800	4,000-4,700
1995 Cabriolet	11,000-12,200	10,000-11,000	6,500-7,400
1996 Cabriolet	13,000-14,500	12,000-13,000	8,000-9,000
1997 Cabriolet	16,000-17,500	14,500-16,000	10,000-11,000
1998 Cabriolet	19,000-20,500	17,500-19,000	12,000-13,000

AVERAGE REPLACEMENT COSTS

A/C Compressor	$1,040	Clutch, Pressure Plate, Bearing	975
Alternator	640	Constant Velocity Joints	680
Automatic Transmission or Transaxle	1,220	Exhaust System	550
Brakes	300	Exhaust System	450
Shocks and/or Struts	1,410	Timing Chain or Belt	240

TROUBLE SPOTS

• **Steering noise.** A clunk from the front when the steering wheel is turned is caused by a heat shield on the left motor mount that may be striking the bracket. (1993-94)

• **Climate control.** Intermittent climate control operation can be caused by a loose wire on the control center. (1993-94)

• **Oil leak.** On any model with the V6 engine, the rear main seal may leak. (1993-94)

• **Cruise control.** The cruise control may not maintain speed due to a defective vacuum servo unit. (1995)

• **Wipers.** The wiper blades skip or jerk across the windshield, which may damage the blades or scratch the windshield. (1993-96)

RECALL HISTORY

1993: Some airbag sensors do not comply with Audi's durability standards. **1993-95 w/V6 engine:** Internal seal of fuel injector can malfunction, allowing fuel leakage. **1994-96:** Defective ignition switch can cause some accessories (turn signals, lamps, wipers) to malfunction when engine is started. **1995-97:** Discharge of static electricity in low humidity conditions can activate driver's airbag when driver enters or exits car.

1996-01 AUDI A4

FOR Ride • Handling • Build quality • Optional all-wheel drive • Automatic transmission performance

AGAINST Rear-seat room • Steering feel

EVALUATION Despite changing little for 1996, Audi's V6 felt like a new engine when installed in the A4—smoother, quieter, and a lot more responsive. Although it's not the most potent V6 in the "near-luxury" league, it feels energetic most of the time and gets the job done nicely. Performance with the more potent dual-cam V6, installed in 1997, isn't dramatically better. Gear changes with the new 5-speed automatic transmission are so smooth that they virtually set new standards for the entire industry. Downshifts occur

1998 Audi A4 2.8 4-door sedan

promptly for passing, too. Tiptronic on the 1998 and beyond models makes an already-smooth transmission even better. Best bet for the turbocharged model is manual shift, though acceleration is adequate with automatic. With either engine, the manual gearbox is easy to operate. As for economy, an A4 1.8T Quattro yielded nearly 24 mpg on a long highway trip. On the downside, the turbo engine growls at higher speeds. Audi's Quattro all-wheel-drive system works without any driver input to provide excellent traction in slippery conditions. Still, front-drive models offer better gas mileage and have sufficient traction for most drivers. Road noise is generally pleasing in the A4, in contrast to the old 90. However, the car's aggressive high-performance tires generate considerable sound on rough pavement. Riding smoothly on rough roads, the A4's suspension easily soaks up dips and bumps. Body lean is well-controlled in hard cornering, with good tire grip and stable handling. An optional Sport Package, with a firmer suspension and higher-performance tires, sacrifices ride comfort for a small extra measure of cornering grip and handling agility. As for negative aspects, there are mainly two: over-assisted, somewhat numb power steering, and brakes that seem touchy at first. Passenger space is generally good, with plenty of room for large occupants up front. But tall people still don't have an abundance of leg room in back. Furthermore, head room all around is only adequate with the optional sunroof installed. Gauges and most controls are easy to see and intuitive to use, with the exception of the climate-control panel, which is too small and low for easy reading. Cargo space is good, but not great. Detail finish is superior inside and out. Interior materials are also mostly excellent.

VALUE Audi's A4 has sufficient merits to withstand comparison with the BMW 3-Series, Lexus ES 300, and Mercedes-Benz C-Class, putting it in good company at the low end of the premium sedan market. As for build quality, there's no more solid small sedan on the market than an A4.

SPECIFICATIONS

	4-door sedan	4-door wagon
Wheelbase, in.	103.0	103.0
Overall length, in.	178.0	176.7
Overall width, in.	68.2	68.2
Overall height, in.	55.8	56.7
Curb weight, lbs.	3087	3289
Cargo volume, cu. ft.	13.7	31.0-63.7
Fuel capacity, gals.	16.4	16.4
Seating capacity	5	5
Front head room, in.	38.1	38.1
Max. front leg room, in.	41.3	41.2
Rear head room, in.	36.8	37.8
Min. rear leg room, in.	33.4	33.3

Powertrain layout: longitudinal front-engine/front- or all-wheel drive

ENGINES

	Turbocharged dohc I4	ohc V6	dohc V6	Turbocharged dohc V6
Size, liters/cu. in.	1.8/107	2.8/169	2.8/169	2.7/163
Horsepower	150-170	172	190	250
Torque (lbs./ft.)	155-166	184	207	258
EPA city/highway mpg				
5-speed OD manual	23/25	19/27	20/27	
6-speed OD manual				17/24
5-speed OD automatic	21/30	18/28	18/28	17/24
City/highway mpg (as tested)				
5-speed OD manual	26.3	21.5		
6-speed OD manual				20.0
5-speed OD automatic	23.6		21.5	

Built in Germany

RETAIL PRICES

	GOOD	AVERAGE	POOR
1996 A4 2.8 sedan	$10,500-12,500	$9,500-11,500	$6,500-8,000
1997 A4 1.8T sedan	11,000-13,000	10,000-12,000	6,800-8,200
1997 A4 2.8 sedan	13,000-15,000	11,800-13,700	8,500-9,800
1998 A4 1.8T sedan	13,000-15,000	11,800-13,500	8,500-9,500
1998 A4 2.8 sedan	15,500-17,800	14,200-16,300	10,000-11,500
1998 A4 2.8 Avant wagon	16,800-19,000	15,500-17,500	11,000-12,500
1999 A4 1.8T sedan	15,700-18,500	14,500-17,200	10,200-12,000
1999 A4 2.8 sedan	18,500-21,000	17,000-19,500	12,500-14,500
1999 A4 1.8T Avant wagon	18,500-20,000	17,000-18,500	12,500-13,500
1999 A4 2.8 Avant wagon	21,500-23,500	20,000-22,000	15,000-16,500
2000 A4 1.8T sedan	18,000-20,500	16,700-19,000	12,000-13,800
2000 A4 2.8 sedan	21,000-23,500	19,500-22,000	14,500-16,500
2000 S4 sedan	29,000-31,000	27,000-29,000	20,000-21,500
2000 A4 1.8T Avant wagon	21,000-22,500	19,500-21,000	14,500-15,500
2000 A4 2.8 Avant wagon	24,000-26,000	22,000-24,000	16,500-18,000
2001 A4 1.8T sedan	20,000-22,500	18,500-21,000	—
2001 A4 2.8 sedan	23,000-25,500	21,500-24,000	—
2001 S4 sedan	32,000-34,000	30,000-32,000	—
2001 A4 1.8T Avant wagon	23,500-25,000	22,000-23,500	—
2001 A4 2.8 Avant wagon	26,000-28,000	24,000-26,000	—

AVERAGE REPLACEMENT COSTS

A/C Compressor	$1,065	Clutch, Pressure Plate, Bearing	910
Alternator	615	Constant Velocity Joints	710
Automatic Transmission or Transaxle	1,540	Exhaust System	730
Brakes	280	Radiator	640
Shocks and/or Struts	880	Timing Chain or Belt	280

TROUBLE SPOTS

• **Engine misfire.** If the battery is disconnected, the engine may idle rough or lack power requiring recalibration of the throttle valve control module. (1997)

• **Brakes.** Jump starting a dead battery, or charging the battery with more than 16 volts, may blow the fuse to the ABS system. (1996)

• **Dashboard lights.** The check-engine light may come on with less than three gallons in the fuel tank. This can lead to a lean misfire. (1996)

• **Cruise control.** The cruise control may not hold the set speed requiring replacement of the vacuum servo. (1996)

• **Hard starting.** The engine speed (crankshaft position) sensor can come loose causing the engine to crank, but not start. (1997-98)

• **Fuel gauge.** The fuel gauge may not register full, due to a bad electrical ground connection. (1996)

• **Dashboard lights.** Using cheap gas can cause carbon buildup on the valves, pistons, and combustion chamber, which will cause poor idling and illuminate the check-engine light. (1996)

RECALL HISTORY

1996: Horn may work only intermittently, due to insufficient electrical ground contact. **1996-97:** Discharge of static electricity in low humidity conditions can activate driver's airbag when driver enters or exits car. **1998:** If engine backfires during cold-start, an air screen loosely seated in airflow meter can become damaged; screen pieces could enter intake system and prevent the throttle plate from returning to its full idle position. **1997-99 w/automatic transmission:** Control valve in vacuum hose may not open or close fully at temperatures below -4 degrees (F) under certain conditions; could cause insufficient vacuum to be provided to brake booster. **1998-99:** Some tie rod seals may not seal properly; if moisture and/or dust enters swivel mechanism, bearing could wear over time.

1998-01 AUDI A6

FOR Steering/handling • Passenger room • Cargo room • Side airbags • Standard antilock braking • Build quality • Exterior finish • Interior materials • Acceleration

AGAINST Rear visibility • Climate controls

EVALUATION Thanks to throttle recalibrations and engine tuning, overall acceleration with the base engine is satisfying. Performance is swifter yet from the A6 2.7T and A6 4.2 sedans. Audi claimed 0-60 mph acceleration times below 7 seconds for each of

2000 Audi A6 2.8 sedan

the performance editions, and we wouldn't dispute those figures. They easily rank among the faster cars in the near-luxury class. Fuel economy is good for a near-luxury car. We averaged 22.4 mpg in a front-drive sedan. Heavier weight makes the Quattro editions somewhat less frugal. Firm steering communicates well in turns and helps the car head effortlessly down interstates and straightaways. Few front-drive midsize sedans corner with more poise or grip than an A6. The penalty is a suspension that glides over rough pavement centers, but notices nearly every small bump and tar strip, making for a "busy" ride on many surfaces. On the plus side, the ride is generally supple and quiet. Brakes are strong, with neatly progressive pedal feel. Wind noise is very slight, but tires thump and whine. As for the interior, the A6 cabin is a breezy, sophisticated blend of color-matched surfaces and walnut trim, joined by touches of brightwork on the dashboard, doors, and console. The sedan is roomier than competitive BMW 5-Series or Mercedes-Benz E-Class models. Occupants enjoy an abundance of head, shoulder, and leg room. In back is a supportive bench seat that promises plenty of knee clearance, toe space, and head room. The wagon's 2-place rear seat is sized for preteens. Outside mirrors are small enough to hamper lane changes, but visibility otherwise is quite good. It's even better in the glassy wagon, which also boasts good load-carrying ability. Trunk space is cavernous and easily accessible. Interior storage is also plentiful, including map pockets on every door. Workmanship and materials are top-notch throughout. Panel gaps are precise, inside and out.

VALUE New or used, an A6 costs a lot less than a comparable BMW 528i or Mercedes-Benz E320, yet delivers a similar sense of Teutonic solidity and driving feel. Audi's allroad wagon brings the ride and comfort of an SUV into the mix without sacrificing sophisticated onroad capability. The A6 is a well-made machine that performs admirably on the road. All told, we recommend these great German machines highly, despite their relatively high prices.

SPECIFICATIONS

	4-door sedan	4-door wagon	allroad 4-door wagon
Wheelbase, in.	108.7	108.6	108.5
Overall length, in.	192.0	192	189.4
Overall width, in.	71.3	71.3	76.1
Overall height, in.	57.2	58.2	60.1
Curb weight, lbs.	3759	3947	4167
Cargo volume, cu. ft.	17.2	73.2	73.2
Fuel capacity, gals.	18.5	18.5	18.5
Seating capacity	5.0	5.0	5.0
Front head room, in.	39.3	39.3	37.5
Max. front leg room, in.	41.3	41.3	41.3
Rear head room, in.	37.9	38.7	38.4
Min. rear leg room, in.	37.3	33.2	37.3

Powertrain layout: transverse front-engine/front- or all-wheel drive

ENGINES

	dohc V6	Turbocharged dohc V6	dohc V8
Size, liters/cu. in.	2.8/169	2.7/163	4.2/255
Horsepower	200	250	300
Torque (lbs./ft.)	207	258	295
EPA city/highway mpg			
6-speed OD manual		17/24	
5-speed OD automatic	17/27	17/24	17/24
City/highway mpg (as tested)			
6-speed OD manual		22.0	
5-speed OD automatic	22.4		18.4

Built in Germany

RETAIL PRICES

	GOOD	AVERAGE	POOR
1998 A6 sedan	$17,500-19,000	$16,500-18,000	$13,200-14,500
1998 A6 Quattro sedan	20,000-21,500	18,500-20,000	15,200-16,500
1998 A6 Avant wagon	18,500-20,000	17,200-18,500	13,500-14,700
1998 A6 Quattro Avant	21,000-23,000	19,500-21,500	16,000-17,500
1999 A6 sedan	21,000-22,500	19,500-21,000	15,500-16,700
1999 A6 Quattro sedan	23,500-25,000	22,000-23,500	17,500-18,700
1999 A6 Avant wagon	24,500-26,500	23,000-25,000	18,500-20,000
2000 A6 2.8 sedan	24,000-27,000	22,500-25,500	18,000-20,000
2000 A6 2.7T Quattro sedan	29,500-31,500	27,500-29,500	22,500-24,000
2000 A6 4.2 Quattro sedan	33,000-35,000	31,000-33,000	25,500-28,000
2000 A6 Avant wagon	27,000-29,000	25,000-27,000	20,000-21,500
2001 A6 2.8 sedan	27,000-29,000	255,00 -27,500	—
2001 A6 2.8 Quattro sedan	29,000-31,000	27,500-29,500	—
2001 A6 2.7T Quattro sedan	32,500-34,500	30,500-32,500	—
2001 A6 4.2 Quattro sedan	380,00 -40,000	36,000-42,000	—
2001 A6 Avant wagon	30,000-32,000	28,500-30,500	—
2001 allroad Quattro	35,000-37,000	33,000-35,000	—

AVERAGE REPLACEMENT COSTS

A/C Compressor	$780	Clutch, Pressure Plate, Bearing	800
Alternator	465	Constant Velocity Joints	2,310
Automatic Transmission or Transaxle	1,100	Exhaust System	775
Brakes	745	Radiator	670
Shocks and/or Struts	1,600	Timing Chain or Belt	290

TROUBLE SPOTS

• **Power seats.** The driver's power seat stops working because the electronic module loses its memory. (1998)

• **Paint/body.** The front bumper is low and several owners have complained of damage on parking curbs. (1998-99)

• **Climate control.** The heated steering wheel may not heat up or may not stay warm. (1998-99)

• **Windshield.** The windshield may leak near the top edge. (1998)

RECALL HISTORY

1998: If engine backfires during cold-start, an air screen loosely seated in airflow meter can become damaged; screen pieces could enter intake system and prevent throttle plate from returning to full isle position. **1998-99 w/Quattro:** If car is refueled shortly after engine is started, and is kept running during refueling, fuel vapor recovery system could produce sufficient pressure to expel fuel when nozzle is removed. **1998-99:** Some tie rod seals may not seal properly; if moisture and/or dust particles enter swivel bearing mechanism, bearing could wear over time, diminishing steering control. **1998-99 w/automatic transmission:** Control valve in vacuum hose may not open or close fully at temperatures below -4 degrees (F) under certain conditions; could cause insufficient vacuum to be provided to brake booster. **1998-00:** Sulfur in fuel could cause fuel gauge to read "full" when the tank is actually less than full. **2001 Allroad:** Under a heavy load conditions the wiper blades could become entangled with each other and cease functioning.

2000-01 AUDI TT

FOR Acceleration • Handling/roadholding • Build quality • Interior materials

AGAINST Noise • Visibility • Rear seat entry/exit • Rear-seat room

EVALUATION Racy looks are the main attraction of the TT, whether fitted with a steel or fabric roof. The 180-bhp engine is not all that quick, though 0-60 mph acceleration in 7.4 seconds certainly isn't sluggish. However, the engine needs a lot of revs for quick take-offs and brisk passing. Gas mileage is excellent, but premium fuel is required and Quattro models burn a little more gasoline than front-drivers. With the 225-bhp engine, 0-60 time drops below 7 seconds, but that engine suffers annoying "turbo lag." Handling is sharp and balanced, but the steering wheel can wiggle as the optional 17-inch performance tires travel along deep grooved pavement. On rough surfaces, the ride can grow harsh, and noise levels are on the high side. Civilized for a sports car, the TT offers cozy (but not cramped) seating up front, but the coupe's rear seat is for parcels rather than passengers. An imaginative cabin design makes use of top-notch materials. Visibility is poor to the sides, but not bad to the rear—certainly not as restricted as the low roof and virtual "bathtub" seat posi-

2001 Audi TT 2-door convertible

tion might suggest. Cargo space is good with the coupe's rear seat-backs up, and terrific when they're folded down. Although the Roadster's trunk is small in capacity, it's usefully shaped.

VALUE A TT offers practical sports-car fun, with a style and personality all its own. It's a bit like the New Beetle in terms of differing smartly from the automotive pack, but despite a few drawbacks, the TT delivers a truly sporty experience along with its high style.

SPECIFICATIONS

	2-door convertible	2-door coupe
Wheelbase, in.	95.4	95.4
Overall length, in.	159.1	159.1
Overall width, in.	73.1	73.1
Overall height, in.	53.0	53.0
Curb weight, lbs.	3054	2910
Cargo volume, cu. ft.	7.8	24.2
Fuel capacity, gals.	14.5	14.5
Seating capacity	2	4
Front head room, in.	38.3	37.8
Max. front leg room, in.	41.2	41.2
Rear head room, in.	32.6	—
Min. rear leg room, in.	20.2	—

Powertrain layout: transverse front-engine/front- or 4-wheel drive

ENGINES

	Turbocharged dohc I4	Turbocharged dohc I4
Size, liters/cu. in.	1.8/107	1.8/107
Horsepower	180	225
Torque (lbs./ft.)	173	207

EPA city/highway mpg

5-speed OD manual	22/31	
6-speed OD manual		20/28

City/highway mpg (as tested)

5-speed OD manual	25.3	
6-speed OD manual		24.0

Built in Germany

RETAIL PRICES

	GOOD	AVERAGE	POOR
2000 TT Coupe	$23,000-26,000	$22,000-25,000	$18,000-20,000
2001 TT Coupe	27,000-31,000	25,500-29,500	—
2001 TT Roadster	29,500-34,000	28,000-32,500	—

AVERAGE REPLACEMENT COSTS

A/C Compressor	$801	Clutch, Pressure Plate,	
Alternator	785	Bearing	855
Automatic Transmission or		Constant Velocity Joints	2,635
Transaxle	NA	Exhaust System	950
Brakes	345	Radiator	615
Shocks and/or Struts	1,795	Timing Chain or Belt	345

TROUBLE SPOTS

• **Paint/body.** Hoists or floor jacks may damage early production models' sill panels. Later models are built with hoist lift pads that can be retrofitted. (2000)

• **Audio system.** If the CD player and rear defogger are operated at the same time, a whining noise may come from the audio speakers. This requires a filter on the wiring harness. (2000)

RECALL HISTORY

2000: Small section of fuel line assembly on small number of cars could have been damaged during production; if so, fuel could leak. **2000:** In certain high-speed turns or abrupt lane-change maneuvers at speeds substantially above posted limits, and depending upon road conditions, precise steering response may be demanded to retain directional stability. Dealers will replace front stabilizers in front-drive cars, and front/rear

stabilizers in those equipped with all-wheel drive. A modified control arm will be installed, together with firmer front/rear shock absorbers and a rear spoiler. **2000-01 Quattro:** Rear track control arm mounting bushing and bolt could corrode leading to loss of vehicle control.

1992-98 BMW 318i

1993 BMW 318i 4-door sedan

FOR Ride • Steering/handling • Antilock brakes

AGAINST Wet-weather traction • Rear-seat room

EVALUATION Four-cylinder BMWs target driving enthusiasts, who generally prefer manual shift. Because these engines come alive only at high rpm, they function better with manual shift than with automatic, which robs some of the engine's zest. Around town, though, you can expect to shift the 5-speed frequently. Installation of the larger engine in 1996 did not boost performance appreciably. Fuel mileage has averaged more than 25 mpg with the manual shift. All 3-Series BMWs shine brightest in their sporty handling characteristics. They devour twisting roads with ease, helped by sharply precise yet fluid steering. Quick turns produce more body lean than expected, but the cars feel lithe and surefooted. Though the suspension is firm, ride quality beats many cars with softer suspensions, absorbing plenty of road flaws. Brakes are potent, too. In wet or snowy weather, however, these rear-drivers can get difficult to handle, as the tail slips easily sideways. Traction control is not all that effective. Despite the increased size in this generation, interior space is not much larger than in previous BMWs. Rear space is acceptable only for two small adults, and rear head room is tight in the coupe due to its slightly lower roofline. Cabins are rather austere, with a lot of hard plastic surfaces that seem inappropriate for the car's price. Lack of a tilt feature means the steering wheel sits a bit high, but analog gauges are unobstructed and radio and climate controls are close at hand. Skimpy rear door openings hinder back seat entry into sedans. The trunk floor is flat, and its opening is large.

VALUE Despite high secondhand prices, 4-cylinder BMWs appeal to those who like spirited, high-revving driving enjoyment. For that purpose, they're hard to beat.

SPECIFICATIONS

	2-door convertible	2-door coupe	4-door sedan
Wheelbase, in.	106.3	106.3	106.3
Overall length, in.	174.5	174.5	174.5
Overall width, in.	67.3	67.3	66.8
Overall height, in.	53.1	53.8	54.8
Curb weight, lbs.	3352	2866	2866
Cargo volume, cu. ft.	9.0	14.3	15.4
Fuel capacity, gals.	17.2	17.2	17.2
Seating capacity	4	5	5
Front head room, in.	38.1	36.7	37.8
Max. front leg room, in.	41.2	41.2	40.9
Rear head room, in.	36.3	35.9	37.3
Min. rear leg room, in.	28.1	32.7	34.1

Powertrain layout: longitudinal front-engine/rear-wheel drive

ENGINES

	dohc I4n1	dohc I4	dohc I4
Size, liters/cu. in.	1.8/110	1.8/110	1.9/116
Horsepower	134	138	138
Torque (lbs./ft.)	127	129	133

EPA city/highway mpg

5-speed OD manual	NA	22/32	23/31

	dohc I4n1	dohc I4	dohc I4
4-speed OD automatic	NA	21/29	22/31
City/highway mpg (as tested)			
5-speed OD manual		25.5	
4-speed OD automatic			20.2

1. Used in carryover-styled 1992 convertibles only.

Built in USA, Germany

RETAIL PRICES

	GOOD	AVERAGE	POOR
1992 318i/is	$5,200-5,900	$4,400-6,100	$2,300-2,900
1992 Convertible	7,000-8,000	6,000-7,000	3,200-4,000
1993 318i/is	6,500-7,400	5,600-6,400	3,000-3,700
1994 318i/is	8,000-9,000	7,000-8,000	4,000-4,800
1994 Convertible	10,500-11,500	9,500-10,500	6,000-6,800
1995 318i/is	10,000-11,000	9,000-10,000	5,600-6,400
1995 Convertible	12,500-13,500	11,300-12,200	7,500-8,300
1996 318i/is	12,000-13,000	11,000-12,000	7,200-8,000
1996 Convertible	15,000-16,300	13,700-15,000	9,500-10,500
1997 318i/is	14,000-15,500	12,500-14,000	8,500-9,500
1997 Convertible	17,500-19,000	16,000-17,500	11,500-12,500
1998 318i	16,000-17,500	14,500-16,000	10,000-11,000

AVERAGE REPLACEMENT COSTS

A/C Compressor	$1,200	Clutch, Pressure Plate, Bearing	570
Alternator	420	Exhaust System	1,450
Automatic Transmission or Transaxle	1,150	Radiator	655
Brakes	260	Shocks and/or Struts	1,225
Timing Chain or Belt	820		

TROUBLE SPOTS

• **Air conditioner.** Air conditioners that don't cool well enough may need to have some of the R-12 (Freon®) removed if the system was overcharged. (1991-93)

• **Doors.** If the central locking system unlocks itself after being locked or locks itself after being unlocked, the actuators could be defective or the trunk lock may need to be adjusted. (1992-93)

• **Climate control.** Small flakes may come from the vents or a foul odor may be present when the A/C is operated. (1992-93)

• **Automatic transmission.** The automatic transmission may suffer from delayed engagement after sitting overnight because the fluid drains out of the torque converter. (1992-95)

• **Dashboard lights.** The hazard flashers may begin flashing by themselves and the turn signals may flash at twice the normal speed due to condensation shorting out the circuit board. (1992-94)

• **Starter.** The starter may fail because it keeps running after the engine starts and eventually burns out. The root cause is a sticking ignition switch. The whole lock and switch must be replaced. (1992-94)

RECALL HISTORY

1992: Airbag contact ring locking tab can break without warning, eventually causing broken wiring; airbag would then not deploy in collision, and indicator would illuminate. **1992-93:** Fuel hoses can harden and "set" over time, allowing seepage that could result in fire. **1992-95:** Malfunction or failure of cooling system component can result in significantly increased coolant temperature and system pressure. **1992-97:** Plastic bushing for cruise-control and throttle cables could break, causing throttle valve to remain partially open; car might not decelerate as expected.

1992-98 BMW 325i/328i/323i

1992 BMW 325is 2-door coupe

FOR Acceleration • Ride • Steering/handling • Standard antilock brakes and traction control (later models)

AGAINST Wet-weather traction • Rear-seat room • Fuel economy • Control layout

EVALUATION Acceleration is swift and smooth at higher engine speeds, but early models suffered a shortage in low-end power, feeling somewhat lethargic until they revved past 3000 rpm or more. Performance in general is adequate with automatic, but these cars are best enjoyed with the highly inviting 5-speed manual gearbox. In town, though, that 5-speed needs to be shifted often. Fuel economy averaged 20.4 mpg in a test of a 1992 model with manual shift. Swift turns with the base suspension bring more body roll than expected, but the 3-Series feels tight, lithe, and surefooted. Antilock brakes deliver commendable stopping power and excellent sensitivity. Steering is sharp and precise, road manners nicely balanced. A firm, yet absorbent suspension soaks up road flaws while keeping the body stable. Beware in wet weather, as rear-drivers can get twitchy in rain or snow. Even with the traction control, snow tires are a must in northern climates. Space up front is adequate, but the rear is sufficient only for two on a narrow seat. Rear head room in coupes is tight, due to their slightly lower roofline, and the center rear occupant must straddle the driveline tunnel. Skimpy door openings on sedans hinder back-seat entry. The trunk floor is flat, with a large opening. Interiors are austere, with hard plastic surfaces. Radio and climate controls are close at hand but feature a confusing array of buttons.

VALUE Like their bigger brothers, 3-Series BMWs are far from cheap secondhand, but their many fans are willing to lay out the extra bucks for top-notch roadholding and high-quality materials.

SPECIFICATIONS

	2-door conv.	2-door conv.	2-door coupe	4-door sedan
Wheelbase, in.	101.2	106.3	106.3	106.3
Overall length, in.	175.2	174.5	174.5	174.5
Overall width, in.	64.8	67.3	67.3	66.8
Overall height, in.	53.9	53.1	53.8	54.8
Curb weight, lbs.	2990	3352	2866	2866
Cargo volume, cu. ft.	11.0	9.0	14.3	15.4
Fuel capacity, gals.	16.4	17.2	17.2	17.2
Seating capacity	4	4	5	5
Front head room, in.	NA	38.1	36.7	37.8
Max. front leg room, in.	NA	41.2	41.2	40.9
Rear head room, in.	NA	36.3	35.9	37.3
Min. rear leg room, in.	NA	28.1	32.7	34.1

Powertrain layout: longitudinal front-engine/rear-wheel drive

ENGINES

	ohc I6n1	dohc I6	dohc I6	dohc I6
Size, liters/cu. in.	2.5/152	2.5/152	2.8/170	3.0/182
Horsepower	168	168-189	190	240
Torque (lbs./ft.)	164	181	206	225
EPA city/highway mpg				
5-speed OD manual	17/24	19/28	20/29	19/27
4-speed OD automatic		20/28	19/26	
5-speed OD automatic				19/28
City/highway mpg (as tested)				
5-speed OD manual		20.4		
4-speed OD automatic		17.6	19.8	

1. Used in carryover-styled 1992-93 convertibles only.

Built in USA, Germany

RETAIL PRICES

	GOOD	AVERAGE	POOR
1992 325i/is	$7,000-8,000	$6,000-7,000	$3,200-4,000
1992 Convertible	8,000-9,000	7,000-9,000	4,000-4,800
1993 325i/is	8,500-9,500	7,500-6,500	4,500-5,300
1993 Convertible	10,000-11,000	9,000-10,000	5,500-6,300
1994 325i/is	10,500-11,500	9,500-10,500	6,000-6,800
1994 Convertible	12,500-14,000	11,500-13,000	7,500-8,500
1995 325i/is	12,500-13,700	11,300-12,500	7,300-8,000
1995 Convertible	15,500-17,000	14,000-15,500	9,500-10,500
1995 M3 coupe	145,00 -16,000	13,200-14,700	8,700-9,800
1996 328i/is	15,000-16,300	13,700-15,000	9,500-10,500
1996 Convertible	19,000-21,000	17,500-19,500	12,500-13,500
1996 M3 coupe	17,500-19,000	16,000-17,500	11,000-12,000
1997 328i/is	18,000-19,500	16,500-18,000	11,500-12,500
1997 Convertible	22,500-24,500	21,000-22,500	16,000-17,000
1997 M3 coupe/sedan	21,000-22,500	19,500-21,000	14,500-15,500

	GOOD	AVERAGE	POOR
1998 323is	$17,000-18,500	$15,700-17,000	$11,000-12,000
1998 328i/is	21,000-22,500	19,500-21,000	14,500-15,500
1998 323i Convertible	22,500-24,000	21,000-22,500	15,800-17,000
1998 328i Convertible	26,500-28,500	24,500-26,500	18,500-20,000
1998 M3 coupe/sedan	25,000-27,000	23,000-25,000	17,500-19,000
1998 M3 Convertible	29,500-31,500	27,500-29,500	21,500-23,000

AVERAGE REPLACEMENT COSTS

A/C Compressor	$970	Clutch, Pressure Plate,	
Alternator	590	Bearing	645
Automatic Transmission or		Exhaust System	670
Transaxle	1,190	Exhaust System	790
Brakes	260	Shocks and/or Struts	980
		Timing Chain or Belt	1,265

TROUBLE SPOTS

• **Air conditioner.** Air conditioners that don't cool well enough may need to have some of the R-12 (Freon®) removed if the system was over-charged. (1991-93)

• **Doors.** If the central locking system unlocks itself after being locked or locks itself after being unlocked, the actuators could be defective or the trunk lock may need to be adjusted. (1992-93)

• **Climate control.** Small flakes may come from the vents or a foul odor may be present when the A/C is operated. (1992-93)

• **Automatic transmission.** The automatic transmission may suffer from delayed engagement after sitting overnight because the fluid drains out of the torque converter. (1992-95)

• **Dashboard lights.** The hazard flashers may begin flashing by them-selves and the turn signals may flash at twice the normal speed due to condensation shorting out the circuit board. (1992-94)

• **Starter.** The starter may fail because it keeps running after the engine starts and eventually burns out. The root cause is a sticking ignition switch. The whole lock and switch must be replaced. (1992-94)

RECALL HISTORY

1992: Airbag contact ring locking tab can break without warning, eventually causing broken wiring; airbag would not deploy in colli-sion, and indicator would illuminate. **1992:** Failed to meet safety standard for driver chest injury in crash test. **1992-93:** Fuel hoses can harden and "set" over time. **1992-94 325i/iS:** Brake lights may fail to operate, or be on continuously. **1992-95 325i:** Plastic bushing for cruise-control and throttle cables could break, causing throttle valve to remain partially open; car then might not decelerate as expected. **1992-95:** Malfunction or failure of cooling system compo-nent can result in significantly increased coolant temperature and system pressure. **1993-94 325i/iS:** Replace front transmission crossmember support. **1994 325iC:** Brake lights may fail to operate, or be on continuously. **1995 M3:** Brake lights may fail to operate, or be on continuously. **1995-97 M3:** Plastic bushing for cruise-control and throttle cables could break, causing throttle valve to remain par-tially open; car then might not decelerate as expected. **1997-98 M3:** Side airbag system is unduly sensitive to certain noncrash impacts, such as large potholes or curbs; could deploy without actual side crash. Battery Safety Terminal could also activate, so engine could not be restarted.

1999-01 BMW 3-SERIES

2000 BMW 323Ci 2-door coupe

FOR Head protection system • Acceleration • Steering/handling • Build quality

AGAINST Cargo room (convertible) • Rear-seat entry/exit (coupe/convertible) • Rear-seat room (coupe/convertible) • Ride (M3)

EVALUATION Spirited performance, great handling, high refine-ment, and terrific workmanship mark BMW's compact models, which mimic the feel of the German automaker's larger 5-Series cars. All versions shine for silky engines, solid on-road feel, modest noise levels, and athletic, class-leading rear-drive handling. The 2.5-liter six is a model of smoothness and performs nearly as swiftly as the 328i—which is among the segment's best-accelerating cars. A 328i accelerated to 60 mph in 7.5 seconds, and BMW claimed that the later 330i could do it in 6.4 seconds with manual shift, or 7.0 with automatic. All engines demand premium fuel, but economy is laudable. A 328i averaged 23.5 mpg. Automatic transmissions pro-vide quick, velvety gear changes in normal mode. BMW's forte is ride control and comfort, along with handling balance. Sport sus-pensions (standard on coupes) and bigger tires produce notice-ably sharper grip and steering response, but don't absorb bumps as well as the base tire/suspension setups. They also yield some jiggle on rough pavement and lack grip in snow—despite traction control and antiskid systems. Interiors are cozy, with a rather nar-row cabin feel. Head room is plentiful in front and adequate in back. Rear knee and foot room are tight with front seats moved fully aft. Coupe front seats automatically slide forward to ease entry to the rear, but it's still tricky. Large climate and audio panels are easy to use. Visibility is good, except in top-up convertibles—which are impressively solid, but suffer mild body shake on rough, broken pavement. Trunk volume is unexceptional, but space is usable and the opening is large.

VALUE Unchallenged in sporting character, these are the true "driver's cars" of the near-luxury class. Some rivals offer more interior room, but none are more refined or as sporty. Price is the main drawback, because resale values are strong.

SPECIFICATIONS	2-door conv.	2-door coupe	4-door sedan	4-door wagon
Wheelbase, in.	107.3	107.3	107.3	107.3
Overall length, in.	176.7	176.7	176.0	176.3
Overall width, in.	69.2	69.2	68.5	68.5
Overall height, in.	54.0	53.5	55.7	55.5
Curb weight, lbs.	3560	3020	3153	3351
Cargo volume, cu. ft.	7.7	9.5	10.7	25.7
Fuel capacity, gals.	16.6	16.6	16.6	16.6
Seating capacity	4	4	5	5
Front head room, in.	38.3	37.5	38.4	38.4
Max. front leg room, in.	41.7	41.7	41.4	41.4
Rear head room, in.	36.9	36.5	37.5	37.7
Min. rear leg room, in.	32.0	33.2	34.6	34.0

Powertrain layout: longitudinal front-engine/rear- or all-wheel drive

ENGINES	dohc I6	dohc I6	dohc I6	dohc I6	dohc I6
Size, liters/cu. in.	2.5/152	2.5/152	2.8/170	3.0/182	3.2/192
Horsepower	170	184	193	225	330
Torque (lbs./ft.)	181	175	206	211-214	225
EPA city/highway mpg					
5-speed OD man.	20/29	20/29	20/29	21/30	
6-speed OD man.					16/24
5-speed OD auto.	19/28	19/27	19/27	19/27	
City/highway mpg (as tested)					
5-speed OD man.		23.5		25.4	

Built in Germany

RETAIL PRICES	GOOD	AVERAGE	POOR
1999 323i coupe/sedan	$22,000-23,500	$21,000-22,500	$17,000-18,000
1999 323i convertible	27,000-28,500	25,500-27,000	21,000-22,000
1999 328i coupe/sedan	25,000-26,500	23,500-25,000	19,000-20,500
1999 328i convertible	31,000-33,000	29,000-31,000	24,500-25,500
1999 M3 coupe	30,000-32,000	28,000-30,000	23,500-24,500
1999 M3 convertible	34,500-36,500	32,500-34,500	27,000-28,500
2000 323i coupe/sedan	24,000-26,000	23,000-25,000	19,000-20,000
2000 323i convertible	30,000-32,000	28,500-30,500	24,000-25,000
2000 328i coupe/sedan	27,500-29,000	26,000-27,600	22,000-23,000
2000 328i convertible	34,000-36,000	32,000-34,000	27,000-28,000
2001 325i cpe/sdn/wgn	26,500-29,000	25,000-27,500	—
2001 325i convertible	32,500-34,500	31,000-33,000	—
2001 330i coupe/sedan	30,000-32,000	28,500-30,500	—

	GOOD	AVERAGE	POOR
2001 330Ci convertible	36,500-39,000	34,500-37,000	—
2001 M3 coupe	38,000-40,000	36,000-38,000	—
2001 M3 convertible	45,000-47,500	43,000-45,000	—

AVERAGE REPLACEMENT COSTS

A/C Compressor	$770	Clutch, Pressure Plate, Bearing	725
Alternator	640	Constant Velocity Joints	1,235
Automatic Transmission or Transaxle	810	Exhaust System	895
Brakes	445	Radiator	650
Shocks and/or Struts	1,320	Timing Chain or Belt	415

TROUBLE SPOTS

• **Exhaust system.** BMW issued a voluntary emissions recall to replace faulty crankshaft position sensors. (1999)

• **Transmission leak.** Manual transmissions drain plugs may leak. BMW also suggests replacing the fill plug. (1999-00)

• **Steering noise.** Steering wheel buzzes or vibrates due to poor isolation of the power steering pumg. (1999)

RECALL HISTORY

1999 323i/328i: Retaining clip that secures brake booster pushrod to brake pedal arm could detach from pin, allowing pushrod to disconnect, causing brake failure. **1999:** Side airbag system is unduly sensitive to certain noncrash impacts, such as contacting large potholes or curbs at substantial speed; could deploy without an actual side crash. Battery Safety Terminal could also activate, disconnecting starter cable from battery, so engine could not be restarted after being shut off. **2000 323i/328i:** Brake lamp switch could fail internally, remaining either in "off" or "on" position; brake lamps would then either not operate or be continuously illuminated. **2001 315i/335i:** On some vehicles, tires could lose air suddenly, affecting vehicle control. **2001:** Failure of engine fan motor can cause electrical circuitry to overload and fail, causing fan to stop operating, with consequent engine overheating and possible engine damage. **2001 M3:** Screws could fall into the parking brake drum, reducing effectiveness or making screeching noises.

1990-96 BMW 5-SERIES

1990 BMW 535i 4-door sedan

FOR Antilock brakes • Steering/handling • Acceleration • Ride • Brake performance

AGAINST Fuel economy (V8) • Automatic transmission performance

EVALUATION Acceleration from the 535i is brisk, and passing power impressive, but the automatic transmission does not always cooperate. At times it changes gears too soon and is slow to downshift for passing. All 6-cylinder engines are at their best at high speeds or with a manual transmission. We averaged 16.9 mpg in an automatic 535i, and it requires premium fuel. Handling is fluid and responsive, with ample grip and minimal body roll. The sedans ride tautly but comfortably, and noise levels are low. Stopping power is stunning, helped by all-disc antilock braking. BMW beat the Japanese handily in suspension sophistication. That means suppleness over bumps and taut control at speed, accompanied by precise steering. Driver confidence is enhanced by the no-nonsense dashboard, supportive seats, and fine visibility. These mid-size sedans seat four in comfort, five in a pinch. Rear-seat leg room is not the most generous, whereas head room is adequate all around. Both V8 models are reasonably smooth and provide ample power at all speeds. We clocked a 540i with automatic at 7.1 seconds to 60 mph.

Unfortunately, that car averaged just 15.7 mpg. Six-cylinder cars promise the same enthusiast-oriented road manners as the V8 models, but their engine trades somewhat higher gas mileage for a noticeable loss of acceleration, especially for midrange passing with automatic transmission.

VALUE These midrange BMWs are thoughtfully designed and highly capable. Few sedans can match their supple suspension, comfortable seats, and precise steering. You also get robust construction and excellent detail finish. Yet, these cars lag behind such competitors as Lexus and Infiniti in overall value.

SPECIFICATIONS

	4-door sedan	4-door wagon
Wheelbase, in.	108.7	108.7
Overall length, in.	185.8	185.8
Overall width, in.	68.9	68.9
Overall height, in.	55.6	55.8
Curb weight, lbs.	3484	3760
Cargo volume, cu. ft.	16.2	51.2
Fuel capacity, gals.	21.1	21.1
Seating capacity	5	5
Front head room, in.	36.9	36.8
Max. front leg room, in.	41.6	41.6
Rear head room, in.	36.4	37.7
Min. rear leg room, in.	37.0	34.2

Powertrain layout: longitudinal front-engine/rear-wheel drive

ENGINES

	ohc I6	dohc I6	ohc I6	dohc V8	dohc V8
Size, liters/cu. in.	2.5/152	2.5/152	3.4/209	3.0/183	4.0/243
Horsepower	168	189	208	215	282
Torque (lbs./ft.)	164	181-184	225	214	295
EPA city/highway mpg					
5-speed OD man.	18/25	19/28	15/23	16/24	14/23
4-speed OD auto.	18/23	18/25	16/22		
5-speed OD auto.				17/26	17/25
City/highway mpg (as tested)					
4-speed OD auto.		17.2			
5-speed OD auto.					15.7

Built in Germany

RETAIL PRICES

	GOOD	AVERAGE	POOR
1990 525i	$4,500-5,400	$3,600-4,500	$1,600-2,200
1990 535i	6,000-7,000	5,000-6,000	2,500-3,200
1991 525i	6,000-7,000	5,000-6,000	2,500-3,200
1991 535i	7,500-8,500	6,500-7,500	3,500-4,300
1992 525i	7,500-8,500	6,500-7,500	3,600-4,300
1992 535i	9,000-10,000	8,000-9,000	4,700-5,600
1993 525i	9,000-10,200	8,000-9,000	4,500-5,300
1993 535i	10,500-11,500	9,500-10,500	5,700-6,500
1994 525i	10,500-12,000	9,500-10,800	5,600-6,500
1994 530i	11,200-12,500	10,000-11,200	6,000-7,000
1994 540i	13,000-14,000	11,700-12,500	7,500-8,200
1995 525i	13,000-14,500	11,700-13,000	7,700-8,800
1995 530i	14,000-15,500	12,500-14,000	8,500-9,000
1995 540i	16,000-17,500	14,500-16,000	10,000-11,000
1996 525i	14,500-16,000	13,000-14,500	8,800-9,800
1996 530i	15,500-17,000	14,000-12,500	9,500-10,500
1996 540i	17,500-19,000	16,000-17,500	11,000-12,000

AVERAGE REPLACEMENT COSTS

A/C Compressor	$1,280	Clutch, Pressure Plate, Bearing	875
Alternator	610	Exhaust System	1,015
Automatic Transmission or Transaxle	1,150	Radiator	710
Brakes	255	Shocks and/or Struts	865
Timing Chain or Belt	1,920		

TROUBLE SPOTS

• **Climate control.** Fuse #20 may blow repeatedly and BMW has approved replacing the original 10-amp fuse with a 15-amp fuse. (1993-94)

• **Doors.** If the central locking system unlocks itself after being locked or locks itself after being unlocked, the actuators could be defective or the trunk lock may need to be adjusted. (1992-93)

• **Air conditioner.** Small flakes may come from the vents or a foul odor may be present when the A/C is operated and a redesigned evaporator is available to fix the problem. (1992-93)

- **Dashboard lights.** The hazard flashers may begin flashing by themselves or the turn signals may flash at twice the normal speed due to condensation shorting out the circuit board. (1992-94)

- **Starter.** The starter may fail because it keeps running after the engine starts. The root cause is a sticking ignition switch. The whole lock and switch must be replaced. (1992-94)

RECALL HISTORY

1990: Under certain conditions, front armrest may contact seatbelt buckle, damaging its release button. **1990-92 535i:** Brake lights may fail to operate, or be on continuously. **1990-94 525i:** Brake lights may fail to operate, or be on continuously. **1990-95 525i:** Plastic bushing for cruise-control and throttle cables could break, causing throttle valve to remain partially open; car then might not decelerate as expected. **1990-95:** Malfunction or failure of cooling system component can result in significantly increased coolant temperature and system pressure. **1991 525/535:** Movement of throttle valve may be impeded, preventing car from decelerating. **1991-92 525i/535i/M5:** Airbag contact ring locking tab can break without warning, eventually causing broken wiring; airbag would then not deploy in collision, and indicator would illuminate. **1992 525it:** Airbag contact ring locking tab can break without warning, eventually causing broken wiring; airbag would then not deploy in collision, and indicator would illuminate. **1992-94 525it:** Brake lights may fail to operate, or be on continuously. **1994 530i/it, 540i:** Brake lights may fail to operate, or be on continuously. **1994-95 525:** Double-lock mechanism can engage with key and occupants inside car. **1994-95 530i:** Plastic bushing for cruise-control and throttle cables could break, causing throttle valve to remain partially open; car then might not decelerate as expected.

1996-01 BMW Z3

1997 BMW Z3 2-door convertible

FOR Steering/handling • Acceleration (6-cylinder) • Brake performance

AGAINST Acceleration (4-cylinder/auto) • Noise • Passenger and cargo room

EVALUATION Even though horsepower and torque are greater in a 4-cylinder Z3 than in Mazda's Miata, the BMW roadster does not feel any swifter—partly because it carries more pounds. Automatic is slower yet. Because the Z3's 4-cylinder engine does not develop much power below 3500 rpm, it cannot get an eager jump off the line when you push the gas pedal hard. Past 3500 rpm, acceleration becomes brisk. Performance is better with the 2.8-liter 6-cylinder engine. It doesn't set any records either, however. The 6-cylinder's extra torque is most beneficial because it reduces the amount of shifting when driving in town. A test manual-transmission 2.5i did 0-60 mph in a brisk 7.0 sec and had ample midrange passing punch. The 3.0i/manual hatchback felt more muscular—BMW lists 0-60 at 5.9 sec—but didn't present significantly more usable acceleration on the street than the 2.5i. M-Series roadsters and hatchbacks have exhilarating performance—almost reminiscent of a Corvette. Refinement is where BMW has the edge over the Miata. BMW's 4-cylinder engine is far smoother and quieter than Mazda's. It gets noisy only when working hard. The 6-cylinder engine is quieter yet. Wind noise is intrusive at highway speeds, making it hard for the two occupants to converse in normal tones. Because these are sports cars, noises from the engine, road, and wind increase markedly with speed. Firm suspensions allow little lean in turns, and the Z3 corners as if it's on rails. For a car with such high cornering limits, the ride is supple—more comfortable than the Miata's. Still, it gets jiggly on anything other than glass-smooth surfaces. All told, the Z3 lags behind Mercedes' SLK in smothering bumps. Braking is straight and short. A "panic" stop from 60 mph took about 105 feet. Space is adequate for medium-size adults, but large folks might feel cramped. Trunk space is meager by anything other than sports-car standards. The manual folding top is fairly easy to raise and lower, but the plastic back window is subject to easy wrinkling and scratches, especially if not cared for properly. Like most convertibles, the top's rear quarters are wide enough to restrict visibility over the driver's shoulders. Inside, you'll find a no-frills, Teutonic design—not inappropriate for a sports car. Standard "leatherette" upholstery on the 1.9, however, with its odd pebble-grain pattern, looks rather cheap for a car of this caliber.

VALUE Eye-catching appearance and BMW's reputation for handling prowess make the Z3 tempting. Still, based on performance or equipment, it's difficult to justify paying so much more for a Z3 than a Mazda Miata. M-Series models, on the other hand, perform as promised and just might be worth the extra dollars.

SPECIFICATIONS

	2-door conv.	2-door coupe
Wheelbase, in.	96.3	96.3
Overall length, in.	158.5	158.5
Overall width, in.	66.6	68.5
Overall height, in.	50.7	51.4
Curb weight, lbs.	2701	2943
Cargo volume, cu. ft.	5.0	9.0
Fuel capacity, gals.	13.5	13.5
Seating capacity	2	2
Front head room, in.	37.6	37.6
Max. front leg room, in.	41.8	41.8
Rear head room, in.	—	—
Min. rear leg room, in.	—	—

Powertrain layout: longitudinal front-engine/rear-wheel drive

ENGINES

	dohc I4	dohc I6	dohc I6	dohc I6	dohc I6
Size, liters/cu. in.	1.9/116	2.5/152	2.8/170	3.0/182	3.2/192
Horsepower	138	170-184	193	225	240-315
Torque (lbs./ft.)	133	175-181	206	214	225-251
EPA city/highway mpg					
5-speed OD man.	23/31	19/26	19/27	21/28	19/26
4-speed OD auto.	23/31	19/26	18/25		
5-speed OD auto.				19/27	
City/highway mpg (as tested)					
5-speed OD man.	25.0	18.6	21.1	19.7	
4-speed OD auto.		22.2			

Built in USA

RETAIL PRICES

	GOOD	AVERAGE	POOR
1996 Z3 1.9	$14,000-15,000	$13,000-14,000	$9,500-10,300
1997 Z3 1.9	15,500-17,000	14,300-15,500	10,500-11,500
1997 Z3 2.8	18,500-20,000	17,000-18,500	13,000-14,000
1998 Z3 1.9	17,500-19,000	16,000-17,500	12,000-13,000
1998 Z3 2.8	20,500-22,000	19,000-20,500	14,000-15,000
1998 M-Series	24,500-26,000	23,000-24,500	17,500-18,500
1999 Z3 2.3 Roadster	20,000-22,000	18,500-20,500	13,500-15,000
1999 Z3 2.8 Roadster	23,000-25,000	21,200-23,000	15,500-17,000
1999 Z3 2.8 Coupe	20,000-22,000	18,500-20,500	135,00 -15,000
1999 M-Series Roadster	27,000-29,000	25,000-27,000	19,500-21,000
1999 M-Series Coupe	23,500-25,000	21,500-23,000	15,500-17,000
2000 Z3 2.3 Roadster	23,000-25,000	21,000-23,000	15,500-16,500
2000 Z3 2.8 Roadster	26,000-28,000	24,000-26,000	180,00 -19,500
2000 Z3 2.8 Coupe	23,500-25,000	21,500-23,000	15,500-17,000
2000 M-Series Roadster	30,000-32,500	28,000-30,500	22,000-23,500
2000 M-Series Coupe	27,000-28,500	25,000-26,500	19,000-20,000
2001 Z3 2.5 Roadster	26,000-28,000	24,000-26,000	—
2001 Z3 2.5 Coupe	23,000-25,000	21,000-23,000	—
2001 Z3 3.0 Roadster	29,500-31,500	27,500-29,500	—
2001 Z3 3.0 Coupe	27,500-29,500	25,500-27,500	—
2001 M-Series Roadster	35,000-37,500	33,000-35,000	—
2001 M-Series Coupe	32,000-34,000	30,000-32,000	—

AVERAGE REPLACEMENT COSTS

A/C Compressor	$1,250	Clutch, Pressure Plate, Bearing	570
Alternator	410	Constant Velocity Joints	960
Automatic Transmission or Transaxle	1,150	Exhaust System	1,140
Brakes	295	Radiator	710
Shocks and/or Struts	1,310	Timing Chain or Belt	840

TROUBLE SPOTS

• **Water leak.** A leak may develop between the fabric top and the plastic seal that holds the rear window. (1996-99)

• **Vehicle noise.** Incorrect installation or the wrong mount causes rattles from the rear shock mount. (1996)

• **Windshield.** The black tape on the windshield trim buckles and peels in hot weather. (1996-97)

• **Vehicle noise.** The fuel tank may rattle when it is full because the mounting strap is loose. Additional foam pads must be installed. (1996-97)

• **Water leak.** Water may leak between the convertible top and door windows due to a poor fitting seal. (1996)

RECALL HISTORY

1999: Nut that secures positive cable to battery terminal clamp on some cars was not tightened properly, allowing cable to loosen over time; ultimately, engine could stop or lighting might be shut off. **1999:** Ring gear bolts in differential on some cars were incorrectly torqued and could loosen, leading to noise; if a bolt worked loose fully, rear-axle lockup could occur.

1990-96 BUICK CENTURY

1995 Buick Century Special Edition 4-door sedan

FOR Passenger and cargo room • Antilock brakes (later models) • Acceleration (V6) • Quietness (V6) • Visibility

AGAINST Acceleration (4-cylinder) • Ride • Handling (base suspension)

EVALUATION The rough 2.5-liter 4-cylinder engine is barely adequate for sedans, and weaker yet in the heavier station wagon. A smooth, responsive 3.3-liter V6 delivers ample power at low speeds and a surprisingly strong kick under heavy throttle for brisk highway passing. That engine also is fairly quiet, unlike the noisy standard four. Also, the 2.5-liter four did not prove to be trouble-free, and fuel mileage wasn't much better than the V6. We averaged nearly 20 mpg with a 3.3-liter V6 in mixed city/suburban driving. A four gets only about two mpg more. The 2.2-liter four that replaced the 2.5-liter in 1993 isn't much improvement, lacking the power to move a car this size with any authority. Adding 10 horsepower to the four for '94 didn't make it a tempting choice, either. The 3.1-liter V6 installed in more recent models delivers ample power for passing and spirited takeoffs. Century's Dynaride suspension delivers a soft and reasonably good ride, but handling won't win any awards. The base suspension and narrow standard tires are fine for gentle commuting, but spirited cornering causes the narrow tires to lose their grip. That suspension absorbs most bumps easily, but the front end bounces over wavy surfaces for a floaty, poorly controlled ride. An optional Gran Touring Suspension, with fatter tires, improves cornering ability but results in a harsh ride. Six adults will fit inside, but four will be far more comfortable. Head and leg room are adequate all around, but three cannot fit across without squeezing. Luggage space is ample, with a deep, wide trunk that has a flat floor. Wagons have an optional rear-facing third seat, for 8-passenger capacity. Front brakes tend to wear out quickly. Many early problems, including trouble with the rack-and-pinion power steering system, were eventually corrected on the later models.

VALUE Nothing flashy here, but Century can be a sensible choice for families on a budget. Forget the 4-cylinder models and look for a livelier, quieter V6. That shouldn't be difficult, as most late Centurys were sold with the V6 engine.

SPECIFICATIONS

	2-door coupe	4-door sedan	4-door wagon
Wheelbase, in.	104.9	104.9	104.9
Overall length, in.	189.1	189.1	190.9
Overall width, in.	69.4	69.4	69.4
Overall height, in.	53.7	54.2	54.2
Curb weight, lbs.	2903	2950	3118
Cargo volume, cu. ft.	16.2	16.2	74.4
Fuel capacity, gals.	16.4	16.5	16.5
Seating capacity	6	6	8
Front head room, in.	38.6	38.6	38.6
Max. front leg room, in.	42.1	42.1	42.1
Rear head room, in.	38.3	38.3	38.9
Min. rear leg room, in.	35.9	35.9	34.8

Powertrain layout: transverse front-engine/front-wheel drive

ENGINES

	ohv I4	ohv I4	ohv V6	ohv V6
Size, liters/cu. in.	2.2/133	2.5/151	3.1/191	3.3/204
Horsepower	110-120	110	160	160
Torque (lbs./ft.)	130	135	185	185
EPA city/highway mpg				
3-speed automatic	24/31	22/31		19/26
4-speed OD automatic			20/29	19/30
City/highway mpg (as tested)				
4-speed OD automatic			22.3	19.8

Built in USA

RETAIL PRICES

	GOOD	AVERAGE	POOR
1990 Century	$1,300-2,000	$800-1,400	$100-300
1991 Century	1,600-2,400	1,000-1,800	200-500
1992 Century	1,900-2,700	1,300-2,100	300-700
1993 Century	2,300-3,100	1,600-2,400	400-900
1994 Century	2,800-3,600	2,100-2,800	600-1,100
1995 Century	3,400-4,200	2,600-3,400	800-1,400
1996 Century	4,200-5,000	3,400-4,200	1,200-1,800

AVERAGE REPLACEMENT COSTS

A/C Compressor	$555	Constant Velocity Joints	535
Alternator	195	Exhaust System	450
Automatic Transmission or Transaxle	1,095	Radiator	430
		Shocks and/or Struts	825
Brakes	210	Timing Chain or Belt	350

TROUBLE SPOTS

• **Automatic transmission.** 4T60E transmissions may drop out of drive while cruising, shift erratically, or have no second, third, or fourth gear because of a bad ground connection for the shift solenoids. (1994)

• **Engine noise.** A tick or rattle when the engine is started cold may be due to too much wrist pin-to-piston clearance. (1994-95)

• **Engine noise.** An intermittent rattling noise after starting is often caused by automatic transmission pump starvation or cavitation, or a sticking pressure regulator valve. (1994-95)

• **Engine noise.** Bearing knock was common on many 3.3- and 3.8-liter engines due to too much clearance on the number one main bearing. (1992-93)

• **Engine misfire.** Cars with the 3.1-liter engine may stall, idle roughly, or suffer from tip-in hesitation after extended idling. Additionally, the defroster may not clear the windshield when the temperature is around 40-50 degrees F. The fix is to get a new PROM and a vacuum hose elbow for the PCV system. (1994-95)

• **Automatic transmission.** TH-125 or 440-T4 automatic transmissions may shift late or not upshift at all. The problem is a stuck throttle valve inside the transmission. (1990-94)

• **Oil leak.** The plastic valve covers on 3.1-liter engines were prone to leaks and should be replaced with redesigned aluminum valve covers. (1994-95)

• **Transmission leak.** The right front axle seal at the automatic transaxle is prone to leak and GM issued a revised seal to correct the problem. (1992-94)

• **Steering noise.** The upper bearing mount in the steering column can get loose and cause a snapping or clicking, requiring a new bearing spring and turn signal cancel cam. (1994-96)

RECALL HISTORY

1990-91 w/six-way power seats or power recliner: Short circuit could set seats on fire. **1990-96:** Rear outboard seatbelt anchors may not withstand required load; in a collision, metal may tear and allow anchor to separate from body. **1993:** Right front brake hose on some cars is improperly manufactured and can cause reduced brake effectiveness. **1994:** Water can cause short circuit in power door lock assembly. **1994:** Improperly tightened spindle nut can cause premature wheel bearing failure.

1997-01 BUICK CENTURY

1997 Buick Century Limited

FOR Passenger and cargo room • Entry/exit

AGAINST Steering/handling • Seat comfort

EVALUATION Smooth and reasonably quiet, the V6 engine provides adequate acceleration, but it growls when asked to deliver sufficient action for passing. The automatic transmission shifts smoothly and promptly. Wind and road noise are low at highway speeds. A test Century averaged 28 mpg in mostly highway driving, and 18.5 mpg in urban conditions. Only one suspension is used, and it's too soft for many drivers. Most bumps are absorbed well, but the body continues to bounce long after the initial impact. This limp suspension also allows too much body lean in turns, and makes the Century feel queasy over rough pavement surfaces. Retuning for '99 made the suspension deliver better control in turns, but body lean remains pronounced. Century has a spacious interior that provides adult-size room, front and rear. Four occupants would be happier than five or six, however. Tall, wide doors ease entry and exit. As for luggage, the roomy trunk has a wide, flat floor, but you have to reach over a wide bumper-level shelf for loading and unloading. Instruments are easy to read, but limited to a speedometer and fuel and coolant gauges. Most controls are clearly marked, easy for the driver to reach. Climate controls, however, are mounted low enough so they might interfere with a center passenger's knees. In addition, standard cloth seats are so softly padded that they might not suit everyone.

VALUE Though Century performs admirably, it won't satisfy an enthusiastic driver. Still, it's quiet, comfortable, and economical for a 6-passenger automobile. Modern and well thought out, it retains the no-surprises theme that made the prior Century popular with older buyers.

SPECIFICATIONS

	4-door sedan
Wheelbase, in.	109.0
Overall length, in.	194.6
Overall width, in.	72.7
Overall height, in.	56.6
Curb weight, lbs.	3335
Cargo volume, cu. ft.	16.7
Fuel capacity, gals.	17.0
Seating capacity	6
Front head room, in.	39.3
Max. front leg room, in.	42.4
Rear head room, in.	37.4
Min. rear leg room, in.	37.5

Powertrain layout: transverse front-engine/front-wheel drive

ENGINES

	ohv V6
Size, liters/cu. in.	3.1/191
Horsepower	160-175
Torque (lbs./ft.)	185-195

EPA city/highway mpg

4-speed OD automatic	20/29

City/highway mpg (as tested)

4-speed OD automatic	18.5

Built in Canada

RETAIL PRICES

	GOOD	AVERAGE	POOR
1997 Century	$7,500-8,800	$6,600-7,800	$3,900-4,800
1998 Century	8,500-10,000	7,500-9,000	4,600-5,300
1999 Century	9,700-11,200	8,700-10,200	5,400-6,300
2000 Century	11,000-12,800	10,000-11,800	6,500-8,000
2001 Century	13,000-15,000	12,000-14,000	—

AVERAGE REPLACEMENT COSTS

A/C Compressor	$380	Constant Velocity Joints	1,100
Alternator	320	Exhaust System	400
Automatic Transmission or		Radiator	380
Transaxle	980	Shocks and/or Struts	720
Brakes	330	Timing Chain or Belt	315

TROUBLE SPOTS

• **Suspension noise.** A popping or groaning from the rear of the car is caused by the stabilizer shaft links. Redesigned links are available. (1997-98)

• **Engine noise.** A ticking should in the engine is caused by excessive clearance between the piston bores and wrist pins. Although this should not cause a problem, GM will replace all pistons under normal warranty. (1997-98)

• **Vehicle shake.** In warm weather the engine bounces in its mounts, causing a shaking sensation throughout the whole car. A new transmission mount should be installed under normal warranty. (1997-98)

• **Keyless entry.** The remote keyless entry may not have much range, requiring a new receiver (with foil antenna) to be installed. (1997)

RECALL HISTORY

1997: Windshield wipers may stop working, due to separation between drive pin and crescent in crank arm assembly. **1998:** Vertical headlamp adjusting device may not be calibrated properly. **1999:** ABS motor in some cars "shorts" to its case and grounds through brake fluid pipe; can cause extreme heating of brake pipe, which could melt nearby plastic fuel hose. **2000 w/rear drum brakes:** Bolt heads on rear spindle rod can separate and affected wheel can shift, causing loss of control. **2000:** Clamp that secures flexible fuel fill hose to metal fill tube on a few cars may be loose and could separate, causing fuel leakage. **2000:** Some seatbelt assemblies were not properly heat treated and do not pass the load bearing requirement.

1992-99 BUICK LeSABRE

1994 Buick LeSabre Limited

FOR Antilock brakes • Acceleration • Automatic transmission performance • Passenger and cargo room

AGAINST Steering feel • Fuel economy • Radio and climate controls (early models)

EVALUATION Performance is brisk, from a standing start or on the highway. Transmission shifts go virtually unnoticed, and kickdowns come quickly. The 3800 Series II V6 found in the 1996 LeSabre is not only more powerful, it's also smoother and quieter than previous versions of this engine. It delivers ample acceleration, and it's mated to one of the smoothest transmissions available.Power steering is over-assisted, deleting most of the road feel. Even so, handling and overall road manners best a number of rivals. With the base suspension, the LeSabre retains the smooth "big-car" ride that traditional Buick customers have come to expect. For those wanting less body lean and more precise steering feel, we recommend the optional Gran Touring Package. While the LeSabre's handling will never be mistaken for that of a European sport sedan, the optional handling package is a welcome improvement, making this full-size car much more manageable and athletic. Adults can sit upright easily in back, in a spacious interior. Pre-1995 models have awkward reach to climate/radio controls. Roomy trunk has a wide, flat floor and bumper-height opening.

VALUE Pleasant to look at and to drive, LeSabre offers few surprises but carries on traditional Buick virtues. Buick's popular LeSabre is a roomy family sedan that offers most of the features found in the Park Avenue at a lower price. Along with its siblings at Oldsmobile and Pontiac, it ranks among the best choices in a full-size sedan.

SPECIFICATIONS

	4-door sedan
Wheelbase, in.	110.8
Overall length, in.	200.0
Overall width, in.	74.9
Overall height, in.	55.7
Curb weight, lbs.	3430
Cargo volume, cu. ft.	17.1
Fuel capacity, gals.	18.0
Seating capacity	6
Front head room, in.	38.8
Max. front leg room, in.	42.5
Rear head room, in.	37.8
Min. rear leg room, in.	40.4

Powertrain layout: transverse front-engine/front-wheel drive

ENGINES

	ohv V6	ohv V6
Size, liters/cu. in.	3.8/231	3.8/231
Horsepower	170	205
Torque (lbs./ft.)	225	230
EPA city/highway mpg		
4-speed OD automatic	18/28	19/30
City/highway mpg (as tested)		
4-speed OD automatic	22.0	19.3

Built in USA

RETAIL PRICES

	GOOD	AVERAGE	POOR
1992 LeSabre	$3,000-3,800	$2,300-3,100	$600-900
1993 LeSabre	3,600-4,400	2,900-3,600	1,000-1,400
1994 LeSabre	4,200-5,200	3,400-4,300	1,400-1,800
1995 LeSabre	5,200-6,500	4,400-5,500	2,000-2,800
1996 LeSabre	6,500-8,000	5,500-7,000	2,700-4,000
1997 LeSabre	8,000-9,500	7,000-8,500	3,700-4,700
1998 LeSabre	9,500-11,200	8,500-10,200	4,800-5,800
1999 LeSabre	11,500-13,500	10,500-12,300	6,000-7,500

AVERAGE REPLACEMENT COSTS

A/C Compressor	$500	Constant Velocity Joints	760
Alternator	195	Exhaust System	470
Automatic Transmission or		Radiator	360
Transaxle	1,045	Shocks and/or Struts	840
Brakes	130	Timing Chain or Belt	265

TROUBLE SPOTS

• **Automatic transmission.** 440-T4 automatic transmissions may shift late or not upshift at all. The problem is a stuck throttle valve inside the transmission. (All years)

• **Automatic transmission.** 4T60E transmission may drop out of drive while cruising, shift erratically, or have no second, third, or fourth gear because of a bad ground connection for the shift solenoids. (1992-94)

• **Engine noise.** An intermittent rattling noise at start up is often caused by automatic transmission pump starvation or cavitation, or a sticking pressure regulator valve. (1992-95)

• **Engine knock.** Bearing knock is caused by too much clearance on the number one main bearing. (1992-94)

• **Cruise control.** If the cruise control doesn't stay engaged, or drops out of cruise, the brake switch can usually be adjusted. (1992-95)

• **Engine knock and oil leak.** Models with the 3.8-liter engine are prone to excessive oil consumption often accompanied by spark knock due to failure of the valve stem seals. (1993-95)

• **Automatic transmission.** The 4T60-E automatic transmission can suddenly go into neutral at highway speeds due to a problem with internal shift valves. (1995-96)

• **Transmission leak.** The right front axle seal at the automatic transaxle is prone to leak; GM issued a revised seal to correct the problem. (1992-94)

• **Steering noise.** The upper bearing mount in the steering column can get loose and cause a snapping or clicking, requiring a new bearing spring and turn signal cancel cam. (1994-95)

RECALL HISTORY

1992: Parking brake lever assembly may release one or more teeth when applied, so parking brake might not hold the car. **1992-93:** Transmission cooler line in cars with certain powertrains sold in specified states can separate at low temperature. **1995:** Driver-side headlamp lens has incorrect aim pad number. **1996:** "Key in the Ignition" warning chime, driver seatbelt-unbuckled warning, and other functions may fail to operate properly. **1996-97:** Backfire can break upper intake manifold, resulting in no-start condition and possible fire. **1997:** Seatbelt might not latch properly. **1999:** Clip that secures linkage of transmission detent lever can loosen and disconnect; indicated gear would then differ from actual state of the transmission.

2000-01 BUICK LeSABRE

2001 Buick LeSabre Limited

FOR Ride (base suspension) • Acceleration • Instruments/controls • Automatic transmission performance

AGAINST Ride (Gran Touring option) • Fuel economy • Rear-seat comfort

EVALUATION A generally capable performer, the LeSabre makes few demands on its driver. With a proven powertrain, it takes off smartly with ample passing power and smooth, fairly responsive gear changes. We averaged 17.9 mpg, and the engine takes regular-grade fuel. The base suspension's smooth ride is marred by some body float over big humps and dips. The Gran Touring suspension option does a poor job of absorbing most sharp bumps and rides. Worse, it compromises control by imparting a jittery feeling over all but blemish-free pavement. Directional stability is good with either suspension, but steering feels artificially heavy in directional changes. Handling is competent enough, with moderate body lean in turns and good grip in steady-state cornering. Brakes are easy to modulate, but stopping power fails to impress. Wind and road noise are well-muffled, but tires whine on grooved or pebbled pavement. Quiet while cruising, the engine emits a muted growl during hard acceleration. Thick front pillars and slightly narrowed rear side glass produce a somewhat closed-in sensation. Seats are not wide enough to fit three adults without squeezing. Bucket and bench front seats are both roomy for two, though some folks find the cushions too pillowlike. Rear-seat comfort is disappointing. The cushion is low to the floor and its soft foam provides little thigh or back support. Gauges and controls are large, simple and generally well-positioned. Automatic climate controls on the Limited are hard to adjust while driving. Glossy plastic faces reflect light to obscure some readouts. The interior has a lot of hard plastic surfaces, along with budget-grade upholstery material.

VALUE For its core audience, the LeSabre imparts a feeling of size and substance, with a standard-equipment list that's well planned. Still, subpar rear-seat accommodations and indifferent interior furnishings are letdowns.

SPECIFICATIONS

	4-door sedan
Wheelbase, in.	112.2
Overall length, in.	200.0
Overall width, in.	73.5
Overall height, in.	57.0
Curb weight, lbs.	3567
Cargo volume, cu. ft.	18.0
Fuel capacity, gals.	17.5
Seating capacity	6
Front head room, in.	38.8
Max. front leg room, in.	42.4
Rear head room, in.	37.8
Min. rear leg room, in.	39.9

Powertrain layout: transverse front-engine/front-wheel drive

ENGINES

	ohv V6
Size, liters/cu. in.	3.8/231
Horsepower	205
Torque (lbs./ft.)	230

EPA city/highway mpg

4-speed OD automatic	19/30

City/highway mpg (as tested)

4-speed OD automatic	17.9

Built in USA

RETAIL PRICES

	GOOD	AVERAGE	POOR
2000 LeSabre	$14,500-16,500	$13,500-15,500	$10,000-11,500
2001 LeSabre	17,000-20,500	16,000-19,500	—

AVERAGE REPLACEMENT COSTS

A/C Compressor	$500	Constant Velocity Joints	905
Alternator	380	Exhaust System	445
Automatic Transmission or Transaxle	1,090	Radiator	450
		Shocks and/or Struts	535
Brakes	470	Timing Chain or Belt	505

TROUBLE SPOTS

• **Steering noise.** A countermeasure high-pressure power steering hose will reduce vibrations, shudders or moans from the steering during slow-speed turns. (2000-01)

• **Horn.** If the horn becomes difficult to operate or sounds by itself in cold temperatures, the air bag module will have to be replaced. (2000)

• **Brake noise.** The original equipment rear brake pads cause a humming or moaning noise, especially when the brakes are hot or warm. (2000)

• **Automatic transmission.** Transmission may slip, shift harshly or erratically due to sediment in the pressure control solenoid requiring. (2000)

RECALL HISTORY

2000: Loose inner tie rod nuts on certain cars can result in separation of tie rod, causing unexpected steering input. **2000:** Some cars have internal fluid leaks in brake hydraulic control unit; when rear brake proportioning, antilock braking, traction control, or stability control feature is activated in some driving situations, feature may not perform as designed.

1991-96 BUICK PARK AVENUE

1991 Buick Park Avenue

FOR Antilock brakes • Acceleration • Transmission performance • Passenger and cargo room

AGAINST Fuel economy • Steering/handling (base suspension) • Climate controls (early models)

EVALUATION Although the initial engine in this heavyweight sounds harsh at full throttle, the sedan is fairly brisk and smooth, as the V6 responds quickly. Engine flaws are more noticeable because the transmission shifts so beautifully—and doesn't slip repeatedly into and out of overdrive like so many 4-speed automatics. The Ultra edition's supercharger does its job well, with a noticeable increase in passing ability. Step on the gas and you get a spirited, satisfying response—but in an understated manner with no hint of raucousness. Adding 35 horsepower to the base engine in 1994 gave it ample power for most situations. Neither engine is particularly economical, but they could be worse. A base Park Avenue registered an average of 21.4 mpg in a long trial. Mileage around town, however, was in the 15-18 mpg neighborhood. An Ultra averaged 19.7 mpg, and the supercharged engine demands premium fuel. The Park Avenue's ride is comfortable, even cushy, with a soft feel from the base suspension. The car gets bouncy and floaty over wavy surfaces, and leans heavily in turns, which yield plenty of tire howling. The automatic ride control introduced in '93 reduces the floating sensation. Expect some firmness with the Gran Touring option, which got wide tires for better grip and handling, with only slight sacrifice in ride comfort. Steering in both the base and Ultra editions is too light, and doesn't center well after turns. Four adults sit comfortably in pillowy seats, with generous head and leg room all around. Even six can ride without undue squeezing, helped by space under front seats for rear occupants' feet. Wide doors permit easy entry/exit. Automatic climate controls in the Ultra (optional on base model) are arranged in two rows of seven small buttons, mounted low and away on the dashboard, thus hard to reach. That situation improved in 1994.

VALUE Park Avenue has sold well and is certainly worth a look. Take note, though: LeSabres offer many of the same features at a lower cost.

SPECIFICATIONS

	4-door sedan
Wheelbase, in.	110.8
Overall length, in.	205.9
Overall width, in.	74.1
Overall height, in.	55.1
Curb weight, lbs.	3536
Cargo volume, cu. ft.	20.3
Fuel capacity, gals.	18.0
Seating capacity	6
Front head room, in.	38.9
Max. front leg room, in.	42.7
Rear head room, in.	37.9
Min. rear leg room, in.	40.7

Powertrain layout: transverse front-engine/front-wheel drive

ENGINES

	ohv V6	ohv V6	Supercharged ohv V6
Size, liters/cu. in.	3.8/231	3.8/231	3.8/231
Horsepower	170	205	205-240
Torque (lbs./ft.)	200-225	230	260-280

EPA city/highway mpg

	ohv V6	ohv V6	Supercharged ohv V6
4-speed OD automatic	18/27	19/29	18/27

City/highway mpg (as tested)

4-speed OD automatic	21.4		19.7

Built in USA

RETAIL PRICES

	GOOD	AVERAGE	POOR
1991 Park Avenue	$2,700-3,400	$2,100-2,700	$600-800
1991 Park Avenue Ultra	3,100-3,800	2,500-3,100	800-1,000
1992 Park Avenue	3,400-4,100	2,700-3,300	900-1,200
1992 Park Auenue Ultra	3,900-4,600	3,200-3,800	1,200-1,500
1993 Park Avenue	4,200-5,000	3,400-4,200	1,300-1,700
1993 Park Avenue Ultra	4,800-5,600	4,000-4,800	1,800-2,000
1994 Park Avenue	5,000-5,800	4,200-5,000	2,000-2,200
1994 Park Avenue Ultra	5,700-6,500	4,800-5,800	2,500-3,000
1995 Park Avenue	6,500-7,300	5,500-6,500	3,000-3,500
1995 Park Avenue Ultra	7,300-8,200	6,400-7,300	3,600-4,200
1996 Park Avenue	8,000-9,000	7,000-8,000	4,000-4,800
1996 Park Avenue Ultra	9,000-10,000	8,000-9,000	4,800-5,600

AVERAGE REPLACEMENT COSTS

A/C Compressor	$725	Clutch, Pressure Plate, Bearing	1,010
Alternator	395	Constant Velocity Joints	810
Automatic Transmission or Transaxle	1,270	Exhaust System	610
Brakes	215	Radiator	445
Shocks and/or Struts	955	Timing Chain or Belt	230

TROUBLE SPOTS

• **Automatic transmission.** 4T60E transmissions may drop out of drive while cruising, shift erratically, or have no second, third, or fourth gear because of a bad ground connection for the shift solenoids. (1991-94)

• **Engine noise.** An intermittent rattling noise at start up is often caused by automatic transmission pump starvation or cavitation, or a sticking pressure regulator valve. (1991-95)

• **Engine knock.** Bearing knock was common on many 3.8-liter engines due to too much clearance on the number one main bearing. (1992-94)

• **Cruise control.** Cruise control doesn't stay engaged, or drops out of cruise. (1991-95)

• **Cruise control.** If the cruise control doesn't stay engaged or drops out of cruise, the brake switch can usually be adjusted. (1991-95)

• **Oil consumption and engine knock.** Models with the 3.8-liter engine are prone to excessive oil consumption often accompanied by spark knock during normal driving conditions due to failure of the valve stem seals. (1993-95)

• **Transmission leak.** The right front axle seal at the automatic transaxle is prone to leak and GM issued a revised seal to correct the problem. (1992-94)

• **Steering noise.** The upper bearing mount in the steering column can get loose and cause a snapping or clicking, requiring a new bearing spring and turn signal cancel cam. (1994-96)

RECALL HISTORY

1991: Parking brake lever assembly may release one or more teeth when applied, reducing cable load to rear brakes; parking brake might not hold the vehicle, allowing it to roll. **1992-93:** Transmission cooler line in cars with certain powertrains sold in specified states can separate at low temperature. **1995:** Driver-side headlamp lens has incorrect aim pad number; if headlamps are re-aimed using those numbers, result would be out of specified range. **1996:** Cars were assembled with one or more incorrect safety belt and/or buckle ends, so belt may not latch properly. **1996:** "Key in the Ignition" warning chime, driver seatbelt-unbuckled warning, and other functions may not operate properly. **1996:** Backfire can break upper intake manifold, resulting in possible fire.

1997-01 BUICK PARK AVENUE

1998 Buick Park Avenue Ultra

FOR Acceleration • Passenger room • Cargo room • Steering/handling (Ultra)

AGAINST Fuel economy (supercharged V6) • Steering/handling (base suspension)

EVALUATION Performance is satisfying in basic form—sufficient for most situations—but especially impressive when the engine is supercharged. Acceleration in an Ultra feels much like a small V8, so it makes a strong showing against the 6-cylinder competition. Helped by the automatic transmission's subtle and alert shifting, both models distribute ample, seamless power over a wide range of engine speeds. A base Park Avenue averaged 19.8 mpg using regular-grade fuel, helped by some highway time. Another base model averaged 19.5 mpg with a more even driving mix. Standard steering and suspension settings favor low-effort comfort. Unfortunately, this produces steering that's too light at freeway speeds, as well as floaty body motions over undulating surfaces. The Ultra's suspension is markedly stiffer—possibly too much so for some luxury-car buyers. A Gran Touring suspension setup has been optional on both models. That unit does a fine job of soaking up bumps with little jarring, while maintaining a flat, stable ride. It also quells undue body lean and front-end plowing through corners. Part of that package is magnetic variable-effort steering, which responds quickly with good straight-line stability, but feels a bit numb. Braking power feels strong. Simulated emergency stops can produce pronounced nose dive, but with no loss of stability or control. The Ultra, in particular, does a great job of muffling wind, road, and engine noises. Roomy and comfortable, Park Avenue promises space for adults to relax. Head and leg room are abundant. Six-passenger capacity is a bonus, though everyone will be sitting shoulder-to-shoulder when the car is filled. Seats are comfortable, but not sufficiently contoured to give occupants good lateral support when the road turns twisty. Front lap and shoulder belts are anchored to the seat itself, so they move right along with the seats, fore and aft. Belts are handy to grab and always seem to fit just right. Gauges and switches are generous in size, easy to read and operate. A simple dashboard pull-knob operates the headlights. If a secondhand Park Avenue is equipped with OnStar, the buyer will have to pay a monthly service fee to make use of the system. Park Avenues that were test-driven when new demonstrated good fit and finish, inside and out. One Ultra driven in sub-freezing weather, however, emitted creaks from its suspension when crossing speed bumps or entering driveways.

VALUE What do you get from a Park Avenue? Mainly, traditional American virtues- roominess, power, and amenities—at a sensible price. This domestic sedan is definitely worth a close look, though some of its virtues can be found in Buick's LeSabre for less money. In addition, it must be said that Buick's customer satisfaction ratings have not been as high as those of some foreign competitors.

SPECIFICATIONS

	4-door sedan
Wheelbase, in.	113.8
Overall length, in.	206.8
Overall width, in.	74.7
Overall height, in.	57.4
Curb weight, lbs.	3740
Cargo volume, cu. ft.	19.1
Fuel capacity, gals.	18.5
Seating capacity	6
Front head room, in.	39.8
Max. front leg room, in.	42.4
Rear head room, in.	38.0
Min. rear leg room, in.	41.1

Powertrain layout: transverse front-engine/front-wheel drive

ENGINES

	ohv V6	Supercharged ohv V6
Size, liters/cu. in.	3.8/231	3.8/231
Horsepower	205	240
Torque (lbs./ft.)	220-230	280
EPA city/highway mpg		
4-speed OD automatic	19.29	18/27
City/highway mpg (as tested)		
4-speed OD automatic	19.5	17.5

Built in USA

RETAIL PRICES

	GOOD	AVERAGE	POOR
1997 Park Avenue	$11,000-12,000	$10,000-11,000	$7,000-7,800
1997 Park Avenue Ultra	12,000-13,200	11,000-12,000	7,800-8,700
1998 Park Avenue	13,000-14,500	12,000-13,300	8,500-9,500
1998 Park Avenue Ultra	14,200-15,700	13,000-14,500	9,300-10,300
1999 Park Avenue	15,000-16,500	14,000-15,300	10,000-11,000
1999 Park Avenue Ultra	16,500-18,000	15,000-16,500	11,000-12,000
2000 Park Avenue	18,000-19,500	16,500-18,000	12,300-13,500
2000 Park Avenue Ultra	20,000-21,500	18,500-20,000	14,000-15,000
2001 Park Avenue Ultra	23,500-25,500	22,000-24,000	—

AVERAGE REPLACEMENT COSTS

A/C Compressor	$500	Constant Velocity Joints	750
Alternator	265	Exhaust System	475
Automatic Transmission or		Radiator	450
Transaxle	850	Shocks and/or Struts	900
Brakes	365	Timing Chain or Belt	325

TROUBLE SPOTS

• **Fuel odors.** Fuel spurts out of the filler pipe as the tank reaches full. (1997)

• **Seatbelts/safety.** Some owners have complained of excessive shoulder belt slack. (1997-98)

• **Brake noise.** The brakes make grinding, squealing, growling and other noises, and new brake pads were issued, but new, heftier rotors are also needed. (1997-98)

• **Horn.** The horn sounds by itself, especially in cold weather, requiring replacement of the horn pad assembly. (1997)

• **Oil consumption.** The oil dipstick shows on over-filled level because the original dipstick tube is too short and must be replaced. (1997)

• **Keyless entry.** The trunk pops open because the button on the remote is too sensitive and is easily activated while in a purse or pocket. (1997-98)

RECALL HISTORY

1997: Electronic Brake Control or Brake/Traction Control module can cause antilock brake system to cycle in non-ABS braking; could increase stopping distance. **1997-98:** Front shoulder belts might twist, becoming jammed in retractor. **1999:** A few cars may have been built with incorrect brake components, and could pull to one side during braking. **1999:** Brake booster to pedal assembly attachment nuts on some cars may be loose. **2000:** Due to internal fluid leakage in some cars, rear brake proportioning, ABS, traction control or stability control may not perform as designed.

1990-96 BUICK REGAL

1990 Buick Regal Gran Sport 2-door coupe

FOR Acceleration (3.8-liter V6) • Passenger and cargo room • Antilock brakes (optional until '94) • Ride

AGAINST Fuel economy (3.8-liter V6) • Seat comfort • Steering feel • Engine noise (early models) • Instruments/controls (early models) • Performance (early models)

EVALUATION Front seat room is generous, and the rear is adequate for 6-footers. Both body styles are roomy, but leg and head room are better in the sedan, though the lower cushion feels puny for long-distance comfort. Front shoulder belts in the sedan were anchored to door pillars, so belts could ride on the neck of shorter passengers. Wide front pillars compromise visibility. The initial Regal's lack of power was remedied by the arrival of the 3.8-liter engine in 1992. It gives the car sufficient oomph to accelerate smartly away from stoplights and pass safely. The early 3.1-liter, in contrast, sounds strained when a brisk getaway is called for, generating more noise than power. With the electronically controlled automatic installed in 1993, shifts grew swifter and smoother. Gas mileage is better with the 3.1-liter. We've averaged better than 20 mpg. The 3.8-liter yielded no more than 17-18 mpg. Analog instrumentation in early Regals is not the greatest and some instruments are blocked by the steering wheel. The optional electronic cluster has poorly designed graphics and has to squeeze into the same tight space. Climate controls also are far to the right, but have big buttons. The new

interior for 1995 cured many of these complaints. Ride/handling aren't bad, even with the base suspension. It seems to strike a sensible compromise between soft ride and capable handling, though slanting toward the former. Steering is on the light side, and the car leans heavily in turns. The firmer Gran Sport suspension provides taut handling and a well-controlled ride, but gets a bit harsh when rolling through pavement irregularities. Antilock braking works well, but takes high pedal pressure for a quick stop.

VALUE A Regal might not be much to get excited about, but it's not a bad choice when prices are tempting. About 75 percent of Regals got the 3.8-liter V6, and that's the one that approaches Ford Taurus in appeal.

SPECIFICATIONS

	2-door coupe	4-door sedan
Wheelbase, in.	107.5	107.5
Overall length, in.	193.9	193.7
Overall width, in.	72.5	72.5
Overall height, in.	53.0	54.5
Curb weight, lbs.	3232	3335
Cargo volume, cu. ft.	15.6	15.9
Fuel capacity, gals.	16.5	16.5
Seating capacity	6	6
Front head room, in.	37.6	38.6
Max. front leg room, in.	42.3	42.4
Rear head room, in.	37.0	37.8
Min. rear leg room, in.	34.8	36.2

Powertrain layout: transverse front-engine/front-wheel drive

ENGINES

	ohv V6	ohv V6
Size, liters/cu. in.	3.1/191	3.8/231
Horsepower	135-160	170-205
Torque (lbs./ft.)	180-185	220-230
EPA city/highway mpg		
4-speed OD automatic	20/29	19/30
City/highway mpg (as tested)		
4-speed OD automatic	20.5	17.3

Built in Canada

RETAIL PRICES

	GOOD	AVERAGE	POOR
1990 Regal	$1,400-2,100	$900-1,500	$200-400
1991 Regal	1,700-2,700	1,200-2,100	300-600
1992 Regal	2,200-3,300	1,600-2,600	400-900
1993 Regal	2,700-4,000	2,000-3,200	700-1,300
1994 Regal	3,500-4,800	2,700-4,000	1,100-1,800
1995 Regal	4,500-5,800	3,700-5,000	1,600-2,500
1996 Regal	5,500-7,000	4,500-6,000	2,100-3,100

AVERAGE REPLACEMENT COSTS

A/C Compressor	$555	Constant Velocity Joints	470
Alternator	215	Exhaust System	470
Automatic Transmission or		Radiator	340
Transaxle	1,075	Shocks and/or Struts	1,856
Brakes	200	Timing Chain or Belt	170

TROUBLE SPOTS

• **Automatic transmission.** 440-T4 automatic transmissions may shift late or not upshift at all. The problem is a stuck throttle valve inside the transmission. (1990-92)

• **Automatic transmission.** 4T60E transmissions may drop out of drive while cruising, shift erratically, or have no second, third, or fourth gear because of a bad ground connection for the shift solenoids. (1991-94)

• **Engine noise.** An intermittent rattle at start up may be due to too much wrist pin-to-piston clearance. (1994-95)

• **Engine noise.** An intermittent rattling noise at start up is often caused by automatic transmission pump starvation or cavitation, or a sticking pressure regulator valve. (1991-95)

• **Engine noise.** Bearing knock was common on many 3.8-liter engines due to too much clearance on the number one main bearing. (1992-94)

• **Oil consumption.** Models with the 3.8-liter engine are prone to excessive oil consumption often accompanied by spark knock during normal driving conditions due to failure of the valve stem seals. (1993-95)

• **Valve cover leaks.** The plastic valve covers on 3.1-liter engines were prone to leaks and should be replaced with redesigned aluminum valve covers. (1994-95)

• **Transaxle leak.** The right front axle seal at the automatic transaxle is prone to leak and GM issued a revised seal to correct the problem. (1992-94)

• **Steering noise.** The upper bearing mount in the steering column can get loose and cause a snapping or clicking that can be both heard and felt. (1994-96)

RECALL HISTORY

1990: Brake lights may not illuminate, or will not stay lit all the time when brakes are applied, due to faulty switch. **1990 w/Kelsey-Hayes steel wheels:** Cracks may develop in wheel mounting surface; if severe, wheel could separate from car. **1990:** Front shoulder belt may not properly restrain passenger in an accident. **1990-91:** Steering shaft could separate from steering gear. **1991:** Front door shoulder belt guide loops may be cracked. **1991 in 15 states:** Corrosion due to road salt could allow one or both front engine cradle bolts to pull through their retainers; steering shaft could possibly separate from steering gear. **1992:** Reverse servo apply pin of 4-speed automatic transmission may bind, which could cause loss or slipping of reverse, poor performance, or transmission to remain in reverse while indicator shows neutral. **1993:** Manual recliner mechanisms on some front seats will not latch under certain conditions, causing seatback to recline without prior warning. **1993-95:** Replace clear front side marker bulbs with amber. **1994-95:** Rear brake hoses can contact suspension components and wear through, resulting in loss of brake fluid. **1994-95:** Strained wire can cause intermittent or nonexistent wiper/washer operation. **1995:** On a few cars, steering-column support bolts could vibrate, loosen, or fall out. **1995:** Center rear seatbelt anchor plate could fracture in a crash. **1995:** Seatbelt anchor can fracture during crash. **1996:** Left front brake line can contact transaxle mounting bracket or bolt, causing line to wear through, resulting in loss of fluid and eventual loss of half the brake system. **1996 w/3.8-liter V6:** Backfire can break upper intake manifold, resulting in possible fire. **1995-96:** The driver's airbag could deploy inadvertently and injure the driver.

1997-01 BUICK REGAL

1998 Buick Regal GS

FOR Acceleration • Passenger and cargo room • Ride • Automatic transmission performance

AGAINST Fuel economy (supercharged engine)

EVALUATION Well known for smooth running, GM's 3.8-liter V6 engine feels great when installed in a Regal, furnishing good acceleration at low speeds, as well as plenty of passing power. Performance is better yet with the supercharged edition. Unfortunately, the GS suffers marked torque steer, in which the steering wheel is tugged in one direction during rapid takeoffs. Transmission behavior is absolutely sparkling and mannerly with either engine—just the way all automatic transmissions should function. We averaged between 16.9 and 20.1 mpg with a Regal GS. Gas mileage with an LS is about the same, but that model does not require premium fuel. Although Buick has promoted the Regal as a sports sedan, the car leans more toward comfort than true handling prowess. Steering response is a little slow in quick changes of direction, and the body floats slightly over high-speed dips that European sport sedans would take in stride. Body lean is moderate, however, and the Regal's suspension soaks up large bumps with little intrusion toward occupants. Pleasant inside, the Regal offers ample space in front and rear, though it's better for four adults than five. Comfortable front seats support the occupants nicely even during spirited driving. On the downside, the fold-down center armrest is too low to be of much value, yet its presence restricts outboard passenger space. Climate controls could be simpler, however. Having a trunklid release

inside the car would be handy, too, but there's one only on the remote keyless entry fob. Not only does the lid to the big trunk open to 90 degrees, but its hinges do not intrude on luggage space.

VALUE Regal fails to match the overall refinement or proven reliability record of a Honda Accord or Toyota Camry, and prices are likely to be far higher than for a comparable Ford Taurus or Mercury Sable. Still, Regal's solidity, performance, and ample quantity of equipment make it worth a close look in the mid-size family-sedan league.

SPECIFICATIONS

	4-door sedan
Wheelbase, in.	109.0
Overall length, in.	196.2
Overall width, in.	72.7
Overall height, in.	56.6
Curb weight, lbs.	3447
Cargo volume, cu. ft.	16.7
Fuel capacity, gals.	17.0
Seating capacity	5
Front head room, in.	39.3
Max. front leg room, in.	42.4
Rear head room, in.	31.4
Min. rear leg room, in.	36.9

Powertrain layout: transverse front-engine/front-wheel drive

ENGINES

	ohv V6	Supercharged ohv V8
Size, liters/cu. in.	3.8/231	3.8/231
Horsepower	195-200	240
Torque (lbs./ft.)	220	280

EPA city/highway mpg

4-speed OD automatic	19/30	17/27

City/highway mpg (as tested)

4-speed OD automatic		17.6

Built in Canada

RETAIL PRICES

	GOOD	AVERAGE	POOR
1997 Regal LS	$8,500-9,500	$7,500-8,500	$5,000-5,700
1997 Regal GS	9,500-10,500	8,500-9,500	5,800-6,500
1998 Regal LS	10,000-11,000	9,000-10,000	6,000-6,800
1998 Regal GS	11,200-12,500	10,200-11,500	7,000-8,000
1999 Regal LS	11,500-12,500	10,500-11,500	7,000-7,800
1999 Regal GS	13,000-14,500	12,000-13,500	8,500-9,500
2000 Regal LS	13,000-14,000	12,000-13,000	8,500-9,300
2000 Regal GS	14,500-16,000	13,200-14,500	9,500-10,500
2001 Regal LS	14,500-15,500	13,500-14,500	—
2001 Regal GS	16,500-18,000	15,000-16,500	—

AVERAGE REPLACEMENT COSTS

A/C Compressor	$380	Constant Velocity Joints	1,100
Alternator	240	Exhaust System	470
Automatic Transmission or		Radiator	440
Transaxle	980	Shocks and/or Struts	1,500
Brakes	520	Timing Chain or Belt	315

TROUBLE SPOTS

• **Suspension noise.** A popping or groaning noise from the rear of the car is caused by the stabilizer shaft links. Redesigned links are available. (1997-98)

• **Engine noise.** A ticking sound in the engine is caused by excessive clearance between the piston bores and wrist pins. GM will replace all pistons under normal warranty. (1997-98)

• **Engine misfire.** An engine miss causes rough running and a check engine light. It is due to the spark plug boots cracking and allowing the voltage to jump to ground. (1997-98)

• **Vehicle shake.** In warm weather the engine bounces in its mounts causing a shaking sensation throughout the whole car. A new transmission mount will be installed under normal warranty. (1997-98)

• **Keyless entry.** The remote keyless entry may not have much range, requiring a new receiver (with foil antenna) to be installed. (1997)

RECALL HISTORY

1997: Right front brake line can wear through; can result in fluid loss, and loss of half of braking system. **1997:** Windshield wipers may stop working, due to separation between drive pin and crescent in crank arm assembly. **1998-99:** Vertical headlamp adjusting device may not be calibrated properly. **1999:** Short in ABS motor can cause extreme heating of flexible brake pipe, where it can melt nearby plastic fuel hose. **2000 w/rear drum brakes:** Bolt heads on rear spindle rod can separate and affected wheel can shift, causing loss of control. **2000 w/rear drum brakes:** Bolt heads on rear spindle rod can separate and rear wheel can shift, causing rear steering of vehicle. **2000:** Clamp that secures flexible fuel fill hose to metal fill tube on a few cars may be loose and could separate, causing fuel leakage. **2000:** Some seatbelt assemblies were not properly heat treated and do not pass the load bearing requirement.

1990-93 BUICK RIVIERA

1991 Buick Riveria

FOR   Quietness • Acceleration (1991-93) • Antilock brakes

AGAINST   Fuel economy • Ride (Gran Touring suspension) • Rear-seat room • Rear visibility

EVALUATION   Adding those 11 inches to the Riviera's length for 1989 did not increase interior room. All told, the quiet-running coupe was not as roomy as its exterior dimensions suggest. Sure, you do get plenty of luxury and convenience features in the plush interior; but space is adequate for only four people and their luggage. Climbing into the back also demands maneuvering around the seatbelts and squeezing through a narrow opening. Over-the-shoulder visibility is obscured by wide rear pillars, while the large, heavy doors need a lot of room to open. Acceleration from the Riv's 3.8-liter engine ranges from adequate to peppy and spirited, depending on the circumstances. The early (1990) automatic transmission didn't always respond quickly to the throttle. An improved automatic for '91 yielded passing response that was consistently prompt. The gutsy engine and improved automatic transmission combine for brisk acceleration and smooth power delivery. Fuel-economy tests of a 1990 model averaged 17 mpg: 20 mpg on suburban expressways, but less than 15 in the city. Ride and handling are competent, and the Riviera is quite agile as well, with good high-speed stability. The soft base suspension puts ride comfort over handling ability. A Gran Touring package with its wider tires and stiffer suspension improves handling and yields a more controlled feel, at some cost in ride comfort. Antilock braking produces sure, stable stops, even under slippery conditions. Instruments and controls are far more logical than in earlier Rivieras. Positioning of climate and stereo controls, high on the dash within easy reach of the driver, is another "plus." The Riviera's wide trunk has a flat floor, but isn't very deep, or shaped to hold more than a couple of large suitcases.

VALUE   Despite its enhanced appearance, the early '90s Riviera does nothing exceptional and doesn't stand high on our older luxury-coupe shopping list. Though far beyond earlier Rivs in acceleration, handling, and stability, this version simply doesn't offer quite as much as we'd expect for its still-lofty price.

SPECIFICATIONS

	2-door coupe
Wheelbase, in.	108.0
Overall length, in.	198.2
Overall width, in.	73.1
Overall height, in.	52.9
Curb weight, lbs.	3504
Cargo volume, cu. ft.	14.4
Fuel capacity, gals.	18.8
Seating capacity	5
Front head room, in.	37.8
Max. front leg room, in.	42.7
Rear head room, in.	37.8
Min. rear leg room, in.	35.6

Powertrain layout: transverse front-engine/front-wheel drive

ENGINES

	ohv V6
Size, liters/cu. in.	3.8/231
Horsepower	165-170
Torque (lbs./ft.)	210-220

EPA city/highway mpg

4-speed OD automatic	19/28

City/highway mpg (as tested)

4-speed OD automatic	17.0

Built in USA

RETAIL PRICES

	GOOD	AVERAGE	POOR
1990 Riviera	$2,300-3,000	$1,600-2,400	$400-700
1991 Riviera	3,000-3,800	2,300-3,000	700-1,200
1992 Riviera	3,800-4,600	3,000-3,800	1,100-1,600
1993 Riviera	4,600-5,500	3,800-4,600	1,600-2,200

AVERAGE REPLACEMENT COSTS

A/C Compressor	$465	Constant Velocity Joints	870
Alternator	265	Exhaust System	430
Automatic Transmission or		Radiator	410
Transaxle	985	Shocks and/or Struts	1,300
Brakes	230	Timing Chain or Belt	225

TROUBLE SPOTS

• **Automatic transmission.** 4T60E transmissions may drop out of drive while cruising, shift erratically, or have no second, third, or fourth gear, because of a bad ground connection for the shift solenoids. (1991-93)

• **Water leak.** A leak in the left fender well and firewall area causes water to collect on the left front floor. (1990)

• **Engine noise.** An intermittent rattling noise at start up is often caused by automatic transmission pump starvation or cavitation, or a sticking pressure regulator valve. (1991-93)

• **Engine knock.** Bearing knock was common on many 3.3- and 3.8-liter engines due to too much clearance on the number one main bearing. (1992-93)

• **Cruise control.** Cars equipped with vacuum-operated cruise control (as opposed to the Electro-Motor Cruise Control) may not maintain the proper speed due to a faulty vacuum servo. (1990-92)

• **Engine stalling.** Cars with 3800 engines may stall when decelerating or be hard to start due to a faulty idle air control, which must be replaced. (1990)

• **Automatic transmission.** Model 440-T4 or 700-R4 automatic transmissions may shift late or not upshift at all. The problem is a stuck throttle valve inside the transmission. (1990-93)

• **Oil consumption.** Models with the 3.8-liter engine are prone to excessive oil consumption often accompanied by spark knock during normal driving conditions due to failure of the valve stem seals. (1993)

• **Oil consumption.** Oil leaks may be due to a defect in the oil pan and gasket, and the display may report a false low oil level due to a defective oil level sensor and/or deformed oil pan. (1990)

• **Oil consumption.** The oil pressure gauge may display an intermittent high reading due to a faulty oil pressure sensor. (1990)

• **Transaxle leak.** The right front axle seal at the automatic transaxle is prone to leak and GM issued a revised seal to correct the problem. (1992-93)

RECALL HISTORY

1990: Cable may disengage from transaxle's floor-shift control so driver might be unable to determine which gear is engaged, possibly resulting in unexpected vehicle movement. **1990:** Misaligned rear seatbelt shoulder retractor assemblies could cause pendulum interference, causing belt to remain in locked position or to travel freely without locking, increasing likelihood of injury in panic stop or accident. **1990:** Brake indicator light may not operate when ignition is "on," parking brake is applied, and gear selector is in "Park" or "Neutral." **1990-93:** Front outer shoulder belt web can become stuck in its retractor. **1992:** Intermediate shaft to steering rack lower coupling pinch bolt may be missing on some cars.

1995-99 BUICK RIVIERA

FOR   Antilock brakes • Acceleration • Ride • Steering/handling

AGAINST   Instruments/controls • Rear visibility • Entry/exit • Fuel economy (supercharged)

1995 Buick Riviera

EVALUATION Acceleration, handling, and ride quality are vastly better than in the old Riviera. In performance as well as refinement, this rendition rivals premium coupes that cost much more. Even at highway speeds, noise, vibration, and harshness of any sort are nearly absent. We clocked a supercharged '95 model at a brisk 7.9 seconds to 60 mph. That kind of action sends the Riviera into the same league as some V8 competitors. As for economy, we averaged 17.7 mpg in a supercharged Riviera, commuting through urban areas about two-thirds of the time. The normally aspirated engine offers acceleration that is more than adequate, though less lively. Despite its rather abundant size, this Riviera feels balanced and nimble in turns, exhibiting little body lean and good grip onto the pavement. Buick's suspension teams with the long wheelbase to provide a comfortable ride, even over bumps and broken pavement. Though a front bench is standard, Riviera works best as a 4-seater. An occasional passenger might occupy the middle rear seat. Leg room is sufficient for four 6-footers to stretch out. Head room is generous in front but only adequate in back. Long, heavy doors are cumbersome in tight parking spaces. One big weak spot is the dashboard, which lags in practical considerations. Not only are the speedometer and tachometer too far apart, but the steering wheel blocks the headlamp and cruise control switches. Visibility is generally good, but a high rear parcel shelf and thick rear roof pillars interfere with the driver's view aft and over the shoulders.

VALUE Buick aimed the Riviera against such 2-door contenders as the Acura Legend Coupe, Cadillac Eldorado, Lincoln Mark VIII, and Mercedes E320. If the styling appeals, it's worth a serious test drive. If not, you might prefer to shop elsewhere.

SPECIFICATIONS

	2-door coupe
Wheelbase, in.	113.8
Overall length, in.	207.2
Overall width, in.	75.0
Overall height, in.	55.2
Curb weight, lbs.	3690
Cargo volume, cu. ft.	17.4
Fuel capacity, gals.	20.0
Seating capacity	5/6
Front head room, in.	38.2
Max. front leg room, in.	42.6
Rear head room, in.	36.2
Min. rear leg room, in.	37.3

Powertrain layout: transverse front-engine/front-wheel drive

ENGINES

	ohv V6	Supercharged ohv V6
Size, liters/cu. in.	3.8/231	3.8/231
Horsepower	205	225-240
Torque (lbs./ft.)	230	275-280
EPA city/highway mpg		
4-speed OD automatic	19/28	18/27
City/highway mpg (as tested)		
4-speed OD automatic		17.7

Built in USA

RETAIL PRICES

	GOOD	AVERAGE	POOR
1995 Riviera	$6,500-7,500	$5,500-6,500	$2,800-3,500
1996 Riviera	8,000-9,200	7,000-8,200	3,800-4,600
1997 Riviera	10,000-11,800	9,000-10,800	5,200-6,200
1998 Riviera	13,000-14,500	11,800-13,200	7,700-8,700
1999 Riviera	16,000-17,500	14,500-16,000	10,000-11,000

AVERAGE REPLACEMENT COSTS

A/C Compressor	$685	Exhaust System	235
Alternator	340	Radiator	480
Automatic Transmission or Transaxle	970	Shocks and/or Struts	795
		Timing Chain or Belt	360
Brakes	265		

TROUBLE SPOTS

• **Suspension noise.** A thumping sound from the rear is likely unless the original shock mounts are replaced with redesigned ones. (1995-96)

• **Battery.** Battery venting or an overflow of acid causes the floor pan to rust. (1995-99)

• **Automatic transmission.** The 4T60-E automatic transmission can suddenly go into neutral at highway speeds due to a problem with internal shift valves. (1995-96)

• **Electrical problem.** The door locks may quit working and the instrument panel fuse may blow due to a short circuit caused by a bolt inside either front door chafing the wiring harness. (1995)

• **Climate control.** The heater output on the driver's side may be inadequate because the insulation material may be protruding into the heater duct. (1995-96)

• **Engine misfire.** The idle may be rough when restarting a warm engine (supercharged) and is fixed by replacing the fuel pressure regulator and computer MEM-CAL. (1995)

• **Doors.** The power door locks may not operate due to a rubber bumper falling off of the actuator arm. (1995-96) The locks may malfunction, and the door locks fuse may blow due to a short inside the door. (1995)

• **Starter.** The starter may keep running after the engine starts or the key is turned off due to a short in the wiring. (1995)

RECALL HISTORY

1995: Rear shoulder belts may not retract. **1996:** "Key in the Ignition" chime, driver seatbelt-unbuckled warning, and other functions may fail to operate properly. **1996:** Backfire during engine startup can cause breakage of upper intake manifold, resulting in non-start condition and possible fire.

1991-96 BUICK ROADMASTER

1992 Buick Roadmaster Limited 4-door sedan

FOR Acceleration • Passenger and cargo room • Trailer towing capability • Antilock brakes

AGAINST Fuel economy (city) • Size and weight

EVALUATION More stable than its predecessors, with a firmer suspension than Chevrolet's structurally similar Caprice, the Roadmaster offers capable highway handling for a car of this class. The ride is smooth and steady, with less bounce over bumps and sway in the corners than a Caprice suffers. The big wagon feels stable and is easy enough to control at high speed. Steering is more accurate and the ride more controlled than a Caprice's. Even so, the generously-sized sedan and wagon tend to bound and float over wavy surfaces. Antilock braking works well, with good control. Acceleration with the initial 5.0-liter V8 is good. Snappier yet, especially when passing or merging, is the 5.7-liter V8 that became standard for 1992. Hottest of all: the Corvette-based 260-horsepower V8 tucked into 1994-96 models. Those Roadmasters also contain dual airbags, rather than a driver-only airbag as in earlier models. Gas mileage is barely passable in town, but surprisingly good on the road. We averaged 24 mpg on a highway trip in a Limited sedan with the 180-horsepower engine, but mileage dropped below 16 mpg in city driving. Six fit easily in a sedan, and the wagon's rear-facing third seat holds two youngsters. The fixed-glass "vista roof" manages to brighten the wagon's interior. A roomy Roadmaster with Trailer-Towing Package can haul 5000 pounds. In addition to a large cargo area, the wagon has numerous storage bins and pockets. Sedans offer a huge trunk, but rearward visibility is marred by thick roof pillars. Controls are straightforward. Full analog gauges, including a tachometer, are better than Caprice's. Nine large climate-control buttons may be reached by the driver or front passenger.

VALUE Naturally, not everyone needs a boat this large, but Roadmaster ranks as one of the better examples of this now-extinct breed.

SPECIFICATIONS

	4-door sedan	4-door wagon
Wheelbase, in.	115.9	115.9
Overall length, in.	215.8	217.5
Overall width, in.	78.1	79.9
Overall height, in.	55.9	60.3
Curb weight, lbs.	4211	4572
Cargo volume, cu. ft.	21.0	92.4
Fuel capacity, gals.	23.0	22.0
Seating capacity	6	8
Front head room, in.	39.2	39.6
Max. front leg room, in.	42.1	42.3
Rear head room, in.	38.6	39.4
Min. rear leg room, in.	38.9	37.3

Powertrain layout: longitudinal front-engine/rear-wheel drive

ENGINES

	ohv V8	ohv V8	ohv V8
Size, liters/cu. in.	5.0/305	5.7/350	5.7/350
Horsepower	170	180	260
Torque (lbs./ft.)	255	290-300	330-335
EPA city/highway mpg			
4-speed OD automatic	16/25	16/25	17/26
City/highway mpg (as tested)			
4-speed OD automatic			13.8

Built in USA

RETAIL PRICES

	GOOD	AVERAGE	POOR
1991 Roadmaster wagon	$2,500-3,300	$1,800-2,600	$500-800
1992 Roadmaster sedan	3,000-3,800	2,300-3,000	800-1,200
1992 Roadmaster wagon	4,000-4,800	3,200-4,000	1,200-1,800
1993 Roadmaster sedan	4,000-5,200	3,200-4,400	1,200-2,000
1993 Roadmaster wagon	5,200-6,200	4,300-5,300	2,000-2,700
1994 Roadmaster sedan	5,500-6,800	4,600-5,800	1,800-2,800
1994 Roadmaster wagon	6,700-7,700	5,700-6,700	2,700-3,400
1995 Roadmaster sedan	7,000-8,500	6,000-7,500	2,800-3,800
1995 Roadmaster wagon	8,500-9,800	7,500-8,800	4,000-4,800
1996 Roadmaster sedan	9,000-10,500	8,000-9,500	4,200-5,200
1996 Roadmaster wagon	10,700-12,500	9,500-11,000	5,500-6,500

AVERAGE REPLACEMENT COSTS

A/C Compressor	$460	Exhaust System	410
Alternator	195	Radiator	510
Automatic Transmission or Transaxle	780	Shocks and/or Struts	290
		Timing Chain or Belt	305
Brakes	210	Universal Joints	200

TROUBLE SPOTS

• **Automatic transmission.** Model 700-R4 automatic transmissions may shift late or not upshift at all. The problem is a stuck throttle valve inside the transmission. (All years)

• **Engine noise.** The exhaust valves on the 5.0- and 5.7-liter engines may not get enough lubrication causing a variety of noises. Usually, the same engine consumes excess oil because the valve guide seals on the exhaust valves are bad and have to be replaced. (1994-96)

• **Steering noise.** The upper bearing mount in the steering column can get loose and cause a clicking that can be both heard and felt, requiring a new bearing spring and turn signal cancel cam. (1994-96)

RECALL HISTORY

1991-92: Secondary hood latch assembly can corrode, causing high latch release effort and possibly preventing hood from latching properly. **1991-92:** Shoulder belt guide loop plastic covering may crack and expose steel sub plate; seatbelt webbing could be cut in a crash. **1992:** Antilock brake system modulator can corrode and leak fluid; can reduce brake effectiveness and increase stopping distance. **1994:** Oil cooler inlet hose may be too close to steering gear, causing chafing; could result in oil leakage and fire. **1994:** On a few cars, paint between wheel and brake rotor/drum can cause lug nut to loosen. **1994:** Fuel tank fasteners can detach, eventually allowing tank to sag and strike roadway. **1994-95:** At low temperatures, throttle return spring could fail, and engine speed may not return to idle. **1994-95:** Lower ball joint on a few cars sent to Guam and Puerto Rico can separate. **1995:** Improperly adjusted transmission linkage may permit shifting from "park" position with ignition key removed. **1995-96 station wagon:** Airbag caution label and roof-rack caution label were incorrectly installed on same side of sunvisor. **1995-96:** Wheel lug nuts were not tightened to the proper specification. This could result in wheel loss.

1990-93 CADILLAC DeVILLE/FLEETWOOD

1992 Cadillac Coupe DeVille 2-door coupe

FOR Acceleration • Quietness • Antilock brakes • Passenger and cargo room • Ride • Traction control • Drivability

AGAINST Fuel economy • Electronic instruments (early models) • Rear visibility

EVALUATION Cadillac's 4.5-liter V8 is impressive, moving these luxury heavyweights with authority. You get ample power for brisk takeoffs from stoplights, as well as for safe highway passing. Cadillac estimated a 0-60 mph acceleration time of 9.5 seconds—not bad at all for a big sedan. The 4-speed automatic transmission stays out of overdrive until the car reaches a cruising speed past 40 mph, and downshifts rapidly for passing/merging. The 4.9-liter V8 installed in '91 models turned these cars into some of the most powerful front-drive sedans around. Even if slightly rough at idle, the 4.9 is a fine V8, delivering ample power for quick takeoffs and easy passing. A slicker automatic now complemented the engine with prompt, smooth gear changes. No economy improvement occurred, so expect 25 mpg on the highway but no more than 15 mpg or so around town. We got only 11.3 mpg in the city. Premium fuel is required. Computer Command Ride improves both ride and handling. At speeds past 60 mph, CCR-equipped cars offer a stable, smooth ride with almost none of the bounding and floating of previous models. But CCR feels too soft between 40 and 60 mph, so you get a lot of bobbing up and down over wavy surfaces. With the regular suspension, in particular, handling and roadholding favor conservative driving. Those Cadillacs bounce and float too much at intermediate speeds. Interior space is bountiful, cargo room ample. Even back-seat occupants can stretch out, and the spacious trunk has a flat, uncluttered floor. Occupants enjoy easy-chair softness. Doors are tall and wide, so there's easy entry to the huge cabin. Chunky styling and non-flush glass contribute to noticeable wind noise around roof pillars; otherwise, you cruise in near silence. Thick rear pillars and a narrow back window limit visibility.

VALUE If you're looking for a strong, refined engine plus appealing comfort and a host of convenience features in a full-size front-drive automobile, Cadillac might have just what you seek.

SPECIFICATIONS

	2-door coupe	4-door sedan
Wheelbase, in.	110.8	113.7
Overall length, in.	203.3	206.3
Overall width, in.	73.4	73.4
Overall height, in.	54.8	55.1
Curb weight, lbs.	3519	3605
Cargo volume, cu. ft.	18.1	18.4
Fuel capacity, gals.	18.0	18.0

	2-door coupe	4-door sedan
Seating capacity	6	6
Front head room, in.	39.2	39.3
Max. front leg room, in.	42.0	42.0
Rear head room, in.	37.9	38.1
Min. rear leg room, in.	40.3	43.6

Powertrain layout: transverse front-engine/front-wheel drive

ENGINES

	ohv V8	ohv V8
Size, liters/cu. in.	4.5/273	4.9/300
Horsepower	180	200
Torque (lbs./ft.)	245	275
EPA city/highway mpg		
4-speed OD automatic	16/25	16/25
City/highway mpg (as tested)		
4-speed OD automatic	16.1	

Built in USA

RETAIL PRICES

	GOOD	AVERAGE	POOR
1990 DeVille	$2,000-2,700	$1,400-2,100	$300-600
1990 Fleetwood	2,400-3,100	1,800-2,500	500-800
1991 DeVille	2,500-3,200	1,800-2,500	600-800
1991 Fleetwood	2,900-3,700	2,200-3,000	800-1,100
1992 DeVille	3,200-4,000	2,500-3,200	900-1,100
1992 Fleetwood	3,700-4,800	3,000-4,000	1,200-1,700
1993 DeVille	4,000-5,300	3,200-4,400	1,300-2,000

AVERAGE REPLACEMENT COSTS

A/C Compressor...........	$470	Constant Velocity Joints	875
Alternator......................	270	Exhaust System	429
Automatic Transmission or		Radiator........................	417
Transaxle	1,010	Shocks and/or Struts....	745
Brakes	200	Timing Chain or Belt.....	250

TROUBLE SPOTS

• **Automatic transmission.** 440-T4 automatic transmissions may shift late or not upshift at all. The problem is a stuck throttle valve inside the transmission. (1990-92)

• **Automatic transmission.** 4T60E transmissions may drop out of drive while cruising, shift erratically, or have no second, third, or fourth gear because of a bad ground connection for the shift solenoids. Poor grounds also allow wrong gear starts. (1991-93)

• **Engine noise.** A rattling noise at start up is often caused by automatic transmission pump starvation or cavitation, or a sticking pressure regulator valve. (1991-93)

• **Vehicle noise.** Noises from the front, often mistaken as coming from behind the dash, are due to the front spring coils clashing when driving over bumps requiring sleeves on the lower spring coils. (1991-92)

• **Brakes.** Some early-build models have unexpected ABS brake pedal pulsation below 10mph due to moisture getting into the rear wheel speed sensor(s). (1991)

• **Brakes.** Some models may be hard to shift out of park due to mal-adjustment of the brake-shifter interlock system. (1991)

• **Engine stalling.** The engine may stall when coasting down to a stop due to a faulty throttle position sensor (TPS). (1990-91)

• **Transaxle leak.** The right front axle seal at the automatic transaxle is prone to leak and GM issued a revised seal to correct the problem. (1992-93)

RECALL HISTORY

1991-93: Transaxle oil cooler hose can pull out of coupling, causing oil leak that could result in fire.

1994-99 CADILLAC
DeVILLE/CONCOURS

FOR Antilock brakes • Acceleration • Passenger and cargo room • Interior noise levels • Traction control

AGAINST Fuel economy • Climate control (base and d'Elegance) • Rear visibility

1994 Cadillac Sedan DeVille Concours

EVALUATION Concours is the performance prince, but even a base DeVille boasts impressive acceleration, with brisk passing response. Power is plentiful with the 4.9-liter base engine—and even better with the later Northstar. With any of the Northstar V8s under the hood, you can expect surprisingly sizzling action, which belies the car's heft. A Concours, with the most potent V8 ready and waiting, actually rivals some sports sedans when pushing the pedal to the floor. Even better, Cadillac's 4-speed overdrive automatic transmission shifts with buttery smoothness. Fuel economy is poor. Only on the highway did we average better than 20 mpg. Overall, a Concours averaged just 15.8 mpg in a long-term trial. Worse yet, all engines demand premium gasoline. Because of a stiffer structure and better engine mounts, these two ride much more quietly than in previous years, with less noise and vibration. Both suspensions do a good job of isolating the cabin and keeping bouncing to a minimum. The Road Sensing Suspension does a commendable job of maintaining a stable, comfortable ride and minimizing body lean in turns. Agile may not be an appropriate word to describe either DeVille, but these sizable sedans handle reasonably well for cars in their category. Later models with StabiliTrak feel much more agile in hard driving, with no penalty in ride quality. Road and wind noise are minimal, though not necessarily nonexistent. Brakes are strong and fade-free. Steering is firm and responsive, but lacks true road feel and precision. Inside, you get ample six-passenger seating in a spacious cabin, plus dual airbags. Basic dashboard design is borrowed from the Seville, so climate controls are just to the right of the steering wheel, where they're hard to see and reach. The trunk opens at bumper level and has a wide, flat floor that can hold loads of luggage.

VALUE Don't judge the latest DeVille and Concours just by their conservative styling, which continues to appeal mainly to older drivers. Both Cadillacs offer tempting performance and roomy accommodations, and represent good value for the money.

SPECIFICATIONS

	4-door sedan
Wheelbase, in.	113.8
Overall length, in.	209.7
Overall width, in.	76.6
Overall height, in.	56.3
Curb weight, lbs.	3959
Cargo volume, cu. ft.	20.0
Fuel capacity, gals.	20.0
Seating capacity	6
Front head room, in.	38.5
Max. front leg room, in.	42.6
Rear head room, in.	38.4
Min. rear leg room, in.	43.3

Powertrain layout: transverse front-engine/front-wheel drive

ENGINES

	dohc V8	dohc V8	ohv V8
Size, liters/cu. in.	4.6/279	4.6/279	4.9/300
Horsepower	270-275	300	200
Torque (lbs./ft.)	300	295	275
EPA city/highway mpg			
4-speed OD automatic..........................	17/26	17/26	16/26
City/highway mpg (as tested)			
4-speed OD automatic..........................	15.8	17.2	

Built in USA

RETAIL PRICES

	GOOD	AVERAGE	POOR
1994 DeVille	$6,500-7,500	$5,500-6,500	$3,000-3,700

	GOOD	AVERAGE	POOR
1994 Concours	$7,300-8,300	$6,300-7,300	$3,500-4,200
1995 DeVille	7,800-9,000	6,800-8,000	3,800-4,800
1995 Concours	8,700-10,000	7,700-9,000	4,500-5,400
1996 DeVille	10,000-11,200	9,000-10,200	5,500-6,500
1996 Concours	11,000-12,500	10,000-11,500	6,300-7,300
1997 DeVille	12,500-14,000	11,300-12,700	7,500-8,500
1997 Concours	14,000-15,500	12,500-14,000	8,500-9,500
1998 DeVille	15,000-17,000	13,500-15,500	9,500-11,000
1998 Concours	16,800-18,200	15,300-16,700	11,000-12,200
1999 DeVille	18,000-20,000	16,500-18,500	12,000-13,500
1999 Concours	20,000-22,000	18,500-20,500	13,500-15,000

AVERAGE REPLACEMENT COSTS

A/C Compressor	$475	Constant Velocity Joints	700
Alternator	350	Exhaust System	1,000
Automatic Transmission or		Radiator	490
Transaxle	1,160	Timing Chain or Belt	720
Brakes	210		

TROUBLE SPOTS

• **Engine noise.** A rattling noise from the engine at start up is often caused by automatic transmission pump starvation or cavitation, or a sticking pressure regulator valve. (1994-95)

• **Fuel odors.** Leaks in the vapor recovery system, due to excessively short hoses coming loose, causes fuel odors inside the car. (1997)

• **Blower motor.** The blower motor fails if the spark plug wires are routed too close to the blower motor housing. (1994-97)

• **Steering noise.** The upper bearing mount in the steering column can get loose and cause a snapping or clicking, requiring a new bearing spring and turn signal cancel cam. (1994-96)

RECALL HISTORY

1995: Inadvertent airbag deployment could occur, due to water intrusion. **1996:** Secondary hood latch may be improperly adjusted; if primary latch also is not engaged, hood could open unexpectedly. **1997:** Brake/traction control module can cause antilock brake system to cycle in non-ABS braking; could increase stopping distance. **1998:** Hood hinge pivot bolts can break; could cause either the corner of the hood near the windshield to rise, or one side of hood to be unstable when opened. **1998:** Misrouted canister purge evaporative emissions harness could interfere with cruise control and throttle linkage, preventing return to close throttle position.

2000-01 CADILLAC DeVILLE

2001 Cadillac DeVille DTS

FOR Acceleration • Quietness • Passenger and cargo room • Entry/exit • Build quality

AGAINST Navigation system controls • Fuel economy • Rear visibility

EVALUATION Poised on the road, a DeVille DHS easily holds its own against imported luxury sedans, with a ride that's comfortable yet controlled. Acceleration is outstanding, as a DeVille is able to reach 60 mph in as little as 7 seconds. The refined powertrain features a smooth and responsive automatic transmission. As for gas mileage, a DTS sedan with the 300-bhp engine averaged 14.6 to 16.7 mpg. Cadillac recommends premium fuel, but regular is acceptable and does not affect performance by much. Few sedans are more spacious or comfortable than a DeVille. Front seats provide fine support and stretch-out room in outboard position, though the middle occupant of the front bench is likely to feel squeezed. Leg clearance in back ranks as limousinelike, with a firm, generous cushion that's wide enough for three adults. All doors open exceptionally wide for easy entry/exit. Whether digital or analog, gauges are unobstructed and legible. Though abundant, controls on the dashboard and steering wheel are large and clearly labeled. Outward visibility is generally good, but thick rear roof pillars hamper over-the-shoulder vision. The big trunk opens to bumper level. Cabin materials and workmanship are competitive with imported luxury cars, and notably better than other domestics. Two exceptions are the low-budget plastic in the dashboard center and crude movement of vent adjusters. Cadillac's Night Vision option is most useful in rural areas, displaying a moving image in the windshield that resembles a photographic negative. It does not interfere with normal forward vision, and can be switched off.

VALUE Spacious and powerful, the DeVille is loaded with jet-age gizmos. Priced below most V8 luxury rivals, it has a markedly different appearance than DeVilles of the past, which pleases some potential buyers but may distress others. Ride and handling are on a par with the world's most prestigious luxury sedans, accompanied by energetic performance.

SPECIFICATIONS

	4-door sedan
Wheelbase, in.	115.3
Overall length, in.	207.0
Overall width, in.	74.4
Overall height, in.	56.7
Curb weight, lbs.	3978
Cargo volume, cu. ft.	19.1
Fuel capacity, gals.	18.5
Seating capacity	6
Front head room, in.	39.1
Max. front leg room, in.	43.2
Rear head room, in.	38.3
Min. rear leg room, in.	43.2

Powertrain layout: transverse front-engine/front-wheel drive

ENGINES

	dohc V8	dohc V8
Size, liters/cu. in.	4.6/279	4.6/279
Horsepower	275	300
Torque (lbs./ft.)	300	295
EPA city/highway mpg		
4-speed OD automatic	16/27	16/27
City/highway mpg (as tested)		
4-speed OD automatic		16.7

Built in USA

RETAIL PRICES

	GOOD	AVERAGE	POOR
2000 DeVille	$26,000-27,500	$25,000-26,500	$20,500-21,500
2000 DeVille DHS/DTS	29,000-31,000	27,500-29,500	22,500-24,000
2001 DeVille	29,500-31,000	28,000-29,500	—
2001 DeVille DHS/DTS	34,000-38,000	32,000-36,000	—

AVERAGE REPLACEMENT COSTS

A/C Compressor	$750	Constant Velocity Joints	800
Alternator	550	Exhaust System	500
Automatic Transmission or		Radiator	670
Transaxle	1,190	Shocks and/or Struts	1,755
Brakes	575	Timing Chain or Belt	1,275

TROUBLE SPOTS

• **Climate control.** Due to insufficient tension on the pivots, the shut-off doors in the dashboard may close when the blower is set on high. (2000)

• **Horn.** If the horn becomes difficult to operate or sounds by itself in cold temperatures, the air bag module will have to be replaced. (2000)

• **Brakes.** The original equipment rear brake pads cause a humming or moaning noise, especially when the brakes are hot or warm. (2000)

• **Brakes.** When warm, the front brake pads on may cause the front end and steering wheel to vibrate and shake. Countermeasure pads are available. (2000)

RECALL HISTORY

2000: Some cars have internal fluid leaks in brake hydraulic control unit; when rear brake proportioning, antilock braking, traction control, or stability control feature is activated in some driving situations, feature may not perform as designed.

1992-01 CADILLAC ELDORADO

1993 Cadillac Eldorado Sport Coupe

FOR Acceleration • Steering/handling • Standard antilock brakes • Traction control (later models)

AGAINST Fuel economy • Rear visibility • Climate controls (early models)

EVALUATION Despite the car's weight, Eldo acceleration is brisk with the original 4.9-liter engine. Dropping in one of the Northstar engines turns performance from brisk to nearly blistering—especially in Touring Coupe form. Cadillac claimed that both Northstar engines yielded 0-60 mph acceleration of 7.5 seconds, or nearly two seconds quicker than the base V8. No engine is economical. We averaged 16 mpg in a Touring Coupe and 18 mpg in a Northstar-engined base coupe. Computer Command Ride, which adjusts according to speed, delivers a secure road feel. Unlike prior Eldorados, this one does not bob or wallow over dips and around corners. Steering is precise, and the car is stable at speed and in curves. With a firmer suspension and new touring tires, the Touring Coupe is quieter and more supple than before. Rear space is okay—generous for a coupe—but the rear seatback is too reclined for total comfort. Huge rear pillars impair the over-the-shoulder view. The large trunk has a usable shape. Buttons for heat and air conditioning are hidden behind the steering wheel. That flaw was corrected on 1996 Touring Coupes, but base coupes kept the former layout. Front bucket seats lack some lumbar bolstering, but are otherwise supportive.

VALUE In any guise, these are Cadillac's best premium coupes in a long while—excellent, expertly assembled, domestically built rivals to such imports as the Lexus SC 300/400, and competitive with Lincoln's Mark VIII. A solid structure completes this excellent package, giving the sizable coupe a unified feel, worthy of its price and status.

SPECIFICATIONS

	2-door coupe
Wheelbase, in.	108.0
Overall length, in.	200.2
Overall width, in.	75.5
Overall height, in.	54.0
Curb weight, lbs.	3774
Cargo volume, cu. ft.	15.3
Fuel capacity, gals.	20.0
Seating capacity	5
Front head room, in.	37.4
Max. front leg room, in.	42.6
Rear head room, in.	38.3
Min. rear leg room, in.	36.0

Powertrain layout: transverse front-engine/front-wheel drive

ENGINES

	dohc V8	dohc V8	ohv V8
Size, liters/cu. in.	4.6/279	4.6/279	4.9/300
Horsepower	270-275	295-300	200
Torque (lbs./ft.)	300	290-295	275
EPA city/highway mpg			
4-speed OD automatic	17/26	17/26	16/25
City/highway mpg (as tested)			
4-speed OD automatic	18.0	16.0	

Built in USA

RETAIL PRICES

	GOOD	AVERAGE	POOR
1992 Eldorado	$5,000-5,800	$4,200-5,000	$2,000-2,700
1992 Touring Coupe	5,600-6,500	4,800-5,700	2,500-3,200
1993 Eldorado	6,000-6,900	5,200-6,000	2,800-3,500
1993 Touring Coupe	$6,800-7,700	$6,000-6,800	$3,400-4,000
1994 Eldorado	7,200-8,500	6,300-7,500	3,600-4,500
1994 Touring Coupe	8,000-9,000	7,000-8,000	4,200-5,000
1995 Eldorado	8,500-9,500	7,500-8,500	4,700-5,400
1995 Touring Coupe	9,500-10,800	8,500-9,800	5,300-6,300
1996 Eldorado	11,000-12,500	9,500-11,000	6,200-7,500
1996 Touring Coupe	12,000-13,500	10,500-12,000	7,000-8,300
1997 Eldorado	14,500-16,000	13,000-14,500	9,000-10,000
1997 Touring Coupe	16,000-17,500	14,500-16,000	10,000-11,000
1998 Eldorado	17,500-19,000	16,000-17,500	11,500-12,500
1998 Touring Coupe	19,000-20,500	17,500-19,000	13,500-14,500
1999 Eldorado	21,000-23,000	19,500-21,500	15,000-16,500
1999 Touring Coupe	22,500-24,500	21,000-23,000	16,000-17,500
2000 Eldorado	25,000-27,000	23,500-25,000	18,000-19,000
2000 Touring Coupe	26,500-28,500	25,000-26,500	19,000-20,000
2001 Eldorado	29,500-31,500	27,500-29,500	—
2001 Touring Coupe	31,000-33,000	27,500-31,500	—

AVERAGE REPLACEMENT COSTS

A/C Compressor	$500	Constant Velocity Joints	800
Alternator	350	Exhaust System	1,135
Automatic Transmission or Transaxle	1,160	Shocks and/or Struts	1,225
Brakes	210	Timing Chain or Belt	820

TROUBLE SPOTS

• **Automatic transmission.** 440-T4 automatic transmissions may shift late or not upshift at all. The problem is a stuck throttle valve inside the transmission. (1992)

• **Automatic transmission.** 4T60E transmissions may drop out of drive while cruising, shift erratically, or have no second, third, or fourth gear, because of a bad ground connection for the shift solenoids. Poor grounds also allow wrong gear starts. (1992-93)

• **Engine noise.** A rattling noise at start up is often caused by automatic transmission pump starvation or cavitation, or a sticking pressure regulator valve. (1992-93)

• **Transaxle leak.** The right front axle seal at the automatic transaxle is prone to leak and GM issued a revised seal to correct the problem. (1992-93)

• **Steering noise.** The upper bearing mount in the steering column can get loose and cause a snapping or clicking, requiring a new bearing spring and turn signal cancel cam. (1994-96)

RECALL HISTORY

1992: Intermediate shaft to steering rack lower-coupling pinch bolt may be missing on some cars; disengagement produces loss of steering control. **1993 w/4.6-liter engine:** Fuel feed and return lines to fuel injection system could work loose, causing fuel leakage in engine compartment that could result in fire. **1993-94 w/4.6-liter V8:** If air conditioner compressor clutch assembly contacts auxiliary engine oil cooler hose, that hose may wear through, allowing leakage that could result in fire. **1994:** Throttle cable can disengage and interfere with cam mechanism. **1995:** Inadvertent airbag deployment could occur, due to water intrusion. **1996:** Analog instrument cluster on some cars could have internal short circuit disrupting Pass-Key system, causing failure of gauges and most tell-tale indicators, and possible no-start condition; panel could go black while driving. **1997:** Brake/traction control module can cause antilock system to cycle in non-ABS braking; could increase stopping distance. **1998:** Misrouted canister purge evaporative emissions harness could interfere with cruise control and throttle linkage, preventing return to closed throttle position. **2000:** Inner tie rod nuts on some cars are loose and can result in separation of tie rod, which can cause unexpected steering input.

1993-96 CADILLAC FLEETWOOD

FOR Antilock brakes • Acceleration • Passenger and cargo room • Trailer towing capability • Interior noise levels

AGAINST Fuel economy • Size and weight • Rear visibility

EVALUATION "Fleet" is definitely the word for the 1994-96 Fleetwood, with its Corvette-derived engine. With that powerplant on tap, you get swift takeoffs, as well as vigorous passing—which takes

1993 Cadillac Fleetwood

only a little more pressure on the gas pedal. Cadillac claimed that 0-60 mph acceleration took just 8.5 seconds—two seconds faster than the 1993 model. Fuel economy is no bargain; we averaged only 14.8 mpg. Fleetwood suspensions are firmer than those in a Caprice or Roadmaster, so you don't get the pillowy-soft ride that characterized big Cadillacs of the more distant past. Sure, it filters out fewer bumps, but the massive sedan also wallows less and has better control in turns than its GM siblings. Even so, body lean is excessive and the undeniably soft suspension allows lots of bouncing on wavy roads. Steering is firmer, too, for improved road feel. Traction control is a definite "plus." When actuated, it pushes back gently on the gas pedal, and an indicator light illuminates. Inside, three can sit across, front or rear, but those in the middle won't have much leg room. Adults can stretch their legs at outboard positions. Front seats are "split-frame" design, in which the lower cushion adjusts independently of the backrest. Base-model seat cushions seem firmer and no less comfortable than the multi-adjustable seats in the costlier Brougham. Back seats are nothing short of cavernous, but the cushion lacks thigh support. Drivers face an uncluttered dashboard layout. A huge trunk holds several suitcases.

VALUE   Quite a few traditional-type shoppers regret the fact that Cadillac stopped making these big rear-drive sedans. If you tow a trailer and travel cross-country, a Fleetwood just might be your best practical choice.

SPECIFICATIONS

	4-door sedan
Wheelbase, in.	121.5
Overall length, in.	225.0
Overall width, in.	78.0
Overall height, in.	57.1
Curb weight, lbs.	4477
Cargo volume, cu. ft.	21.1
Fuel capacity, gals.	23.0
Seating capacity	6
Front head room, in.	38.7
Max. front leg room, in.	42.5
Rear head room, in.	39.1
Min. rear leg room, in.	43.9

Powertrain layout: longitudinal front-engine/rear-wheel drive

ENGINES

	ohv V8	ohv V8
Size, liters/cu. in.	5.7/350	5.7/350
Horsepower	185	260
Torque (lbs./ft.)	300	330-335

EPA city/highway mpg

4-speed OD automatic	16/25	17/26

City/highway mpg (as tested)

4-speed OD automatic		14.8

Built in USA

RETAIL PRICES

	GOOD	AVERAGE	POOR
1993 Fleetwood	$5,000-6,000	$4,200-5,100	$2,000-2,700
1994 Fleetwood	6,200-7,200	5,200-6,200	2,800-3,600
1995 Fleetwood	8,000-9,200	7,000-8,200	3,800-4,800
1996 Fleetwood	10,500-12,500	9,500-11,500	5,500-7,000

AVERAGE REPLACEMENT COSTS

A/C Compressor	$485	Exhaust System	420
Alternator	225	Radiator	409
Automatic Transmission or Transaxle	780	Shocks and/or Struts	430
		Timing Chain or Belt	220
Brakes	235	Universal Joints	270

TROUBLE SPOTS

- **Automatic transmission.** 700-R4 automatic transmissions may shift late or not upshift at all. The problem is a stuck throttle valve inside the transmission. (1993)
- **Steering noise.** The upper bearing mount in the steering column can get loose and cause a snapping or clicking, requiring a new bearing spring and turn signal cancel cam, which the manufacturer will warranty. (1994-96)

RECALL HISTORY

1993: Passenger-side airbag in a few cars could experience an inflator ignition delay in an accident; delayed deployment could increase risk of injury. **1994:** Oil cooler inlet hose may be too close to steering gear, causing chafing; could result in leakage and fire. **1994:** On small number of cars, paint between wheel and brake rotor/drum can cause lug nut to loosen. **1994:** Fuel tank strap fasteners can detach, eventually allowing tank to sag. **1994-95:** At low temperatures, throttle return spring could fail. **1994-95:** Lower ball joint on a few cars sent to Guam and Puerto Rico can separate. **1995:** Improperly adjusted transmission linkage may permit shifting from "Park" position with ignition key removed. **1995-96:** Wheel lug nuts were not tightened to the proper specification. This could result in wheel loss.

1992-97 CADILLAC SEVILLE

1992 Cadillac Seville

FOR   Acceleration • Steering/handling • Passenger and cargo room • Standard antilock brakes and traction control (later models)

AGAINST   Fuel economy • Rear visibility • Climate controls (early models) • Ride (later STS)

EVALUATION   More than prior Sevilles, the 1992-96 edition displays fine road manners and a rock-solid feel, thanks to a stiffened chassis. Road noise was reduced, and improved engine-mounting better isolated the V8 from the passenger compartment. Despite the extra bulk, acceleration is brisk with the initial 4.9-liter engine, never lacking for strength whether in the city or on the highway. Shifts are almost imperceptible. The Northstar V8 added for 1993 is smoother and faster yet, but limits its most impressive acceleration to engine speeds above 3500 rpm. That gives the STS terrific performance on the open road. Speed-dependent Computer Command Ride adds to the secure feel of early Sevilles. Sure, the base-model ride is a bit soft at lower speeds (under 45 mph or so), but the bounce is nearly gone at highway velocities, and the sedan cruises with commendable stability and comfort. At low speeds, the 1993-up STS's Road Sensing Suspension floats less than the base setup. It's also more absorbent at higher speeds, and handles better on bumpy pavement. Steering is firm and precise, and the sedan remains stable through corners. Stiff tires give the later STS impressive handling, but a harsh, even jittery ride. Softer tires on the base (SLS) sedan transmit less impact and generate less noise. The '96 STS adopted softer tires, reducing the contrast between models. Head room is ample, front and rear. Adult knees aren't likely to press into the front seatback. Wide rear doors make entry/exit a snap, but thick roof pillars hamper over-the-shoulder visibility. Dashboards are well laid out, but climate-control buttons are hidden to the right of the steering wheel. That flaw was corrected in the 1996 STS, but the SLS kept the prior layout. The roomy trunk has a flat floor that's wide at the rear and stretches well forward. Its lid opens nearly from bumper height for easy loading.

VALUE   Especially in STS trim, the Seville is Cadillac's best premium sedan in ages, scoring strongly against such imported rivals as the BMW 740iL, Lexus LS 400, and Infiniti Q45.

SPECIFICATIONS

	4-door sedan
Wheelbase, in.	111.0
Overall length, in.	204.1

	4-door sedan
Overall width, in.	74.2
Overall height, in.	54.5
Curb weight, lbs.	3832
Cargo volume, cu. ft.	14.4
Fuel capacity, gals.	20.0
Seating capacity	5
Front head room, in.	38.0
Max. front leg room, in.	43.0
Rear head room, in.	38.3
Min. rear leg room, in.	39.1

Powertrain layout: transverse front-engine/front-wheel drive

ENGINES

	dohc V8	dohc V8	ohv V8
Size, liters/cu. in.	4.6/279	4.6/279	4.9/300
Horsepower	270-275	295-300	200
Torque (lbs./ft.)	300	290-295	275
EPA city/highway mpg			
4-speed OD automatic	17/26	17/26	16/25
City/highway mpg (as tested)			
4-speed OD automatic	15.9	16.8	

Built in USA

RETAIL PRICES

	GOOD	AVERAGE	POOR
1992 Seville	$4,500-5,300	$3,600-4,500	$1,600-2,200
1992 Seville STS	5,000-5,800	4,200-5,000	2,000-2,700
1993 Seville	5,500-6,500	4,600-5,600	2,300-3,000
1993 Seville STS	6,200-7,200	5,300-6,300	2,800-3,600
1994 Seville SLS	7,000-8,300	6,100-7,300	3,500-4,400
1994 Seville STS	7,800-8,800	6,800-7,800	4,000-4,700
1995 Seville SLS	9,000-10,300	8,000-9,300	5,000-5,900
1995 Seville STS	10,000-11,500	9,000-10,500	5,800-6,800
1996 Seville SLS	12,000-13,500	10,800-12,200	7,000-8,000
1996 Seville STS	13,200-14,500	12,000-13,200	8,000-9,000
1997 Seville SLS	15,500-17,500	14,000-16,000	9,500-11,000
1997 Seville STS	17,000-18,500	15,500-17,000	10,500-11,500

AVERAGE REPLACEMENT COSTS

A/C Compressor	$465	Constant Velocity Joints	810
Alternator	295	Exhaust System	998
Automatic Transmission or Transaxle	1,085	Radiator	375
		Shocks and/or Struts	1,360
Brakes	210	Timing Chain or Belt	265

TROUBLE SPOTS

• **Transaxle leak.** 440-T4 automatic transmissions may shift late or not upshift at all. The problem is a stuck throttle valve inside the transmission. (1992)

• **Automatic transmission.** 4T60E transmissions may drop out of drive while cruising, shift erratically, or have no second, third, or fourth gear, because of a bad ground connection for the shift solenoids. Poor grounds also allow wrong gear starts. (1991-93)

• **Engine noise.** A rattling noise at start up is often caused by automatic transmission pump starvation or cavitation, or a sticking pressure regulator valve. (1992-93)

• **Transaxle leak.** The right front axle seal at the automatic transaxle is prone to leak and GM issued a revised seal to correct the problem. (1992-93)

• **Steering noise.** The upper bearing mount in the steering column can get loose and cause a snapping or clicking, requiring a new bearing spring and turn signal cancel cam. (1994-96)

RECALL HISTORY

1992: Intermediate shaft to steering rack lower-coupling pinch bolt may be missing on some cars; disengagement of shaft produces loss of steering control. **1993 w/4.6-liter V8:** Fuel feed and return lines to fuel injection system could work loose, causing fuel leakage in engine compartment. **1993-94 w/4.6-liter V8:** If air conditioner compressor clutch assembly contacts auxiliary engine oil cooler outlet hose, that hose may wear through. **1994:** Throttle cable can disengage and interfere with cam mechanism; car could accelerate unexpectedly. **1995:** Airbag could deploy inadvertently, due to water intrusion. **1996:** Analog instrument cluster on some cars could have internal short circuit disrupting Pass-Key system, causing failure of gauges and most tell-tale indicators, and possible no-start condition; panel could go black while driving. **1997:** Brake/traction control module can cause antilock system to cycle in non-ABS braking; could increase stopping distance.

1998-01 CADILLAC SEVILLE

1998 Cadillac Seville STS

FOR Acceleration • Handling/roadholding • Interior storage space • Automatic transmission performance • Interior materials

AGAINST Fuel economy • Rear visibility

EVALUATION Seville again ranks among the class leaders in acceleration, courtesy of the unaltered Northstar V8 engines and little-changed curb weights. Behavior of the smooth 4-speed automatic transmission is beyond reproach—smooth and responsive. The SLS sedan focuses on low-speed acceleration, whereas the STS emphasizes high-speed responses. Both engines are on the thirsty side, achieving only 14.8 mpg in our tests. At least, the 2000 models manage on regular gasoline. The SLS feels appropriately soft without being sloppy—nicely composed during directional changes. With its tauter suspension, aggressive tire tread, and lower ride height, an STS responds more quickly to steering inputs and corners with a greater degree of flatness. The STS also is prone to irritating steering-wheel tug in hard takeoffs, and its magnetic power steering can lag behind driver inputs. Cadillac has claimed that Seville was as quiet as a Lexus LS 400. That's almost true, but not quite. Despite the 5-passenger claim, four adults is the comfortable limit inside a Seville. At that, back-seat riders must tuck their legs and swivel their ankles to negotiate narrow door bottoms. Front-seat space is generous. Rear-seat room ranks only as adequate. Tall riders' heads are likely to brush the headliner. Optional adaptive seats in the STS are comfortable, if not vastly more so than the regular seats. A new instrument panel, illuminated by fluorescent back-lighting and LED needles, gives the gauges outstanding definition. If desired, the driver can eliminate the illumination, leaving only a digital speed display. Switchgear is logically arranged, except that the climate controls sit low. Wide rear roof pillars and a tall trunk limit the driver's view, both aft and over both shoulders. The trunk is spacious. Inside, the Seville boasts a class-leading array of 19 separate pockets, boxes, and a pouch.

VALUE Sevilles seem solid and well assembled, and interior materials are top-notch. However, one test model suffered a wind leak around the driver's window, ill-fitting rear-door seals, and a wiring harness dangling beneath the driver's seat—not quite what's expected in this price league. Were it not for such questionable details, Seville would be easy to recommend on the grounds of performance, features, and solidity. We give a higher rating to the SLS, which does a fine job balancing performance and comfort.

SPECIFICATIONS

	4-door sedan
Wheelbase, in.	112.2
Overall length, in.	201.0
Overall width, in.	75.0
Overall height, in.	55.7
Curb weight, lbs.	3972
Cargo volume, cu. ft.	15.7
Fuel capacity, gals.	18.6
Seating capacity	5
Front head room, in.	38.1
Max. front leg room, in.	42.5
Rear head room, in.	38.0
Min. rear leg room, in.	38.2

Powertrain layout: transverse front-engine/front-wheel drive

ENGINES

	dohc V8	dohc V8
Size, liters/cu. in.	4.6/279	4.6/279
Horsepower	275	300
Torque (lbs./ft.)	300	295
EPA city/highway mpg		
4-speed OD automatic	17/26	17/26
City/highway mpg (as tested)		
4-speed OD automatic	19.4	14.9

Built in USA

RETAIL PRICES

	GOOD	AVERAGE	POOR
1998 Seville SLS	$19,500-21,000	$18,000-19,500	$13,500-14,500
1998 Seville STS	21,000-22,500	19,500-21,000	14,500-15,500
1999 Seville SLS	22,500-24,000	21,000-22,500	16,000-17,000
1999 Seville STS	24,500-26,000	23,000-24,500	17,500-18,500
2000 Seville SLS	26,500-28,500	24,500-26,500	19,000-205,00
2000 Seville STS	29,000-31,000	27,000-29,000	21,000-22,500
2001 Seville SLS	30,000-32,500	28,000-30,000	—
2001 Seville STS	33,000-36,000	31,000-34,000	—

AVERAGE REPLACEMENT COSTS

A/C Compressor	$730	Constant Velocity Joints	1,050
Alternator	735	Exhaust System	595
Automatic Transmission or		Radiator	520
Transaxle	1,350	Shocks and/or Struts	1,350
Brakes	570	Timing Chain or Belt	1,090

TROUBLE SPOTS

• **Paint/body.** On white cars, the door handles turn yellow from the lock cylinder grease staining them. The company will replace the cylinders under warranty and there is a colorless grease available for service. (1998-99)

• **Audio system.** The company is replacing radios that have poor AM reception or FM bleed into the AM band. (1998-99)

• **Engine knock.** The engine makes ticking noises and knocking noises that sound like main bearing knock, often due to cylinder carbon buildup. (1998-99)

• **Brake noise.** The front brakes make noises (squeals, grinding, groaning, etc.) requiring new brake pads and redesigned rotors. (1998)

• **Fuel gauge.** The fuel gauge reads empty or swings between empty and full due to problem with the in-tank sender. (1998)

• **Poor transmission shift.** Transmission is slow to engage between drive and reverse, often accompanied by a clunk requiring a transmission rebuild under warranty. (1998)

RECALL HISTORY

1998: Windshield wiper "Low" speed function can become inoperative if motor is switched from "High" to "Low." **1998-99:** Electrical short can develop in generator, even when engine is off. **2000:** Inner tie rod nuts on some cars are loose and can result in separation of tie rod, which can cause unexpected steering input. **2000:** Due to internal fluid leakage in some cars, rear brake proportioning, ABS, traction control or stability control may not perform as designed. **2001 w/235/55R17 tires:** These vehicles can have an incorrect tire pressure label.

1990-01 CHEVROLET ASTRO

1991 Chevrolet Astro AWD extended length

FOR Antilock brakes • Optional AWD traction • Passenger and cargo room • Trailer towing capability

AGAINST Fuel economy • Entry/exit • Ride

EVALUATION Spacious inside, Astro vans can be fitted to tow up to three tons and seat up to eight. The penalty that must be paid for its brawn is a rough, bouncy ride—definitely less car-like than front-drive minivans, which serve as replacements for the traditional old family station wagon. Clumsy handling also ranks as subpar. Even the least-potent V6 engine has plenty of torque for hauling heavy loads and towing, but that muscle does not translate into brisk acceleration. As for economy, we averaged just 14.5 mpg in an early AWD, regular-length Astro. Expect around 15 mpg in urban driving, and not a whole lot more on the highway. Another demerit: Servicing isn't so easy. Entry/exit to the front seats is hampered by doorways that are narrow at the bottom. There's also a tall step-up to get inside. Interiors offer loads of passenger and cargo room, though front-seat riders must deal with uncomfortably narrow footwells. The dashboard, as revised for 1996, has a convenient layout with plenty of built-in storage space. With eight seats, a regular-length Astro has little rear cargo room. All-wheel drive offers better rain/snow traction, but with even more thirst for gas. It also makes the Astro an inch higher, adding to step-in height.

VALUE Like the now-extinct Ford Aerostar, the Astro and its GMC Safari cousin are truck-based vehicles, better suited to heavy-duty work than are front-drive minivans. Trucklike behavior could be a turnoff unless you need Astro's brand of brawniness for towing or other demanding applications.

SPECIFICATIONS

	3-door van	3-door van	3-door van
Wheelbase, in.	111.0	111.0	111.0
Overall length, in.	176.8	186.8	189.8
Overall width, in.	77.5	77.5	77.5
Overall height, in.	76.2	76.2	76.2
Curb weight, lbs.	3897	3987	3998
Cargo volume, cu. ft.	151.8	170.4	170.4
Fuel capacity, gals.	27.0	27.0	27.0
Seating capacity	8	8	8
Front head room, in.	39.2	39.2	39.2
Max. front leg room, in.	41.6	41.6	41.6
Rear head room, in.	37.9	37.9	37.9
Min. rear leg room, in.	36.5	36.5	36.5

Powertrain layout: longitudinal front-engine/rear- or all-wheel drive

ENGINES

	ohv V6	ohv V6
Size, liters/cu. in.	4.3/262	4.3/262
Horsepower	150-165	175-200
Torque (lbs./ft.)	230-235	250-260
EPA city/highway mpg		
4-speed OD automatic	16/21	16/20
City/highway mpg (as tested)		
4-speed OD automatic	14.5	

Built in USA

RETAIL PRICES

	GOOD	AVERAGE	POOR
1990 Astro 2WD	$1,600-2,700	$1,000-2,000	$200-500
1990 Astro AWD	2,000-3,200	1,400-2,500	400-700
1991 Astro 2WD	2,100-3,400	1,500-2,700	500-600
1991 Astro AWD	2,600-3,900	1,900-32,00	600-1,000
1992 Astro 2WD	2,600-4,000	1,900-3,300	700-1,100
1992 Astro AWD	3,200-4,600	2,500-3,800	900-1,400
1993 Astro 2WD	3,100-4,800	2,400-4,000	800-1,600
1993 Astro AWD	3,700-5,400	3,000-4,600	1,200-2,200
1994 Astro 2WD	3,800-5,600	3,000-4,800	1,200-2,300
1994 Astro AWD	4,500-6,500	3,700-5,700	1,600-3,000
1995 Astro 2WD	4,500-6,400	3,700-5,500	1,600-2,900
1995 Astro AWD	5,600-7,200	4,700-6,300	2,200-3,400
1996 Astro 2WD	5,700-7,500	4,800-6,500	2,300-3,500
1996 Astro AWD	7,000-8,500	6,000-7,500	3,000-4,200
1997 Astro 2WD	7,000-9,000	6,000-8,000	3,000-4,500
1997 Astro AWD	8,200-10,200	7,200-9,200	3,800-5,200
1998 Astro 2WD	8,500-10,500	7,500-9,500	4,000-5,400
1998 Astro AWD	10,000-12,000	9,000-11,000	5,200-6,500
1999 Astro 2WD	10,500-12,500	9,500-11,500	5,500-6,900
1999 Astro AWD	12,000-14,000	11,000-13,000	7,000-8,500
2000 Astro 2WD	12,500-14,500	11,300-13,000	7,200-8,500
2000 Astro AWD	14,000-16,000	12,800-14,500	8,200-9,500

	GOOD	AVERAGE	POOR
2001 Astro 2WD	$14,500-16,500	$13,000-15,000	—
2001 Astro AWD	16,000-18,000	14,500-16,500	—

AVERAGE REPLACEMENT COSTS

A/C Compressor	$515	Clutch, Pressure Plate,	
Alternator	245	Bearing	555
Automatic Transmission or		Exhaust System	320
Transaxle	770	Radiator	420
Brakes	225	Shocks and/or Struts	247
Timing Chain or Belt	255	Universal Joints	153

TROUBLE SPOTS

• **Engine knock.** A knocking sound may be due to three possible causes and may be fixed with either an oil filter having a built-in check valve, a revised PROM or replacement of the main bearings. (1990-95)

• **Engine noise.** An engine noise might be caused by the exhaust valves sticking in their guides. New valve guide seals should correct the problem if the guides are not worn. (1996)

• **Transmission leak.** Fluid may leak from the pump body on 4L60-E transmissions due to the pump bushing walking out of the valve body. (1995-96)

• **Doors.** Improper adjustment of the sliding door can make it hard to open or close. (1990-93)

• **Engine misfire.** New valve guide seals should eliminate the blue smoke from the tailpipe during cold starting. (1990-93)

• **Engine misfire.** The fuel injector wires tend to get pinched when the air filter is reinstalled. (1990-93)

• **Transmission leak.** The rear seal on the transmission (extension housing seal) may leak on vans with a one-piece drive shaft. (1990-94)

RECALL HISTORY

1990-91: Bucket seat's knob-type recliner mechanism with foam or vinyl "soft joint" may loosen and cause bolt failure, allowing seatback to recline suddenly; could produce loss of control. **1995 w/L35 engine:** Fuel lines at tank were improperly tightened and could loosen, allowing leakage and possible fire. **1995:** On a few vans, left lower control arm bolt could loosen, fatigue, and break. **1996-97:** Outboard seatbelt webbing on right rear bucket seat can separate during crash. **1996-98 w/integrated child seats:** Seatbelt retractor clutch spring and/or pawl spring in child seat may be missing.

1990-96 CHEVROLET BERETTA

1990 Chevrolet Beretta GTZ

FOR Antilock brakes (1992-96) • Acceleration (V6 and Quad 4) • Handling/roadholding (GT, GTZ, Z26) • Value

AGAINST Control layout • Engine noise (4-cylinder) • Acceleration (early 4-cylinder) • Rear-seat room

EVALUATION The V6 engines, standard on the GT, are more powerful than the noisy and anemic four. A GT, in fact, delivered the best mix of performance, looks, and value. In any model, an automatic transmission beats the imprecise 5-speed. Four-cylinder Berettas with base suspension and standard narrow tires furnish few thrills, even with the extra horsepower in later models. Weak in performance when connected to automatic, that 2.2-liter engine is noisy with either transmission. A V6 delivers lively acceleration and works well with the smoother 4-speed automatic transmission. Adding the GTZ in 1990 took performance a serious step forward. Even its sport suspension and 16-inch tires cannot prevent the GTZ from getting weak-kneed in really fast driving, but it offers quite a lot of driving

pleasure for the money. On the other hand, the GTZ's unsupportive sport bucket seats and uncoordinated suspension detract from the fun on twisty roads. The Quad 4 engine in later Z26 coupes is quick but noisy, demands expensive premium fuel, and, like the GTZ, came only with the rough-shifting manual transmission. Front seats are roomy and the rear is passable. Average-size adults aren't likely to complain about brief rides back there—though getting in and out can be a challenge. Gauges are clearly marked, but cumbersome rotary dials for headlights and wipers cannot be operated without taking your hands off the wheel. Climate controls are too low to operate easily while driving.

VALUE By its final years, Beretta lagged behind its rivals in style and image. On the other hand, a Beretta offers more interior space than most sport coupes and was among the few to offer a V6 engine option.

SPECIFICATIONS

	2-door coupe
Wheelbase, in.	103.4
Overall length, in.	187.3
Overall width, in.	67.9
Overall height, in.	53.0
Curb weight, lbs.	2756
Cargo volume, cu. ft.	13.1
Fuel capacity, gals.	15.2
Seating capacity	5
Front head room, in.	37.6
Max. front leg room, in.	43.4
Rear head room, in.	36.6
Min. rear leg room, in.	32.6

Powertrain layout: transverse front-engine/front-wheel drive

ENGINES

	ohv I4	dohc I4	ohv V6
Size, liters/cu. in.	2.2/133	2.3/138	3.1/191
Horsepower	95-120	170-180	135-160
Torque (lbs./ft.)	120-130	150-160	180-185
EPA city/highway mpg			
5-speed OD manual	25/27	21/31	19/28
3-speed automatic	24/31		20/28
4-speed OD automatic			21/29
City/highway mpg (as tested)			
5-speed OD manual	27.6		
3-speed automatic	22.3		
4-speed OD automatic			21.9

Built in USA

RETAIL PRICES

	GOOD	AVERAGE	POOR
1990 Beretta	$1,100-1,600	$600-1,000	$100-200
1990 Beretta GT	1,500-2,000	900-1,400	200-300
1991 Beretta	1,300-1,900	700-1,300	200-300
1991 Beretta GT	2,000-2,500	1,300-1,800	400-600
1992 Beretta	1,600-2,300	1,000-1,600	300-500
1992 Beretta GT	2,300-3,000	1,600-2,300	500-800
1993 Beretta	2,000-2,700	1,400-2,000	400-700
1993 Beretta GT	2,700-3,400	2,000-2,700	700-900
1994 Beretta	2,400-3,100	1,800-2,400	500-8,00
1994 Beretta Z26	3,000-3,700	2,300-3,000	900-1,200
1995 Beretta	3,000-3,700	2,300-3,000	900-1,200
1995 Beretta Z26	3,800-4,500	3,100-3,800	1,300-1,700
1996 Beretta	3,800-4,500	3,100-3,800	1,300-1,700
1996 Beretta Z26	4,600-5,400	3,800-4,600	1,800-2,300

AVERAGE REPLACEMENT COSTS

A/C Compressor	$590	Clutch, Pressure Plate,	
Alternator	280	Bearing	625
Automatic Transmission or		Constant Velocity Joints	500
Transaxle	510	Exhaust System	315
Brakes	225	Radiator	375
Shocks and/or Struts	505	Timing Chain or Belt	255

TROUBLE SPOTS

• **Engine noise.** A rattling noise on cold start ups could be due to oil pump starvation and cavitation in the automatic transmission. (1994-95)

• **Transmission leak.** A revised transmission oil seal (green in color) was created to correct a leak at the right front (drive) axle. (1992-94)

• **Engine noise.** Ticking noise from the engine after start up may be due to loose piston wrist pins requiring replacement of all six pistons and pins. (1994-95)

• **Water leak.** Water leaks onto the right front floor through a gap between the air inlet screen at the bottom of the windshield. (1991-94)

RECALL HISTORY

1991: Steering wheel nut may not have been properly tightened, allowing steering wheel to separate from column, causing loss of control and potential for crash without warning. **1994-95:** Reinforcement panel was omitted from right-side rocker assembly, reducing occupant protection in a side-impact collision. **1996:** Interior lamps might come on unexpectedly while vehicle is being driven.

1995-01 CHEVROLET BLAZER

1995 Chevrolet Blazer 4-door wagon

FOR Antilock brakes • Acceleration • Passenger and cargo room • Ride • 4WD traction

AGAINST Rear seat comfort • Fuel economy

EVALUATION Acceleration is above average for a sport-utility, livelier than a V6 Explorer from a standstill, with stronger passing power. Unfortunately, the automatic transmission pauses a moment before downshifting. Naturally, too, the Blazer's V6 cannot hope to match an Explorer's V8 when hitting the gas pedal hard. Fuel economy wins no prizes. A long-term test of a 4-door 4WD Blazer averaged 15.2 mpg. A variety of suspension choices have been offered, tailoring the ride from off-road firm to suburban-street soft. Of all the suspension packages available, we prefer the "premium ride" version, which absorbs most bumps easily and produces a comfortable, stable highway ride. In fact, that Blazer rides more like a car than a truck. Blazers actually steer and handle much like a midsize sedan. Body lean is moderate in tight corners. Steering feels more precise than on the old S10 Blazer. Stopping power is adequate, though our test vehicle suffered a mushy brake-pedal feel, as well as substantial nosedive in quick stops. Things improved with the 4-wheel disc brakes on the '98 model. Passenger space is about the same as before. That translates to good room for four adults in both body styles. In a pinch, five or even six can fit into the bigger 4-door. However, the rear seat has a short, hard backrest—bolt upright and uncomfortable. Cargo room is ample, improved in the 4-door by mounting the spare tire beneath the rear end. Visibility is fine in the 4-door, but obstructed by the 3-door's sloped roof pillars as well as the spare tire. The modern-looking dashboard has clear gauges and easy-to-use controls. Power window and lock buttons are large and helpfully backlit. The climate system uses rotary switches for selecting mode and temperature. Some engine roar remains in hard acceleration, but road and wind noise now are well-muffled, ranking as moderate.

VALUE Blazers are competitive with the Explorer and Jeep Grand Cherokee in most areas, and beat them on price when new. Good buys also can be found in the secondhand market.

SPECIFICATIONS

	2-door wagon	4-door wagon
Wheelbase, in.	100.5	107.0
Overall length, in.	174.7	181.2
Overall width, in.	67.8	67.8
Overall height, in.	66.9	67.0
Curb weight, lbs.	3867	4071
Cargo volume, cu. ft.	66.9	74.1
Fuel capacity, gals.	20.0	19.0
Seating capacity	4	6
Front head room, in.	39.6	39.6
Max. front leg room, in.	42.5	42.5
Rear head room, in.	38.2	38.2
Min. rear leg room, in.	36.3	36.2

Powertrain layout: longitudinal front-engine/rear- or 4-wheel drive

ENGINES

	ohv V6
Size, liters/cu. in.	4.3/262
Horsepower	190-195
Torque (lbs./ft.)	250-260

EPA city/highway mpg

5-speed OD manual	17/22
4-speed OD automatic	16/21

City/highway mpg (as tested)

4-speed OD automatic	15.2

Built in USA

RETAIL PRICES

	GOOD	AVERAGE	POOR
1995 Blazer 2-dr 2WD	$4,000-5,500	$3,200-4,600	$1,400-2,400
1995 Blazer 2-dr 4WD	5,500-7,000	4,600-6,000	2,400-3,500
1995 Blazer 4-dr 2WD	5,000-7,000	4,000-6,000	1,900-3,500
1995 Blazer 4-dr 4WD	6,000-7,500	5,000-6,500	2,700-3,800
1996 Blazer 2-dr 2WD	5,200-7,000	4,200-6,200	2,100-3,400
1996 Blazer 2-dr 4WD	6,700-8,200	5,700-7,200	3,200-4,300
1996 Blazer 4-dr 2WD	6,000-8,000	5,000-7,000	2,500-4,000
1996 Blazer 4-dr 4WD	7,500-9,000	6,500-8,000	3,700-4,800
1997 Blazer 2-dr 2WD	6,500-8,300	5,500-7,300	2,900-4,200
1997 Blazer 2-dr 4WD	8,000-9,800	7,000-8,800	4,000-5,300
1997 Blazer 4-dr 2WD	7,500-9,000	6,500-8,000	3,700-4,800
1997 Blazer 4-dr 4WD	9,000-10,500	8,000-9,500	4,800-5,800
1998 Blazer 2-dr 2WD	8,000-10,000	7,000-9,000	4,000-5,300
1998 Blazer 2-dr 4WD	9,500-12,000	8,500-10,800	5,200-6,500
1998 Blazer 4-dr 2WD	9,300-11,000	8,300-10,000	5,100-6,000
1998 Blazer 4-dr 4WD	10,500-12,000	9,300-10,500	5,800-6,600
1999 Blazer 2-dr 2WD	9,500-11,000	8,500-9,800	5,200-6,200
1999 Blazer 2-dr 4WD	11,000-12,500	9,800-11,000	6,200-7,100
1999 Blazer 4-dr 2WD	11,000-13,000	9,800-11,500	6,200-7,500
1999 Blazer 4-dr 4WD	12,500-14,500	11,000-13,000	7,000-8,300
2000 Blazer 2-dr 2WD	11,500-13,000	10,000-11,500	6,200-7,500
2000 Blazer 2-dr 4WD	13,000-14,500	11,500-13,000	7,300-8,300
2000 Blazer 4-dr 2WD	13,000-15,000	11,500-13,500	7,300-8,600
2000 Blazer 4-dr 4WD	14,500-16,500	13,000-15,000	8,500-9,800
2001 Blazer 2-dr 2WD	13,000-14,500	11,500-130,00	—
2001 Blazer 2-dr 4WD	14,500-16,000	13,000-14,500	—
2001 Blazer 4-dr 2WD	14,500-16,000	13,000-14,500	—
2001 Blazer 4-dr 4WD	16,000-17,500	14,500-16,000	—
2001 Blazer 2-dr Xtreme	14,000-15,000	12,500-13,500	—

AVERAGE REPLACEMENT COSTS

A/C Compressor	$520	Clutch, Pressure Plate,	
Alternator	225	Bearing	800
Automatic Transmission or		Exhaust System	485
Transaxle	850	Radiator	450
Brakes	220	Shocks and/or Struts	410
Timing Chain or Belt	230	Universal Joints	270

TROUBLE SPOTS

• **Engine noise.** Engine knock at startup is usually eliminated by using an oil filter with a check valve. However, GM has revised PROMs and may even replace the main bearings if no other solution is found. (1995)

• **Engine noise.** Exhaust valves may not get enough lubrication causing a variety of noises. Usually, the same engine consumes excess oil because the valve guide seals on the exhaust valves are bad. (1996)

• **Transmission leak.** Fluid may leak from the pump body on 4L60-E transmissions due to the pump bushing walking out of the valve body. (1995-96)

• **Engine misfire.** The powertrain control module may cause a lack of power, early upshifts, late shifting in the 4WD-Low range. (1996)

RECALL HISTORY

1995: Brake pedal bolt on some vehicles might disengage, causing loss of braking. **1995 w/4WD:** A few upper ball joint nuts were under-torqued; stud can loosen and fracture, resulting in loss of steering control. **1995 w/air conditioning:** Fan blade rivets can break and allow blade to separate from hub. **1995-96 w/AWD/4WD:** During development testing, prop shaft contacted inboard side of fuel tank, rupturing the tank; fuel leakage was beyond permissible level. **1995-96:** Windshield wipers may work intermittently. **1995-96 w/4WD and ABS:** Under certain conditions, stopping distances in 2WD mode could be excessive. **1995-96 w/4WD and EBC4 ABS:** Increased stopping distances can occur during ABS stops while in 2WD mode. **1996-97 2-door w/manual locking recliner bucket seats:** Outboard seatbelt webbing can separate during frontal impact. **1996-97:** Failure of an upper and lower control arm ball joint assembly could occur due to corrosion, resulting in impaired steering or steering loss, or a partial or complete collapse of the front suspension. **1998:** Daytime running lights do not meet FMVSS No. 108 requirements. **1998:** Fatigue fracture of rear-axle brake pipe can occur, causing slow fluid leak and resulting in soft brake pedal; if pipe breaks, driver would face sudden loss of rear-brake performance. **1998 w/4WD or AWD:** On a few vehicles, one or both attaching nuts for lower control arm could separate from frame, resulting in loss of control. **2000 w/2WD:** On certain vehicles, right-hand ABS module feed pipe and/or brake crossover pipe tube nuts could have been tightened improperly; seal could have been broken, causing leakage and increasing stopping distance. **2000:** Some seatbelt assemblies were not properly heat treated and do not pass the load bearing requirement.

1992-00 CHEVROLET BLAZER/TAHOE

1995 Chevrolet Tahoe C1500 4-door wagon

FOR Driver-side and dual airbags (later models) • Acceleration (5.7-liter) • Passenger and cargo room • Ride • Trailer towing capability

AGAINST Fuel economy • Ride (2-door) • Entry/exit (2-door and 4WD)

EVALUATION Blazers and their Tahoe successors are brawny but civilized, both on-road and off. Acceleration with Blazer/Tahoe gasoline V8s ranks as robust, and these models can pull a heavy trailer with ease. As for economy, an early 2-door Tahoe averaged 12.5 mpg in mostly city driving. Vortec engines of 1996-97 might be a bit more frugal. A 4-door 4WD returned 14.3 mpg.Road behavior isn't bad, though body lean is still noticeable—but not as much as in earlier models. When loaded, at least, the big Blazer handles rough pavement with less bouncing and pitching than before. Unladen, the tail still tends to judder sideways over closely spaced bumps. Steering is a bit overassisted, but precise, and this version is quieter on the road than its predecessors. Step-up into the interior isn't as high as before, and you get plenty of space for three abreast, with bountiful head and leg room. Dashboards have easy-to-read gauges and handy controls. Rear doors of the 4-door create unprecedented access to the back seat, but door openings are narrow at the bottom, and step-in height is tall. Cargo room in the 4-door benefits from the under-chassis location of the spare tire. Three-door models carry their spares inside.

VALUE Sure, a compact sport-utility is more sensible and economical for everyday driving. But if you require real muscle, especially for towing, try the 4-door Tahoe and also Ford's Expedition.

SPECIFICATIONS

	2-door wagon	4-door wagon
Wheelbase, in.	111.5	117.5
Overall length, in.	188.5	199.1
Overall width, in.	77.1	76.4
Overall height, in.	72.4	70.2
Curb weight, lbs.	4731	5134
Cargo volume, cu. ft.	99.4	122.9
Fuel capacity, gals.	30.0	30.5
Seating capacity	6	6
Front head room, in.	39.9	39.9
Max. front leg room, in.	41.9	41.7
Rear head room, in.	37.8	38.9
Min. rear leg room, in.	36.4	36.7

Powertrain layout: longitudinal front-engine/rear- or 4-wheel drive

ENGINES

	ohv V8	ohv V8	Turbodiesel ohv V8
Size, liters/cu. in.	5.7/350	5.7/350	6.5/400
Horsepower	210	250-255	180
Torque (lbs./ft.)	300-310	330-335	360
EPA city/highway mpg			
5-speed OD manual	12/16		
4-speed OD automatic	12/15	13/17	15/18
City/highway mpg (as tested)			
4-speed OD automatic	12.5	14.3	

Built in USA, Mexico

RETAIL PRICES	GOOD	AVERAGE	POOR
1992 Blazer 4WD	$5,000-7,000	$4,200-6,200	$1,700-3,000
1993 Blazer 4WD	6,000-8,000	5,100-7,000	2,400-4,000
1994 Blazer 4WD	7,200-9,000	6,200-8,000	3,200-4,700
1995 Tahoe 2WD	7,000-8,300	6,000-7,300	3,000-4,000
1995 Tahoe 4WD	8,500-10,000	7,500-9,000	4,000-5,000
1995 Tahoe LS, LT 2WD	8,500-9,500	7,500-8,500	4,000-4,800
1995 Tahoe LS, LT 4WD	9,500-10,800	8,500-9,800	4,800-5,800
1996 Tahoe 2WD	7,500-9,000	6,500-8,000	3,500-4,500
1996 Tahoe 4WD	9,500-10,500	8,500-9,500	4,800-5,500
1996 Tahoe LS, LT 2WD	8,500-10,000	7,500-9,000	4,200-5,000
1996 Tahoe LS, LT 4WD	11,000-12,500	9,800-11,200	5,800-6,800
1997 Tahoe 2WD	9,000-11,500	8,000-10,500	4,500-6,200
1997 Tahoe 4WD	11,000-13,000	10,000-11,800	6,000-7,200
1997 Tahoe LS, LT 2WD	10,500-12,500	9,500-11,300	5,500-6,500
1997 Tahoe LS, LT 4WD	12,500-14,000	11,200-12,500	7,000-8,000
1998 Tahoe 2WD	10,500-13,500	9,500-12,000	5,500-7,200
1998 Tahoe 4WD	12,500-15,000	11,300-13,500	7,000-8,000
1998 Tahoe LS, LT 2WD	12,500-15,000	11,300-13,500	7,000-8,000
1998 Tahoe LS, LT 4WD	14,000-16,000	12,500-14,500	8,000-9,300
1999 Tahoe 2WD	12,000-15,000	10,800-13,500	6,700-8,000
1999 Tahoe 4WD	14,000-16,500	12,500-15,000	8,000-9,800
1999 Tahoe LS, LT 2WD	14,000-17,000	12,500-15,500	8,000-10,000
1999 Tahoe LS, LT 4WD	16,000 -18,000	14,500-16,500	9,300-10,800
2000 Tahoe Limited	22,000-24,000	18,500-22,500	14,000-19,000
2000 Tahoe Z51	22,500-25,000	19,000-23,000	15,000-20,000

AVERAGE REPLACEMENT COSTS

A/C Compressor	$555	Clutch, Pressure Plate,	
Alternator	220	Bearing	730
Automatic Transmission or		Exhaust System	380
Transaxle	750	Radiator	650
Brakes	260	Shocks and/or Struts	340
Timing Chain or Belt	415	Universal Joints	225

TROUBLE SPOTS

• **Automatic transmission.** Automatic transmissions may suffer harsh or shuddering shifts between first and second or may buzz or vibrate in park or neutral. (1992)

• **Transmission leak.** Fluid may leak from the pump body on 4L60-E transmissions due to the pump bushing walking out of the valve body. (1995-96)

• **Dashboard lights.** The oil pressure gauge may read high, move erratically, or not work because the oil pressure sensor is defective. (1990-93)

• **Climate control.** The temperature control lever may slide from hot to cold, usually when the blower is on high speed. (1992-94)

RECALL HISTORY

1995 w/M30/MT1 automatic transmission: When shift lever is placed in "Park" position, its indicator light may not illuminate. **1995-96 w/gasoline engine:** Throttle cable may contact dash mat and bind; engine speed might then not return to idle. **1998:** On some vehicles, one or both front brake rotor/hubs may have out-of-spec gray iron that can fail during life of vehicle. **1998 C10706:** Rear brake line can contact left front fender wheelhouse inner panel; a hole could be worn in brake line, allowing loss of fluid and reducing rear brake effectiveness. **1998:** Lower steering pinch bolt may be "finger loose" or missing, resulting in off-center steering wheel or separation of shaft from steering gear. **1999:** In a crash, right front passenger restraint systems may not meet neck extension requirements.

1990-98 CHEVROLET C/K PICKUP

1995 Chevrolet C1500 Work Truck regular cab

FOR Antilock brakes • Acceleration (V8) • Cargo room • Visibility • Cargo and towing ability • Interior room

AGAINST Fuel economy • Control layout • Ride quality

EVALUATION The V6 feels adequate with manual shift, but a 5.0- or 5.7-liter V8 would be wiser for any significant work, especially with automatic transmission. Short-bed Sportsides have a more sporty appearance and, with a larger V8, move impressively. A K2500 4x4 with 5.7-liter V8 and automatic averaged 13.3 mpg, and yielded strong low-end pulling power as well as good passing response. Braking can be a problem with rear antilocking, when the bed is unladen. Four-wheel ABS on later models is a better bet. Acceleration in a 454 SS is actually neck-snapping, and its wide tires and sports suspension make it the best-handling full-size pickup you're likely to find. Visibility is good from a wide, spacious cab that has ample room for even the largest occupants. Gauges are unobstructed but can be hard to read in sunlight, and electronic heat/vent controls are complicated. Gloveboxes are tiny. Ride quality is better than in prior pickups, but higher-capacity models don't take bumps so well when the box is unloaded. Only the short-wheelbase 4x4 with off-road suspension rides really harshly. Engine improvements for '96 were impressive. The V6 still isn't ideal for heavy work, but the 5.0-liter V8 is now a smooth, capable choice (except for serious towing or hauling). The 5.7 V8 feels much livelier, furnishing robust acceleration and fine pulling power.

VALUE Chevrolet's C/K models are an excellent choice in the full-size pickup field. Trucks equipped with the 5.7-liter V8 are still our top choice.

SPECIFICATIONS

	ext. cab long bed	ext. cab short bed	reg. cab long bed	reg. cab short bed
Wheelbase, in.	155.5	141.5	131.5	117.5
Overall length, in.	236.6	217.9	213.4	194.5
Overall width, in.	76.8	76.8	76.8	76.8
Overall height, in.	73.8	70.6	70.4	70.4
Curb weight, lbs.	4387	4140	4001	3849
Fuel capacity, gals.	34.0	34.0	34.0	25.0
Seating capacity	6	6	3	3
Front head room, in.	39.9	39.9	39.9	39.9
Max. front leg room, in.	41.7	41.7	41.7	41.7
Rear head room, in.	37.5	37.5	NA	NA
Min. rear leg room, in.	34.8	34.8	NA	NA

Powertrain layout: longitudinal front-engine/rear- or 4-wheel drive

ENGINES

	ohv V6	ohv V6	ohv V8	ohv V8
Size, liters/cu. in.	4.3/262	4.3/262	5.0/305	5.7/350
Horsepower	160-165	200	175-230	200-255
Torque (lbs./ft.)	235	255	270-285	300-335

EPA city/highway mpg

	ohv V6	ohv V6	ohv V8	ohv V8
4-speed manual	18/20			
5-speed OD manual		17/22	15/20	14/19
3-speed automatic	17/19		15/17	14/19
4-speed OD automatic		16/21	15/19	15/19

	ohv V6	ohv V6	ohv V8	ohv V8
4-speed OD automatic			14.5	13.0

ENGINES

	Diesel ohv V8	Diesel ohv V8[1]	ohv V8
Size, liters/cu. in.	6.2/379	6.5/400	7.4/454
Horsepower	140-143	155-180	230-290
Torque (lbs./ft.)	255	360	385-410

EPA city/highway mpg

	Diesel ohv V8	Diesel ohv V8[1]	ohv V8
4-speed manual	19/21		
5-speed OD manual	NA		
4-speed OD automatic	18/24	15/18	10/12

1. Naturally aspirated (155 horsepower); turbodiesel (180 horsepower).

Built in USA, Canada

RETAIL PRICES

	GOOD	AVERAGE	POOR
1990 C 1500 2WD	$2,000-3,800	$1,400-3,100	$300-1,300
1990 C 2500 2WD	2,700-4,200	2,000-3,500	600-1,600
1990 K 1500 4WD	2,800-4,500	2,100-3,800	700-1,800
1990 K 2500 4WD	3,400-4,900	2,700-4,200	1,100-2,100
1991 C 1500 2WD	2,500-4,800	1,900-4,100	500-1,900
1991 C 2500 2WD	3,600-5,200	2,900-4,400	1,300-2,300
1991 K 1500 4WD	3,400-5,400	2,800-4,600	1,200-2,500
1991 K 2500 4WD	4,400-6,000	3,700-5,200	1,800-2,900
1992 C 1500 2WD	3,000-5,500	2,400-4,800	800-2,500
1992 C 2500 2WD	4,100-6,000	3,400-5,200	1,500-2,800
1992 K 1500 4WD	3,800-5,500	3,100-4,700	1,300-2,500
1992 K 2500 4WD	5,000-7,200	4,200-6,300	2,100-3,800
1993 C 1500 2WD	3,500-6,500	2,800-5,700	1,000-3,200
1993 C 2500 2WD	4,700-7,000	4,000-6,200	1,800-3,600
1993 K 1500 4WD	4,600-7,600	3,900-6,800	1,700-4,100
1993 K 2500 4WD	6,000-8,000	5,200-7,200	2,700-4,400
1994 C 1500 2WD	4,200-8,000	3,500-7,200	1,400-4,000
1994 C 2500 2WD	6,500-8,500	7,700-7,700	3,100-4,700
1994 K 1500 4WD	5,900-9,000	5,200-8,200	2,700-5,200
1994 K 2500 4WD	7,500-9,800	6,500-8,800	3,700-5,700
1995 C 1500 2WD	5,000-9,200	4,200-8,300	1,800-5,000
1995 C 2500 2WD	7,400-10,000	6,500-9,000	3,700-5,800
1995 K 1500 4WD	6,800-10,000	6,000-9,000	3,300-5,800
1995 K 2500 4WD	9,000-11,500	8,000-10,500	4,500-6,500
1996 C 1500 2WD	6,000-11,000	5,000-10,000	2,500-5,500
1996 C 2500 2WD	8,300-11,500	7,400-10,500	3,900-5,900
1996 K 1500 4WD	7,700-12,000	6,800-11,000	3,600-6,500
1996 K 2500 4WD	10,000-13,000	9,000-12,000	5,200-7,300
1997 C 1500 2WD	7,000-12,500	6,000-11,300	3,300-6,500
1997 C 2500 2WD	10,000-13,000	9,000-12,000	5,200-7,300
1997 K 1500 4WD	8,500-13,500	7,500-12,300	4,000-7,500
1997 K 2500 4WD	11,500-15,000	10,300-13,500	6,200-8,500
1998 C 1500 2WD	8,500-14,000	7,500-12,700	4,000-7,800
1998 C 2500 2WD	11,000-14,000	10,000-12,800	6,000-8,000
1998 K 1500 4WD	10,000-15,000	9,000-13,700	5,200-8,600
1998 K 2500 4WD	13,000-16,500	11,500-15,000	7,200-9,500

AVERAGE REPLACEMENT COSTS

A/C Compressor	$560	Clutch, Pressure Plate, Bearing	595
Alternator	378	Exhaust System	420
Automatic Transmission or Transaxle	725	Radiator	350
Brakes	230	Shocks and/or Struts	335
Timing Chain or Belt	210		

TROUBLE SPOTS

• **Automatic transmission.** 700-R4 automatic transmissions may shift late or not upshift at all. The problem is a stuck throttle valve inside the transmission. (1990-92)

• **Clutch.** A grinding noise during clutch engagement and difficulty shifting into first or reverse is caused by a clutch master cylinder pushrod that is too long. (1992-93)

• **Engine knock.** Engine knock at startup on 4.3- 5.7- or 7.4-liter engines is usually eliminated by using an oil filter with a check valve. If this does not fix it, GM has revised PROMs for the computers and will even replace the main bearings if all else fails. (1990-95)

• **Cruise control.** The cruise control cuts out and won't reset unless the key is turned off because the cruise control module is too sensitive to vibrations at the brake pedal. (1994-95)

• **Engine noise.** The exhaust valves on 4.3-, 5.0-, or 5.7-liter engines may not get enough lubrication causing a variety of noises. Usually, the same engine consumes excess oil because the valve guide seals on the exhaust valves are bad and have to be replaced. (1996)

• **Automatic transmission.** Trucks with the 6.5L engine may have a transmission shudder when the torque converter clutch applies and releases. (1991-94)

RECALL HISTORY

1990 diesel: Fuel lines can contact automatic transmission linkage shaft and/or propshaft. **1990, '92:** Brake-pedal pivot bolt could disengage. **1992 extended-cab w/high-back bucket seats:** Seat recliner-to-frame bolts can loosen, fatigue, and fracture, allowing seatback to recline suddenly. **1994:** Reversed polarity of brake switch can cause contacts to wear prematurely; may result in loss of brake lights without warning. **1994:** Some drivers' seats could loosen. **1994:** Brake pedal retainer may be missing, mispositioned, or poorly seated. **1994-95 extended-cab C10/15 w/gas engine or 6.5-liter H.O. turbodiesel:** If lap- and shoulder-belt energy-management loops on front seatbelt assemblies release at or near the same time, acceleration forces can cause release mechanism to activate and allow buckle to separate from latch. Also, a few trucks lack those loops. **1994-95 extended-cab C10/15 w/high-back front bucket seats or 60/40 split bench seat:** Recliner-to-frame bolts could loosen, fatigue, and fracture, allowing seatback to recline suddenly. **1994-96 C10:** Solder joints can crack, causing windshield wipers to work intermittently. **1995:** Steering-column shaft nut could loosen and detach. **1995-96 w/gasoline engine:** Throttle cable may contact dash mat, which could bind the throttle; engine speed might then not return to idle. **1995-97 extended-cab w/Easy-Entry:** Pinch point in recliner mechanism can trap and pinch a person's hand or fingers when Easy-Entry feature is activated. **1995-98 crew-cab:** Front inner corner of fuel tank can contact body sill, wearing a hole in or cracking the tank; can result in fuel leakage. **1996 C10/15 w/7.4-liter engine:** Fuel rail assemblies may have improperly crimped end retainer clip that results in leak. **1996:** Four U-bolts on either side of rear axle were under-torqued and could loosen and eventually fall off; could result in sudden loss of control. **1997 C10/20:** On some trucks, one or two front seat mounting bolts were not installed. **1998 C10 extended-cab and 4-door utility:** Steering gear bolt can loosen and fall out, resulting in separation of shaft from gear. **1998:** On some trucks, one or both front brake rotor/hubs may have out-of-spec gray iron that can fail during life of vehicle. **1998 C10753 extended-cab:** Rear brake line can contact left front fender wheelhouse inner panel; a hole could be worn in brake line, allowing loss of fluid and reducing rear brake effectiveness.

1993-01 CHEVROLET CAMARO

1993 Chevrolet Camaro Z28 2-door hatchback

FOR Airbags • Antilock brakes • Acceleration (Z28) • Handling • Control layout

AGAINST Fuel economy (Z28) • Ride (Z28) • Tire noise (Z28) • Wet-weather traction • Visibility • Noise • Rear-seat comfort

EVALUATION This latest Camaro generation beats its predecessor in two notable ways: ride quality and dashboard layout. Both the base model and the Z28 have softer suspensions, which reduces the harsh impacts commonly endured in prior models. Z28s are still quite harsh over rough pavement, but more easygoing than before, though optional high-performance tires generate too much noise at highway speeds. Both models retain their well-known handling prowess. Gauges are easily visible through the steering wheel. Radio and climate controls are high-mounted, easy to reach and see. Climbing inside can be a chore because of low seats. Wide rear roof pillars still obscure the view to sides and rear quarters. A hump in the right-front floorboard intrudes into passenger leg room. Rear head room is a tad better than before, but the cushion is narrow and knee space extremely limited. A deep cargo well doesn't hold much luggage. The low seating position hinders visibility. Though somewhat gruff and noisy under acceleration, the 3.4-liter V6 performs nicely—especially with 5-speed manual shift. Acceleration in a Z28 is strong with either transmission, but the V8 demands premium fuel. We averaged only 13.2 mpg in mostly urban driving. Adding the 3.8-liter V6 narrowed the performance gap between the two modes. The 200-horsepower engine matches the 4.6-liter V8 in Ford Mustangs when the gas pedal hits the floor. Poor wet-weather traction remains a problem. Traction control wasn't optional until 1995.

VALUE This generation of Camaro is the best ever, but we feel that it forces too many compromises to be a daily driver for anyone but the performance enthusiast.

SPECIFICATIONS

	2-door conv.	2-door hatchback
Wheelbase, in.	101.1	101.1
Overall length, in.	193.2	193.2
Overall width, in.	74.1	74.1
Overall height, in.	52.0	51.3
Curb weight, lbs.	3440	3306
Cargo volume, cu. ft.	7.6	12.9-33.7
Fuel capacity, gals.	15.5	15.5
Seating capacity	4	4
Front head room, in.	38.0	37.2
Max. front leg room, in.	43.0	43.0
Rear head room, in.	39.0	35.3
Min. rear leg room, in.	26.8	26.8

Powertrain layout: longitudinal front-engine/rear-wheel drive

ENGINES

	ohv V6	ohv V6	ohv V8	ohv V8
Size, liters/cu. in.	3.4/207	3.8/231	5.7/350	5.7/346
Horsepower	160	200	275-310	305-325
Torque (lbs./ft.)	200	225	325-340	335-350
EPA city/highway mpg				
6-speed OD manual			16/27	17/25
4-speed OD automatic	19/28	19/29	17/25	18/27
5-speed OD automatic	19/28	19/30		
City/highway mpg (as tested)				
6-speed OD manual			13.2	
4-speed OD automatic		18.6	17.4	15.1

Built in Canada

RETAIL PRICES

	GOOD	AVERAGE	POOR
1993 Camaro Coupe	$3,600-4,300	$3,000-3,600	$800-1,200
1993 Z28 Coupe	4,800-5,500	4,000-4,700	1,400-1,800
1994 Camaro Coupe	4,200-4,900	3,600-4,200	1,100-1,600
1994 Conv., Z28 Coupe	5,200-6,200	4,500-5,400	1,800-2,300
1994 Z28 Convertible	6,600-7,600	5,800-6,700	2,400-3,000
1995 Camaro Coupe	5,500-6,200	4,800-5,500	1,800-2,300
1995 Conv., Z28 Coupe	6,800-7,700	6,000-6,900	2,300-3,000
1995 Z28 Convertible	8,500-9,500	7,600-8,500	3,600-4,300
1996 Camaro Coupe	7,000-8,000	6,300-7,200	2,700-3,300
1996 Conv., Z28 Coupe	8,500-9,700	7,500-8,700	3,500-4,400
1996 Z28 Convertible	10,500-11,500	9,500-10,500	4,800-5,600
1997 Camaro Coupe	8,500-9,800	7,600-8,800	3,600-4,400
1997 Conv., Z28 Coupe	10,000-11,500	9,000-10,500	4,800-5,800
1997 Z28 Convertible	12,500-13,500	11,500-12,500	6,500-7,300
1998 Camaro Coupe	10,000-11,000	9,000-10,000	4,800-5,500
1998 Conv., Z28 Coupe	11,700-13,000	10,500-11,800	5,800-7,000
1998 Z28 Convertible	14,500-16,000	13,200-14,500	8,200-9,200
1999 Camaro Coupe	11,500-12,800	10,500-11,500	6,000-6,700
1999 Conv., Z28 Coupe	13,200-15,000	12,000-13,500	7,000-8,000
1999 Z28 Convertible	16,500-18,000	15,000-16,500	9,500-10,500
2000 Camaro Coupe	13,000-14,500	12,000-13,200	7,200 -7,800
2000 Conv., Z28 Coupe	14,700-16,700	13,500-15,200	8,500-9,700
2000 Z28 Convertible	18,500-20,000	17,000-18,500	11,000-12,000
2001 Camaro Coupe	14,500-16,000	13,200-14,500	—
2001 Conv., Z28 Coupe	16,500-18,500	15,000-17,000	—
2001 Z28 Convertible	21,500-23,500	20,000-22,000	—

AVERAGE REPLACEMENT COSTS

A/C Compressor	$535	Clutch, Pressure Plate,	
Alternator	290	Bearing	775
Automatic Transmission or		Exhaust System	470
Transaxle	775	Radiator	410
Brakes	255	Shocks and/or Struts	527
Timing Chain or Belt	330	Universal Joints	200

TROUBLE SPOTS

• **Cruise control.** Because of oversensitivity, the cruise control cuts out and won't reset unless the key is turned off. GM will replace the cruise control module. (1993-95)

• **Automatic transmission.** TH-200 or 700-R4 automatic transmissions may shift late or not upshift at all. The problem is a stuck throttle valve inside the transmission. (1993)

• **Heater core.** The seal on the heater core case gets loose and cold air enters, which reduces the heater performance. (1993-94)

• **Steering noise.** The upper bearing mount in the steering column can get loose and cause a snapping or clicking, requiring a new bearing spring and turn signal cancel cam. (1994-96)

• **Rear axle noise.** Under warranty, the company will replace the entire rear axle (excluding brake rotors on cars with rear disc brakes) on a complete exchange basis. (1995)

RECALL HISTORY

1994: Misrouted V8 fuel line may contact "air" check valve; heat could damage line, which could leak fuel into engine compartment. **1995:** Lower coupling of steering intermediate shaft could loosen and rotate, resulting in loss of control. **1997:** Seatbelt retractors on some cars can lock-up on slopes. **1999 w/manual transmission:** Clutch master cylinder on a few cars may have incorrect retaining ring, preventing clutch from disengaging.

1991-96 CHEVROLET CAPRICE/IMPALA SS

1994 Chevrolet Caprice Classic 4-door sedan

FOR Acceleration • Passenger and cargo room • Trailer towing capability • Antilock brakes

AGAINST Fuel economy • Steering feel (Caprice) • Ride/handling/roadholding (Caprice w/base suspension) • Wind noise

EVALUATION Despite the new look for 1991, not much changed in this full-size sedan and wagon. Caprice's traditional soft ride is distressingly bouncy and floaty with the base suspension. Qualifying as virtually aquatic, the car leans way over in turns and wallows over wavy roads. Loose, vague steering impairs quick maneuvers. An optional F41 Ride/Handling suspension offers a slightly more assured feel, without much comfort loss. The sporty LTZ sedan option drew praise, and its stiffer suspension tightens handling considerably. The entertaining Impala SS of 1994-96 offers quite a secure feel on the road, leaning little in curves, its big tires grasping the pavement tenaciously. Wagon suspensions are firmer than those in sedans. The 5.0-liter V8 is understressed and quiet, with good low-end torque for easy merging/passing as well as brisk getaways. Still, it doesn't respond quickly to sharp jabs at the gas pedal. Gas mileage is nothing to boast about, either: We averaged only 16 mpg in a '91 sedan. A 5.7-liter V8 is quicker without guzzling much more fuel. The Corvette-based V8 introduced in 1994 is swifter yet, and none of the V8s demand premium gasoline. Mechanical noise while cruising is low, but wind roars constantly around the thick side pillars, detracting from the quiet ride. A

Caprice is roomy, soft, and plush; though the bulky transmission tunnel robs leg room from center passengers, front and rear. The trunk is sizable. Controls are logical. Antilock braking is a welcome addition, but the nose dives too much in hard stops.

VALUE GM's front-drive full-size sedans (Buick LeSabre, Olds Eighty Eight, Pontiac Bonneville) handle better and consume less fuel, but can't match Caprice's towing ability.

SPECIFICATIONS

	4-door sedan	4-door wagon
Wheelbase, in.	115.9	115.9
Overall length, in.	214.1	217.3
Overall width, in.	77.5	79.6
Overall height, in.	55.7	60.9
Curb weight, lbs.	4061	4473
Cargo volume, cu. ft.	20.4	92.7
Fuel capacity, gals.	23.1	21.0
Seating capacity	6	8
Front head room, in.	39.2	39.6
Max. front leg room, in.	42.2	42.2
Rear head room, in.	37.4	39.4
Min. rear leg room, in.	39.5	38.0

Powertrain layout: longitudinal front-engine/rear-wheel drive

ENGINES

	ohv V8	ohv V8	ohv V8	ohv V8
Size, liters/cu. in.	4.3/265	5.0/305	5.7/350	5.7/350
Horsepower	200	170	180	260
Torque (lbs./ft.)	235-245	255	300	330
EPA city/highway mpg				
4-speed OD automatic	18/26	17/26	16/25	17/26
City/highway mpg (as tested)				
4-speed OD automatic		16.0		17.0

Built in USA

RETAIL PRICES	GOOD	AVERAGE	POOR
1991 Caprice sedan	$2,200-3,000	$1,600-2,300	$300-600
1991 Caprice wagon	3,000-3,700	2,300-3,000	700-1,100
1992 Caprice sedan	2,700-3,600	2,000-2,900	400-900
1992 Caprice wagon	3,700-4,500	2,900-3,700	800-1,200
1993 Caprice sedan	3,400-4,500	2,700-3,700	700-1,200
1993 Caprice wagon	4,500-5,300	3,700-4,500	1,300-1,800
1994 Caprice sedan	4,200-5,600	3,500-4,800	1,200-1,900
1994 Caprice wagon	5,500-6,500	4,700-5,600	1,800-2,400
1994 Impala SS	10,000-11,000	9,000-10,000	5,000-5,800
1995 Caprice sedan	5,500-6,500	4,700-5,600	1,800-2,400
1995 Caprice wagon	7,000-8,000	6,200-7,100	2,700-3,400
1995 Impala SS	12,000-13,500	11,000-12,300	6,500-7,500
1996 Caprice sedan	7,000-8,000	6,100-7,000	2,700-3,400
1996 Caprice wagon	8,500-10,000	7,500-9,000	3,600-4,600
1996 Impala SS	14,500-16,500	13,000-15,000	8,000-9,300

AVERAGE REPLACEMENT COSTS

A/C Compressor	$465	Exhaust System	460
Alternator	280	Radiator	480
Automatic Transmission or		Shocks and/or Struts	250
Transaxle	780	Timing Chain or Belt	305
Brakes	220	Universal Joints	260

TROUBLE SPOTS

• **Automatic transmission.** TH-700-R4 automatic transmissions may shift late or not upshift at all. The problem is a stuck throttle valve inside the transmission. (1991-93)

• **Engine noise.** The exhaust valves on the 4.3- or 5.7-liter engines may not get enough lubrication causing a variety of noises. Usually, the same engine consumes excess oil because the valve guide seals on the exhaust valves are bad and have to be replaced. (1994-96)

• **Steering noise.** The upper bearing mount in the steering column can get loose and cause a snapping or clicking, requiring a new bearing spring and turn signal cancel cam. (1994-96)

RECALL HISTORY

1991: Shoulder belt guide loop plastic covering may crack and expose the steel subplate; in a crash, seatbelt webbing can be cut. **1991-92:** Secondary hood latch assembly can corrode. **1991-96**

police/taxi: Rear lower control arm can crack. **1992:** Antilock brake system modulator can corrode and leak fluid; may reduce brake effectiveness and increase stopping distance. **1992 w/special-order 4.3-liter engine:** Engine-mounted fuel feed and return pipes on some cars may fracture. **1994:** Oil cooler inlet hose may be too close to steering gear, causing chafing that could result in leakage and fire. **1994:** On small number of cars, paint between wheel and brake rotor/drum can cause lug nut to loosen. **1994:** Fuel tank strap fasteners can detach, eventually allowing tank to sag. **1994-95:** At low temperatures, throttle return spring could fail due to excess friction. **1994-95:** Lower ball joint on a few cars sent to Guam and Puerto Rico can separate (also applies to 1995-96 police/taxi/limo). **1995:** Improperly adjusted transmission linkage may permit shifting from "Park" position with ignition key removed. **1995-96 station wagon:** Airbag caution label and roof-rack caution label were incorrectly installed on same side of sunvisor. **1995-96:** Wheel lug nuts were not tightened to the proper specification. This could result in wheel loss.

1990-94 CHEVROLET CAVALIER

1994 Chevrolet Cavalier 4-door sedan

FOR Acceleration (V6) • Fuel economy (4-cylinder) • Handling/roadholding (Z24) • Price • Antilock brakes

AGAINST Acceleration (4-cylinder) • Rear-seat comfort • Engine noise (4-cylinder)

EVALUATION Early 4-cylinder engines give only adequate performance, but decent mileage. However, the automatic transmission eats sharply into acceleration figures. Later fours, with extra horsepower, perform a bit better. The 3-speed automatic also trails 4-speed units, used by some Cavalier competitors, in fuel economy and quiet running. The Z24 with V6 power ranks as a minimuscle car, exhibiting brisk performance as well as styling flair. The 3.1-liter V6 also is a sensible choice for a station wagon. Gas mileage is great with the 4-cylinder, but those engines sound harsh and crude during hard acceleration. A 5-speed VL averaged 23.1 mpg in rush-hour commuting, hitting 33.8 mpg on the highway. Cavaliers ride reasonably comfortably. Capable handling/roadholding grows more athletic with an optional sport suspension. For truly spirited cornering, search for a Z24 coupe or convertible. Updating of the dashboard for 1991 made controls easier to see and reach, though the turn-signal lever is still too short. Lack of an airbag is a drawback, especially since many rivals had one sometime in this period. Coupes and sedans offer adequate space up front, but rear compartments are cramped. Convertibles offer decent rear space for two, as well as a convenient power top.

VALUE Neither as roomy nor as technically sophisticated as Japanese subcompacts of the same period, Cavaliers have always offered good value. Convertibles add some flair, but also cost far more than their solid-topped mates.

SPECIFICATIONS

	2-door conv.	2-door coupe	4-door sedan	4-door wagon
Wheelbase, in.	101.3	101.3	101.3	101.3
Overall length, in.	182.3	182.3	182.3	181.1
Overall width, in.	66.3	66.3	66.3	66.3
Overall height, in.	52.0	52.0	53.6	52.8
Curb weight, lbs.	2678	2509	2520	2623
Cargo volume, cu. ft.	10.7	13.2	13.0	64.4
Fuel capacity, gals.	15.2	15.2	15.2	15.2
Seating capacity	4	5	5	5
Front head room, in.	37.8	37.8	39.1	38.9
Max. front leg room, in.	42.2	42.6	42.1	42.1
Rear head room, in.	37.3	36.1	37.4	38.5

	2-door conv.	2-door coupe	4-door sedan	4-door wagon
Min. rear leg room, in.	32.0	31.2	32.0	32.5

Powertrain layout: transverse front-engine/front-wheel drive

ENGINES

	ohv I4	ohv V6
Size, liters/cu. in.	2.2/133	3.1/191
Horsepower	95-120	135-140
Torque (lbs./ft.)	120-130	180-185
EPA city/highway mpg		
5-speed OD manual	25/36	19/28
3-speed automatic	23/33	20/28
City/highway mpg (as tested)		
5-speed OD manual	23.1	
3-speed automatic	25.3	

Built in USA

RETAIL PRICES

	GOOD	AVERAGE	POOR
1990 Cavalier	$1,000-1,600	$500-1,000	$100-200
1990 Cavalier Z24	1,700-2,300	1,100-1,700	300-500
1991 Cavalier	1,200-1,800	700-1,200	200-400
1991 Convertible	2,000-2,600	1,400-1,900	400-700
1991 Cavalier Z24	2,100-2,700	1,500-2,000	400-700
1992 Cavalier	1,400-2,000	900-1,400	200-500
1992 Convertible	2,200-2,900	1,600-2,200	400-700
1992 Cavalier Z24	2,400-3,100	1,800-2,400	500-800
1992 Z24 Convertible	2,900-3,600	2,200-2,900	700-1,100
1993 Cavalier	1,700-2,500	1,100-1,800	300-600
1993 Convertible	2,700-3,400	2,000-2,700	600-900
1993 Cavalier Z24	3,000-3,700	2,400-3,000	800-1,100
1993 Z24 Convertible	3,400-4,100	2,700-3,400	1,000-1,300
1994 Cavalier	2,100-2,800	1,500-2,100	400-700
1994 Convertible	3,000-3,700	2,300-3,000	700-1,100
1994 Cavalier Z24	3,300-4,000	2,600-3,300	900-1,200
1994 Z24 Convertible	4,200-6,000	3,500-4,200	1,300-1,700

AVERAGE REPLACEMENT COSTS

A/C Compressor	$540	Clutch, Pressure Plate, Bearing	620
Alternator	190	Constant Velocity Joints	545
Automatic Transmission or Transaxle	865	Exhaust System	350
Brakes	210	Radiator	240
Shocks and/or Struts	315	Timing Chain or Belt	255

TROUBLE SPOTS

• **Automatic transmission.** TH-125 automatic transmissions may shift late or not upshift at all. The problem is a stuck throttle valve inside the transmission. (1990-94)

• **Ignition switch.** The ignition switch may not return from the start to the run position and the accessories may not work because the screws that hold the switch in place were overtightened. (1991-94)

• **Transaxle leak.** The right front axle seal at the automatic transaxle is prone to leak. GM issued a revised seal to correct the problem. (1992-94)

RECALL HISTORY

1991: Front door interlock striker may fail, causing door frame collapse and insufficient strength for shoulder belt anchorage. **1991:** Front door shoulder belt guide loops may be cracked; occupant faces increased risk of injury in sudden stop or accident. **1992:** Secondary hood latch spring in some cars is improperly installed or missing. **1993:** Rear brake hoses on some cars are improperly manufactured and can cause reduced brake effectiveness. **1994:** On small number of cars, drive axle spindle nuts may be overtorqued; can result in separation of steering knuckle tire-wheel assembly from axle.

1995-01 CHEVROLET CAVALIER

FOR Airbags • Standard antilock brakes • Instruments/controls • Fuel economy • Acceleration (Twin Cam engine) • Visibility

AGAINST Rear-seat head room • Seat comfort • Entry/exit (2-door models)

EVALUATION An improved suspension, lengthened wheelbase,

1995 Chevrolet Cavalier LS 4-door sedan

and stiffer structure combine to furnish a comfortable ride that absorbs most bumps easily, without floating or wallowing on wavy surfaces. Base and LS models lean considerably in turns, however, and respond lazily to quick steering changes. For tight control, look into the Z24, which also rides quite well on most pavement surfaces. Base-engine acceleration is adequate with either transmission, but the engine feels coarse under hard throttle. Fortunately, that engine noise settles down to a peaceful level at cruising speed. Wind and road noise are moderate. As for economy, we averaged 23.8 mpg with a base Cavalier sedan with the automatic transmission. We'd expect more than 30 mpg on the highway. The 2.4-liter Twin Cam unit is a better match to the automatic transmission than are some rival dual-cam engines, because it produces slightly more torque over a broader range of engine speeds. Gauges are clear and controls easy to reach and use, in a well-designed dashboard. Visibility is good to all angles. Six-footers have adequate room in front, though seats lack lower-back support. Rear leg room is okay, but head room suffices only for shorter folks. Getting in and out of the rear on 2-doors is tough. Trunk space is ample, but a small opening makes it difficult to load bulky items. A one-piece folding rear seatback is standard.

VALUE Compared with its most natural rival, the sportier-natured Dodge/Plymouth Neon, the refined Cavalier puts comfort and utility ahead of performance and style. All told, however, it doesn't match the refinement of the Toyota Corolla. For a reasonable sum, however, you get a car with dual airbags and antilock braking, even if it isn't quite as much fun to drive as a Neon.

SPECIFICATIONS

	2-door conv.	2-door coupe	4-door sedan
Wheelbase, in.	104.1	104.1	104.1
Overall length, in.	180.3	180.3	180.3
Overall width, in.	67.4	67.4	67.4
Overall height, in.	53.2	53.2	54.8
Curb weight, lbs.	2838	2617	2676
Cargo volume, cu. ft.	13.2	13.2	13.2
Fuel capacity, gals.	15.2	15.2	15.2
Seating capacity	4	5	5
Front head room, in.	38.8	37.6	39.0
Max. front leg room, in.	42.4	42.3	42.3
Rear head room, in.	38.5	36.6	37.2
Min. rear leg room, in.	32.8	33.2	34.6

Powertrain layout: transverse front-engine/front-wheel drive

ENGINES

	ohv I4	dohc I4	dohc I4
Size, liters/cu. in.	2.2/132	2.3/138	2.4/146
Horsepower	115-120	150	150
Torque (lbs./ft.)	130	145	150
EPA city/highway mpg			
5-speed OD manual	25/37	22/32	23/33
3-speed automatic	24/31	21/31	
4-speed OD automatic			22/32
City/highway mpg (as tested)			
5-speed OD manual		25.7	
3-speed automatic	23.8		
4-speed OD automatic			23.4

Built in USA

RETAIL PRICES

	GOOD	AVERAGE	POOR
1995 Cavalier	$3,000-3,700	$2,400-3,000	$800-1,200
1995 Cavalier Z24	4,000-4,700	3,300-4,000	1,300-1,800
1995 LS Convertible	4,200-5,000	3,500-4,200	1,500-2,000
1996 Cavalier	3,800-4,500	3,200-3,800	1,200-1,600
1996 Cavalier Z24	4,800-5,600	4,100-4,800	1,800-2,400
1996 LS Convertible	5,000-5,800	4,300-5,000	2,000-2,500
1997 Cavalier	$4,800-5,600	$4,100-4,900	$1,800-2,400
1997 Cavalier Z24	6,300-7,100	5,500-6,300	2,900-3,400
1997 LS Convertible	6,600-7,500	5,800-6,600	3,100-3,600
1998 Cavalier	5,800-6,600	5,000-5,800	2,500-3,100
1998 Cavalier Z24	7,800-8,800	6,900-7,800	3,900-4,500
1998 Z24 Convertible	8,500-9,500	7,500-8,500	4,200-4,900
1999 Cavalier	6,800-7,700	6,000-6,900	3,200-3,700
1999 Cavalier Z24	9,000-10,000	8,000-9,000	4,500-5,200
1999 Z24 Convertible	10,000-11,000	9,000-10,000	5,300-6,000
2000 Cavalier	8,000-9,000	7,100-8,100	3,800-4,400
2000 Cavalier Z24	10,000-11,500	9,000-10,300	5,300-6,000
2000 Z24 Convertible	11,500-13,000	10,500-11,800	6,500-7,200
2001 Cavalier	9,200-10,500	8,200-9,500	—
2001 Cavalier Z24	11,600-12,800	10,500-11,500	—

AVERAGE REPLACEMENT COSTS

A/C Compressor	$555	Clutch, Pressure Plate, Bearing	550
Alternator	270	Constant Velocity Joints	480
Automatic Transmission or Transaxle	895	Exhaust System	320
Brakes	210	Radiator	347
Shocks and/or Struts	640	Timing Chain or Belt	315

TROUBLE SPOTS

• **Traction control indicator light.** The ETC warning light may glow and the cruise control stops working, but there is no problem with the systems. No current fix. (1996)

• **Brake wear.** The front brakes wear out prematurely because of the friction compound. GM and several aftermarket companies have brakes with lining that will last longer. (1995)

RECALL HISTORY

1995: Missing welds in lower front suspension control arms assemblies can result in separation of front bushing sleeve subassembly from control arm, resulting in loss of vehicle control. **1995-96:** Front and/or rear hazard warning lamps might not work. **1996:** Accelerator cable in a few cars could be kinked, causing high pedal effort, or sticking or broken cable. **1996:** Interior lamps might come on unexpectedly while vehicle is being driven. **1996-97:** Airbag could deploy inadvertently during low-speed crash or when an object strikes the floor pan. **1996-97:** Rear suspension trailing arm bolts can fatigue and break. **1997:** Driver's wiper blades on a few cars are 17 inches long instead of the required 22 inches. **1997:** Spare tire on small number of cars may have incorrect rim. **1999:** Instrument-panel backlighting on some cars may not function after driver adjusts interior light intensity.

1990-96 CHEVROLET CORSICA

1991 Chevrolet Corsica LT 4-door sedan

FOR Antilock brakes (1992-96) • Acceleration (V6) • Price

AGAINST Control layout • Engine noise (4-cylinder) • Rear-seat room • Acceleration (early 4-cylinder)

EVALUATION

See the 1990-96 Chevrolet Beretta.

VALUE

See the 1990-96 Chevrolet Beretta.

SPECIFICATIONS

	4-door hatchback	4-door sedan
Wheelbase, in.	103.4	103.4
Overall length, in.	183.4	183.4

	4-door hatchback	4-door sedan
Overall width, in.	68.2	68.2
Overall height, in.	56.2	56.2
Curb weight, lbs.	2706	2638
Cargo volume, cu. ft.	39.1	13.5
Fuel capacity, gals.	15.6	15.6
Seating capacity	5	5
Front head room, in.	38.1	38.1
Max. front leg room, in.	43.4	43.4
Rear head room, in.	37.4	37.4
Min. rear leg room, in.	35.0	35.0

Powertrain layout: transverse front-engine/front-wheel drive

ENGINES

	ohv I4	ohv V6
Size, liters/cu. in.	2.2/133	3.1/191
Horsepower	95-120	135-160
Torque (lbs./ft.)	120-130	185

EPA city/highway mpg

5-speed OD manual	25/34	19/28
3-speed automatic	24/31	20/28
4-speed OD automatic		21/29

City/highway mpg (as tested)

3-speed automatic	22.7
4-speed OD automatic	23.4

Built in USA

RETAIL PRICES

	GOOD	AVERAGE	POOR
1990 Corsica	$1,000-1,500	$500-900	$100-200
1991 Corsica	1,200-1,700	700-1,200	100-300
1992 Corsica	1,400-2,000	900-1,400	200-400
1993 Corsica	1,700-2,300	1,200-1,700	200-500
1994 Corsica	2,200-2,900	1,600-2,300	300-600
1995 Corsica	2,700-3,400	2,000-2,700	500-800
1996 Corsica	3,400-4,100	2,700-3,300	800-1,100

AVERAGE REPLACEMENT COSTS

See the 1990-96 Chevrolet Beretta.

TROUBLE SPOTS

See the 1990-96 Chevrolet Beretta.

RECALL HISTORY

1991: Steering wheel nut may not have been properly tightened, allowing steering wheel to separate from column, causing loss of control and potential for crash without warning.

1991-96 CHEVROLET CORVETTE

1994 Chevrolet Corvette 2-door hatchback

FOR Acceleration • Antilock brakes • Steering/handling

AGAINST Ride • Fuel economy • Noise • Entry/exit • Price

EVALUATION Since the beginning, Corvettes have been cars for those who enjoy life in the fast lane—and are willing to sacrifice some comfort for the privilege. Improved assembly has greatly reduced the number of squeaks and rattles. The '90s suspension no longer jars your teeth while passing over bumps, but it's still quite firm. Corvettes offer great grip and ultra-quick reflexes, though bumpy roads upset the composure of the stiff suspension. On the positive side, wide tires, a firm suspension, and a low center of gravity allow Corvettes to handle like a race car as long as the pavement is reasonably smooth. Getting in and out of the deep bucket seats in the pitlike cabin tends to be a challenge. Luggage space and interior room are at a premium, and visibility could be better. Noise levels are high. A husky exhaust note is prominent at all times, accompanied by abun-

dant tire noise at highway speeds. Acceleration is sheer magnificence: lusty and bold, whether from the standard LT1 engine in 1992-96 models, the prior L98, or the super-powered ZR-1. Each engine delivers a seamless rush of power from virtually any speed, causing the car to vault ahead under moderate to hard throttle. An LT1 pushes you back in your seat all the way to its 5500-rpm redline and feels discernably smoother than its predecessor. Fuel economy is nothing to boast about. There's an undeniable performance advantage in the ZR-1 package, but not enough to justify the huge prices that model still commands. Acceleration Slip Regulation in 1992-96 models squelches the wheel spin that nearly incapacitated earlier Corvettes when accelerating on slippery surfaces.

VALUE Rivals such as a Nissan 300ZX Turbo and Toyota Supra are more refined, but simply cannot match a Corvette's all-American macho flavor. To those who love them, there's simply nothing like a Corvette.

SPECIFICATIONS

	2-door conv.	2-door coupe
Wheelbase, in.	96.2	96.2
Overall length, in.	178.5	178.5
Overall width, in.	73.1	70.7
Overall height, in.	47.3	46.3
Curb weight, lbs.	3360	3298
Cargo volume, cu. ft.	6.6	12.6
Fuel capacity, gals.	20.0	20.0
Seating capacity	2	2
Front head room, in.	37.0	36.5
Max. front leg room, in.	42.0	42.0
Rear head room, in.	—	—
Min. rear leg room, in.	—	—

Powertrain layout: longitudinal front-engine/rear-wheel drive

ENGINES

	ohv V8	ohv V8	dohc V8
Size, liters/cu. in.	5.7/350	5.7/350	5.7/350
Horsepower	245	300-330	375-405
Torque (lbs./ft.)	340	330-340	370-385

EPA city/highway mpg

6-speed OD manual	16/25	16/27	17/25
4-speed OD automatic	16/24	17/25	

City/highway mpg (as tested)

4-speed OD automatic	16.6

Built in USA

RETAIL PRICES

	GOOD	AVERAGE	POOR
1991 Corvette	$9,500-10,500	$8,500-9,500	$5,500-6,300
1991 Convertible	11,000-12,000	10,000-11,000	6,800-7,600
1991 Corvette ZR-1	17,000-19,000	15,500-17,500	12,000-13,200
1992 Corvette	10,800-12,000	9,800-11,000	6,600-7,600
1992 Convertible	12,200-13,500	11,000-12,300	7,600-8,600
1992 Corvette ZR-1	19,500-21,500	18,000-20,000	14,000-15,500
1993 Corvette	12,000-13,500	10,700-12,000	7,300-83,000
1993 Convertible	13,500-15,000	12,000-13,500	8,400-9,400
1993 Corvette ZR-1	23,000-25,000	21,500-23,000	17,000-18,500
1994 Corvette	13,500-15,000	12,000-13,500	8,400-9,400
1994 Convertible	15,500-17,000	14,000-15,500	10,000-11,000
1994 Corvette ZR-1	26,000-29,000	24,000-27,000	19,500-21,500
1995 Corvette	15,000-16,500	13,500-15,000	9,500-10,500
1995 Convertible	17,500-19,000	16,000-17,500	11,500-13,500
1995 Corvette ZR-1	30,000-33,000	28,000-31,000	23,000-25,000
1996 Corvette	16,500-18,500	15,000-17,000	10,500-12,000
1996 Convertible	19,500-21,500	18,000-20,000	13,500-14,800

AVERAGE REPLACEMENT COSTS

A/C Compressor	$820	Clutch, Pressure Plate, Bearing	785
Alternator	280	Exhaust System	995
Automatic Transmission or Transaxle	890	Radiator	495
Brakes	365	Shocks and/or Struts	730
Timing Chain or Belt	990	Universal Joints	305

TROUBLE SPOTS

• **Transmission leak.** Fluid may leak from the pump body on 4L60-E transmissions due to the pump bushing walking out of the valve body. (1995-96)

• **Engine misfire.** If the engines with a manual 6-speed transmission surge or sag at engine speeds below 2500 rpm, there is a revised PROM to correct it. (1995)

• **Climate control.** The CD player may skip when driving on rough roads unless foam tape was applied to the top and bottom of the radio. (1991-94)

• **Engine misfire.** The distributor vacuum vent wiring harness might rub the power steering pulley. This can be fixed by tie-strapping the harness to the throttle body coolant hose. (1995)

• **Automatic transmission.** Unless the shift detent ball roller has been replaced, it may be hard to shift the manual 6-speed into reverse. (1995)

RECALL HISTORY

1992-93 w/LT1 engine: Power steering gear inlet hose can fracture, causing flammable fluid to spray into engine compartment.

1997-01 CHEVROLET CORVETTE

1997 Chevrolet Corvette hatchback

FOR Acceleration • Steering/handling • Instruments/controls • Standard antilock braking • Standard traction control

AGAINST Fuel economy • Ride (Continuously Variable Real Time Damping Suspension) • Rear visibility

EVALUATION Simply put, the "C5" Corvette is one of the world's fastest cars—accelerating to 60 miles per hour in a fierce 4.7 seconds. Gas mileage is about as expected for a performance machine. We've averaged 16.5 mpg with an automatic-transmission coupe, and 16.4 in an automatic convertible. Steering and smooth-road handling are race car-sharp. Unlike some prior models, however, the tail is now less likely to skitter sideways when encountering bumps during a turn. It can still tail-hop in bumpy corners, however. A stiffened chassis allowed engineers to fit softer springs to this Corvette, so ride quality is good enough to qualify it as everyday transportation. Three suspensions have been available, and we recommend the base setup as best all-around choice, furnishing a firm but not punishing ride. The Z51 suspension is harsh for everyday driving. Chevrolet's Continuously Variable Real Time Damping option tends to feel either too soft or too rigid. Corvettes are not quiet. You can expect a booming exhaust note, plenty of engine roar during hard acceleration, plus copious tire noise. Because of its inner-lined soft top, at least the convertible is hardly noisier overall than the coupe. Entering an earlier Corvette could be difficult, due to their tall door-frame sills. Those are gone in this generation. So, getting in and out is about as easy as with certain less-racy sport coupes—though it's still essentially a crouch-and-crawl proposition. Space is generous for two adults. Instruments and controls are sensibly designed and conveniently located. The convertible's soft roof folds neatly beneath a hard tonneau, which flows into an intriguing body-colored panel between the seats. Thick roof pillars impair visibility to all corners, but a low cowl creates a clear field of vision straight ahead. Both bodies have sufficient cargo room to hold two sets of golf clubs. Cockpit storage is limited to a tiny glovebox and a minuscule center console compartment. Test Corvettes have had solid structures, but detail flaws have turned up repeatedly even when the cars were close to new.

VALUE Big, bold, and brawny. That's the kind of high-performance driving you get from a Corvette. If that sounds appealing, there's no better all-around performance value, whether new or used. On the downside, some of the trim isn't really finished with sufficient richness for a car in the Corvette's price league.

SPECIFICATIONS

	2-door conv.	2-door coupe	2-door hatchback
Wheelbase, in.	104.5	104.5	104.5
Overall length, in.	179.7	179.7	179.7
Overall width, in.	73.6	73.6	73.6
Overall height, in.	47.7	47.7	47.7
Curb weight, lbs.	3246	3245	3212
Cargo volume, cu. ft.	13.9	24.8	24.8
Fuel capacity, gals.	19.1	19.1	18.5
Seating capacity	2	2	2.0
Front head room, in.	37.6	37.8	37.9
Max. front leg room, in.	42.8	42.7	42.7
Rear head room, in.	—	—	—
Min. rear leg room, in.	—	—	—

Powertrain layout: longitudinal front-engine/rear-wheel drive

ENGINES

	ohv V8	ohv V8
Size, liters/cu. in.	5.7/346	5.7/346
Horsepower	345-350	405
Torque (lbs./ft.)	350-375	400

EPA city/highway mpg

6-speed OD manual	18/28	19/28
4-speed OD automatic	17/25	

City/highway mpg (as tested)

6-speed OD manual		19.0
4-speed OD automatic	16.5	

Built in USA

RETAIL PRICES

	GOOD	AVERAGE	POOR
1997 Corvette coupe	$24,000-25,000	$22,500-23,500	$17,000-18,000
1998 Corvette coupe	27,000-28,500	25,500-27,000	20,000-21,000
1998 Corvette convertible	31,500-33,500	29,500-31,500	23,000-24,000
1999 Corvette coupe	30,000-32,000	28,500-30,000	22,500-23,500
1999 Corvette convertible	35,500-37,500	33,500-35,500	27,500-28,500
2000 Corvette coupe	33,000-35,000	31,000-33,000	24,500-26,000
2000 Corvette convertible	39,000-41,000	37,000-39,000	30,500-32,000
2001 Corvette coupe	36,000-38,000	34,000-36,000	—
2001 Corvette Z06 coupe	42,000-44,000	40,000-42,000	—
2001 Corvette convertible	41,500-43,500	39,500-41,500	—

AVERAGE REPLACEMENT COSTS

A/C Compressor	$550	Clutch, Pressure Plate,	
Alternator	300	Bearing	1,640
Automatic Transmission or		Constant Velocity Joints	1,190
Transaxle	1,350	Exhaust System	1,500
Brakes	900	Radiator	710
Shocks and/or Struts	2,395	Timing Chain or Belt	870

TROUBLE SPOTS

• **Paint/body.** On white cars, the door handles turn yellow from the lock cylinder grease staining them. The company will replace the cylinders under warranty and there is a colorless grease available for service. (1997-99)

• **Doors.** The audible key reminder continues to sound after the key is removed from the ignition accompanied by power door locks not working due to a problem in the lock cylinder. (1997-99)

• **Climate control.** The rear defroster fails because the Velcro that holds the wires in place does not hold. (1998)

• **Engine noise.** The serpentine belt is noisy due to a problem with the idler pulley and/or the belt tensioner. (1997-99)

• **Water leak.** Water leaks from above the door windows. (1997-98 coupe, 1998 convertible)

RECALL HISTORY

1997: Torn fuel tank seal can cause fuel odor and/or leakage. **1997:** Seatbelt's energy management loop is inadequate. **1997-00:** Lap belt webbing can twist, allowing webbing to become jammed in retractor.

2000-01 CHEVROLET IMPALA

FOR Passenger and cargo room • Instruments and controls • Handling/roadholding

AGAINST Road noise • Rear-seat comfort

EVALUATION Even though the modern-day Impala is a far cry from the V8-powered Super Sport of the distant past, or the Impala SS of the early '90s, the sedan acquits itself nicely in most respects. Power is adequate with the base engine, while the 3.8-liter delivers usefully stronger takeoffs and passing response. An alert, smooth-shifting automatic transmission helps, but neither engine sounds

2000 Chevrolet Impala LS

smooth or refined when pushed hard. A 3.8-liter LS averaged 20.1 mpg, with a lot of highway mileage. In a more even mix of driving, a 3.4-liter Impala got 19.8 mpg. A good ride/handling balance makes this family four-door pleasing to drive. Even the Ride and Handling suspension that accompanies the bigger engine absorbs most bumps well, while tempering much of the floatiness and wallow that plague the base suspension over high-speed dips. Any Impala furnishes good grip and balance, along with authoritative steering feel. Stopping power is good, though pedal feel could be firmer. Wind noise is low, but tire roar intrudes somewhat on coarse pavement. Space is sufficient for 6-footers to ride in tandem without cramping of legs. Still, there's not quite enough seat width for three large adults. The back-seat cushion is far too soft and short, lacking in contour for satisfying comfort. Head room is good all around, even with an optional moonroof. Entry/exit is big-car easy, but tall-tail styling impedes rearward vision. The ample flat-floor trunk has a long, wide opening, but the glovebox is puny.

VALUE A clear alternative to the Ford Taurus (as redesigned for 2000), the Impala promises comfort-oriented American style as opposed to the Taurus's import-influenced approach. Impala beats Taurus in powertrain response, while Ford leads in safety features and back-seat comfort. Both offer more room and equipment for the price than an equivalent Accord or Camry, though Japanese-brand rivals are more polished all-around.

SPECIFICATIONS

	4-door sedan
Wheelbase, in.	110.5
Overall length, in.	200.0
Overall width, in.	73.0
Overall height, in.	57.5
Curb weight, lbs.	3389
Cargo volume, cu. ft.	17.6
Fuel capacity, gals.	17.0
Seating capacity	6
Front head room, in.	39.2
Max. front leg room, in.	42.2
Rear head room, in.	36.8
Min. rear leg room, in.	38.4

Powertrain layout: transverse front-engine/front-wheel drive

ENGINES

	ohv V6	ohv V6
Size, liters/cu. in.	3.4/205	3.8/231
Horsepower	180	200
Torque (lbs./ft.)	205	225
EPA city/highway mpg		
4-speed OD automatic	20/32	20/29
City/highway mpg (as tested)		
4-speed OD automatic	19.8	20.1

Built in Canada

RETAIL PRICES

	GOOD	AVERAGE	POOR
2000 Impala	$12,500-14,500	$11,500-13,500	$8,000-9,000
2001 Impala	14,500-17,000	13,500-16,000	—

AVERAGE REPLACEMENT COSTS

A/C Compressor	$525	Constant Velocity Joints	750
Alternator	275	Exhaust System	565
Automatic Transmission or		Radiator	450
Transaxle	895	Shocks and/or Struts	975
Brakes	485	Timing Chain or Belt	325

TROUBLE SPOTS

• **Battery.** A problem with the ground circuit of the trunk light causes the battery to go dead. (2000-01)

• **Vehicle noise.** Banging, clunking, or popping noises from the front under acceleration or braking require shims between the engine cradle and frame. (2000)

• **Vehicle noise.** Fuel makes banging and sloshing noises in the tank when less than half full. (2000)

• **Automatic transmission.** The column-mounted shift lever is hard to move out of park due to the interlock cable being too long. (2000)

• **Brakes.** The rear brakes make squealing or moaning noises. Countermeasure brake pads are available. (2000-01)

RECALL HISTORY

2000 w/TRW seatbelt buckle assemblies: Seat-belt buckle assemblies fail to conform to federal requirements, because buckle base was not properly heat treated. **2001:** On certain cars, airbag sensing and diagnostic modules could experience a memory error, and airbags might not deploy during a crash.

1990-94 CHEVROLET LUMINA

1990 Chevrolet Lumina 4-door sedan

FOR Acceleration (3.4-liter V6) • Handling (Euro, Z34) • Passenger and cargo room • Antilock brakes (later models)

AGAINST Instruments/controls • Ride • Steering feel • Acceleration (4-cylinder)

EVALUATION Lumina's base 2.5-liter 4-cylinder engine delivers only so-so action. The 2.2-liter of 1993 isn't sufficient, either. The 3.1-liter V6 is snappier, especially with 4-speed automatic transmission. However, the automatic's aversion to downshifts makes the car feel sluggish. Acceleration off-the-line is quick, but once underway, a heavy throttle foot is needed to overcome the transmission's reluctance. Highway cruising is quiet and relaxed, however. The twin-cam 3.4-liter engine, available from 1991 onward delivers outstanding acceleration, but most of its power is concentrated at high engine speeds. Body lean in turns is well-controlled. While the suspension absorbs most bumps without much disturbance, freeway dips set the body to jouncing. Steering feel is imprecise and heavy, contributing to the car's ponderous feel in urban driving. All-disc brakes have good stopping power, but the pedal is too firm and hard to modulate. Non-Euros lag a bit in performance and handling, though both versions deliver a solid feel on the road. For competent handling, the Euro's sport suspension and bigger tires are a necessity. Even so, Euros have proved to be disappointing. Their suspensions fail to filter out the bumps well, and still allow too much bounce over wavy surfaces. With its sport suspension, the Z34 is quick but rides rougher than its more sedate mates. Gauges are not easy to read at a glance, and some controls are hard to reach. Climate controls are large and simple. Luminas are roomy inside for adults, front and rear, with plenty of cargo space on a flat trunk floor. Rear seat cushions are too short for long-distance comfort. Every door has a map pocket, and the center storage console is handy, but the glovebox is tiny.

VALUE Though quiet and capable cruisers, Luminas don't quite match Taurus in overall style, features, or performance. On the other hand, a reasonable secondhand price can overcome at least a few of those objections.

SPECIFICATIONS

	2-door coupe	4-door sedan
Wheelbase, in.	107.5	107.5
Overall length, in.	198.3	198.3
Overall width, in.	71.7	71.0
Overall height, in.	53.3	53.6
Curb weight, lbs.	3269	3333
Cargo volume, cu. ft.	15.7	15.7

	2-door coupe	4-door sedan
Fuel capacity, gals.	16.5	16.5
Seating capacity	6	6
Front head room, in.	37.5	38.7
Max. front leg room, in.	42.4	42.4
Rear head room, in.	37.1	38.0
Min. rear leg room, in.	34.8	36.9

Powertrain layout: transverse front-engine/front-wheel drive

ENGINES

	ohv I4	ohv I4	ohv V6	dohc V6
Size, liters/cu. in.	2.2/133	2.5/151	3.1/191	3.4/207
Horsepower	110	105-110	135-140	200-210
Torque (lbs./ft.)	130	135	180-185	215
EPA city/highway mpg				
5-speed OD manual				17/27
3-speed automatic	21/29	21/28	19/27	
4-speed OD automatic			19/29	17/26
City/highway mpg (as tested)				
4-speed OD automatic			20.1	17.6

Built in Canada

RETAIL PRICES

	GOOD	AVERAGE	POOR
1990 Lumina	$1,100-1,600	$600-1,100	$100-200
1991 Lumina	1,300-1,800	700-1,200	100-300
1991 Lumina Z34	2,300-3,000	1,600-2,300	300-800
1992 Lumina	1,600-2,300	1,000-1,700	200-400
1992 Lumina Z34	2,600-3,300	1,900-2,600	600-1,000
1993 Lumina	2,100-2,900	1,400-2,200	300-600
1993 Lumina Z34	3,200-4,000	2,500-3,300	900-1,300
1994 Lumina	2,800-3,500	2,100-2,800	500-800
1994 Lumina Z34	3,900-4,700	3,200-4,000	1,100-1,600

AVERAGE REPLACEMENT COSTS

A/C Compressor	$550	Clutch, Pressure Plate, Bearing	670
Alternator	200	Constant Velocity Joints	485
Automatic Transmission or Transaxle	1,150	Exhaust System	360
Brakes	189	Radiator	310
Shocks and/or Struts	865	Timing Chain or Belt	325

TROUBLE SPOTS

• **Automatic transmission.** 4T60E transmissions may drop out of drive while cruising, shift erratically, or have no second, third, or fourth gear because of a bad ground connection for the shift solenoids. Poor grounds also allow wrong gear starts. (1991-94)

• **Engine noise.** A rattling noise at startup is often caused by automatic transmission pump starvation or cavitation, or a sticking pressure regulator valve. (1991-94)

• **Engine noise.** An engine rattle at startup may be due to too much wrist-pin-to-piston clearance. (1993-95)

• **Automatic transmission.** TH-125 or 440-T4 automatic transmissions may shift late or not upshift at all. The problem is a stuck throttle valve inside the transmission. (1991-93)

• **Oil leak.** The plastic valve covers on 3.1-liter engines were prone to leaks and should be replaced with redesigned aluminum valve covers. (1995)

• **Transaxle leak.** The right front axle seal at the automatic transaxle is prone to leak. GM issued a revised seal to correct the problem. (1992-94)

• **Steering noise.** The upper bearing mount in the steering column can get loose and cause a snapping or clicking, requiring a new bearing spring and turn signal cancel cam. (1994)

RECALL HISTORY

1990: Front seatbelt may not properly restrain passenger in an accident. **1990:** Front shoulder safety belt webbing may separate at upper guide loops on either side of front seat. **1990:** Brake lights may not illuminate or, in some cases, will not stay illuminated all the time when brakes are applied, due to faulty stoplight switch. **1990:** Cracks may develop in mounting surface of certain Kelsey-Hayes steel wheels; wheel will separate from vehicle. **1990-91:** Due to corrosion at front subframe, steering shaft could separate from steering gear, resulting in crash. **1990-91 in 15 states:** Corrosion due to road salt could permit one or both front engine

cradle bolts to pull through retainer; could result in steering-gear separation. **1991:** Front door shoulder belt guide loops may be cracked and not in compliance with federal standard; occupant faces increased risk of injury in a sudden stop or accident. **1992:** Reverse servo apply pin of 4-speed automatic transmission may bind, which could cause loss or slipping of reverse, poor performance, or transmission to remain in "Reverse" while the indicator shows "Neutral" position. **1993:** Some front seatbacks may recline without prior warning.

1990-96 CHEVROLET LUMINA APV/MINIVAN

1995 Chevrolet Lumina APV

FOR Acceleration (3.8-liter V6) • Noise • Passenger and cargo room • Ride

AGAINST Acceleration (3.1-liter) • Visibility • Steering feel

EVALUATION The long sloping snout with steep windshield cuts into interior space and looks oddly daunting from the driver's seat—almost like you're steering from the back seat. Most people quickly get used to that, but it's still difficult to see the front end while maneuvering. Even after the snout was shortened for 1994, forward visibility could be a problem. Don't be dissuaded by appearances, as the APV has several notable virtues. This minivan drives much like a passenger car, cornering with commendable control and absorbing most bumps without harshness or wallowing. Smooth and quiet on the road, the minivan leans modestly in turns and offers good rain/snow traction, but steering feels much too light. Lack of power is a major drawback in early models, especially at passing speeds when fully loaded. The 3.1-liter V6 simply runs out of breath in a hurry. So, give yourself plenty of time and room to merge into traffic or overtake other vehicles. Once at highway speed, on the other hand, the minivan settles in for fine cruising. An optional 165-horsepower "3800" V6 with 4-speed automatic, offered since '92, moves more quickly and gives the Lumina performance to match or exceed its rivals from Ford and Chrysler. The 3.4-liter V6 installed in final Minivans feels stronger than the 3.1, but less lively than the 3.8-liter. Undersized climate controls are the only serious flaw on the dashboard. Storage bins are everywhere, and there's no engine hump to hinder passage to the rear. Versatile interiors seat up to seven, using modular seats that weigh just 34 pounds each and remove in seconds. With all seats installed, there's little room for cargo, but each rear seatback folds down to create a 4x6-foot load space. The optional power sliding door is convenient.

VALUE If you need cargo space but demand the smooth ride and handling of a car, and don't like boxy vans, look no further. Dodge and Plymouth have long been the class leaders, but Luminas tend to be cheaper.

SPECIFICATIONS

	4-door van
Wheelbase, in.	109.8
Overall length, in.	191.5
Overall width, in.	73.9
Overall height, in.	65.7
Curb weight, lbs.	3686
Cargo volume, cu. ft.	112.6
Fuel capacity, gals.	20.0
Seating capacity	7
Front head room, in.	39.2
Max. front leg room, in.	40.0
Rear head room, in.	39.0
Min. rear leg room, in.	36.1

Powertrain layout: transverse front-engine/front-wheel drive

ENGINES

	ohv V6	ohv V6	ohv V6
Size, liters/cu. in.	3.1/191	3.4/207	3.8/231

	ohv V6	ohv V6	ohv V6
Horsepower	120	180	165-170
Torque (lbs./ft.)	170-175	205	220-225
EPA city/highway mpg			
3-speed automatic...................	19/23		
4-speed OD automatic...............		19/26	17/25
City/highway mpg (as tested)			
3-speed automatic...................	17.4		
4-speed OD automatic...............		17.5	16.5

Built in USA

RETAIL PRICES	GOOD	AVERAGE	POOR
1990 Lumina APV	$1,400-2,100	$900-1,500	$100-400
1991 Lumina APV	1,800-2,500	1,200-1,900	300-600
1992 Lumina APV	2,300-3,000	1,700-2,300	500-900
1993 Lumina APV	2,800-3,400	2,200-2,700	800-1,200
1994 Lumina Minivan	3,500-4,200	2,800-3,500	1,200-1,600
1995 Lumina Minivan	4,300-5,000	3,600-4,200	1,600-2,000
1996 Lumina Minivan	5,500-6,500	4,700-5,600	2,300-2,900

AVERAGE REPLACEMENT COSTS

A/C Compressor...........	$565	Constant Velocity Joints	505
Alternator......................	280	Exhaust System	310
Automatic Transmission or		Radiator........................	430
Transaxle..................	1,095	Shocks and/or Struts....	430
Brakes	230	Timing Chain or Belt.....	310

TROUBLE SPOTS

• **Automatic transmission.** 4T60E transmissions may drop out of drive while cruising, shift erratically, or have no second, third, or fourth gear because of a bad ground connection for the shift solenoids. Poor grounds also allow wrong gear starts. (1992-94)

• **Engine noise.** A rattling noise at startup is often caused by automatic transmission pump starvation or cavitation, or a sticking pressure regulator valve. (1992-95)

• **Engine knock.** Bearing knock on many 3.3- and 3.8-liter engines is due to too much clearance on the number one main bearing requiring it to be replaced with a 0.001-inch undersize bearing. (1992-94)

• **Automatic transmission.** TH-125 automatic transmissions may shift late or not upshift at all. The problem is a stuck throttle valve inside the transmission. (1990-94)

• **Oil consumption.** The 3.8-liter engine is prone to excessive oil consumption often accompanied by spark knock due to failure of the valve stem seals. (1993-95)

• **Transaxle leak.** The right front axle seal at the automatic transaxle is prone to leak. GM issued a revised seal to correct the problem. (1992-94)

• **Steering noise.** The upper bearing mount in the steering column can get loose and cause a snapping or clicking, requiring a new bearing spring and turn signal cancel cam. (1994-96)

RECALL HISTORY

1990: Rear modular seat frame hold-down hooks on some vans may not meet the required pull force at rear seat anchorage. **1990-91:** Due to corrosion, steering shaft could separate from steering gear. **1992-93:** Seatbelt for left third-row seat of six-passenger van, or center second-row seat of seven-passenger van, may lock up. **1992-95:** Transmission cooler line in cars with certain powertrains, sold in specified states, can separate at low temperature. **1993-94 w/optional power sliding door:** Second-row, right-hand shoulder belt can become pinched, unable to retract properly. **1994:** Pawl spring may be missing from retractors for rear center lap belts. **1994:** Third-row seatbelt retractors may lock up when van is on a slope. **1995:** On some vehicles, brake pedal arm can fracture during braking. **1995 w/3.1-liter engine:** Throttle cable support brackets could contact throttle-lever system and inhibit throttle return; engine speed would then decrease more slowly than anticipated.

1995-00 CHEVROLET LUMINA/MONTE CARLO

FOR Antilock brakes • Passenger and cargo room • Ride • Automatic transmission performance

1995 Chevrolet Lumina LS

AGAINST Steering feel • Fuel economy (3.4-liter) • Engine noise (3.4-liter) • Rear visibility (Monte Carlo) • Rear-seat entry/exit (Monte Carlo)

EVALUATION Performance is adequate from the 3.1-liter engine, though it feels a little slow initially. The 4-speed automatic transmission changes gears smoothly and downshifts promptly when passing power is needed. We've averaged 20.1 mpg in a Lumina with the base engine, with about half of the driving on expressways. Expect a few mpg less with the stronger 3.4-liter engine. That one has more potent passing punch, but gets louder during hard acceleration. The smooth 3.8-liter on some later models is even more powerful—especially around town. An absorbent suspension on the Lumina soaks up bumpy pavement without harshness or excessive bouncing. Steering in the Lumina is light and has little road feel. As many as six people can fit in a Lumina—though everyone will be squeezed somewhat. There's ample room for four in the Monte Carlo, but a fifth might feel unwelcome. The Monte Carlo requires plenty of room to fully open its wide doors, and climbing into the back seat demands some bending. Thick rear pillars hurt over-the-shoulder visibility in the Monte Carlo, whereas relatively narrow pillars and deep side windows in the Lumina help give a good view to all directions. Dashboards have a clean, contemporary design. Simple controls are easy to see and reach while driving. Trunks in both models are roomy, with a flat floor that reaches well forward.

VALUE The Lumina is a pleasant, competent family sedan, which deserves consideration if you're shopping in the midsize field. Monte Carlo shares most of its pluses and minuses, in 2-door coupe form.

SPECIFICATIONS	2-door coupe	4-door sedan
Wheelbase, in.	107.5	107.5
Overall length, in.	200.7	200.9
Overall width, in.	72.5	72.5
Overall height, in.	55.2	53.8
Curb weight, lbs.	3306	3330
Cargo volume, cu. ft.	15.7	15.7
Fuel capacity, gals.	17.1	17.1
Seating capacity	6	6
Front head room, in.	38.4	37.9
Max. front leg room, in.	42.4	42.4
Rear head room, in.	37.4	36.9
Min. rear leg room, in.	36.6	34.9

Powertrain layout: transverse front-engine/front-wheel drive

ENGINES	ohv V6	dohc V6	ohv V6
Size, liters/cu. in.	3.1/191	3.4/207	3.8/231
Horsepower	160-175	210-215	200
Torque (lbs./ft.)	185-190	215-220	225
EPA city/highway mpg			
4-speed OD automatic...............	20/29	17/26	19/30
City/highway mpg (as tested)			
4-speed OD automatic...............	20.1		19.1

Built in Canada

RETAIL PRICES	GOOD	AVERAGE	POOR
1995 Monte Carlo	$4,500-5,400	$3,800-4,700	$1,600-2,200
1995 Lumina	3,500-4,200	2,800-3,500	900-1,300
1996 Monte Carlo	5,500-6,500	4,700-5,700	2,000-2,600
1996 Lumina	4,200-5,000	3,500-4,200	1,300-1,800
1997 Monte Carlo	6,700-7,800	5,900-7,000	3,000-3,600
1997 Lumina	5,400-6,500	4,600-5,700	1,900-2,500
1998 Monte Carlo	8,200-9,500	7,300-8,500	4,000-4,700
1998 Lumina	6,900-8,200	6,000-7,200	3,000-3,800
1999 Monte Carlo	9,500-10,800	8,500-9,800	4,800-5,600

	GOOD	AVERAGE	POOR
1999 Lumina	$8,300-9,700	$7,300-8,700	$4,000-4,800
2000 Lumina	9,700-11,000	8,700-10,000	5,000-5,800
2001 Lumina	11,000-12,200	10,000-11,200	—

AVERAGE REPLACEMENT COSTS

A/C Compressor	$525	Shocks and/or Struts	665
Alternator	200	Constant Velocity Joints	915
Automatic Transmission or		Exhaust System	385
Transaxle	1,180	Radiator	430
Brakes	270	Timing Chain or Belt	450

TROUBLE SPOTS

• **Suspension noise.** A popping noise from the front end is caused by a problem with the struts and can be corrected with an additional jounce bumper. (1995-96)

• **Fuel pump.** Excess material in the plastic fuel tank can collect on the fuel pickup filter and restrict fuel flow. (1995-96)

• **Oil leak.** Some cars have high oil consumption that is corrected by replacing the PCV harness as well as the valve cover, spark plugs and wires, and oil fill cap. (1995)

• **Engine temperature.** The engine may overheat due to a problem with the heater hoses, which swell, then loosen from the heater core pipes and leak. (1996)

• **Hard starting.** There is a new Flash PROM available to correct hard starting and stalling under high-load, slow-speed operation. (1996)

RECALL HISTORY

1995: Right lower control arm ball-joint mounting hole was incorrectly positioned. **1995:** Seatbelt anchor can fracture in a crash. **1995:** Center rear seatbelt anchor plate could fracture in a crash. **1995:** Wiper/washer operation may be intermittent or nonexistent. **1995 Lumina:** Steering-column bracket bolts on some cars may not be tightened. **1995:** Strained or separated windshield wiper/washer switch wire can cause intermittent or nonexistent wash/wipe operation. **1996:** Brake booster tab is improperly located; if stopping distance is short, crash could occur. **1996 Lumina:** Left front brake line can contact transaxle bracket or bolt and wear through. **2000 Lumina:** Passenger airbag modules on a few cars have undersized inflator orifice, so module could explode during a crash. **2000 Lumina w/rear drum brakes:** Bolt heads on rear spindle rod can separate and affected wheel can shift, causing loss of control. **2000 Lumina:** Clamp that secures flexible fuel fill hose to metal fill tube on a few cars could be loose and might separate, causing fuel leakage. **2000 Lumina:** Right front brake hose on a few cars is incorrectly routed and could be cut or separated. **2000 Lumina:** Some seatbelt assemblies were not properly heat treated and do not pass the load bearing requirement.

1997-01 CHEVROLET MALIBU

1997 Chevrolet Malibu

FOR Passenger room • Cargo room • Ride • Fuel economy (4-cylinder) • Standard antilock braking • Build quality

AGAINST Engine noise (4-cylinder) • Steering feel

EVALUATION Acceleration is good with the 4-cylinder engine—more than sufficient for most owners. On the downside, the four gets loud when accelerating hard. A Malibu with the substantially smoother V6 is stronger off the line and around town, but does not feel markedly more energetic at highway speeds. The automatic transmission shifts without jarring, but does not always downshift promptly to furnish suitable passing power. A 4-cylinder Malibu averaged 22.5 mpg in a mix of city and expressway driving. A Malibu V6 returned about 19 mpg. Malibu feels agile, maneuverable, and secure, but charging down a freeway off-ramp produces substantial body lean, as well as tire scrubbing. Malibus ride comfortably and stably on the highway. But there's a lot of suspension and tire thumping over ruts and potholes. Wind noise is tolerable, but the level of engine and tire noise yields less-than-serene cruising. Braking power is adequate, with good pedal modulation and moderate nosedive in hard braking. Malibu is spacious for its size. Front head room is generous. Leg room is more than adequate all around. Rear head room is sufficient for folks under 6 feet tall. Front bucket seats are firm and nicely contoured, but the rear bench is harder and flatter than it should be. Malibu's dashboard is a gently curved model of efficiency. A tasteful blend of fabrics, plastics, and padded surfaces gives Malibu the feel of a more expensive automobile. Interior storage space ranks above average and trunk space is generous, helped by a flat floor, huge opening, and near-bumper-level sill to ease loading. Thin roof pillars and large outside mirrors offer good visibility. However, the rear parcel shelf is high enough to block the driver's view of the trunk while backing up.

VALUE Offering an admirable blend of utility, driving fun, and features, Malibu is an intermediate-sized sedan that warrants serious consideration.

SPECIFICATIONS

	4-door sedan
Wheelbase, in.	107.0
Overall length, in.	190.4
Overall width, in.	69.4
Overall height, in.	56.4
Curb weight, lbs.	3100
Cargo volume, cu. ft.	17.0
Fuel capacity, gals.	15.0
Seating capacity	5
Front head room, in.	39.4
Max. front leg room, in.	41.9
Rear head room, in.	37.6
Min. rear leg room, in.	38.0

Powertrain layout: transverse front-engine/front-wheel drive

ENGINES

	dohc I4	ohv V6
Size, liters/cu. in.	2.4/146	3.1/191
Horsepower	150	155-170
Torque (lbs./ft.)	155	180-190
EPA city/highway mpg		
4-speed OD automatic	23/32	20/29
City/highway mpg (as tested)		
4-speed OD automatic	22.5	18.9

Built in USA

RETAIL PRICES

	GOOD	AVERAGE	POOR
1997 Malibu	$6,000-7,200	$5,300-6,500	$2,700-3,400
1998 Malibu	7,000-8,200	6,300-7,400	3,400-4,100
1999 Malibu	8,200-9,500	7,500-8,600	4,200-4,900
2000 Malibu	9,500-11,000	8,600-10,000	5,000-5,900
2001 Malibu	11,000-12,800	10,000-11,500	—

AVERAGE REPLACEMENT COSTS

A/C Compressor	$500	Constant Velocity Joints	750
Alternator	265	Exhaust System	475
Automatic Transmission or		Radiator	450
Transaxle	850	Shocks and/or Struts	900
Brakes	365	Timing Chain or Belt	325

TROUBLE SPOTS

• **Antenna.** Because of the way it is routed, a passenger can accidentally disconnect the antenna so the cable must be rerouted. (1997-99)

• **Suspension noise.** Noises from the front end (clunks, rattles, squeaks) may require replacement of the lower control arms or rack-and-pinion assembly or both. (1997-98)

• **Paint/body.** On white cars, the door handles turn yellow from the lock cylinder grease staining them. The company will replace the cylinders under warranty and there is a colorless grease available for service. (1997-99)

• **Doors.** The key reminder continues to sound after the key is removed from the ignition accompanied by power door locks not working due to a problem in the lock cylinder. (1997-99)

• **Seat.** The leather on the bucket seat back wears prematurely and the company will replace the seat cover and install extra padding under warranty. (1997-99)

• **Doors.** The power door locks fail, but still work manually, due to a rubber part breaking on the actuator arm inside the door. (1997)

RECALL HISTORY

1997: If airbag deploys, module could separate from instrument panel, striking and injuring occupant. **1997-98:** A buildup of snow or ice restricts the movement of the passenger-side windshield wiper arm, the pivot housing can crack and the wipers will not operate. **2000:** Fuel fill fitting is improperly secured to fuel tank and could leak an excessive amount of fuel, especially after refueling or when tank is more than half full.

2000-01 CHEVROLET MONTE CARLO

2000 Chevrolet Monte Carlo LS

FOR Acceleration (SS) • Steering/handling (SS) • Instruments and controls

AGAINST Engine noise • Road noise • Rear-seat entry/exit

EVALUATION Modest handling skills are the rule for the LS version of this relatively large coupe, but it feels reasonably balanced and secure in corners. The SS edition shines on twisty roads, showing minimal body lean and great grip. Stable during highway cruising, both offer firm, accurate steering and a comfortable ride. A responsive automatic transmission works with the base V6 to furnish adequate acceleration. Although the SS is no muscle car, its bigger V6 provides brisk takeoffs and ready power for freeway merging and backroad passing. Both engines are loud and gruff in hard acceleration, and tire roar is prominent on coarse surfaces. Even the firm SS suspension is compliant enough on bumpy urban streets. Brakes feel strong and have good pedal modulation, but hard stops induce excessive nosedive. Midsize dimensions give the Monte a big advantage in interior space, compared to most coupes on the market. Two adults can stretch out in front, and rear leg room is adequate for average-size adults. Head room gets tight with an optional sunroof, but there's far more clearance than in, say, a Mercury Cougar or Dodge Stratus. The cabin feels roomier than an Accord or Solara. The trunk is tall, wide, and deep, with convenient bumper-height liftover. The driver gets a comfortable bucket seat with plenty of lateral bolstering, but thick rear roof pillars impede over-the-shoulder vision. Gauge groupings and graphics are excellent, controls handy.

VALUE Roomier than other sports coupes, the Monte trounces models like the Avenger in size, comfort, and performance. New or used, it beats an Accord or Solara in features for the price. Though less poised than Japanese-brand rivals, it has its own American character. Resale value has not been strong, which can be a bonus for used-car shoppers.

SPECIFICATIONS

	2-door coupe
Wheelbase, in.	110.5
Overall length, in.	197.9
Overall width, in.	72.7
Overall height, in.	55.2
Curb weight, lbs.	3340
Cargo volume, cu. ft.	15.8
Fuel capacity, gals.	17.0
Seating capacity	5
Front head room, in.	38.1
Max. front leg room, in.	42.4
Rear head room, in.	36.5
Min. rear leg room, in.	35.8

Powertrain layout: transverse front-engine/front-wheel drive

ENGINES

	ohv V6	ohv V6
Size, liters/cu. in.	3.4/205	3.8/231
Horsepower	180	200
Torque (lbs./ft.)	205	225
EPA city/highway mpg		
4-speed OD automatic	20/32	19/29
City/highway mpg (as tested)		
4-speed OD automatic	21.0	21.0

Built in Canada

RETAIL PRICES

	GOOD	AVERAGE	POOR
2000 Monte Carlo LS	$13,500-14,500	$12,500-13,500	$9,000-10,000
2000 Monte Carlo SS	15,500-16,500	14,500-15,500	11,500-12,500
2001 Monte Carlo LS	15,200-17,000	14,200-16,000	—
2001 Monte Carlo SS	18,000-19,500	17,000-18,500	—

AVERAGE REPLACEMENT COSTS

A/C Compressor	$525	Constant Velocity Joints	750
Alternator	275	Exhaust System	565
Automatic Transmission or Transaxle	895	Radiator	450
		Shocks and/or Struts	975
Brakes	485	Timing Chain or Belt	325

TROUBLE SPOTS

• **Vehicle noise.** Banging, clunking, or popping noises from the front under acceleration or braking require shims between the engine cradle and frame. (2000)

• **Vehicle noise.** Fuel makes banging and sloshing noises in the tank when less than half full. (2000)

• **Brakes.** The rear brakes make squealing or moaning noises. Countermeasure brake pads are available. (2000-01)

RECALL HISTORY

2000 w/TRW seat-belt buckle assemblies: Seat-belt buckle assemblies fail to conform to federal requirements, because buckle base was not properly heat treated. **2001:** On certain cars, airbag sensing and diagnostic modules could experience a memory error, and airbags might not deploy during a crash.

1998-01 CHEVROLET PRIZM

1998 Chevrolet Prizm

FOR Fuel economy • Ride • Optional antilock braking • Optional side airbags

AGAINST Rear-seat room • Automatic transmission performance

EVALUATION

See the 1998-01 Toyota Corolla.

VALUE

See the 1998-01 Toyota Corolla.

SPECIFICATIONS

	4-door sedan
Wheelbase, in.	97.0
Overall length, in.	174.2
Overall width, in.	66.7
Overall height, in.	53.7
Curb weight, lbs.	3330
Cargo volume, cu. ft.	12.1
Fuel capacity, gals.	13.2
Seating capacity	5
Front head room, in.	39.3
Max. front leg room, in.	42.5
Rear head room, in.	36.9
Min. rear leg room, in.	33.2

Powertrain layout: transverse front-engine/front-wheel drive

ENGINES

	dohc I4
Size, liters/cu. in.	1.8/110
Horsepower	120-125
Torque (lbs./ft.)	112-125

EPA city/highway mpg

5-speed OD manual	31/37
4-speed OD automatic	28/36

City/highway mpg (as tested)

5-speed OD manual	29.2
4-speed OD automatic	24.8

Built in USA

RETAIL PRICES

	GOOD	AVERAGE	POOR
1998 Prizm	$6,000-6,800	$5,300-6,100	$2,700-3,200
1999 Prizm	7,200-8,000	6,400-7,200	3,500-4,200
2000 Prizm	8,500-9,500	7,600-8,500	4,200-4,900
2001 Prizm	9,800-11,000	8,900-10,000	—

AVERAGE REPLACEMENT COSTS

See the 1998-01 Toyota Corolla.

TROUBLE SPOTS

• **None.** There are no discernible trouble spots for this vehicle at this time.

1990-94 CHEVROLET S10 BLAZER

1993 Chevrolet S10 Blazer LT 4-door wagon

FOR Antilock brakes • Acceleration • 4WD traction • Passenger and cargo room • Ride (4-door)

AGAINST Rear-seat comfort • Fuel economy • Noise • Ride (2-door models)

EVALUATION The 4.3-liter engine develops considerable torque at low engine speeds, yielding strong acceleration around town, plus plenty of towing power. Sadly, it's also noisy. Suspensions are among the least compliant in their class, but the 4-door's longer wheelbase improves ride quality. With a 2-door, you can expect to bounce and bang over bumpy roads. Body lean in turns isn't bad, but Blazers don't match the smaller Jeep Cherokee in urban nimbleness. Interior room is good, but not as spacious as an Explorer or Grand Cherokee. Dashboard layout also is pleasing on the whole, but some controls are a long reach, and radio buttons are small. Interior noise gets bothersome on the highway. Back seats are hard to get at in 2-doors. Four-door models, with their extra 6.5 inches of wheelbase, boast vastly improved access. Rear leg room is identical in each body style, but the 4-door's longer wheelbase allowed the back seat to be fitted ahead of rear wheelwells, for 15 inches more hip room than the 2-door. Shift-on-the-fly 4WD and 4-wheel ABS are particularly appealing features.

VALUE By 1993, when Jeep launched its Grand Cherokee with a driver-side airbag and available V8, the Blazer was showing its age. Grand Cherokee and Explorers beat the Blazer in refinement, but the S10 Blazer still is a good choice in a smaller sport-utility.

SPECIFICATIONS

	2-door wagon	4-door wagon
Wheelbase, in.	100.5	107.0
Overall length, in.	170.3	176.8
Overall width, in.	65.4	65.4
Overall height, in.	64.1	64.3
Curb weight, lbs.	3536	3776
Cargo volume, cu. ft.	67.3	74.3
Fuel capacity, gals.	20.0	20.0
Seating capacity	4	6
Front head room, in.	39.1	39.1
Max. front leg room, in.	42.5	42.5
Rear head room, in.	38.7	38.8
Min. rear leg room, in.	35.5	36.5

Powertrain layout: longitudinal front-engine/rear- or 4-wheel drive

ENGINES

	ohv V6	ohv V6
Size, liters/cu. in.	4.3/262	4.3/262
Horsepower	160-165	200
Torque (lbs./ft.)	230-235	260

EPA city/highway mpg

5-speed OD manual	16/21	
4-speed OD automatic	17/22	16/22

City/highway mpg (as tested)

4-speed OD automatic	16.2	15.3

Built in USA

RETAIL PRICES

	GOOD	AVERAGE	POOR
1990 S10 Blazer 2WD	$1,300-2,100	$700-1,500	$100-300
1991 S10 Blazer 2WD	1,600-2,600	1,000-2,000	200-600
1992 S10 Blazer 2WD	1,900-3,500	1,300-2,800	300-900
1992 S10 Blazer 4WD	2,900-4,800	2,200-4,000	700-1,800
1993 S10 Blazer 2WD	2,400-4,200	1,700-3,500	500-1,300
1993 S10 Blazer 4WD	3,400-5,500	2,600-4,700	1,000-2,200
1994 S10 Blazer 2WD	3,000-5,000	2,300-4,200	800-1,800
1994 S10 Blazer 4WD	4,000-6,200	3,200-5,300	1,300-2,600

AVERAGE REPLACEMENT COSTS

A/C Compressor	$365	Clutch, Pressure Plate, Bearing	390
Alternator	195	Exhaust System	405
Automatic Transmission or Transaxle	735	Radiator	415
Brakes	210	Shocks and/or Struts	275
Timing Chain or Belt	205	Universal Joints	160

TROUBLE SPOTS

• **Engine knock.** Knock in the 4.3-liter engine is usually eliminated by using an oil filter with a check valve. If this does not fix it, GM has revised PROMs for the computers and will even replace the main bearings. (1990-94)

• **Automatic transmission.** TH-700-R4 automatic transmissions may shift late or not upshift at all. The problem is a stuck throttle valve inside the transmission. (1990-94)

RECALL HISTORY

1990-91: Fuel tank sender seal may be out of position, which could result in fuel leakage. **1990-92 w/2.5-liter engine and no air conditioning:** Fan blades could break off while engine is running. **1991:** Rear seatbelt buckle release button can stick in unlatched position, under certain conditions. **1991-94 w/4WD and EBC4 ABS:** Increased stopping distances can occur during ABS stops while in 2WD mode. **1993:** Rear seatbelts may not meet government requirements. **1994 w/VR4 weight-distribution trailer hitch option:** Trailer hitch attaching bolts were not tightened adequately.

1999-01 CHEVROLET SILVERADO

FOR Acceleration (V8) • Instruments and controls

AGAINST Rear-seat entry/exit (extended-cab) • Fuel economy • Ride

EVALUATION Silverado and GMC Sierra pickups perform better than their predecessors, though not always by a lot. New V8s are smooth and capable, but have slightly less torque than the previous engines, so acceleration and throttle response are similar. The Tow/Haul mode and optional adjustable suspension are welcome features, since most big pickups haul or tow at times. All-around performance easily matches Ford's F-150. Although

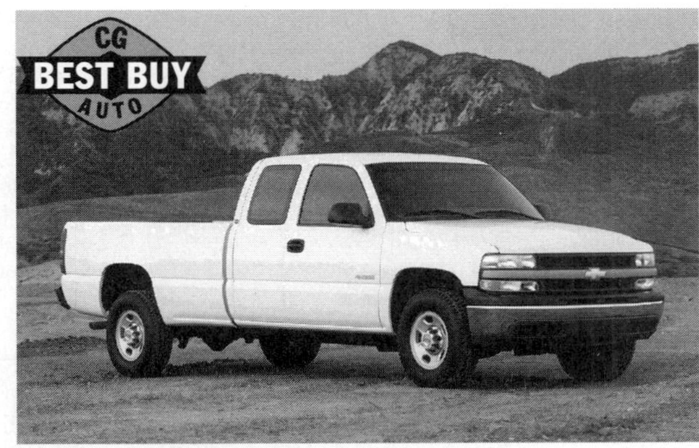

2001 Chevrolet Silverado 1500 extended cab

the V6 struggles under heavy loads or up long grades, it's a smooth runner. The 5.3-liter V8 offers good power in all conditions, though it trails Ford's 5.4-liter in torque. An alert, fuss-free automatic transmission helps get the most out of any engine. A 4WD extended-cab with the 5.3 V8 averaged 13.7 mpg. Brakes offer good stopping power and firm, progressive pedal action, beating the previous model's mushy feel. Steering is more precise, but overboosted. A stiffer structure helps improve ride quality, which is more compliant than Ford's, though the tail still stutters over bumps when the bed is empty. Road, wind, and engine noise levels are unobjectionable. The biggest improvements lie inside. In design, feel, and location, gauges and controls are best-in-class. GM also was the first to supplement the odometer with an engine-hour meter. Front seats are roomy and supportive, with integrated seatbelts that move comfortably. Both GM makes soundly trounce Ford and Dodge pickups in rear-seat accommodations, with more leg clearance. A contoured cushion and reclined backrest approach sedan levels of comfort. Doors open wider, too.

VALUE GM earns credit for refining its big pickups while introducing a host of worthy improvements. No extended-cabs are more comfortable. Though a step behind Ford in innovation, GM pickups deliver high value for performance, comfort, and design, and beat Ford in 4WD convenience.

SPECIFICATIONS	ext. cab long bed	ext. cab short bed	reg. cab long bed	reg. cab short bed
Wheelbase, in.	157.5	143.5	133.0	119.0
Overall length, in.	246.7	227.5	222.0	203.3
Overall width, in.	78.5	78.5	78.5	78.5
Overall height, in.	70.8	71.2	71.0	71.2
Curb weight, lbs.	4442	4235	4032	3923
Fuel capacity, gals.	34.0	26.0	34.0	26.0
Seating capacity	6	6	3	3
Front head room, in.	41.0	41.0	41.0	41.0
Max. front leg room, in.	41.3	41.3	41.3	41.0
Rear head room, in.	38.4	38.4	—	—
Min. rear leg room, in.	33.7	33.7	—	—

Powertrain layout: longitudinal front-engine/rear- or 4-wheel drive

ENGINES	ohv V6	ohv V8	ohv V8
Size, liters/cu. in.	4.3/262	4.8/292	5.3/325
Horsepower	200	255-270	270-285
Torque (lbs./ft.)	260	285	315-325
EPA city/highway mpg			
5-speed OD manual	17/23	16/20	
4-speed OD automatic	16/20	16/21	16/20
City/highway mpg (as tested)			
4-speed OD automatic			13.7

Built in Mexico

RETAIL PRICES	GOOD	AVERAGE	POOR
1999 Silverado 1500 2WD	$11,400-16,000	$10,400-15,000	$7,500-10,000
1999 Silverado 1500 4WD	13,400-18,000	12,400-17,000	8,500-11,500
2000 Silverado 1500 2WD	12,900-18,000	11,900-17,000	8,200-11,500
2000 Silverado 1500 4WD	14,800-20,000	13,800-18,800	9,800-13,000
2001 Silverado 1500 2WD	14,400-200,00	13,400-18,500	—
2001 Silverado 1500 4WD	16,300-23,000	15,200-21,500	—

AVERAGE REPLACEMENT COSTS

A/C Compressor	$390	Clutch, Pressure Plate,	
Alternator	325	Bearing	455
Automatic Transmission or		Constant Velocity Joints	890
Transaxle	1,115	Exhaust System	455
Brakes	375	Radiator	555
Shocks and/or Struts	665	Timing Chain or Belt	610

TROUBLE SPOTS

• **Vehicle shake.** Extended cab, long box models shudder when accelerating from a stop requiring replacement of the two-piece driveshaft with a one-piece driveshaft. (1999-2001)

• **Manual transmission.** Manual transmissions tend to pop out of first gear because the transmissions were built without a detent ball and spring. These parts will be installed under warranty,. (1999-2000)

• **Automatic transmission.** The front wheels slip while in 4WD requiring replacement of the clutch plates as well as the use of synthetic gear oil. (1999-2001)

RECALL HISTORY

1999-2000: Clearance between front right-hand brake pipe and body cross sill could decrease to the point of allowing contact, which could result in damage and loss of brake fluid and pressure. **2000 w/4-wheel disc brakes:** Out-of-spec spring clip in antilock brake system could allow motor bearing to become misaligned; eventually, ABS would be non-functional and Dynamic Rear Proportioning system would become inoperative.

1994-01 CHEVROLET S-SERIES

1994 Chevrolet S10 SS regular cab

FOR Passenger room • Acceleration (V6) • Instruments/controls • Ride (2WD models) • Optional third door (1996-later) • Handling

AGAINST Fuel economy • Ride (4WD models) • Rear-seat room (extended cab)

EVALUATION Pleasant to drive, the S-Series is a solid-feeling truck. Cabins feel roomier than before, with more rearward seat travel and storage space. Extra glass area gives great visibility and an airy feel. Wind noise is reduced. Acceleration is good with the V6. Automatic-transmission gear changes are smooth, though downshifts might be delayed for low-speed passing. An extended-cab V6 LS averaged 17.2 mpg in a long-term trial. When cold, however, that engine ran somewhat roughly, and its fan was intrusively loud. If you prefer a 4-cylinder pickup, your best bet is manual shift. An extended-cab 2WD LS delivered ride quality as smooth as many cars. These pickups easily absorb most bumps, and take dips with minimal bouncing, but some optional tire/suspension setups are rougher. When the cargo bed is empty, the tail tends to hop over sharp bumps and ridges. Body lean is evident in turns, but the truck feels balanced and poised in directional changes. Standard antilock brakes prevent lock-up during simulated panic stops, but brake-pedal feel on early models is disturbingly spongy.

VALUE In their latest form, these compact pickups rank among the best in overall performance, ergonomics, and refinement. A Dodge Dakota has heftier hauling ability and an available V8 engine, but most buyers will be pleased with the Chevrolet. It outsells the Dakota and is a worthy contender to the sales-leading Ford Ranger.

SPECIFICATIONS	reg. cab short bed	reg. cab long bed	ext. cab	crew cab
Wheelbase, in.	108.3	117.9	122.9	122.9
Overall length, in.	188.6	204.6	203.3	204.8

	reg. cab short bed	reg. cab long bed	ext. cab	crew cab
Overall width, in.	67.9	67.9	67.9	67.9
Overall height, in.	62.1	62.1	62.2	63.4
Curb weight, lbs.	2822	2874	3081	4039
Fuel capacity, gals.	19.0	19.0	19.0	18.0
Seating capacity	3	3	5	5
Front head room, in.	39.5	39.5	39.5	39.4
Max. front leg room, in.	43.2	43.2	43.2	42.4
Rear head room, in.	—	—	—	38.2
Min. rear leg room, in.	—	—	—	34.6

Powertrain layout: longitudinal front-engine/rear- or 4-wheel drive

ENGINES

	ohc I4	ohv V6	ohv V6
Size, liters/cu. in.	2.2/134	4.3/262	4.3/262
Horsepower	118-120	155-180	180-195
Torque (lbs./ft.)	130-140	235-245	245-260
EPA city/highway mpg			
5-speed OD manual...............................	23/30	18/25	18/25
4-speed OD automatic...........................	20/27	20/24	20/24
City/highway mpg (as tested)			
5-speed OD manual...............................	22.3		
4-speed OD automatic...........................		18.4	18.0

Built in USA

RETAIL PRICES

	GOOD	AVERAGE	POOR
1994 S10 2WD	$3,000-4,800	$2,400-4,100	$700-1,700
1994 S10 4WD	4,200-6,300	3,500-5,500	1,500-2,800
1995 S-Series 2WD	3,500-6,500	2,800-5,800	1,000-2,800
1995 S-Series 4WD	5,000-8,500	4,200-7,700	2,000-4,200
1996 S-Series 2WD	4,300-7,500	3,600-6,800	1,500-3,600
1996 S-Series 4WD	6,000-9,700	52,00 -8,700	2,500-5,200
1997 S-Series 2WD	5,100-8,200	4,300-7,400	2,000-4,100
1997 S-Series 4WD	7,000-11,000	6,200-10,000	3,000-6,200
1998 S-Series 2WD	6,000-9,000	5,200-8,100	2,500-4,800
1998 S-Series 4WD	8,000-12,000	7,000-11,000	3,600-6,900
1999 S-Series 2WD	7,000-10,000	6,200-9,000	3,000-5,500
1999 S-Series 4WD	9,000-13,000	8,000-11,800	4,300-7,500
2000 S-Series 2WD	8,000-11,500	7,000-10,500	3,500-6,000
2000 S-Series 4WD	10,000-14,000	9,000-12,800	5,000-7,500
2001 S-Series 2WD	9,200-12,500	8,200-11,500	—
2001 S-Series 4WD	11,500-15,500	10,300-14,000	—

AVERAGE REPLACEMENT COSTS

A/C Compressor...........	$550	Clutch, Pressure Plate,	
Alternator......................	255	Bearing	545
Automatic Transmission or		Exhaust System	460
Transaxle	750	Radiator.........................	410
Brakes :........................	210	Shocks and/or Struts....	345
Timing Chain or Belt.....	420	Universal Joints.............	190

TROUBLE SPOTS

• **Engine knock.** Knock in the 4.3-liter engine is usually eliminated by using an oil filter with a check valve. If this does not fix it, GM has revised PROMs for the computers and will even replace the main bearings. (1990-95)

RECALL HISTORY

1994 w/2.2-liter engine: Vacuum hose can detach from power brake booster check valve, as a result of engine backfire. **1994-95 Postal Vehicle:** Loose/worn steering shaft can result in separation from steering gear. **1994-96 w/4WD and EBC4 ABS:** Increased stopping distances can occur during ABS stops while in 2WD mode. **1994-97:** Seatbelt webbing on certain models can separate during frontal impact. **1995 w/air conditioning and V6 engine:** Rivet can break and allow fan blade to separate from hub. **1996:** Top coat of paint on a few trucks peels severely. **1996 2WD manual-shift w/2.2-liter engine:** Drive wheels could seize and lock while truck is moving. **1996-97 w/V6 engine:** Front brake line can contact oil pan, causing wear that may result in fluid loss. **1997-98 electric:** Fuel-fired heater pipe ground strap contacts rear brake pipe, leading to premature corrosion and eventual loss of brake pipe integrity. **1998:** Fatigue fracture of rear-axle brake pipe can occur, causing slow fluid leak and resulting in soft brake pedal; if pipe breaks, driver would face sudden loss of rear-brake performance. **1998:** Wiring-harness clip can melt and drip onto exhaust manifold, possibly resulting in fire. **1998:** Daytime running lights do not meet FMVSS No. 108 requirements. **2000 w/2WD:** On certain vehicles, right-hand ABS module feed pipe and/or brake crossover pipe tube nuts could have been tightened improperly; seal could have been broken, causing leakage and increasing stopping distance. **2000 w/all-disc brakes:** Out-of-spec spring clip in ABS motor could allow bearing to become misaligned; eventually, ABS and Dynamic Rear Proportioning system would become inoperative. **2000:** Some seatbelt assemblies were not properly heat treated and do not pass the load bearing requirement.

1992-99 CHEVROLET SUBURBAN

1993 Chevrolet Suburban C1500

FOR Antilock brakes • Passenger and cargo room • Highway ride • Acceleration (7.4-liter) • Visibility • Trailer towing capability

AGAINST Acceleration (early models) • Fuel economy • Rear-seat entry/exit • Maneuverability • Handling

EVALUATION Evolved from GM pickup trucks, full-size Suburbans might be fitted to haul either cargo or passengers. Step-in height is a lot lower than in earlier Suburbans. Even so, it's tough to get in and out from the back because the opening between door pillar and seat is narrow, and step-in height of 4WD Suburbans is still quite tall. Access to the optional third seat demands some serious stooping. Three can easily sit abreast, but there's not as much stretch-out leg room for adults in the back seats as the vehicle's size would suggest. Folding the 70/30 split middle bench is a two-step procedure, and a handy carpeted panel hinges down to create a flat load floor from front seatbacks to the front of the rear-most bench. Unfortunately, the rear bench's seatback does not fold flat. Though it's removable, that seat is heavy and cumbersome. Visibility is fine, from a carlike seating position. Controls are within easy reach, though the climate and radio buttons suffer from a haphazard layout. Cargo space is cavernous and loading is easy, because the load floor is more than two feet off the ground. Acceleration with the early 5.7-liter V8 is only adequate in town, and the transmission is reluctant to downshift. With its extra 50 horsepower, the Vortec gas V8 introduced for 1996 gives the Suburban a much-needed boost. That one is more lively off the line, and teams with an improved transmission to furnish better power for passing and climbing long grades. No longer is it necessary to push the pedal to the floor to induce a downshift. Fuel economy is no bonus, with any engine. Don't expect much more than the miserable 10.7 mpg achieved in mixed driving with a K1500. The big 7.4-liter engine is the choice for truly heavy towing, but most shoppers will be satisfied with a 5.7-liter V8. Suburbans are smooth and capable on the highway. Bumps are absorbed well, with only moderate floating over freeway dips—though turns at any speed are accompanied by noticeable body lean. Simulated panic stops induce pronounced nosedive, and occasionally a bit of rear-wheel lockup (despite the antilock braking system).

VALUE Through the early '90s, Suburbans were virtually unchallenged in the full-size wagon segment. GM's Tahoe/Yukon offers much of the Suburban's brawn in a more manageable size. Still, those two cannot match the Suburban's payload ratings and towing ability. Neither can they seat more than six—a feat that's possible, however, in a Ford Expedition with third-row seating, as well as in a full-size van. Sales declined during 1996, for the first time in this generation. Some potential Suburban buyers evidently gravitated to the smaller Tahoe/Yukon. No rival can match the Suburban's 149.5-cubic-foot cargo capacity. Also, no engine is as powerful as the muscular 7.4-liter V8.

SPECIFICATIONS

	4-door wagon
Wheelbase, in.	131.5
Overall length, in.	220.0
Overall width, in.	76.7
Overall height, in.	70.2
Curb weight, lbs.	4634
Cargo volume, cu. ft.	149.5
Fuel capacity, gals.	42.0
Seating capacity	9
Front head room, in.	39.9
Max. front leg room, in.	41.3
Rear head room, in.	38.9
Min. rear leg room, in.	26.2

Powertrain layout: longitudinal front-engine/rear- or 4-wheel drive

ENGINES

	ohv V8	ohv V8	ohv V8	Turbodiesel ohv V8
Size, liters/cu. in.	5.7/350	5.7/350	7.4/454	6.5/400
Horsepower	190-210	250-255	230-290	190
Torque (lbs./ft.)	300-310	330-335	265-410	385

EPA city/highway mpg				
4-speed OD automatic	13/17	12/16	NA	15/18

City/highway mpg (as tested)				
4-speed OD automatic	10.7	13.9		

Built in USA, Mexico

RETAIL PRICES

	GOOD	AVERAGE	POOR
1992 Suburban 2WD	$5,800-6,500	$5,100-5,700	$2,500-3,000
1992 Suburban 4WD	6,500-7,200	5,800-6,500	3,000-3,500
1992 LS, LT 2WD	6,200-7,000	5,300-6,100	2,700-3,200
1992 LS, LT 4WD	7,200-8,200	6,400-7,400	3,600-4,300
1993 Suburban 2WD	7,000-8,000	6,200-7,200	3,400-4,000
1993 Suburban 4WD	7,700-8,700	6,800-7,800	3,900-4,600
1993 LS, LT 2WD	7,500-8,500	6,700-7,600	3,800-4,500
1993 LS, LT 4WD	8,700-9,700	7,800-8,800	4,700-5,500
1994 Suburban 2WD	8,000-9,000	7,000-8,000	4,700-5,500
1994 Suburban 4WD	9,000-10,000	8,000-9,000	4,700-5,500
1994 LS, LT 2WD	8,800-9,800	7,800-8,800	4,500-5,300
1994 LS, LT 4WD	9,800-10,800	8,800-9,800	5,200-6,000
1995 Suburban 2WD	9,000-10,000	8,000-9,000	4,800-5,500
1995 Suburban 4WD	10,200-11,500	9,200-10,300	5,500-6,200
1995 LS, LT 2WD	10,000-11,500	9,000-10,300	5,300-6,200
1995 LS, LT 4WD	11,200-12,500	10,000-11,200	6,000-7,000
1996 Suburban 2WD	10,200-11,500	9,200-10,300	5,500-6,200
1996 Suburban 4WD	11,500-13,900	10,300-11,500	6,300-7,300
1996 LS, LT 2WD	11,000-13,000	9,800-11,500	6,000-7,200
1996 LS, LT 4WD	12,500-14,000	11,300-12,500	7,000-8,000
1997 Suburban 2WD	11,500-13,000	10,300-11,500	6,500-7,500
1997 Suburban 4WD	13,000-14,500	11,800-13,000	7,500-8,400
1997 LS, LT 2WD	12,500-14,500	11,300-13,000	7,100-8,400
1997 LS, LT 4WD	14,000-16,000	12,500-14,500	8,000-9,500
1998 Suburban 2WD	13,500-15,000	12,000-13,500	8,000-9,000
1998 Suburban 4WD	15,500-17,000	14,000-15,500	8,700-10,500
1998 LS, LT 2WD	150,00 -17,000	13,500-15,500	8,700-10,500
1998 LS, LT 4WD	16,500-18,500	15,000-17,000	10,000-11,500
1999 Suburban 2WD	16,000-18,000	14,500-16,500	9,700-11,500
1999 Suburban 4WD	18,000-20,000	16,500-18,500	11,500-13,000
1999 LS, LT 2WD	18,000-20,000	16,500-18,500	11,500-13,000
1999 LS, LT 4WD	19,500-21,500	18,000-20,000	12,500-14,000

AVERAGE REPLACEMENT COSTS

A/C Compressor	$520	Clutch, Pressure Plate,	
Alternator	225	Bearing	800
Automatic Transmission or		Exhaust System	485
Transaxle	850	Radiator	450
Brakes	220	Shocks and/or Struts	410
Timing Chain or Belt	230	Universal Joints	270

TROUBLE SPOTS

• **Transmission leak.** Fluid may leak from the pump body on 4L60-E transmissions due to the pump bushing walking out of the valve body. (1995-96)

• **Brake wear.** Front brake linings wear rapidly. Replacing the proportioning valve and the rear shoes with a different friction materia prolongs front brake life. (1992-99)

• **Hard starting.** No-starts, hard starting, or rough idle may be due to some gasolines dissolving compounds in the fuel filler pipe that then clog the fuel injectors. (1997-99)

• **Oil leak.** Oil loss and fouled spark plugs result from intake manifold gasket leaks. (1996-98)

• **Clutch.** The clutch may fail to engage or disengage, or become noisy due to overtravel of the clutch damper on trucks with the 6.5-liter diesel engine. Revised parts are available to prevent recurrence. (1992-99)

• **Fuel pump.** The electronic injection pump on diesel engines is prone to failures and may be covered under an extended warranty up to 11 years or 120,000 miles.

• **Dashboard lights.** The oil pressure gauge may read high, move erratically, or not work because the oil pressure sensor is defective. (1992-93)

• **Doors.** The rear cargo doors may be hard to open because the hinges corrode requiring the hinge pins and bushings to be replaced. (1992-97)

RECALL HISTORY

1992: Brake-pedal pivot bolt can disengage. **1994:** Reversed polarity of brake switch can cause contacts to wear prematurely; may result in loss of brake lights without warning. **1994-96:** Solder joints can crack, causing windshield wipers to work intermittently. **1995 w/M30/MT1 automatic transmission:** When shift lever is placed in "Park" position, its indicator light may not illuminate. **1995 w/4180-E automatic transmission:** External transmission leak can occur. **1995-96 w/gasoline engine:** Throttle cable may contact dash mat and bind. **1998:** On some vehicles, one or both front brake rotor/hubs may have out-of-spec gray iron that can fail during life of vehicle. **1999:** In a crash, right front passenger restraint systems may not meet neck extension requirements.

2000-01 CHEVROLET TAHOE AND SUBURBAN

2000 Chevrolet Tahoe LT

FOR Passenger and cargo room • Trailer towing ability

AGAINST Fuel economy • Rear-seat entry/exit

EVALUATION Tahoe/Suburban advances were mainly evolutionary, but they yielded some noticeable improvements. New V8s feel slightly smoother than the engines they replaced, but not dramatically stronger. Acceleration is adequate, aided by the smooth automatic's astute shifting, but the 4.8-liter feels strained in towing or heavy hauling. Gas mileage is dismal. A Tahoe 4x4 with the 5.3-liter V-8 averaged 12.9 mpg, while a similar Suburban got 11.5 mpg. These big SUVs don't corner like cars, but handling is better than their size might suggest. They feel balanced in directional changes, and are fairly easy to maneuver. Steering is reasonably precise, but road feel is only adequate. At lower speeds, the speed-variable assist makes steering too light for some tastes. Biggest improvements are in ride quality and brake feel. The suspension absorbs bumps well and is surefooted on rough pavement. Stopping power is strong, with firm, progressive pedal action. Wind rush is noticeable but not intrusive. Tire noise is low for a full-size SUV, but audible at highway speeds. The dashboard layout is logical and handy, with clear gauges and easily accessed controls. Drivers get a commanding view, while moving the spare tire beneath the rear undercarriage improved visibility and cargo space. Suburbans have ample head, shoulder, and leg room for two grownups, but leg and head clearance in the Tahoe's third-row seat suggests children and occasional use. Entry/exit is somewhat hampered by modest back-door openings, especially on Tahoes. A Tahoe has only enough room for a single row of grocery bags behind the third row, but Suburbans are more sizable. Third-row seats fold easily, and have wheels for removal. The Suburban's heavy bench takes two people to remove, while the Tahoe's third row is in two sections.

VALUE GM's impressive new full-size SUVs are capable, comfortable, and easy to live with. Though too big for a lot of buyers, their size fits nicely into the gap between Ford's Expedition and Excursion. Don't buy a big SUV without trying a Chevrolet or GMC.

SPECIFICATIONS

	4-door wagon[1]	4-door wagon[2]
Wheelbase, in.	116.0	130.0
Overall length, in.	198.9	219.3
Overall width, in.	78.9	78.8
Overall height, in.	74.0	73.3
Curb weight, lbs.	5050	5123
Cargo volume, cu. ft.	108.2	138.4
Fuel capacity, gals.	26.0	33.0
Seating capacity	9	9
Front head room, in.	40.7	40.7
Max. front leg room, in.	41.3	41.3
Rear head room, in.	39.4	39.0
Min. rear leg room, in.	38.6	39.1

1. Tahoe. 2. Suburban.

Powertrain layout: longitudinal front-engine/rear- or 4-wheel drive

ENGINES

	ohv V8	ohv V8	ohv V8	ohv V8
Size, liters/cu. in.	4.8/292	5.3/325	6.0/364	8.1/496
Horsepower	275	285	300-320	285
Torque (lbs./ft.)	290	325	355-360	455
EPA city/highway mpg				
4-speed OD automatic	15/20	14/18	NA	NA
City/highway mpg (as tested)				
4-speed OD automatic		12.9	9.8	

Built in USA

RETAIL PRICES

	GOOD	AVERAGE	POOR
2000 Tahoe 1500 2WD	$20,500-24,500	$19,500-23,000	$15,000-18,000
2000 Tahoe 1500 4WD	22,500-26,500	21,000-25,000	16,500-19,500
2000 Suburban 1500 2WD	21,500-26,500	20,000-25,000	15,500-19,500
2000 Suburban 1500 4WD	23,500-28,500	22,000-27,000	17,000-21,000
2000 Suburban 2500 2WD	23,000-28,000	21,500-26,500	16,500-20,500
2000 Suburban 2500 4WD	25,000-30,000	23,500-28,500	18,000-22,000
2001 Tahoe 1500 2WD	22,500-26,500	21,000-25,000	—
2001 Tahoe 1500 4WD	25,000-29,000	23,500-27,500	—
2001 Suburban 1500 2WD	23,500-29,000	22,000-27,500	—
2001 Suburban 1500 4WD	26,000-31,000	24,500-29,500	—
2001 Suburban 2500 2WD	25,500-31,000	24,000-29,500	—
2001 Suburban 2500 4WD	28,000-33,000	26,500-31,500	—

AVERAGE REPLACEMENT COSTS

A/C Compressor	$390	Constant Velocity Joints	890
Alternator	325	Exhaust System	455
Automatic Transmission or Transaxle	1,115	Radiator	555
		Shocks and/or Struts	665
Brakes	375	Timing Chain or Belt	610

TROUBLE SPOTS

• **Oil leak.** An oil leak may be created by the front driveshaft hitting the oil filter on 4x4 models with the 7.4L engine. An adapter will relocate the filter. (2000)

• **Climate control.** Low output of the rear heater in very cold weather is due to a restrictor in the T-coupling. A revised coupling is offered. (2000-01)

RECALL HISTORY

2000: Clearance between front right-hand brake pipe and body cross sill could decrease to the point of allowing contact, which could result in damage and loss of brake fluid and pressure. **2000-01:** Rear wheelhouse plugs may be loose or missing, allowing exhaust gases to flow forward under certain conditions and accumulate in rear wheelhouse. **2001:** Outboard seatbelt retractors for the 2nd and 3rd row of seats could be cracked. With repeated actuation of the locking mechanism, the crack could spread to the point such that the seatbelt would no longer lock.

1999-01 CHEVROLET TRACKER

2001 Chevrolet Tracker ZR2 4-door wagon

FOR Maneuverability • Cargo room

AGAINST Rear-seat room • Acceleration

EVALUATION Both 4-cylinder engines feel weak and gruff when worked hard—which is necessary most of the time, even for ordinary driving. In the convertible, power is only passable; in the wagon, lethargic. No ball of fire itself, the V6 at least adds a welcome dose of oomph. Automatic transmissions are well behaved, but the manual gearbox suffers vague shift action. Gas mileage is no bargain. A 4-cylinder 4x4 convertible with the 5-speed averaged 20.2 mpg. Ride and handling are nothing to shout about, either. Even on fairly smooth roads, Trackers are prone to fore-aft pitching, though they absorb most bumps without jarring. Cornering grip is only so-so. A CR-V or Forester is far more composed and comfortable. Tracker is the better off-road choice, however, thanks to its low-range gearing and truck-style construction. Rear space is tight, and rear entry/exit tricky. Up front, however, two occupants get more pleasing space and comfort. Relatively low seats mean drivers don't get so commanding a forward view. Tall rear headrests and an outside spare tire hamper rearward vision. Step-in height is moderate, but narrow rear doors make it hard to get into wagons. The convertible's back seat is cramped and park-bench hard. Stereo and climate controls are too low for easy adjusting on the move, and the radio has annoyingly tiny buttons. Neither body style has much cargo space, and the tailgate swings to the right, which hampers curbside loading.

VALUE Despite some off-road prowess, Tracker is an also-ran among mini-SUVs. A CR-V, RAV4 or Forester is more pleasant, spacious, and enjoyable for the kind of driving that most folks do. Because the Tracker's resale value is lower, it costs less secondhand.

SPECIFICATIONS

	2-door conv.	2-door wagon
Wheelbase, in.	86.6	97.6
Overall length, in.	151.8	162.8
Overall width, in.	67.3	67.3
Overall height, in.	66.5	66.3
Curb weight, lbs.	2723	2987
Cargo volume, cu. ft.	33.7	44.7
Fuel capacity, gals.	14.8	17.4
Seating capacity	4	5
Front head room, in.	40.9	39.9
Max. front leg room, in.	41.4	41.4
Rear head room, in.	39.5	39.6
Min. rear leg room, in.	35.9	35.9

Powertrain layout: longitudinal front-engine/rear- or 4-wheel drive

ENGINES

	ohc I4	dohc I4	dohc V6
Size, liters/cu. in.	1.6/97	2.0/121	2.5/152
Horsepower	97	127	155
Torque (lbs./ft.)	100	134	160
EPA city/highway mpg			
5-speed OD manual	25/28	23/25	
4-speed OD automatic		24/26	18/20
City/highway mpg (as tested)			
5-speed OD manual	—	20.2	—
4-speed OD automatic	—	—	17.9

Built in Canada

RETAIL PRICES

	GOOD	AVERAGE	POOR
1999 Tracker 2WD	$6,000-7,500	$5,200-6,700	$2,800-3,800
1999 Tracker 4WD	7,500-9,500	6,500-8,500	4,000-5,000

	GOOD	AVERAGE	POOR
2000 Tracker 2WD	$7,500-9,000	$6,600-8,000	$3,800-4,800
2000 Tracker 4WD	9,300-11,000	8,300-10,000	5,200-6,500
2001 Tracker 2WD	9,000-11,000	8,000-10,000	—
2001 Tracker 4WD	10,800-12,000	9,800-11,000	—

AVERAGE REPLACEMENT COSTS

A/C Compressor	$430	Clutch, Pressure Plate, Bearing	430
Alternator	590	Constant Velocity Joints	430
Automatic Transmission or Transaxle	715	Exhaust System	210
Brakes	220	Radiator	400
Shocks and/or Struts	525	Timing Chain or Belt	275

TROUBLE SPOTS

• **Engine noise.** 2.0L or 2.5L engine make a ticking noise when cold started due to problems with the valve lifters. (1999-2001)

• **Manual transmission.** 4WD transfer case shifter may be hard to move because the shift synchronizers have too much grab. New synchros, blocking rings, and front shift shaft are required. (1999-2000)

• **Water leak.** Convertible tops leak from a gap between the retainer and hem, through a gap in the quarter trim panel, from the top joint trim molding, over the top of the trim, through the vent in the rear quarter panel, and through the rear quarter trim panel brace. (1999)

• **Air conditioner.** It the air conditioner loses refrigerant, the O-rings must be replaced at the compressor, evaporator, and condenser. (1999-2000)

• **Automatic transmission.** Slow upshifts or downshifts while driving with the cruise control engaged are due to a faulty cruise control servo. (1999-2000)

• **Pedals.** The throttle valve cable (for the automatic transmission) corrodes inside the casing causing the accelerator pedal to become very stiff.

RECALL HISTORY

1999: Brake lights on some vehicles may be inoperative when brake pedal is depressed. On vehicles equipped with automatic transaxle, this failure may also prevent shifting out of "Park." **2001 4-dr:** Mislabeled seatbelts intended for 2-door models were installed in some 4-door vehicles, and do not work properly.

1997-01 CHEVROLET VENTURE

1998 Chevrolet Venture

FOR Ride • Passenger and cargo room • Antilock brakes • Automatic transmission performance

AGAINST Fuel economy • Rear-seat comfort

EVALUATION In terms of interior space utilization, General Motors designers did their job well. Even with the minivan's split-bench seats, they managed to retain the flexibility of the convenient modular seating concept. At the same time, they added innovative storage helpers throughout the interior, and the Venture's optional driver-side sliding door opens wide enough to permit access to the third row of seats. Chevrolet's minivan feels somewhat sportier than those from Ford or Chrysler. Steering is precise and accurately communicates the action of the front tires. Body lean is moderate in turns, and the minivan's all-season tires grip securely. The suspension absorbs most bumps with ease and delivers a comfortable, stable highway ride. Test Ventures halted with good control and a progressive pedal feel. Wind noise around the mirrors has been prominent at highway speeds, but road and engine sounds tend to be well-muffled. The 3.4-liter V6 engine produces sufficient acceleration for near-

ly every usage. On the other hand, both Ford and Chrysler have offered optional engines with higher torque ratings, which are better able to cope with full loads of cargo and/or passengers. The automatic transmission keeps unnecessary gear changes to a minimum. It also reacts quickly when a downshift is needed to pass or merge. As for economy, we averaged 15.3 mpg with an early Venture, in a blend of city/suburban commuting and freeway travel—just about average in the minivan league. A later test of an extended-length model averaged 17.6 mpg.

VALUE Critical shoppers are likely to find a lot to like about the GM trio of minivans, despite the discomfort endured by some backseat riders due to the low seats.

SPECIFICATIONS	3-door van	4-door van	4-door van
Wheelbase, in.	112.0	120.0	112.0
Overall length, in.	186.9	200.9	186.9
Overall width, in.	72.0	72.0	72.0
Overall height, in.	67.4	68.1	67.4
Curb weight, lbs.	3699	3838	3699
Cargo volume, cu. ft.	126.6	148.3	119.8
Fuel capacity, gals.	20.0	25.0	20
Seating capacity	7	7	7
Front head room, in.	39.9	39.9	39.9
Max. front leg room, in.	39.9	39.9	39.9
Rear head room, in.	39.3	39.3	39.3
Min. rear leg room, in.	36.9	39.0	36.9

Powertrain layout: transverse front-engine/front-wheel drive

ENGINES

	ohv V6
Size, liters/cu. in.	3.4/207
Horsepower	180-185
Torque (lbs./ft.)	205-210

EPA city/highway mpg
4-speed OD automatic	18/25

City/highway mpg (as tested)
4-speed OD automatic	15.3

Built in USA

RETAIL PRICES	GOOD	AVERAGE	POOR
1997 Venture regular	$7,500-8,700	$6,600-7,700	$3,600-4,300
1997 Venture extended	8,500-9,500	7,500-8,500	4,200-4,900
1998 Venture regular	9,000-10,200	8,000-9,200	4,500-5,300
1998 Venture extended	10,000-11,500	9,000-10,500	5,300-6,200
1999 Venture regular	10,500-12,000	9,500-11,000	5,700-6,700
1999 Venture extended	12,500-14,000	11,300-12,700	7,300-8,000
2000 Venture regular	12,000-14,500	10,800-13,200	6,800-8,500
2000 Venture extended	14,000-16,000	12,500-14,500	8,000-9,500
2000 Warner Brothers	17,500-19,000	16,000-17,500	11,500-12,500
2001 Venture regular	13,500-16,000	12,200-14,500	—
2001 Venture extended	16,000-18,000	14,500-16,500	—
2001 Warner Brothers	21,000-23,000	19,500-21,500	—

AVERAGE REPLACEMENT COSTS

A/C Compressor	$635	Constant Velocity Joints	490
Alternator	380	Exhaust System	330
Automatic Transmission or Transaxle	1,160	Radiator	450
Brakes	240	Shocks and/or Struts	460
		Timing Chain or Belt	345

TROUBLE SPOTS

• **Vehicle noise.** A rattling noise from the rear on long wheelbase models equipped with electronic level control requires replacement shock absorbers. (1997-98)

• **Air conditioner.** If the air conditioning is insufficient, the engine cooling fan and the air conditioning orifice tube may have to be replaced. (1997)

• **Windows.** If the "auto-down" feature of the power window quits, the integrated circuit that controls this function must be replaced. (1997)

• **Brakes.** The brake pedal may not return causing the brakes to drag, get hot and wear out prematurely. The cause may be misadjusted brake or cruise control switches of a defective brake pedal assembly. (1997)

• **Climate control.** The heater may not be adequate in cold weather requiring a revised heater core and possibly a new distribution duct. (1997)

• **Windshield.** The windshield may crack in cold weather. (1997)

RECALL HISTORY

1997-98: Windshield wiper linkage arm can contact brake line connected to traction-control modulator valve; brake line can chafe, resulting in brake fluid leakage. **1997-98 w/bucket seats or split bench seat in second or third row:** Seat latch mechanism does not have protective covers; when activating release mechanism to roll a bucket seat forward, finger(s) could be severely injured or severed, if they are not kept clear. **1997-2001 w/passenger-side power doors:** Door closes but may not be latched. If this happens, the sliding door can open while the vehicle is in motion. **1998:** Broken shift cable fitting or loose shift linkage can occur; moving shift lever to "Park" position may not shift the transmission to "Park," and vehicle could roll. **1998-01 w/passenger-side sliding door:** Front passenger-side sliding doors may have inadequate welds. Actuator can jam in the unlatched position and, when the sliding door closes, it will not be latched. **1999:** Front lower insulator to cradle sleeve on small number of minivans may collapse, which could result in steering-shaft separation. **2000 w/extended wheelbase:** Small number of vehicles have inoperative fuel tank rollover valves. **2000:** Some seatbelt assemblies were not properly heat treated and do not pass the load bearing requirement. **2001:** Passenger airbag inflator modules may have been built without the correct amount of explosive. Airbag explosion or failure could occur.

1999-01 CHRYSLER 300M/LHS

2000 Chrysler 300M

FOR Acceleration • Ride/handling • Passenger and cargo room

AGAINST Trunk liftover • Rear visibility

EVALUATION Because LHS and 300M sedans have more horsepower than any 6-cylinder near-luxury rivals, acceleration and throttle response are a match for any direct competitor—and a clear step ahead of a Concorde or Intrepid. In overall refinement, however, both fall short of such import-brand models as the Lexus GS 300 and Acura TL. Chrysler's engine isn't quite as smooth. Road and wind noise, while not objectionable, aren't as well isolated. Fuel economy is no bargain, either. A test LHS averaged 17.7 mpg when new and 21.6 mpg in long-term testing, whereas a 300M averaged 18.6 mpg in mostly highway driving. Road manners are impressive. The LHS offers competent handling and a well-controlled ride. A 300M steers and turns with genuine assertiveness, yet the base suspension absorbs bumps well. Brakes on both are strong, with fine pedal feel. On rough pavement, the ride can get jarring in a 300M with the Performance Handling Group. No near-luxury rival equals their generous interior volume, though the 300M's slight rear legroom deficiency, compared to the LHS, is apparent. Rear-seat entry on both is hampered by elongated doors. Instruments are tastefully designed and imaginatively illuminated, but nighttime readability could be better. Controls are well-positioned and have good tactile feel. The driving position is easily tailored. Models with light-colored dashboard tops suffer annoying reflections in the windshield, and narrow back windows mean poor rearward visibility. The trunk is large on the LHS, with a wide opening. Cargo volume and opening are both smaller on the 300M.

VALUE Although these two give up a measure of refinement to their top competitors, and cabin decor is less sophisticated, they deliver more interior space and comparable performance at hard-to-match prices. Neither has established a track record for reliability and customer service. Still, Chrysler's flagships show promise.

SPECIFICATIONS

	4-door sedan[1]	4-door sedan[2]
Wheelbase, in.	113.0	113.0
Overall length, in.	197.8	207.7
Overall width, in.	74.4	74.4
Overall height, in.	56.0	56.0
Curb weight, lbs.	3567	3564
Cargo volume, cu. ft.	16.8	18.7
Fuel capacity, gals.	17.2	17.2
Seating capacity	5	5
Front head room, in.	38.3	38.3
Max. front leg room, in.	42.2	42.2
Rear head room, in.	37.2	37.1
Min. rear leg room, in.	39.1	42.2

1. 300M. 2. LHS.

Powertrain layout: transverse front-engine/front-wheel drive

ENGINES

	ohc V6
Size, liters/cu. in.	3.5/215
Horsepower	253
Torque (lbs./ft.)	255

EPA city/highway mpg
4-speed OD automatic 18/27

City/highway mpg (as tested)
4-speed OD automatic 17.7

Built in Canada

RETAIL PRICES

	GOOD	AVERAGE	POOR
1999 300M	$17,000-18,000	$16,000-17,000	$12,500-13,500
1999 LHS	16,000-17,000	15,000-16,000	11,500-12,500
2000 300M	19,200-20,500	18,200-19,500	14,200-15,200
2000 LHS	17,700-19,000	16,700-18,000	12,700-13,700
2001 300M	22,000-24,000	21,000-22,500	—
2001 LHS	20,500-22,000	19,500-20,500	—

AVERAGE REPLACEMENT COSTS

A/C Compressor	$530	Constant Velocity Joints	950
Alternator	425	Exhaust System	480
Automatic Transmission or		Radiator	555
Transaxle	1,670	Shocks and/or Struts	1,390
Brakes	360	Timing Chain or Belt	250

TROUBLE SPOTS

• **Vehicle noise.** Front end makes a squeaking noise when going over speed bumps, etc. due to problem with MacPherson struts' striker caps.

• **Steering problems.** Loose or sloppy steering feel may be due to bad inner tie-rod bushings. (1999-2001)

• **Steering noise.** Pinhole leaks in the rubber bellows of the steering gear may cause a rattle from the front end. (1999-2000)

• **Electrical problem.** The interior lights may not work (or may stay on) and/or the overhead courtesy lights may flicker due to damaged wiring near the trunk light or bad terminal in the courtesy light connector. (1999)

• **Keyless entry.** The range of the optional automatic garage door opener is poor. A replacement antenna is available. (2000)

RECALL HISTORY

1999 LHS: Front seatbelt retractor on certain vehicles does not work properly. **1999 LHS:** The front seatbelt retractor does not comply with the requirements of the standard. If the retractor does not work properly, it will not adequately protect occupants in the event of a crash. **1999-00:** Inadequately manufactured seatbelt shoulder height adjustable turning loop top mounting bolt may not withstand sufficient force to function properly in certain impacts. **2000 300M:** Passenger airbag inflator assembly in small number of cars contains incorrect inflator charge amount, which could increase risk of passenger injury under certain crash conditions. **2000:** Manufacturing molding error can prevent operation of G-lock and tilt lock functions on some driver's side seatbelt retractors. **2000-01:** Some owner's manuals are missing full instructions for properly attaching a child restraint system's tether strap. **2000-01:** In the event of a crash, there is a potential for injury if the occupant's head were to contact the B-pillar. Owners will be sent a storage bin accessory unit that can be attached to the B-pillar along with installation instructions.

1995-00 CHRYSLER CIRRUS

1996 Chrysler Cirrus LXi

FOR Antilock brakes • Ride • Steering/handling • Passenger and cargo room • Instruments/controls

AGAINST Road noise • Rear visibility

EVALUATION
See the 1995-00 Dodge Stratus.

VALUE
See the 1995-00 Dodge Stratus.

SPECIFICATIONS

	4-door sedan
Wheelbase, in.	108.0
Overall length, in.	186.0
Overall width, in.	71.0
Overall height, in.	54.1
Curb weight, lbs.	3150
Cargo volume, cu. ft.	15.7
Fuel capacity, gals.	16.0
Seating capacity	5
Front head room, in.	38.1
Max. front leg room, in.	42.3
Rear head room, in.	36.8
Min. rear leg room, in.	37.8

Powertrain layout: transverse front-engine/front-wheel drive

ENGINES

	dohc I4	ohc V6
Size, liters/cu. in.	2.4/148	2.5/152
Horsepower	150	168
Torque (lbs./ft.)	165-167	170

EPA city/highway mpg

4-speed OD automatic	20/29	20/28

City/highway mpg (as tested)

4-speed OD automatic	21.0

Built in USA

RETAIL PRICES

	GOOD	AVERAGE	POOR
1995 Cirrus	$4,200-5,000	$3,600-4,300	$1,600-2,100
1996 Cirrus	5,200-6,000	4,500-5,300	2,200-2,700
1997 Cirrus	6,500-7,600	5,800-6,800	3,000-3,700
1998 Cirrus	7,800-8,800	6,900-7,800	3,700-4,400
1999 Cirrus	9,000-10,000	8,000-9,000	4,400-5,100
2000 Cirrus	10,000-11,500	9,000-10,500	5,200-6,000

AVERAGE REPLACEMENT COSTS
See the 1995-00 Dodge Stratus.

TROUBLE SPOTS
See the 1995-00 Dodge Stratus.

RECALL HISTORY
1995: Rear seatbelt anchors will not withstand loading required by Federal standard. **1995-96:** Brake master cylinder can leak fluid, due to damaged seal; warning light will signal impairment prior to partial brake-system loss. **1995-96:** Corrosion of ABS hydraulic control unit can cause solenoid valves to stick open, so car tends to pull from a straight stop when brakes are applied. **1995-96 w/2.4-liter:** Oil leakage could cause engine-compartment fire. **1995-97:** Lower ball joint can separate due to loss of lubrication; could cause loss of control. **1995-98 w/automatic transmission:** If operator presses button to shift out of "Park" with key in locked position, pin can break; "ignition-park" interlock would then be non-functional. **1996-97:** Secondary hood latch spring can disengage if hood is slammed. **1998-99:** Right rear brake tube can contact exhaust system

clamp and wear a hole in it; tube could then leak, reducing braking effectiveness. **2000:** Incorrect child lock instruction labels could cause confusion as to whether the childproof safety lock was activated. **2000:** The right front-brake tube may get damaged. **2000:** Some of the owner's manuals for these vehicles are missing instructions for properly attaching a child restraint system's tether strap to the tether anchorage.

1998-01 CHRYSLER CONCORDE

1998 Chrysler Concorde LXi

FOR Passenger room • Cargo room • Ride • Steering/handling • Traction control (optional) • Fuel economy (2.7-liter)

AGAINST Rear visibility • Trunk liftover

EVALUATION
See the 1998-01 Dodge Intrepid.

VALUE
See the 1998-01 Dodge Intrepid.

SPECIFICATIONS

	4-door sedan
Wheelbase, in.	113.0
Overall length, in.	209.1
Overall width, in.	74.5
Overall height, in.	55.9
Curb weight, lbs.	3446
Cargo volume, cu. ft.	18.7
Fuel capacity, gals.	17.0
Seating capacity	5-6
Front head room, in.	38.3
Max. front leg room, in.	42.1
Rear head room, in.	37.2
Min. rear leg room, in.	41.6

Powertrain layout: transverse front-engine/front-wheel drive

ENGINES

	dohc V6	ohc V6
Size, liters/cu. in.	2.7/167	3.2/197
Horsepower	200	222-225
Torque (lbs./ft.)	190	222-225

EPA city/highway mpg

4-speed OD automatic	21/30	19/29

City/highway mpg (as tested)

4-speed OD automatic	21.0

Built in Canada

RETAIL PRICES

	GOOD	AVERAGE	POOR
1998 Concorde	$10,000-11,500	$9,000-10,500	$5,300-6,300
1999 Concorde	11,500-13,200	10,500-12,000	6,300-7,500
2000 Concorde	13,000-15,000	11,800-13,500	7,500-9,000
2001 Concorde	15,000-17,000	13,500-15,500	—

AVERAGE REPLACEMENT COSTS
See the 1998-01 Dodge Intrepid.

TROUBLE SPOTS
See the 1998-01 Dodge Intrepid.

RECALL HISTORY
1999: The front seatbelt retractor does not comply with the requirements of the standard. If the retractor does not work properly, it will not adequately protect occupants in the event of a crash. **1999-00:** Inadequately manufactured mounting bolt for seatbelt shoulder height adjustable turning loop may not withstand sufficient force to function properly in certain impact situations. **2000:** Molding flash on primary lever may prevent operation of G-lock and tilt lock functions on some driver's side retractors,

which could reduce driver protection during a frontal crash **2000:** Passenger airbag inflator assembly on some cars contains incorrect inflator charge amount. **2000 w/o ABS:** Brake master cylinder piston retainer snap ring may be bent inward, which could result in brake drag condition. **2000-01:** Some of the owner's manuals for these vehicles are missing instructions for properly attaching a child restraint system's tether strap to the tether anchorage. **2000-01:** In the event of a crash, there is a potential for injury if the occupant's head were to contact the B-pillar. Owners will be sent a storage bin accessory unit that can be attached to the B-pillar along with installation instructions.

1993-97 CHRYSLER CONCORDE/NEW YORKER/LHS

1993 Chrysler Concorde

FOR Antilock brakes • Acceleration (3.5-liter) • Passenger and cargo room • Steering/handling • Ride

AGAINST Climate controls • Acceleration (3.3-liter) • Rear visibility (LHS/New Yorker)

EVALUATION

See the 1993-97 Dodge Intrepid.

VALUE

See the 1993-97 Dodge Intrepid.

SPECIFICATIONS

	4-door sedan[1]	4-door sedan[2]
Wheelbase, in.	113.0	113.0
Overall length, in.	201.5	207.4
Overall width, in.	74.4	74.5
Overall height, in.	56.3	55.9
Curb weight, lbs.	3492	3587
Cargo volume, cu. ft.	16.6	17.9
Fuel capacity, gals.	18.0	18.0
Seating capacity	6	6
Front head room, in.	38.4	38.9
Max. front leg room, in.	42.3	42.3
Rear head room, in.	37.3	37.8
Min. rear leg room, in.	38.7	41.7

Powertrain layout: longitudinal front-engine/front-wheel drive

1. Concorde. 2. New Yorker.

ENGINES

	ohv V6	ohc V6
Size, liters/cu. in.	3.3/201	3.5/215
Horsepower	153-161	214
Torque (lbs./ft.)	181	221
EPA city/highway mpg		
4-speed OD automatic	19/27	18/26
City/highway mpg (as tested)		
4-speed OD automatic		19.1

Built in Canada

RETAIL PRICES

	GOOD	AVERAGE	POOR
1993 Concorde	$2,500-3,200	$1,800-2,500	$500-900
1994 Concorde	3,200-4,000	2,500-3,200	800-1,400
1994 New Yorker	3,400-4,100	2,700-3,400	1,000-1,600
1994 LHS	3,900-4,600	3,200-3,900	1,300-1,900
1995 Concorde	4,000-4,800	3,300-4,000	1,300-1,800
1995 New Yorker	4,300-5,000	3,600-4,200	1,500-2,000
1995 LHS	5,300-6,000	4,500-5,100	2,000-2,700
1996 Concorde	5,000-6,000	4,200-5,200	1,800-2,500
1996 New Yorker	5,400-6,200	4,600-5,400	2,100-2,600
1996 LHS	6,500-7,500	5,500-6,500	2,500-3,300
1997 Concorde	6,500-7,800	5,700-6,800	2,600-3,400
1997 LHS	8,000-9,200	7,000-8,200	3,400-4,200

AVERAGE REPLACEMENT COSTS

See the 1993-97 Dodge Intrepid.

TROUBLE SPOTS

See the 1993-97 Dodge Intrepid.

RECALL HISTORY

1993 w/3.3-liter engine: Deterioration of O-rings at fuel-injector tubes can cause fuel leakage, with potential for fire. **1993-95 Concorde, LHS:** Lower control arm attaching brackets on some cars can crack due to fatigue and separate from engine cradle; transmission half-shaft could then pull out of transaxle. **1993-97 w/3.5-liter engine:** Fuel injection system can leak from O-rings or hairline cracks in fuel-injection rail. **1994:** Right steering tie rod can rub through automatic-transmission wiring harness, causing short circuit; may result in stalling, or allow engine to start when selector is not in "Park" position.

1990-95 CHRYSLER LeBARON COUPE/CONVERTIBLE

1990 Chrysler LeBaron 2-door convertible

FOR Acceleration (V6 and turbo) • Antilock brakes • Instruments/controls

AGAINST Rear-seat room • Road noise (convertible) • Cargo room • Engine noise (4-cylinder) • Automatic transmission performance

EVALUATION With a Mitsubishi V6 beneath the hood, the shapely LeBarons gained refined power to match their sharp looks. Both the base 4-cylinder engine and its turbocharged counterparts are gruff and noisy, while the Mitsubishi-built V6 provides smoother performance. Sure, it has less power and torque than either of the turbocharged fours, but it's much quieter and delivers its strength in a far more linear manner. If you simply must have a turbocharged engine, note that the 2.5-liter turbo is less raucous than the earlier 2.2, which disappeared after 1990. We averaged 22.9 mpg with a V6 convertible in city/highway driving. Regardless of engine choice, automatic transmissions shift sloppily. Convertibles lag somewhat in solidity. Even minor bumps cause the body to twist and flex more than most open cars. For anything beyond merely competent handling and roadholding, look for a GTC with its performance suspension and tires. But be prepared for a choppy ride over rough pavement. Abundant road noise can make it difficult to talk in normal tones at highway speeds. The new, modern interior installed for 1990 is a vast improvement over prior dashboards, positioning controls closer to the driver. Gauges are easy to see, controls easy to use. Climate and radio controls are readily accessible. Six-footers are likely to be comfortable in front. Backseats are bigger than in most coupes, but insufficient for adults on long drives. Trunks are small.

VALUE Though not devoid of flaws, LeBarons still look sharp and perform reasonably well—at least with the smooth V6 engine.

SPECIFICATIONS

	2-door conv.	2-door coupe
Wheelbase, in.	100.6	100.5
Overall length, in.	184.8	184.8
Overall width, in.	69.2	69.2
Overall height, in.	52.4	53.3
Curb weight, lbs.	3010	2863
Cargo volume, cu. ft.	10.3	14.4
Fuel capacity, gals.	14.0	14.0
Seating capacity	4	5
Front head room, in.	38.3	37.6
Max. front leg room, in.	42.5	42.5
Rear head room, in.	37.0	36.3

	2-door conv.	2-door coupe
Min. rear leg room, in.	33.0	33.0

Powertrain layout: transverse front-engine/front-wheel drive

ENGINES

	Turbocharged ohc I4	ohc I4	Turbocharged ohc I4	ohc V6
Size, liters/cu. in.	2.2/135	2.5/153	2.5/153	3.0/181
Horsepower	174	100	152	141
Torque (lbs./ft.)	210	135	210-211	171

EPA city/highway mpg

	Turbocharged ohc I4	ohc I4	Turbocharged ohc I4	ohc V6
5-speed OD manual	20/28	24/34	20/27	19/28
3-speed automatic		23/28	19/24	21/27
4-speed OD automatic				20/29

City/highway mpg (as tested)

	ohc I4	ohc V6
5-speed OD manual	25.1	
3-speed automatic	22.5	
4-speed OD automatic		22.9

Built in USA

RETAIL PRICES

	GOOD	AVERAGE	POOR
1990 LeBaron Coupe	$1,200-1,700	$700-1,100	$100-200
1990 Convertible	1,500-2,100	1,000-1,500	200-400
1991 LeBaron Coupe	1,600-2,200	1,000-1,600	200-300
1991 Convertible	2,000-2,600	1,400-1,900	400-500
1992 LeBaron Coupe	2,000-2,600	1,400-1,900	300-500
1992 Convertible	2,500-3,200	1,800-2,500	500-800
1993 LeBaron Coupe	2,500-3,200	1,800-2,500	500-700
1993 Convertible	3,000-3,700	2,300-3,000	800-1,100
1994 Convertible	3,600-4,400	2,800-3,600	800-1,200
1995 Convertible	4,500-5,500	3,600-4,600	1,200-1,800

AVERAGE REPLACEMENT COSTS

A/C Compressor...........	$450	Clutch, Pressure Plate, Bearing	515
Alternator......................	315	Constant Velocity Joints	375
Automatic Transmission or Transaxle	905	Exhaust System	325
Brakes	240	Radiator.........................	315
Shocks and/or Struts....	340	Timing Chain or Belt.....	345

TROUBLE SPOTS

• **Cold starting problems.** 2.2- or 2.5-liter engines may idle rough or stumble when first started below freezing temperatures unless a revised intake manifold (with an "X" cast into the number 1 runner) was installed (1992), a revised computer (PCM) was installed (1992-93), or the computer was reprogrammed (1994).

• **Automatic transmission.** 41TE or 42LE automatic transaxles could take several seconds to engage at startup because of a problem with the valve body. (1993-95)

• **Automatic transmission.** Bad seals in the transmission lead to premature friction component wear, which causes shudder when starting from a stop, a bump when coasting to a stop, and slipping between gears. (1993-95)

• **Oil consumption.** High oil consumption and smoke from the exhaust at idle and deceleration on 3.0-liter engines is caused by exhaust valve guides that slide out of the heads. (1990-93)

• **Air conditioner.** If the air conditioner gradually stops cooling and/or the airflow from the vents decreases, the computer (PCM) may not be sending a signal to the compressor clutch relay to cycle off, which causes the AC evaporator to freeze up. (1991-95)

• **Engine noise.** The motor mount on the left side of the engine tends to break. (1992-93)

• **Automatic transmission.** Transmission shudder under light to moderate acceleration could be due to a worn bushing, which requires replacement of the pump as well as the torque converter. (1990-95)

• **Alternator belt.** Unless a shield is installed under the engine on the right side, deep snow could knock the serpentine belt off the pulleys of a 3.0-liter engine. (1991-95)

RECALL HISTORY

1990: Engine valve cover gasket may dislocate and allow oil leak, which could cause a fire. **1991:** Front disc brake caliper guide pin bolts may not be adequately tightened and could loosen. **1991:** On small number of cars, mismatched parking brake cable to rear wheels may reduce braking capability to one wheel, possibly allowing inadvertent roll-away. **1992:** Zinc plating of some upper steering column shaft coupling bolts caused hydrogen embrittlement and breakage of the bolt. **1992:** Hood latch assembly may not have been properly installed and secondary latch may be prevented from engaging when hood is closed.

1990-94 CHRYSLER LeBARON SEDAN

1990 Chrysler LeBaron

FOR Acceleration • Antilock brakes (optional) • Quietness • Passenger and cargo room • Visibility

AGAINST Automatic transmission performance

EVALUATION Quiet and competent, the luxurious compact LeBaron sedan is quite a pleasant surprise. Handling is reasonably good and the ride is pleasing, helped by a touring-type suspension. Acceleration with the 6-cylinder engine, at least, is smooth and responsive. On the downside, early automatic transmissions downshift too sluggishly for easy passing on the highway. Brake feel and control are good, too, though the nose dives a bit in hard stops. A tauter handling suspension might be found on later models, and LeBarons had a choice of several fixed and split bench seats. On the whole, though, new LeBarons did not come with the suspension and seating choices that faced buyers of the Dodge Spirit. Chrysler promised more rear leg room than any domestic sedan in its class. Roomy interiors offer top-notch visibility. Bench seats are comfortable in the traditional mode, if not quite sufficiently supportive to suit everyone. The LeBaron's big, flat-floored trunk is easy to load.

VALUE No, there's nothing startling about a 4-door LeBaron, but these are solid, capable family sedans offering entry-level luxury and a likable persona, plus a distinctive appearance. Although they lag behind Japanese rivals in overall quality, they're also cheaper secondhand.

SPECIFICATIONS

	4-door sedan
Wheelbase, in.	103.5
Overall length, in.	182.7
Overall width, in.	68.1
Overall height, in.	55.9
Curb weight, lbs.	2971
Cargo volume, cu. ft.	14.4
Fuel capacity, gals.	16.0
Seating capacity	6
Front head room, in.	38.4
Max. front leg room, in.	41.9
Rear head room, in.	37.9
Min. rear leg room, in.	38.3

Powertrain layout: transverse front-engine/front-wheel drive

ENGINES

	ohc I4	ohc V6
Size, liters/cu. in.	2.5/153	3.0/181
Horsepower	100	141
Torque (lbs./ft.)	135	171

EPA city/highway mpg

	ohc I4	ohc V6
3-speed automatic	23/28	
4-speed OD automatic		20/28

City/highway mpg (as tested)

	ohc V6
4-speed OD automatic	21.6

Built in USA, Mexico

RETAIL PRICES

	GOOD	AVERAGE	POOR
1990 LeBaron	$1,100-1,500	$600-900	$100-200
1991 LeBaron	1,400-1,900	800-1,200	100-300
1992 LeBaron	1,800-2,300	1,200-1,600	200-400

	GOOD	AVERAGE	POOR
1993 LeBaron	$2,200-2,800	$1,600-2,100	$300-600
1994 LeBaron	2,700-3,400	2,000-2,700	500-800

AVERAGE REPLACEMENT COSTS

A/C Compressor	$450	Shocks and/or Struts	340
Alternator	315	Constant Velocity Joints	375
Automatic Transmission or		Exhaust System	310
Transaxle	905	Radiator	315
Brakes	240	Timing Chain or Belt	345

TROUBLE SPOTS

• **Cold starting problems.** 2.2- or 2.5-liter engines may idle rough or stumble when first started below freezing temperatures unless a revised intake manifold (with an "X" cast into the number 1 runner) was installed (1992), a revised computer (PCM) was installed (1992-93), or the computer was reprogrammed (1994).

• **Automatic transmission.** 41TE or 42LE automatic transaxles could take several seconds to engage at startup because of a problem with the valve body. (1993-94)

• **Oil consumption.** High oil consumption and smoke from the exhaust at idle and deceleration on 3.0-liter engines is caused by exhaust valve guides that slide out of the heads. (1990-93)

• **Air conditioner.** If the air conditioner gradually stops cooling and/or the airflow from the vents decreases, the computer (PCM) may not be sending a signal to the compressor clutch relay to cycle off, which causes the AC evaporator to freeze up. (1991-94)

• **Engine noise.** The motor mount on the left side of the engine tends to break. (1992-93)

• **Alternator belt.** Unless a shield is installed under the engine on the right side, deep snow could knock the serpentine belt off the pulleys of 3.0-liter engines. (1991-94)

RECALL HISTORY

1990: Engine valve cover gasket may dislocate and allow oil leak, which could cause a fire. **1990:** On cars with grey interior, airbag inflator modules may not contain diffuser holes between ignitor and propellant chambers, so airbag would not deploy in an impact, which could lead to driver injury. **1991:** Front disc brake caliper guide pin bolts may not be adequately tightened and could loosen, which could cause reduced braking effectiveness that might result in accident. **1991:** Both airbag system front impact sensors may not be secured to mounting brackets, so airbag would not deploy in a frontal collision. **1991:** Front outboard seatbelt may become difficult to latch and/or unlatch; latch may then open during accident or sudden stop, increasing risk of injury. **1992:** Zinc plating of some upper steering column shaft coupling bolts could cause hydrogen embrittlement and breakage of the bolt. **1994:** Seatbelt assembly on small number of cars may fail in accident.

1995-00 CHRYSLER SEBRING

1997 Chrysler Sebring LX 2-door coupe

FOR Passenger and cargo room • Acceleration (4-cylinder manual, V6) • Steering/handling • Antilock brakes (optional on some)

AGAINST Rear visibility • Radio controls • Noise • Acceleration (2.0-liter automatic)

EVALUATION Coupes have plenty of performance when equipped with the 4-cylinder and 5-speed manual transmission, but things slow down considerably with the automatic. Acceleration is decent with the V6, but it lacks low-speed torque and the automatic transmission is slow to downshift for passing. All told, though, it's a better choice than the 4-cylinder. Both engines promise excellent gas mileage, especially on the highway. Handling limits are good, and the coupe's ride is firm but not harsh, apart from some lumpiness over coarse pavement. While wind noise is hushed, road and engine noise are high on the highway, which tends to make long drives more tiring. The coupe's interior is just as roomy as Chrysler claims, with ample room for four adults to stretch out, in front and rear. The trunk is quite large, too. Coupe controls are easy to reach while driving, but the stereo is too low in the center of the dashboard to adjust without a long look away from the road. Coupes also have poor rear visibility, because of wide rear pillars and a high parcel shelf. Convertible acceleration is more than adequate with the V6 engine, though it can run low on vigor during a corner. Like the coupe, its ride is controlled and devoid of coarseness, if a tad jittery over washboard surfaces. Interiors are roomy, with impressive space for two adults in the back seat. Side windows drop as the power top is actuated, which happens without a hitch. With the top down, occupants can talk in normal tones at highway speeds. Unfortunately, the convertible does not feel as solid as some rivals. In addition, despite large rear-quarter glass, the fabric top has wide rear "pillars" and a narrow back window, causing an over-the-shoulder blind spot that's big enough to hide another car. Convertibles have a different dashboard than coupes, with more convenient controls. Their front seats have integrated seatbelts, so you don't have to grope for a buckle.

VALUE All told, this stylish open car is also practical for all seasons, offering the expected virtues of the ragtop breed and only a few of the familiar vices. For an appealing combination of sport and practicality, these well-designed automobiles deserve a close look—despite a few drawbacks.

SPECIFICATIONS

	2-door conv.	2-door coupe
Wheelbase, in.	106.0	103.7
Overall length, in.	193.0	187.4
Overall width, in.	69.2	69.7
Overall height, in.	54.2	53.0
Curb weight, lbs.	3350	2908
Cargo volume, cu. ft.	11.3	13.1
Fuel capacity, gals.	16.0	16.0
Seating capacity	4	5
Front head room, in.	38.7	39.1
Max. front leg room, in.	42.4	43.3
Rear head room, in.	37.0	36.5
Min. rear leg room, in.	35.2	35.0

Powertrain layout: transverse front-engine/front-wheel drive

ENGINES

	dohc I4	dohc I4	ohc V6
Size, liters/cu. in.	2.0/122	2.4/148	2.5/152
Horsepower	140	150	155-168
Torque (lbs./ft.)	130	167	170
EPA city/highway mpg			
5-speed OD manual	22/31		
4-speed OD automatic	21/30	20/29	20/27
City/highway mpg (as tested)			
4-speed OD automatic			25.6

Built in USA, Mexico

RETAIL PRICES

	GOOD	AVERAGE	POOR
1995 Sebring coupe	$5,000-6,000	$4,300-5,200	$2,100-2,700
1996 Sebring coupe	6,000-7,200	5,300-6,400	2,800-3,500
1996 Convertible	7,000-8,500	6,200-7,500	3,500-4,300
1997 Sebring coupe	7,500-8,800	6,600-7,900	3,600-4,500
1997 Convertible	8,500-10,000	7,500-9,000	4,300-5,200
1998 Sebring coupe	9,000-10,500	8,000-9,500	4,500-5,500
1998 Convertible	10,000-11,800	9,000-10,800	5,400-6,500
1999 Sebring coupe	10,500-12,000	9,500-10,800	5,700-6,700
1999 Convertible	12,000-13,800	10,800-12,500	6,500-7,800
2000 Sebring coupe	12,000-13,700	10,800-12,500	6,500-7,700
2000 Convertible	14,000-16,000	12,500-14,500	8,000-9,500

AVERAGE REPLACEMENT COSTS

A/C Compressor	$730	Clutch, Pressure Plate,	
Alternator	230	Bearing	575
Automatic Transmission or		Constant Velocity Joints	375
Transaxle	905	Exhaust System	285
Brakes	255	Radiator	570
Shocks and/or Struts	490	Timing Chain or Belt	220

CONSUMER GUIDE®

TROUBLE SPOTS

- **Hard starting.** A corroded connector behind the left headlight may cause hard starting, intermittently flashing "Check Engine" light, and radiator/condenser fan that will not run. (1995)

- **Hard starting.** Intermittent no-starts may be due to a damaged wire near the transaxle shift lever. (1995)

- **Engine misfire.** Rough idle, hesitation, and hard restarts during cold weather are due to a defective engine control computer. (1995)

- **Sunroof/moonroof.** The pivot pin in the power sunroof may come out, or the plastic tabs on the control unit may cause interference, preventing the sunroof from closing completely. (1995) The sunroof may open by itself if water shorts the control unit. (1995-96)

- **Alarm system.** The theft alarm may go off randomly, most often in high winds, and is often due to a misaligned hood. (1995-96)

- **Automatic transmission.** Transmission tends to default to second gear only for no apparent reason requiring the transmission control computer to be reprogrammed. (1996)

RECALL HISTORY

1995-96: Rubber boots on lower ball joint can become damaged, allowing dirt and water intrusion, which can cause excessive wear and possible separation. **1995-97:** Lower ball joint can separate due to loss of lubrication; could cause loss of control. **1996 JX w/2.5-liter engine:** Disconnected vacuum hose may cause increase in engine idle speed and loss of braking power assist. **1996 convertible:** Electrical contacts of power mirror switch can accumulate road salt, which may result in fire. **1996-98 w/automatic transmission:** If operator presses button to shift out of Park with key in locked position, pin can break; "ignition-park" interlock would then be nonfunctional. **1997 coupe:** On small number of cars, improperly welded head restraint support bracket on passenger side can break. **1998:** Dash panel pad can shift, interfering with throttle cable control.

1991-95 CHRYSLER TOWN & COUNTRY

1991 Chrysler Town & Country

FOR Acceleration (3.8-liter V6) • Passenger and cargo room • Ride/handling • Entry/exit • Antilock brakes

AGAINST Fuel economy

EVALUATION

See the 1991-95 Dodge Caravan.

VALUE

See the 1991-95 Dodge Caravan.

SPECIFICATIONS

	3-door van
Wheelbase, in.	119.3
Overall length, in.	192.8
Overall width, in.	72.0
Overall height, in.	66.7
Curb weight, lbs.	3955
Cargo volume, cu. ft.	141.3
Fuel capacity, gals.	20.0
Seating capacity	7
Front head room, in.	39.1
Max. front leg room, in.	38.3
Rear head room, in.	38.4
Min. rear leg room, in.	37.6

Powertrain layout: transverse front-engine/front- or all-wheel drive

ENGINES

	ohv V6	ohv V6
Size, liters/cu. in.	3.3/201	3.8/232
Horsepower	147-150	162
Torque (lbs./ft.)	183-185	213
EPA city/highway mpg		
4-speed OD automatic	18/23	17/23
City/highway mpg (as tested)		
4-speed OD automatic	17.6	15.9

Built in USA

RETAIL PRICES

	GOOD	AVERAGE	POOR
1991 Town & Country	$2,600-3,300	$2,000-2,600	$600-1,000
1992 Town & Country	3,300-4,000	2,600-3,300	800-1,400
1993 Town & Country	4,000-4,800	3,300-4,000	1,200-1,700
1994 Town & Country	4,800-6,000	4,000-5,200	1,700-2,400
1995 Town & Country	5,700-7,000	4,800-6,100	2,300-3,000

AVERAGE REPLACEMENT COSTS

See the 1991-95 Dodge Caravan.

TROUBLE SPOTS

See the 1991-95 Dodge Caravan.

RECALL HISTORY

1991 w/ABS: High-pressure hose in antilock braking system may leak or detach at crimped end fitting, resulting in discharge of hydraulic fluid. **1991 w/ABS:** High-pressure pump of antilock braking system may be porous, resulting in brake fluid leakage. **1991, 93-94:** Liftgate support attaching bolts can break, resulting in liftgate falling unexpectedly. **1991-92:** The steering wheel mounting armature can develop cracks and separate from the center hub attachment to the steering column. This can result in loss of vehicle control. **1991-93 w/ABS:** ABS hydraulic control unit can experience excessive actuator piston seal wear, causing pump-motor deterioration; ABS could fail, and power assist might be reduced. **1991-93:** Left windshield wiper pivot drive arm was not mechanically staked to shaft; arm could disengage, causing loss of wiper function. **1991-93:** Seatbelt release button can stick inside cover, so buckle is only partly latched; also, center rear belt anchor clip can disconnect. **1992:** Zinc plating of some upper steering column shaft coupling bolts caused hydrogen embrittlement and breakage of the bolt. **1992:** Improperly bent fuel tank flanges may not allow specified clearance for mounting straps and fuel lines, both of which could be damaged; a broken strap would cause tank to drop, while damaged fuel line may leak fuel. **1993-94:** 15-inch stamped steel wheels in some vans have malformed lug nut seat configuration, which causes poor nut-to-wheel contact and centering of wheel during installation; could lead to possible loss of wheel and loss of vehicle control. **1993-95:** Electrical short could cause airbags to deploy inadvertently.

1996-00 CHRYSLER TOWN & COUNTRY

1996 Chrysler Town & Country LXi

FOR Antilock brakes • Acceleration (3.8-liter) • Ride • Passenger and cargo room

AGAINST Fuel economy • Wind noise

EVALUATION

See the 1996-00 Dodge Caravan.

VALUE
See the 1996-00 Dodge Caravan.

SPECIFICATIONS

	4-door van	4-door van
Wheelbase, in.	113.3	119.3
Overall length, in.	186.3	199.6
Overall width, in.	75.6	75.6
Overall height, in.	68.5	68.5
Curb weight, lbs.	3863	3951
Cargo volume, cu. ft.	141.9	167.0
Fuel capacity, gals.	20.0	20.0
Seating capacity	7	7
Front head room, in.	39.8	39.8
Max. front leg room, in.	41.2	41.2
Rear head room, in.	40.1	39.6
Min. rear leg room, in.	35.2	37.3

Powertrain layout: transverse front-engine/front- or all-wheel drive

ENGINES

	dohc I4	ohv V6	ohv V6
Size, liters/cu. in.	2.4/153	3.3/201	3.8/230
Horsepower	150	158	166
Torque (lbs./ft.)	167	203	245
EPA city/highway mpg			
3-speed automatic	20/26		
4-speed OD automatic		17/24	17/24
City/highway mpg (as tested)			
4-speed OD automatic		17.4	15.1

Built in USA

RETAIL PRICES

	GOOD	AVERAGE	POOR
1996 Town & Country	$7,200-8,500	$6,400-7,600	$3,400-4,200
1996 Town & Country LXi	8,500-9,800	7,500-8,800	4,100-5,000
1997 Town & Country	9,000-10,500	8,000-9,500	4,500-5,500
1997 Town & Country LXi	10,500-12,000	9,500-11,000	5,500-6,500
1998 Town & Country	11,500-13,500	10,200-12,000	6,000-7,400
1998 Town & Country LXi	13,500-15,000	12,000-13,500	7,500-8,500
1999 Town & Country	14,000-16,000	12,500-14,500	7,800-9,200
1999 LXi, Limited	16,500-18,500	15,000-17,000	9,500-11,000
2000 Town & Country	16,500-18,500	15,000-17,000	10,000-11,500
2000 LXi, Limited	18,500-21,000	17,000-19,500	11,500-13,500

AVERAGE REPLACEMENT COSTS
See the 1996-00 Dodge Caravan.

TROUBLE SPOTS
See the 1996-00 Dodge Caravan.

RECALL HISTORY
1996: Fuel tank rollover valve can allow fuel to enter vapor canister, creating potential for leakage and fire. **1996:** On certain minivans, fuel can leak from tank at interface of fuel pump module attachment. **1996:** On a few minivans, bolts holding integrated child seat modules to seat frame can break. **1996:** Static charge could cause spark as tank is filled; vapors could ignite. **1996-97 w/integrated child seats:** Shoulder harness restraint on child seat can be difficult to release when latch plate becomes contaminated. **1997:** Certain master cylinder seals will not seal adequately, allowing hydraulic fluid to be drawn into power-assist vacuum reservoir; brake warning lamp will then illuminate. **1998 w/integrated child seats:** Shoulder harness webbing was incorrectly routed around reinforcement bar; can fail to restrain child properly.

1995-00 DODGE AVENGER

FOR Passenger and cargo room • Acceleration (V6) • Steering/handling • Available antilock brakes

AGAINST Acceleration (4-cylinder automatic) • Radio controls • Road noise • Rear visibility

EVALUATION Front bucket seats offer plenty of head and leg space for two adults. Rear seats are equally pleasing, with space for two adults. However, large people may not want to spend long periods in back, and getting in and out can be a chore. Avenger's trunk has a wide, flat floor, plus split-folding rear seatbacks. Although you sit relatively low, visibility is generally good in all directions. However, a narrow back window, tall parcel shelf, and wide roof pillars make it

1995 Dodge Avenger ES

difficult to see what's directly behind the car. Instruments are easy to read, though auxiliary gauges are small. Most controls are easy to reach while driving. However, the radio is mounted too low and has too many small buttons. Both engines provide adequate acceleration from a stop, but the 4-cylinder is noisy and slowed by the automatic transmission. Four-cylinder pickup is acceptable with manual shift. The V6 is smooth and more powerful, and fairly lively, but it doesn't produce much torque at low speeds. Step on the gas, and there might be a rather long pause before the automatic transmission downshifts. Each model handles adeptly, zipping around corners and through curves with good grip and only moderate body lean. Roadholding is good overall, and the car responds well to steering inputs. Ride quality from the firm suspension is on the choppy side, and when encountering certain pavement separators. Road, engine, and wind noise might all become intrusive at high speeds.

VALUE Attractively styled and capable on the road, the Avenger has a lot going for it: proven mechanical elements, reasonable prices, and wholly adequate room for four.

SPECIFICATIONS

	2-door coupe
Wheelbase, in.	103.7
Overall length, in.	187.2
Overall width, in.	68.5
Overall height, in.	53.0
Curb weight, lbs.	2879
Cargo volume, cu. ft.	13.1
Fuel capacity, gals.	16.0
Seating capacity	5
Front head room, in.	39.1
Max. front leg room, in.	43.3
Rear head room, in.	36.5
Min. rear leg room, in.	35.0

Powertrain layout: transverse front-engine/front-wheel drive

ENGINES

	dohc I4	ohc V6
Size, liters/cu. in.	2.0/122	2.5/152
Horsepower	140	155-163
Torque (lbs./ft.)	130	160-170
EPA city/highway mpg		
5-speed OD manual	22/31	
4-speed OD automatic	21/30	20/27
City/highway mpg (as tested)		
4-speed OD automatic		23.6

Built in USA

RETAIL PRICES

	GOOD	AVERAGE	POOR
1995 Avenger	$4,200-4,800	$3,500-4,000	$1,500-1,900
1995 Avenger ES	5,000-5,600	4,300-4,800	2,000-2,500
1996 Avenger	5,500-6,300	4,800-5,500	2,200-2,700
1996 Avenger ES	6,300-7,000	5,500-6,200	2,700-3,200
1997 Avenger	6,800-7,500	6,000-6,700	2,900-3,400
1997 Avenger ES	7,700-8,600	6,900-7,700	3,500-4,100
1998 Avenger	8,200-9,000	7,300-8,100	3,600-4,200
1998 Avenger ES	9,400-10,200	8,600-9,300	4,300-5,100
1999 Avenger	9,500-10,500	8,500-9,500	4,500-5,200
1999 Avenger ES	10,700-11,700	9,700-10,700	5,500-6,300
2000 Avenger	11,000-12,000	10,000-11,000	5,800-6,600
2000 Avenger ES	12,500-13,800	11,300-12,300	6,800-7,700

AVERAGE REPLACEMENT COSTS

A/C Compressor	$400	Clutch, Pressure Plate,	
Alternator	315	Bearing	560
Automatic Transmission or		Constant Velocity Joints	370
Transaxle	905	Exhaust System	320
Brakes	265	Radiator	530
Shocks and/or Struts	375	Timing Chain or Belt	190

TROUBLE SPOTS

• **Hard starting.** A corroded connector behind the left headlight may cause hard starting, an intermittently flashing "Check Engine" light, or make inoperative the radiator/condenser fan. (1995)

• **Engine misfire.** Engines that idle rough, hesitate, stall, or are hard to restart during cold weather may require a new engine control computer. (1995)

• **Hard starting.** Intermittent no-starts may be due to a damaged wire near the transaxle shift lever. (1995)

• **Sunroof/moonroof.** The pivot pin in the power sunroof may come out, or the plastic tabs on the control unit may cause interference. (1995) The sunroof may open by itself if water shorts the control unit. (1995-96)

• **Alarm system.** The theft alarm may go off randomly due to a mis-aligned hood. (1995-96)

• **Automatic transmission.** Transmission may shudder when accelerating from a stop, thump when coasting down to a stop, or slip when shifting. (1995)

• **Automatic transmission.** Transmission tends to default to second gear only requiring the transmission control computer to be reprogrammed. (1996)

RECALL HISTORY

1995-96: Rubber boots on lower ball joint can become damaged, allowing dirt and water intrusion, which can cause excessive wear and possible separation. **1997:** On a small number of cars, improperly welded head restraint support bracket on passenger side can break. **1998:** Dash panel pad can shift, interfering with throttle cable control.

1991-95 DODGE CARAVAN

1994 Dodge Grand Caravan ES

FOR Passenger and cargo room • Ride

AGAINST Fuel economy • Acceleration (4-cylinder)

EVALUATION With the Caravan, avoid the weak 4-cylinder engine and balky 5-speed manual transmission. They are more trouble than the initial savings you might make in a lower purchase price. The 3.0- and 3.3-liter V6 engines provide adequate acceleration, but the 3.8-liter V6 delivers the best action in all situations. It's also the quietest. With any of the V6 engines, don't expect to get more than 20 mpg. The standard front-wheel drive provides sufficient traction for most situations; however, the effective AWD system is a boon in the snow belt. But beware: AWD makes the ride rougher, hurts acceleration, and lessens fuel economy. The Caravan's ride is carlike and secure, but there's too much body lean and not enough traction for these vehicles to score as anything other than minivans when it comes to handling. Though the regular-length versions can seat seven people, it gets crowded if everyone is an adult. In addition, cargo room is only adequate with all the seats in place. Grand Caravans have more space for everyone and ample cargo room. Though the middle and rear seats can be removed, they are quite heavy. The dashboard has a convenient design, and climate and radio controls are easy to use. However, front-seat occupants might find themselves craving more leg room.

VALUE The Caravan's initial basic design lasted more than a decade, and most of the bugs were worked out in the first generation. With so much versatility, these vans are an exceptional second-hand value. If you're shopping for a minivan, Caravan and its twins should be first on your list.

SPECIFICATIONS

	3-door van	3-door van
Wheelbase, in.	112.3	119.3
Overall length, in.	178.1	192.8
Overall width, in.	72.0	72.0
Overall height, in.	66.0	66.7
Curb weight, lbs.	3305	3573
Cargo volume, cu. ft.	117.0	141.3
Fuel capacity, gals.	20.0	20.0
Seating capacity	7	7
Front head room, in.	39.1	39.1
Max. front leg room, in.	38.3	38.3
Rear head room, in.	38.5	38.4
Min. rear leg room, in.	37.6	37.7

Powertrain layout: transverse front-engine/front- or all-wheel drive

ENGINES

	ohc I4	ohc V6	ohv V6	ohv V6
Size, liters/cu. in.	2.5/153	3.0/181	3.3/202	3.8/230
Horsepower	100	141-142	150-162	162
Torque (lbs./ft.)	135	173	194	213
EPA city/highway mpg				
5-speed OD manual	19/25			
3-speed automatic	20/30	19/24		
4-speed OD automatic		19/25	18/23	17/23
City/highway mpg (as tested)				
5-speed OD manual	21.6			
3-speed automatic	19.9	18.2		
4-speed OD automatic		19.7	18.5	18.5

Built in USA, Canada

RETAIL PRICES

	GOOD	AVERAGE	POOR
1991 Caravan	$1,500-2,600	$1,000-2,000	$200-600
1991 Grand Caravan	1,800-2,700	1,200-2,000	300-600
1991 Grand LE/ES	2,400-3,100	1,800-2,400	500-900
1992 Caravan	1,800-2,900	1,200-2,200	300-700
1992 Grand Caravan	2,100-3,000	1,500-2,300	500-800
1992 Grand LE/ES	2,900-3,600	2,200-2,900	800-1,200
1993 Caravan	2,100-3,400	1,500-2,700	400-900
1993 Grand Caravan	2,500-3,300	1,800-2,600	600-900
1993 Grand LE/ES	3,400-4,100	2,700-3,300	1,100-1,500
1994 Caravan	2,500-4,000	1,800-3,200	600-1,200
1994 Grand Caravan	2,800-4,000	2,100-3,200	700-1,200
1994 Grand LE/ES	4,000-5,000	3,200-4,200	1,400-1,800
1995 Caravan	3,200-5,000	2,500-4,200	900-1,700
1995 Grand Caravan	3,600-4,800	2,800-4,000	1,100-1,600
1995 Grand LE/ES	5,000-6,000	4,200-5,000	1,900-2,500

AVERAGE REPLACEMENT COSTS

A/C Compressor	$455	Constant Velocity Joints	385
Alternator	310	Exhaust System	400
Automatic Transmission or		Radiator	325
Transaxle	1,040	Shocks and/or Struts	230
Brakes	275	Timing Chain or Belt	265

TROUBLE SPOTS

• **Cold starting problems.** 2.2- or 2.5-liter engines idle rough or stumble when first started below freezing temperatures unless a revised intake manifold (with an "X" cast into the number 1 runner) was installed (1992) or a revised computer (PCM) was installed (1992-93) or the computer was reprogrammed (1994).

• **Automatic transmission.** 41TE or 42LE automatic transaxles could take several seconds to engage at startup because of a problem with the valve body. (1993-95)

• **Automatic transmission.** Any minivan with the 3.3-liter engine may have late, harsh, or erratic automatic transmission shifts that are not transmission related, but caused by a defective throttle position sensor. (1994)

• **Automatic transmission.** Bad seals in the transmission lead to premature friction component wear, which causes shudder when starting from a stop, a bump when coasting to a stop, and slipping between gears. (1993-95)

• **Alternator belt.** Deep snow could knock the serpentine belt off the pulleys of a 3.0-liter engine. Installation of a shield fixes the problem. (1991-95)

• **Air conditioner.** If the air conditioner gradually stops cooling and/or the airflow from the vents decreases, the computer (PCM) may not be sending a signal to the compressor clutch relay to cycle off, which causes the AC evaporator to freeze up. (1991-95)

• **Automatic transmission.** If the transmission shudders under light to moderate acceleration, the transmission front pump could be leaking due to a worn bushing. (1990-95)

• **Oil consumption.** Oil consumption and smoke from the exhaust at idle and deceleration on 3.0-liter engines is caused by exhaust valve guides that slide out of the heads. (1990-93)

• **Engine noise.** The motor mount on the left side of the engine tends to break. (1992-93)

RECALL HISTORY

1991 w/ABS: High-pressure hose in antilock braking system may leak or detach, which increases likelihood of brake lockup. **1991 w/ABS:** High-pressure pump of antilock braking system may be porous, resulting in increased stopping distances. **1991, 93-94:** Liftgate support attaching bolts can break, resulting in liftgate falling unexpectedly. **1991-92:** Steering wheel mounting armature can develop cracks and separate from the center hub attachment to the steering column. This can result in loss of vehicle control. **1991-93 w/ABS:** Piston seal in control unit can wear excessively; ABS could fail, and power assist might be reduced. **1991-93:** Left windshield wiper pivot drive arm was not mechanically staked to shaft; arm could disengage, causing loss of wiper function. **1991-93:** Seatbelt release button can stick inside cover, so buckle is only partly latched; also, center rear belt anchor clip can disconnect. **1992:** Zinc plating of some upper steering column shaft coupling bolts caused hydrogen embrittlement and breakage. **1992:** Brake pedal pad attachment to pedal arm may not have adequate strength. **1992:** Fuel tank may drop or lines may rupture near fuel tank, leading to possible fire. **1992:** Brake pedal pad attachment arm on small number of vehicles could break. **1992:** Bolts that attach gas strut to rear liftgate can accumulate fatigue damage, if loose; liftgate could fall suddenly. **1993-94:** Lug nuts on optional 15-inch stamped steel wheels may have been improperly installed, which could lead to wheel separation. **1993-95:** Electrical short could cause airbags to deploy inadvertently.

1996-00 DODGE CARAVAN

1996 Dodge Grand Caravan ES

FOR Antilock brakes • Acceleration (3.8-liter) • Ride • Passenger and cargo room

AGAINST Fuel economy • Wind noise • Road noise

EVALUATION These highly impressive second-generation Caravans are a clear step ahead of the hugely popular 1984-95 minivans. Among other bonuses, you get more space in all seating positions. Design features included a lower dashboard and larger windows for improved visibility, and a 1.4-inch lower step-in height for easier entry and exit. A driver-side sliding door also helps on that latter score. The new dashboard has a more user-friendly layout, putting most controls within easy reach of the driver. Illuminated markers for the power window switches and other controls make them easier to find in the dark. The innovative removable seats are handy, but each seat weighs about 90 pounds, so it might take two people to lift one in and out. You also get an assortment of storage bins,

nooks, and crannies for stashing miscellaneous items. Performance with the 3.3-liter engine is adequate in daily driving, but the 3.8-liter is better yet, giving the Caravan enough power to pass and merge easily. Gas mileage should run 15-17 mpg in the city, and just above 20 on the highway. The 4-cylinder engine has nearly as much power as the 3.0-liter V6, but both are taxed by a full load of passengers. Quieter and even more carlike than before, these minivans handle more like large sedans than vans, rolling along with a stable, comfortable attitude. Caravans hold the road well and lean moderately in tight turns. Road and wind noise grow obtrusive at higher speeds, but otherwise these minivans are great for long-distance cruising.

VALUE This assessment is simple: Caravans and their Chrysler-Plymouth cousins rank at the head of their class, just as their predecessors did.

SPECIFICATIONS

	3-door van	3-door van
Wheelbase, in.	113.3	119.3
Overall length, in.	186.3	199.6
Overall width, in.	75.6	75.6
Overall height, in.	68.5	68.5
Curb weight, lbs.	3528	3680
Cargo volume, cu. ft.	146.2	172.3
Fuel capacity, gals.	20.0	20.0
Seating capacity	7	7
Front head room, in.	39.8	39.8
Max. front leg room, in.	41.2	41.2
Rear head room, in.	40.1	40.0
Min. rear leg room, in.	36.6	39.6

Powertrain layout: transverse front-engine/front- or all-wheel drive

ENGINES

	dohc I4	ohc V6	ohv V6	ohv V6
Size, liters/cu. in.	2.4/148	3.0/181	3.3/201	3.8/230
Horsepower	150	150	158	166
Torque (lbs./ft.)	167	176	203	227

EPA city/highway mpg

3-speed automatic	20/26	19/25		
4-speed OD automatic		18/26	18/24	17/24

City/highway mpg (as tested)

4-speed OD automatic			19.2	17.7

Built in USA, Canada

RETAIL PRICES

	GOOD	AVERAGE	POOR
1996 Caravan	$5,000-7,500	$4,200-6,500	$2,000-3,800
1996 Grand Caravan	6,000-7,300	5,200-6,300	2,700-3,600
1996 Grand LE/ES	8,000-9,000	7,000-8,000	4,000-4,800
1997 Caravan	6,000-9,000	5,100-8,000	2,700-4,700
1997 Grand Caravan	7,000-9,000	6,000-8,000	3,300-4,700
1997 Grand LE/ES	9,500-10,500	8,500-9,500	5,200-6,000
1998 Caravan	7,500-11,000	6,500-10,000	3,500-6,000
1998 Grand Caravan	9,000-11,000	8,000-10,000	4,700-6,000
1998 Grand LE/ES	11,500-13,000	10,500-11,800	6,500-7,300
1999 Caravan	9,000-12,500	8,000-11,200	4,700-7,200
1999 Grand Caravan	11,000-13,000	9,800-11,500	5,800-7,400
1999 Grand LE/ES	13,500-15,000	12,000-13,500	7,500-8,500
2000 Caravan	10,500-13,500	9,500-12,200	5,800-8,000
2000 Grand Caravan	12,500-15,000	11,000-13,500	6,800-9,000
2000 Grand LE/ES	15,000-16,500	13,500-15,000	8,800-10,000

AVERAGE REPLACEMENT COSTS

A/C Compressor	$490	Clutch, Pressure Plate, Bearing	605
Alternator	310	Constant Velocity Joints	385
Automatic Transmission or Transaxle	1,040	Exhaust System	330
Brakes	390	Radiator	480
Shocks and/or Struts	330	Timing Chain or Belt	230

TROUBLE SPOTS

• **Vehicle noise.** A thud or thump, which comes from the rear when accelerating or stopping, is caused by fuel sloshing in the tank. A foam pad and strap kit does not always fix the problem. (1996-97)

• **Blower motor.** Blower motors make a whine in low and second speed. (1996)

• **Doors.** Sliding door and/or liftgate power locks fail to lock or unlock both manually or electrically. (1996)

- **Brakes.** The antilock brakes may activate at speeds under 10 mph due to one or more faulty wheel speed sensors. (1996)
- **Dashboard lights.** The instrument cluster, minitrip computer, and/or compass may show incorrect information or go completely blank due to a bad relay for the heated backlight. (1997)
- **Radiator.** The radiator fan may run after the key is turned off, or may not run, leading to overheating because the fan relay attaching screws break and the relay overheats. (1996-97)
- **Automatic transmission.** Transmission may shudder when accelerating from a stop, thump when coasting down to a stop, or slip when shifting. (1996)
- **Wipers.** Windshield wipers come on by themselves or fail to stop when the switch is turned off due to a problem with the multifunction switch. (1996)

RECALL HISTORY

1996: Fuel tank rollover valve can allow fuel to pass into vapor canister, resulting in potential for leakage and fire. **1996:** Static charge could cause spark as tank is being filled; vapors could ignite. **1996:** On a few minivans, bolts holding integrated child seat modules to seat frame can break. **1996:** On certain minivans, fuel can leak from tank at interface of fuel pump module attachment. **1996 w/bench seats, built at Windsor plant ("R" in 11th position of VIN):** Rear-seat bolts can fracture; in an accident, seat could break away. **1996-97 w/integrated child seats:** Shoulder harness restraint on child seat can be difficult to release when latch plate becomes contaminated. **1997:** Certain master cylinder seals will not seal adequately, allowing hydraulic fluid to be drawn into power-assist vacuum reservoir; brake warning lamp will then illuminate. **1997:** Wheels on small number of minivans were damaged by equipment used for mounting. **1997 w/P215/65R15 Goodyear Conquest tires on steel wheels:** Tires were damaged, and may lose pressure suddenly. **1998 w/integrated child seats:** Shoulder harness webbing was incorrectly routed around reinforcement bar; can fail to restrain child properly. **1999:** The front seatbelt retractor does not comply with the requirements of the standard. If the retractor does not work properly, it will not adequately protect occupants in the event of a crash.

1990-96 DODGE DAKOTA

1994 Dodge Dakota Sport 4WD regular cab

FOR Passenger room • Acceleration (V6, V8)

AGAINST Interior storage space • Acceleration (4-cylinder)

EVALUATION Regular cabs have ample space for three adults, but neither the bench seat nor the available buckets are particularly comfortable (1993 and later buckets are better). Not much storage space is available behind the seat, unless you opt for the Club Cab. But it's hard to get into the rear seat, which isn't sufficient for three and has limited knee room. The floor-mounted 4WD lever is low and sits well forward, so you have to reach under the dash to shift from 2WD to 4WD High. Other controls are easy to reach. The base 4-cylinder engine is adequate, but not a wise choice unless you rarely carry cargo. Relaxed at highway speeds, the husky early V6 develops enough low-speed torque to haul heavy loads, but it's still no fireball when pushing hard. The "Magnum" V6 introduced for 1992 yields better acceleration (Dodge claimed a 0-60 mph time of 8.3 seconds), but engine and exhaust noise are more noticeable under hard throttle. Acceleration is more robust yet with the V8, which is the choice for towing. Dakotas handle competently and ride well considering their size, though the ride gets bouncy when the cargo box is empty. Despite ABS, rear wheels tend to lock prematurely in hard

stops. We'd prefer a later model with the optional 4-wheel antilock braking.

VALUE Solid and robust, a Dakota makes a good practical choice. A long-wheelbase version with the 8-foot bed might serve nearly as well as a full-size pickup.

SPECIFICATIONS

	reg. cab short bed	reg. cab long bed	ext. cab
Wheelbase, in.	111.9	123.9	130.9
Overall length, in.	189.0	207.5	208.0
Overall width, in.	69.4	69.4	69.4
Overall height, in.	65.0	65.0	65.6
Curb weight, lbs.	3042	3124	3528
Fuel capacity, gals.	15.0	15.0	15.0
Seating capacity	3	3	6
Front head room, in.	39.5	39.5	39.5
Max. front leg room, in.	41.8	41.8	41.8
Rear head room, in.	—	—	37.9
Min. rear leg room, in.	—	—	24.8

Powertrain layout: longitudinal front-engine/rear- or 4-wheel drive

ENGINES

	ohc I4	ohc V6	ohv V8
Size, liters/cu. in.	2.5/153	3.9/239	5.2/318
Horsepower	99-120	125-180	165-230
Torque (lbs./ft.)	132-145	195-225	250-295
EPA city/highway mpg			
5-speed OD manual	21/25	16/22	14/20
4-speed OD automatic		16/20	14/18
City/highway mpg (as tested)			
5-speed OD manual	20.2		15.4
4-speed OD automatic			13.9

Built in USA

RETAIL PRICES

	GOOD	AVERAGE	POOR
1990 Dakota 2WD	$1,200-2,600	$700-2,000	$100-500
1990 Dakota 4WD	1,700-2,300	1,100-1,700	300-500
1991 Dakota 2WD	1,500-3,000	900-2,300	200-700
1991 Dakota 4WD	2,100-3,500	1,500-2,800	500-1,000
1992 Dakota 2WD	1,700-3,500	1,100-2,800	300-1,000
1992 Dakota 4WD	2,400-4,200	1,800-3,500	700-1,400
1993 Dakota 2WD	2,000-4,200	1,400-3,500	500-1,400
1993 Dakota 4WD	3,000-5,200	2,300-4,400	800-1,900
1994 Dakota 2WD	2,300-5,000	1,700-4,200	600-1,800
1994 Dakota 4WD	3,400-6,200	2,600-5,200	900-2,500
1995 Dakota 2WD	2,800-6,000	2,100-5,200	800-2,400
1995 Dakota 4WD	4,100-8,000	3,300-7,000	1,300-3,600
1996 Dakota 2WD	3,600-8,000	2,800-7,000	1,000-3,500
1996 Dakota 4WD	5,000-9,500	4,200-8,500	1,900-4,500

AVERAGE REPLACEMENT COSTS

A/C Compressor	$415	Clutch, Pressure Plate, Bearing	525
Alternator	295	Exhaust System	310
Automatic Transmission or Transaxle	790	Radiator	405
Brakes	315	Shocks and/or Struts	190
Timing Chain or Belt	190	Universal Joints	130

TROUBLE SPOTS

- **Transaxle leak.** Automatic transmission fluid leaks from the speed sensor in the transmission. (1994)
- **Rough idle.** Because of a problem with the idle air control motor, the engine idles rough, stalls at low speeds or when decelerating, especially in warm weather. (1992-94)
- **Exhaust backfire.** Exhaust backfire and/or a popping noise in the exhaust may be caused by a defective Powertrain Control Module. (1994-95)
- **Air conditioner.** If the air conditioner gradually stops cooling and/or the airflow from the vents decreases, the computer (PCM) may not be sending a signal to the compressor clutch relay to cycle off, which causes the AC evaporator to freeze up. (1991-95)
- **Automatic transmission.** If the transmission will not engage when first started, chances are the torque converter is draining down. Chrysler will correct the problem by installing a check valve. (1993)
- **Automatic transmission.** If the transmission won't upshift in cool weather, it is probably due to defective cast iron seal rings in the gover-

nor drive. (1992-94)

• **Engine fan noise.** In warm weather, the fan makes a roaring sound. Dodge will replace the fan, the fan clutch, and, on max cooling systems, the radiator cap. (All)

• **Oil leak.** Oil leak at the filter on 3.9-, 5.2-, and 5.9-liter engines is likely due to a warped adapter plate. (1995)

• **Oil pump.** Oil pump gear wear results in bucking and surging when the engine is warm and lack of lubrication when the engine is cold. (1992-93)

• **Oil leak.** Rear main seals on 2.5- and 4.0-liter engines are prone to leakage. To prevent future failures, Chrysler has a rubber plug available that goes in a hole above the starter that protects the rear main seal. (1996)

• **Water leak.** The roof seams leak water that seeps down behind the dashboard onto the floor. (1993-95)

RECALL HISTORY

1990: Valve cover gasket may allow oil leakage. **1990 light-duty 4x2 and club-cab w/V8:** Frame can crack at steering gear attachment and/or mounting bolts can fracture, allowing steering gear to separate. **1991 w/4-speed automatic:** Fuel hose may contact wiring harness, resulting in leakage. **1991:** Premium steering wheel could crack and separate from hub. **1991 2WD:** Right front brake hose may rub against tire during full-left turn. **1991-92 w/A500 automatic transmission:** Inadvertent placement of shift lever in "Reverse" can occur when driver believes it has been placed in "Park." **1993:** ABS could become inoperative when hard pedal effort is applied. **1996 w/2.5-liter engine:** Power brake vacuum hose in some trucks could be improperly installed; disconnected hose can cause increase in idle speed and loss of power assist.

1997-01 DODGE DAKOTA

1998 Dodge Dakota Sport regular cab

FOR Acceleration (V8) • Quietness • Ride (2WD)

AGAINST Fuel economy (V8) • Acceleration (4-cylinder) • Rear seat room/comfort (ext. cab)

EVALUATION The stiffer frame on this generation of Dakota evidently made a noticeable difference, as a 2WD Club Cab model proved to be impressively solid on rough roads. Ride quality was also pleasing. The suspension provided a comfortable and stable ride, with only a little bouncing on wavy surfaces. A 4-wheel-drive model, on the other hand, does not feel as stable or comfortable, jiggling more over bumps. The 5.2-liter V8 is smoother and quieter than before, delivering strong acceleration and passing power. Gas mileage is another story. We averaged only 13.3 mpg with the V8, though that included mainly urban commuting. The overhead-cam 4.7-liter V8 that replaced the 5.2 in 2000 also furnishes strong acceleration. The base 4-cylinder engine is simply too weak for a vehicle of this size and weight. The V6 makes a sensible compromise. The Dakota R/T delivers impressive acceleration, but is hampered by a rough ride and lack of 4-wheel drive. Although the Dakota is roomier than rival compact pickups, the rear bench seat in Club Cab models lacks sufficient leg room for adults. Getting into the rear seat is a squeeze, too. As a bonus, the rear-seat cushion folds up to reveal a couple of handy, flat-topped storage compartments. Rear doors on the Quad Cab are not technically full-size, but they open independently of the front doors and make entry/exit a lot more convenient. The Quad Cab also has more rear leg room than any rival's extended cab, though long-legged adults still will find their knees pressed into the front seatback. This Dakota's dashboard looks more modern, but it's covered with flimsy plastic. Inside door panels are made of cheap-looking molded plastic that does not look or feel durable. In general, though, materials are comparable to those in most rival trucks. Visibility is good all around. Radio and climate controls are easy to reach. Two cupholders are molded into the center console.

VALUE Dakota offers a bit more interior space and towing capacity than compact pickup rivals, and a significant advantage in payload capacity. If you like the styling, the rest of the truck probably won't be disappointing.

SPECIFICATIONS

	reg. cab short bed	reg. cab long bed	ext. cab
Wheelbase, in.	111.9	123.9	131.0
Overall length, in.	195.8	215.1	214.8
Overall width, in.	71.5	71.5	71.5
Overall height, in.	65.6	65.3	65.6
Curb weight, lbs.	3481	3556	3733
Fuel capacity, gals.	15.0	15.0	15.0
Seating capacity	3	3	6
Front head room, in.	40.0	40.0	40.0
Max. front leg room, in.	41.9	41.9	41.9
Rear head room, in.	—	—	38.0
Min. rear leg room, in.	—	—	22.1

Powertrain layout: longitudinal front-engine/rear- or 4-wheel drive

ENGINES

	ohv I4	ohv V6	ohv V8	ohv V8	ohc V8
Size, liters/cu. in.	2.5/150	3.9/239	5.2/318	5.9/360	4.7/287
Horsepower	120	175	230	250	230-235
Torque (lbs./ft.)	145	225	300	345	295
EPA city/highway mpg					
5-speed OD man.	20/25	16/22	14/19		14/18
4-speed OD auto.		16/21	14/18	12/16	14/17
City/highway mpg (as tested)					
4-speed OD auto.		16.5	13.3	13.3	

Built in USA

RETAIL PRICES

	GOOD	AVERAGE	POOR
1997 Dakota 2WD	$5,500-9,500	$4,800-8,500	$2,400-5,300
1997 Dakota 4WD	7,000-11,500	6,000-10,500	3,200-6,700
1998 Dakota 2WD	6,500-10,700	5,500-9,500	2,900-6,000
1998 Dakota 4WD	8,500-12,500	7,500-11,200	4,300-7,400
1999 Dakota 2WD	7,500-12,000	6,500-11,000	3,500-6,800
1999 Dakota 4WD	10,000-14,000	9,000-12,500	5,000-8,000
1999 Dakota R/T	11,000-125,00	10,000-11,500	6,000-7,000
2000 Dakota 2WD	9,000-14,500	8,000-13,000	4,500-8,300
2000 Dakota 4WD	11,000-16,500	9,800-15,000	5,700-9,800
2000 Dakota R/T	12,500-14,500	11,000-13,000	7,000-8,000
2001 Dakota 2WD	11,000-17,000	9,800-15,500	—
2001 Dakota 4WD	13,200-18,500	12,000-17,000	—
2001 Dakota R/T	14,500-16,500	13,000-15,000	—

AVERAGE REPLACEMENT COSTS

A/C Compressor	$525	Clutch, Pressure Plate, Bearing	610
Alternator	355	Exhaust System	510
Automatic Transmission or Transaxle	990	Radiator	400
Brakes	305	Shocks and/or Struts	330
Timing Chain or Belt	205	Universal Joints	180

TROUBLE SPOTS

• **Vehicle noise.** A popping noise can come from the rear of the cab because the sleeves in the cab isolators are too long and must be ground down. (1997-98)

• **Engine misfire.** Engine bucking at about 5300 rpm may occur when many electrical devices are in use. Noise from the generator affects the transmission governor pressure sensor delaying upshifts. (1997-98)

• **Keyless entry.** If the remote keyless entry transmitter batteries die in less than two months, there is a problem with the transmitter and it will be replaced under warranty. (1997-98)

• **Paint/body.** "Radiant Red Metallic" paint suffers chipping problems because antichip primer was not applied during production. (1997)

• **Exhaust system.** The exhaust manifold studs on the 2.5-liter engine tend to break. (1997-98)

• **Dashboard lights.** The gauges and overhead console quit working because a fuse tends to blow. (1997)

• **Engine noise.** The timing chain makes a rattling noise, which requires a replacement chain, sprockets, and tensioner. (1997)

RECALL HISTORY

1997: Airbag could deploy inadvertently when ignition is shut off. **1997 w/131-inch wheelbase:** Some vehicles may have inadequate clearance between fuel line and cab underbody. **1997-00 w/2.5-liter engine:** Some vehicles may have inadequate clearance between left front brake tube and power steering hose. **1997-00:** Some vehicles may have inadequate clearance between rear axle vent hose and brake hose. **1997-2000:** Sound-deadening material inside the steering wheel could become detached from the cover and housing causing the driver airbag system to become disabled. The airbag warning lamp will illuminate on the instrument panel. **1998 2WD:** Front brake hoses or antilock brake system sensor wire may be abraded at front wheels by contact with wheelhouse splash shield; prolonged contact with hose can cause partial braking loss. **1998:** Bolts used to attach cab and core support to frame may have been improperly hardened; can allow cab to separate from frame. **1999:** The front seatbelt retractor does not comply with the requirements of the standard. If the retractor does not work properly, it will not adequately protect occupants in the event of a crash. **2000 w/4.7-liter engine and automatic:** Automatic transmission may expel fluid from fill tube during normal temperature operation. **2000-01:** Some of the owner's manuals for these vehicles are missing instructions for properly attaching a child restraint system's tether strap to the tether anchorage. **2001 w/4WD:** Electric shift transfer case may not fully engage into gear, causing the transfer case to end up in the neutral position. **2001 Quad Cab:** Front outboard lower seatbelt anchor bolts may not be tightened correctly. An improperly tightened seatbelt anchor may not provide the anticipated level of occupant restraint in a crash.

1990-93 DODGE DAYTONA

1990 Dodge Daytona Shelby

FOR Antilock brakes (optional) • Acceleration (V6, turbo) • Handling/roadholding

AGAINST Ride • Engine noise (turbo) • Rear-seat room

EVALUATION Replacing an earlier 2.2-liter 4-cylinder, the 2.5-liter base engine delivers modest performance and good gas mileage. Turbo model's acceleration rivals that of V8s, with equally impressive handling, but its exhaust is loud, and the stiff suspension turns a city drive into a jarring trek. The V6 isn't as quick as a top turbo, but makes its power with less work and in a smoother, more linear fashion. So, it's the most satisfying choice all around. All engines perform best with a 5-speed, which delivers top-notch action but works with a stiff clutch. Base and ES coupes promise competent handling, but the IROC's stiff suspension and wide tires sharpen reflexes considerably. Ride quality ranges from willowy on the base model, to slightly firmer on an ES, to unforgiving on IROC coupes. Front head room is just adequate for tall drivers, but seats are low and combine with thick roof pillars for a closed-in feel. Fold-down rear seats create a generous cargo area but are small for passengers. Long doors and low front seats make entry/exit a chore.

VALUE Daytonas cannot match the refinement or assembly quality of import rivals. Still, you get decent performance at a reasonable price. Our favorite is the V6 IROC, which is quicker and quieter than base four.

SPECIFICATIONS

	2-door hatchback
Wheelbase, in.	97.2
Overall length, in.	179.0
Overall width, in.	69.3
Overall height, in.	51.8
Curb weight, lbs.	2779
Cargo volume, cu. ft.	33.0
Fuel capacity, gals.	14.0
Seating capacity	4

	2-door hatchback
Front head room, in.	37.1
Max. front leg room, in.	42.5
Rear head room, in.	34.3
Min. rear leg room, in.	30.0

Powertrain layout: transverse front-engine/front-wheel drive

ENGINES

	ohc I4	Turbocharged ohc I4	Turbocharged ohc I4	Turbocharged dohc I4	ohc V6
Size, liters/cu. in.	2.5/153	2.5/153	2.2/135	2.2/135	3.0/181
Horsepower	100	150-152	174	225	141
Torque (lbs./ft.)	135	180-210	210	217	171

EPA city/highway mpg

	ohc I4	Turbocharged ohc I4	Turbocharged ohc I4	Turbocharged dohc I4	ohc V6
5-speed OD man.	25/32	21/27	20/28	19/27	19/27
3-speed autom.	23/28	18/24			
4-speed OD auto.					21/28

City/highway mpg (as tested)

	ohc I4	Turbocharged ohc I4	Turbocharged ohc I4	Turbocharged dohc I4	ohc V6
5-speed OD man.			20.8		21.2

Built in USA

RETAIL PRICES

	GOOD	AVERAGE	POOR
1990 Daytona	$1,000-1,600	$600-1,000	$100-200
1990 Daytona Shelby	1,400-1,900	900-1,300	200-300
1991 Daytona	1,300-1,900	700-1,300	100-300
1991 Daytona Shelby/IROC	1,900-2,500	1,300-1,900	300-500
1992 Daytona	1,800-2,400	1,200-1,700	200-400
1992 Daytona IROC	2,500-3,300	1,900-2,600	500-800
1993 Daytona	2,400-3,000	1,700-2,300	400-700
1993 Daytona IROC	3,000-3,700	2,300-3,000	700-1,100

AVERAGE REPLACEMENT COSTS

A/C Compressor	$405	Clutch, Pressure Plate, Bearing	665
Alternator	320	Constant Velocity Joints	550
Automatic Transmission or Transaxle	905	Exhaust System	230
Brakes	290	Radiator	355
Shocks and/or Struts	335	Timing Chain or Belt	145

TROUBLE SPOTS

• **Engine misfire.** Blue exhaust smoke at idle or during deceleration indicates bad exhaust valve guide seals on 3.0-liter engines. (1990-93)

• **Engine stalling.** Serpentine drive belt can be knocked off the pulleys when driven through deep snow. Fix requires installation of a shield. (1991-93)

• **Steering noise.** Squeaks when turning require replacement of the strut mount assemblies. (1992-93)

• **Suspension noise.** Sway bar bushing wear causes a squeaking noise from the front suspension. (1992-93)

• **Air conditioner.** The A/C evaporator freezes up because the compressor does not cycle off causing a lack of cooling. (1991-93)

• **Automatic transmission.** Transaxle may have delayed shift when car is started. Fix requires replacement of the valve body and filter. (1993)

• **Windshield washer.** Windshield washer nozzles that freeze up are repaired by installing a check valve in the fluid reservoir. (1990-93)

RECALL HISTORY

1990: Engine valve cover gasket may dislocate and allow oil leak. **1990:** On cars with gray interior, airbag inflator modules may not contain diffuser holes between igniter and propellant chambers, so airbag would not deploy in an impact. **1992-93:** Spot welds that attach front rails to dash panel may suffer structural damage (such as interference with opening of doors), which could reduce occupant protection during an accident.

1998-01 DODGE DURANGO

FOR Passenger room • Cargo room • Acceleration (5.9-liter V8) • Optional antilock braking

AGAINST Fuel economy • Acceleration (V6) • Rear-seat comfort

EVALUATION Durango feels more like a large car than a truck, delivering a ride that's absorbent and composed even on bumpy roads, with little bouncing. Despite the usual SUV body lean and nose-plowing in quick turns, Durango does not feel ponderous.

1998 Dodge Durango

Directional stability is generally good, though steering is vague around center and a lot of correction may be needed to stay on course at highway speeds. V8 engines are smooth and quiet. Vigor is adequate with the 4.7- and 5.2-liter, but they lack a strong punch at low speeds for quick getaways. The 5.9-liter V8 has a huskier tone and feels stronger off the line and in passing situations. In city/highway driving, we got a modest 12.4 mpg from a Durango with the 5.2-liter V8. A Durango with the 5.9-liter V8 managed only 11.2 mpg. Durango uses its size well, providing generous shoulder width and head room. Squeezing eight seats into a vehicle the size of a midsize car is no small feat, but Dodge managed it in the Durango. Be warned, though: The third seat is better for children than adults. Second-row seats have thin padding that is less supportive than the more-substantial cushions used by many rivals. Cargo space behind the third seat, measuring 18.8 cubic feet, is adequate for a few small suitcases or a week's worth of groceries. Center and rear seats fold flat in seconds, for a handy alternative to removable seats that opens up ample cargo room. All 4WD models have a floor-mounted transfer case lever, which is something of a stretch for the driver. The dashboard is simple and convenient, but thick side pillars and rear headrests impede rear vision. Also on the negative side, the climate-control system will not feed air to floor and face vents simultaneously. Workmanship is solid and thorough, but black plastic trim over the gauge cluster and main dashboard controls feels cheap and flimsy, and the inside door panels look plain.

VALUE Despite a few demerits, Durango is a well-designed truck that approaches full-size models for brawn and space, and therefore deserves strong consideration as a late-model, secondhand SUV.

SPECIFICATIONS

	4-door wagon
Wheelbase, in.	115.9
Overall length, in.	193.3
Overall width, in.	71.5
Overall height, in.	72.0
Curb weight, lbs.	4513
Cargo volume, cu. ft.	88.0
Fuel capacity, gals.	25.0
Seating capacity	8
Front head room, in.	39.8
Max. front leg room, in.	41.9
Rear head room, in.	40.4
Min. rear leg room, in.	37.3

Powertrain layout: longitudinal front-engine/rear- or 4-wheel drive

ENGINES

	ohv V6	ohc V8	ohv V8	ohv V8
Size, liters/cu. in.	3.9/239	4.7/287	5.2/318	5.9/360
Horsepower	175	235	230	245
Torque (lbs./ft.)	225	295	300	335
EPA city/highway mpg				
4-speed OD automatic	15/18	14/17	13/17	12/16
City/highway mpg (as tested)				
4-speed OD automatic		12.1	12.4	11.2

Built in USA

RETAIL PRICES

	GOOD	AVERAGE	POOR
1998 Durango 4WD	$14,000-15,500	$13,000-14,500	$9,000-10,000
1999 Durango 2WD	14,000-15,500	13,000-14,500	9,000-10,000
1999 Durango 4WD	16,500-18,000	15,000-16,500	10,500-11,500
2000 Durango 2WD	16,500-18,000	15,000-16,500	10,500-11,500
2000 Durango 4WD	19,000-21,000	17,500-19,500	12,500-14,000
2000 Durango R/T	$21,000-22,500	$19,500-21,000	$14,000-15,200
2001 Durango 2WD	19,000-21,000	17,500-19,500	—
2001 Durango 4WD	21,500-23,000	20,000-21,500	—
2001 Durango R/T	24,000-26,000	22,000-24,000	—

AVERAGE REPLACEMENT COSTS

A/C Compressor	$415	Clutch, Pressure Plate, Bearing	610
Alternator	400	Exhaust System	385
Automatic Transmission or Transaxle	615	Radiator	560
Brakes	450	Shocks and/or Struts	490
Timing Chain or Belt	615	Universal Joints	215

TROUBLE SPOTS

• **Engine misfire.** If the spark plug wires are misrouted, the engine may knock, the cylinders may misfire and the vehicle surges (which may feel like a transmission problem) around 45 mph. (1998-99)

• **Vehicle noise.** Squeaks from the front wheels may be caused by a loose spindle retaining nut. (1999)

• **Air conditioner.** The air conditioner gradually become less effective, which may require a new evaporator. (1998-99)

• **Keyless entry.** The remote keyless entry system doesn't work due to a problem with the transmitter case. (1999)

• **Steering noise.** The steering column makes popping noises and feels rough during parking maneuvers. (1998-00)

RECALL HISTORY

1998: Fastener that secures generator cable has insufficient clamp load, resulting in a loose connection and electrical arcing; could result in fire. **1998-2000:** Sound-deadening material inside the steering wheel could become detached from the cover and housing causing the the driver airbag system to become disabled. The airbag warning lamp will illuminate on the instrument panel. **1998:** Rear brake tube can contact underbody crossmember, eventually wearing a hole in the tube that could reduce braking from rear wheels. **1998-99:** Fuel tank strap can separate due to fatigue during vehicle operation, causing tank to be unsupported. **1999:** The front seatbelt retractor does not comply with the requirements of the standard. If the retractor does not work properly, it will not adequately protect occupants in the event of a crash. **2000-01:** Some of the owner's manuals for these vehicles are missing instructions for properly attaching a child restraint system's tether strap to the tether anchorage. **2001 w/4WD:** Electric shift transfer case may not fully engage into gear, causing the transfer case to end up in the neutral position.

1993-97 DODGE INTREPID

1994 Dodge Intrepid ES

FOR Antilock brakes • Acceleration (3.5-liter) • Passenger and cargo room • Steering/handling • Ride (base suspension)

AGAINST Road noise • Ride (Performance Handling Group) • Climate controls • Acceleration (3.3-liter) • Rear visibility

EVALUATION Acceleration is adequate with the 3.3-liter V6, but it's not too snappy for quick passing. For that reason, an early ES is the better choice with the larger V6 engine and touring suspension employing 16-inch tires. This combination offers fine overall performance, including precise handling and cornering. But watch out for an ES with the optional Performance Handling Group, which yields a stiff ride. By 1994, all Intrepids had the touring suspension as standard, delivering a satisfying level of handling precision without much loss in comfort. Even base Intrepids with that suspension handle as well as some smaller sports sedans, zipping through tight turns with little body lean and commendable grip. The ride is firm, but not harsh.

Gas mileage with an ES sedan averaged 22 mpg in a long-term trial, including considerable highway mileage—not quite a miser, but better than some all-out full-size automobiles. Even stop-and-go commuting usually resulted in 16-18 mpg economy. Three adults fit in back without crowding. Head room is good in front and adequate in back. Ergonomics are great. Instruments and controls are logically arranged and convenient, except for climate controls that are mounted too low for easy access. Lightweight plastic on the dashboard and door panels does not feel too durable. Cargo space is fine and the trunk opens at bumper level for easier loading of luggage. Road noise is prominent at highway speeds, even with the sound insulation added for 1996. Wind noise is low. Workmanship is generally tight and solid, but some cars have suffered minor creaks, rattles, or assembly flaws—even when new.

VALUE Intrepid is an impressive and worthy family sedan with a healthy helping of flair, offering good value for the money. However, full-size General Motors cars, such as the Oldsmobile Eighty-Eight and Pontiac Bonneville, may have the edge in terms of overall quality.

SPECIFICATIONS

	4-door sedan
Wheelbase, in.	113.0
Overall length, in.	201.7
Overall width, in.	74.4
Overall height, in.	56.3
Curb weight, lbs.	3318
Cargo volume, cu. ft.	16.7
Fuel capacity, gals.	18.0
Seating capacity	6
Front head room, in.	38.4
Max. front leg room, in.	42.4
Rear head room, in.	37.5
Min. rear leg room, in.	38.8

Powertrain layout: longitudinal front-engine/front-wheel drive

ENGINES

	ohv V6	ohc V6
Size, liters/cu. in.	3.3/201	3.5/215
Horsepower	153-161	214
Torque (lbs./ft.)	177-181	221
EPA city/highway mpg 4-speed OD automatic	19/27	18/26
City/highway mpg (as tested) 4-speed OD automatic	21.9	22.0

Built in Canada

RETAIL PRICES

	GOOD	AVERAGE	POOR
1993 Intrepid	$2,300-2,900	$1,700-2,200	$500-800
1994 Intrepid	2,800-3,500	2,200-2,800	700-1,100
1995 Intrepid	3,500-4,400	2,800-3,600	1,000-1,500
1996 Intrepid	4,500-5,500	3,800-4,500	1,600-2,100
1997 Intrepid	5,700-6,800	4,900-5,800	2,300-2,800

AVERAGE REPLACEMENT COSTS

A/C Compressor	$365	Constant Velocity Joints	310
Alternator	190	Exhaust System	418
Automatic Transmission or Transaxle	1,089	Radiator	350
		Shocks and/or Struts	480
Brakes	250	Timing Chain or Belt	230

TROUBLE SPOTS

• **Automatic transmission.** 41TE or 42LE automatic transaxle could take several seconds to engage at startup because of a problem with the valve body. (1993-95)

• **Automatic transmission.** A defective throttle positions sensor could be the cause of late, erratic, or harsh shifting. (1994)

• **Automatic transmission.** Bad seals in the transmission lead to premature friction component wear, which causes a shudder when starting from a stop, a bump when coasting to a stop, and slipping between gears. (1993-95)

• **Cold starting problems.** Hard starting and a miss at idle can be traced to defective fuel rails. (1993-94)

• **Air conditioner.** If the air conditioner is intermittent or quits altogether, but the refrigerant charge is OK, the pressure transducer is probably malfunctioning. (All)

• **Air conditioner.** The air conditioner lines are prone to leak at the compressor because of nicks and sharp edges on the A/C line grooves for the O-rings, making it necessary to replace the lines. (1993-94)

• **Engine noise.** The motor mount on the left side of the engine tends to break. (1993)

• **Automatic transmission.** Transmission front pump could be leaking due to a worn bushing, which requires replacement of the pump as well as the torque converter. (1993-96)

RECALL HISTORY

1993: Lower control arm washers in front suspension of some cars can crack and fall off due to hydrogen embrittlement; will cause clunking sound during braking and eventually result in loss of steering control. **1993 w/3.3-liter engine:** O-rings used to seal interface of fuel-injector tubes are insufficiently durable; deterioration can cause fuel leakage, with potential for fire. **1993-95:** Lower control arm attaching brackets on some cars can crack due to fatigue and separate from engine cradle; transmission half-shaft could then pull out of transaxle. **1993-97 w/3.5-liter engine:** Fuel injection system can leak from O-rings or hairline cracks in fuel-injection rail. **1994:** Right steering tie rod can rub through automatic-transmission wiring harness, causing short circuit; may result in stalling, or allow engine to start when selector is not in "Park" position.

1998 Dodge Intrepid ES

FOR Passenger room • Cargo room • Ride • Steering/handling

AGAINST Rear visibility • Trunk liftover

EVALUATION The Intrepid's suspension is firm and stable at highway speeds, without growing harsh on rough pavement. Suspensions of the two models are tuned identically, but the wider tires on the ES provide slightly sharper feel in directional changes. Brakes provide short, straight stops from high speeds, with fine pedal modulation. Although the 2.7-liter engine moves this full-size sedan with adequate swiftness, acceleration is hardly neck-snapping. Though it's no powerhouse, the stronger 3.2-liter V6 can chirp the tires during rapid takeoffs, and delivers a quicker burst of power for passing and merging. Autostick helps the ES scoot through traffic, and produce more confident passing and merging. Both engines are smooth and quiet, and road noise is less noticeable than in earlier Intrepids. Wind noise is noticeable but not excessive. As for economy, a test ES averaged 20.7 mpg. Head room is generous in front, though the Intrepid's sloping roofline puts the heads of taller back-seaters right up to the headliner. Leg space is sufficient for 6-footers to be comfortable in all seats. Most gauges and controls, including those for the climate system, are easy to see and reach. Radio controls are more difficult to reach, and demand some study to decipher. Intrepid has a much larger rear window than the Concorde, allowing the driver to see the trunk for parking and enjoy a better view of surrounding traffic. A high rear parcel shelf does impair visibility, however. Cargo space is ample, and split folding rear seats increases that total capacity.

VALUE When first seen as 1998 models, both the Intrepid and the Chrysler Concorde made other full-size automobiles look—and feel—dated. Roomy, athletic, and eye-catching, handling much like European sport sedans, Intrepids also offer plenty of interior space. Long-term mechanical reliability is still a question mark, but these stylish sedans can be good value, whether new or used.

SPECIFICATIONS

	4-door sedan
Wheelbase, in.	113.0
Overall length, in.	203.7
Overall width, in.	74.7
Overall height, in.	55.9

	4-door sedan
Curb weight, lbs.	3422
Cargo volume, cu. ft.	18.4
Fuel capacity, gals.	17.0
Seating capacity	5-6
Front head room, in.	38.3
Max. front leg room, in.	42.2
Rear head room, in.	37.4
Min. rear leg room, in.	39.1

Powertrain layout: transverse front-engine/front-wheel drive

ENGINES

	dohc V6	ohc V6	ohc V6
Size, liters/cu. in.	2.7/167	3.2/197	3.5/215
Horsepower	200	225	242
Torque (lbs./ft.)	190	225	248
EPA city/highway mpg			
4-speed OD automatic	21/30	19/29	18/26
City/highway mpg (as tested)			
4-speed OD automatic		20.7	

Built in Canada

RETAIL PRICES

	GOOD	AVERAGE	POOR
1998 Intrepid	$8,500-9,800	$7,600-8,800	$4,300-5,200
1999 Intrepid	10,000-11,300	9,000-10,000	5,300-6,000
2000 Intrepid	11,500-13,000	10,500-11,800	6,500-7,500
2000 Intrepid R/T	14,000-16,000	12,500-14,500	8,300-9,800
2001 Intrepid	13,000-15,000	11,800-13,500	—
2001 Intrepid R/T	16,000-18,000	14,500-16,500	—

AVERAGE REPLACEMENT COSTS

A/C Compressor	$440	Constant Velocity Joints	1,300
Alternator	360	Exhaust System	425
Automatic Transmission or		Radiator	430
Transaxle	775	Shocks and/or Struts	1,505
Brakes	615	Timing Chain or Belt	360

TROUBLE SPOTS

• **Steering problems.** Drivability problems occur when the speed sensor wires pull out of the transmission. (1999)

• **Electrical problem.** Moisture getting inside the car behind the kick panels makes the windows, door locks, and power mirrors operate by themselves. (1998)

• **Electrical problem.** The interior lights will not go out or will not come on because of a blown fuse due to a damaged wiring harness in the roof area. (1998-99)

• **Oil leak.** The oil filter adapter may come out of the engine block when the filter is removed on 3.2L and 3.5L engines. When this happens the adapter must be replaced, not reinstalled. (1998-99)

RECALL HISTORY

1998: A few passenger airbag module assemblies are missing some required components, so airbag would not deploy during a crash. **1999:** The front seatbelt retractor does not comply with the requirements of the standard. If the retractor does not work properly, it will not adequately protect occupants in the event of a crash. **1999-00:** Inadequately manufactured mounting bolt for seatbelt shoulder height adjustable turning loop may not withstand sufficient force to function properly in certain impact situations. **2000:** Molding flash on primary lever may prevent operation of G-lock and tilt lock functions on some driver's side retractors, which could reduce driver protection during a frontal crash. **2000:** Passenger airbag inflator assembly on some cars contains incorrect inflator charge amount. **2000:** Seatbelt shoulder height adjustable turning loop bolt may not withstand sufficient force in certain impact situations. **2000:** Brake master cylinder piston retainer snap ring may be bent inward, which could result in brake drag condition. **2000-01:** Some of the owner's manuals for these vehicles are missing instructions for properly attaching a child restraint system's tether strap to the tether anchorage. **2000-01:** In the event of a crash, there is a potential for injury if the occupant's head were to contact the B-pillar. Owners will be sent a storage bin accessory unit that can be attached to the B-pillar along with installation instructions.

1995-99 DODGE NEON

1995 Dodge Neon 2-door coupe

FOR Antilock brakes (optional) • Passenger and cargo room • Steering/handling • Ride • Fuel economy • Instruments/controls

AGAINST Engine noise • Automatic transmission performance

EVALUATION The base engine is quick off the line with either transmission, but it growls loudly under hard throttle. Even so, it transmits little vibration to the car's interior and cruises quietly. The automatic transmission shifts abruptly during brisk acceleration, and tends to be oversensitive to the throttle. It also downshifts unexpectedly. Although the available dual-cam four is livelier than the base engine, the difference isn't big enough to make it a priority, and it's no quieter, either. Fuel economy is commendable. We averaged 31 mpg with a 5-speed base engine model in a mix of city and highway driving. A Sport Neon with the base engine and automatic averaged 24.2 mpg, with most driving in and around urban areas. Neons feel solid and well-planted on the road. The firm suspension soaks up bumps with little harshness, and neither floats nor bottoms out, though bad pavement can deliver a few jolts. Handling is sporty, even with the base model. Steering is firm, feels natural, and centers quickly, producing agile response on winding roads. Brakes have strong stopping power, too. Passenger space is impressive for such a small vehicle. There's enough head and leg room to seat four 6-footers without squeezing, though rear doors are too small to allow easy entry and exit. The modern dashboard layout offers simple, convenient controls. The Neon's trunk opens at bumper level to a wide, flat cargo floor that reaches well forward to yield good luggage space.

VALUE In all, Neon offers a solid domestic alternative to the imports. Whether to pick a Dodge or Plymouth is a matter of individual choice; except for the insignia on the body, they're exactly the same car.

SPECIFICATIONS

	2-door coupe	4-door sedan
Wheelbase, in.	104.0	104.0
Overall length, in.	171.8	171.8
Overall width, in.	67.5	67.5
Overall height, in.	53.0	52.8
Curb weight, lbs.	2385	2416
Cargo volume, cu. ft.	11.8	11.8
Fuel capacity, gals.	11.2	11.2
Seating capacity	5	5
Front head room, in.	39.6	39.6
Max. front leg room, in.	42.5	42.5
Rear head room, in.	36.5	36.5
Min. rear leg room, in.	35.1	35.1

Powertrain layout: transverse front-engine/front-wheel drive

ENGINES

	ohc I4	dohc I4
Size, liters/cu. in.	2.0/122	2.0/122
Horsepower	132	150
Torque (lbs./ft.)	129	130-133
EPA city/highway mpg		
5-speed OD manual	28/38	28/38
3-speed automatic	25/33	25/33
City/highway mpg (as tested)		
5-speed OD manual	31.0	25.4
3-speed automatic	23.6	

Built in USA, Mexico

RETAIL PRICES

	GOOD	AVERAGE	POOR
1995 Neon	$2,600-3,200	$2,000-2,600	$500-900
1995 Neon Sport	2,900-3,500	2,300-2,800	700-1,000

	GOOD	AVERAGE	POOR
1996 Neon	$3,200-3,900	$2,500-3,200	$800-1,200
1996 Neon Sport	3,600-4,400	3,000-3,700	1,100-1,500
1997 Neon	4,200-4,900	3,500-4,200	1,400-1,800
1998 Neon	5,300-6,000	4,600-5,200	2,000-2,500
1999 Neon	6,400-7,200	5,600-6,400	2,700-3,300

AVERAGE REPLACEMENT COSTS

A/C Compressor	$400	Clutch, Pressure Plate,	
Alternator	300	Bearing	535
Automatic Transmission or		Constant Velocity Joints	345
Transaxle	555	Exhaust System	290
Brakes	295	Radiator	375
Shocks and/or Struts	450	Timing Chain or Belt	190

TROUBLE SPOTS

• **Air conditioner.** A lack of cooling caused by the A/C evaporator freezing up because the compressor does not cycle off. (1995)

• **Battery.** Batteries that go dead may be the result of one or more of the following: a glove box without a raised pad that closes the light switch, misaligned doors, a faulty trunk lid switch and lamp assembly, or a missing door-ajar bumper pad. (1995)

• **Rough idle.** Faulty valve springs on the 2.0-liter DOHC engine cause rough idle, misfires. (1997-99)

• **Brakes.** If the ABS warning light stays on, which disables the ABS, the ABS controller needs to be replaced. (1995)

• **Climate control.** In cold weather, ice may form in the blower motor housing, which prevents the blower from moving and blows the fuse. The drain tube must be rerouted, the blower motor replaced, and a new fuse installed. (1995-97)

• **Brakes.** The front brakes wear abnormally fast on cars with four wheel studs, so heavy-duty linings should be used to replace them. (All)

• **Steering noise.** Unless the power steering fluid is replaced with a revised fluid, the steering system makes noise for the first few minutes when started in cold weather. (1995-98)

RECALL HISTORY

1995: Fuel and rear-brake tubes can experience accelerated corrosion between metallic tubes and rubber isolator; may lead to brake fluid or fuel leakage. **1995:** Steering column coupler can become disconnected when vehicle sustains underbody impact. **1995-96 w/ACR competition package:** Brake master cylinder can leak fluid due to damaged seal; warning light will signal impairment prior to partial brake-system loss. **1996:** Wiring harness in Mexican-built cars could short circuit; can cause various malfunctions, including stalling. **1996 built in Toluca, Mexico:** Engine wiring harness can short-circuit due to contact with exhaust gas recirculation tube; can cause various malfunctions, including engine stalling. **1997:** Airbag could deploy inadvertently when ignition is shut off. **1998:** Rear suspension crossmember on some cars may be missing spot welds; can result in structural cracks in body, and reduced rear-impact crash protection. **1999:** Inadequate welding on some cars could allow pivot tube to separate from lower control arm in front suspension.

2000-01 DODGE NEON

2000 Dodge Neon

FOR Steering/handling • Fuel economy

AGAINST Noise • Automatic transmission performance

EVALUATION Compared to the 1995-99 generation, this Neon is an improvement, but modest acceleration remains a weak point. Though lively enough with manual shift, highway passing typically demands a downshift from fifth gear to third. Standing-start pickup is a lot duller with the automatic transmission. Most rival models have 4-speed automatics, which quicken takeoffs. Gas mileage is a bonus. A new test Neon average 24 mpg with an automatic transmission in mostly highway driving, and 25.3 with manual shift in a mix of city/highway travel. Neon suspensions absorb most bumps well. Sporty steering and handling carry on the car's basic fun-to-drive character. Wind and road noise are noticeable, but the real sound culprit is the engine, which groans loudly under hard throttle. For a subcompact, the Neon is roomy and reasonably comfortable. The driver sits in an alert, upright position. Both front buckets are comfortable, with plenty of head room. Leg room is sufficient in the back, where seat comfort is adequate, but head clearance is tight for anyone over 5-foot-8 or so. Generously-sized gauges look dressy, but they lose contrast in dim light when the headlights are on. A high parcel shelf restricts the driver's view directly to the rear. Seat fabrics feel rich, and despite a surplus of hard plastic on doors and dashboard, nothing looks or feels cheap. Doorways are fairly large, but the rear-door shape hinders entry/exit. Trunk volume is good for this class, but liftover is high and the lid's hinges cut into load space. Acceleration is good with the R/T and ACR editions that were added for 2001, but fewer of those are on sale.

VALUE Tepid acceleration aside, the regular Neon is a capable, fairly refined and well-equipped subcompact at an appealing price—perhaps even more tempting when secondhand than as a new car. Sales have been sluggish in new-car showrooms, which helps to keep prices down.

SPECIFICATIONS

	4-door sedan
Wheelbase, in.	105.0
Overall length, in.	174.4
Overall width, in.	67.4
Overall height, in.	56.0
Curb weight, lbs.	2559
Cargo volume, cu. ft.	13.1
Fuel capacity, gals.	12.5
Seating capacity	5
Front head room, in.	39.1
Max. front leg room, in.	42.4
Rear head room, in.	36.8
Min. rear leg room, in.	34.8

Powertrain layout: transverse front-engine/front-wheel drive

ENGINES

	ohc I4	ohc I4
Size, liters/cu. in.	2.0/122	2.0/122
Horsepower	132	150
Torque (lbs./ft.)	130	135
EPA city/highway mpg		
5-speed OD manual	28/35	28/35
3-speed OD automatic	25/31	
City/highway mpg (as tested)		
5-speed OD manual	25.3	
3-speed OD automatic	24.0	

Built in USA

RETAIL PRICES

	GOOD	AVERAGE	POOR
2000 Neon	$8,000-9,000	$7,200-8,100	$5,500-6,200
2001 Neon	9,500-11,000	8,500-10,000	—

AVERAGE REPLACEMENT COSTS

A/C Compressor	$495	Clutch, Pressure Plate,	
Alternator	360	Bearing	570
Automatic Transmission or		Constant Velocity Joints	770
Transaxle	1,110	Exhaust System	370
Brakes	360	Radiator	450
Shocks and/or Struts	490	Timing Chain or Belt	280

TROUBLE SPOTS

• **Air conditioner.** A clunk or hooting sound from the A/C compressor can be corrected with a new expansion valve. (2000-01)

• **Vehicle shake.** A countermeasure motor mount on the right side eliminates a shake in the steering wheel or seat. (2000)

• **Climate control.** Leaves, etc. getting inside the plenum and rubbing on the blower squirrel cage causes noises when the blower is running. Installing seals near the hood hinges, and screens in the cowl, will keep debris out. (2000)

• **Steering problems.** Power steering moan or groan is caused by low fluid levels air in the system. A revised cap/dipstick was also released to increase the fluid level in the reservoir. (2000-01)

- **Vehicle noise.** Snapping noises from the front suspension, particularly on rough roads, is often due to loose front crossmember mounting bolts. (2000)

- **Antenna.** The threads for the antenna get stripped when someone tries to tighten it because there is a gap between the antenna and base. (2000-01)

RECALL HISTORY

2000 Neon: Vapors from PCV system on certain cars can condense and freeze inside throttle body, when operated in cold ambient temperatures; throttle might not return fully to idle. **2000:** Some front (passenger-side) airbags may not inflate properly in a crash. **2000-01:** Brake booster vacuum hose could swell and loosen from intake manifold, causing loss of power brake assist and increased engine idle speed. **2000-01:** Some owner's manuals are missing full instructions for properly attaching a child restraint system's tether strap. **2001 w/R/T pkg. and 16-inch wheels:** Certain vehicles have an incorrect tire placard, indicating that 14- and 15-inch tires are recommended.

1994-01 DODGE RAM PICKUP

1996 Dodge Ram 1500 4WD Club Cab extended cab

FOR Acceleration (V8, V10) • Interior room • Cargo and towing ability • Optional 4-wheel antilock brakes

AGAINST Acceleration (V6) • Ride • Noise • Fuel economy

EVALUATION Acceleration is more than adequate with the 5.2-liter V8, which delivered average fuel economy of 14.4 mpg. We don't recommend a V6 for heavy-duty work. A burly Cummins turbodiesel is also available, but not too many folks really need that much pull. You don't get neck-snapping pickup with the V10, but it does propel the Ram with more authority than any V8, and generates less noise than expected. Gas mileage is dismal, however: just 10 mpg in mostly city travel. A turbodiesel delivered 14.6 mpg, but is slower in standing-start acceleration than a gas engine, and idles as roughly as a big rig. Even with a base suspension, a Ram 1500 can get bouncy over dips and bumps when the bed is empty. Turns may be taken with good grip and balance, and gusty crosswinds have little effect on directional stability. Ride quality in a 2500-series is undeniably stiff. Four-wheel antilock braking brings this pickup to a halt with fine control. Engine and road noise are modest for a truck, but wind roar around front roof pillars is a problem. Space is ample for three-across seating. The cab has plenty of space behind the seat, making it possible to recline seatbacks—a rarity in full-size pickups. The seatback center folds into an armrest that doubles as a compartmented console. Opening the large padded lid to gain access to the compartments, however, is not so easy while driving. Three can sit abreast in the back of a Club Cab, but the seat cushion is too short to offer real thigh support, and rear leg room is no better than in a compact car. Gauges are plainly marked; controls near at hand and logical. Three simple knobs operate the climate control. Most controls are lit at night. A slide-out holder is big enough to carry two 16-ounce beverage containers, but it obstructs the radio controls when in use.

VALUE All told, the impressive Ram is as accommodating and refined as any Ford or General Motors rival. Even if you're leaning toward another brand, it's a good idea to test-drive a Ram before buying any full-size pickup.

SPECIFICATIONS

	reg. cab short bed	reg. cab long bed	ext. cab short bed	ext. cab long bed
Wheelbase, in.	118.7	134.7	138.7	154.7
Overall length, in.	204.1	224.1	224.0	244.0
Overall width, in.	79.4	79.4	79.4	79.4
Overall height, in.	71.9	71.8	71.6	71.5
Curb weight, lbs.	4009	4180	4529	4549
Fuel capacity, gals.	26.0	35.0	26.0	35.0
Seating capacity	3	3	6	6
Front head room, in.	40.2	40.2	40.2	40.2
Max. front leg room, in.	41.0	41.0	41.0	41.0
Rear head room, in.	—	—	39.4	39.4
Min. rear leg room, in.	—	—	31.6	31.6

Powertrain layout: longitudinal front-engine/rear- or 4-wheel drive

ENGINES

	ohv V6	ohv V8	ohv V8	Turbodiesel ohv I6	ohv V10
Size, liters/cu. in.	3.9/239	5.2/318	5.9/360	5.9/360	8.0/488
Horsepower	170-175	220	230-235	160-215	300
Torque (lbs./ft.)	230	300	330	420-440	440-450
EPA city/highway mpg					
5-speed OD man.	16/20	14/19	12/16	NA	NA
4-speed OD auto.	14/18	13/17	12/17	NA	NA
City/highway mpg (as tested)					
4-speed OD auto.		14.4		14.6	10.0

Built in USA, Mexico

RETAIL PRICES

	GOOD	AVERAGE	POOR
1994 Ram 1500 pickup	$3,700-6,500	$3,000-5,700	$1,100-3,000
1994 Ram 2500 pickup	6,200-8,500	5,500-7,700	2,800-4,500
1995 Ram 1500 pickup	4,500-9,000	3,800-8,200	1,500-5,000
1995 Ram 2500 pickup	7,000-11,000	6,100-10,000	3,300-6,200
1996 Ram 1500 pickup	5,300-10,500	4,500-9,500	2,000-6,000
1996 Ram 2500 pickup	7,900-12,500	7,000-11,500	4,000-7,300
1997 Ram 1500 pickup	6,200-12,000	5,300-11,000	2,700-7,200
1997 Ram 2500 pickup	9,000 -14,000	8,000-13,000	4,700-8,500
1998 Ram 1500 pickup	7,200-13,500	6,200-12,300	3,300-8,200
1998 Ram 2500 pickup	10,200-16,000	9,200-14,500	5,400-9,500
1999 Ram 1500 pickup	8,300-15,000	7,300-13,500	4,000-9,000
1999 Ram 2500 pickup	11,000-17,000	10,000-15,500	6,000-10,200
2000 Ram 1500 pickup	9,400-16,500	8,300-15,000	4,800-10,000
2000 Ram 2500 pickup	12,500-18,000	11,200-16,500	7,000-11,200
2001 Ram 1500 pickup	10,500-18,000	9,300-16,500	—
2001 Ram 2500 pickup	14,000-20,000	12,500-18,500	—

AVERAGE REPLACEMENT COSTS

A/C Compressor...........	$380	Clutch, Pressure Plate,	
Alternator....................	295	Bearing	610
Automatic Transmission or		Exhaust System	260
Transaxle	795	Radiator.......................	325
Brakes	295	Shocks and/or Struts....	230
Timing Chain or Belt.....	235	Universal Joints............	225

TROUBLE SPOTS

- **Suspension noise.** A rattle or clunk from the front can often be traced to the sway bar links where they attach to the sway bar. (1994-95)

- **Transmission leak.** Automatic transmission fluid leaks from the speed sensor in the transmission. (1994)

- **Air conditioner.** If the air conditioner gradually stops cooling and/or the airflow from the vents decreases, the computer (PCM) may not be sending a signal to the compressor clutch relay to cycle off, which causes the A/C evaporator to freeze up. (1994-95)

- **Automatic transmission.** If the transmission will not engage when first started, chances are the torque converter is draining down. A check valve in the fluid line leading to the transmission cooler will fix the problem. (1994)

- **Automatic transmission.** If the transmission won't upshift in cool weather, it is probably due to defective cast iron seal rings in the governor drive. (1994)

RECALL HISTORY

1994: Component within passenger-side seatbelt buckle assembly shatters, causing belt to release. **1994:** Seatback release latch lever might remain in released position. **1994 BR1500/2500 w/no rear bumpers:** Does not meet rear-impact test requirements, and increases the risk of fuel spill. **1994 4WD:** Front suspension attachment to axle may not be adequately tightened; can cause axle vibration. **1994-95:** While making a turn, extra keys in keyring can lodge in holes in back of steering wheel. **1994-99:** Secondary hood latch rod can bind and prevent engagement. **1994-95 2500/3500:** Front spring/shock towers on certain trucks can crack and eventually separate from vehicle frame. **1994-95:** Lower steering shaft can separate from upper shaft if the retaining plastic pins and metal clip break; can result in loss of vehicle control. **1994-96 w/gasoline engine:** Valve on fuel tank can allow fuel to leak onto ground; could result in fire. **1994-96 w/diesel:** The throttle cable could unravel (fray) or break, resulting in a loss of throttle control. **1994-96:** Ignition switch and wiring on certain trucks could overheat. **1994-97:** Under certain high-load conditions, fluid line could separate from transmission; fluid may then spray onto exhaust manifold. **1994-99 w/V10 engine, manual transmission, 4WD:** Under sustained maximum load, while driving up steep grade in 4WD low range in hot ambient conditions, hydraulic clutch line temperature can become excessive and possibly rupture. **1995-96 w/diesel engine:** Vacuum hose may deteriorate and partially collapse, possibly reducing power-brake assist. **1996 w/6800- or 9000-pound GVW rating:** Tire/wheel specification information on certification label indicates smaller tire than is required. **1997 w/diesel engine:** Exhaust pipe may contact, or be too near, dash panel silencer pad, causing smoldering and igniting of adjacent materials. **1997-2001:** Sound-deadening material inside the steering wheel could become detached from the cover and housing causing the the the driver airbag system to become disabled. The airbag warning lamp will illuminate on the instrument panel. **1998:** Brake rotor material strength on some trucks is not sufficient, causing hub fatigue fracture that can result in crack propagation and, ultimately, in wheel separation. **1998:** Front seatbelt buckles were not properly riveted to support strap. **1998 w/V10 or heavy-duty 5.9-liter gas V8:** Exhaust system heat shield attaching screw is too close to fuel line, which can rub against the screw, possibly causing fuel leakage. **1998 w/5.9-liter diesel engine:** Low-pressure supply tube between filter and high-pressure pump can fracture, allowing fuel to leak. **1998 w/5.9-liter diesel engine:** Intermittent high engine-idle condition can occur, due to malfunction of vehicle speed sensor. **1998:** Bolts used to attach cab and core support to frame may have been improperly hardened; can allow cab to separate from frame. **1998-00 w/optional trailer hitch:** Trailer hitch side brackets may lack sufficient strength, and could fatigue and fracture in area where hitch mounts to frame. **1999:** Underbody hydraulic clutch line heat shield on some trucks is too short, allowing line material to be directly exposed to exhaust temperatures. **1999:** The front seatbelt retractor does not comply with the requirements of the standard. If the retractor does not work properly, it will not adequately protect occupants in the event of a crash. **2000:** Welds at right lower control arm bracket to axle-tube attachment on a few trucks may have inadequate fatigue life; could result in separation. **2000:** During full lock turns, it is possible for the tire or wheel to contact the brake hose/ABS sensor wire assembly. Continued contact can result in wire damage and/or a hole in the brake line and reduced braking effectiveness. **2000-01:** Some of the owner's manuals for these vehicles are missing instructions for properly attaching a child restraint system's tether strap to the tether anchorage. **2001 Quad Cab w/camper:** Spacer plate could lead to deformation of the upper spring plate during assembly of the axle to the vehicle, resulting in a soft joint and possible loss of vehicle control.

1990-94 DODGE SHADOW

1994 Dodge Shadow ES 2-door coupe

FOR Acceleration (V6, Turbo) • Cargo room • Antilock brakes • Ride/handling

AGAINST Rear-seat room • Engine noise (4-cylinder)

EVALUATION Performance is listless with the basic 2.2-liter engine, which is on the noisy side. Action is somewhat better—and smoother—with the 2.5-liter four, which doesn't consume much more

fuel, either. It's a better choice with automatic, in particular, but by no means devoid of noise. Either turbo engine delivers swift acceleration, but it's accompanied by plenty of raucous behavior beneath the hood. The V6 engine is smooth and flexible, making a Shadow downright frisky when coupled to manual shift. Lacking an overdrive gear, the 3-speed automatic isn't the best choice for highway gas mileage and quiet cruising. The standard suspension is firm for a domestic car. Handling beats most small cars, even in base form, and Shadows produce a stable highway ride. An ES version is tauter, but not harsh over most pavement surfaces. Quick-ratio power steering has good feel and centers well. Interiors are nicely packaged, with reclining front bucket seats, tachometer, and gauges. Rear-seat room could be better but folding the seatbacks creates a generous cargo hold. Convertibles displayed some cowl shake and body flex even when new, but not to a troubling degree.

VALUE Assembly quality doesn't match that of Japanese competitors, and Shadows aren't the most refined small cars around. Some might call even them mechanically crude. Still, Dodge's subcompact is a solid vehicle that looks good, performs well, and costs considerably less.

SPECIFICATIONS

	2-door conv.	2-door hatchback	4-door hatchback
Wheelbase, in.	97.0	97.2	97.2
Overall length, in.	171.7	171.9	171.9
Overall width, in.	67.3	67.3	67.3
Overall height, in.	52.6	52.7	52.7
Curb weight, lbs.	2916	2613	2884
Cargo volume, cu. ft.	13.2	33.3	33.3
Fuel capacity, gals.	14.0	14.0	14.0
Seating capacity	4	5	5
Front head room, in.	38.3	38.3	38.3
Max. front leg room, in.	42.0	42.0	42.0
Rear head room, in.	37.4	37.4	37.4
Min. rear leg room, in.	33.7	33.7	33.7

Powertrain layout: transverse front-engine/front-wheel drive

ENGINES

ENGINES	ohc I4	Turbocharged ohc I4	ohc I4	Turbocharged ohc I4	ohc V6
Size, liters/cu. in.	2.2/135	2.2/135	2.5/153	2.5/153	3.0/181
Horsepower	93	174	100	150-152	141
Torque (lbs./ft.)	122	210	135	180	171
EPA city/highway mpg					
5-speed OD man.	26/33	20/28	24/29	20/26	19/28
3-speed auto.	23/30		22/27	19/23	
4-speed OD auto.					19/24
City/highway mpg (as tested)					
5-speed OD man.	25.2	19.8			
4-speed OD auto.					21.7

Built in USA

RETAIL PRICES

RETAIL PRICES	GOOD	AVERAGE	POOR
1990 Shadow	$1,000-1,500	$600-1,000	$100-200
1991 Shadow	1,200-1,800	700-1,200	100-200
1991 Shadow Convertible	1,700-2,200	1,100-1,600	300-500
1992 Shadow	1,400-2,100	900-1,500	200-300
1992 Shadow Convertible	2,100-2,700	1,500-2,000	500-800
1993 Shadow	1,700-2,400	1,100-1,800	300-500
1993 Shadow Convertible	2,800-3,500	2,200-2,800	800-1,300
1994 Shadow	2,100-2,800	1,500-2,200	400-700

AVERAGE REPLACEMENT COSTS

A/C Compressor	$450	Clutch, Pressure Plate, Bearing	625
Alternator	280	Constant Velocity Joints	445
Automatic Transmission or Transaxle	675	Exhaust System	260
Brakes	250	Radiator	325
Shocks and/or Struts	330	Timing Chain or Belt	150

TROUBLE SPOTS

• **Cold starting problems.** 2.2- or 2.5-liter engines may idle rough or stumble when first started unless a revised intake manifold (with an "X" cast into the number 1 runner) was installed (1992) or a revised computer (PCM) was installed (1992-93) or the computer was reprogrammed (1994).

• **Automatic transmission.** 41TE or 42LE automatic transaxles could take several seconds to engage at startup because of a problem with the valve body. (1993-94)

• **Automatic transmission.** Bad seals in the transmission lead to premature friction component wear. (1993-94)

• **Alternator belt.** Deep snow could knock the serpentine belt off the pulleys of a 3.0-liter engine. Installing a shield will solve the problem. (1991-94)

• **Air conditioner.** If the air conditioner gradually stops cooling and/or the airflow from the vents decreases, the computer (PCM) may not be sending a signal to the compressor clutch relay to cycle off, which causes the A/C evaporator to freeze up. (1991-94)

• **Oil consumption.** Oil consumption and smoke from the exhaust at idle and deceleration on 3.0-liter engines is caused by exhaust valve guides that slide out of the heads. (1992-93)

• **Engine noise.** The motor mount on the left side of the engine tends to break. (1992-93)

• **Automatic transmission.** Transmission shudder under light to moderate acceleration could be caused by a leaking front trans pump due to a worn bushing. (1990-94)

RECALL HISTORY

1991: Front disc brake caliper guide pin bolts may not be adequately tightened and could loosen, which could cause reduced braking effectiveness that might result in an accident. **1991:** Both airbag system front impact sensors may not be secured to mounting brackets, so airbag would not deploy. **1991-92:** Steering wheel mounting armature can develop cracks and separate from the center hub attachment to the steering column; can result in loss of vehicle control. **1991-92:** Lower driver's seatback attaching bolt can fail and separate. **1991-94 2-door:** Bolt that attaches recliner mechanism to driver's seatback on certain cars could break; may result in seatback suddenly reclining. **1992:** Zinc plating of some upper steering column shaft coupling bolts caused hydrogen embrittlement and breakage of the bolt.

1990-95 DODGE SPIRIT

1991 Dodge Spirit ES

FOR Antilock brakes (optional later models) • Passenger and cargo room • Acceleration (V6, Turbo)

AGAINST Engine noise (4-cylinder) • Road noise • Wind noise • Ride • Rear-seat comfort

EVALUATION Acceleration with the base four is barely adequate and particularly meager when passing/merging. But gas mileage is impressive—a 4-cylinder Spirit averaged 22.3 mpg in mixed expressway/highway driving. The V6 is smooth and responsive, but its 4-speed automatic transmission shifts too quickly into higher gears, and also holds backs on downshifts when trying to pass. A 3-speed automatic is less frugal, but operates more dependably. Some turbos suffer lag that detracts from initial acceleration, but they're strong and swift after that opening period. Revisions for 1991 improved low-speed response, but the engine is noisy and coarse. Takeoffs are smooth and vigorous with the Spirit R/T, which suffers minimal turbo lag and offers balanced performance. Firmer shock absorbers than those used on base and midlevel Acclaims yield a tauter ride and sharper steering/handling. The suspension does a good job of controlling bouncing on wavy roads, but bangs and clunks on rough surfaces. Road and wind noise intrude at highway speeds, too. Roomy interiors for a car this size offer top-notch visibility. Getting in and out is a snap, and the big trunk with a flat floor is easy to load. Gauges are readable on a dashboard that's nicely laid out. Front seats feel fine, and rear head/knee room is adequate; but rear cushions are too low and short for comfort.

VALUE Solid, spacious, and competent, a Spirit might fail to stimulate anyone's spirit—unless it happens to be the wheel-twisting R/T, that is. Even in tamer form, Dodge's practical domestic sedan is worth a look.

SPECIFICATIONS

	4-door sedan
Wheelbase, in.	103.3
Overall length, in.	181.2
Overall width, in.	68.1
Overall height, in.	53.5
Curb weight, lbs.	2863
Cargo volume, cu. ft.	14.4
Fuel capacity, gals.	16.0
Seating capacity	6
Front head room, in.	38.4
Max. front leg room, in.	41.9
Rear head room, in.	37.9
Min. rear leg room, in.	38.3

Powertrain layout: transverse front-engine/front-wheel drive

ENGINES

	Turbocharged ohc I4	ohc I4	Turbocharged ohc I4	ohc V6
Size, liters/cu. in.	2.2/135	2.5/153	2.5/153	3.0/181
Horsepower	224	100-101	150-152	141-142
Torque (lbs./ft.)	217	135-140	210	171

EPA city/highway mpg

5-speed OD manual	24/34	24/29	19/27	21/26
3-speed automatic	23/27	22/28		
4-speed OD automatic				19/24

City/highway mpg (as tested)

5-speed OD manual	21.2
3-speed automatic	22.3

Built in USA, Mexico

RETAIL PRICES

	GOOD	AVERAGE	POOR
1990 Spirit	$1,000-1,500	$600-1,000	$100-200
1991 Spirit	1,200-1,800	700-1,200	100-300
1991 Spirit R/T	1,800-2,400	1,200-1,700	400-600
1992 Spirit	1,400-2,000	900-1,400	200-400
1992 Spirit R/T	2,000-2,800	1,400-2,100	500-800
1993 Spirit	1,700-2,300	1,200-1,700	300-500
1994 Spirit	2,200-2,800	1,600-2,200	400-700
1995 Spirit	2,800-3,500	2,200-2,800	600-900

AVERAGE REPLACEMENT COSTS

A/C Compressor	$415	Constant Velocity Joints	660
Alternator	315	Exhaust System	320
Automatic Transmission or Transaxle	905	Radiator	335
		Shocks and/or Struts	340
Brakes	250	Timing Chain or Belt	290

TROUBLE SPOTS

• **Cold starting problems.** 2.2- or 2.5-liter engines may idle rough or stumble unless a revised intake manifold (with an "X" cast into the number 1 runner) was installed (1992), or a revised computer (PCM) was installed (1992-93), or the computer was reprogrammed. (1994)

• **Automatic transmission.** 41TE or 42LE automatic transaxles could take several seconds to engage at startup because of a problem with the valve body. (1993-95)

• **Automatic transmission.** Bad seals in the transmission lead to premature friction component wear. (1993-95)

• **Alternator belt.** Deep snow could knock the serpentine belt off the pulleys of the 3.0-liter engine. Installing a shield will solve the problem. (1991-95)

• **Air conditioner.** If the air conditioner gradually stops cooling and/or the airflow from the vents decreases, the computer (PCM) may not be sending a signal to the compressor clutch relay to cycle off, which causes the AC evaporator to freeze up. (1991-95)

• **Oil consumption and exhaust smoke.** Oil consumption and smoke from the exhaust at idle and deceleration on 3.0-liter engines is caused by exhaust valve guides that slide out of the heads. (1990-93)

• **Engine noise.** The motor mount on the left side of the engine tends to break. (1992-93)

• **Automatic transmission.** Transmission shudder under light to moderate acceleration could be caused by a leaking front trans pump due to a worn bushing. (1990-95)

RECALL HISTORY

1991: Front disc brake caliper guide pin bolts may not be adequately tightened and could loosen. **1991:** Both airbag system front impact sensors may not be secured to mounting brackets, so airbag would not deploy. **1992:** Zinc plating of some upper steering column shaft coupling bolts caused hydrogen embrittlement and breakage of the bolt. **1994:** Seatbelt assembly on small number of cars may fail in accident, increasing risk of injury.

1991-96 DODGE STEALTH

1996 Dodge Stealth R/T Turbo

FOR Acceleration • Handling/roadholding • Antilock brakes • All-wheel-drive traction (R/T Turbo)

AGAINST Fuel economy (R/T Turbo) • Rear-seat room • Cargo room • Ride (R/T Turbo)

EVALUATION An R/T Turbo is frightfully fast. All told, a base or ES Stealth makes more sense for most drivers. Both feel more responsive in daily driving with manual shift. Far lighter in weight, they don't suffer the flagship model's turbo lag or stiff ride. Front-drive Stealths suffer only minimal torque steer, and run quieter. Sadly, the optional automatic transmission keeps the V6 from revving high enough. Turbo gas mileage is marginal, but not bad for a car with such strong performance and so many pounds to haul. An early test Turbo averaged 18.8 mpg. Still, the aero gimmicks on either R/T do not justify their higher prices. Stealths suffer a rather claustrophobic 2+2 cockpit that isn't so easy to enter or leave. Elbow room is greater than a Talon or Eclipse, but rear seats are next to useless. Cargo space is scant, too. All-wheel drive on the R/T Turbo is a bonus on wet pavement, though front-drive Stealths also provide fine grip. Four-wheel steering subtly does its part toward that top Stealth's tenacious roadholding. On the other hand, the difference isn't great, and 4WS can communicate a nervous detachment, unlike the satisfying precision of regular steering on other Stealths.

VALUE Appealing more because of its style and performance than its practical virtues, Dodge's sports coupe scores high on that level. But a Stealth is not nearly as successful as a daily driver.

SPECIFICATIONS

	2-door hatchback
Wheelbase, in.	97.2
Overall length, in.	179.5
Overall width, in.	72.4
Overall height, in.	49.1
Curb weight, lbs.	3064
Cargo volume, cu. ft.	11.1
Fuel capacity, gals.	19.8
Seating capacity	4
Front head room, in.	37.1
Max. front leg room, in.	44.2
Rear head room, in.	34.1
Min. rear leg room, in.	28.5

Powertrain layout: transverse front-engine/front- or all-wheel drive

ENGINES	ohc V6	dohc V6	Turbocharged dohc V6
Size, liters/cu. in.	3.0/181	3.0/181	3.0/181
Horsepower	164	222	300-320
Torque (lbs./ft.)	185	201	307-315
EPA city/highway mpg			
4-speed OD automatic	18/23	18/24	
5-speed OD manual	19/24	19/25	19/25
6-speed OD manual			18/24

City/highway mpg (as tested)

5-speed OD manual		18.8
4-speed OD automatic	19.2	

Built in Japan

RETAIL PRICES	GOOD	AVERAGE	POOR
1991 Stealth, R/T	$2,600-4,000	$1,900-3,300	$500-1,300
1991 Stealth R/T Turbo	4,500-5,400	3,700-4,500	1,200-1,700
1992 Stealth, R/T	3,300-4,800	2,600-4,000	700-1,700
1992 Stealth R/T Turbo	5,500-6,500	4,500-5,500	1,600-2,400
1993 Stealth, R/T	4,200-5,600	3,400-4,800	1,100-2,400
1993 Stealth R/T Turbo	6,500-7,500	5,500-6,500	2,400-3,200
1994 Stealth, R/T	5,500-6,800	4,700-6,000	1,800-3,200
1994 Stealth R/T Turbo	8,000-9,500	7,000-8,500	3,300-4,200
1995 Stealth, R/T	7,000-8,500	6,000-7,500	2,800-4,200
1995 Stealth R/T Turbo	10,000-11,500	9,000-10,200	4,800-5,600
1996 Stealth, R/T	8,500-10,500	7,500-9,500	3,700-5,000
1996 Stealth R/T Turbo	12,000-13,500	10,500-12,000	5,800-6,800

AVERAGE REPLACEMENT COSTS

A/C Compressor	$760	Clutch, Pressure Plate, Bearing	485
Alternator	690	Constant Velocity Joints	490
Automatic Transmission or Transaxle	1,025	Exhaust System	420
Brakes	245	Radiator	530
Shocks and/or Struts	720	Timing Chain or Belt	295

TROUBLE SPOTS

• **Automatic transmission.** Hard shifting and gear clash can be eliminated by installing revised synchronizer components. (1991)

• **Automatic transmission.** No second gear and/or a loud tapping noise when shifted into or out of any forward range. (1991-96)

• **Dashboard lights.** The check engine light comes on, and will set a code for a bad camshaft sensor. The fix is to replace the engine control computer. (1996)

• **Doors.** The door window weatherstrip pulls out when the glass is moved up or down. A revised weatherstrip has been released to replace it. (1994)

RECALL HISTORY

1991: Front seatbelt release button can break, causing improper operation. **1991 R/T Turbo:** Oil might leak from AWD transfer case, causing bearing damage and failure. **1991-94:** In conditions of full-lock steering and full suspension travel, front brake hose can crack, resulting in brake fluid leakage.

1995-00 DODGE STRATUS

1995 Dodge Stratus ES

FOR Antilock brakes (ES) • Acceleration • Ride • Steering/handling • Passenger and cargo room

AGAINST Noise • Rear visibility

EVALUATION Although Stratus has the exterior dimensions of a compact car, it offers the interior room of a midsize model. In fact, there's plenty of leg space fore and aft, and sufficient rear-seat width for three medium-size adults to travel without feeling like sardines. Visibility is great to all angles except the rear. The high rear parcel shelf makes it hard to see out the back window. A large trunk with a flat floor and low liftover gives the Stratus good cargo-carrying ability. The driving position is comfortable, and the dashboard layout logical. The sedan's abundant, airy interior is well-designed; however, some trim pieces on the dashboard and door panels look and feel cheap. Of the several engine choices, we recommend the V6s for their smoother running and livelier acceleration. It's not the quietest engine around, but the 2.5-liter V6 takes off from a standstill with spirit. However, you're likely to experience a long pause before the automatic transmission downshifts for passing. Despite being shy two cylinders, the 2.4-liter 4-cylinder offers nearly as much punch as the V6, though at the expense of some refinement. The 2.0-liter four is noisier and a trifle slower, but gets great mileage with the 5-speed manual. Stratus rides and handles more like a sports sedan than a typical American car. That means more interior noise and road vibrations than people may be used to. You benefit from agile handling with little body lean and good grip, making it easy to thread along twisting roads. An ES, in particular, takes corners and curves adeptly. Ride comfort is generally good on both models, despite the firmer suspension on the ES, and the Stratus does feel smoother than a Ford Contour.

VALUE Overall, the large, comfortable interior; moderate price; and attractive styling make the well-equipped Stratus a good buy. Our only reservation might be Chrysler's past reputation for poor build quality.

SPECIFICATIONS

	2-door coupe	4-door sedan
Wheelbase, in.	103.7	108.0
Overall length, in.	190.2	186.0
Overall width, in.	70.3	71.7
Overall height, in.	53.7	54.1
Curb weight, lbs.	3012	2899
Cargo volume, cu. ft.	16.3	15.7
Fuel capacity, gals.	16.3	16.0
Seating capacity	5	5
Front head room, in.	38.5	38.1
Max. front leg room, in.	42.3	42.3
Rear head room, in.	36.0	36.8
Min. rear leg room, in.	34.0	37.8

Powertrain layout: transverse front-engine/front-wheel drive

ENGINES

	ohc I4	dohc I4	ohc V6	ohc I4
Size, liters/cu. in.	2.0/122	2.4/148	2.5/152	2.4/143
Horsepower	132	150	164-168	147
Torque (lbs./ft.)	129	165-167	161-170	158
EPA city/highway mpg				
5-speed OD manual	25/36			22/30
4-speed OD automatic		20/29	20/28	20/30
City/highway mpg (as tested)				
5-speed OD manual	24.7			
4-speed OD automatic		20.3		

Built in USA

RETAIL PRICES

	GOOD	AVERAGE	POOR
1995 Stratus	$3,500-4,100	$2,900-3,400	$1,000-1,400
1995 Stratus ES	3,700-4,300	3,000-3,600	1,100-1,500
1996 Stratus	4,300-5,000	3,600-4,300	1,400-1,800
1996 Stratus ES	4,700-5,400	4,000-4,700	1,700-2,100
1997 Stratus	5,300-6,000	4,500-5,200	2,000-2,400
1997 Stratus ES	5,800-6,500	5,100-5,700	2,400-2,800
1998 Stratus	6,500-7,300	5,600-6,300	2,700-3,200
1998 Stratus ES	7,100-8,000	6,300-7,200	3,200-3,700
1999 Stratus	7,700-8,700	6,700-7,700	3,600-4,200
1999 Stratus ES	8,700-9,700	7,700-8,700	4,200-4,800
2000 Stratus SE	9,000-10,000	8,000-9,000	4,300-5,000
2000 Stratus ES	10,000-11,000	9,000-10,000	5,000-5,700

AVERAGE REPLACEMENT COSTS

A/C Compressor	$425	Clutch, Pressure Plate,	
Alternator	300	Bearing	545
Automatic Transmission or		Constant Velocity Joints	345
Transaxle	1,115	Exhaust System	290
Brakes	325	Radiator	440
Shocks and/or Struts	375	Timing Chain or Belt	190

TROUBLE SPOTS

• **Air conditioner.** Air conditioning compressor fails on cars with 2.5-liter engine. (1995-96)

• **Air conditioner.** Air conditioning may be intermittent or stop due to failed pressure transducer. (1995)

• **Headlights.** Poor illumination from headlights corrected by replacing both headlamp modules. (1996-97)

• **Automatic transmission.** Transmission may shudder when accelerating from a stop, thump when coasting down to a stop, or slip when shifting. (1995)

• **Water leak.** Water leaks in between the door and interior door trim panel or from the cowl/plenum/floor/A-pillar seams. (1995-96)

RECALL HISTORY

1995: Rear seatbelt anchors will not withstand loading required by federal standard. **1995-96 w/ABS:** Corrosion of ABS hydraulic control unit can cause solenoid valves to stick open, so car tends to pull from a straight stop when brakes are applied. **1995-96:** Brake master cylinder can leak fluid, due to damaged seal; warning light will signal impairment prior to partial brake-system loss. **1995-96 w/2.4-liter:** Oil leakage could cause engine-compartment fire. **1995-97:** Lower ball joint can separate due to loss of lubrication; could cause loss of control. **1995-98 w/automatic transmission:** If operator presses button to shift out of Park with key in locked position, pin can break; "ignition-park" interlock would then be nonfunctional. **1996-97:** Secondary hood latch spring can disengage if hood is slammed. **1998-99:** Right rear brake tube can contact exhaust system clamp and wear a hole in it; tube could then leak, reducing braking effectiveness. **2000:** Incorrect child lock instruction label could cause confusion as to whether the childproof safety lock was activated. **2000:** The right front-brake tube may get damaged. **2000:** Some of the owner's manuals for these vehicles are missing instructions for properly attaching a child restraint system's tether strap to the tether anchorage.

1992-96 EAGLE SUMMIT WAGON

1992 Eagle Summit 4-door wagon AWD

FOR Passenger and cargo room • Antilock brakes (optional) • All-wheel-drive traction (AWD)

AGAINST Acceleration (automatic) • Noise

EVALUATION Compact size, great visibility, and good maneuverability at low speeds make the Summit Wagon a good urban vehicle. On the downside, you get lots of body lean in quick turns because of the vehicle's tall body and narrow track. Grip is poor with the base model's skinny tires, but improves with the LX wagon's wider rubber, and with the AWD version. Even if tight corners produce marked body roll and tire squealing, the Summit Wagon's ride is pliant—good over all surfaces. Braking feels strong and balanced, even without antilocking. Acceleration is adequate—but no more—with the base engine and manual shift, but that engine lacks sufficient torque to keep the automatic transmission from frequent gear-hunting. It feels particularly underpowered with automatic when the wagon is loaded with passengers and cargo. The stronger 2.4-liter engine is a better all-around choice, with more torque for better throttle response and pulling power. The standard 5-speed manual gearbox shifts smoothly, and has a light clutch. The wagon's automatic transmission downshifts quickly to maintain speed on hills or to pass, but its gear changes are rather harsh. Noise levels are high, which makes highway driving more tiring. Wind noise and road rumble are problems. Base models, in particular, are not well insulated against engine and wind sounds. Entry and exit are eased by the wagon's low step-in height. The minivan-style sliding right-rear passenger door opens and closes via a unique inner-rail mechanism, which eliminates the bodyside channel that's necessary with traditional sliding doors. Passenger room is plentiful. Cargo space behind the backseat is tight, but the rear bench folds flat and tumbles forward to create a flat load floor ahead of the tailgate. Seating positions are comfortably chairlike for great visibility out of an expansive greenhouse. However, the driver's seat might be too high for some shorter drivers.

Gauges and controls are simple and logically laid out.

VALUE This versatile "mini-minivan" is worth a look if you need more practical utility than a small station wagon can provide, but don't want a regular compact van.

SPECIFICATIONS

	4-door wagon
Wheelbase, in.	99.2
Overall length, in.	168.5
Overall width, in.	66.7
Overall height, in.	62.1
Curb weight, lbs.	2734
Cargo volume, cu. ft.	79.0
Fuel capacity, gals.	14.5
Seating capacity	5
Front head room, in.	40.0
Max. front leg room, in.	40.8
Rear head room, in.	38.6
Min. rear leg room, in.	36.1

Powertrain layout: transverse front-engine/front- or all-wheel drive

ENGINES

	ohc I4	ohc I4
Size, liters/cu. in.	1.8/112	2.4/144
Horsepower	113-119	116-136
Torque (lbs./ft.)	116	136-145
EPA city/highway mpg		
5-speed OD manual	26/33	20/24
4-speed OD automatic	26/33	20/26
City/highway mpg (as tested)		
5-speed OD manual		22.8
4-speed OD automatic	25.3	

Built in Japan

RETAIL PRICES

	GOOD	AVERAGE	POOR
1992 Summit Wagon	$2,000-2,600	$1,400-2,000	$200-400
1992 AWD Wagon	2,500-3,100	1,800-2,400	300-500
1993 Summit Wagon	2,500-3,100	1,900-2,400	300-500
1993 AWD Wagon	3,200-4,000	2,500-3,300	600-1,000
1994 Summit Wagon	3,000-3,600	2,300-2,900	500-800
1994 AWD Wagon	3,700-4,400	3,000-3,600	900-1,300
1995 Summit Wagon	3,600-4,300	2,900-3,500	800-1,200
1995 AWD Wagon	4,300-5,000	3,600-4,200	1,200-1,600
1996 Summit Wagon	4,300-5,000	3,600-4,200	1,200-1,600
1996 AWD Wagon	5,000-5,800	4,200-5,000	1,600-2,200

AVERAGE REPLACEMENT COSTS

A/C Compressor	$915	Clutch, Pressure Plate,	
Alternator	770	Bearing	475
Automatic Transmission or		Constant Velocity Joints	710
Transaxle	960	Exhaust System	500
Brakes	260	Radiator	390
Shocks and/or Struts	700	Timing Chain or Belt	165

TROUBLE SPOTS

• **Automatic transmission.** Delayed shifts from second to third, or third to fourth when the transmission fluid is cold, may appear to be a malfunction, but it is not. (1993-94)

• **Information stickers/paperwork.** Replacement Vehicle Emission Control Information decals were sent to original owners because the original 1.8-liter engine valve clearance specs were wrong on vehicles built before mid December 1992. (1993)

• **Suspension noise.** The front stabilizer ball joint is prone to premature wear causing a rattling or popping noise while driving. (1992-93)

• **Doors.** The sliding door goes out of adjustment causing it to hit the rear of the front door. Installing shims will fix the problem. (1992)

• **Doors.** The sliding doors may be hard to open due to a variety of problems including a faulty latch connecting rod clip, rear door lock holder, or striker that is out of adjustment. (1992-95)

RECALL HISTORY

1992-93: Over time, abrading force on the lower edges of the chamber for the moving cable that controls driver's shoulder belt may be sufficient to allow cable to drop; could cause shoulder-belt anchorage to become stuck. **1992-96 w/AWD:** Lockup of transfer case can occur, due to insufficient lubrication.

1990-94 EAGLE TALON

1992 Eagle Talon

FOR Acceleration (except 1.8-liter) • Handling/roadholding • AWD traction (TSi AWD) • Antilock brakes (optional)

AGAINST Rear-seat room • Visibility • Cargo room • Engine noise • Road noise

EVALUATION

See the 1990-94 Mitsubishi Eclipse.

VALUE

See the 1990-94 Mitsubishi Eclipse.

SPECIFICATIONS

	2-door hatchback
Wheelbase, in.	97.2
Overall length, in.	172.4
Overall width, in.	66.7
Overall height, in.	51.4
Curb weight, lbs.	2549
Cargo volume, cu. ft.	25.7
Fuel capacity, gals.	15.8
Seating capacity	4
Front head room, in.	37.9
Max. front leg room, in.	43.9
Rear head room, in.	34.1
Min. rear leg room, in.	28.5

Powertrain layout: transverse front-engine/front- or all-wheel drive

ENGINES

	ohc I4	dohc I4	Turbocharged dohc I4
Size, liters/cu. in.	1.8/107	2.0/122	2.0/122
Horsepower	92	135	180-195
Torque (lbs./ft.)	105	125	203
EPA city/highway mpg			
5-speed OD manual	23/32	22/29	21/28
4-speed OD automatic	23/30	22/27	19/23
City/highway mpg (as tested)			
5-speed OD manual			20.4
4-speed OD automatic		22.6	

Built in USA

RETAIL PRICES

	GOOD	AVERAGE	POOR
1990 Talon	$1,400-1,900	$900-1,300	$100-200
1990 Talon TSi	1,700-2,300	1,100-1,600	200-400
1991 Talon	1,600-2,200	1,000-1,600	200-400
1991 Talon TSi	1,900-2,500	1,300-1,800	300-500
1992 Talon	1,900-2,600	1,300-1,900	300-600
1992 Talon TSi	2,200-2,900	1,600-2,200	500-800
1993 Talon	2,300-3,000	1,700-2,300	600-900
1993 Talon TSi	2,700-3,400	2,100-2,700	800-1,100
1994 Talon	2,800-3,500	2,100-2,800	800-1,200
1994 Talon TSi	3,500-4,200	2,800-3,500	1,100-1,600

AVERAGE REPLACEMENT COSTS

See the 1990-94 Mitsubishi Eclipse.

TROUBLE SPOTS

See the 1990-94 Mitsubishi Eclipse.

RECALL HISTORY

1990: Operation of factory-installed sunroof in "nonstandard" manner may cause hinge disengagement. **1990:** Diluted primer may have been used on windshield opening flanges of a few cars, which would not provide required retention of glass. **1990-91:** Front seatbelt release button can break and pieces can fall inside. **1990-94 w/AWD:** Lockup of transfer case can occur, due to insufficient lubrication.

1995-98 EAGLE TALON

1995 Eagle Talon ESi

FOR Acceleration (TSi, TSi AWD) • Steering/handling • AWD traction (AWD models) • Antilock brakes (optional)

AGAINST Acceleration (base/ESi auto.) • Rear-seat room • Road noise

EVALUATION

See the 1995-98 Mitsubishi Eclipse.

VALUE

See the 1995-98 Mitsubishi Eclipse.

SPECIFICATIONS

	2-door hatchback
Wheelbase, in.	98.8
Overall length, in.	172.2
Overall width, in.	68.3
Overall height, in.	51.0
Curb weight, lbs.	2789
Cargo volume, cu. ft.	16.6
Fuel capacity, gals.	15.9
Seating capacity	4
Front head room, in.	37.9
Max. front leg room, in.	43.3
Rear head room, in.	34.1
Min. rear leg room, in.	28.4

Powertrain layout: transverse front-engine/front- or all-wheel drive

ENGINES

	dohc I4	Turbocharged dohc I4
Size, liters/cu. in.	2.0/122	2.0/122
Horsepower	140	205-210
Torque (lbs./ft.)	130	214

EPA city/highway mpg

5-speed OD manual	22/32	20/27
4-speed OD automatic	20/30	23/31

City/highway mpg (as tested)

5-speed OD manual	23.6

Built in USA

RETAIL PRICES

	GOOD	AVERAGE	POOR
1995 Talon ESi	$4,300-5,000	$3,600-4,300	$1,500-1,900
1995 Talon TSi	5,000-5,800	4,300-5,000	2,000-2,400
1996 Talon/ESi	5,000-5,800	4,300-5,000	2,000-2,400
1996 Talon TSi	6,200-7,000	5,400-6,200	2,700-3,200
1997 Talon/ESi	6,200-7,000	5,500-6,200	2,800-3,300
1997 Talon TSi	7,800-8,800	6,800-7,800	3,500-4,200
1998 Talon/ESi	7,500-8,500	6,600-7,500	3,400-4,100
1998 Talon TSi	9,200-10,500	8,200-9,500	4,400-5,200

AVERAGE REPLACEMENT COSTS

See the 1995-98 Mitsubishi Eclipse.

TROUBLE SPOTS

See the 1995-98 Mitsubishi Eclipse.

RECALL HISTORY

1995-96: Rubber boots on lower ball joint may be damaged, allowing dirt and water intrusion, which can cause excessive wear and possible separation. **1995-96:** Tank gaskets for fuel pump and/or gauge unit could

have been incorrectly installed, allowing fuel or fumes to escape. **1995-98 w/AWD:** Lockup of transfer case can occur, due to insufficient lubrication. **1997:** On small number of cars, improperly welded head restraint support bracket on passenger side can break. **1998:** Dash panel pad can shift, interfering with throttle cable control.

1990-97 FORD AEROSTAR

1991 Ford Aerostar XL

FOR Trailer towing capability • Optional AWD traction • Passenger room • Cargo room (extended-length)

AGAINST Fuel economy • Entry/exit • Ride

EVALUATION The 3.0-liter engine produces adequate muscle, but the extra grunt of a 4.0-liter V6 is welcome, helping to haul around the hardware of the available 4-wheel-drive system. Don't expect great gas mileage with either engine: around 15 mpg in city/suburban driving, or low 20s on the highway. Poor traction can be a problem in rain or snow with the rear-drive Aerostar. Ride quality is another drawback, even with the Aerostar's long wheelbase. Suspensions are not very compliant, producing a rather harsh experience over bumps, though an Aerostar is stable and well-controlled. Cabins are roomy. Seven people can sit without squeezing, and the XLT and Eddie Bauer models contain plush and comfortable interior furnishings. Getting into the front seats requires a high step up. Cargo space is unimpressive in standard-size models, when all seats are in place.

VALUE Aerostar and the Chevrolet Astro/GMC Safari are better suited to heavy-duty work, such as hauling hefty payloads or towing trailers (up to 4800 pounds), than the league-leading front-drive Chrysler minivans.

SPECIFICATIONS

	3-door van	3-door van
Wheelbase, in.	118.9	118.9
Overall length, in.	174.9	190.3
Overall width, in.	71.7	72.0
Overall height, in.	72.2	72.3
Curb weight, lbs.	3374	3478
Cargo volume, cu. ft.	141.4	170.0
Fuel capacity, gals.	21.0	21.0
Seating capacity	7	7
Front head room, in.	39.5	39.5
Max. front leg room, in.	41.4	41.4
Rear head room, in.	38.8	38.3
Min. rear leg room, in.	39.5	40.5

Powertrain layout: longitudinal rear-engine/rear- or all-wheel drive

ENGINES

	ohv V6	ohv V6
Size, liters/cu. in.	3.0/182	4.0/244
Horsepower	135-145	152-155
Torque (lbs./ft.)	160-165	215-230

EPA city/highway mpg

4-speed OD automatic	17/23	17/23
5-speed OD automatic		16/22

City/highway mpg (as tested)

4-speed OD automatic	13.5	14.6

Built in USA

RETAIL PRICES

	GOOD	AVERAGE	POOR
1990 Aerostar regular	$1,400-2,100	$900-1,500	$100-300
1990 Aerostar extended	1,700-2,500	1,100-1,800	300-600
1991 Aerostar regular	1,700-2,400	1,100-1,800	300-600
1991 Aerostar extended	2,000-2,900	1,400-2,200	400-800
1992 Aerostar regular	2,000-2,900	1,400-2,200	400-800
1992 Aerostar extended	2,300-3,500	1,600-2,800	500-1,100

	GOOD	AVERAGE	POOR
1993 Aerostar regular	$2,300-3,200	$1,700-2,500	$500-1,000
1993 Aerostar extended	2,600-3,800	1,900-3,000	600-1,100
1994 Aerostar regular	2,800-4,000	2,200-3,300	700-1,200
1994 Aerostar extended	3,100-4,800	2,400-4,000	800-1,500
1995 Aerostar regular	3,600-4,600	2,900-3,900	1,000-1,500
1995 Aerostar extended	4,100-5,300	3,400-4,500	1,300-1,900
1996 Aerostar regular	4,700-5,700	4,000-5,000	1,800-2,400
1996 Aerostar extended	5,300-6,500	4,600-5,700	2,200-2,800
1997 Aerostar regular	6,000-7,000	5,200-6,100	2,400-3,000
1997 Aerostar extended	6,700-8,000	5,800-7,000	2,800-3,500

AVERAGE REPLACEMENT COSTS

A/C Compressor	$410	Clutch, Pressure Plate,	
Alternator	315	Bearing	450
Automatic Transmission or		Exhaust System	445
Transaxle	775	Radiator	360
Brakes	305	Shocks and/or Struts	255
Timing Chain or Belt	400	Universal Joints	160

TROUBLE SPOTS

• **Steering noise.** A clanging noise comes from the power steering cooler. A replacement will eliminate the noise. (1990-96)

• **Engine noise.** A hammering noise and erratic temperature gauge reading is caused by a weak water pump. A revised pump is available. (1994-97)

• **Air conditioner.** Air conditioner compressors are prone to failure if there is not enough A/C oil in the system. (1994-97)

• **Engine noise.** The dash panel rattles or buzzes due to interference between the trim on the front pillar and the side quarter glass. (1992-96)

• **Audio system.** Whining noises in the radio speakers is caused by the gas tank fuel pump. An electronic noise filter must be installed on the fuel pump. (1990-96)

RECALL HISTORY

1990: With quad captain's chairs, tilt-forward latch of right-hand seat in second row may release under severe frontal impact. **1990:** Inability to maintain pressure in master cylinder could increase brake-pedal travel. **1990 registered in specified states:** Upper portion of fuel tank can develop cracks due to extended exposure to high ambient temperatures; fuel vapor or leakage could occur. **1990-91:** Ignition switch could short-circuit, causing smoke and possible fire. **1990-91:** When automatic transmission is in Park position, pawl does not always engage park gear. **1992 w/AWD:** Powertrain bending resonance or transfer case output shaft bushing displacement can result in structural failure leading to fluid expulsion, driveshaft separation, or loss of vehicle drive. **1992-97:** During startup, arcing could potentially cause pitting, which, over time, might create short circuit that leads to overheating and potential fire. **1992-97 w/all-wheel drive:** Structural failure of transmission and/or transfer case can occur, resulting in fluid expulsion, driveshaft separation, or loss of drive. **1994-95:** Heat generation in wiring harness to fuel pump assembly can cause electrical short; vehicle could experience loss of power and become immobilized, fuel gauge may be erratic, and possible heat damage could lead to fire. **1995:** Underbody spare tire can contact brake lines, resulting in fracture of line. **1996:** When in secondary latched position, driver's door may not sustain specified load. **1996:** Certification label shows incorrect rear tire inflation pressure. **1997 w/3.0-liter engine:** Accelerator cable may be kinked during installation, causing the core wires to eventually fray with wire strands breaking one at a time.

1990-96 FORD BRONCO

FOR Trailer towing capability • Cargo room • 4WD traction

AGAINST Fuel economy • Ride/handling • Maneuverability

EVALUATION Even the 6-cylinder engine provides sufficient power for adequate acceleration, though we prefer V8s for their stronger performance. Best all-around choice is the 5.0-liter, providing satisfying acceleration and relaxed cruising ability, without using much more fuel than a six. Gas mileage with either V8 is poor. A light throttle foot is needed to keep from dipping into single-digit figures in city driving, and 20 mpg on the open road is about the best most drivers can hope for. Four-wheel antilock braking is safer than 2-wheel, maintaining better steering control in panic stops. It works when the

1991 Ford Bronco 4WD

vehicle is in 4WD, when conditions may make it most beneficial. Capping the rear portion of the Bronco's cabin with a fiberglass shell promoted squeaks, and offered much less isolation from road and wind noise than the full-metal body of a Blazer or Yukon. Space for six adults, ample cargo capacity, heavy-duty towing power, and rugged off-road capabilities are Bronco's main attractions. Minuses include unwieldy size (clumsy in urban driving), a jouncy ride, and poor fuel economy. Tall and bulky, a Bronco is difficult to maneuver through dense traffic. Occupants also face a rather tall step-up into the interior.

VALUE With only two side doors, a Bronco is less convenient for family use than a 4-door Grand Wagoneer or smaller Cherokee/Wagoneer.

SPECIFICATIONS

	2-door wagon
Wheelbase, in.	104.7
Overall length, in.	183.6
Overall width, in.	79.1
Overall height, in.	74.4
Curb weight, lbs.	4616
Cargo volume, cu. ft.	101.4
Fuel capacity, gals.	32.0
Seating capacity	6
Front head room, in.	41.2
Max. front leg room, in.	41.1
Rear head room, in.	39.3
Min. rear leg room, in.	37.7

Powertrain layout: longitudinal front-engine/rear- or 4-wheel drive

ENGINES

	ohv I6	ohv V8	ohv V8
Size, liters/cu. in.	4.9/300	5.0/302	5.8/351
Horsepower	145-150	185-205	200-210
Torque (lbs./ft.)	260-265	270-275	300-328
EPA city/highway mpg			
5-speed OD manual	14/17	14/17	
3-speed automatic	NA	NA	NA
City/highway mpg (as tested)			
4-speed OD automatic	14/18	13/17	12/16

Built in USA

RETAIL PRICES	GOOD	AVERAGE	POOR
1990 Bronco	$2,000-3,500	$1,400-2,800	$300-800
1991 Bronco	2,700-4,300	2,000-3,600	500-1,100
1992 Bronco	3,500-5,300	2,800-4,500	800-1,500
1993 Bronco	4,500-6,500	3,700-5,500	1,300-2,000
1994 Bronco	5,800-7,800	5,000-6,800	2,000-2,900
1995 Bronco	7,200-9,500	6,200-8,500	3,000-4,000
1996 Bronco	8,700-11,500	7,500-10,000	4,000-5,300

AVERAGE REPLACEMENT COSTS

A/C Compressor	$405	Clutch, Pressure Plate,	
Alternator	280	Bearing	580
Automatic Transmission or		Exhaust System	325
Transaxle	830	Radiator	415
Brakes	280	Shocks and/or Struts	240
Timing Chain or Belt	210	Universal Joints	280

TROUBLE SPOTS

• **Engine knock.** A knocking noise on vehicles with the 4.9-liter engine may be due to insufficient oil requiring a new filter mounting insert and antidrainback oil filter. (1990-95)

• **Engine knock.** A knocking sound on startup on 5.8-liter engines is likely due to a problem with the secondary air pump. (1995-96)

• **Automatic transmission.** Shifting problems occur when water seeps into the sensor that reports the position of the shift lever. A service kit is available to fix it. (1990-94)

• **Engine noise.** The drive belt on 5.0- and 5.8-liter engines chirps because of misalignment caused by the water pump pulley. (1990-94)

• **Brakes.** The parking brake pedal spontaneously drops to the floor because the adjustment pawl does not engage. (1992-94)

• **Brakes.** The transmission may be able to shift out of park without the brakes being applied if the center high-mount stoplamp is burned out or missing. (1994-95)

• **Audio system.** Whining noises in the radio speakers are caused by the gas tank fuel pump. An electronic noise filter must be installed on the fuel pump. (1990-96)

RECALL HISTORY

1990-91: Ignition switch could short-circuit, causing smoke and possible fire. **1992:** Door latch mechanism may malfunction in below-freezing temperatures. **1992-94 w/manual shift:** Parking brake pawl can slip; brake might not hold. **1993 w/Touch Drive:** Transfer case can slip out of 4x4 high-gear position during coasting in forward gears or with power applied in reverse.

1995-00 FORD CONTOUR

1995 Ford Contour

FOR Acceleration (V6) • Steering/handling • Automatic transmission performance • Optional antilock brakes and traction control

AGAINST Engine noise (4-cylinder) • Rear-seat room • Radio controls

EVALUATION Smooth, responsive, and lively in acceleration, the 170-horsepower V6 is more than adequate for all ordinary driving situations. During testing, a V6 Contour accelerated to 60 mph in 9.3 seconds. The 190-horsepower SVT engine is even more powerful, but you really have to work the transmission to get the extra power. By contrast, the noisy 4-cylinder engine feels sluggish when going uphill and requires a heavy throttle foot for brisk acceleration. A V6 Contour with automatic averaged 21.7 mpg. Under similar conditions, the 4-cylinder with automatic did only a little better: 23 mpg, to be exact. Road noise has been prominent on all models. Precise steering, sporty handling, and a firm ride make a Contour feel more German than American. Most road-testers praised the sporty SE, in particular, for its fun-to-drive qualities, though a few were less enthusiastic about its ride quality. Front leg room is ample, but back-seat space for adults is barely adequate in 1995 Contours. That shortage of space was slightly improved in '96 models, but remains a drawback. Head room is generous in front and adequate in back. The modern, attractive dashboard is well-designed, but the stereo has too many small buttons that are difficult to decipher. Large gauges are easy to read. The climate system is controlled by three rotary dials that are clearly labeled and easy to use.

VALUE Ford took a huge step forward in performance, refinement, and overall execution with its compact sedan. All told, Contour is a formidable rival to Japanese compacts and to the Chrysler Cirrus and Dodge Stratus.

SPECIFICATIONS

	4-door sedan
Wheelbase, in.	106.5
Overall length, in.	183.9
Overall width, in.	69.1
Overall height, in.	54.5
Curb weight, lbs.	2769
Cargo volume, cu. ft.	13.9
Fuel capacity, gals.	14.5
	4-door sedan
Seating capacity	5
Front head room, in.	39.0
Max. front leg room, in.	42.4
Rear head room, in.	36.7
Min. rear leg room, in.	34.3

Powertrain layout: transverse front-engine/front-wheel drive

ENGINES

	dohc I4	dohc V6	dohc V6
Size, liters/cu. in.	2.0/121	2.5/155	2.5/155
Horsepower	125	170	195
Torque (lbs./ft.)	130	165	165
EPA city/highway mpg			
5-speed OD manual	24/34	21/31	20/29
4-speed OD automatic	23/32	21/30	
City/highway mpg (as tested)			
5-speed OD manual			24.3
4-speed OD automatic	21.7	23.0	

Built in USA, Mexico

RETAIL PRICES

	GOOD	AVERAGE	POOR
1995 Contour	$3,000-3,600	$2,400-3,000	$700-1,100
1995 Contour SE	3,700-4,400	3,000-3,700	1,100-1,500
1996 Contour	3,800-4,500	3,200-3,800	1,200-1,600
1996 Contour SE	4,600-5,300	3,900-4,600	1,600-2,100
1997 Contour	4,800-5,600	4,200-4,900	1,800-2,300
1997 Contour SE	5,800-6,500	5,000-5,700	2,200-2,700
1998 Contour	6,000-7,000	5,200-6,200	2,400-3,000
1998 Contour SE	6,500-7,500	5,700-6,700	2,800-3,300
1998 Contour SVT	9,500-10,500	8,500-9,500	4,800-5,500
1999 Contour	7,200-8,200	6,300-7,200	3,200-3,700
1999 Contour SE	7,700-8,700	6,800-7,700	3,500-4,100
1999 Contour SVT	11,000-12,500	10,000-11,200	6,000-6,800
2000 Contour	8,500-9,500	7,500-8,500	4,000-4,600
2000 Contour SVT	12,500-14,000	11,500-12,500	7,000-7,800

AVERAGE REPLACEMENT COSTS

A/C Compressor	$360	Clutch, Pressure Plate, Bearing	750
Alternator	455	Constant Velocity Joints	465
Automatic Transmission or Transaxle	800	Radiator	345
Brakes	290	Shocks and/or Struts	700
Shocks and/or Struts	345	Timing Chain or Belt	175

TROUBLE SPOTS

• **Dashboard lights.** A slipping drive belt causes a lack of power steering and the charge warning light to glow. A new belt, idler pulley, and a splash kit are needed. (1995-97)

• **Transmission noise.** Gear clash going into third on the manual transmission can be remedied by a rebuilt input gear shaft and a new shift fork. (1995-97)

• **Brakes.** Ice in the parking brake cables will not allow the parking brake to release or release fully. (1995-97)

• **Steering problems.** It the steering wheel vibrates while idling with the transmission engaged and the A/C running, the steering mass damper, airbag module, and radiator mounts must be replaced. (1995-97)

• **Engine misfire.** Lack of acceleration in below 32°F on the 2.5-liter engine is often due to ice on the throttle plate. A revised engine computer prevents the problem. (1995)

• **Automatic transmission.** The transmission may go into limp-in mode due to a faulty manual lever position sensor. (1995)

RECALL HISTORY

1995: If right rear door window breaks, glass fragments will exceed allowable size. **1995:** Fuel tank filler reinforcement can leak. **1995:** Metal shield on plastic fuel filler pipe can develop static charge during refueling; could serve as ignition source. **1995:** Passenger airbag's inflator body is cracked and may not inflate properly. **1995:** Front seatbelt anchor tabs may be cracked. **1995-96 w/traction control:** Throttle cables were damaged during assembly, leading to fraying or separation; could prevent engine from returning to idle. **1995-96 w/V6:** Tightening of the engine cooling fan motor bearings can result in increased motor torque and higher than normal motor current and accompanying high motor temperatures. **1995-98:** Automatic-transmission control can be damaged if subjected to certain interior cleaning products; gear indicator can deteriorate and incorrectly indicate actual gear position. **1996:** Fuel filler pipe vent hose may have less than intended level of ozone resistance, which could result in brittleness and cracking. **1996-97 w/bi-fuel engine:** If natural-gas fuel line is damaged in a collison, gas leakage could occur. **1996-98 w/o ABS:** Pressure reducing valve in rear brakes may be subject to corrosion, which could result in malfunction when operated in areas that use salt compounds for de-icing or dust control. **1996-98:** Overheating at headlamp and wiring-harness terminals could result in open circuit for instrument lights, parking lamps, and taillamps. **1996-98:** An open circuit in the wiring harness could lead to electrical arcing that could melt the connector housing material, increasing the potential for a fire. **1998:** Airbag sensor wiring insulation can become brittle and crack over time; could cause airbag warning light to illuminate and disable airbag system. **1998:** Text and/or graphics for headlamp aiming instructions, provided in owner guides, are not sufficiently clear. **1998:** Front coil springs may fracture as a result of corrosion in high corrosion environments. **1998:** Accelerator cable may have burr that could fray the core wire; cable could stick, bind, or cause high engine rpm. **1999 w/automatic transmission:** Ignition key can be rotated to "Lock" position and removed, without shift lever being in "Park" position. **2000:** Improper label was installed on some cars, with incorrect instructions for activation of childproof safety locks.

1992-01 FORD CROWN VICTORIA

1992 Ford Crown Victoria

FOR   Acceleration • Passenger and cargo room • Trailer towing capability • Optional antilock brakes

AGAINST   Fuel economy • Steering feel • Radio controls (early models)

EVALUATION   The Crown Vic's extra-smooth V8 sets the heavy sedan into motion swiftly enough, and past highway traffic without delay. Midrange response is more sluggish, however, worsened by the fact that the transmission seems reluctant to downshift. Gas mileage is nothing to boast about. One early test LX Crown Victoria averaged an impressive 19.9 mpg. Later, an LX yielded only 15.3 mpg. Handling and stability are fine for a big sedan. The base suspension absorbs bumps nicely, yet doesn't wallow or float past pavement swells. The handling/performance option delivers a jittery ride, aggravated by too-light, numb power steering that easily turns twitchy. Traction can be a problem in the snow belt. You're likely to hear virtually no road, wind, or engine noise. Expansive seating for six is marred only by a lack of lateral support in the driver's seat. Controls are grouped logically and work smoothly, though tiny horn buttons are an annoyance. Visibility is fine and the trunk ranks as close to cavernous, but a large well in the center of the floor could induce a little back strain when loading heavy objects.

VALUE   Vastly more impressive than the prior generation, this Crown Vic mixes traditional values with contemporary virtues—a good choice if you like rear drive in a body-on-frame vehicle. Crown Vic and Mercury's Grand Marquis are the last of their kind.

SPECIFICATIONS

	4-door sedan
Wheelbase, in.	114.4
Overall length, in.	212.0
Overall width, in.	77.8
Overall height, in.	56.8
Curb weight, lbs.	3780
Cargo volume, cu. ft.	20.6
Fuel capacity, gals.	20.0
Seating capacity	6
Front head room, in.	39.4
Max. front leg room, in.	42.5
Rear head room, in.	38.0
Min. rear leg room, in.	39.6

Powertrain layout: longitudinal front-engine/rear-wheel drive

ENGINES

	ohv V8
Size, liters/cu. in.	4.6/281
Horsepower	190-235
Torque (lbs./ft.)	260-285

EPA city/highway mpg
4-speed OD automatic	17/25

City/highway mpg (as tested)
4-speed OD automatic	15.3

Built in Canada

RETAIL PRICES

	GOOD	AVERAGE	POOR
1992 Crown Victoria	$2,300-3,100	$1,700-2,400	$300-700
1993 Crown Victoria	2,800-3,600	2,200-2,900	600-1,000
1994 Crown Victoria	3,500-4,200	2,800-3,500	1,000-1,400
1995 Crown Victoria	4,500-5,300	3,800-4,500	1,500-1,900
1996 Crown Victoria	6,000-7,000	5,200-6,200	2,200-2,700
1997 Crown Victoria	7,500-8,500	6,600-7,500	3,200-3,700
1998 Crown Victoria	9,200-10,500	8,200-9,500	4,200-4,900
1999 Crown Victoria	11,000-12,500	10,000-11,300	5,400-6,400
2000 Crown Victoria	13,000-14,500	12,000-13,200	7,000-8,000
2001 Crown Victoria	15,000-17,000	13,500-15,500	—

AVERAGE REPLACEMENT COSTS

A/C Compressor	$380	Exhaust System	353
Alternator	375	Radiator	380
Automatic Transmission or Transaxle	870	Shocks and/or Struts	505
		Timing Chain or Belt	330
Brakes	275	Universal Joints	125

TROUBLE SPOTS

• **Vehicle noise.** A broken gusset or weld separation at the frame crossmember causes a rattle from the rear of the car. (1992)

• **Vehicle noise.** A chattering noise that can be felt, and sometimes heard, coming from the rear during tight turns after highway driving is caused by a lack of friction modifier or over-shimming of the clutch packs in the Traction-Lok (limited-slip) differential. (1992-96)

• **Air springs.** Air springs are prone to leaks caused by the bag rubbing against the axle or control arm. (1992-96)

• **Hard starting.** If the engine does not start or cranks for a long time then stalls, the idle air control valve may be sticking. (1996)

• **Automatic transmission.** The automatic transmission is notorious for shuddering or vibrating under light acceleration or when shifting between third and fourth gear. It requires that the transmission fluid (including fluid in the torque converter) be changed. (1992-94)

• **Hard starting.** The connector at the starter solenoid tends to corrode resulting in a "no crank" condition. (1992-94)

• **Engine noise.** The drive belt tensioner pulley or idler pulley bearings are apt to make a squealing noise when the engine is started in cold weather. (1993-96)

• **Oil leak.** The oil filter balloons and leaks because the oil pump relief valve sticks. Higher than recommended viscosity oils cause wear to the valve bore. (1992-94)

• **Automatic transmission.** The transmission may slip and the engine may flare when the transmission shifts into fourth gear, which can be traced to a bad TR/MLP sensor. (1992-95)

RECALL HISTORY

1992: "Antilock" brake warning lights in small number of cars will not actuate. **1992-93:** Speed control deactivation switch can develop a short, which could potentially result in fire even if engine is not running. **1992-99 police/fleet/natural gas:** Bearing within lower ball joint can weaken slowly during use and eventually crack; could result in separation, allowing control arm to drop to the ground. **1993-94 w/police option:** Upper control arm bolts can loosen and fracture, causing substantial negative camber and steering pull; fracture at both holes could result in loss of control. **1994:** Nuts and bolts that attach rear brake adapter to axle flange can loosen and eventually separate. **1995:** On some cars, passenger airbag's inflator body is cracked and may not inflate properly; also, igniter end cap can separate. **1995:** Seal material between fuel filler pipe and tank may not have been fully cured, which could allow fuel to leak. **1995:** In the event of short-circuit or overload, both headlamps can go out without warning. **1995:** Rivet heads holding rear outboard seatbelt D-rings may fracture under load, reducing belt's restraining capability. **1995-96 fleet cars only:** Corrosion of inadequately lubricated Pitman arms can cause abnormal wear of joint, resulting in separation. **1996:** Driver's door, when closed only to secondary latched position, may not sustain specified load. **1996-00:** Replacement seatbelts made by TRW and sold by Ford may not restrain occupant in a collision. **1998-00:** Incorrect jacking instructions may cause personal injury. **2000:** During high-load conditions (ice, snow, or other debris), windshield wipers could become inoperative with no advance wiring. **2000:** Loose module on a few cars could result in delayed airbag deployment. **2000:** Left rear seatbelt retractor bolts were incorrectly tightened on a few cars. **2001:** A restraint control module (RCM) or a side or front crash sensor may have been assembled with one or more of the screws that mount the circuit board in the housing missing. **2001:** Driver's and/or outboard front passenger's seatbelt buckle may not fully latch. In the event of a crash, the restraint system may not provide adequate occupant protection.

1991-96 FORD ESCORT

1992 Ford Escort 4-door sdan

FOR Fuel economy • Ride • Acceleration (GT, LX-E) • Antilock brakes (optional)

AGAINST Engine noise • Road noise • Rear-seat room

EVALUATION In hard acceleration, either engine causes the automatic transmission to jolt between gears. With automatic, there's just not enough low-end power for quick getaways. Acceleration to 60 mph took a leisurely 12.5 seconds. Though more powerful, the GT's engine gets lazy below 3500 rpm; but it runs smoother than the 1.9-liter. Both engines vibrate at idle, and are noisy while cruising. Gas mileage is great. An early automatic LX averaged 25.9 mpg. A later edition did better yet, averaging 26.8 mpg even while commuting. Stable and well-controlled at highway speeds, the Escort's suspension is surprisingly absorbent on harsher pavement. A GT handles crisply, courtesy of its sport suspension and 15-inch tires. The same cannot be said of Pony and LX hatchbacks, whose 13-inch rubber easily loses grip in brisk cornering. Standard 4-wheel disc brakes on the GT bring the Escort to a swift, sure stop. Wind and road noise are noticeable, especially at highway speeds. Visibility is good from the Escort's airy cabin. Head room isn't bad for a subcompact, unless it has the optional sunroof. Leg room is adequate, but three in back is a squeeze. The cargo area of hatchbacks and wagons is quite narrow between wheelwells, but wider at the rear. Controls are logically positioned, simply marked, operating with smooth precision that belies the car's modest roots.

VALUE With Escort you get plenty of practical value. Though the Escort can't match a Honda Civic or Toyota Corolla for refinement, it does give the impression of true quality in the subcompact field.

SPECIFICATIONS

	2-door hatchback	4-door hatchback	4-door sedan	4-door wagon
Wheelbase, in.	98.4	98.4	98.4	98.4
Overall length, in.	170.0	170.0	170.9	171.3
Overall width, in.	66.7	66.7	66.7	66.7
Overall height, in.	52.5	52.5	52.7	53.6
Curb weight, lbs.	2355	2385	2404	2451
Cargo volume, cu. ft.	35.2	36.0	12.1	66.9
Fuel capacity, gals.	11.9	11.9	11.9	11.9
Seating capacity	5	5	5	5

	2-door hatchback	4-door hatchback	4-door sedan	4-door wagon
Front head room, in.	38.4	38.4	38.4	38.4
Max. front leg room, in.	41.7	41.7	41.7	41.7
Rear head room, in.	37.6	37.6	37.4	38.5
Min. rear leg room, in.	34.6	34.6	34.5	34.6

Powertrain layout: transverse front-engine/front-wheel drive

ENGINES

	ohc I4	dohc I4
Size, liters/cu. in.	1.9/114	1.8/109
Horsepower	88	127
Torque (lbs./ft.)	108	114

EPA city/highway mpg

	ohc I4	dohc I4
5-speed OD manual	31/38	25/31
4-speed OD automatic	26/34	23/29

City/highway mpg (as tested)

	ohc I4	dohc I4
5-speed OD manual		21.6
4-speed OD automatic	25.9	

Built in USA, Mexico

RETAIL PRICES

	GOOD	AVERAGE	POOR
1991 Escort	$1,100-1,600	$600-1,000	$100-200
1991 Escort GT	1,400-1,900	800-1,300	100-300
1992 Escort	1,300-2,000	700-1,400	100-300
1992 Escort GT	1,800-2,400	1,200-1,800	300-400
1993 Escort	1,600-2,400	1,000-1,800	200-400
1993 Escort GT	2,200-2,800	1,600-2,200	400-600
1994 Escort	1,900-2,700	1,300-2,100	400-600
1994 Escort GT	2,500-3,200	1,800-2,500	600-800
1995 Escort	2,400-3,100	1,800-2,400	600-800
1995 Escort GT	3,100-3,800	2,500-3,100	800-1,200
1996 Escort	3,000-3,800	2,400-3,100	800-1,200
1996 Escort GT	3,800-4,500	3,100-3,800	1,200-1,500

AVERAGE REPLACEMENT COSTS

A/C Compressor	$470	Clutch, Pressure Plate, Bearing	275
Alternator	370	Constant Velocity Joints	585
Automatic Transmission or Transaxle	1,160	Exhaust System	375
Brakes	260	Radiator	382
Shocks and/or Struts	620	Timing Chain or Belt	145

TROUBLE SPOTS

• **Vehicle noise.** A grinding noise while turning is most likely due to dirt accumulating in the top strut-mount bushing. (1991-92)

• **Engine knock.** Carbon build-up on the pistons causes a knocking noise. Sometimes solved by cleaning the carbon from the pistons using carburetor cleaner, often pistons must be replaced with redesigned ones. (1991-93)

• **Transmission noise.** If a whine comes from the transmission during coast-down, it is probably because the idler gear teeth were not machined properly. (1995-96)

• **Hard starting.** If the engine does not start or cranks for a long time then stalls, the idle air control valve may be sticking. (1995-96)

• **Horn.** Sometimes the horn will not work due to a poor ground circuit in the steering column. (1995-96)

• **Blower motor.** Squeaking or chirping blower motors are the result of defective brush holders. (1993-94)

• **Brakes.** There is a redesigned brake master cylinder and brake booster available that provides better pedal feel and travel. (1993-95)

• **Fuel pump.** Under general campaign number 94B55, Ford will install a fused jumper harness in the fuel pump electrical circuit to prevent erratic fuel gauge readings, stalling, or wiring damage. (1991-94)

• **Brake noise.** Wear spots and ridges on the front brake caliper sleeves cause a knocking noise when gently applying the brakes. (1991-96)

RECALL HISTORY

1991: Interference may occur between bolt that secures fuel line shield to lower dash and gas pedal, causing pedal to stick wide open. **1991:** Pins securing ignition lock can separate or move out of position; cylinder may disengage, causing steering column to lock up. **1991-92:** On some cars, fatigue crack can develop in solder joint between fuel return tube and fuel pump sending unit; fuel vapor could escape when tank is full, and small amount may leak. **1991-93:** On small number of front suspension units made by Dana Corp., the offset toe adjusting pin may fracture under certain conditions, resulting in loss of control. **1993:** Driver's seat in some cars may not engage fully in its track in positions near midpoint; could move in event of crash. **1994-95:** On a few cars, driver-side airbag may deploy improperly and expel hot gases. **1995:** Two bolts that attach passenger-side airbag may be missing; in frontal impact, the airbag could fail to restrain the passenger. **1995 cars in certain states:** Cracks can develop in plastic fuel tank, resulting in leakage.

1997-01 FORD ESCORT/ZX2

1998 Ford Escort LX 4-door sedan

FOR Fuel economy • Optional antilock brakes • Price

AGAINST Rear-seat room • Road noise (ZX2) • Wind noise (ZX2)

EVALUATION Because the new Escort weighs about 120 pounds more than its predecessor, the increase of 22 horsepower does not result in inspiring performance. Acceleration is merely adequate, as before, but the new engine is smoother and quieter. The automatic transmission feels smoother with the new engine, and also downshifts faster for passing and merging. We averaged 23.9 mpg in an LX sedan with automatic, but most of that trial consisted of urban driving. On the highway, we'd expect well over 30 mpg. Manual-transmission Escorts feel livelier, as expected, and also get better gas mileage than cars with automatic. A well-tuned suspension helps the Escort absorb bumps better than most subcompacts. Handling on sedans and wagons is competent rather than sporting, though steering feels natural in turns and its on-center sense contributes to stable cruising. Visibility is generally good, but the sedan's rear roof pillars are thick enough to block the driver's over-the-shoulder view. Road and wind noise are noticeable on the highway, but sedans and wagons aren't much noisier than a Honda Civic. The ZX2 coupe suffers from a lot more road and wind sound—enough to cause annoyance. Partly due to the extra punch of its stronger engine, the ZX2 drives in a sporty manner. Here too, manual shift is quicker, but the 5-speed gets the engine turning at a buzzy 3000 rpm when traveling at 65 mph. We averaged an impressive 29 mpg with an automatic ZX2, which is at home on twisting roads, where grip and stability have proved to be good. Body roll in the ZX2 is well-controlled, too. Harder driving in a manual-shift ZX2 averaged 24.5 mpg. Front head room is generous, even for tall occupants. Leg space is adequate for adults. Rear knee room is tight, as is head room in the coupe. The new dashboard puts gauges directly ahead of the driver. Audio and climate controls sit in an oval "integrated control panel." Interior storage is adequate, consisting of small door map pockets, a console with cupholders, and a small glovebox. Cargo space also ranks as adequate, and the wagon qualifies as a versatile hauler. The rear seatback folds for additional space, but does not lie totally flat.

VALUE Sensible design, competent road manners, and reasonable prices put both Escort and Tracer high on our list of desirable subcompacts, but we're less impressed by the noisier ZX2 coupe.

SPECIFICATIONS

	2-door coupe	4-door sedan	4-door wagon
Wheelbase, in.	98.4	98.4	98.4
Overall length, in.	175.2	174.7	172.7
Overall width, in.	67.4	67.0	67.0
Overall height, in.	52.3	53.3	53.9
Curb weight, lbs.	2478	2468	2531
Cargo volume, cu. ft.	11.8	12.8	63.4
Fuel capacity, gals.	12.8	12.8	12.8
Seating capacity	5	5	5
Front head room, in.	38.0	39.0	38.7
Max. front leg room, in.	42.5	42.5	42.5
Rear head room, in.	35.1	36.7	39.1
Min. rear leg room, in.	33.4	34.0	34.0

Powertrain layout: transverse front-engine/front-wheel drive

ENGINES

	ohc I4	dohc I4
Size, liters/cu. in.	2.0/121	2.0/121
Horsepower	110	130
Torque (lbs./ft.)	125	127
EPA city/highway mpg		
5-speed OD manual	28/37	26/33
4-speed OD automatic	26/34	25/33
City/highway mpg (as tested)		
5-speed OD manual		24.5
4-speed OD automatic	23.9	29.0

Built in USA, Mexico

RETAIL PRICES

	GOOD	AVERAGE	POOR
1997 Escort sedan	$4,000-4,700	$3,400-4,000	$1,400-1,800
1997 Escort wagon	4,500-5,200	3,800-4,500	1,700-2,100
1998 Escort sedan	5,000-5,800	4,300-5,000	2,000-2,400
1998 Escort ZX2	5,500-6,300	4,800-5,600	2,300-2,800
1998 Escort wagon	5,600-6,400	4,900-5,600	2,400-2,800
1999 Escort sedan	6,000-6,800	5,300-6,000	2,600-3,100
1999 Escort ZX2	6,600-7,300	5,900-6,500	3,000-3,500
1999 Escort wagon	6,800-7,700	6,000-6,900	3,100-3,700
2000 Escort sedan	7,200-8,000	6,300-7,000	3,200-3,700
2000 Escort ZX2	7,600-8,400	6,700-7,300	3,500-3,900
2001 Escort sedan	8,500-9,500	7,500-8,500	—
2001 Escort ZX2	9,000-10,000	8,000-9,000	—

AVERAGE REPLACEMENT COSTS

A/C Compressor	$665	Clutch, Pressure Plate, Bearing	665
Alternator	475	Constant Velocity Joints	540
Automatic Transmission or Transaxle	1,175	Exhaust System	430
Brakes	320	Radiator	430
Shocks and/or Struts	770	Timing Chain or Belt	805

TROUBLE SPOTS

• **Audio system.** Electrical noise caused by the electric fuel pump in the tank can cause a buzzing noise when the AM band of the radio is selected. (1997-98)

• **Hard starting.** If the engine will not start or the cooling fan does not shut off in cold weather. The integrated relay control module needs to be replaced. (1997-98)

• **Oil leak.** In cold weather, moisture can freeze in the PCV system. When the engine is started, the dipstick pops out of its tube and oil leaks out. (1997-98)

• **Vehicle noise.** The blower motor may chirp or squeak at low speeds. This can be corrected with a replacement motor. (1997)

• **Doors.** The dome light may come on while driving or fail to come on when the door is opened. (1997-98)

• **Fuel gauge.** The gas gauge may have an error of about ⅛ tank, may drop from full too fast, and the tank may take fuel slowly due to a problem with the fuel sending unit or slosh module. (1998)

• **Automatic transmission.** The transmission may not engage right away when the car has been parked overnight because the torque converter drains down. (1997)

RECALL HISTORY

1999 w/S/R option: Manual-transmission shift pattern for some cars is not displayed.

1997-01 FORD EXPEDITION

FOR Acceleration (5.4-liter) • Passenger and cargo room • Visibility • Trailer towing capability

AGAINST Fuel economy • Entry/exit (4WD)

EVALUATION On the road Expedition does not seem as large as the rival Tahoe and Yukon, partly because Expedition's deep side

1997 Ford Expedition

and rear windows—and sloping hood—provide good visibility to all directions. Not really agile, but easy enough to drive for a vehicle of this size, it corners with moderate body lean so long as speeds are modest. With 2WD, the ride is stable, well-controlled and relatively soft—less trucklike than some rival SUVs. Most bumps are easily absorbed, and the Expedition delivers an impressively solid feel. Ride quality is a little stiffer and more jiggly in a 4WD model, but not jarring. Any model with the 5.4-liter V8 will accelerate smartly from a standstill, passing quickly and safely at highway speeds. A 2WD version with the smaller engine performs nearly as well off-the-line, but passing power falls short of snappy. The additional weight of 4WD puts a noticeable burden on the 4.6-liter V8. Both engines are smooth and fairly quiet, but the 5.4-liter V8 is the better choice for towing. As for economy, a 2WD Eddie Bauer edition got only 14.3 mpg in a mix of urban commuting and highway cruising. A 4WD Expedition with the 5.4-liter engine managed a measly 12 mpg. In the cavernous, well-designed interior, space is ample for front and middle rows, which have reclining seatbacks. Front shoulder room is expansive, and three adults can ride in back in genuine comfort. A nearly flat floor means no one has to straddle a hump. The optional third seat is more for children than adults, however. Behind the third seat (if so equipped), the cargo area amounts to little more than a foot-long trench. Without that seat, cargo space is long and wide. Entry/exit is easy on 2WD models, with wide doorways and a moderate step up to the interior. 4WD versions sit much higher off the ground, so you have to hoist yourself up with the aid of an inside grab handle.

VALUE Competitively priced when new, the impressive Expedition has also been a popular model on the used-vehicle market. All told, it's a good alternative to GM's SUVs—more modern and refined, and well worth a close look. In fact, Expedition ranks as a trend-setter.

SPECIFICATIONS

	4-door wagon
Wheelbase, in.	119.1
Overall length, in.	204.6
Overall width, in.	78.6
Overall height, in.	76.6
Curb weight, lbs.	4850
Cargo volume, cu. ft.	118.3
Fuel capacity, gals.	26.0
Seating capacity	5[1]
Front head room, in.	39.8
Max. front leg room, in.	40.9
Rear head room, in.	39.8
Min. rear leg room, in.	38.9

1. Up to 9 passengers with optional seats.

Powertrain layout: longitudinal front-engine/rear- or 4-wheel drive

ENGINES

	ohc V8	ohc V8
Size, liters/cu. in.	4.6/281	5.4/330
Horsepower	215-240	230-260
Torque (lbs./ft.)	290-293	325-345
EPA city/highway mpg		
4-speed OD automatic	14/18	13/17
City/highway mpg (as tested)		
4-speed OD automatic	14.3	12.0

Built in USA

RETAIL PRICES

	GOOD	AVERAGE	POOR
1997 Expedition XLT	$12,000-14,000	$11,000-13,000	$7,000-8,500
1997 Eddie Bauer	13,500-15,500	12,300-14,000	8,000-9,200
1998 Expedition XLT	14,500-16,500	13,000-15,000	9,000-10,500
1998 Eddie Bauer	16,500-18,500	15,000-17,000	10,500-12,000
1999 Expedition XLT	$16,500-18,800	$15,000-17,300	$10,500-12,000
1999 Eddie Bauer	19,000-21,500	17,500-20,000	12,500-14,300
2000 Expedition XLT	19,000-21,000	17,500-19,500	12,500-14,000
2000 Eddie Bauer	22,000-24,500	20,500-23,000	15,000-17,000
2001 Expedition XLT	21,500-23,500	20,000-22,000	—
2001 Eddie Bauer	24,500-27,000	23,000-25,500	—

AVERAGE REPLACEMENT COSTS

A/C Compressor	$545	Radiator	430
Automatic transmission	930	Shocks and/or Struts	445
Alternator	515	Timing Chain or Belt	380
Brakes	320	Universal Joints	260
Exhaust System	485		

TROUBLE SPOTS

• **Climate control.** Cold air may come out of the heater vents at the floor due to a door in the duct not sealing properly. (1997)

• **Audio system.** Electrical noise caused by the electric fuel pump in the tank can cause a buzzing noise when the AM band of the radio is selected. (1997-98)

• **Automatic transmission.** If water gets into the transfer case, the mode switch can be shorted out making it impossible to select a different range. (1997)

• **Engine misfire.** The engine may run rough or idle roughly if condensation from the air conditioning drips onto the oxygen sensor. (1997-98)

• **Seat.** The front leather seats may wear out quickly because the foam sticks to the leather. New seat covers should be installed. (1997-98)

• **Automatic transmission.** Transmission fluid can leak from the transmission into the transfer case. The low transmission fluid level causes shifting and engagement problems. (1997)

• **Dashboard lights.** Water in the spark plug wells may cause the ignition spark to jump to ground causing a misfire and illuminating the check engine light. (1997)

RECALL HISTORY

1997: Rear axle track bar bracket can separate from frame due to missing welds or inadequate weld penetration; axle can move laterally until tires contact frame or wheelhouse. **1997-98:** Main battery cable could short circuit, causing loss of electrical supply, or fire. **1997-98:** Due to insufficient clamp load, lug nuts could loosen and studs could fatigue and fail, creating potential for wheel to separate. **1997-98:** Certain off-lease vehicles, Canadian in origin but sold in the U.S., have daytime running lights that do not meet U.S. specifications. **1997-00:** Bolts that attach trailer hitch assembly to frame could lose their clamp load; hitch could then separate from vehicle. **1999:** Fuel line assemblies on some vehicles may have been damaged by supplier during manufacture, and could leak. **1999:** Retainer clip that holds master cylinder pushrod to brake pedal arm may be missing or partially installed, causing increased stopping distances. **1999:** Contact area between wheel and hug can deform, resulting in loss of lug nut torque that can cause vibration or separation of wheel/tire from vehicle. **1999 w/4WD and 17-inch chrome steel wheels:** Due to insufficient wheel contact area with hub, loss of lug nut torque can cause vibration or separation of wheel. **2000-01:** Some of the owner's manuals for these vehicles are missing instructions for properly attaching a child restraint system. **2000-01:** A switch located in the plastic cover of the wiper motor gear case could malfunction and overheat, potentially resulting in loss of wiper function or fire. **2001:** Driver's and/or outboard front passenger's seatbelt buckle may not fully latch. In the event of a crash, the restraint system may not provide adequate occupant protection.

1991-01 FORD EXPLORER/ SPORT TRAC/SPORT

FOR Acceleration (V8) • Passenger and cargo room • 4WD traction • Antilock brakes (optional later models) • Visibility

AGAINST Fuel economy • Engine noise (ohv V6) • Wind noise

EVALUATION Explorers are easy to enter and depart from, due to a relatively low step-in height. Head room is generous all around. Rear leg space is adequate. There's plenty of space for three abreast in the back of a 4-door. Split front seat backs fold flat to create a long

1996 Ford Explorer V8 4-door wagon

load floor that suffers little intrusion from the rear wheels. There's no spare tire in the way of cargo, either. Controls are simple, analog gauges clearly legible; visibility fine through deep side and rear windows. Acceleration is adequate from the ohv V6 engine, but it is sluggish and rough when first stomping the pedal and averaged a low 15.9 mpg. Eight-cylinder engines provide outstanding acceleration, and equally depressing fuel economy. The new ohc V6 is probably the best option. It offers ample acceleration and averaged 20.4 mpg. Though smoother and quieter than the ohv unit, the ohc V6 engine feels a little rough and sounds gruff at low speeds. The automatic transmission responds neatly, and shifts nearly flawlessly— quick and unobtrusive. The relatively long, wide stance gives either Explorer reasonable stability in turns, though you get a choppy ride from the shorter-wheelbase 3-door. Steering precisely, cornering confidently, an Explorer suffers less body lean than Chevrolet's Blazer.

VALUE Not cheap, an Explorer offers the utility of a minivan and the hauling power of a truck. If you're a likely prospect for a smaller sport-utility, best not to buy until you've test-driven Ford's compact. But try a Chevy Blazer and Jeep Grand Cherokee, too. We do like the added versatility of the Sport Trac's crew cab design.

SPECIFICATIONS

	2-door wagon	4-door wagon	crew cab
Wheelbase, in.	101.7	111.5	125.9
Overall length, in.	178.6	188.5	205.9
Overall width, in.	68.2	70.2	71.8
Overall height, in.	67.5	67.3	70.1
Curb weight, lbs.	3690	3915	4323
Cargo volume, cu. ft.	69.4	81.6	—
Fuel capacity, gals.	17.5	21.0	20.5
Seating capacity	4	6	5
Front head room, in.	39.8	39.8	39.4
Max. front leg room, in.	42.4	42.4	42.4
Rear head room, in.	39.1	39.3	38.9
Min. rear leg room, in.	36.6	37.7	37.8

Powertrain layout: longitudinal front-engine/rear- or 4-wheel drive

ENGINES

	ohv V6	ohc V6	ohv V8
Size, liters/cu. in.	4.0/245	4.0/245	5.0/302
Horsepower	145-160	205-210	210-215
Torque (lbs./ft.)	220-225	240-250	280-288

EPA city/highway mpg

	ohv V6	ohc V6	ohv V8
5-speed OD manual	16/20		
4-speed OD automatic	15/20		14/18
5-speed OD automatic		15/20	

City/highway mpg (as tested)

	ohv V6	ohc V6	ohv V8
5-speed OD manual	16.1		
4-speed OD automatic	15.9		12.4
5-speed OD automatic		20.4	

Built in USA

RETAIL PRICES

	GOOD	AVERAGE	POOR
1991 Explorer 2WD	$1,800-3,800	$1,200-3,100	$200-1,100
1991 Explorer 4WD	2,300-4,500	1,700-3,800	500-1,600
1992 Explorer 2WD	2,300-4,300	1,600-3,600	400-1,500
1992 Explorer 4WD	2,900-5,000	2,200-4,300	700-2,000
1993 Explorer 2WD	2,800-4,800	2,100-4,000	600-1,800
1993 Explorer 4WD	3,500-5,500	2,800-4,700	1,000-2,300
1994 Explorer 2WD	3,400-5,500	2,700-4,700	900-2,300
1994 Explorer 4WD	4,200-6,200	3,400-5,400	1,400-2,800
1995 Explorer 2WD	4,200-6,500	3,500-5,700	1,500-3,000
1995 Explorer 4WD	5,000-7,500	4,200-6,600	1,900-35,00
1996 Explorer 2WD	$5,500-8,500	$4,700-7,600	$2,200-4,000
1996 Explorer 4WD	6,500-9,500	5,500-8,500	2,700-4,500
1997 Explorer 2WD	7,000-10,000	6,000-9,000	3,000-5,000
1997 Explorer 4WD	8,500-11,500	7,500-10,200	4,000-5,800
1998 Explorer 2WD	8,800-11,500	7,800-10,500	4,200-6,000
1998 Explorer 4WD	10,500-13,000	9,500-11,500	5,400-6,800
1999 Explorer 2WD	10,500-13,500	9,500-12,200	5,400-7,200
1999 Explorer 4WD	12,000-15,000	10,800-13,500	6,500-8,500
2000 Explorer 2WD	12,500-16,500	11,000-15,000	6,700-10,000
2000 Explorer 4WD	14,000-18,000	12,500-16,500	7,800-11,000
2001 Explorer 2WD	14,500-19,000	13,000-17,500	—
2001 Explorer 4WD	16,200-21,000	14,700-19,500	—

AVERAGE REPLACEMENT COSTS

A/C Compressor	$505	Clutch, Pressure Plate, Bearing	435
Alternator	280	Exhaust System	295
Automatic Transmission or Transaxle	840	Radiator	440
Brakes	265	Shocks and/or Struts	175
Timing Chain or Belt	400	Universal Joints	105

TROUBLE SPOTS

• **Vehicle noise.** A chattering noise that can be felt coming from the rear during tight turns after highway driving is caused by a lack of friction modifier or over-shimming of the clutch packs in the Traction-Lok differential. (1991-96)

• **Hard starting.** If the engine does not start or cranks for a long time then stalls, the idle air control valve may be sticking. (1996)

• **Vehicle noise.** Loose frame rivets should be replaced with bolts (welding is not approved). (1991-96)

• **Vehicle noise.** Synthetic rubber radius arm bushings separate internally, causing noise and degraded steering control. (All)

• **Radiator.** The radiator may leak in cold weather because of a bad seal between the tank and core. (1995-96)

• **Air conditioner.** Water may drip onto the floor when the air conditioner is operated because the evaporator strip seals were not properly positioned. (1995-96)

RECALL HISTORY

1991: Seatbelts may be defective, resulting in insufficiently latched or unlatched belt. **1991:** Front heat shield may contact plastic fuel tank, causing damage to the extent of penetration. **1991:** Hot weld that attaches vapor vent valve carrier to plastic fuel tank may partially fracture, allowing escape of fuel vapor. **1991 w/A4LD automatic transmission:** Vehicle may appear to be in "Park" position, when gear is not truly engaged. **1991-93 w/factory sunroof:** Sunroof glass panel assembly can separate while vehicle is moving. **1991-94:** On cars sold or registered in specified southern California counties, studs that attach master cylinder to power brake booster assembly can develop stress corrosion cracking after extended period; fractures could cause separation of master cylinder when brakes are applied. **1992-93:** Bracket welds for liftgate's hydraulic lift cylinders can fracture. **1992-94:** Short circuit can occur in remote power mirror switch's circuit board; overheated board and other plastic and elastomeric components can result in smoke or fire. **1993-94 w/manual shift:** Parking brake self-adjust pawl does not line up properly and can slip. **1993-95:** Some hydraulic lift cylinder bracket welds could fracture, resulting in potential for liftgate bracket to gradually bend, allowing ball stud to disengage. **1995:** Passenger-side airbag's inflator body may be cracked and not inflate properly; also, igniter end cap can separate, causing hot gases to be released. **1995:** Inner tie rod assemblies can fracture, resulting in shaking or shimmy at low speeds. **1995 2-door:** Brake tubes in some models were misrouted, resulting in excessive stopping distance. **1995-97:** Front stabilizer bar link stud can fracture from bending fatigue. **1996:** Driver's door, when closed only to secondary latched position, may not sustain specified load. **1996:** Gas cylinder bracket may not properly support rear liftgate. **1996:** Certification label shows incorrect rear tire inflation pressure. **1996-97 in 15 northern states:** After operation at highway speeds, at below -20 degrees (F), engine may not return to idle. **1997-98:** Certain off-lease vehicles, Canadian in origin but sold in the U.S., have daytime running lights that do not meet U.S. specifications. **1997-98 w/SOHC 4.0-liter engine:** Fuel lines can be damaged and fire could result if vehicle is jump-started and ground cable is attached to fuel line bracket near battery. **1997-98 w/4.0-**

liter engine: A gap between the plate and bore of throttle body was too narrow, causing the throttle pedal to stick. **1997-99:** Speed control cable on certain vehicles can interfere with servo pulley, preventing throttle from returning to idle when disengaging the speed control. **1998 Eddie Bauer and Limited:** Key-in-ignition/door-open warning chime may not function properly. **1998-99:** Secondary hood latch on certain vehicles may corrode and stick in open position. **1999:** Right front brake line to hydraulic control unit connection could separate, causing leakage when brake pedal is applied. **1999-00 w/4.0-liter engine and AWD:** Generic electronic module could "lock-up," so various functions (front wipers, interior lights, 4x4 system, etc.) could not be turned on or off. **1999-2000 w/3.27 or 3.55 rear axle:** Powertrain Control Module could allow the vehicle to exceed the design intent top speed. **2000 w/side airbags:** Side airbags could deploy if ignition key is in "run" position and seatbelt webbing is extracted from locked retractor with jerking motion. **2000-01 Sport and Sport Trac:** Hood striker could fracture causing the hood could fly open while the vehicle is being driven.

1990-96 FORD F-150/250 PICKUP

1990 Ford F-150 regular cab

FOR Acceleration (V8) • Passenger and cargo room • Trailer-towing capability

AGAINST Fuel economy • Noise • Handling • Interior storage space

EVALUATION Even though the 6-cylinder engine nearly matches torque output of a 5.0-liter V8, we prefer gasoline V8 models on the basis of their impressive acceleration and passing ability. That was our appraisal of an F-150 XLT with the 5.0 and 4-speed automatic. The 5.0 was just about as responsive as a 5.8-liter, in fact, but both returned horrid gas mileage: around 12.5 mpg in a city/highway mix. Some 4-speed automatics have demonstrated slurred, lurching gear changes, plus sluggish downshifting for passing. Tall and square, Ford trucks can be blown around in heavy crosswinds, but otherwise hold the road well—even with an empty cargo box. Steering feels looser than in a GM or Dodge pickup, and requires a bit more correction on the highway. An unloaded short-wheelbase 4x4 rides harshly over city streets, but longer-wheelbase models cope much better with bumps. Engine noise and tire rumble can annoy, though wind noise is modest. Regular-cab models easily hold three adults, though the center rider straddles the transmission tunnel. Dashboards are better after 1991, with an easy-to-use climate system and audio controls grouped near the driver. All trucks have plenty of head room. The steering wheel sits near the driver's chest, and pedals are close to the chair-height seat cushion. SuperCab rear seats are a convenience, but have minimal knee and foot space.

VALUE If you're in the market for a pickup in this league, also look at the Chevrolet C/K and Dodge Ram. But we put the F-Series at the top of our list in terms of room, power, payload, and trailer-towing ability.

SPECIFICATIONS

	reg. cab short bed	reg. cab long bed	ext. cab short bed	ext. cab long bed
Wheelbase, in.	116.8	133.0	138.8	155.0
Overall length, in.	197.1	213.3	219.1	235.3
Overall width, in.	79.0	79.0	79.0	79.0
Overall height, in.	71.0	71.0	71.9	74.0
Curb weight, lbs.	3886	3982	4186	4316
Fuel capacity, gals.	34.7	37.2	34.7	37.1
Seating capacity	3	3	6	6
Front head room, in.	40.3	40.3	39.9	39.9
Max. front leg room, in.	41.1	41.1	41.0	41.0
Rear head room, in.	—	—	37.6	37.6
Min. rear leg room, in.	—	—	28.8	28.8

Powertrain layout: longitudinal front-engine/rear- or 4-wheel drive

ENGINES

	ohv I6	ohv V8	ohv V8	ohv V8	Diesel ohv V8
Size, liters/cu. in.	4.9/300	5.0/302	5.8/351	7.5/460	7.3/444
Horsepower	145	185-205	200-210	245-250	185-210
Torque (lbs./ft.)	265	270-275	300-325	400-410	360-425

EPA city/highway mpg

4-speed man.			15/16		
5-speed OD man.	15/19	15/19	NA	NA	NA
3-speed auto.	NA		NA	NA	NA
4-speed OD auto.	14/18	14/19	12/17	NA	NA

City/highway mpg (as tested)

4-speed OD auto.		15.2		12.9	

Built in USA, Mexico, Canada

RETAIL PRICES

	GOOD	AVERAGE	POOR
1990 F-150	$2,000-3,500	$1,400-2,800	$200-900
1990 F-150 SuperCab	2,300-3,800	1,600-3,100	300-1,100
1990 F-250	2,600-3,900	1,900-3,200	500-1,100
1990 F-250 SuperCab	3,000-4,200	2,300-3,400	700-1,200
1991 F-150	2,400-4,500	1,800-3,800	300-1,300
1991 F-150 SuperCab	2,800-5,000	2,200-4,300	500-1,600
1991 F-250	3,300-5,000	2,600-4,200	800-1,600
1991 F-250 SuperCab	3,800-5,500	3,000-4,500	1,000-1,800
1992 F-150	2,800-5,300	2,200-4,600	500-1,900
1992 F-150 SuperCab	3,400-6,000	2,600-5,100	800-2,200
1992 F-250	3,900-5,900	3,100-5,000	1,000-2,100
1992 F-250 SuperCab	4,500-6,500	3,700-5,700	1,400-2,600
1993 F-150	3,200-6,200	2,500-5,400	700-2,500
1993 F-150 SuperCab	4,200-6,800	3,400-6,000	1,200-2,800
1993 F-250	4,200-6,700	3,400-5,900	1,200-2,700
1993 F-250 SuperCab	5,000-7,500	4,200-6,600	1,700-3,200
1994 F-150	3,700-7,000	3,000-6,200	1,000-3,000
1994 F-150 SuperCab	4,800-8,000	4,000-7,200	1,500-3,700
1994 F-250	5,500-8,000	4,700-7,200	2,000-3,700
1994 F-250 SuperCab	6,200-9,500	5,300-8,500	2,400-4,500
1995 F-150	4,200-8,000	3,400-7,100	1,300-3,600
1995 F-150 SuperCab	5,500-9,500	4,500-8,500	1,900-4,500
1995 F-250	6,000-8,500	5,200-7,500	2,300-3,800
1995 F-250 SuperCab	7,000-10,500	6,000-9,500	2,800-5,200
1996 F-150	4,900-9,500	4,000-8,500	1,800-4,800
1996 F-150 SuperCab	6,500-11,000	5,500-10,000	2,500-5,800
1996 F-250	7,000-10,000	6,000-9,000	2,800-5,000
1996 F-250 SuperCab/Crew	9,000-12,500	8,000-11,200	4,000-6,500

AVERAGE REPLACEMENT COSTS

A/C Compressor	$395	Clutch, Pressure Plate, Bearing	515
Alternator	290	Exhaust System	375
Automatic Transmission or Transaxle	560	Radiator	425
Brakes	295	Shocks and/or Struts	160
Timing Chain or Belt	200	Universal Joints	175

TROUBLE SPOTS

• **Vehicle noise.** A chattering noise that can be felt coming from the rear during tight turns after highway driving is caused by a lack of friction modifier or over-shimming of the clutch packs in the Traction-Lok differential. (1990-96)

• **Suspension problems.** Front tire cupping is common with Twin Axle suspension. Often new springs will help, but sometimes other suspension parts must also be replaced. Regular alignment is crucial. (All)

• **Hard starting.** Hesitation, miss, stumble, no-start, or stalling could be due to a short in the wiring harness for the powertrain control module (PCM). (1993-95)

• **Alternator belt.** If the accessory drive belt on 4.9-liter engines chirps, the pulley for the power steering may be misaligned on the pump or the A/C compressor may have to be repositioned. If the belt squeals, the automatic tensioner must be replaced. (1990-94)

• **Hard starting.** If the engine does not start or cranks for a long time then stalls, the idle air control valve may be sticking. (1995-96)

• **Automatic transmission.** If the transmission does not shift from second to third, the valve body separator plate may be distorted. (1990-94)

• **Ball joints.** If water gets into the ball joints, they will wear out early and have to be replaced. (1990-96)

• **Vehicle noise.** Loose frame rivets should be replaced with bolts (welding is not approved). (1990-96)

• **Manual transmission.** On trucks with a diesel engine, the clutch may not release due to a leaking slave cylinder. (1993-95)

• **Suspension problems.** The front leaf springs are prone to sag over time and must be replaced. (1991-94)

• **Automatic transmission.** The transmission may slip and the engine may flare when the transmission shifts into fourth gear, which can often be traced to a bad TR/MLP sensor. (1994-95)

RECALL HISTORY

1990 4x2 w/one-piece driveshaft and E40D transmission: Under certain conditions, snap ring may fracture and park gear would not engage. **1990 w/dual fuel tanks:** Supply and return fuel lines may be crossed on some trucks. **1990-91 F-250/350 w/7.3/.5 liter engine, and 4x4 w/5.8-liter:** Brake fluid may overheat, diminishing braking effectiveness. **1990-91:** Ignition switch could short-circuit and overheat, causing smoke and possible fire. **1990-93 w/dual fuel tanks:** Portion of unused fuel from one tank may be returned to the second, causing spillage. **1992 F-250/350 diesel:** Sound insulation can contact exhaust manifold. **1992:** Door latch may malfunction in below-freezing temperatures. **1992-94 w/manual shift:** Parking brake pawl can slip; brake might not hold. **1993 F-150 w/Touch Drive:** Transfer case can slip out of 4x4 high gear during coasting or with power applied in reverse. **1993 w/dual fuel tanks:** Fuel pressure regulator in the fuel system can wear out during the life of the vehicle, causing high fuel system pressure. **1994 F-150/250:** Airbag and its warning light might not function; or, airbag might deploy when passenger door is slammed while key is turned to start position. **1994-95 Super Cab w/40/20/40 power driver's seat:** Wiring harness for power lumbar support could overheat, leading to melting, smoke, or possible ignition of surrounding materials. **1996 Super/F-250/F-350:** Fuel tank strap could loosen or disconnect. **1996 F-250/F-350/Super Duty:** Undersized fasteners on a few trucks can separate, causing fuel-tank strap to become disconnected. **1996-97 F-250:** Certification label shows incorrect rear tire inflation pressure.

1997-01 FORD F-150

1998 Ford F-150 SuperCab extended cab

FOR Trailer towing capability • Passenger room • Cargo room

AGAINST Acceleration (V6) • Fuel economy • Engine noise (V6) • Rear-seat comfort

EVALUATION Ford's base V6 engine is noisy at idle, and grows raucous under hard throttle. Acceleration is adequate only in lighter-weight models with little cargo aboard. Both V8 engines are smoother and more powerful, but don't offer quite as much low-speed muscle as the bigger overhead-valve V8 from GM and Dodge. For most applications, a V8 is the wiser choice—and the bigger, the better. For most light-duty work, however, the 4.6-liter would suffice. It feels lively when accelerating from a standstill (at least with an empty cargo bed), but is a little short of power when you punch the gas quickly in the 25-40 mph range—especially in a heavier model. Passing response is ample at highway speeds, however. An F-150 SuperCab 4x4 averaged only 12.5 mpg in a mix of city and highway driving, and managed 16.2 mpg on a highway journey. On the highway, an F-150 delivers a stable and comfortable ride, with little of the bounciness or pitching that's common to most pickups. When going through bumpy pavement, the suspension absorbs the worst of the rough stuff. In addition, the rear axle resists juddering even when the cargo bed is empty. Wind and road noise are moderate for a pickup truck. Depending on the model and option package—and there's a vast selection available—interior furnishings range from stark to utterly luxurious. All F-150s have a modern, convenient dashboard with handy controls. Cupholders pop out from the dashboard, and large map pockets are mounted on doors. Head, leg, and shoulder room up front are generous. Because 4WD models sit high off the ground, entry and exit demand more effort than in the 2WD versions. The SuperCab's passenger-side rear door makes life easier. You get plenty of head room but marginal leg space in the rear seat. Getting into the back is definitely easier with the 1999 SuperCab's rear half-doors. And the 2001 SuperCrew is plenty roomy and comfortable for three adults, with a high step in but large crew-cab door openings.

VALUE All told, we rate the latest F-150 tops in its class, even with the arrival of new challengers for 1999: the redesigned Chevrolet Silverado and GMC Sierra.

SPECS

	reg. cab short bed	reg. cab long bed	ext. cab short bed	ext. cab long bed	crew cab
Wheelbase, in.	119.9	138.5	138.5	157.1	138.5
Overall length, in.	202.2	220.8	220.8	239.4	225.9
Overall width, in.	78.4	78.4	78.4	78.4	79.1
Overall height, in.	72.4	72.1	72.6	72.4	73.9
Curb weight, lbs.	4028	4339	4575	4558	4644
Fuel capacity, gals.	25.0	30.0	25.0	30.0	25.0
Seating capacity	3	3	6	6	6
Front head room, in.	40.8	40.8	40.8	40.8	39.8
Max. front leg room, in.	40.9	40.9	40.9	40.9	41.0
Rear head room, in.	—	—	37.8	37.8	39.8
Min. rear leg room, in.	—	—	32.2	32.2	36.8

Powertrain layout: longitudinal front-engine/rear- or 4-wheel drive

ENGINES

	ohv V6	ohc V8	ohc V8	Supercharged ohc V8
Size, liters/cu. in.	4.2/256	4.6/281	5.4/330	5.4/330
Horsepower	205-210	220	235-260	380
Torque (lbs./ft.)	250-255	290	330-345	450
EPA city/highway mpg				
5-speed OD manual	17/22	16/21		
4-speed OD automatic	17/22	16/21	14/18	12/16
City/highway mpg (as tested)				
4-speed OD automatic		12.5	12.0	

Built in USA, Canada

RETAIL PRICES

	GOOD	AVERAGE	POOR
1997 F-150 2WD	$6,000-11,000	$5,200-10,000	$2,700-6,000
1997 F-150 4WD	8,000-13,000	7,000-12,000	3,700-7,500
1998 F-150 2WD	7,200-12,500	6,200-11,500	3,300-7,200
1998 F-150 4WD	9,200-14,500	8,200-13,000	4,500-8,200
1999 F-150 2WD	8,500-12,000	7,500-11,000	4,200-6,700
1999 F-150 4WD	10,500-14,000	9,300-12,500	5,500-7,700
1999 SuperCab 2WD	11,000-14,000	9,500-12,500	5,700-7,700
1999 SuperCab 4WD	13,000-16,500	11,500-15,000	7,500-9,500
1999 Lightning	19,000-21,000	17,500-19,500	13,000-14,500
2000 F-150 2WD	10,000-13,200	8,800-12,000	5,000-8,000
2000 F-150 4WD	12,000-15,500	10,700-14,000	6,800-9,000
2000 SuperCab 2WD	12,500-16,000	11,000-14,500	7,000-9,000
2000 SuperCab 4WD	14,000-17,500	13,000-16,000	8,000-10,500
2000 Lightning	22,000-24,000	20,500-22,500	15,500-17,000
2000 Harley-Davidson	22,500-24,500	21,000-23,000	16,000-17,500
2001 F-150 2WD	11,500-14,000	10,200-12,500	—
2001 F-150 4WD	13,500-16,500	12,000-15,000	—
2001 SuperCab 2WD	14,000-17,500	12,500-16,000	—
2001 SuperCab 4WD	15,500-19,500	14,000-18,000	—
2001 Lightning	25,000-27,000	23,000-25,000	—
2001 Harley-Davidson	26,000-28,000	24,000-26,000	—
2001 SuperCrew 2WD	18,000-21,500	16,500-20,000	—
2001 SuperCrew 4WD	20,500-24,000	19,000-22,500	—

AVERAGE REPLACEMENT COSTS

A/C Compressor	$300	Clutch, Pressure Plate, Bearing	620
Alternator	315	Exhaust System	515
Automatic Transmission or Transaxle	930	Radiator	510
Brakes	320	Shocks and/or Struts	575
Timing Chain or Belt	380	Universal Joints	260

TROUBLE SPOTS

• Climate control. Cold air may come out of the heater vents at the floor due to a door in the duct not sealing properly. (1997)

• Audio system. Electrical noise caused by the electric fuel pump in the tank can cause a buzzing noise when the AM band of the radio is selected. (1997)

• Automatic transmission. If water gets into the transfer case, the mode switch can be shorted out making it impossible to select a different range. (1997)

• Engine noise. Piston slap on cold startup due to faulty pistons in 5.4-liter engine. (1998)

• Engine misfire. The engine may run rough or idle roughly if condensation from the air conditioning drips onto the oxygen sensor. (1997-98)

• Automatic transmission. Transmission fluid can leak from the transmission into the transfer case. The low transmission fluid level causes shifting and engagement problems. (1997)

• Dashboard lights. Water in the spark plug wells may cause the ignition spark to jump to ground causing a misfire and illuminating the check engine light. (1997)

RECALL HISTORY

1997: Retainer clip that holds master cylinder pushrod to brake pedal arm could be missing, causing loss of braking. **1997:** Separation of transmission bracket fitting from cable can result in inability to shift into "Park." **1997 in 10 northern states:** Operation at highway speeds in winter conditions can cause PVC fitting to freeze; throttle plate could then remain in cruising position after pedal is released. **1997:** Seatbelt anchorage attachments are missing or misinstalled. **1997-98:** Certain off-lease vehicles, Canadian in origin but sold in the U.S., have daytime running lights that do not meet U.S. specifications. **1997-98 w/4WD:** If vehicle is overloaded, rear leaf springs can fracture. **1997-98 w/automatic transmission:** Shift cable assembly might not be fully attached to steering column bracket and could come out, preventing shifting into "Park" even though indicator shows it is in "Park." **1997-98:** Lug nuts may loosen and studs may experience fatigue failure, with potential for wheel separation. **1997-98 w/V6, in any of 23 states:** Throttle is unable to return to idle due to ice forming in throttle body. **1997-98:** Main battery cable can contact body panel in trunk, resulting short circuit. **1999 4x4 w/Off Road package and 4x2 w/Sport package:** Tire and rim identification information is incorrect on certification labels. **1999:** Fuel pressure regulator O-ring may have been damaged, allowing fuel vapor leakage. **1999:** Speed control cable on certain vehicles can interfere with pulley, preventing throttle from returning to idle when disengaging the speed control. **1999-00 Super Duty w/5.4-liter V8 and manual transmission:** Accelerator cable core wire on certain trucks can wear the conduit end fitting; could lead to separation of strands, which could prevent throttle from returning to idle. **2000-01:** Some of the owner's manuals for these vehicles are missing instructions for properly attaching a child restraint system. **2000-01:** A switch located in the plastic cover of the wiper motor gear case could malfunction and overheat, potentially resulting in loss of wiper function or fire. **2001:** Driver's and/or outboard front passenger's seatbelt buckle may not fully latch. In the event of a crash, the restraint system may not provide adequate occupant protection.

2000-01 FORD FOCUS

2000 Ford Focus 4-door sedan

FOR Cargo room (wagon) • Handling/roadholding • Control layout • Fuel economy

AGAINST Acceleration • Rear-seat entry/exit (hatchback) • Engine noise

EVALUATION Terrific road manners are tempered by mediocre engine performance. A Focus tackles twisty roads with linear, communicative steering, well-controlled body lean, and outstanding grip from the 15-inch tires that are standard on most models. Firm suspensions yield a flat, wallow-free highway ride, but bumps register with a thump. Honda's Civic rides softer and is quieter. Antilock braking feels strong and stable, with only moderate nose-dive in simulated "panic" stops. Delivering slightly better acceleration, the twincam engine is a better choice than the tepid base 4-cylinder. Even with manual shift, though, both are merely adequate at merging with fast-moving traffic or pulling steadily up long grades. Automatic dulls off-the-line punch, but provides fuss-free gear changes. A 5-speed ZTS reached 60 mph in a so-so 9.5 seconds, and averaged 26.2 mpg. A ZTS with automatic averaged 23.2 mpg. Wind rush is noticeable, but noise is acceptable otherwise and engines are tolerably smooth. Few subcompacts are roomier than a Focus. Occupants sit comfortably upright on chair-like cushions, enjoying bountiful head clearance and plenty of rear leg space, though rear head room is less generous. Controls are conspicuous and smooth-operating, and the air conditioner operates in all vent modes. No gauge is unobstructed, but the tachometer in the ZX3 and ZTS lacks a redline. Large front-door frames ease entry/exit, but rear doors don't open all that far. Cargo holds are generous, and rear seats flip/fold flat. Liftovers are low, and the sedan's trunklid hinges don't intrude into luggage space. Some test models have had poor-fitting interior panels.

VALUE Less refined than a class-leading Honda Civic and not as polished as the more conservative Toyota Corolla, the Civic offers more room, style, and body types than any competitor. Despite timid engines, it's also fun to drive. Word of advice: Don't buy a small car without checking out the Focus.

SPECIFICATIONS

	2-door hatchback	4-door sedan	4-door wagon
Wheelbase, in.	103.0	103.0	103.0
Overall length, in.	168.1	174.9	178.2
Overall width, in.	66.9	66.9	66.9
Overall height, in.	56.3	56.3	57.0
Curb weight, lbs.	2551	2564	2707
Cargo volume, cu. ft.	18.5	12.9	55.3
Fuel capacity, gals.	13.2	13.2	13.2
Seating capacity	5	5	5
Front head room, in.	39.3	39.3	39.3
Max. front leg room, in.	43.1	43.1	43.1
Rear head room, in.	38.7	38.5	40.0
Min. rear leg room, in.	37.6	37.6	37.6

Powertrain layout: transverse front-engine/front-wheel drive

ENGINES

	ohc I4	dohc I4
Size, liters/cu. in.	2.0/121	2.0/121
Horsepower	110	130
Torque (lbs./ft.)	125	135
EPA city/highway mpg		
5-speed OD manual	28/38	25/34
4-speed OD automatic	27/35	24/32
City/highway mpg (as tested)		
5-speed OD manual		26.5
4-speed OD automatic		23.2

Built in Mexico

RETAIL PRICES

	GOOD	AVERAGE	POOR
2000 Focus ZX3, LX	$8,800-10,000	$8,000-9,100	$5,700-6,500
2000 Focus SE, ZTS	9,700-10,700	8,900-9,700	6,300-7,000
2001 Focus ZX3, LX	10,300-11,300	9,300-10,300	—
2001 Focus SE, ZTS	11,200-12,500	10,200-11,500	—

AVERAGE REPLACEMENT COSTS

A/C Compressor	$650	Clutch, Pressure Plate, Bearing	410
Alternator	410		
Automatic Transmission or Transaxle	1,200	Constant Velocity Joints	850
		Exhaust System	650
Brakes	455	Radiator	475
Shocks and/or Struts	130	Timing Chain or Belt	350

TROUBLE SPOTS

- **Fuel pump.** The fuel hose between the filler neck and tank may flake and clog. In-tank fuel filter and hoses are being replaced under a recall. (2000)

- **Vehicle noise.** The right motor mount could break due to defective hardware resulting in noise, vibration, and possible driveshaft damage. Redesigned mounts were being installed under a recall. (2000)

- **Climate control.** The ventilation system may make fluttering noises when using the panel/defrost setting due to a problem with the linkage or whistle when the blower is running due to a gap on the resistor mounting. (2000)

RECALL HISTORY

2000 Focus: Hub retaining nuts can loosen, allowing left rear wheel and brake drum assembly to separate. **2000 w/speed control:** Control cable core wire could catch on sleeve at cable end during wide-open throttle acceleration, preventing throttle from returning to idle. **2000 w/speed control:** Speed-control cable end fitting can allow water to enter servo assembly; corrosion could develop and cause intermittent operation or prevent throttle from returning to idle. **2000:** Decklid wire harness on certain cars can fatigue and develop broken wires, resulting in loss of individual lamp functions or electrical short. **2000-01 Focus wagon and hatchback wagon and hatchback:** In certain vehicles with folding 60/40 second seat, when the 60-percent portion is folded down and load is applied to front edge of load floor, outboard hinge pivot could disengage. **2000-01:** A switch located in the plastic cover of the wiper motor gear case could malfunction and overheat, potentially resulting in loss of wiper function or fire. **2001:** Seatback recliner handle spring on some vehicles could be damaged, causing seatback to be loose or to recline unexpectedly.

1990-93 FORD MUSTANG

1992 Ford Mustang GT 2-door convertible

FOR Handling/roadholding • Acceleration (V8 models)

AGAINST Fuel economy (V8) • Rear-seat room • Noise • Ride • Acceleration (4-cylinder)

EVALUATION Best to skip the weak, noisy 4-cylinder engine, with its poor repair record. For reliable and strong performance choose the V8, but watch out for its notorious poor wet-weather traction and dismal fuel economy, especially in town. Four-cylinder models average in the low twenties. Ride quality is well-controlled on base models. In the GT, you can definitely expect to jiggle and jounce over harsh pavement, courtesy of an admittedly stiff suspension. However, it is that suspension that makes the GT model handle so well, while the base model leans over heavily even in modest turns. Brakes are one of the bigger bugaboos. Front-disc/rear-drum brakes are simply not up to par for a car of this caliber. Passenger space is fine up front but tight in back. Hatchbacks offer plenty of cargo space with the rear seatback folded down. Convertibles are fun, of course, but bodies are likely to be loose and rattly. Controls are small and some awkwardly placed, but overall better than a Chevy Camaro.

VALUE To be frank, few other cars offer as much bang for the buck as a Mustang. Only the Chevrolet Camaro and Pontiac Firebird rank as true rivals. Despite high insurance rates and poor gas mileage, Mustangs still deliver good overall value, new or used.

SPECIFICATIONS

	2-door conv.	2-door coupe	2-door hatchback
Wheelbase, in.	100.5	100.5	100.5
Overall length, in.	179.6	179.6	179.6
Overall width, in.	68.3	68.3	68.3
Overall height, in.	52.1	52.1	52.1
Curb weight, lbs.	2996	2775	2834
Cargo volume, cu. ft.	6.4	10.0	30.0
Fuel capacity, gals.	15.4	15.4	15.4
Seating capacity	4	4	4
Front head room, in.	37.6	37.0	37.0
Max. front leg room, in.	41.7	41.7	41.7
Rear head room, in.	37.0	35.9	35.7
Min. rear leg room, in.	30.7	30.7	30.7

Powertrain layout: longitudinal front-engine/rear-wheel drive

ENGINES

	ohc I4	ohc I4	ohv V8	ohv V8
Size, liters/cu. in.	2.3/140	2.3/140	5.0/302	5.0/302
Horsepower	88	105	205-225	245
Torque (lbs./ft.)	132	135	275-300	320
EPA city/highway mpg				
5-speed OD manual	23/29	22/30	17/24	NA
4-speed OD automatic		22/29	17/24	
City/highway mpg (as tested)				
5-speed OD manual			15.3	
4-speed OD automatic		19.8		

Built in USA

RETAIL PRICES

	GOOD	AVERAGE	POOR
1990 Mustang LX	$1,500-2,300	$900-1,700	$100-300
1990 LX Convertible	2,300-3,200	1,700-2,500	500-900
1990 Mustang GT	2,500-3,400	1,900-2,700	600-1,000
1990 GT Convertible	3,500-4,300	2,800-3,600	1,000-1,500
1991 Mustang LX	1,800-2,700	1,200-2,000	200-500
1991 LX Convertible	2,800-3,500	2,100-2,700	600-1,100
1991 Mustang GT	3,400-4,100	2,700-3,300	900-1,400
1991 GT Convertible	4,200-5,000	3,500-4,200	1,300-1,800
1992 Mustang LX	2,300-3,300	1,700-2,600	400-800
1992 LX Convertible	3,200-4,000	2,500-3,200	800-1,200
1992 Mustang GT	3,900-4,700	3,200-3,900	1,100-1,600
1992 GT Convertible	4,800-5,500	4,100-4,700	1,600-2,000
1993 Mustang LX	2,800-3,800	2,200-3,100	500-1,100
1993 LX Convertible	3,800-4,800	3,100-4,000	1,000-1,500
1993 Mustang GT	4,600-5,300	3,900-4,500	1,400-1,800
1993 GT Convertible	5,500-6,300	4,700-5,500	2,000-2,500

AVERAGE REPLACEMENT COSTS

A/C Compressor	$410	Clutch, Pressure Plate, Bearing	480
Alternator	535	Exhaust System	565
Automatic Transmission or Transaxle	675	Radiator	360
Brakes	245	Shocks and/or Struts	435
Timing Chain or Belt	215	Universal Joints	95

TROUBLE SPOTS

- **Vehicle noise.** A chattering noise that can be felt coming from the rear during tight turns after highway driving is caused by a lack of friction modifier or over-shimming of the clutch packs in the Traction-Lok differential. (1990-93)

- **Wipers.** Because water commonly seeps past the hood seal onto the wiper motor, the wipers may be erratic or quit working. (1990-93)

- **Suspension problems.** It may be impossible to align the front end and get the camber correct due to the dimensions of the crossmember across the spring seats. (1990-93)

- **Blower motor.** Squeaking or chirping blower motors are the result of defective brush holders. (1993)

RECALL HISTORY

1990-93: Ignition switch could short-circuit and overheat, causing smoke and possible fire. **1991:** Park rod assembly of automatic overdrive transmission may contain a cam with inadequate surface hardness, which could lead to disengagement or nonengagement when lever is placed in "Park" position; with parking brake off, vehicle could then roll away.

1994-01 FORD MUSTANG

FOR Acceleration (V8) • Handling/roadholding • Antilock brakes (optional)

AGAINST Fuel economy (V8) • Rear-seat room • Ride (GT)

1994 Ford Mustang GT 2-door coupe

EVALUATION

All Mustangs take quick corners smartly, but because of a softened suspension, base cars ride with only modest jarring—considerably less shocking than in the past. A more stiffly suspended GT, on the other hand, grows harsh, actually crashing and banging over broken surfaces. Cobras are stiffer-suspended yet, as expected, but their ride quality isn't noticeably worse. Acceleration is adequate with the V6 and either transmission, though automatic downshifts tend to be delayed when dashing uphill. Obviously, the V8 is the choice for performance, though increased weight in this generation makes that engine seem a little less peppy than before. Fuel economy is good with a V6, but not with V8 power. The 4.6-liter V8 in later models yields little acceleration improvement, but it's smoother and more refined. Thrilling is the operative word for a session behind the wheel of a Cobra, savoring the feel of the 5-speed gearbox and high-performance engine. Wet-weather traction continues to be a problem on all Mustangs, especially V8s. All-disc brakes are fine, but we'd look for a Mustang with the optional antilocking. Entry/exit is easy enough, courtesy of the Mustang's relatively upright stance (compared to Camaro, at any rate). Backseat space is truly tight, but the cockpit has an open, airy feel. Instruments are unobstructed, controls near at hand, and the dual airbags are a safety bonus.

VALUE

Cobras can be pricey, and don't expect discounts on the limited-production Bullitt. Overall, though, Mustang delivers sporty performance at a reasonable price—especially in base and GT form. A major improvement over its predecessor, and more user-friendly for everyday driving than Chevy's Camaro, the current Mustang is well worth a test drive.

SPECIFICATIONS

	2-door conv.	2-door coupe
Wheelbase, in.	101.3	101.3
Overall length, in.	181.5	181.5
Overall width, in.	71.8	71.8
Overall height, in.	52.8	52.9
Curb weight, lbs.	3257	3077
Cargo volume, cu. ft.	7.7	10.9
Fuel capacity, gals.	15.4	15.4
Seating capacity	4	4
Front head room, in.	37.9	38.1
Max. front leg room, in.	42.6	42.6
Rear head room, in.	35.8	35.9
Min. rear leg room, in.	30.3	30.3

Powertrain layout: longitudinal front-engine/rear-wheel drive

ENGINES

	ohv V6	ohv V8	ohc V8	dohc V8
Size, liters/cu. in.	3.8/232	5.0/302	4.6/281	4.6/281
Horsepower	145-190	215-240	215-260	305-320
Torque (lbs./ft.)	215-220	285	285-302	300-317
EPA city/highway mpg				
5-speed OD manual	20/30	17/25	18/27	18/26
4-speed OD automatic	20/20	17/24	17/24	
City/highway mpg (as tested)				
5-speed OD manual			17.5	14.0
4-speed OD automatic		16.5	15.7	

Built in USA

RETAIL PRICES

	GOOD	AVERAGE	POOR
1994 Mustang	$4,000-4,800	$3,300-4,000	$1,200-1,600
1994 Conv., GT Coupe	5,200-6,000	4,400-5,200	2,000-2,700
1994 GT Convertible	7,000-8,000	6,100-7,000	3,300-3,800
1995 Mustang	5,000-5,800	4,200-5,000	1,800-2,400
1995 Conv., GT Coupe	6,300-7,200	5,500-6,300	2,800-3,300
1995 GT Convertible	$8,200-9,200	$7,300-8,200	$3,400-3,900
1996 Mustang	6,200-7,000	5,400-6,100	2,700-3,200
1996 Conv., GT Coupe	7,800-8,800	6,900-7,800	3,800-4,500
1996 GT Convertible	9,500-10,800	8,500-9,800	4,800-5,600
1996 Mustang Cobra	11,500-12,500	10,500-11,500	6,500-7,200
1996 Cobra Convertible	13,500-15,000	12,300-13,500	7,500-8,500
1997 Mustang	7,500-8,500	6,500-7,500	3,500-4,200
1997 Conv., GT Coupe	9,000-10,000	8,100-9,000	4,500-5,100
1997 GT Convertible	11,500-12,500	10,500-11,500	6,500-7,200
1997 Mustang Cobra	13,500-15,000	12,000-13,500	7,300-8,500
1997 Cobra Convertible	15,500-17,000	14,000-15,500	9,000-10,000
1998 Mustang	8,800-9,800	7,800-8,800	4,300-5,000
1998 Conv., GT Coupe	10,500-12,000	9,500-11,000	5,500-6,500
1998 GT Convertible	13,500-14,500	12,500-13,300	7,500-8,100
1998 Mustang Cobra	15,500-17,000	14,000-15,500	9,000-10,000
1998 Cobra Convertible	17,800-19,300	16,300-17,800	11,000-12,300
1999 Mustang	10,200-11,200	9,200-10,200	5,200-5,900
1999 Conv., GT Coupe	12,300-13,500	11,000-12,000	7,000-7,700
1999 GT Convertible	15,500-17,000	14,000-15,500	9,000-10,000
1999 Mustang Cobra	18,000-19,500	16,500-18,000	11,000-12,000
1999 Cobra Convertible	20,000-21,500	18,500-20,000	12,500-13,500
2000 Mustang	11,500-12,500	10,500-11,500	6,000-6,700
2000 Conv., GT Coupe	14,000-15,500	12,500-14,000	7,500-8,500
2000 GT Convertible	17,500-19,500	16,000-17,500	11,000-12,000
2001 Mustang	13,000-14,000	12,000-12,800	—
2001 Conv., GT Coupe	16,000-17,500	14,500-16,000	—
2001 Bullitt Coupe	21,000-23,000	19,500-21,500	—
2001 GT Convertible	19,500-21,000	18,000-19,500	—
2001 Mustang Cobra	22,000-23,500	20,500-22,000	—
2001 Cobra Convertible	24,500-26,000	23,000-24,500	—

AVERAGE REPLACEMENT COSTS

A/C Compressor	$410	Clutch, Pressure Plate, Bearing	435
Alternator	535	Exhaust System	830
Automatic Transmission or Transaxle	675	Radiator	480
Brakes	245	Shocks and/or Struts	435
Timing Chain or Belt	215	Universal Joints	95

TROUBLE SPOTS

• **Vehicle noise.** A chattering noise that can be felt coming from the rear during tight turns after highway driving is caused by a lack of friction modifier or over-shimming of the clutch packs in the Traction-Lok differential. (1994-96)

• **Hard starting.** If the engine does not want to start or cranks for a long time then stalls, the idle air control valve may be sticking. (1995-96)

• **Blower motor.** Squeaking or chirping blower motors are the result of defective brush holders. (1994)

• **Automatic transmission.** The automatic transmission is notorious for shuddering or vibrating under light acceleration or when shifting between third and fourth gear above 35 mph. It requires that the transmission fluid be changed and that only Mercon® fluid be used. (1994)

• **Alternator belt.** The drive belt tensioner pulley or idler pulley bearings are apt to make a squealing noise when the engine is started in cold weather. (1994-96)

• **Automatic transmission.** The transmission may slip and the engine may flare when the transmission shifts into fourth gear, which can often be traced to a bad TR/MLP sensor. (1994-95)

RECALL HISTORY

1994 GT w/power lumbar adjustment: Electrical short can result in overheating, melting, smoke, and ignition of surrounding materials. **1994-96:** Tearing of bond between inner and outer hood panels during minor front-end collision can result in gap at leading edge of hood; could result in separation of outer panel. **1994-97:** Replacement driver-side airbag modules might not properly deploy in a crash. **1995:** On some cars, passenger airbag's inflator body is cracked and may not inflate properly; also, igniter end cap can separate, causing hot gases to be released. **1995:** Some outer tie rod ends can fracture within 50,000 miles; may result in shake or shimmy and cause wheel to tuck inward or outward. **1998 w/V8 engine:** Some cars have missing or inadequately brazed joints between fuel rail body and mounting brackets; separation can result in leakage. **1998:** Some rack-and-pinion steering gears may have damaged shaft bearings. **1998-99:** Speed control cable on certain vehicles can interfere with servo pulley, preventing throttle from returning to idle when disengaging the speed control. **1999-00 Cobra R:** Ball joint assembly could cause knuckle casting to fail. If this occurs, the lower control arm could contact the inside of the rear wheel. In some cases, steering of the vehicle could be reduced. **1999-00:** Seatbelt retractor may have incorrectly formed pin shaft that could, in some circumstances, prevent seatbelt webbing from being extracted. **2000 GT (w/4.6-liter engine):** A coolant flow blockage exists at the intake manifold heater core nipple, resulting in no coolant flow to the heater and, therefore, no warm air flow from the heater or windshield defroster.

1993-97 FORD PROBE

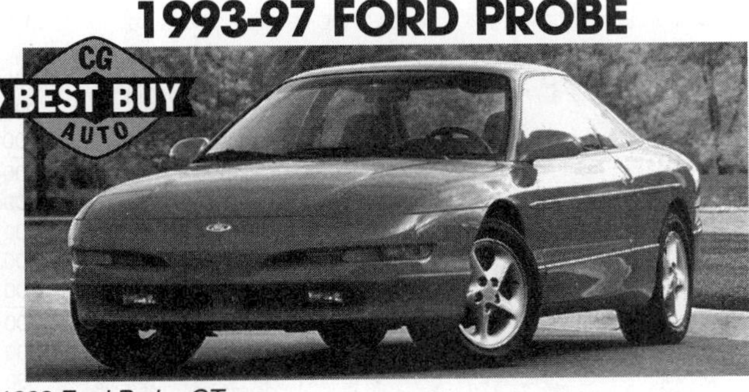

1993 Ford Probe GT

FOR Acceleration (V6) • Steering/handling (GT) • Visibility • Antilock brakes (optional) • Cargo room

AGAINST Rear-seat room • Automatic transmission performance • Ride (GT)

EVALUATION Acceleration is excellent with the GT's V6 and standard 5-speed gearbox. Action from the 4-cylinder engine is adequate, at least with manual shift. Performance lags with optional 4-speed automatic, which is also slow to downshift. The engine's low-end torque simply isn't sufficient to move the car off with any degree of real vigor. Even the V6 engine feels somewhat sluggish with automatic. Base-model handling is secure and sporty. Firm suspension tuning and low-profile tires give the GT sharp, agile handling and a secure grip. In exchange, you can expect to endure a harsher, more jittery ride. A Probe GT jiggles on roads that feel smooth in the MX-6 LS. That level of roughness can lead to fatigue on a long trip. Base Probes are softer suspended for a better ride, without losing much handling competence. Ford softened the GT's suspension for 1996, but tires are still stiff so the ride isn't a whole lot better. Visibility is better than in most sport coupes, due to the low cowl and relatively slim roof pillars. Space is adequate up front. Space is scant in back for grownups. Cargo room ranks as generous, especially with the split rear seatback folded down, though the rear sill is quite tall. The modern dashboard is neatly laid out, though climate and radio controls don't fall too easily to hand.

VALUE Significantly improved over the first (1989-92) generation, the latest Probe delivers plenty of punch and prowess for its price.

SPECIFICATIONS

	2-door hatchback
Wheelbase, in.	102.8
Overall length, in.	178.7
Overall width, in.	69.8
Overall height, in.	51.6
Curb weight, lbs.	2690
Cargo volume, cu. ft.	18.0
Fuel capacity, gals.	15.5
Seating capacity	4
Front head room, in.	37.8
Max. front leg room, in.	43.1
Rear head room, in.	34.8
Min. rear leg room, in.	28.5

Powertrain layout: *transverse front-engine/front-wheel drive*

ENGINES

	dohc I4	dohc V6
Size, liters/cu. in.	2.0/122	2.5/153
Horsepower	115-118	164
Torque (lbs./ft.)	124-127	156-160
EPA city/highway mpg		
5-speed OD manual	26/33	21/27
4-speed OD automatic	23/31	20/26
City/highway mpg (as tested)		
4-speed OD automatic	22.2	

Built in USA

RETAIL PRICES

	GOOD	AVERAGE	POOR
1993 Probe	$2,400-3,000	$1,800-2,300	$500-800
1993 Probe GT	2,800-3,500	2,200-2,800	600-1,000
1994 Probe	3,000-3,800	2,300-3,100	700-1,100
1994 Probe GT	3,600-4,200	2,900-3,500	1,000-1,400
1995 Probe	3,600-4,300	2,900-3,500	1,000-1,400
1995 Probe GT	4,400-5,100	3,600-4,300	1,300-1,700
1996 Probe	4,500-5,200	3,800-4,400	1,400-1,800
1996 Probe GT	5,500-6,500	4,600-5,500	2,000-2,400
1997 Probe	5,500-6,300	4,700-5,400	1,900-2,300
1997 Probe GT	6,600-7,600	5,600-6,600	2,400-3,000

AVERAGE REPLACEMENT COSTS

A/C Compressor	$875	Clutch, Pressure Plate, Bearing	590
Alternator	380	Constant Velocity Joints	780
Automatic Transmission or Transaxle	1,075	Exhaust System	485
Brakes	275	Radiator	430
Shocks and/or Struts	770	Timing Chain or Belt	180

TROUBLE SPOTS

• **Transmission leak.** Automatic transmission fluid leaks from the vent and gives the appearance of a leak at the cooler lines or main control cover. (1994-96)

• **Engine stalling.** If the engine stalls when the transmission is shifted into drive, the problem may be a cracked mass airflow snorkel tube. (1993-94)

• **Fuel gauge.** The fuel gauge may only read 3/4 full when the tank is full because the fuel return line is bent and interferes with the sender in the tank. (1995-96)

RECALL HISTORY

1993: Lower pivot pin that joins liftgate gas strut to body can separate from mounting bracket due to undersized rivet head; liftgate could descend suddenly, resulting in potential injury. **1994:** Passenger-side airbag on small number of cars can detach from, and deform, the mounting bracket if it deploys during an accident and no one is occupying that seating position. **1995:** On some cars, passenger airbag may not inflate properly; also, igniter end cap can separate, causing hot gases to be released. **1996:** Supplementary inflatable restraint caution label on driver's sunvisor does not contain proper warning that rearward-facing child safety seats should not be installed in front passenger seat position. **1997:** External spring in timing belt tensioner can break, get caught in belt, and result in engine stalling.

1993-97 FORD RANGER

1993 Ford Ranger XL Sport SuperCab extended cab

FOR Acceleration (V6) • Reliability • Ride

AGAINST Fuel economy (V6) • Control layout

EVALUATION Acceleration is about the same as in the prior generation. Though adequate with a 5-speed, the 4-cylinder engine labors under a heavy load and generally feels lethargic with automatic. Ranger's 4.0-liter V6 uses only slightly more fuel than the 3.0-liter, and delivers good low-speed punch; but the 4.0 is somewhat coarse and noisy. A 4.0 should perform most tasks with relative ease, and it works well with the automatic to furnish prompt passing power.

We averaged 16.5 mpg in a 4WD Splash SuperCab with the 4.0-liter V6. Rangers ride nicely and handle well (for a truck, that is). The suspension absorbs most big bumps without jarring, and the truck is stable in turns. Steering feedback and response are top-notch, and the Ranger has a notably solid feel overall. Gauges are unobstructed, and the climate controls and radio are grouped efficiently. However, some buttons on optional stereos are too small, and climate controls demand quite a reach around the steering wheel. A regular-cab interior lacks space behind the seat. Also, the steering wheel protrudes too far, leaving no surplus of space for larger drivers.

VALUE Ford sought a more carlike look and feel for its Ranger—and succeeded. Some rugged truck characteristics may have been gone, but we view the changes as improvements. Ranger remained one of the best in its class, but we recommend that you shop all three domestic brands—including the Dodge Dakota and Chevrolet S-Series—before deciding.

SPECIFICATIONS

	reg. cab short bed	reg. cab long bed	ext. cab
Wheelbase, in.	107.9	113.9	125.2
Overall length, in.	184.3	196.3	198.2
Overall width, in.	69.4	69.4	69.4
Overall height, in.	64.0	64.0	64.1
Curb weight, lbs.	2970	3010	3300
Fuel capacity, gals.	17.0	17.0	20.5
Seating capacity	3	3	5
Front head room, in.	39.1	39.1	39.3
Max. front leg room, in.	42.4	42.4	42.4
Rear head room, in.	—	—	35.6
Min. rear leg room, in.	—	—	41.2

Powertrain layout: longitudinal front-engine/rear- or 4-wheel drive

ENGINES

	ohc I4	ohv V6	ohv V6
Size, liters/cu. in.	2.3/140	3.0/182	4.0/245[1]
Horsepower	98-112	140-147	160
Torque (lbs./ft.)	130-135	162-170	220
EPA city/highway mpg			
5-speed OD manual	22/27	19/25	18/23
4-speed OD automatic	20/25	18/24	17/23
5-speed OD automatic			16/22
City/highway mpg (as tested)			
5-speed OD manual		17.8	16.5
4-speed OD automatic			14.2

1. Rangers with the 4.0-liter V6 switched from a 4-speed to a 5-speed automatic for '97.

Built in USA

RETAIL PRICES

	GOOD	AVERAGE	POOR
1993 Ranger	$2,400-4,000	$1,800-3,300	$400-1,200
1993 Ranger SuperCab	3,400-5,000	2,700-4,200	900-1,700
1994 Ranger	2,800-5,200	2,100-4,400	600-1,800
1994 Ranger SuperCab	4,000-6,500	3,200-5,600	1,200-2,700
1995 Ranger	3,300-6,200	2,600-5,400	800-2,400
1995 Ranger SuperCab	4,500-7,400	3,700-6,500	1,500-2,900
1996 Ranger	4,000-7,500	3,300-6,600	1,100-3,000
1996 Ranger SuperCab	5,500-9,000	4,500-8,000	1,900-4,000
1997 Ranger	4,800-8,800	4,000-7,800	1,500-3,800
1997 Ranger SuperCab	6,800-10,800	5,800-9,800	2,500-5,000

AVERAGE REPLACEMENT COSTS

A/C Compressor	$425	Clutch, Pressure Plate,	
Alternator	280	Bearing	390
Automatic Transmission or		Exhaust System	215
Transaxle	745	Radiator	340
Brakes	300	Shocks and/or Struts	285
Timing Chain or Belt	395	Universal Joints	90

TROUBLE SPOTS

• **Vehicle noise.** A chattering noise that can be felt coming from the rear during tight turns after highway driving is caused by a lack of friction modifier or over-shimming of the clutch packs in the Traction-Lok differential. (1993-96)

• **Hard starting.** If the engine does not want to start or cranks for a long time then stalls, the idle air control valve may be sticking. (1995-96)

• **Vehicle noise.** Loose frame rivets should be replaced with bolts (welding is not approved). (1993-96)

1993-94 w/manual shift: Parking brake might not hold. **1993-94 sold or currently registered in specified southern California counties:** Studs that attach master cylinder to power brake booster assembly can develop stress corrosion cracking after extended period; if one or both studs fractures, master cylinder could separate from booster when brakes are applied, preventing brakes from activating. **1993-94 w/2.3-liter engine, registered in AK, ME, MI (upper peninsula), MN, MT, ND, NH, NY, VT, or WI:** During extreme cold in northern winters, ice can form in throttle body, causing throttle plate to remain in highway cruising position after accelerator is released or speed control is deactivated. **1993-94 w/V6 engine:** Flexible hose in front fuel line is susceptible to cracking. **1996:** Certification label shows incorrect rear tire inflation pressure.

1998-01 FORD RANGER

1998 Ford Ranger

FOR Acceleration (4.0-liter V6) • Ride • Handling • Optional ABS (XLT, Splash)

AGAINST Acceleration (4-cylinder) • Interior room (regular cab) • Rear-seat comfort

EVALUATION Four-cylinder Rangers struggle to gain speed, especially with an automatic transmission. We recommend the 4.0-liter V6, which uses only slightly more fuel than the 3.0 V6 and costs only slightly more. Although the 4.0-liter is a bit coarse and noisy, it offers plenty of low-speed torque and should perform most tasks with ease. That engine also works well with Ford's 5-speed automatic transmission and furnishes prompt passing power. None of these engines is quiet, though the sixes are slightly smoother than the four. Gas mileage is passable, too. We averaged 15.6 mpg in a long-term test of a 4WD SuperCab with the 4.0 and automatic. Like its Mazda B-Series cousin, Ranger rides and handles admirably for a truck. Yes, it jiggles more on rough roads than most cars. Still, the suspension absorbs most bumps without jarring the occupants, and provides stable cornering with moderate body lean. Slightly roomier than before, with more behind-the-seat storage space, Ranger's regular-cab interior is still not spacious. The longer regular cab allows the seatback to be tilted farther back than before, but taller drivers may find the SuperCab a necessity for comfort. Some shorter drivers may declare the bottoms of the bucket seats to be too long, catching them behind the knees. The 4-door SuperCab option is a big plus, but those rear-hinged back doors are narrow and cannot be opened unless the front door has been opened first. Even with a bench seat, three adults would be a tight squeeze up front. Entry/exit borders on awkward in the higher-riding 4x4s and 2WD Edge models. SuperCabs have a pair of child-sized rear seats that flip down from the sidewalls, but that area is more useful for cargo than people. Controls are positioned within easy reach, in a carlike interior, though the climate panel is recessed too much for quick adjustment. Radio controls are easier to use than in the past. Solid in build, Rangers use better quality interior materials than might be expected in a compact pickup.

VALUE Yes, Ranger lacks a few features available on rivals, including a third door (on extended-cab GM pickups) and the V8 option of a Dodge Dakota. Nevertheless, the Ranger is refined, well built, and priced sensibly. No wonder Ranger has been the top-selling compact truck. Because Mazda's B-Series does not sell as well, however, prices might be a bit lower without the Ford badge.

SPECIFICATIONS

	reg. cab short bed	reg. cab long bed	ext. cab short bed
Wheelbase, in.	111.6	117.5	125.7
Overall length, in.	187.5	200.7	202.9
Overall width, in.	69.4	69.4	69.4
Overall height, in.	68.2	68.2	68.2
Curb weight, lbs.	3060	3100	3280
Fuel capacity, gals.	17.0	20.0	20.0
Seating capacity	3	3	5
Front head room, in.	39.2	39.2	39.2
Max. front leg room, in.	42.2	42.2	42.2
Rear head room, in.	—	—	NA
Min. rear leg room, in.	—	—	NA

Powertrain layout: longitudinal front-engine/rear- or 4-wheel drive

ENGINES

	ohc I4	dohc I4	ohv V6	ohv V6	ohc V6
Size, liters/cu. in.	2.5/152	2.3/138	3.0/182	4.0/245	4.0/245
Horsepower	117-119	135	145-150	158-160	207
Torque (lbs./ft.)	146-149	153	178-190	223-225	238

EPA city/highway mpg

5-speed OD man.	22/27	24/28	17/23	16/21	18/22
4-speed OD auto.	20/25	21/25	17/22		
5-speed OD auto.				17/21	

City/highway mpg (as tested)

4-speed OD auto.	18.2	
5-speed OD auto.		16.4

Built in USA

RETAIL PRICES

	GOOD	AVERAGE	POOR
1998 Ranger 2WD	$5,800-7,800	$5,000-7,000	$2,500-3,800
1998 Ranger 4WD	7,500-10,000	6,500-9,000	3,500-5,000
1998 SuperCab 2WD	8,000-10,000	7,000-9,000	4,000-5,000
1998 SuperCab 4WD	10,000-12,000	9,000-11,000	5,500-7,000
1999 Ranger 2WD	6,800-7,900	6,000-7,000	3,100-3,800
1999 Ranger 4WD	8,800-10,500	7,800-9,500	4,500-5,500
1999 SuperCab 2WD	9,300-10,500	8,300-9,500	4,800-5,500
1999 SuperCab 4WD	11,300-12,800	10,000-11,300	6,200-7,200
2000 Ranger 2WD	7,900-9,000	7,000-8,000	3,800-5,000
2000 Ranger 4WD	10,000-11,500	9,000-10,500	5,500-6,500
2000 SuperCab 2WD	10,500-12,000	9,500-11,000	5,800-6,800
2000 SuperCab 4WD	12,500-14,200	11,000-12,700	7,000-8,000
2001 Ranger 2WD	9,000-10,500	8,100-9,500	—
2001 Ranger 4WD	13,000-14,500	11,500-13,000	—
2001 SuperCab 2WD	11,000-13,000	9,800-11,500	—
2001 SuperCab 4WD	13,000-16,000	11,500-14,500	—

AVERAGE REPLACEMENT COSTS

A/C Compressor	$450	Clutch, Pressure Plate, Bearing	415
Alternator	250	Exhaust System	245
Automatic Transmission or Transaxle	580	Radiator	430
Brakes	420	Shocks and/or Struts	445
Timing Chain or Belt	95	Universal Joints	145

TROUBLE SPOTS

- **Vehicle noise.** A hammering noise occurs due to steam forming in the cooling system requiring a coolant bypass retrofit kit. (1998-00)

- **Engine misfire.** Hesitation or surging when accelerating is caused by a faulty mass airflow sensor. (1998-99)

- **Air conditioner.** The air conditioner hose may rub against the radiator hose and one, or both, develop leaks. (1998)

- **Battery.** The battery tray may have burrs that cut into the battery causing it to leak and eventually fail. (1998)

- **Audio system.** The in-tank fuel pump causes a whining or buzzing noise to come through the radio speakers. (1998-99)

- **Engine misfire.** The truck may feel like it is thumping or jerking under acceleration due to a problem with the driveshaft requiring replacement. (1998-99)

RECALL HISTORY

1998 w/4.0-liter engine: Flexible section of chassis-mounted fuel line on some trucks could contact exhaust manifold; might potentially result in damage to fuel line or, in some cases, cause a fuel leak. **1998 4-wheel drive w/off-road option:** Tire and rim identification information is incorrect. **1998-99:** Cruise-control cable can interfere with servo pulley and not allow throttle to return to idle. **1999 w/3.0-liter engine:** O-ring seal in fuel injection pulse damper to fuel rail joint could be damaged, allowing fuel leakage. **2000 w/2.5-liter engine:** Engine coolant circulation through heater circuit is prevented by plugged return tube at water pump. **2000-01:** Hood striker could fracture causing the hood could fly open while the vehicle is being driven. **2001:** Driver's and/or outboard front passenger's seatbelt buckle may not fully latch. In the event of a crash, the restraint system may not provide adequate occupant protection.

1990-95 FORD TAURUS

1995 Ford Taurus SE 4-door sedan

FOR Ride • Passenger and cargo room • Acceleration (V6) • Handling/roadholding • Antilock brakes (optional)

AGAINST Acceleration (4-cylinder) • Fuel economy (V6) • Radio controls

EVALUATION Taurus feels composed over bumps and in corners. Steering is precise, and suspension movements are well-controlled. Taurus is surefooted and agile, with balanced handling in turns and minimal body lean. The firm, Euro-style ride is just right, even if you can expect a few bumps on rougher surfaces. The weak, noisy 4-cylinder engine just isn't strong enough to power a Taurus. A 3.0-liter V6 promises much brisker passing, and the optional 3.8-liter V6 noticeably stronger acceleration from a standstill, plus better midrange response. Harsh shifts from the automatic transmission do occur occasionally in low-speed driving. Neither V6 is frugal: One Taurus averaged just 17.9 mpg in commuting and expressway driving. For excitement behind the wheel of a seemingly sedate midsize sedan, SHO is the way to go. Acceleration rivals that of the world's leading sports sedans. Variable-assist power steering was modified in 1992, resulting in a less-precise feel at highway speed. Also on the downside, Taurus tires thump loudly over bumps. Head room is ample all around, and sedans have a deep, wide trunk. Analog gauges are clearly marked, but the stereo sits low and has small, poorly marked controls.

VALUE We rank the early '90s Taurus/Sable among the most impressive domestic cars: solid, roomy, great to look at, and a joy to drive.

SPECIFICATIONS

	4-door sedan	4-door wagon
Wheelbase, in.	106.0	106.0
Overall length, in.	192.0	193.1
Overall width, in.	70.7	70.7
Overall height, in.	54.1	55.5
Curb weight, lbs.	3118	3285
Cargo volume, cu. ft.	18.0	83.1
Fuel capacity, gals.	16.0	16.0
Seating capacity	6	8
Front head room, in.	38.3	38.5
Max. front leg room, in.	41.7	41.7
Rear head room, in.	37.6	38.1
Min. rear leg room, in.	37.7	36.9

Powertrain layout: transverse front-engine/front-wheel drive

ENGINES

	ohv I4	ohv V6	dohc V6	dohc V6	ohv V6
Size, liters/cu. in.	2.5/153	3.0/182	3.0/182	3.2/195	3.8/232
Horsepower	90-105	140	220	220	140
Torque (lbs./ft.)	130-140	160-165	200	215	215

EPA city/highway mpg

5-speed OD man.			18/26		
3-speed auto.	21/27				
4-speed OD auto.		20/30		18/26	19/28

City/highway mpg (as tested)

4-speed OD automatic	17.9

Built in USA

RETAIL PRICES

	GOOD	AVERAGE	POOR
1990 Taurus	$1,000-1,700	$500-1,100	$100-200
1990 Taurus SHO	1,700-2,300	1,100-1,600	200-400
1991 Taurus	1,300-2,100	700-1,500	100-300
1991 Taurus SHO	2,100-2,800	1,500-2,100	400-700
1992 Taurus	1,700-2,500	1,100-1,900	200-400
1992 Taurus SHO	2,500-3,200	1,800-2,500	600-1,000
1993 Taurus	2,100-3,000	1,500-2,300	400-700
1993 Taurus SHO	3,000-3,800	2,300-3,100	800-1,200
1994 Taurus	2,600-3,500	2,000-2,800	600-1,000
1994 Taurus SHO	3,500-4,300	2,800-3,500	1,000-1,400
1995 Taurus	3,200-4,200	2,500-3,500	800-1,400
1995 Taurus SHO	4,500-5,400	3,700-4,600	1,400-1,800

AVERAGE REPLACEMENT COSTS

A/C Compressor	$455	Constant Velocity Joints	505
Alternator	440	Exhaust System	365
Automatic Transmission or		Radiator	525
Transaxle	930	Shocks and/or Struts	495
Brakes	230	Timing Chain or Belt	210

TROUBLE SPOTS

• **Vehicle noise.** A popping noise comes from the front due to the strut rod bushing mountings moving in the frame. (1990-95)

• **Oil leak.** Ford extended the warranty on the 3.8-liter Taurus to 7/100,000 and may compensate owners for repairs related to head gasket failures. (1994-95)

• **Hard starting.** If the engine does not start or cranks for a long time then stalls, the idle air control valve may be sticking. (1995)

• **Tire wear.** Inner edge of rear tires wear excessively from camber problems corrected with a revised rear suspension adjuster kit. (1990-95)

• **Tire wear.** Premature tire wear and cupping is caused by rear wheel misalignment. (1990-95)

• **Blower motor.** Squeaking or chirping blower motors are the result of defective brush holders. (1990-94)

• **Engine noise.** The motor mounts are prone to wear out prematurely so Ford has issued a voluntary recall (number 92M77) to replace the right front and right rear mounts. The coverage is 6 years or 60,000 miles. (1992-93)

• **Suspension problems.** The stabilizer bar links wear rapidly due to lack of grease fittings, especially if a technician is careless when servicing the MacPherson struts. (1990-95)

RECALL HISTORY

1990-91: Front brake rotors on cars sold in 14 northeastern and Great Lakes states may suffer severe corrosion, resulting in reduced braking effectiveness. **1990-95 sold or registered in 24 states or D.C.:** Rear lower subframe mount plate nut can experience corrosion cracking if subjected to long-term exposure to road salt; can result in fracture. **1991-95 w/3.8-liter engine in 23 states:** Water can accumulate within speed-control conduit; if cable has frozen, throttle can stick and not return to idle. **1992 wagon:** Children can accidentally lock themselves in footwell area of rear-facing third seat or in storage compartment in wagons that lack optional third seat; self-latching assembly should be replaced with a unit that can be closed only with a key. **1992 wagon:** Secondary liftgate latch mechanism on some cars may not function, possibly allowing liftgate to open while car is in motion. **1992-93:** On cars sold in 14 Midwestern and Northeastern states, body mounts at rear subframe corners (which support engine/transmission) may detach due to corrosion, allowing subframe to drop; could result in clunking noise or altered steering-wheel alignment or, if both corners drop, could make steering very difficult. **1992-95 w/3.0- or 3.8-liter engine, in AK, IA, MN, NE, ND, or SD:** During high winds, heavy snow, and low temperatures, engine fan may become blocked or frozen; can cause smoke/flame. **1993:** Controllers intended for rear-drive vehicles (instead of front-drive) may have been installed in a few cars with optional antilock braking. **1993 in 21 states:** Front coil springs can fracture as a result of corrosion in combination with small cracks. **1993-94:** Headlights can flash intermittently as a result of a circuit-breaker opening. **1995:** On some cars, retainer that holds master cylinder pushrod to brake pedal arm is missing or not fully installed; can result in loss of braking.

1996-99 FORD TAURUS

1997 Ford Taurus SHO 4-door sedan

FOR Optional antilock brakes • Acceleration (LX, SHO) • Steering/handling • Passenger and cargo room

AGAINST Transmission performance (G, GL) • Rear visibility • Ride (SHO)

EVALUATION An LX accelerates with greater authority than its less-potent G/GL siblings. That 200-horsepower engine is smooth, refined, and potent at higher engine speeds. Low-speed torque is lacking, however, so you must floor the throttle to achieve brisk passing. The LX transmission shifts smoothly. Not only is the G/GL V6 engine less powerful, but it's noisier, rougher, and slower. Its transmission often stumbles, shifts roughly, and is slow to downshift for passing. Low-speed power is also lacking in the SHO's V8, though it's plenty potent at higher speeds. You simply have to wait until engine speed reaches 3000 rpm or so before much happens. Steering is light and precise. Both models corner with good grip and commendable composure. Ride quality has improved somewhat, but the suspension does not absorb bumps well and feels too stiff on rough roads. Beware: The SHO's ride is stiff at all times. Wind and road noise have been reduced compared to previous Tauruses. The modern-looking control panel for the climate and audio systems is easy to see and reach, but buttons are overly abundant and many look alike. With optional automatic air conditioning, that control pad gets packed full. Interior space is better all around than before, especially in the rear, where leg room has grown substantially. Sitting three across, however, will crowd everyone—in both front and rear. The sedan trunk is roomy—wide, deep, and reaching well forward. The driver enjoys a clear view to the front and sides, but it's difficult to see the trunk of the sedan.

VALUE Though not perfect, Taurus is roomy, well-built, and enjoyable to drive. Prices went up for this generation, but Tauruses remained a good value and an excellent choice, new or used.

SPECIFICATIONS

	4-door sedan	4-door wagon
Wheelbase, in.	108.5	108.5
Overall length, in.	197.5	199.6
Overall width, in.	73.0	73.0
Overall height, in.	55.1	57.6
Curb weight, lbs.	3326	3480
Cargo volume, cu. ft.	15.8	81.3
Fuel capacity, gals.	16.0	16.0
Seating capacity	6[1]	8[2]
Front head room, in.	39.2	39.3
Max. front leg room, in.	42.6	42.6
Rear head room, in.	36.2	38.9
Min. rear leg room, in.	38.9	38.5

1. 5 with front bucket seats. 2. 6 without optional third row seat.

Powertrain layout: transverse front-engine/front-wheel drive

ENGINES

	ohv V6	dohc V6	dohc V8
Size, liters/cu. in.	3.0/182	3.0/181	3.4/207
Horsepower	145	200	235
Torque (lbs./ft.)	170	200	230
EPA city/highway mpg			
4-speed OD automatic	20/28	19/28	17/26
City/highway mpg (as tested)			
4-speed OD automatic	18.3	17.1	16.5

Built in USA

RETAIL PRICES

	GOOD	AVERAGE	POOR
1996 Taurus sedan	$4,200-5,300	$3,500-4,600	$1,500-2,100
1996 Taurus wagon	4,800-5,700	4,100-4,900	1,800-2,300
1996 Taurus SHO	7,500-8,500	6,500-7,500	3,500-4,200
1997 Taurus sedan	5,500-6,700	4,800-6,000	2,400-3,200
1997 Taurus wagon	6,200-7,200	5,400-6,300	2,800-3,400
1997 Taurus SHO	9,000-10,500	8,000-9,500	4,500-5,500
1998 Taurus sedan	7,000-8,000	6,200-7,100	3,200-3,800
1998 Taurus wagon	8,000-9,000	7,100-8,000	3,700-4,300
1998 Taurus SHO	11,000-12,500	10,000-11,300	6,000-7,000
1999 Taurus sedan	8,500-9,500	7,500-8,500	4,200-4,900
1999 Taurus wagon	9,500-10,500	8,500-9,500	4,800-5,600
1999 Taurus SHO	13,000-14,500	11,800-13,000	7,500-8,500

AVERAGE REPLACEMENT COSTS

A/C Compressor	$440	Shocks and/or Struts	600
Alternator	350	Constant Velocity Joints	605
Automatic Transmission or		Exhaust System	415
Transaxle	1,115	Radiator	585
Brakes	280	Timing Chain or Belt	350

TROUBLE SPOTS

• **Tire wear.** Inner edge of rear tires wear excessively from camber problems corrected with a revised rear suspension adjuster kit. (1996-97)

• **Vehicle noise.** Noises from the front end (popping, clunking, knocking) result from worn sway bar links. Countermeasure links have been issued by the carmaker. (1996-97)

• **Vehicle noise.** Rattling and buzzing from under the car is common due to loose heat shields on the catalytic converter and/or muffler. (1996-97)

• **Tire wear.** Rear tires wear prematurely due to incorrect rear alignment (toe and camber). (1996-97)

• **Air conditioner.** The air conditioning may not cool properly because the lines leak at the spring-lock couplings. Larger O-rings are available. (1996-97)

• **Dashboard lights.** The check engine light comes on for a variety of reasons including bad gasoline, a wobbling accessory drive pulley, or bad spark plugs. (1996-97)

• **Steering problems.** The power steering gets harder to turn when decelerating from about 50 miles per hour or when shifting form reverse to drive requiring replacement of the control module and/or transmission range sensors. (1996)

• **Suspension noise.** The sway bar links wear prematurely causing a clunking noise. Revised parts are available. (1996-97)

• **Automatic transmission.** Vehicles with the AX4S automatic transmission may shift harshly from first to second gear. (1996-97)

• **Water leak.** Water leaks onto the front floor because of poor sealing of the cabin air filter cowl inlet. (1996-98)

RECALL HISTORY

1996: Automatic-transmission "park" pawl shaft may not be free to rotate; vehicle could then roll as if in neutral, with shift lever in "park" position. **1996:** Vacuum diaphragm in fuel pressure regulator was damaged during manufacture; if it tears or ruptures, liquid fuel could be released from air cleaner assembly or exhaust system. **1996:** Brake fluid indicator can malfunction. **1996 w/AX4S automatic transaxle:** "Park" pawl shaft was improperly positioned; pawl may occasionally fail to engage when selector lever is placed in "park" position, allowing vehicle to roll if parking brake has not been applied. **1996-97:** "Park" pawl abutment bracket has sharp edge, which can cause pawl to hang up and not engage gear; vehicle can then move, even though indicator shows "Park." **1997 w/AX4S automatic transaxle:** Low/intermediate servo cover can separate while vehicle is moving, allowing transmission fluid to contact the hot catalytic converter. **1997-98:** Headlamp aiming instruction in owner's manual is not sufficiently clear. **1998-99 w/manual seat tracks:** Front seatbelt buckle attaching stud may have been improperly heat-treated, resulting in cracks. **1999:** Retainer clip can disengage from accelerator cable and fall into pedal arm pivot area; engine may not fully return to idle, and insulator could interfere with cable. **1999 w/"California" emissions pkg.:** Incorrect transmission oil cooler line was installed, which contacts ABS module bracket and, over time, can wear and develop a leak. **1999:** Seatbelt retractor may have incorrectly formed pin shaft that could, in some circumstances, prevent seatbelt webbing from being extracted.

2000-01 FORD TAURUS

2000 Ford Taurus 4-door sedan

FOR Handling/roadholding • Rear-seat comfort • Cargo room

AGAINST Acceleration (ohv V6)

EVALUATION Taurus delivers plenty of performance for a mainstream midsize car, though it lacks class-leading acceleration. Both engines run smoothly, but neither moves all that swiftly beyond midrange speeds. Each V6 can accelerate suitably from a standstill, but a Chevrolet Impala with the base engine responds better to the throttle than a Taurus, at 25-50 mph. Fuel economy with the twincam engine averaged 18.4 mpg. Road manners are another story. Taurus feels balanced, secure, and predictable even in rapid directional changes. Steering has fine on-center sense, but turning effort is not as linear as some drivers might like. Resistance to wallow and float is impressive, but rough-road ride is not. Stopping power feels strong and easily modulated. Family-focused space is a strong point, including excellent back-seat room and comfort. Rear head clearance is generous, helped by the revised roof shape. Leg/foot space also is plentiful. The back seat is substantial and comfortably contoured, but the wagon's fold-away rear-racing third seat is for children under 80 pounds. Front outboard seating positions are uncrowded, but the bench's center spot is mighty snug. The new adjustable pedals work easily via a control on the seat bottom. Shorter drivers can sit farther from the steering-wheel airbag. Gauges are unobstructed, but their analog markings are small. On bucket-seat models, the only gear indicator is near the console floor shift. Audio and climate controls are easy to see and use, but lack selectable air conditioning or recirculation modes. Luggage space is generous in either body style.

VALUE Taurus returned to its roots as family transportation with the 2000 redesign. Fully contemporary in styling, a Taurus delivers fine road manners, great utility, and an appealing array of safety features, at competitive prices. Despite acceleration limitations and imperfect ride comfort, Taurus deserves a place on any midsize-car shopping list.

SPECIFICATIONS

	4-door sedan	4-door wagon
Wheelbase, in.	108.5	108.5
Overall length, in.	197.6	197.6
Overall width, in.	73.0	73.0
Overall height, in.	56.1	58.0
Curb weight, lbs.	3328	3486
Cargo volume, cu. ft.	17.0	81.3
Fuel capacity, gals.	16.0	16.0
Seating capacity	6	8
Front head room, in.	40.0	39.3
Max. front leg room, in.	42.2	42.2
Rear head room, in.	38.1	38.7
Min. rear leg room, in.	38.9	38.5

Powertrain layout: transverse front-engine/front-wheel drive

ENGINES

	ohv V6	dohc V6
Size, liters/cu. in.	3.0/182	3.0/181
Horsepower	155	200
Torque (lbs./ft.)	185	200
EPA city/highway mpg		
4-speed OD automatic	19/28	20/28
City/highway mpg (as tested)		
4-speed OD automatic		18.4

Built in USA

RETAIL PRICES

	GOOD	AVERAGE	POOR
2000 Taurus 4-dr sedan	$10,500-12,300	$9,500-11,300	$6,500-7,500
2000 Taurus 4-dr wagon	11,700-12,700	10,700-11,700	7,500-8,300

	GOOD	AVERAGE	POOR
2001 Taurus 4-dr sedan	$12,000-14,300	$11,000-13,300	—
2001 Taurus 4-dr wagon	13,200-14,500	12,200-13,500	—

AVERAGE REPLACEMENT COSTS

A/C Compressor	$405	Constant Velocity Joints	990
Alternator	535	Exhaust System	300
Automatic Transmission or		Radiator	405
Transaxle	1,120	Shocks and/or Struts	1,100
Brakes	240	Timing Chain or Belt	180

TROUBLE SPOTS

• **Fuel odors.** Gasoline odor is probably due to a bad gasket on the lower intake manifold on the 3.0-L Duratec engine. (2000-01)

• **Vehicle shake.** Harsh downshifts or shudder, especially on curves, can be caused by the transmission fluid level being below the fullest level as shown on the dipstick. (2000)

• **Audio system.** Noise (whine or buzz) in the radio speakers is probably due to interference from the in-tank fuel pump requiring a RFI filter on the pump assembly. (2000-01)

RECALL HISTORY

2000: On certain vehicles, "vehicle capacity weight" and "designated seating capacity" information was not printed on safety certification labels. **2000:** Headlamp switch knob can fracture and separate from the headlamp switch. **2000-01:** CHMSL can illuminate (at reduced intensity) even though the service brakes have not been applied. **2000-01 w/adjustable pedals:** Grease from the adjustable pedal assembly enters the stop lamp switch and can contaminate the contacts leading to carbon build up, and potentially, a short circuit. **2000-01:** A switch located in the plastic cover of the wiper motor gear case could malfunction and overheat, potentially resulting in loss of wiper function or fire. **2001:** Owner guides may not identify center rear seating position as having LATCH-compatible lower anchorages. **2001:** Child Safety Seat Anchor Latch (ISO-fix anchor) fasteners on certain vehicles do not have adequate residual torque; road vibrations could cause a nut to loosen and separate.

1990-97 FORD THUNDERBIRD

1990 Ford Thunderbird

FOR Acceleration (SC and V8) • Ride • Handling/roadholding • Antilock brakes (optional)

AGAINST Acceleration (V6) • Fuel economy (SC and V8) • Entry/exit

EVALUATION Substantially heavier than prior T-Birds, the stylish but portly '90s edition is roomier inside. Three can fit into the rear, but head room is limited and the center occupant straddles a wide driveline tunnel. Controls are clear and easy to reach, analog gauges easy to read on a cockpit-style dash. The optional electronic dashboard isn't so easy. As with most coupes of this size, the big, heavy doors are a chore to open and demand a lot of room. Though smooth-running and capable, the base V6 sets no acceleration records. The Super Coupe, on the other hand, is one swift cruiser. Unfortunately, the 5-speed manual gearshift gets balky, making automatic the better choice for an SC. A V8 engine is the sensible choice for those who like performance, but don't need the all-out muscle of the Super Coupe. The V8 delivers a smooth power flow, not neck-snapping takeoffs. A V8 Thunderbird reached 60 mph in 8.8 seconds. The 4.6-liter V6 is quieter, smoother than the older 5.0-liter, but yields unimpressive throttle response in the 30-50-mph range. Fuel economy is tempting only on base (V6) models. A late LX V8 got 18.2 mpg (just 15 in urban commuting). An automatic-transmission SC averaged 15.2 mpg. All Thunderbirds have competent road manners. Base and LX models handle well and ride comfortably, but

do tend to float and bound over dips as speed rises. SCs hug the road tightly, but heavy weight keeps even that Thunderbird from feeling truly agile, and the Super Coupe suffers from an overly firm ride. Even in its softest mode, the SC's standard adjustable suspension is on the harsh side. The Sport model (available only briefly) gives you V8 power and a tauter ride than the base car. Thunderbirds can suffer poor traction on wet/slick pavement even with traction control.

VALUE Standard Thunderbirds are pretty and pleasant compared to front-drive GM coupes, such as the Chevrolet Monte Carlo and Pontiac Grand Prix. You get a solid feel, quiet ride, and modern appearance.

SPECIFICATIONS

	2-door coupe
Wheelbase, in.	113.0
Overall length, in.	200.3
Overall width, in.	72.7
Overall height, in.	52.5
Curb weight, lbs.	3536
Cargo volume, cu. ft.	15.1
Fuel capacity, gals.	18.0
Seating capacity	5
Front head room, in.	38.1
Max. front leg room, in.	42.5
Rear head room, in.	37.5
Min. rear leg room, in.	35.8

Powertrain layout: longitudinal front-engine/rear-wheel drive

ENGINES

	ohv V6	Supercharged ohv V6	ohc V8	ohv V8
Size, liters/cu. in.	3.8/232	3.8/232	4.6/281	5.0/302
Horsepower	140-145	210-230	203-205	200
Torque (lbs./ft.)	215	315-330	265-280	275
EPA city/highway mpg				
5-speed OD manual		18/26	17/25	
4-speed OD automatic	19/26	18/24	17/24	17/24
City/highway mpg (as tested)				
5-speed OD manual		15.8	18.2	
4-speed OD automatic		15.2	15.1	15.1

Built in USA

RETAIL PRICES

	GOOD	AVERAGE	POOR
1990 Thunderbird	$1,500-2,200	$1,000-1,600	$200-400
1990 Super Coupe	2,200-3,000	1,600-2,300	400-800
1991 Thunderbird	2,000-2,700	1,400-2,000	400-700
1991 Super Coupe	3,000-3,800	2,300-3,000	800-1,200
1992 Thunderbird	2,500-3,200	1,900-2,500	600-900
1992 Super Coupe	3,500-4,200	2,800-3,400	1,000-1,400
1993 Thunderbird	3,000-3,700	2,300-3,000	800-1,100
1993 Super Coupe	4,000-4,800	3,200-3,900	1,200-1,600
1994 Thunderbird	3,500-4,200	2,800-3,400	1,000-1,400
1994 Super Coupe	4,600-5,300	3,800-4,500	1,600-2,000
1995 Thunderbird	4,200-5,000	3,500-4,200	1,400-1,800
1995 Super Coupe	5,500-6,500	4,600-5,500	2,000-2,600
1996 Thunderbird	5,400-6,300	4,700-5,500	2,000-2,600
1997 Thunderbird	6,800-7,800	5,900-6,800	2,600-3,200

AVERAGE REPLACEMENT COSTS

A/C Compressor	$365	Exhaust System	275
Alternator	445	Radiator	405
Automatic Transmission or		Shocks and/or Struts	285
Transaxle	810	Timing Chain or Belt	340
Brakes	235	Universal Joints	265

TROUBLE SPOTS

• **Vehicle noise.** A chattering noise that can be felt coming from the rear during tight turns after highway driving is caused by a lack of friction modifier or over-shimming of the clutch packs in the Traction-Lok differential. (1990-96)

• **Blower motor.** Squeaking or chirping blower motors are the result of defective brush holders. (1993-94)

• **Automatic transmission.** The automatic transmission is notorious for shuddering or vibrating under light acceleration or when shifting between third and fourth gear. It requires that the transmission fluid (including fluid in the torque converter) be changed and that only Mercon® fluid be used. (1994)

- **Alternator belt.** The drive belt tensioner pulley or idler pulley bearings are apt to make a squealing noise when the engine is started in cold weather. (1993-96)
- **Oil leak.** The oil filter balloons and leaks because the oil pump relief valve sticks. Higher than recommended viscosity oils cause wear to the valve bore. (1992-94)
- **Automatic transmission.** The transmission may slip and the engine may flare when shifting into fourth gear. This can often be traced to a bad TR/MLP sensor. (1994-95)
- **Air conditioner.** Water drips onto the floor when the air conditioner is operated and may be due to over a half-dozen potential leak sources, including seals and bad seams in the evaporator case or heater core. (1990-96)

RECALL HISTORY

1990-91: Nuts that hold windshield wiper motor may loosen or come off. **1990-93:** Ignition switch could suffer short circuit, which can cause overheating, smoke, and possibly fire in steering-column area. **1991:** Park rod assembly of automatic overdrive transmission may contain a cam with inadequate surface hardness, which could lead to disengagement or nonengagement when lever is placed in "Park" position. **1992-93 w/foglights:** Headlights may go out for various intervals as a result of circuit breaker opening. **1992-93 cars in specified states:** Movement of fuel lines can result in leakage. **1996:** Driver's door, when closed only to secondary latched position, may not sustain the specified 1000-pound transverse load. **1996 w/semiautomatic temperature-control:** Under certain conditions, blower does not operate as intended.

1995-98 FORD WINDSTAR

1995 Ford Windstar

FOR Antilock brakes • Passenger and cargo room • Ride/handling

AGAINST Fuel economy • Instruments/controls • Rear-seat entry/exit • Steering feel

EVALUATION Start-up acceleration with the 3.8-liter engine is okay, but the relatively heavy Windstar fails to feel truly lively. The automatic transmission typically pauses before downshifting to pass, and often shifts roughly. The stronger 1996 version of the 3.8-liter doesn't improve performance dramatically, but its extra passing power is appreciated. The 3.0-liter V6 has to struggle, and feels sluggish when passing. Gas mileage is not the greatest either way. We averaged 15.9 mpg with one Windstar and just 13.8 with another. A 3.0-liter Windstar averaged 16 mpg in urban driving and 20-21 mpg on the highway. The absorbent suspension delivers a comfortable, stable ride at highway speeds and also on bumpy urban streets. Body lean is moderate, and tires grip well in spirited cornering. On the downside, steering feels loose and imprecise. Getting in and out of the front seats is just about as easy as in most passenger cars. Climbing into the rear requires ducking around a shoulder belt for the middle seat. The rear seat must be pushed all the way back on its 7-inch track to produce adequate leg space. Major controls are backlit at night, and the dashboard is conveniently laid out. The stereo is easy to reach, but controls are small and hard to decipher. Round dials for the climate system are easy to use. With all seats in place, Windstar offers 16 cubic feet of cargo room—more than a Grand Caravan/Voyager.

VALUE Windstars haven't proven to be quite as successful as Ford had hoped, but Ford's front-drive model equals or beats Chrysler's minivans in key areas of performance and accommodations. Therefore, Windstar is well worth a try.

SPECIFICATIONS

	3-door van
Wheelbase, in.	120.7
Overall length, in.	201.2
Overall width, in.	75.4
Overall height, in.	68.0
Curb weight, lbs.	3800
Cargo volume, cu. ft.	144.0
Fuel capacity, gals.	20.0
Seating capacity	7
Front head room, in.	39.3
Max. front leg room, in.	40.7
Rear head room, in.	38.9
Min. rear leg room, in.	39.2

Powertrain layout: transverse front-engine/front-wheel drive

ENGINES

	ohv V6	ohv V6
Size, liters/cu. in.	3.0/182	3.8/232
Horsepower	150	155-200
Torque (lbs./ft.)	170	220-230
EPA city/highway mpg		
4-speed OD automatic	17/25	17/24
City/highway mpg (as tested)		
4-speed OD automatic	20.9	15.9

Built in Canada

RETAIL PRICES

	GOOD	AVERAGE	POOR
1995 Windstar GL	$4,000-4,800	$3,300-4,000	$1,400-1,800
1995 Windstar LX	4,800-5,800	4,000-5,000	1,900-2,500
1996 Windstar GL	5,500-6,500	4,700-5,700	2,300-2,800
1996 Windstar LX	6,300-7,300	5,500-6,500	2,800-35,00
1997 Windstar, GL	7,000-8,000	6,200-7,000	3,300-3,800
1997 Windstar LX	8,000-9,500	7,200-8,500	4,000-5,000
1998 Windstar 3.0L, GL	9,000-10,000	8,100-9,000	4,500-5,200
1998 Windstar LX	10,500-12,000	9,500-11,000	5,500-6,500
1998 Windstar Limited	115,00 -12,800	10,300-11,500	6,000-6,800

AVERAGE REPLACEMENT COSTS

A/C Compressor	$380	Exhaust System	425
Alternator	430	Radiator	425
Brakes	320	Shocks and/or Struts	515
Constant Velocity Joints	476	Timing Chain or Belt	520

TROUBLE SPOTS

- **Engine noise.** A clunk heard and/or felt from the floor on acceleration, deceleration, or turns is caused by movement between the body and subframe, which is corrected by installing revised insulators. (1995-96)
- **Airbags.** Diagnostic trouble codes for the airbag system flash intermittently requiring reprogramming. (1995)
- **Oil leak.** Ford extended the warranty on 3.8-liter Windstars to 7/100,000 and may compensate owners for repairs related to head gasket failures. (1995)
- **Air conditioner.** Moaning air conditioners are repaired by replacing the A/C compressor clutch and pulley. (1995-97)
- **Brakes.** The parking brake may fail to release because the release rod breaks. (1995-98)
- **Poor transmission shift.** Vehicles with the AX4S automatic transmission may shift harshly from first to second gear. (1996-97)
- **Audio system.** Whining noises in the radio speakers are caused by the fuel pump in the gas tank. An electronic noise filter must be installed on the fuel pump. (1995-96)

RECALL HISTORY

1995: Wiring harness insulation can abrade on a brace between instrument panel and cowl, resulting in short-circuit and possible fire. **1995:** Some passenger airbags may not inflate properly; also, igniter end cap can separate, releasing hot gases. **1995:** Improperly tightened alternator output wire may result in overheating and possible fire. **1995 in certain hot-weather states:** Cracks can develop in standard 20-gallon fuel tank. **1995-96:** Tearing of bond between inner and outer hood panels during minor front-end collisions can result in gap at leading edge of hood; could lead to total separation of outer hood panel. **1996:** Due to improperly torqued fasteners, driver's seat on a few minivans may not hold properly in an accident. **1996 w/AX4S automatic transmission:** Park pawl shaft was improperly positioned; pawl may occasionally fail to engage when selector lever is placed in Park position, allowing vehicle to roll if parking brake has not been applied. **1996:** Park pawl abutment bracket has sharp edge, which can cause pawl to hang up and not engage gear; vehicle can move even though indicator shows Park. **1996-98:** Certain off-lease vehicles, Canadian in origin but sold in the U.S., have daytime running lights that do not meet U.S. specifications. **1996-99:** Brake master cylinder on certain vehicles is oriented so warning statements are not entirely visible by direct view. **1997:** Servo cover can separate, causing transmission fluid to leak and contact catalytic converter; could result in fire. **1997-98:** Front coil springs could fracture as a result of corrosion. Some tires have deflated due to contact with a broken spring. **1998:** Damaged bearings on a few minivans can increase steering effort.

1999-01 FORD WINDSTAR

2001 Ford Windstar SE Sport

FOR Passenger and cargo room

AGAINST Fuel economy

EVALUATION Windstar has been, and continues to be, one of the better all-around minivan performers. The 3.0-liter engine struggles to provide adequate acceleration, making the quieter, smoother 3.8-liter V6 a stronger and better choice. That engine furnishes sufficient power even with a full load of passengers, and should not consume much more fuel than the overworked 3.0-liter. Both engines are gruff under hard throttle. With the longest wheelbase of any minivan, Windstar provides a stable, carlike ride, though it does not absorb bumps quite as well as a Toyota Sienna. Handling is confident and better than Sienna's. Even so, steering feels artificial and does not respond as quickly as General Motors minivans or the Honda Odyssey. Brake-pedal feel is good, but overall stopping power is about average. One test SEL exhibited annoying torque steer in brisk take-offs. A friendly dashboard and comfortable, roomy seating carry over from the previous (1995-98) Windstar, with improvements evident in several areas. Power sliding doors are a true convenience. Even the manual sliders are unusually easy to open and close, thanks to easy-to-grip interior handles. Rear hatches raise and lower easily, though separate-opening rear glass was not available. Substantial, supportive seats are heavy, so removal and installation demand muscle and technique, despite new rear rollers. Seatbacks do fold forward and recline, allowing great cargo and passenger versatility. Audio controls are too "busy," but the climate system's ability to run air conditioning in all vent modes is a benefit. If installed, the Reverse Sensing System is a valuable safeguard against unseen objects directly behind. That's helpful, because the base of the Windstar's rear window is not visible to the driver, complicating backing up.

VALUE Chrysler, Honda, and Toyota minivans have been ranked Best Buys, but the solid, easy-driving Windstar also is a fine choice, boasting some significant new safety and convenience features.

SPECIFICATIONS

	3-door van	4-door van
Wheelbase, in.	120.7	120.7
Overall length, in.	200.9	200.9
Overall width, in.	76.6	76.6
Overall height, in.	66.1	65.8
Curb weight, lbs.	3890	4194
Cargo volume, cu. ft.	145.7	148.5
Fuel capacity, gals.	26.0	26.0
Seating capacity	7	7
Front head room, in.	39.3	39.3
Max. front leg room, in.	40.7	40.7
Rear head room, in.	41.1	40.7
Min. rear leg room, in.	36.8	38.6

Powertrain layout: transverse front-engine/front-wheel drive

ENGINES

	ohv V6	ohv V6
Size, liters/cu. in.	3.0/182	3.8/232
Horsepower	150	200
Torque (lbs./ft.)	186	240

EPA city/highway mpg

4-speed OD automatic	17/23	17/23

City/highway mpg (as tested)

4-speed OD automatic	14.8

Built in Canada

RETAIL PRICES

	GOOD	AVERAGE	POOR
1999 Windstar	$11,500-14,000	$10,500-13,000	$7,000-8,000
1999 Windstar SEL	16,000-17,000	14,800-15,800	10,000-11,000
2000 Windstar	13,000-16,500	12,000-15,500	8,200-10,000
2000 SEL Limited	18,000-20,000	16,700-18,500	12,500-13,500
2001 Windstar	15,000-19,000	14,000-18,000	—
2001 SEL Limited	20,000-22,500	18,500-21,000	—

AVERAGE REPLACEMENT COSTS

A/C Compressor	$415	Constant Velocity Joints	990
Alternator	535	Exhaust System	320
Automatic Transmission or Transaxle	1,120	Radiator	395
		Shocks and/or Struts	1,200
Brakes	240	Timing Chain or Belt	180

TROUBLE SPOTS

• **Doors.** Corroded relay contacts in the controller prevent the power sliding door from closing. (1999-2000)

• **Seat.** Driver's weighing more than 275 lbs. can pinch the electrical harness between the seat and frame shorting out the power seat circuit and blowing the fuse. (1999)

• **Engine knock.** Engine knock may be due to oil getting into the intake manifold leading to a buildup of carbon in the cylinders. A redesigned valve cover alleviates the problem. (1999-2000)

• **Air conditioner.** Insufficient air conditioning may be due to a loose fitting at the condenser allowing the refrigerant to escape. (1999)

• **Climate control.** Lack of climate control temperature adjustment may be due a defective heater control head or binding blend door. (1999)

RECALL HISTORY

1999: On certain vehicles, brake-fluid warning statement embossed on top of filler cap, and also on side of master-cylinder reservoir body, is not entirely visible by direct view. **1999-00:** Certain instrument clusters without a "message center" fail to comply with Federal safety requirements. **1999-2001:** Wiper motor gear case could malfunction and overheat, causing loss of wiper function or fire. **1999-2001:** Auxiliary air conditioning blower motor stops turning while in the medium-low blower speed setting, there is the potential that the resistor may become hot and smoke. **2000:** Some minivans may have incorrect urethane, resulting in an adhesive bond rather than the intended molecular bond for the front windshield and rear liftgate glass. If the bond deteriorates, it could provide less than the intended level of glass retention in a crash. **2000:** Certain minivans may have incorrect fuel line end forms that result in insufficient pull-apart force for the fuel line connection. **2000-01 w/adjustable pedals:** Driver's floor mat could interfere with accelerator pedal, potentially resulting in stuck throttle. **2001:** Driver's and/or outboard front passenger's seatbelt buckle may not fully latch. **2001:** Restraint control module or crash sensor may have one or more screws missing, which could affect performance of occupant restraint. **2001:** Certain vehicles were built with a newly designed restraint control module that, in some cases, does not recognize certain system faults that could result in airbag or seatbelt pretensioner unexpectedly activating during the self-test sequence at start-up time.

1993-97 GEO PRIZM

FOR Ride • Fuel economy • Acceleration (1.8-liter) • Quietness • Antilock brakes (optional)

AGAINST Rear-seat room • Radio controls

EVALUATION

See the 1993-97 Toyota Corolla.

1994 Geo Prizm LSi

VALUE

See the 1993-97 Toyota Corolla.

SPECIFICATIONS

	4-door sedan
Wheelbase, in.	97.0
Overall length, in.	173.0
Overall width, in.	66.3
Overall height, in.	53.3
Curb weight, lbs.	2359
Cargo volume, cu. ft.	12.7
Fuel capacity, gals.	13.2
Seating capacity	5
Front head room, in.	38.5
Max. front leg room, in.	41.7
Rear head room, in.	36.4
Min. rear leg room, in.	33.1

Powertrain layout: transverse front-engine/front-wheel drive

ENGINES

	dohc I4	dohc I4
Size, liters/cu. in.	1.6/97	1.8/110
Horsepower	100-108	105-115
Torque (lbs./ft.)	100-105	115-117
EPA city/highway mpg		
5-speed OD manual	28/34	29/34
3-speed automatic	26/30	
4-speed OD automatic		27/34
City/highway mpg (as tested)		
5-speed OD manual		29.7
4-speed OD automatic		27.1

Built in USA

RETAIL PRICES

	GOOD	AVERAGE	POOR
1993 Prizm	$2,300-3,000	$1,700-2,300	$400-700
1994 Prizm	2,800-3,500	2,200-2,800	600-900
1995 Prizm	3,400-4,200	2,800-3,500	900-1,200
1996 Prizm	4,000-4,800	3,300-4,000	1,200-1,600
1997 Prizm	4,800-5,800	4,100-5,000	1,600-2,100

AVERAGE REPLACEMENT COSTS

See the 1993-97 Toyota Corolla.

TROUBLE SPOTS

See the 1993-97 Toyota Corolla.

RECALL HISTORY

1993-95: If liquid is spilled in console box area, airbag warning light can illuminate during normal driving conditions and cause airbag to malfunction, deploying inadvertently. **1994:** Anchor straps in certain seatbelt assemblies made by Quality Safety Systems were improperly heat treated and can break. **1995:** Battery may have defective weld inside terminal, which can result in no-start condition or explosion. **1997:** If airbag computer experiences mechanical shock within very short time after engine is started, airbag can deploy inadvertently.

1995-00 GEO/CHEVROLET METRO

FOR Optional antilock brakes • Fuel economy • Maneuverability • Visibility

AGAINST Passenger room • Ride • Noise

EVALUATION Metro's light weight remains evident in the way it drives. Bumps jar the suspension and create kickback through the steering wheel. On the plus side, the Metro is more composed on the road than before. A switch to 13-inch tires (from the former 12-inchers) helps,

1995 Geo Metro LSi 2-door hatchback

but cornering grip remains modest, and the Metro suffers plenty of body lean. Only the 4-cylinder/manual shift combination provides suitable acceleration for both city and highway driving—lively. Step on the gas and the Metro delivers considerable noise, but not so much progress. With an automatic transmission or the 3-cylinder engine, a Metro moves out slowly and requires plenty of room for safe passing. An LSi 4-door with automatic averaged 25.8 miles per gallon, with nearly all city and suburban commuting. That's good, but not really great. Leg room is adequate in front, but getting four adults aboard requires pushing the front seats forward. Head and leg room in the rear are adequate for two. Getting in or out of the back is difficult, on either body style. The rear seat is firm and flat. Controls are easy to see and reach. The dashboard layout is convenient, but the steering wheel sits uncomfortably high and does not adjust. Tall windows and slim roof pillars combine to produce a great view in all directions. Cargo space is generous for the car's size, and the interior offers an airy feeling. Though quieter now, a Metro is still noisy compared to most cars.

VALUE All told, we rank Metro ahead of Ford's Aspire in the minicar field. It's worth a look if price is your top priority.

SPECIFICATIONS

	2-door hatchback	4-door sedan
Wheelbase, in.	93.1	93.1
Overall length, in.	149.4	164.0
Overall width, in.	62.6	62.6
Overall height, in.	54.7	55.7
Curb weight, lbs.	1808	1940
Cargo volume, cu. ft.	21.9	10.3
Fuel capacity, gals.	10.6	10.6
Seating capacity	4	4
Front head room, in.	39.1	39.3
Max. front leg room, in.	42.5	42.5
Rear head room, in.	36.0	37.3
Min. rear leg room, in.	32.8	32.8

Powertrain layout: transverse front-engine/front-wheel drive

ENGINES

	ohc I3	ohc I4
Size, liters/cu. in.	1.0/61	1.3/79
Horsepower	55	70-79
Torque (lbs./ft.)	58	74-75
EPA city/highway mpg		
5-speed OD manual	44/49	39/43
3-speed automatic		30/34
City/highway mpg (as tested)		
5-speed OD manual		32.8
3-speed automatic		25.8

Built in Canada

RETAIL PRICES

	GOOD	AVERAGE	POOR
1995 Metro	$1,700-2,400	$1,100-1,800	$200-400
1996 Metro	2,100-3,000	1,500-2,300	300-600
1997 Metro	2,600-3,500	2,000-2,800	500-900
1998 Metro	3,300-4,300	2,600-3,600	700-1,200
1999 Metro	4,300-5,300	3,600-4,600	1,100-1,600
2000 Metro	5,400-6,500	4,700-5,800	1,700-2,400

AVERAGE REPLACEMENT COSTS

A/C Compressor	$780	Clutch, Pressure Plate,	
Alternator	470	Bearing	580
Automatic Transmission or		Constant Velocity Joints	640
Transaxle	480	Exhaust System	310
Brakes	230	Radiator	420
Shocks and/or Struts	905	Timing Chain or Belt	105

TROUBLE SPOTS

• **Brakes.** Antilock Brake System (ABS) light comes on, especially in hot or humid weather, due to binding in the ABS motor pack. (1995-97)

• **Doors.** The rear doors may not open from the outside due to a problem with the latch. (1995)

• **Brakes.** Vehicle is susceptible to brake pedal vibrations from warped rotor caused by uneven lug nut torque. (1995)

RECALL HISTORY

1995 hatchback w/o ABS: On some cars, rear brake drums were incorrectly machined, causing fatigue failure of wheel studs; wheel could then separate from vehicle. **1997 w/automatic:** Shift lever might appear to be in "Park," but could easily be moved to another position without use of the key, transaxle lever detent button, or depressing the brake pedal.

1990-98 GEO/CHEVROLET TRACKER

1993 Geo Tracker 2-door wagon

FOR 4WD traction (4WD) • Fuel economy

AGAINST Ride • Noise • Rear-seat room

EVALUATION The initial 80-horsepower engine has sufficient power for decent acceleration and passing on the 2-door model. With automatic, you have to push the pedal to the floor often to keep up with traffic. That's true even with the 95-horsepower engine. In addition, four-doors are so sluggish with automatic that passing maneuvers have to be planned with care. Gas mileage is fine. We've averaged 24 mpg in a 4-wheel-drive convertible and 28.6 mpg with 2-wheel drive. Tall and narrow, a Tracker must be driven with care through turns due to a high center of gravity. Even if it's not quite as precarious as it may seem while cornering, the abundant body lean quickly grows frightening. The ride is undeniably choppy, and noise levels are high. Two-wheel-drive Trackers are softer suspended for easier going on rough pavement, but even they get choppy. A Tracker's interior is roomy for two in front, but the back seat is best for children. The driver's seat lacks much rearward travel, and suffers minimal space past one's left shoulder. Cargo space behind the rear seat is minuscule, but at least you can fold the seat forward if a load of parcels has to be transported. Controls operate smoothly; gauges are simple. Four-door wagons offer lots of head room, adequate rear leg space, and ample cargo area.

VALUE More modern and refined than the paramilitary Jeep Wrangler, Trackers are appealing in many ways. Still, Trackers and Suzuki Sidekicks are just too rough and noisy for service as daily drivers.

SPECIFICATIONS

	2-door conv.	4-door wagon
Wheelbase, in.	86.6	97.6
Overall length, in.	143.7	158.7
Overall width, in.	64.2	64.4
Overall height, in.	64.3	65.7
Curb weight, lbs.	2246	2434
Cargo volume, cu. ft.	32.9	45.9
Fuel capacity, gals.	11.1	14.5
Seating capacity	4	4
Front head room, in.	39.5	40.5
Max. front leg room, in.	42.1	42.1
Rear head room, in.	39.0	40.0
Min. rear leg room, in.	31.6	32.7

Powertrain layout: longitudinal front-engine/rear- or 4-wheel drive

ENGINES

	ohc I4
Size, liters/cu. in.	1.6/97
Horsepower	80-95
Torque (lbs./ft.)	94-98

EPA city/highway mpg

5-speed OD manual	24/26
3-speed automatic	23/24
4-speed OD automatic	22/25

City/highway mpg (as tested)

5-speed OD manual	24.8
4-speed OD automatic	24.0

Built in Japan, Canada

RETAIL PRICES

	GOOD	AVERAGE	POOR
1990 Tracker 2WD	$1,100-1,700	$600-1,100	$100-200
1990 Tracker 4WD	1,400-2,000	800-1,400	100-300
1991 Tracker 2WD	1,300-2,000	700-1,400	100-300
1991 Tracker 4WD	1,700-2,300	1,100-1,700	300-500
1992 Tracker 2WD	1,500-2,200	900-1,600	200-400
1992 Tracker 4WD	2,000-2,700	1,400-2,100	400-700
1993 Tracker 2WD	1,800-2,600	1,200-1,900	300-500
1993 Tracker 4WD	2,300-3,000	1,600-2,300	500-800
1994 Tracker 2WD	2,300-3,100	1,700-2,400	400-700
1994 Tracker 4WD	2,900-3,600	2,200-2,900	600-1,000
1995 Tracker 2WD	2,800-3,600	2,200-2,900	600-900
1995 Tracker 4WD	3,500-4,200	2,800-3,500	900-1,200
1996 Tracker 2WD	3,300-4,200	2,600-3,500	800-1,200
1996 Tracker 4WD	4,000-4,800	3,300-4,000	1,200-1,600
1997 Tracker 2WD	3,800-4,700	3,100-4,000	1,000-1,500
1997 Tracker 4WD	4,500-5,400	3,800-4,600	1,500-1,900
1998 Tracker 2WD	4,500-5,500	3,800-4,800	1,400-1,900
1998 Tracker 4WD	5,400-6,500	4,700-5,700	1,800-2,300

AVERAGE REPLACEMENT COSTS

A/C Compressor	$980	Clutch, Pressure Plate, Bearing	600
Alternator	395	Exhaust System	475
Automatic Transmission or Transaxle	740	Radiator	665
Brakes	370	Shocks and/or Struts	270
Timing Chain or Belt	210	Universal Joints	175

TROUBLE SPOTS

• **Automatic transmission.** Automatic transmission hunting may be caused by a torque converter clutch that applies and releases too rapidly. (1990-95)

• **Manual transmission.** Because of the rubber compound used to make the shifter boots, some vehicles may not go into four-wheel drive or they may pop out of 4WD. The boot will be replaced with one having softer rubber, at no charge. (1995)

• **Automatic transmission.** The Hydramatic (3L30) automatic transmission causes bucking and jerking due to a problem with the torque converter applying and releasing if the carmaker's modification kit is not installed. (1990-95)

• **Keys.** The original keys were made with a soft metal compound that causes them to break. (1990)

• **Engine misfire.** The PCV breather hose may freeze up while driving in cold weather causing a loss of oil and engine damage. (1990)

• **Exhaust system.** The two-piece muffler/tailpipe may rust out prematurely. If the tailpipe rusts through, heat can damage the rear floor and carpet. GM will install a heat shield over the exhaust system. (1990-91)

RECALL HISTORY

1990-91: Front seatbelt release button can break and pieces can fall inside, causing improper operation. **1995:** Steering wheel hub to spoke weld on some vehicles can fracture, allowing steering wheel to separate. **1996 4-door:** Fuel tank can puncture during rear-end collision.

1990-94 GMC JIMMY

FOR Acceleration • 4WD traction • Passenger room • Antilock rear brakes

1992 GMC Jimmy SLT 4-door wagon

AGAINST Fuel economy • Noise • Ride • Rear-seat entry/exit (2-doors)

EVALUATION
See the 1990-94 Chevrolet S-10 Blazer.

VALUE
See the 1990-94 Chevrolet S-10 Blazer.

SPECIFICATIONS

	2-door wagon	4-door wagon
Wheelbase, in.	100.5	107.0
Overall length, in.	170.3	176.8
Overall width, in.	65.4	65.4
Overall height, in.	64.3	64.3
Curb weight, lbs.	3536	3776
Cargo volume, cu. ft.	67.3	74.3
Fuel capacity, gals.	20.0	20.0
Seating capacity	4	6
Front head room, in.	39.1	39.1
Max. front leg room, in.	42.5	42.5
Rear head room, in.	38.7	38.8
Min. rear leg room, in.	35.5	36.5

Powertrain layout: longitudinal front-engine/rear- or 4-wheel drive

ENGINES

	ohv V6	ohv V6	Turbocharged ohv V6
Size, liters/cu. in.	4.3/262	4.3/262	4.3/262
Horsepower	160-165	200	280
Torque (lbs./ft.)	230-235	260	350
EPA city/highway mpg			
5-speed OD manual	16/21		
4-speed OD automatic	17/22	16/21	15/19

Built in USA

RETAIL PRICES

	GOOD	AVERAGE	POOR
1990 Jimmy 2WD	$1,300-2,100	$700-1,500	$100-300
1990 Jimmy 4WD	2,200-3,000	1,600-2,300	400-800
1991 Jimmy 2WD	1,600-2,600	1,000-2,000	200-600
1991 Jimmy 4WD	2,500-4,000	1,800-3,200	500-1,400
1992 Jimmy 2WD	2,000-3,500	1,400-2,800	300-900
1992 Jimmy 4WD	2,900-4,800	2,200-4,000	700-1,800
1992 Typhoon	7,500-9,000	6,000-7,500	3,000-4,000
1993 Jimmy 2WD	2,500-4,200	1,800-3,500	500-1,300
1993 Jimmy 4WD	3,400-5,500	2,600-4,700	1,000-2,200
1993 Typhoon	8,000-9,500	7,000-8,500	4,000-5,000
1994 Jimmy 2WD	3,000-5,000	2,300-4,200	800-1,800
1994 Jimmy 4WD	4,000-6,200	3,200-5,300	1,300-2,600

AVERAGE REPLACEMENT COSTS
See the 1990-94 Chevrolet S-10 Blazer.

TROUBLE SPOTS
See the 1990-94 Chevrolet S-10 Blazer.

RECALL HISTORY
1990-91: Fuel tank sender seal may be out of position; could result in fuel leakage. **1991:** Rear seatbelt buckle release button can stick n unlatched position. **1991-94 4WD w/EBC4 ABS:** Increased stopping distances can occur during ABS stops while in 2WD mode. **1993:** Rear seatbelts may not meet government requirements. **1994 w/VR4 weight-distribution trailer hitch option:** Trailer hitch attaching bolts were not tightened adequately.

1995-01 GMC JIMMY/ENVOY

CG BEST BUY AUTO

1995 GMC Jimmy 4-door wagon

FOR Acceleration • Passenger and cargo room • Ride • 4WD traction • Antilock brakes

AGAINST Rear-seat comfort • Fuel economy

EVALUATION
See the 1995-01 Chevrolet Blazer.

VALUE
See the 1995-01 Chevrolet Blazer.

SPECIFICATIONS

	2-door wagon	4-door wagon
Wheelbase, in.	100.5	107.0
Overall length, in.	175.1	181.2
Overall width, in.	67.8	67.8
Overall height, in.	66.9	67.0
Curb weight, lbs.	3825	4007
Cargo volume, cu. ft.	66.9	74.1
Fuel capacity, gals.	20.0	19.0
Seating capacity	4	6
Front head room, in.	39.6	39.6
Max. front leg room, in.	42.5	42.5
Rear head room, in.	38.2	38.2
Min. rear leg room, in.	36.3	36.3

Powertrain layout: longitudinal front-engine/rear- or 4-wheel drive

ENGINES

	ohv V6
Size, liters/cu. in.	4.3/262
Horsepower	190-195
Torque (lbs./ft.)	250-260
EPA city/highway mpg	
5-speed OD manual	17/22
4-speed OD automatic	16/21
City/highway mpg (as tested)	
4-speed OD automatic	16.4

Built in USA

RETAIL PRICES

	GOOD	AVERAGE	POOR
1995 Jimmy 2WD	$4,100-7,000	$3,300-6,000	$1,400-3,200
1995 Jimmy 4WD	5,600-7,500	4,700-6,500	2,400-3,500
1996 Jimmy 2WD	5,300-8,000	4,300-7,000	2,100-4,000
1996 Jimmy 4WD	6,800-9,000	5,800-8,000	3,200-4,800
1997 Jimmy 2WD	6,600-9,000	5,600-8,000	2,900-4,800
1997 Jimmy 4WD	8,100-10,500	7,100-9,500	4,000-5,800
1998 Jimmy 2WD	8,100-11,000	7,100-10,000	4,000-6,000
1998 Jimmy 4WD	9,600-12,000	8,600-10,500	5,200-6,600
1998 Envoy	13,000-14,500	11,800-13,000	7,500-8,500
1999 Jimmy 2WD	9,600-13,000	8,600-11,500	5,200-7,500
1999 Jimmy 4WD	11,200-14,500	10,000-13,000	6,200-8,300
1999 Envoy	14,500-16,000	13,200-14,500	8,500-9,800
2000 Jimmy 2WD	11,700-15,000	10,200-13,500	6,200-8,600
2000 Jimmy 4WD	13,200-16,500	11,700-15,000	7,300-9,900
2000 Envoy	16,500-18,500	15,000-17,000	10,000-11,500
2001 Jimmy 2WD	13,100-16,000	11,600-14,500	—
2001 Jimmy 4WD	14,600-17,500	13,100-16,000	—

AVERAGE REPLACEMENT COSTS
See the 1995-01 Chevrolet Blazer.

TROUBLE SPOTS
See the 1995-01 Chevrolet Blazer.

RECALL HISTORY

1995: Brake pedal bolt on some vehicles might disengage, causing loss of braking. **1995 4WD:** A few upper ball joint nuts were under-torqued; stud can loosen and fracture. **1995 w/air conditioning:** Fan blade rivets can break and allow blade to separate from hub. **1995-96 AWD/4WD:** During testing, prop shaft contacted fuel tank, rupturing the tank; fuel leakage was beyond permissible level. **1995-96:** Windshield wipers may work intermittently. **1995-96 4WD w/EBC4 ABS:** Increased stopping distances can occur during ABS stops while in 2WD mode. **1996-97 2-door w/manual locking recliner bucket seats:** Outboard seatbelt webbing can separate during frontal impact. **1996-97:** Failure of an upper and lower control arm ball joint assembly could occur due to corrosion, resulting in impaired steering or steering loss, or a partial or complete collapse of the front suspension. **1998:** Fatigue fracture of rear-axle brake pipe can occur, causing slow fluid leak and resulting in soft brake pedal; if pipe breaks, driver would face sudden loss of rear-brake performance. **1998 w/4WD or AWD:** On a few vehicles, one or both attaching bolts for lower control arm could separate from frame, resulting in loss of control. **1998:** Daytime running lights are not deactivated when turn signal or hazard lamps are activated. **2000 w/2WD:** Right ABS module feed pipe and/or brake crossover pipe tube nuts on certain vehicles could have been improperly tightened; seals could have been broken, resulting in leakage. **2000:** Some seatbelt assemblies were not properly heat treated and do not pass the load bearing requirement.

	GOOD	AVERAGE	POOR
1992 Safari	$2,600-4,000	$1,900-3,300	$700-1,100
1992 Safari AWD	3,200-4,600	2,500-3,800	900-1,400
1993 Safari	3,100-4,800	2,400-4,000	800-1,600
1993 Safari AWD	3,700-5,400	3,000-4,600	1,200-2,200
1994 Safari	3,800-5,600	3,000-4,800	1,200-2,300
1994 Safari AWD	4,500-6,500	3,700-5,700	1,600-3,000
1995 Safari	4,600-6,400	3,800-5,500	1,600-2,900
1995 Safari AWD	5,600-7,200	4,700-6,300	2,200-3,400
1996 Safari	5,800-7,500	4,900-6,500	2,300-3,500
1996 Safari AWD	7,000-8,500	6,000-7,500	3,000-4,200
1997 Safari	7,100-9,000	6,100-8,000	3,000-4,500
1997 Safari AWD	8,300-10,200	7,300-9,200	3,800-5,200
1998 Safari	8,500-10,700	7,500-9,700	4,000-5,500
1998 Safari AWD	10,000-12,200	9,000-11,200	5,200-6,600
1999 Safari	10,500-12,500	9,500-11,500	5,500-6,900
1999 Safari AWD	12,000-14,000	11,000-13,000	7,000-8,500
2000 Safari	12,600-14,500	11,400-13,000	7,200-8,500
2000 Safari AWD	14,000-16,000	12,800-14,500	8,200-9,500
2001 Safari	14,500-16,500	13,000-15,000	—
2001 Safari AWD	16,000-18,000	14,500-16,500	—

AVERAGE REPLACEMENT COSTS

See the 1990-01 Chevrolet Astro.

TROUBLE SPOTS

See the 1990-01 Chevrolet Astro.

RECALL HISTORY

1990-91: Bucket seat's knob recliner mechanism may loosen and cause bolt failure, allowing seatback to recline suddenly. **1995 w/L35 engine:** Fuel lines at tank were improperly tightened and could loosen. **1995:** On a few vans, left lower control arm bolt could loosen, fatigue, and break. **1996-97:** Outboard seatbelt webbing on right rear bucket seat can separate during crash. **1996-98 w/integrated child seats:** Seatbelt retractor clutch spring and/or pawl spring in child seat may be missing.

1990-01 GMC SAFARI

1996 GMC Safari

FOR Antilock brakes • Optional all-wheel-drive traction • Passenger room • Trailer towing capability • Cargo room (extended-length)

AGAINST Fuel economy • Entry/exit • Ride

EVALUATION

See the 1990-01 Chevrolet Astro.

VALUE

See the 1990-01 Chevrolet Astro.

SPECIFICATIONS	3-door van	3-door van	3-door van
Wheelbase, in.	111.0	111.0	111.0
Overall length, in.	176.8	186.8	189.8
Overall width, in.	77.0	77.0	77.0
Overall height, in.	76.4	76.4	76.1
Curb weight, lbs.	3960	3960	4068
Cargo volume, cu. ft.	151.8	170.4	170.4
Fuel capacity, gals.	27.0	27.0	27.0
Seating capacity	8	8	8
Front head room, in.	39.2	39.2	39.2
Max. front leg room, in.	41.6	41.6	41.6
Rear head room, in.	37.9	37.9	37.9
Min. rear leg room, in.	36.5	36.5	36.5

Powertrain layout: longitudinal front-engine/rear- or all-wheel drive

ENGINES	ohv V6	ohv V6
Size, liters/cu. in.	4.3/262	4.3/262
Horsepower	150-165	175-200
Torque (lbs./ft.)	230-235	230-260
EPA city/highway mpg		
4-speed OD automatic	16/21	16/20
City/highway mpg (as tested)		
4-speed OD automatic	14.5	18.3

Built in USA

RETAIL PRICES	GOOD	AVERAGE	POOR
1990 Safari	$1,600-2,700	$1,000-2,000	$200-500
1990 Safari AWD	2,000-3,200	1,400-2,500	400-700
1991 Safari	2,100-3,400	1,500-2,700	500-600
1991 Safari AWD	2,600-3,900	1,900-3,200	600-1,000

1990-98 GMC SIERRA

1992 GMC Sierra

FOR Antilock brakes (later models) • Acceleration (V8) • Trailer towing capability • Visibility • Passenger and cargo room

AGAINST Fuel economy • Climate controls (early) • Ride • Noise

EVALUATION

See the 1990-99 Chevrolet C/K.

VALUE

See the 1990-99 Chevrolet C/K.

SPECIFICATIONS	reg. cab short bed	reg. cab long bed	ext. cab short bed	ext. cab long bed
Wheelbase, in.	117.5	131.5	141.5	155.55
Overall length, in.	194.5	213.4	21`8.4	237.1
Overall width, in.	76.8	76.8	76.8	76.8
Overall height, in.	70.4	70.4	70.4	74.9
Curb weight, lbs.	3849	4001	4140	7387
Fuel capacity, gals.	34.0	34.0	34.0	25.0
Seating capacity	3	3	6	6
Front head room, in.	40.0	40.0	40.0	40.0
Max. front leg room, in.	41.7	41.7	41.7	41.7
Rear head room, in.	—	—	37.5	37.5
Min. rear leg room, in.	—	—	34.8	34.8

Powertrain layout: longitudinal front-engine/rear- or 4-wheel drive

ENGINES

	ohv V6	ohv V8	ohv V8	ohv V8
Size, liters/cu. in.	4.3/262	5.0/305	5.7/350	7.4/454
Horsepower	160-200	175-230	200-255	230-290
Torque (lbs./ft.)	235-255	270-285	300-335	285-410
EPA city/highway mpg				
4-speed manual..............	18/20		13/16	
5-speed OD manual........	17/22	15/20	14/20	
4-speed OD automatic....	17/22	15/19	15/19	10/12
City/highway mpg (as tested)				
4-speed OD automatic....		14.5	13.0	

ENGINES

	diesel ohv V6	diesel ohv V8	turbodiesel ohv V8
Size, liters/cu. in.	6.2/379	6.5/400	6.5/400
Horsepower	140	155	180-190
Torque (lbs./ft.)	255	255	360
EPA city/highway mpg			
4-speed manual	19/21		
5-speed OD manual		19/23	
4-speed OD automatic	18/24	17/22	16/21

Built in USA, Canada

RETAIL PRICES

	GOOD	AVERAGE	POOR
1990 Sierra 1500 2WD	$2,000-3,900	$1,400-3,200	$300-1,300
1990 Sierra 2500 2WD	2,700-4,300	2,000-3,600	600-1,600
1990 Sierra 1500 4WD	2,800-4,600	2,100-3,900	700-1,800
1990 Sierra 2500 4WD	3,400-5,000	2,700-4,300	1,100-2,100
1991 Sierra 1500 2WD	2,500-4,800	1,900-4,100	500-1,900
1991 Sierra 2500 2WD	3,600-5,200	2,900-4,400	1,300-2,300
1991 Sierra 1500 4WD	3,300-5,300	2,700-4,500	1,100-2,500
1991 Sierra 2500 4WD	4,300-5,900	3,600-5,100	1,700-2,900
1992 Sierra 1500 2WD	3,000-5,500	2,400-4,800	800-2,500
1992 Sierra 2500 2WD	4,100-6,000	3,400-5,200	1,500-2,800
1992 Sierra 1500 4WD	3,700-5,800	3,000-5,000	1,200-2,700
1992 Sierra 2500 4WD	4,900-7,100	4,100-6,200	2,000-3,700
1993 Sierra 1500 2WD	3,600-6,500	2,900-5,700	1,100-3,200
1993 Sierra 2500 2WD	4,700-7,100	4,000-6,300	1,800-3,600
1993 Sierra 1500 4WD	4,600-7,700	3,900-6,900	1,700-4,100
1993 Sierra 2500 4WD	6,100-8,100	5,300-7,300	2,800-4,500
1994 Sierra 1500 2WD	4,200-8,200	3,500-7,400	1,400-4,100
1994 Sierra 2500 2WD	6,600-8,500	5,800-7,700	3,100-4,700
1994 Sierra 1500 4WD	5,900-9,200	5,200-8,400	2,700-5,300
1994 Sierra 2500 4WD	7,600-9,800	6,600-8,800	3,700-5,700
1995 Sierra 1500 2WD	5,000-9,500	4,200-8,500	1,800-5,200
1995 Sierra 2500 2WD	7,400-10,200	6,500-9,200	3,700-6,000
1995 Sierra 1500 4WD	6,800-10,200	6,000-9,200	3,300-6,000
1995 Sierra 2500 4WD	9,000-11,700	8,000-10,700	4,500-6,600
1996 Sierra 1500 2WD	6,100-11,300	5,100-10,300	2,500-5,700
1996 Sierra 2500 2WD	8,400-11,800	7,500-10,800	4,000-6,100
1996 Sierra 1500 4WD	7,800-12,300	6,900-11,300	3,700-6,500
1996 Sierra 2500 4WD	10,100-13,300	9,100-12,300	5,300-7,500
1997 Sierra 1500 2WD	7,200-12,800	6,200-11,600	3,400-6,700
1997 Sierra 2500 2WD	10,000-13,300	9,000-12,300	5,200-7,500
1997 Sierra 1500 4WD	8,500-13,800	7,500-12,600	4,000-7,700
1997 Sierra 2500 4WD	11,500-15,300	10,300-13,800	6,200-8,700
1998 Sierra 1500 2WD	8,500-14,300	7,500-13,000	4,000-8,000
1998 Sierra 2500 2WD	11,000-14,400	10,000-13,200	6,000-8,300
1998 Sierra 1500 4WD	10,000 -15,300	9,000-14,000	5,200-8,800
1998 Sierra 2500 4WD	13,000-16,800	11,500-15,300	7,200-9,700

AVERAGE REPLACEMENT COSTS

See the 1990-99 Chevrolet C/K.

TROUBLE SPOTS

See the 1990-99 Chevrolet C/K.

RECALL HISTORY

1990 diesel: Fuel lines can contact automatic transmission linkage shaft or propshaft. **1990, '92:** Brake-pedal bolt could disengage. **1994:** Brake pedal retainer may be missing or mispositioned. **1994:** Brake switch contacts can wear prematurely; may result in loss of brake lights without warning. **1994:** Some driver's seats could loosen. **1994-95:** Extended C10/15 with high-back buckets or 60/40 bench: Seatback might recline suddenly. **1994-96 C15:** Solder joints can crack, causing windshield wipers to work intermittently. **1995:** Steering-column nut could detach. **1995-96 w/gas engine:** Throttle cable may contact dash mat and bind. **1995-98 C15 crew-cab:** Front inner corner of fuel tank can contact body sill, wearing a hole in or cracking the tank; can result in fuel leakage. **1996 C-10/15 w/7.4-liter engine:** Fuel may leak. **1996:** Rear-axle U-bolts could loosen and eventually fall off. **1997 C-15/25:** One or two of the front seat mounting bolts were not installed; seat will not protect occupant properly in the event of a crash. **1998 extended-cab and 4-door utility:** Steering-gear bolt can loosen and fall out, resulting in separation of shaft from gear. **1998:** On some trucks, one or both front brake rotor/hubs may have out-of-spec gray iron that can fail during life of vehicle. **1998 C10753 extended-cab:** Rear brake line can contact left front fender wheelhouse inner panel; a hole could be worn in brake line, allowing loss of fluid and reducing rear brake effectiveness.

1999-01 GMC SIERRA

2001 GMC Sierra 1500 SLT extended cab

FOR Acceleration (V8) • Instruments and controls

AGAINST Fuel economy • Ride

EVALUATION

See the 1990-99 Chevrolet C/K.

VALUE

See the 1990-99 Chevrolet C/K.

SPECIFICATIONS

	reg. cab short bed	reg. cab long bed	ext. cab short bed	ext. cab long bed
Wheelbase, in.	119.0	133.0	143.5	157.5
Overall length, in.	203.2	222.1	227.5	246.6
Overall width, in.	78.5	78.5	78.5	78.5
Overall height, in.	71.2	71.0	71.2	70.8
Curb weight, lbs.	3956	4066	4289	4511
Fuel capacity, gals.	26.0	34.0	26.0	34.0
Seating capacity	3	3	6	6
Front head room, in.	41.0	41.0	41.0	41.0
Max. front leg room, in.	41.3	41.3	41.0	41.0
Rear head room, in.	—	—	38.4	38.4
Min. rear leg room, in.	—	—	33.7	33.7

Powertrain layout: longitudinal front-engine/rear- or 4-wheel drive

ENGINES

	ohv V6	ohv V8	ohv V8	ohv V8
Size, liters/cu. in.	4.3/262	4.8/294	5.3/325	6.0/364
Horsepower	200	255-270	270-285	325
Torque (lbs./ft.)	260	285	315-325	370
EPA city/highway mpg				
5-speed OD manual	17/23	16/20		
4-speed OD automatic	16/20	16/21	16/20	NA
City/highway mpg (as tested)				
4-speed OD automatic			12.6	

Built in Canada

RETAIL PRICES

	GOOD	AVERAGE	POOR
1999 Sierra 1500 2WD	$11,500-16,000	$10,500-15,000	$7,000-10,000
1999 Sierra 1500 4WD	13,500-18,000	12,500-17,000	8,500-11,500
2000 Sierra 1500 2WD	13,000-18,000	12,000-17,000	8,200-11,500
2000 Sierra 1500 4WD	15,000-20,000	14,000-18,800	9,800-13,000
2001 Sierra 1500 2WD	14,500-21,000	13,500-19,500	—
2001 Sierra 1500 4WD	16,500-23,000	15,300-21,500	—
2001 Sierra 1500 C3 AWD	26,000-28,000	24,500-26,500	—

AVERAGE REPLACEMENT COSTS

See the 1999-01 Chevrolet C/K.

TROUBLE SPOTS

See the 1999-01 Chevrolet C/K.

RECALL HISTORY

1999-2000: Clearance between front right-hand brake pipe and body cross sill could decrease and allow contact, which could result in damage and loss of brake fluid and pressure. **2000 w/4-wheel disc brakes:** Out-of-spec spring clip in antilock brake system could allow motor bearing to become misaligned; eventually, ABS would be nonfunctional and Dynamic Rear Proportioning system would become inoperative.

1994-01 GMC SONOMA

1994 GMC Sonoma regular cab

FOR Passenger room • Acceleration (V6) • Instruments/controls • Optional third door (later models)

AGAINST Seat comfort (front passenger) • Ride (some models) • Rear-seat room

EVALUATION

See the 1994-01 Chevrolet S-Series

VALUE

See the 1994-01 Chevrolet S-Series

SPECIFICATIONS

	reg. cab short bed	reg. cab long bed	ext. cab	crew cab
Wheelbase, in.	108.3	117.9	122.9	122.9
Overall length, in.	189.0	205.0	203.7	205.3
Overall width, in.	67.9	67.9	67.9	67.8
Overall height, in.	62.1	62.1	62.2	63.4
Curb weight, lbs.	2930	2983	3168	4039
Fuel capacity, gals.	20.0	20.0	20.0	18.0
Seating capacity	3	3	5	5
Front head room, in.	39.5	39.5	39.5	39.6
Max. front leg room, in.	43.2	43.2	43.2	42.4
Rear head room, in.	—	—	NA	38.2
Min. rear leg room, in.	—	—	NA	34.6

Powertrain layout: longitudinal front-engine/rear- or 4-wheel drive

ENGINES

	ohv I4	ohv V6	ohv V6
Size, liters/cu. in.	2.2/134	4.3/262	4.3/262
Horsepower	118-120	155-180	180-195
Torque (lbs./ft.)	130-140	235-245	245-260
EPA city/highway mpg			
5-speed OD manual	23/30	18/25	18/25
4-speed OD automatic	20/27	19/24	20/24
City/highway mpg (as tested)			
5-speed OD manual	22.3		
4-speed OD automatic		18.4	18.0

Built in USA

RETAIL PRICES

	GOOD	AVERAGE	POOR
1994 Sonoma 2WD	$3,100-4,900	$2,500-4,200	$700-1,700
1994 Sonoma 4WD	4,300-6,400	3,600-5,600	1,500-2,800
1995 Sonoma 2WD	3,600-6,600	2,900-5,900	1,000-2,800
1995 Sonoma 4WD	5,100-8,600	4,300-7,800	2,000-4,200
1996 Sonoma 2WD	4,500-7,300	3,800-6,600	1,600-3,500
1996 Sonoma 4WD	6,100-9,500	5,300-8,500	2,500-5,100
1997 Sonoma 2WD	5,300-8,300	4,500-7,500	2,100-4,100
1997 Sonoma 4WD	7,200-11,100	6,400-10,100	3,100-6,300
1998 Sonoma 2WD	6,200-9,100	5,400-8,200	2,600-4,800
1998 Sonoma 4WD	8,200-12,100	7,200-11,100	3,700-6,900
1999 Sonoma 2WD	7,200-10,100	6,400-9,100	3,100-5,500
1999 Sonoma 4WD	9,200-13,000	8,200-11,800	4,400-7,500
2000 Sonoma 2WD	8,200-11,500	7,200-10,500	3,600-6,000
2000 Sonoma 4WD	10,200-14,000	9,200-12,800	5,100-7,500
2001 Sonoma 2WD	$9,400-12,500	$8,400-11,500	—
2001 Sonoma 4WD	11,600-15,500	10,400-14,000	—

AVERAGE REPLACEMENT COSTS

See the 1994-01 Chevrolet S-Series

TROUBLE SPOTS

See the 1994-01 Chevrolet S-Series

RECALL HISTORY

1994 w/2.2-liter engine: Vacuum hose can detach from power brake booster check valve as a result of backfire. **1994-96 4WD w/EBC4 ABS:** Increased stopping distances can occur during ABS stops while in 2WD mode. **1994-97:** Seatbelt webbing on certain models can separate during frontal impact. **1995 w/air conditioning and 4.3-liter engine:** Rivets can break and allow fan blade to separate from hub; if hood were open, a person could be struck by blade and be injured. **1995-96:** Windshield wipers may work intermittently. **1995-2000:** When the hazard-flasher switch is used to turn the hazard flashers on or off, the retained accessory power feature can be activated without a key in the ignition. **1996:** Top coat of paint on a few trucks peels severely. **1996 2WD manual shift w/2.2-liter engine:** Drive wheels could seize and lock while truck is moving. **1996-97 w/4.3-liter engine:** Front brake line can contact oil pan, causing wear that may result in fluid loss. **1997 w/4.3-liter engine:** Front brake line can contact oil pan, causing wear that may result in fluid loss. **1998:** Fatigue fracture of rear-axle brake pipe can occur, causing slow fluid leak and resulting in soft brake pedal; if pipe breaks, driver would face sudden loss of rear-brake performance. **1998:** Daytime running lights do not comply with FMVSS No. 108 requirements. **1998:** Wiring-harness clip can melt and drip onto exhaust manifold, possibly resulting in fire. **1998-2000:** Left-hand safety belt retractor may not meet the retractor locking requirements of the standard. **2000 w/2WD:** Right ABS module feed pipe and/or brake crossover pipe tube nuts on certain vehicles could have been improperly tightened; seal could have been broken, resulting in leakage. **2000 w/all-disc brakes:** Out-of-spec spring clip in ABS motor could allow bearing to become misaligned; ABS and Dynamic Rear Proportioning system would become inoperative.

1992-99 GMC SUBURBAN

1992 GMC Suburban

FOR Acceleration (7.4-liter) • Passenger and cargo room • Trailer towing capability • Highway ride

AGAINST Acceleration (early models) • Fuel economy • Rear-seat entry/exit

EVALUATION

See the 1990-99 Chevrolet Suburban.

VALUE

See the 1990-99 Chevrolet Suburban.

SPECIFICATIONS

	4-door wagon
Wheelbase, in.	131.5
Overall length, in.	220.0
Overall width, in.	76.7
Overall height, in.	70.2
Curb weight, lbs.	4634
Cargo volume, cu. ft.	149.5
Fuel capacity, gals.	42.0
Seating capacity	9
Front head room, in.	39.9
Max. front leg room, in.	41.3
Rear head room, in.	38.8
Min. rear leg room, in.	26.2

Powertrain layout: longitudinal front-engine/rear- or 4-wheel drive

ENGINES	ohv V8	ohv V8	ohv V8	Turbodiesel ohv V8
Size, liters/cu. in.	5.7/350	5.7/350	7.4/454	6.5/400
Horsepower	190-210	250-255	230-290	190
Torque (lbs./ft.)	300-310	330-335	365-410	385

EPA city/highway mpg				
4-speed OD automatic	13/17	12/16	NA	15/18

City/highway mpg (as tested)		
4-speed OD automatic	10.7	13.9

Built in USA, Mexico

RETAIL PRICES	GOOD	AVERAGE	POOR
1992 Suburban 2WD	$5,800-7,800	$5,100-7,000	$2,500-3,800
1992 Suburban 4WD	6,500-8,500	5,800-7,600	3,000-4,300
1993 Suburban 2WD	7,000-9,000	6,200-8,000	3,400-4,500
1993 Suburban 4WD	7,700-9,500	6,800-8,500	3,900-4,800
1994 Suburban 2WD	8,000-10,000	7,000-9,000	4,000-5,200
1994 Suburban 4WD	9,000-11,000	8,000-10,000	4,700-5,800
1995 Suburban 2WD	9,000-11,500	8,000-10,500	4,800-6,300
1995 Suburban 4WD	10,200-12,700	9,200-11,500	5,500-7,000
1996 Suburban 2WD	10,300-13,000	9,300-11,800	5,500-7,000
1996 Suburban 4WD	11,600-14,200	10,400-12,700	6,300-7,800
1997 Suburban 2WD	11,600-14,500	10,400-13,000	6,500-8,200
1997 Suburban 4WD	13,000-16,000	11,800-14,500	7,500-9,200
1998 Suburban 2WD	13,700-16,500	12,200-15,000	8,100-9,800
1998 Suburban 4WD	15,700-18,500	14,200-17,000	9,300-11,300
1999 Suburban 2WD	16,200-19,000	14,700-17,500	9,800-11,500
1999 Suburban 4WD	18,200-22,000	16,700-20,500	11,600-13,500

AVERAGE REPLACEMENT COSTS

See the 1990-99 Chevrolet Suburban.

TROUBLE SPOTS

See the 1990-99 Chevrolet Suburban.

RECALL HISTORY

1992: Brake-pedal pivot bolt can disengage. **1994:** Brake switch contacts can wear prematurely; may result in loss of brake lights without warning. **1994-96:** Solder joints can crack, causing windshield wipers to work intermittently. **1995 w/M30/MT1 automatic transmission:** When shift lever is placed in Park position, its indicator light may not illuminate. **1995 w/4180-E automatic transmission:** External transmission leak can occur. **1995-96 w/gasoline engine:** Throttle cable may contact dash mat and bind. **1998:** On some vehicles, one or both front brake rotor/hubs may have out-of-spec gray iron that can fail during life of vehicle. **1999:** In a crash, right front passenger restraint systems may not meet neck extension requirements.

1992-00 GMC YUKON/DENALI

1992 GMC Yukon 2-door wagon

FOR Antilock brakes • Ride (4-door) • Quietness • Passenger and cargo room • Trailer towing capability

AGAINST Fuel economy • Maneuverability • Ride (2-door) • Entry/exit (2-door & 4WD)

EVALUATION Until it added 50 horsepower for 1996, the 5.7-liter V8 was on the sluggish side, especially when passing or climbing hills. Improved transmission shift quality helped, though the automatic still is slow to downshift. Gas mileage is no bonus. In tests, we've barely topped 14 miles per gallon, even when driving mainly on the highway. Quieter-running than before, Yukon offers improved

behavior on the road. Suspensions of 4-door models are tuned for on-the-road comfort, resulting in an absorbent ride. The 2-door's ride is more choppy, tending toward rocking-horse motions. Though overassisted, steering is precise. Body lean in curves is still noticeable, but less troubling. Grip in corners is reassuring. Antilock brakes are a bonus, but you can expect severe nosedive in hard stops. Occupants enjoy plenty of space to sit three abreast, with lots of head and leg room. A 4-door, in particular, offers interior space and towing power that's simply not available from compact sport-utility vehicles. Climbing aboard is easier than it used to be, too. The dashboard and control layout is modern and convenient. All controls are well-positioned, with large buttons that are easy to use while driving.

VALUE Yukons offer the strength and toughness of a full-size truck, but carlike comfort and a full load of convenience features. Before turning to Yukon or Tahoe, however, take a look at Ford's Expedition.

SPECIFICATIONS	2-door wagon	4-door wagon
Wheelbase, in.	111.5	117.5
Overall length, in.	188.5	199.1
Overall width, in.	77.1	76.4
Overall height, in.	72.4	70.2
Curb weight, lbs.	4731	5134
Cargo volume, cu. ft.	99.4	122.9
Fuel capacity, gals.	30.5	30.5
Seating capacity	6	6
Front head room, in.	39.9	39.9
Max. front leg room, in.	41.9	41.7
Rear head room, in.	37.8	38.9
Min. rear leg room, in.	36.3	36.7

Powertrain layout: longitudinal front-engine/rear- or 4-wheel drive

ENGINES	ohv V8	ohv V8	Turbodiesel ohv V8
Size, liters/cu. in.	5.7/350	5.7/350	6.5/400
Horsepower	200-210	250-255	180
Torque (lbs./ft.)	300	330-335	360

EPA city/highway mpg			
5-speed OD manual..............................	12/16		
4-speed OD automatic..........................	12/15	14/17	15/18

City/highway mpg (as tested)		
4-speed OD automatic..........................	12.5	14.3

Built in USA, Mexico

RETAIL PRICES	GOOD	AVERAGE	POOR
1992 Yukon 4WD	$5,000-7,000	$4,200-6,200	$1,700-3,000
1993 Yukon 4WD	6,000-8,000	5,100-7,000	2,400-4,000
1994 Yukon 4WD	7,200-9,000	6,200-8,000	3,200-4,700
1995 Yukon 2WD 4-door	7,100-8,500	6,100-7,500	3,000-4,000
1995 Yukon 4WD	8,600-10,800	7,600-9,800	4,000-5,800
1996 Yukon SL 2WD	7,600-9,100	6,600-8,100	3,500-4,500
1996 Yukon SL 4WD	9,600-10,600	8,600-9,600	4,800-5,600
1996 SLE, SLT 2WD	8,600-10,000	7,600-9,000	4,200-5,000
1996 SLE, SLT 4WD	11,100-12,500	9,900-11,200	5,800-6,800
1997 Yukon SL 2WD	9,200-11,500	8,200-10,500	4,600-6,200
1997 Yukon SL 4WD	11,200-13,100	10,200-11,900	6,100-7,200
1997 SLE, SLT 2WD	10,700-12,500	9,700-11,300	5,600-6,500
1997 SLE, SLT 4WD	12,700-14,000	11,400-12,500	7,100-8,000
1998 Yukon 2WD	12,500-14,500	11,500-13,200	7,200-8,300
1998 Yukon 4WD	14,000-16,000	12,500-14,500	8,000-9,500
1998 Denali 4WD	18,000-20,000	16,500-18,500	11,500-13,000
1999 Yukon 2WD	14,000-16,000	12,800-14,500	8,300-9,500
1999 Yukon 4WD	16,000-18,000	14,500-16,500	9,500-10,800
1999 Denali 4WD	21,000-23,000	19,500-21,500	14,000-15,500

AVERAGE REPLACEMENT COSTS

A/C Compressor..........	$555	Clutch, Pressure Plate,	
Alternator.....................	220	Bearing	730
Automatic Transmission or		Exhaust System	380
Transaxle	750	Radiator......................	650
Brakes	260	Shocks and/or Struts....	340
Timing Chain or Belt.....	415	Universal Joints............	225

TROUBLE SPOTS

• **Engine misfire.** A problem with the powertrain control module may cause a lack of power, early upshifts, late shifting in the 4WD-Low range, and otherwise erratic performance. (1996)

• **Automatic transmission.** Automatic transmissions may suffer harsh or shuddering shifts between first and second or may buzz or vibrate in park or neutral. (1992)

• **Engine knock.** Engine knock is usually eliminated by using an oil filter with a check valve. If this does work, GM has revised PROMs for the computers, or engine may require main bearings. (1995)

• **Engine noise.** The exhaust valves may not get enough lubrication causing a variety of noises. Usually, the same engine consumes excess oil because the valve guide seals on the exhaust valves are bad. (1996)

• **Dashboard lights.** The oil pressure gauge may read high, move erratically, or not work because of a defective oil pressure sensor. (1992-93)

• **Climate control.** The temperature control lever may slide from hot to cold, usually when the blower is on high speed. (1992-94)

RECALL HISTORY

1992: Brake-pedal pivot bolt can disengage, resulting in loss of brake control. **1994-96:** Solder joints can crack, causing windshield wipers to work intermittently. **1995 w/M30/MT1 automatic transmission:** When shift lever is placed in Park position, indicator may not illuminate. **1995-96 w/gas engine:** Throttle cable may contact dash mat and bind; engine speed might then not return to idle. **1998:** Lower steering pinch bolt may be "finger loose" or missing, allowing bolt to loosen and fall out; can result in off-center steering wheel and separation of shaft from steering gear. **1998:** On some vehicles, one or both front brake rotor/hubs may have out-of-spec gray iron that can fail during life of vehicle. **1998 C10706:** Rear brake line can contact left front fender wheelhouse inner panel; a hole could be worn in brake line, allowing loss of fluid and reducing rear brake effectiveness. **1999:** In a crash, right front passenger restraint systems may not meet neck extension requirements.

2000-01 GMC YUKON/DENALI

2001 GMC Yukon

FOR Acceleration (Denali) • Passenger and cargo room • Trailer towing

AGAINST Entry/exit (Denali) • Steering feel • Fuel economy

EVALUATION Though mainly evolutionary, Yukon advances brought some noticeable improvements. New V8s feel slightly smoother than the engines they replaced, but not much stronger. Acceleration is adequate, aided by the smooth automatic's astute shifting, but the 4.8-liter feels strained in towing or heavy hauling. Gas mileage is dismal. A Denali XL averaged only 9.8 mpg, though models with smaller engines will do a little better. Big SUVs don't corner like cars, but handling is better than their size might suggest. They feel balanced in directional changes, and are fairly easy to maneuver. Steering is reasonably precise, but road feel is only adequate. Ride quality and brake feel are the most noted improvements. The suspension absorbs bumps well and is surefooted on rough pavement. Stopping power is strong, with firm, progressive pedal action. Wind rush is not intrusive. Tire noise is low for a full-size SUV, but audible at highway speeds. The dashboard layout is logical and handy, with clear gauges and easily accessed controls. Drivers get a commanding view, while moving the spare tire beneath the rear undercarriage improved visibility and cargo space. Front and second-row space is generous. Differences between regular and XL Yukons are most evident in the third row. XLs have ample head, shoulder, and leg room for two grownups, but leg and head clearance in the shorter Yukon's third-row seat suggests children and occasional use. Entry/exit is somewhat hampered by modest backdoor openings. A Yukon has only enough room for a single row of grocery bags behind the third row, but Yukon XLs are more sizable. Third-row seats fold easily, and have wheels for removal. The XL's heavy bench takes two people to remove, while the Yukon's third row

is in two sections.

VALUE GM's impressive new full-size SUVs are capable, comfortable, and easy to live with. Though too big for a lot of buyers, their size fits nicely into the gap between Ford's Expedition and Excursion. Don't buy a big SUV without trying a GMC or Chevrolet.

SPECIFICATIONS

	4-door wagon[1]	4-door wagon[2]
Wheelbase, in.	116.0	130.0
Overall length, in.	198.8	219.3
Overall width, in.	78.8	78.9
Overall height, in.	76.5	75.7
Curb weight, lbs.	5050	5123
Cargo volume, cu. ft.	104.6	138.4
Fuel capacity, gals.	26.0	32.5
Seating capacity	9	9
Front head room, in.	40.7	40.7
Max. front leg room, in.	41.3	41.3
Rear head room, in.	39.4	39.0
Min. rear leg room, in.	38.6	39.1

1. Yukon. 2. Yukon XL.

Powertrain layout: longitudinal front-engine/rear- or 4-wheel drive

ENGINES

	ohv V8	ohv V8	ohv V8	ohv V8
Size, liters/cu. in.	4.8/294	5.3/325	6.0/364	8.1/496
Horsepower	275	285	300-320	340
Torque (lbs./ft.)	290	325	355-360	455
EPA city/highway mpg				
4-speed OD automatic	14/17	14/16	12/16	NA
City/highway mpg (as tested)				
4-speed OD automatic			9.8	

Built in USA

RETAIL PRICES

	GOOD	AVERAGE	POOR
2000 Yukon 2WD	$22,500-24,500	$21,500-23,500	$17,000-19,000
2000 Yukon 4WD	24,500-26,500	23,300-25,300	18,500-20,300
2000 Yukon XL 1500 2WD	23,000-26,000	21,800-24,500	17,300-20,000
2000 Yukon XL 1500 4WD	25,000-28,000	23,500-26,500	18,800-22,000
2000 Yukon XL 2500 2WD	24,500-27,500	23,300-26,000	18,500-21,000
2000 Yukon XL 2500 4WD	26,500-29,500	25,000-28,000	19,800-23,800
2001 Yukon 2WD	25,000-27,000	23,500-25,500	—
2001 Yukon 4WD	27,000-29,000	25,500-27,500	—
2001 Yukon XL 1500 2WD	25,500-27,500	24,000-26,000	—
2001 Yukon XL 1500 4WD	27,500-30,000	26,000-28,500	—
2001 Yukon XL 2500 2WD	27,500-29,500	26,000-28,000	—
2001 Yukon XL 2500 4WD	29,500-32,000	28,000-30,500	—
2001 Yukon Denali	35,000-37,000	33,000-35,000	—
2001 Yukon XL Denali	37,500-39,500	35,500-37,500	—

AVERAGE REPLACEMENT COSTS

A/C Compressor	$390	Constant Velocity Joints	890
Alternator	325	Exhaust System	455
Automatic Transmission or Transaxle	1,115	Radiator	555
		Shocks and/or Struts	665
Brakes	375	Timing Chain or Belt	610

TROUBLE SPOTS

• **Manual transmission.** Manual transmissions tend to pop out of first gear because the transmissions were built without a detent ball and spring. These parts will be installed under warranty. (2000)

RECALL HISTORY

2000: Clearance between front right-hand brake pipe and body cross sill could decrease to the point of allowing contact, which could result in damage and loss of brake fluid and pressure. **2000-01:** Rear wheelhouse plugs may be loose or missing, allowing exhaust gases to flow forward under certain conditions and accumulate in rear wheelhouse. **2001:** Misrouted positive battery cable assembly could come in contact with the steering shaft universal joint. Over time, this contact could cause a wear-through of the cable assembly conduit and cable insulation, exposing the wire core and resulting in intermittent electrical shorting or battery discharge. **2001:** Outboard seatbelt retractors for the 2nd and 3rd row of seats could be cracked. With repeated actuation of the locking mechanism, the crack could spread to the point such that the seatbelt would no longer lock.

1990-93 HONDA ACCORD

1990 Honda Accord EX 2-door coupe

FOR Antilock brakes (later models) • Passenger and cargo room • Fuel economy • Handling • Ride

AGAINST Automatic transmission performance • Rear-seat room • Road noise

EVALUATION Spacious inside, Honda's midsize sedan promises an excellent ride and capable handling talents. Four-cylinder engines are both smoother and quieter in this generation, but take-offs and passing response are not brisk enough to match the V6 engines offered by rivals. In addition, the automatic transmission can be jerky at times, and occasionally harsh. On the plus side, fuel economy should be exceptional with any model. We have consistently averaged over 20 mpg in every Accord tested. Despite its added length, there is only modest rear-seat room (for a midsize car), and below-average head room in both sedans and coupes. The wagon is also smaller when compared with the Taurus and Camry, providing the least cargo room of the three. However, front seat room is good for above-average sized adults and the dashboard design is both thoughtful and useful.

VALUE Pluses tend to outnumber this Honda's minuses. The Accord generally makes up for perceived deficiencies with high levels of overall quality, refinement, and performance when compared with the competition. Blessed with outstanding ride quality, high reliability, and sensible controls nestled in an airy, low-cowl cabin that's become a Honda trademark, the Accord continues to impress.

SPECIFICATIONS

	2-door coupe	4-door sedan	4-door wagon
Wheelbase, in.	107.1	107.1	107.1
Overall length, in.	184.8	185.2	186.8
Overall width, in.	53.9	67.1	67.5
Overall height, in.	54.1	54.7	55.1
Curb weight, lbs.	2738	2733	3139
Cargo volume, cu. ft.	14.4	14.4	64.6
Fuel capacity, gals.	17.0	17.0	17.0
Seating capacity	5	5	5
Front head room, in.	38.8	38.9	39.0
Max. front leg room, in.	42.9	42.6	42.7
Rear head room, in.	36.5	37.5	37.6
Min. rear leg room, in.	32.3	34.3	34.1

Powertrain layout: transverse front-engine/front-wheel drive

ENGINES

	ohc I4	ohc I4	ohc I4
Size, liters/cu. in.	2.2/132	2.2/132	2.2/132
Horsepower	125	130	140
Torque (lbs./ft.)	137	142	142

EPA city/highway mpg

5-speed OD manual	24/30	24/30	22/27
4-speed OD automatic	22/28	22/28	22/28

City/highway mpg (as tested)

4-speed OD automatic		21.5	21.2

Built in USA, Japan

RETAIL PRICES

	GOOD	AVERAGE	POOR
1990 Accord	$1,800-3,000	$1,200-2,400	$300-900
1990 Accord EX	2,400-3,400	1,800-2,700	500-1,000
1991 Accord	2,300-3,800	1,700-3,100	600-1,200
1991 Accord EX, SE	3,100-4,500	2,400-3,800	800-1,600
1992 Accord	2,800-4,000	2,200-3,300	700-1,300
1992 Accord EX	3,800-4,600	3,100-3,900	1,200-1,700
1993 Accord	3,500-4,800	2,800-4,000	1,000-1,800
1993 Accord EX, SE	4,500-5,700	3,800-4,900	1,700-2,400

AVERAGE REPLACEMENT COSTS

A/C Compressor	$530	Clutch, Pressure Plate, Bearing	550
Alternator	355	Constant Velocity Joints	670
Automatic Transmission or Transaxle	1,055	Exhaust System	465
Brakes	250	Radiator	485
		Shocks and/or Struts	545

TROUBLE SPOTS

• **Engine noise.** A squealing noise from under the hood is likely to be caused by a worn alternator bearing, and it may have failed because the belt tension was too great. (1990-93)

• **Automatic transmission.** Cars with high mileage may begin to shift more harshly, which may be corrected by adding a bottle of Lubeguard conditioner to the automatic transmission fluid. (1990-93)

• **Audio system.** If the CD changer in the trunk will not eject, the company will exchange the CD magazines with a redesigned one. (All)

• **Steering noise.** If there is a squeak or squeal in the steering, especially when making a slow, tight turn, look for a label on the power steering reservoir that says PSF-V additive was added. If the noise is still there after additive was installed, the right-side end seal on the steering rack will have to be replaced. (1990-93)

• **Brakes.** The parking brake may not fully release because a rivet on the brake rod is too tight. (1993)

RECALL HISTORY

1990-91: Front seatbelt release button can break and pieces can fall inside. **1991 wagon:** Improperly attached washer in cargo area light may have fallen inside during assembly; if tailgate is open and switch is in its middle position, washer can cause short circuit that causes switch to overheat, resulting in fire. **1991-93 wagon:** Rear outside seatbelts may lock-up at angles other than those required by federal standard; could increase risk of injury in sudden stop or accident. **1992:** Left seatbelt assemblies on a few cars were installed on the right side; belt cannot be pulled out of the retractor, making it unusable.

1994-97 HONDA ACCORD

1996 Honda Accord EX 4-door sedan

FOR Acceleration (V6) • Passenger and cargo room • Ride • Steering/handling

AGAINST Acceleration (4-cylinder) • Road noise • Antilock brakes (limited availability)

EVALUATION The 1994 to '96 models feel much more substantial than their predecessor. Four-cylinder performance is adequate for most driving needs, but the V6's added punch comes in quite handy in passing situations. The automatic transmission still lags behind the competition in shift quality, but it's now at least acceptable. Steering is firm and the car tracks effortlessly. There's also less wind noise than before, though tires whine at expressway speeds.The body, now three inches wider than before, significantly increases the interior's feeling of spaciousness. Leg room is good both front and rear, but head room is only average at best. The driver's seat provides a commanding view of the road, thanks to thin pillars and a low cowl. A wider trunk opening is also greatly appreciated. And while the rear seatback drops forward to allow the transport of large and bulky objects, it does not fold fully flat.

VALUE Overall, the Accord continues to be a fine, solid-feeling family car with a refined, sporty manner. In fact, this was the best Accord to date. The new V6 was most welcome, but long overdue. There was much stronger competition among midsize family sedans today than ever before, with Honda's rivals making noticeable strides in the areas of styling, powertrain sophistication, chassis dynamics, ergonomics, and creature comforts. Yet, Accord came through in fine fashion.

SPECIFICATIONS

	2-door coupe	4-door sedan	4-door wagon
Wheelbase, in.	106.9	106.9	106.9
Overall length, in.	185.6	185.6	188.4
Overall width, in.	70.1	70.1	70.1
Overall height, in.	54.7	55.1	55.9
Curb weight, lbs.	2855	2855	3053
Cargo volume, cu. ft.	13.0	13.0	25.7
Fuel capacity, gals.	17.0	17.0	17.0
Seating capacity	5	5	5
Front head room, in.	39.4	39.4	39.8
Max. front leg room, in.	42.9	42.7	42.7
Rear head room, in.	36.4	37.6	39.0
Min. rear leg room, in.	31.3	34.3	34.1

Powertrain layout: transverse front-engine/front-wheel drive

ENGINES

	ohc I4	ohc I4	ohc V6
Size, liters/cu. in.	2.2/132	2.2/132	2.7/163
Horsepower	130	145	170
Torque (lbs./ft.)	139	147	165

EPA city/highway mpg

5-speed OD manual	25/32	25/31	
4-speed OD automatic	23/31	23/29	19/25

City/highway mpg (as tested)

4-speed OD automatic		23.3	21.0

Built in USA, Japan

RETAIL PRICES

	GOOD	AVERAGE	POOR
1994 Accord	$4,500-6,000	$3,700-5,200	$1,600-2,500
1994 Accord EX	5,800-6,700	5,000-5,900	2,600-3,200
1995 Accord	5,500-7,200	4,700-6,300	2,300-3,400
1995 Accord EX	6,800-8,200	6,000-7,300	3,200-3,900
1996 Accord	6,700-8,700	5,900-7,800	3,100-4,300
1996 Accord EX	8,500-10,000	7,500-9,000	4,200-5,000
1997 Accord	8,000-10,800	7,000-9,800	4,000-5,600
1997 Accord EX	10,000-12,000	9,000-11,000	5,300-6,500

AVERAGE REPLACEMENT COSTS

A/C Compressor	$530	Clutch, Pressure Plate, Bearing	550
Alternator	380	Constant Velocity Joints	670
Automatic Transmission or Transaxle	1,055	Exhaust System	540
Brakes	250	Radiator	485
Shocks and/or Struts	545	Timing Chain or Belt	350

TROUBLE SPOTS

• **Vehicle noise.** A noise coming from the passenger footwell is most likely due to the air conditioning high pressure line vibrating against the power steering fluid line. (1995)

• **Automatic transmission.** Cars with high mileage may begin to shift more harshly, which may be corrected by adding a bottle of Lubeguard conditioner to the automatic transmission fluid. (1994-96)

• **Audio system.** If the CD changer in the trunk will not eject, the company will exchange the CD magazines with a redesigned one. (All)

• **Manual transmission.** If the transmission grinds when shifting into fifth gear, the fork, sleeve set, and mainshaft gear must be replaced. (1994-95)

• **Fuel gauge.** The fuel gauge may not read full even though the tank is filled due to excessive resistance in the sending unit in the tank. (1994-95)

• **Engine noise.** The gasket for the midexhaust pipe sticks, causing a buzzing noise. (1994-95)

• **Dashboard lights.** The heater control panel lights do not glow when the switch is pressed because of breaks in the circuit board solder joints. (1994-95)

• **Brakes.** The parking brake may not fully release because a rivet on the brake rod is too tight. (1994)

RECALL HISTORY

1994: Some tire valve stems were damaged during assembly, resulting in sudden loss of air pressure and/or loss of control. **1995:** Some sup-

plemental restraint system electronic control units can cause unexpected airbag deployment. **1995-97 except DC and V6 models:** Improperly routed wire harness for factory-installed air conditioner can allow wires to rub against each other, which can eventually cause short circuit that may lead to overheating, smoke, and possible fire. **1997:** Certain ball joints can wear out prematurely and, in worst case, would separate, causing front suspension to collapse.

1998-01 HONDA ACCORD

1998 Honda Accord LS V6 4-door sedan

FOR Acceleration (V6) • Instruments/controls • Steering/handling

AGAINST Automatic transmission performance

EVALUATION Engines are silky, revvy, quiet, and packed with punch. The V6 provides quick getaways and ample passing power. Much of the time, you also get smooth and responsive downshifts for passing or merging. At times, though, the automatic shifts with a jerk and can be painfully slow to drop down a gear for passing. Gas mileage is a bonus, especially with the 4-cylinder engine. Our test 5-speed coupe averaged 23.8 mpg in hard urban driving. An automatic 4-cylinder got 24.7 mpg. Test sedans with the V6 engine averaged 24.0 and 20.7 mpg. The ride is comfortable and controlled. Handling, on the other hand, is noticeably more precise than before, with less body lean and better grip in tight corners. You can expect little wind noise in any model, though some tire hum is audible on coarse pavement. Overall, noise levels rank about average. An Accord sedan is just as roomy inside as a Toyota Camry or Ford Taurus. Like those competitors, too, Accords are more comfortable for four adults than for five. In any of those models, the center rear position lacks sufficient width for an average-sized grown-up. Seat comfort ranks as first-rate, especially up front. Wider doors ease entry/exit on sedans, but rear access in coupes demands a certain amount of crouching and crawling. Dashboards are models of functional simplicity. Power window and lock switches are not illuminated, however. Sedans have a deep, wide trunk with a flat floor and a large lid, which opens to bumper level. Liftover is a bit higher in coupes, which also have slightly less trunk volume. All models have a handy split-folding rear seat.

VALUE If you're in the market for a top-notch midsize family sedan (or coupe), don't buy until you've test-driven an Accord. Resale values tend to be on the high side, however, so don't expect fantastic bargains.

SPECIFICATIONS

	2-door coupe	4-door sedan
Wheelbase, in.	105.1	106.9
Overall length, in.	186.8	188.8
Overall width, in.	70.3	70.3
Overall height, in.	55.1	56.9
Curb weight, lbs.	2943	2888
Cargo volume, cu. ft.	13.6	14.1
Fuel capacity, gals.	17.1	17.1
Seating capacity	5	5
Front head room, in.	39.7	40.0
Max. front leg room, in.	42.6	42.1
Rear head room, in.	36.5	37.6
Min. rear leg room, in.	32.4	37.9

Powertrain layout: transverse front-engine/front-wheel drive

ENGINES

	ohc I4	ohc I4	ohc V6
Size, liters/cu. in.	2.3/137	2.3/137	3.0/183
Horsepower	135	150	200
Torque (lbs./ft.)	145	152	195

EPA city/highway mpg

5-speed OD manual	25/31	25/31	

	ohc I4	ohc I4	ohc V6
4-speed OD automatic	22/29	22/30	21/28
City/highway mpg (as tested)			
4-speed OD automatic	21.5	24.7	20.7

Built in USA

RETAIL PRICES

	GOOD	AVERAGE	POOR
1998 Accord DX	$9,500-10,500	$8,500-9,500	$4,900-5,500
1998 Accord LX	11,000-12,500	10,000-11,500	6,000-7,000
1998 Accord EX	12,500-15,000	11,300-13,700	7,100-8,600
1999 Accord DX	10,500-11,500	9,500-10,500	5,700-6,400
1999 Accord LX	12,000-13,500	11,000-12,500	7,000-8,000
1999 Accord EX	13,800-16,500	12,600-15,000	8,600-10,500
2000 Accord DX	11,700-13,000	10,700-12,000	6,700-7,600
2000 Accord LX, SE	13,500-15,000	12,500-14,000	8,500-9,500
2000 Accord EX	15,300-18,000	14,000-16,500	9,500-11,200
2001 Accord DX	13,000-14,500	12,000-13,500	—
2001 Accord LX	14,800-16,500	13,500-15,000	—
2001 Accord EX	16,800-19,000	15,500-17,500	—

AVERAGE REPLACEMENT COSTS

A/C Compressor...........	$775	Clutch, Pressure Plate,	
Alternator......................	460	Bearing	845
Automatic Transmission or		Constant Velocity Joints	1,405
Transaxle	1,110	Exhaust System	610
Brakes	520	Radiator.......................	585
Shocks and/or Struts....	920	Timing Chain or Belt.....	475

TROUBLE SPOTS

• **Paint/body.** If the car is driven on rough roads, the spoiler on the trunk can rub through the paint unless spacer pads are installed between the spoiler and trunk lid. (1998)

• **Suspension noise.** Loose nuts on the rear stabilizer bar cause it to rattle. (1998)

• **Vehicle noise.** Noises come from the top of the windshield and rear window because the teeth for the glass fasteners aren't engaged. The teeth must be trimmed and a wool felt installed. (1998)

• **Brakes.** The brake light may not go off. The cause is a saturated float in the master cylinder that should be replaced under warranty or beyond. (1998)

RECALL HISTORY

1998: Irregularity in transmission cover can allow car to roll down an incline while transmission is in "Park." **2000:** Rear suspension lower arms and/or control arms could break, due to improper welding.

1992-95 HONDA CIVIC

1992 Honda Civic Si 2-door hatchback

FOR Fuel economy • Acceleration (EX and Si) • Ride (4-door) • Handling/roadholding

AGAINST Acceleration (CX and VX) • Rear-seat room (hatchback) • Noise (hatchback) • Cargo room (hatchback)

EVALUATION All four engines are weak on low-end torque, lacking in zest. Although they pull smoothly enough in the middle gears, they fail to exhibit much overall gusto—especially with automatic transmissions. To climb hills and keep up with highway traffic you'll have to shift gears often and push hard on the gas pedal. Automatic transmissions shift neatly, lacking the harsh jolt of earlier models. Fuel economy is great. Over a long-term trial, a 5-speed EX sedan averaged 29.6 mpg. Wind and exhaust sounds are reduced, especially in sedans, though tire noise is a problem. Civics ride smoothly

for a subcompact, although sedans have a much better ride than coupe and hatchback models. Handling can best be described as modest, if agile, with the narrow tires and softer suspension leaning over in tight turns. The steering and brakes work well. Interior room is surprisingly good for a subcompact. Four adults can stretch out in modest comfort. Interior controls are thoughtfully designed and easy to use. Cargo space is good as well, but the hatchbacks' split-opening makes loading and unloading difficult.

VALUE You pay a hefty price for a nice Civic, but in this case the expenditure might well be worth it. Flaws are few in these refined, quietly impressive subcompacts, overwhelmed by some highly tempting virtues. Civics stand apart from the crowd because of their nimble handling, smooth running, enjoyable operation, and miserly gas mileage.

SPECIFICATIONS

	2-door coupe	2-door hatchback	4-door sedan
Wheelbase, in.	103.2	101.3	103.2
Overall length, in.	172.8	160.2	173.0
Overall width, in.	66.9	66.9	66.9
Overall height, in.	50.9	50.7	51.7
Curb weight, lbs.	2231	2108	2213
Cargo volume, cu. ft.	11.8	13.3	12.4
Fuel capacity, gals.	11.9	11.9	11.9
Seating capacity	5	5	5
Front head room, in.	38.5	38.6	39.1
Max. front leg room, in.	42.5	42.5	42.5
Rear head room, in.	34.9	36.5	37.2
Min. rear leg room, in.	31.1	30.5	32.8

Powertrain layout: transverse front-engine/front-wheel drive

ENGINES

	ohc I4	ohc I4	ohc I4	ohc I4
Size, liters/cu. in.	1.5/91	1.5/91	1.5/91	1.6/97
Horsepower	70	92	102	125
Torque (lbs./ft.)	90	97	98	106
EPA city/highway mpg				
5-speed OD manual	42/46	47/56	34/40	29/35
3-speed automatic				
4-speed OD automatic			29/36	26/34
City/highway mpg (as tested)				
5-speed OD manual				29.6

Built in USA, Canada, Japan

RETAIL PRICES

	GOOD	AVERAGE	POOR
1992 Civic	$1,600-3,000	$1,000-2,400	$200-900
1992 Civic EX	3,000-3,800	2,300-3,100	700-1,200
1992 Civic Si	2,300-2,900	1,700-2,200	500-800
1993 Civic	2,100-3,500	1,500-2,800	400-1,100
1993 Civic EX	4,000-4,700	3,300-3,900	1,200-1,600
1993 Civic Si	3,000-3,800	2,300-3,000	700-1,200
1994 Civic	2,600-4,200	2,000-3,500	600-1,500
1994 Civic EX	4,600-5,300	3,900-4,500	1,700-2,100
1994 Civic Si	4,000-4,800	3,300-4,000	1,400-1,800
1995 Civic	3,200-5,400	2,500-4,600	800-2,200
1995 Civic EX	5,500-6,300	4,700-5,400	2,300-2,800
1995 Civic Si	5,000-5,800	4,200-5,000	1,900-2,500

AVERAGE REPLACEMENT COSTS

A/C Compressor...........	$470	Clutch, Pressure Plate,	
Alternator......................	310	Bearing	455
Automatic Transmission or		Constant Velocity Joints	550
Transaxle	750	Exhaust System	428
Brakes	180	Radiator.......................	360
Shocks and/or Struts....	580	Timing Chain or Belt.....	190

TROUBLE SPOTS

• **Automatic transmission.** Cars with high mileage may begin to shift more harshly, which may be corrected by adding a bottle of Lubeguard conditioner to the automatic transmission fluid. (1992-95)

• **Air conditioner.** If the air conditioner belt repeatedly comes off, the splash shield under the engine is probably knocking it off when the car goes over a parking curb, etc. (1992-95)

• **Audio system.** If the CD changer in the trunk will not eject, the company will exchange the CD magazines with a redesigned one. (All)

• **Water leak.** There may be water leaking into the passenger footwell because of insufficient sealer on the seam at the firewall. Look for rust on the floor pan and run water over the right lower corner of the windshield to watch for water leaks before buying the car. (1992-95)

• **Trunk latch.** There may not be sufficient clearance on the trunk latch making it hard to open with the key. (1992-95)

RECALL HISTORY

1992-94: Retaining clip at automatic transmission can come off, so position of lever does not match actual transmission gear range. **1994:** Passenger-side airbag module on small number of cars may contain incorrect inflator, therefore unable to provide adequate protection.

1996-00 HONDA CIVIC

1997 Honda Civic LX 4-door sedan

FOR Antilock brakes • Fuel economy • Ride • Visibility

AGAINST Road noise • Rear-seat entry/exit

EVALUATION Based on interior volume, the sedan now qualifies as a compact car, whereas the coupe and hatchback rank as subcompacts. Rear space in any body style is adequate for most people (up to about 6 feet tall) to fit without squeezing. Hatchbacks gained the most interior space. Thinner roof pillars and a bigger back window improved visibility on all body styles. The driver faces a low steering wheel and easy-to-read gauges. Split-folding rear seatbacks on all Civics expanded cargo capacity. The '01 redesign brought obvious gains in space, refinement, and comfort. Acceleration is liveliest with the EX, but all Civics perform at least adequately. Gas mileage also is a bonus: An EX with automatic reached 36 mpg on the highway, averaging 29 mpg in suburban commuting. Engine noise has been quieted, but road noise is still prominent at highway speeds. Except for some overreaction to wavy surfaces, ride comfort is pleasing—well above average for a small car, with few jolts and minimal bounciness. Easy to maneuver, stable and well-controlled on the highway, the Civic delivers superior steering feedback and excellent response.

VALUE This generation continues Civic's long-standing tradition of reliability and durability. Largely for that reason—coupled with the high new-car prices of LX and EX models, in particular—their resale prices as used vehicles tend to stay high.

SPECIFICATIONS	2-door coupe	2-door hatchback	4-door sedan
Wheelbase, in.	103.2	103.2	103.2
Overall length, in.	175.1	164.5	175.1
Overall width, in.	67.1	67.1	67.1
Overall height, in.	54.1	54.1	54.7
Curb weight, lbs.	2262	2222	2319
Cargo volume, cu. ft.	11.9	13.4	11.9
Fuel capacity, gals.	11.9	11.9	11.9
Seating capacity	5	5	5
Front head room, in.	38.8	38.8	39.8
Max. front leg room, in.	42.7	42.7	42.7
Rear head room, in.	36.2	37.2	37.6
Min. rear leg room, in.	34.1	34.1	34.1

Powertrain layout: transverse front-engine/front-wheel drive

ENGINES	ohc I4	ohc I4	ohc I4	dohc I4
Size, liters/cu. in.	1.6/97	1.6/97	1.6/97	1.6/97
Horsepower	106	115	127	160
Torque (lbs./ft.)	103	104	107	111
EPA city/highway mpg				
5-speed OD manual	33/38	39/45	30/36	16/31
4-speed OD automatic	29/36		28/35	
City/highway mpg (as tested)				
5-speed OD manual			33.8	
4-speed OD automatic			31.4	

Built in USA, Canada

RETAIL PRICES	GOOD	AVERAGE	POOR
1996 Civic	$4,400-6,800	$3,700-6,100	$1,600-3,000
1996 Civic EX	7,000-8,000	6,200-7,000	3,300-3,800
1997 Civic	5,200-7,800	4,500-7,000	2,200-3,700
1997 Civic EX	8,200-9,200	7,500-8,400	4,200-4,800
1998 Civic	6,300-9,000	5,500-8,100	2,900-4,400
1998 Civic EX	9,500-10,500	8,500-9,500	4,800-5,500
1999 Civic	7,400-10,200	6,600-9,200	3,500-5,200
1999 Civic EX	10,500-12,000	9,500-11,000	5,600-6,400
1999 Civic Si	12,000-13,000	11,000-12,000	7,000-7,700
2000 Civic	8,500-11,000	7,600-10,000	4,200-5,800
2000 Civic EX	11,800-13,000	10,800-12,000	6,800-7,500
2000 Civic Si	13,500-15,000	12,500-13,800	8,500-9,300

AVERAGE REPLACEMENT COSTS

A/C Compressor	$465	Clutch, Pressure Plate,	
Alternator	310	Bearing	470
Automatic Transmission or		Constant Velocity Joints	590
Transaxle	800	Exhaust System	405
Brakes	185	Radiator	515
Shocks and/or Struts	690	Timing Chain or Belt	185

TROUBLE SPOTS

• **Audio system.** Installing an aftermarket radio can result in loss of dome lights and keyless entry. Those two systems are tied into the Honda radio. (1997)

• **Seatbelts/safety.** Seatbelts may not retract or may retract slowly. Also, the button that keeps the seatbelt tongue from sliding down breaks. The belts should be serviced under the Honda Lifetime Seat Belt Limited Warranty. (1996-97)

• **Cupholders.** The cupholder lid sticks closed or will not close due to missing latch. (1996-97)

• **Water leak.** Water leaks onto the front floor (either or both sides) due to insufficient sealer on body seams. (1996-97)

RECALL HISTORY

1996: Soapy lubricant used to insert brake booster check valve into vacuum hose causes sticky valve and loss of power assist. **1996-98 w/accessory floormats:** Mispositioned floormat could interfere with accelerator pedal. **1997-98:** Some passenger airbag modules were improperly assembled; could prevent proper deployment.

1997-01 HONDA CR-V

1998 Honda CR-V

FOR Entry/exit • Passenger and cargo room

AGAINST Acceleration • Rear-seat comfort

EVALUATION Performance is not a "plus" with the CR-V, at least with an automatic transmission. Acceleration to 60 mph in an early model with automatic took a leisurely 11.3 seconds, with only the driver aboard. Manual shift cuts about a second from that figure. Go-power sags even further when climbing steep upgrades, or with a full load. Overall gas mileage of 19.7 mpg fell short of expectations, too. CR-V is pleasantly (and predictably) carlike to drive. Wind noise is unusually well-suppressed at cruising speeds, and tire sounds are minor. Even though the engine begins to boom above 4000 rpm or so, it's never throbby or irritating. Body lean ranks as modest through tight turns, so the CR-V can be tossed around much like any small wagon. Ride comfort is generally good, but some road undulations result in an annoying tendency to wheel-hop. Head and leg room are ample, but three adults don't fit comfortably in back. Step-in is low despite an 8-inch ground clearance, so entry/exit is easy, although rear doors are narrow for larger people. Though rather buslike, the driving stance is accommodating, thanks to a standard tilt steering wheel and manual seat-height adjuster. The column-mounted shifter sits awkwardly behind the wiper stalk, but otherwise the driving environment is simple and convenient—quite similar to riding in a Civic. The CR-V's 50/50 split rear seat can fold down to form a flat load floor. With the seat in use, you have space for about 10 grocery bags. Cargo bay access isn't the best, however, as you have to get past an external spare-tire carrier, glass liftgate, and swing-out tailgate. Solid, rattle-free construction has been evident during test drives, even when rolling through rough surfaces. Panel fit and paint finish have been excellent, inside and out.

VALUE Except for a lack of power, the CR-V almost approaches perfection. As it stands, this is a handy and well-built compact wagon with carlike manners and a 4WD system that never needs to be thought about. Even though it can't match the space or brawn of bigger SUVs, Honda's CR-V is clearly the nicest of the "baby-size" 4x4s.

SPECIFICATIONS

	4-door wagon
Wheelbase, in.	103.1
Overall length, in.	176.4
Overall width, in.	68.9
Overall height, in.	65.9
Curb weight, lbs.	3150
Cargo volume, cu. ft.	34.3
Fuel capacity, gals.	15.3
Seating capacity	5
Front head room, in.	40.5
Max. front leg room, in.	41.5
Rear head room, in.	39.2
Min. rear leg room, in.	36.7

Powertrain layout: transverse front-engine/front- or 4-wheel drive

ENGINES

	dohc I4
Size, liters/cu. in.	2.0/122
Horsepower	126-146
Torque (lbs./ft.)	126-133

EPA city/highway mpg

5-speed OD manual	22/25
4-speed OD automatic	22/25

City/highway mpg (as tested)

5-speed OD manual	20.5
4-speed OD automatic	19.2

Built in Japan

RETAIL PRICES

	GOOD	AVERAGE	POOR
1997 CR-V 4WD	$10,500-11,500	$9,500-10,500	$5,700-6,400
1998 CR-V 2WD	11,000-12,000	10,000-11,000	6,000-6,700
1998 CR-V 4WD	11,700-13,000	10,700-11,800	6,700-7,500
1999 CR-V 2WD	12,000-13,000	11,000-12,000	7,000-7,700
1999 CR-V 4WD	13,000-14,500	12,000-13,300	8,000-8,800
2000 CR-V 2WD	13,500-14,500	12,500-13,500	8,500-9,200
2000 CR-V 4WD	14,500-16,500	13,300-15,000	9,200-10,300
2001 CR-V 2WD	15,000-16,500	14,000-15,300	—
2001 CR-V 4WD	16,000-18,000	15,000-16,500	—

AVERAGE REPLACEMENT COSTS

A/C Compressor	$705	Clutch, Pressure Plate, Bearing	840
Alternator	600	Constant Velocity Joints	930
Automatic Transmission or Transaxle	1,265	Exhaust System	415
Brakes	280	Radiator	495
Shocks and/or Struts	940	Timing Chain or Belt	545

TROUBLE SPOTS

• **Brakes.** The ABS light comes on because one (or both) of the rear wheel speed sensors fails. Revised sensors are available to replace them. (1997)

• **Headlights.** The fog light housing is prone to cracking and, when this happens, the lens falls out. (1997)

• **Mirrors.** The power mirrors were not properly sealed to the body on some vehicles causing wind noise. (1997)

RECALL HISTORY

1998-99: Improperly routed under-dash wire harness on some vehicles could be damaged by contact with brake light switch, possibly resulting in blown fuse.

1995-98 HONDA ODYSSEY

1995 Honda Odyssey

FOR Ride • Steering/handling • Entry/exit • Antilock brakes

AGAINST Engine noise • Road noise • Acceleration (full load)

EVALUATION Odyssey departs from the minivan herd by virtue of its fully independent suspension, versus beam-type rear axles for most of the competition. It corners with little body lean and has good stability. Ride quality is also commendable: steady and firm at highway speeds; smoothly absorbent and comfortable when traversing bumpy urban pavement. Braking is nearly faultless. Power from either the 2.2- or 2.3-liter engine is adequate, but the engines are loud when flooring the throttle. Also, when passing or engaging in quick sprints onto expressways, the Odyssey can feel underpowered. Gas mileage is great, more than 21 mpg in city/expressway driving. As in the Accord, Odyssey's automatic transmission delivers prompt shifts that are usually smooth. Full-throttle downshifts, on the other hand, can induce an unwanted lunge forward. Because the Odyssey minivan is three to five inches narrower than rivals, cargo space is somewhat limited. There's also little walk-through room. On the plus side, the rear seat easily folds flush, and it's an easy minivan to park. The interior features plenty of space for six, but an extra person in the center seat of the 7-passenger version could be squeezed. Rear entry/exit is somewhat hampered by doors that don't open as wide as they should. Driving position in the Odyssey is comfortable; visibility good all around. The dashboard is attractive and well-organized.

VALUE Well-built, well-equipped, and likely to be reliable, Odyssey is worth a look—provided that it's big enough to meet your needs. Lack of a V6 and modest dimensions tend to limit its appeal, however, against the league-leading Chrysler minivans and Ford's Windstar.

SPECIFICATIONS

	4-door van
Wheelbase, in.	111.4
Overall length, in.	187.2
Overall width, in.	70.6
Overall height, in.	64.6
Curb weight, lbs.	3450
Cargo volume, cu. ft.	102.5
Fuel capacity, gals.	17.2
Seating capacity	7
Front head room, in.	40.1
Max. front leg room, in.	40.7
Rear head room, in.	39.3
Min. rear leg room, in.	40.2

Powertrain layout: transverse front-engine/front-wheel drive

ENGINES

	ohc I4	dohc I4
Size, liters/cu. in.	2.2/132	3.2/140
Horsepower	140	150
Torque (lbs./ft.)	145	152

EPA city/highway mpg		ohc I4	dohc I4
4-speed OD automatic		20/24	21/26
City/highway mpg (as tested)			
4-speed OD automatic		21.5	21.3

Built in Japan

RETAIL PRICES	GOOD	AVERAGE	POOR
1995 Odyssey	$7,500-8,800	$6,600-7,800	$3,600-4,300
1996 Odyssey	9,500-11,000	8,500-10,000	5,000-6,000
1997 Odyssey	11,500-13,000	10,300-11,500	6,400-7,100
1998 Odyssey	13,500-15,500	12,000-14,000	8,000-9,200

AVERAGE REPLACEMENT COSTS

A/C Compressor	$510	Clutch, Pressure Plate,	
Alternator	280	Bearing	485
Automatic Transmission or		Constant Velocity Joints	620
Transaxle	965	Exhaust System	510
Brakes	220	Radiator	415
Shocks and/or Struts	550	Timing Chain or Belt	290

TROUBLE SPOTS

• **Engine noise.** A problem with the power brakes' vacuum booster check valve causes a buzzing noise when idling in gear. (1995)

• **Seatbelts/safety.** Seatbelts may not retract or may retract slowly. Also, the button that keeps the seatbelt tongue from sliding down breaks. The belts should be serviced under the Honda Lifetime Seat Belt Limited Warranty. (1995-97)

• **Cupholders.** The cigarette lighter/cupholder comes loose. (1995-96)

• **Fuel gauge.** The fuel gauge on some vehicles does not go all the way to "F" because the arm on the sending unit is too long. (1995)

• **Glove box.** The glove box door pops off because the latch assembly falls apart. (1995)

RECALL HISTORY

1997-98: Certain ball joints can wear out prematurely and, in worst case, would separate, causing front suspension to collapse.

1999-01 HONDA ODYSSEY

2000 Honda Odyssey EX

FOR Entry/exit • Passenger and cargo room • Acceleration

AGAINST Navigation system controls • Rear visibility

EVALUATION Honda's competent minivan has a lot to offer. Standing-start acceleration is spirited. Passing maneuvers are aided by a transmission that generally shifts promptly and smoothly—if a bit slow to downshift at full throttle from low and midrange speeds. A test EX reached 60 mph in a bit over 9 seconds. Only Toyota's Sienna offers a more refined powertrain. The new engine is smooth and quiet. Premium fuel is recommended, but Honda has said it will run on regular with only a slight power loss. An absorbent but taut ride is coupled with alert, confident handling that's at or near the top of the minivan class, resulting in excellent road manners. Steering has good feel but is slightly heavy at low speeds, lightening up quickly and feeling very communicative. Even at highway speeds, little engine, road, or wind noise intrudes. Braking is strong and stable. Drivers enjoy a comfortable, commanding position. Other seating positions enjoy plenty of head room. Middle seats offer enough leg space for average adults, but rear seats are most appropriate for chil-

dren, who will have an easier time climbing into the back. A versatile seating arrangement allows for numerous combinations of people and cargo. The fold-away rear seat is especially handy. Easy front and second-row access is provided, via low step-in and large doorways. Gauges and controls are well placed. A headrest for every seating position leaves few clear sight lines to sides and rear, but most minivans have a similar setup. The "space-saver" spare tire is housed in a covered well, ahead of the middle-row seats. If one of the full-size tires goes flat, it will have to be transported in the rear cargo area.

VALUE When Honda finally broke into the minivan mainstream, sales took off in a hurry. A solid value, it's roomy, refined, and performs well. Odysseys ranked as virtual bargains when new, but resale values are on the high side.

SPECIFICATIONS

	4-door van
Wheelbase, in.	118.1
Overall length, in.	201.2
Overall width, in.	76.3
Overall height, in.	66.1
Curb weight, lbs.	4233
Cargo volume, cu. ft.	146.1
Fuel capacity, gals.	20.0
Seating capacity	7
Front head room, in.	41.2
Max. front leg room, in.	41.0
Rear head room, in.	40.0
Min. rear leg room, in.	40.0

Powertrain layout: transverse front-engine/front-wheel drive

ENGINES

	ohc V6
Size, liters/cu. in.	3.5/212
Horsepower	210
Torque (lbs./ft.)	229
EPA city/highway mpg	
4-speed OD automatic	18/25
City/highway mpg (as tested)	
4-speed OD automatic	18.6

Built in Canada

RETAIL PRICES	GOOD	AVERAGE	POOR
1999 Odyssey LX	$18,000-19,500	$17,000-18,500	$13,500-14,500
1999 Odyssey EX	20,000-21,500	19,000-20,500	15,000-16,000
2000 Odyssey LX	20,000-21,500	19,000-20,500	15,000-16,000
2000 Odyssey EX	22,000-24,000	21,000-23,000	16,500-18,000
2001 Odyssey LX	22,500-24,000	21,300-22,500	—
2001 Odyssey EX	25,000-27,000	23,500-25,500	—

AVERAGE REPLACEMENT COSTS

A/C Compressor	$775	Constant Velocity Joints	1,290
Alternator	410	Exhaust System	775
Automatic Transmission or		Radiator	700
Transaxle	1,305	Shocks and/or Struts	1,555
Brakes	745	Timing Chain or Belt	710

TROUBLE SPOTS

• **Doors.** A replacement fuel door clip may be required if the left sliding door will not stay locked. (1999)

• **Doors.** If the junction switch in the B-pillar is not properly grounded, the sliding door alarm may sound when driving on rough roads. (1999-2000)

• **Engine misfire.** The EGR port in the intake manifold clogs requiring installation of a revised PCV hose and manifold end cap. (1999)

RECALL HISTORY

1999: On certain LX and EX models, in cold, wet weather, ice can form in throttle body, preventing return to idle position even though driver's foot is no longer on accelerator pedal. **1999:** On certain LX and EX models, sliding doors could open unexpectedly while vehicle is in motion. **1999 EX:** Excessive grease in remote power-lock actuator could cause slow return of lever to proper latching position, preventing sliding door from latching. **1999-00:** Dimmer control for instrument panel lights on certain minivans can fail. **1999-00:** Wire harness in engine compartment could be damaged by contact with metal pipe, possibly resulting in blown fuse; if fuse blows, engine power, or operation of any or all electrical components (including lights, wipers, horn, and antilock function of brakes) can be lost. **1999-00:** Sliding doors on some minivans may not latch properly because latches were not correctly riveted.

1994-97 HONDA PASSPORT

1995.5 Honda Passport EX

FOR 4WD traction (optional) • Optional antilock brakes • Passenger and cargo room

AGAINST Fuel economy • Noise • No shift-on-the-fly

EVALUATION

See the 1991-97 Isuzu Rodeo.

VALUE

See the 1991-97 Isuzu Rodeo.

SPECIFICATIONS

	4-door wagon
Wheelbase, in.	108.7
Overall length, in.	176.5
Overall width, in.	66.5
Overall height, in.	66.5
Curb weight, lbs.	3545
Cargo volume, cu. ft.	74.9
Fuel capacity, gals.	21.9
Seating capacity	6
Front head room, in.	38.0
Max. front leg room, in.	42.5
Rear head room, in.	38.0
Min. rear leg room, in.	36.0

Powertrain layout: longitudinal front-engine/rear- or 4-wheel drive

ENGINES

	ohc I4	ohc V6
Size, liters/cu. in.	2.6/156	3.2/193
Horsepower	120	175-190
Torque (lbs./ft.)	150	188

EPA city/highway mpg

5-speed OD manual	18/22	16/19
4-speed OD automatic		15/18

City/highway mpg (as tested)

4-speed OD automatic	14.6

Built in USA

RETAIL PRICES

	GOOD	AVERAGE	POOR
1994 Passport 2WD	$4,500-5,700	$3,800-4,900	$1,700-2,400
1994 Passport 4WD	6,000-7,000	5,200-6,000	2,700-3,200
1995 Passport 2WD	5,500-7,500	4,800-6,700	2,500-3,700
1995 Passport 4WD	7,000-8,300	6,000-7,300	3,200-4,000
1996 Passport 2WD	6,700-9,000	5,800-8,000	3,100-4,500
1996 Passport 4WD	8,700-10,000	7,700-9,000	4,300-5,100
1997 Passport 2WD	8,500-10,800	7,500-9,800	4,200-5,700
1997 Passport 4WD	10,500-12,000	9,500-11,000	5,600-6,500

AVERAGE REPLACEMENT COSTS

See the 1991-97 Isuzu Rodeo.

TROUBLE SPOTS

See the 1991-97 Isuzu Rodeo.

RECALL HISTORY

1994: Camshaft seal end plug can become dislodged from cylinder head, allowing oil to leak; can cause engine damage and fire. **1994:** Latch in seatbelt buckle could engage only partially, causing tongue to come out during collision or hard braking.

1998-01 HONDA PASSPORT

1998 Honda Pasport

FOR Passenger room • Cargo room • Acceleration • Antilock brakes

AGAINST Road noise • Fuel economy

EVALUATION

See the 1998-01 Isuzu Rodeo.

VALUE

See the 1998-01 Isuzu Rodeo.

SPECIFICATIONS

	4-door wagon
Wheelbase, in.	106.4
Overall length, in.	177.4
Overall width, in.	70.4
Overall height, in.	67.9
Curb weight, lbs.	3860
Cargo volume, cu. ft.	81.1
Fuel capacity, gals.	21.1
Seating capacity	5
Front head room, in.	38.9
Max. front leg room, in.	42.1
Rear head room, in.	38.3
Min. rear leg room, in.	35.0

Powertrain layout: longitudinal front-engine/rear- or 4-wheel drive

ENGINES

	dohc V6
Size, liters/cu. in.	3.2/193
Horsepower	205
Torque (lbs./ft.)	214

EPA city/highway mpg

5-speed OD manual	18/20
4-speed OD automatic	16/20

Built in USA

RETAIL PRICES

	GOOD	AVERAGE	POOR
1998 Passport LX	$10,500-12,000	$9,500-11,000	$5,700-6,600
1998 Passport EX	12,000-13,500	11,000-12,500	7,000-8,000
1999 Passport LX	12,500-14,500	11,500-13,200	7,500-8,500
1999 Passport EX	14,000-16,200	13,000-15,000	8,800-10,200
2000 Passport LX	15,000-16,800	13,700-15,300	9,500-10,500
2000 Passport EX	16,500-18,500	15,000-17,000	10,500-11,800
2001 Passport LX	18,000-20,500	16,500-19,000	—
2001 Passport EX	20,000-23,000	18,500-21,500	—

AVERAGE REPLACEMENT COSTS

See the 1998-01 Isuzu Rodeo.

TROUBLE SPOTS

See the 1998-01 Isuzu Rodeo.

RECALL HISTORY

1998: Improperly crimped ground connection terminal in engine wiring harness can eventually cause stress fracture, causing powertrain control module to receive an erroneous signal that may result in "no-start" condition or possible engine stalling. **1998-99:** Insufficient paint hardness on rear axles, due to uneven application, could result in loosening of nut for lower link bracket bolt, possibly leading to separation of link from axle.

1992-96 HONDA PRELUDE

FOR Antilock brakes (except S) • Acceleration • Steering/handling

AGAINST Passenger and cargo room • Instruments/controls

1995 Honda Prelude SE

EVALUATION Space up front is okay, but split-back rear seats really are tight—best left to toddlers—and the Prelude's skimpy trunk is tinier than before. Controls are conveniently placed and typically Honda-friendly, but Prelude instruments are annoyingly odd. Warning lights stretch all across the dashboard top, sitting too far to the right for easy checking while underway. Vacuum-fluorescent fuel and temperature gauges are near the center, difficult to read. On the plus side, expect strong performance and good fuel economy. All engines are turbine-smooth. While a base-model Prelude's acceleration is only adequate, the Si feels snappy, and the VTEC is sports-car quick. The automatic transmission hurts performance only slightly, but it has poor shift quality and seems to wander haphazardly through the gears at highway speeds. Test stick-shift Si Preludes have yielded a reasonably frugal 23.1 mpg in daily driving. Cornering is flat and grippy, handling poised and responsive. Stopping ability is commendable, but lack of antilock braking on the S model is unfortunate. We haven't found that 4-wheel steering helps much, yielding only a small gain in maneuvering ease. Not many are around, anyway.

VALUE Expensive? Sure it is; but for buyers who value fine workmanship, refinement, and a solid, reassuring feel, Prelude deserves a trial.

SPECIFICATIONS

	2-door coupe
Wheelbase, in.	100.4
Overall length, in.	174.8
Overall width, in.	69.5
Overall height, in.	50.8
Curb weight, lbs.	2809
Cargo volume, cu. ft.	7.9
Fuel capacity, gals.	15.9
Seating capacity	4
Front head room, in.	38.0
Max. front leg room, in.	44.2
Rear head room, in.	35.1
Min. rear leg room, in.	28.1

Powertrain layout: transverse front-engine/front-wheel drive

ENGINES

	ohc I4	dohc I4	dohc I4
Size, liters/cu. in.	2.2/132	2.3/138	2.2/132
Horsepower	135	160	190
Torque (lbs./ft.)	142	156	158
EPA city/highway mpg			
5-speed OD manual	24/29	22/27	22/26
4-speed OD automatic	22/27	21/26	
City/highway mpg (as tested)			
5-speed OD manual		23.1	21.9
4-speed OD automatic	24.6		

Built in Japan

RETAIL PRICES

	GOOD	AVERAGE	POOR
1992 Prelude	$3,500-4,500	$2,800-3,800	$1,000-1,600
1993 Prelude	4,500-5,800	3,800-5,000	1,700-2,400
1994 Prelude	5,500-6,700	4,700-5,900	2,300-3,000
1994 Prelude 4WS/VTEC	6,700-7,700	5,800-6,700	3,100-3,700
1995 Prelude	6,700-8,000	5,900-7,000	3,100-3,800
1995 Prelude SE/VTEC	8,300-9,300	7,400-8,300	4,200-4,800
1996 Prelude	8,000-9,500	7,000-8,500	3,800-4,900
1996 Prelude VTEC	10,000-11,500	9,000-10,500	5,300-6,200

AVERAGE REPLACEMENT COSTS

A/C Compressor	$370	Clutch, Pressure Plate,	
Alternator	410	Bearing	520
Automatic Transmission or		Constant Velocity Joints	675
Transaxle	965	Exhaust System	670
Brakes	210	Radiator	480
Shocks and/or Struts	845	Timing Chain or Belt	250

TROUBLE SPOTS

• **Seatbelts/safety.** Seatbelts may not retract or may retract slowly. Also, the button that keeps the seatbelt tongue from sliding down breaks. The belts should be serviced under the Honda Lifetime Seat Belt Limited Warranty. (1992-96)

• **Steering problems.** The car may drift to the right on flat roads due to a faulty spool valve in the power steering system. (1992-93)

• **Brakes.** The parking brake may not fully release because a rivet was installed too snugly. (1993-94)

• **Transmission noise.** The transmission grinds when shifting into fifth gear due to mismanufactured shift fork. (1992-95)

RECALL HISTORY

1996: Certain ball joints can wear out prematurely and, in worst case, would separate, causing front suspension to collapse.

1997-01 HONDA PRELUDE

1998 Honda Prelude SH

FOR Acceleration • Steering/handling • Build quality

AGAINST Rear-seat room • Cargo room

EVALUATION This Prelude rides more softly and muffles the VTEC engine better than the old one did, so it doesn't feel—or sound—as sporty this time around. On the other hand, the new Prelude drives more securely through turns and over lumpy surfaces. There's also a satisfying exhaust note when the engine revs high—which it definitely likes to do. The ride is reasonably supple for a sports coupe, though uneven surfaces induce notable jiggle. Engine, wind, and road noise are low while cruising, but "tire slap" might be heard even in around-town driving. Acceleration is lively with either transmission. Our test Preludes accelerated from 0-60 mph in 8.5 seconds with SportShift, and a swifter-yet 7.6 seconds with the 5-speed manual gearbox in an SH. While the you-do-it SportShift gear changes are crisp and immediate, high-rpm downshifts usually occur with a jerky lunge. On the plus side, SportShift's manual-shift capability gives the driver helpful control over engine speeds. Prelude's 5-speed is a slick-shifting, sheer delight, mating masterfully to smooth and easy clutch action. An SH averaged only 19.4 mpg, though a base car with automatic got a more appealing 23.2 mpg. Premium fuel is mandatory either way. The current Prelude is not usefully bigger in size. A longer wheelbase adds some rear foot room, but no more functional backseat space than in prior Preludes. Therefore, the rear seat is again best used to carry children or parcels—though it's no worse than most rivals. Visibility is uncluttered all around. The new dashboard features simple, logically grouped analog gauges.

VALUE New styling gave this Prelude an airier cabin than before, and the base model has been better equipped than its predecessor. Workmanship is pleasing, but the interior decor is closer to economy-car basic than to suave sports machine. Still, energetic performance on the road can help make a Prelude appealing.

SPECIFICATIONS

	2-door coupe
Wheelbase, in.	101.8
Overall length, in.	178.0
Overall width, in.	69.0
Overall height, in.	51.8
Curb weight, lbs.	2954
Cargo volume, cu. ft.	8.7
Fuel capacity, gals.	15.9
Seating capacity	4-5
Front head room, in.	37.9
Max. front leg room, in.	43.0
Rear head room, in.	35.3
Min. rear leg room, in.	28.1

Powertrain layout: transverse front-engine/front-wheel drive

ENGINES

	dohc I4
Size, liters/cu. in.	2.2/132
Horsepower	190-200
Torque (lbs./ft.)	156

EPA city/highway mpg

5-speed OD manual	22/26
4-speed OD automatic	21/26

City/highway mpg (as tested)

5-speed OD manual	19.4
4-speed OD automatic	23.2

Built in Japan

RETAIL PRICES

	GOOD	AVERAGE	POOR
1997 Prelude	$12,000-13,000	$11,000-12,000	$7,000-7,700
1997 Prelude SH	12,800-13,800	11,800-12,800	7,800-8,500
1998 Prelude	13,500-14,500	12,500-13,500	8,500-9,200
1998 Prelude SH	14,400-15,400	13,400-14,400	9,300-10,000
1999 Prelude	15,000-16,000	14,000-15,000	9,700-10,400
1999 Prelude SH	16,000-17,200	15,000-16,000	10,500-11,200
2000 Prelude	17,000-18,200	15,800-17,000	10,800-11,600
2000 Prelude SH	18,300-19,500	17,000-18,200	12,000-12,800
2001 Prelude	19,000-20,500	17,500-19,000	—
2001 Prelude SH	20,500-22,000	19,000-20,500	—

AVERAGE REPLACEMENT COSTS

A/C Compressor	$390	Clutch, Pressure Plate, Bearing	540
Alternator	425	Constant Velocity Joints	680
Automatic Transmission or Transaxle	1,035	Exhaust System	685
Brakes	270	Radiator	505
Shocks and/or Struts	855	Timing Chain or Belt	250

TROUBLE SPOTS

• **Manual transmission.** Because of a manufacturing defect in the shift fork, the transmission may grind going into fifth gear. (1997)

• **Vehicle noise.** Rattles or buzzing from under the car may because the heat shield is too close to the active torque transfer system (ATTS). (1997)

• **Dashboard lights.** The active torque transfer system (ATTS) light may come on and the system will shut down. A revised control unit is available to replace the original one. (1997)

• **Seatbelts/safety.** The button on the seatbelt that prevents the male half of the buckle breaks and the buckle slides down to the floor. (1997-98)

• **Dashboard lights.** The malfunction indicator light comes on because the transmission control module is damaged by electrical spikes from the ignition switch. (1997)

• **Vehicle noise.** The rear corners of the headliner rub against the rear window causing a rattle, especially on rough roads. (1997)

RECALL HISTORY

1997-98: Certain ball joints can wear out prematurely and, in worst case, would separate, causing front suspension to collapse.

1995-99 HYUNDAI ACCENT

1995 Hyundai Accent 4-door sedan

FOR Fuel economy • Visibility • Optional antilock brakes • Instruments/controls

AGAINST Noise • Passing power • Driving position

EVALUATION Acceleration from the base engine is adequate around town with either manual or automatic shift. Highway passing, on the other hand, requires a long stretch of open road. The engine also strains hard when going up even small hills. Automatic-transmission

downshifts are not harsh, and only seldom abrupt at all. Although the GT's engine, with 13 extra horsepower, performs with greater spirit, it does not transform the Accent into anything approaching a mini hot rod. Gas mileage is great. We've averaged more than 30 miles per gallon. Hyundai made great strides in improving the suspension. The ride is now above average for a small automobile. The suspension absorbs most bumps well and has good stability at highway speeds. Large bumps produce a loud thump; but most smaller obstacles are taken in stride. Handling ability is adequate, but the Accent's skinny tires easily lose their grip. Interior space is good in front for adults, but the back seat is too small for anyone taller than 5-foot-10. The dashboard is neat and legible, with easy-to-read gauges and logical controls, but some drivers find the fixed-position steering wheel to be too high for comfort. Outward visibility is good on both body styles. A large glovebox and long door pockets help with interior storage.

VALUE Because an Accent is also more satisfying to drive than some rivals, it can be a reasonable buy, provided that you can get beyond the interior noise problem. Reliability is also a question. All told, we recommend something larger for everyday transportation.

SPECIFICATIONS

	2-door hatchback	4-door sedan
Wheelbase, in.	94.5	94.5
Overall length, in.	161.5	162.1
Overall width, in.	63.8	63.8
Overall height, in.	54.9	54.9
Curb weight, lbs.	2101	2105
Cargo volume, cu. ft.	16.2	10.7
Fuel capacity, gals.	11.9	11.9
Seating capacity	5	5
Front head room, in.	38.7	38.7
Max. front leg room, in.	42.6	42.6
Rear head room, in.	37.8	38.0
Min. rear leg room, in.	32.7	32.7

Powertrain layout: transverse front-engine/front-wheel drive

ENGINES

	ohc I4	dohc I4
Size, liters/cu. in.	1.5/91	1.5/91
Horsepower	92	105
Torque (lbs./ft.)	96	101

EPA city/highway mpg

5-speed OD manual	28/37	27/35
4-speed OD automatic	27/36	26/34

City/highway mpg (as tested)

4-speed OD automatic	—	29.4

Built in South Korea

RETAIL PRICES

	GOOD	AVERAGE	POOR
1995 Accent	$1,500-2,100	$1,000-1,500	$100-300
1996 Accent	2,100-3,000	1,500-2,400	200-400
1997 Accent	2,700-3,600	2,100-2,900	400-700
1998 Accent	3,400-4,500	2,700-3,800	600-1,100
1999 Accent	4,200-5,400	3,500-4,600	900-1,500

AVERAGE REPLACEMENT COSTS

A/C Compressor	$595	Clutch, Pressure Plate, Bearing	300
Alternator	315	Constant Velocity Joints	330
Automatic Transmission or Transaxle	810	Exhaust System	250
Brakes	190	Radiator	390
Shocks and/or Struts	550	Shocks and/or Struts	550

TROUBLE SPOTS

• **Automatic transmission.** Automatic transmission may flare between second and third or downshift poorly. There is a modified transmission control module available. (1996-97)

• **Hard starting.** Hard starting may be due to a cracked in-tank fuel line. (1995-97)

• **Poor transmission shift.** Harsh 4-3 downshifts when coming to a stop below 10 mph due to build problems with the original transmission. (1995-96)

• **Automatic transmission.** If the transmission slips or will not go into fourth gear, the end clutch needs to be replaced. (1995-96)

• **Steering problems.** The power steering bracket may interfere with the coolant reservoir causing a buzzing noise or possible reservoir damage.

A new bracket is available. (1995-97)

RECALL HISTORY

1995 w/manual shift: Engine control module wiring harness can be contacted by clutch pedal assembly; insulation damage can cause fuse to blow and engine to stall. **1995-96 cars sold/used in Puerto Rico:** Through contact with road hazards and curbs, lower control arm can shift from original position. **1995-97 in 20 "salt belt" states:** Road salt can result in corrosion that causes pits to form on lower coil of front springs, allowing cracks to develop and possible breakage. **1996-97:** Wipers may not operate, due to contamination in contacts. **1999 w/automatic transmission:** Pressure control solenoid valve seals can allow transmission fluid to leak, resulting in slippage.

1992-95 HYUNDAI ELANTRA

1992 Hyundai Elantra

FOR Visibility • Control layout • Passenger and cargo room

AGAINST Noise • Ride • Radio controls

EVALUATION Early Elantras with the smaller engine exhibit fairly spirited performance with manual shift. But with the automatic transmission, you must use a heavy foot to keep up with traffic. Performance is better with the 1.8-liter engine that debuted for 1993. Though relatively smooth, the 1.6-liter engine isn't truly quiet. The 1.8-liter engine is smoother but not much quieter. Gas mileage isn't as great as might be expected. An automatic GLS averaged only 22.5 mpg. Road and wind noise is excessive for a modern small car. Elantras have a floaty ride. The suspension does not absorb bumps well, and the ride can get rough over broken pavement. Wavy surfaces yield a bouncy and disjointed sensation. Body lean is excessive in sharp directional changes, and the front tires tend to resist turning. Brakes are adequate, if a bit over-assisted. The addition of optional antilock braking for 1994 was a sensible move, though ABS was available only on the GLS. Passenger space is generous for a car in this class. Six-footers can sit comfortably in back, though the seat is too narrow for three adults. Head room is adequate all around. Except for low-mounted radio gauges, controls are well laid out. Visibility is good to all directions. Out back, the large trunk has a low, bumper-height liftover.

VALUE Overall, Elantra rates no higher than average, but came better equipped than most competitors. Workmanship cannot match that of most rivals, so be sure any Elantra is inspected carefully before you make a purchase.

SPECIFICATIONS

	4-door sedan
Wheelbase, in.	98.4
Overall length, in.	172.8
Overall width, in.	66.1
Overall height, in.	52.0
Curb weight, lbs.	2500
Cargo volume, cu. ft.	11.8
Fuel capacity, gals.	13.7
Seating capacity	5
Front head room, in.	38.4
Max. front leg room, in.	42.6
Rear head room, in.	37.6
Min. rear leg room, in.	33.4

Powertrain layout: transverse front-engine/front-wheel drive

ENGINES

	dohc I4	dohc I4
Size, liters/cu. in.	1.6/97	1.8/110
Horsepower	105-113	124
Torque (lbs./ft.)	102	116

EPA city/highway mpg	dohc I4	dohc I4
5-speed OD manual	22/29	21/28
4-speed OD automatic	22/29	22/29

City/highway mpg (as tested)	
4-speed OD automatic	22.5

Built in South Korea

RETAIL PRICES

	GOOD	AVERAGE	POOR
1992 Elantra	$900-1,500	$500-1,000	$100-200
1993 Elantra	1,100-1,700	600-1,100	100-300
1994 Elantra	1,400-2,000	800-1,400	200-300
1995 Elantra	1,800-2,400	1,200-1,800	300-400

AVERAGE REPLACEMENT COSTS

A/C Compressor	$565	Clutch, Pressure Plate, Bearing	310
Alternator	315	Constant Velocity Joints	355
Automatic Transmission or Transaxle	810	Exhaust System	295
Brakes	190	Radiator	390
Shocks and/or Struts	595	Timing Chain or Belt	195

TROUBLE SPOTS

• **Hard starting.** A cold-start repair kit can aid 1.6-liter engines that do not start in temperatures below 10 degrees Farenheit. (1992-94)

• **Brakes.** Brake pedal pulsation is often due to brake disc thickness variations. (1992-95)

• **Hard starting.** Hard starting may be due to a cracked in-tank fuel line. (1992-95)

• **Automatic transmission.** If the transmission slips or will not go into fourth gear, the end clutch needs to be replaced. (1992-95)

• **Engine misfire.** In cool weather, the engine may stall or run rough. A replacement computer might fix the problem. (1992)

• **Manual transmission.** Manual transaxles may grind when attempting to shift into reverse due to a problem with either the reverse idle gear bushing and reverse shift lever, reverse synchronizer, or a weak wave spring. (1992-94)

• **Automatic transmission.** The transmission may shift poorly between first and second or develop harsh shifting. It can be corrected by adjusting the kickdown servo. (1992-95)

RECALL HISTORY

1994-95: Driver-side airbag warning light could illuminate because of increased electrical resistance; might prevent airbag from activating during a crash.

1996-00 HYUNDAI ELANTRA

1996 Hyundai Elantra 4-door sedan

FOR Fuel economy • Optional antilock brakes • Dual airbags • Passenger room

AGAINST Passing power (automatic) • Small trunk opening • Noise

EVALUATION Hyundai's second-generation Elantra took a giant leap forward in roominess, quiet running, and all-around competence on the road. Not only is this version quieter than the prior Elantra at highway speeds, but the engine becomes raucous only when pushed hard. Acceleration is good with either transmission, and passing power is brisk in around-town driving. On the downside, the automatic transmission shifts abruptly at times, and passing power above 60 mph is meager. Fuel economy is good. We averaged more than 25 mpg. The suspension absorbs most bumps neatly, providing a stable highway ride. Unfortunately, you must cope with an abundance of suspension and tire thumping. Steering feels a trifle loose, but an Elantra handles competently, maneuvering nimbly with good grip. Brakes have a solid pedal feel, but a panic stop in an Elantra without ABS produced plenty of tire squeal and even a threat to swerve. Visibility is clear in all directions. Head and leg room are generous in front for medium-sized adults. Backseat space is adequate, with acceptable head and leg room, but not enough width to hold three occupants comfortably. Sedans have passable trunk space, but a small opening, so loading of bulky items could be easier. The split-rear seatback on the GLS model folds for additional cargo space. The station wagon's rear seatback folds to a flat cargo floor.

VALUE Value-conscious shoppers might want to take a close look at this latest, greatly improved Elantra, which flaunts a friendly demeanor. Though not flawless, moderate secondhand prices can make it tempting.

SPECIFICATIONS

	4-door sedan	4-door wagon
Wheelbase, in.	100.4	100.4
Overall length, in.	174.0	175.2
Overall width, in.	66.9	66.9
Overall height, in.	54.9	58.8
Curb weight, lbs.	2458	2619
Cargo volume, cu. ft.	11.4	63.0
Fuel capacity, gals.	14.5	14.5
Seating capacity	5	5
Front head room, in.	38.6	38.6
Max. front leg room, in.	43.2	43.2
Rear head room, in.	37.6	38.9
Min. rear leg room, in.	34.6	34.8

Powertrain layout: transverse front-engine/front-wheel drive

ENGINES

	dohc I4	dohc I4
Size, liters/cu. in.	1.8/110	2.0/122
Horsepower	130	140
Torque (lbs./ft.)	122	133
EPA city/highway mpg		
5-speed OD manual	24/32	24/33
4-speed OD automatic	23/31	22/31
City/highway mpg (as tested)		
4-speed OD automatic		25.0

Built in South Korea

RETAIL PRICES

	GOOD	AVERAGE	POOR
1996 Elantra	$2,500-3,400	$1,900-2,700	$500-900
1997 Elantra	3,500-4,700	2,800-4,000	1,000-1,600
1998 Elantra	4,700-5,900	4,000-5,200	1,700-2,300
1999 Elantra	6,000-7,200	5,200-6,300	2,300-2,900
2000 Elantra	7,400-8,400	6,600-7,400	3,300-3,800

AVERAGE REPLACEMENT COSTS

A/C Compressor	$565	Clutch, Pressure Plate, Bearing	295
Alternator	315	Constant Velocity Joints	355
Automatic Transmission or Transaxle	810	Exhaust System	355
Brakes	170	Radiator	390
Shocks and/or Struts	595	Timing Chain or Belt	195

TROUBLE SPOTS

• **Automatic transmission.** Automatic transmissions may flare between second and third or downshift poorly. There is a modified transmission control module available. (1996-97)

• **Hard starting.** Hard starting may be due to a cracked in-tank fuel line. (1996-97)

• **Automatic transmission.** If the transmission slips or will not go into fourth gear, the end clutch probably needs to be replaced. (1996)

RECALL HISTORY

1996-97: Wipers may not operate, due to contamination. **1996-97:** Evaporative emissions control system can apply excessive vacuum to fuel tank, resulting in minor tank distortion; small crack could develop, allowing fuel to escape. **1999 w/automatic transmission:** Pressure control solenoid valve seals can allow transmission fluid to leak, resulting in slippage.

1995-98 HYUNDAI SONATA

1995 Hyundai Sonata

FOR Optional antilock brakes • Passenger and cargo room • Acceleration (V6) • Ride

AGAINST Automatic transmission performance • Wind noise

EVALUATION The V6 engine furnishes more than adequate acceleration from a standing start, capable of reaching 60 mph in just over 9 seconds and delivering welcome passing response. A 4-cylinder Sonata with automatic is sluggish, but gets excellent fuel economy—a credible 23.8 mpg, versus 20.5 mpg for a V6 sedan. Wind noise is prominent around the side windows at highway speeds, making long drives more fatiguing. Ride quality is impressive. The suspension is firm enough to provide a stable, comfortable highway ride and absorbent enough to soak up most bumps. On the other hand, the ride can get jumpy when rolling over bad roads. A Sonata is easy to drive, but handling ranks just about average—acceptable, that is, but nothing to boast about. While the previous Sonata was spacious, this one is noticeably roomier. Partly due to its longer wheelbase, the Sonata's backseat looks huge compared to space inside some competitors. Expect plenty of head, leg, and elbow room up front, and also in the rear. Cargo space is generous. The new dashboard has a more convenient design than its predecessor, with easy-to-read gauges and an ample-size glovebox. Panel fit isn't always top-notch, but Sonatas appear to be tight and well-built.

VALUE Anyone seeking a low-priced family car with plenty of interior space should look over a Sonata before deciding on a purchase. Just don't expect it to shine above the competition.

SPECIFICATIONS

	4-door sedan
Wheelbase, in.	106.3
Overall length, in.	185.0
Overall width, in.	69.7
Overall height, in.	55.3
Curb weight, lbs.	3025
Cargo volume, cu. ft.	13.2
Fuel capacity, gals.	17.2
Seating capacity	5
Front head room, in.	38.5
Max. front leg room, in.	43.3
Rear head room, in.	37.7
Min. rear leg room, in.	36.6

Powertrain layout: transverse front-engine/front-wheel drive

ENGINES

	dohc I4	ohc V6
Size, liters/cu. in.	2.0/122	3.0/181
Horsepower	137	142
Torque (lbs./ft.)	129	168
EPA city/highway mpg		
5-speed OD manual	22/28	
4-speed OD automatic	21/29	18/24
City/highway mpg (as tested)		
4-speed OD automatic	23.8	20.5

Built in South Korea

RETAIL PRICES

	GOOD	AVERAGE	POOR
1995 Sonata	$2,200-3,000	$1,600-2,400	$400-800
1996 Sonata	3,000-3,800	2,400-3,100	700-1,200
1997 Sonata	4,000-5,200	3,300-4,400	1,300-1,900
1998 Sonata	5,500-6,700	4,700-5,800	2,200-2,700

AVERAGE REPLACEMENT COSTS

A/C Compressor	$950	Clutch, Pressure Plate,	
Alternator	365	Bearing	325
Automatic Transmission or		Constant Velocity Joints	650
Transaxle	1,010	Exhaust System	345
Brakes	170	Radiator	420
Shocks and/or Struts	760	Timing Chain or Belt	285

TROUBLE SPOTS

• **Automatic transmission.** Automatic transmissions may suffer shift shock or harsh shifting when accelerating from a stop due to a problem with the transmission control module. (1995-97)

• **Automatic transmission.** If the transmission slips or will not go into fourth gear, the end clutch needs to be replaced. (1995-96)

• **Manual transmission.** Manual transaxles may grind when attempting to shift into reverse. The problem is corrected with a new reverse idle gear bushing and reverse shift lever (1995) or reverse synchronizer. (1995-96)

• **Engine misfire.** Rough idle, speed vacillations, shock shifting from park, and hard upshifts and downshifts may result from misadjusted throttle position sensor and idle switch. (1995-97)

• **Brakes.** The brakes may pulsate under light application. A revised set of brake pads plus a hardware kit are available. (1995-97)

RECALL HISTORY

1995: On 356 cars with gas-filled shock absorbers, one or both lower rear spring seats are not securely attached. **1996-97:** Wipers may not operate, due to contamination in contacts.

1999-01 HYUNDAI SONATA

2000 Hyundai Sonata GLS

FOR Cargo room • Ride

AGAINST Automatic transmission performance • Rear-seat comfort

EVALUATION Sonata's suspension easily irons out most bumps, and the sedan rivals larger, more costly cars for overall comfort. Poor control of body motions is the penalty to be paid, a result of soft damping. Dips and creases can induce moderate bounding, and lane changes at highway speeds are sloppy. Nosedive also is significant, in emergency stops. Off-the-line punch with the V6 is decent. With automatic, a test V6 Sonata accelerated to 60 mph in 9 seconds, but passing power is modest. In addition, the automatic transmission is reluctant to kick down for passing, and "hunts" too much between gears in hilly terrain. As for economy, a V6 GLS averaged 22.4 mpg. All-disc brakes in a GLS provide stabile, reasonably short stops even without ABS. Tire thrum is noticeable on coarse pavement and some wind noise is evident, but otherwise the Sonata is fairly quiet. Front seats are sufficiently roomy and supportive for this sedan's class. Rear leg room is good but head room only adequate for 6-footers, who occupy a short, low cushion that compels a knees-up stance. The driving position is comfortably high and sufficiently adaptable, with good visibility except for rear corners. Entry/exit is easy up front but tight in the back. Switches are easy to see and use, but audio controls are on the small side. Interior storage includes front-door map pockets, a decently sized glovebox, and a useful center console. Trunk space is ample, with a low sill. Standard folding rear seatbacks are handy, though the trunk pass-through isn't very large.

VALUE Though uninspiring, the Sonata is a well-equipped sedan, straddling the line between compact and midsize, which offers fair value. Despite several drawbacks, including tepid acceleration and unsporty handling, it's worth a try. Mediocre resale value translates to appealing prices on the secondhand market.

SPECIFICATIONS

	4-door sedan
Wheelbase, in.	106.3
Overall length, in.	185.4
Overall width, in.	71.6
Overall height, in.	55.5
Curb weight, lbs.	3065
Cargo volume, cu. ft.	13.2
Fuel capacity, gals.	17.2
Seating capacity	5
Front head room, in.	39.3
Max. front leg room, in.	43.3
Rear head room, in.	37.6
Min. rear leg room, in.	36.2

Powertrain layout: transverse front-engine/front-wheel drive

ENGINES

	dohc I4	dohc V6
Size, liters/cu. in.	2.4/146	2.5/152
Horsepower	149	170
Torque (lbs./ft.)	156	166
EPA city/highway mpg		
5-speed OD manual	21/30	20/29
4-speed OD automatic	21/28	20/28
City/highway mpg (as tested)		
4-speed OD automatic		22.4

Built in South Korea

RETAIL PRICES

	GOOD	AVERAGE	POOR
1999 Sonata	$7,800-9,000	$7,000-8,100	$4,500-5,300
2000 Sonata	9,000-11,000	8,100-10,000	5,500-6,500
2001 Sonata	11,000-13,000	10,000-12,000	—

AVERAGE REPLACEMENT COSTS

A/C Compressor	$880	Clutch, Pressure Plate,	
Alternator	370	Bearing	435
Automatic Transmission or		Constant Velocity Joints	1,040
Transaxle	710	Exhaust System	775
Brakes	260	Radiator	465
Shocks and/or Struts	850	Timing Chain or Belt	190

TROUBLE SPOTS

• **Manual transmission.** A countermeasure synchronizer, first and second gear and shift-fork kit is required to correct hard shifting manual transmissions. (1999-2000)

• **Fuel pump.** A restriction in the on-board vapor recovery line may cause the gas station fuel pumps to click off when refueling. (1999-2000)

• **Automatic transmission.** Automatic transmissions may not go into drive or reverse after the car has been parked several hours because the torque converter drains down through the front pump. Hyundai was replacing the transmission under warranty. (1999)

• **Audio system.** If the CD player locks up, it can be reset by removing the "short connector" in the fuse panel for ten seconds or longer. (1999)

RECALL HISTORY

1999-2000: Certain sedans with 2.5-liter V6 engines may experience intermittent low-speed engine stalling. **1999-2001:** Unusual motion of the side impact airbag wiring harness and side impact airbag wiring harness connector can cause the airbag warning light could illuminate.

1991-96 INFINITI G20

1996 Infiniti G20t

FOR Acceleration (manual) • Steering/handling • Antilock brakes

AGAINST Acceleration (early automatic transmission) • Engine noise • Road noise • Ride (early models) • Climate controls

EVALUATION The 5-speed gearbox blends neatly with the fast-revving engine for a lively feel, whether off the line or meandering through tight, twisty roads. However, the automatic transmission cuts rather sharply into performance, shifting too often even on moderate uphill grades and impairing standing-start action. As for economy, we averaged 21.7 mpg with an automatic G20. Though wind noise is low, road and engine noise can be a problem. However, the G20 suffers a stiff, jolting ride as soon as any big bumps appear. On the plus side, softer suspension bushings, introduced in mid 1993, deliver a ride that's still firm, but no longer too stiff on bumpy roads. In any year, body lean is minimal, power steering is quick and responsive, and brakes respond eagerly. Space is more than adequate for four adults, and the handsome dashboard is well-organized. Gauges are clearly marked; controls handy, except for a low heat/vent panel. A low beltline and thin roof pillars contribute to a commanding driving position and good visibility. Firm front bucket seats offer good support. Six-footers can ride in back without feeling cramped. The ample trunk has a long, flat floor, and its lid opens from bumper height to more than 90 degrees.

VALUE Though capable and well-designed, the small Infiniti's lack lies in its engine department—neither as quiet nor as quick as expected, especially with automatic—and in the overly taut suspension. Even so, it's a spirited machine with a sensible design, thus worth a test-drive.

SPECIFICATIONS

	4-door sedan
Wheelbase, in.	100.4
Overall length, in.	174.8
Overall width, in.	66.7
Overall height, in.	54.7
Curb weight, lbs.	2977
Cargo volume, cu. ft.	14.2
Fuel capacity, gals.	15.9
Seating capacity	5
Front head room, in.	38.8
Max. front leg room, in.	42.0
Rear head room, in.	37.3
Min. rear leg room, in.	32.2

Powertrain layout: transverse front-engine/front-wheel drive

ENGINES

	dohc I4
Size, liters/cu. in.	2.0/122
Horsepower	140
Torque (lbs./ft.)	132

EPA city/highway mpg

5-speed OD manual	24/32
4-speed OD automatic	22/28

City/highway mpg (as tested)

4-speed OD automatic	21.7

Built in Japan

RETAIL PRICES	GOOD	AVERAGE	POOR
1991 G20	$1,900-2,500	$1,300-1,800	$300-600
1992 G20	2,600-3,300	1,900-2,600	600-900
1993 G20	3,400-4,100	2,700-3,300	900-1,200
1994 G20	4,300-5,000	3,600-4,200	1,500-1,800
1995 G20	5,500-6,200	4,800-5,400	2,300-2,700
1996 G20	6,800-7,700	6,000-6,800	3,100-3,600

AVERAGE REPLACEMENT COSTS

A/C Compressor	$710	Clutch, Pressure Plate, Bearing	485
Alternator	790		
Automatic Transmission or Transaxle	940	Constant Velocity Joints	430
		Exhaust System	520
Brakes	200	Radiator	480
Shocks and/or Struts	820	Timing Chain or Belt	615

TROUBLE SPOTS

• **Automatic transmission.** A campaign was conducted to improve automatic transmission life by installing an in-line filter and auxiliary oil cooler. (1991)

• **Fuel odors.** Fuel odors on cold start can be solved by a free repair that may include new fuel injectors, hoses, fuel rails, regulator, and wiring. (1991-92)

• **Engine stalling.** If a cold engine stalls when coming to a stop and is hard to restart, replacing the hydraulic valve lash adjusters may restore performance. (1991-92)

• **Transmission noise.** If the automatic transmission chirps when shifting from second to third, a redesigned input shaft and high clutch assembly with an improved friction material should eliminate the problem. (1991)

• **Dashboard lights.** If the check engine light comes on, but the technician can find no faulty components, there may be inductive interference on the wiring harness leading to the onboard computer. Separating and isolating the wires from one another cures the problem. (1994-95)

• **Automatic transmission.** If the transmission won't upshift to third or fourth or slips on acceleration, the high clutch assembly may be burnt and debris gets lodged in the valve body. (1991-93)

• **Automatic transmission.** The dropping resistor on the inner left fender can be damaged by rain or windshield washer fluid causing harsh, noisy, or jerky transmission shifts. A new resistor, with a protective cover, is required to fix the problem. (1994)

• **Trunk latch.** The electric trunk release solenoid may stick in the open position, preventing the trunk from closing properly. (1992-94)

RECALL HISTORY

1991-92: Rear seatbelt buckle may engage only partially. **1991-96 19 states and D.C.:** Fuel filler tube assembly can corrode, resulting in leakage. **1993-95:** Harness connector protector near seatbelt pretensioner can ignite, due to proximity to combustion gas generated by pretensioner when device is triggered; fire can then occur in passenger compartment.

1996 Infiniti I30t

FOR Antilock brakes • Acceleration • Steering/handling

AGAINST Rear-seat comfort • Fuel economy • Rear visibility

EVALUATION The V6 engine produces plenty of torque at low speeds, yielding quick takeoffs and brisk passing sprints. Accelerating to 60 mph takes about 8 seconds. Fuel economy is disappointing. Our test I30 averaged under 19 mpg, and premium gasoline is recommended. The basic I30's suspension is firm, yet soaks up most bumps easily. Rear-seat passengers actually feel bumps and tar strips more than those seated in front. Steering is firm and precise, offering good feedback. Stable front-drive competence lets an I30 take high-speed corners with little body lean and taut road grip. Because the I30t has a firmer suspension than other models, coupled with high-performance tires, its handling is more responsive—quite agile for a big car. The I30t also suffers a stiffer ride, however, as well as greater tire noise at highway speeds. Gauges and controls are well-marked and easy to reach while driving. Visibility is good to the front and sides, but large rear headrests block the view directly backward. Interior space is ample for four adults. Rear-seat backrests are too inclined to suit some passengers. The trunk is spacious, and is augmented by a folding pass-through section.

VALUE With more standard features than a Maxima, the I30 is well-equipped and a good alternative to the more expensive Lexus ES 300—a superior road car for long trips.

SPECIFICATIONS

	4-door sedan
Wheelbase, in.	106.3
Overall length, in.	189.6
Overall width, in.	69.7
Overall height, in.	55.7
Curb weight, lbs.	3001
Cargo volume, cu. ft.	14.1
Fuel capacity, gals.	18.5

	4-door sedan
Seating capacity	5
Front head room, in.	40.1
Max. front leg room, in.	43.9
Rear head room, in.	37.4
Min. rear leg room, in.	34.3

Powertrain layout: transverse front-engine/front-wheel drive

ENGINES

	dohc V6
Size, liters/cu. in.	3.0/181
Horsepower	190
Torque (lbs./ft.)	205

EPA city/highway mpg

5-speed OD manual	21/26
4-speed automatic	21/28

City/highway mpg (as tested)

5-speed OD manual	22.3
4-speed automatic	17.3

Built in Japan

RETAIL PRICES

	GOOD	AVERAGE	POOR
1996 I30	$10,000-11,000	$9,000-10,000	$5,300-6,000
1997 I30	12,000-13,000	11,000-12,000	7,000-7,700
1998 I30	14,000-15,400	12,800-14,000	8,700-9,500
1999 I30	16,500-17,800	15,000-16,300	10,500-11,500

AVERAGE REPLACEMENT COSTS

A/C Compressor	$800
Alternator	410
Automatic Transmission or Transaxle	920
Brakes	210
Shocks and/or Struts	1,140
Clutch, Pressure Plate, Bearing	650
Constant Velocity Joints	1,150
Exhaust System	445
Radiator	475
Timing Chain or Belt	690

TROUBLE SPOTS

• **Dashboard lights.** Some cars with the California emissions package may ingest water into the evaporative emissions canister, which triggers the check engine light. (1996)

• **Engine knock.** Spark knock, or ping may result from a defective onboard computer. (1996-97)

• **Engine fan noise.** The mounting flange for the fan (on the water pump) can come loose after service if the fan pulley is not installed properly during repairs. (1996-97)

• **Automatic transmission.** The original automatic transmission (model F04) shift solenoids allowed slipping and premature wear. (1997)

• **Brake noise.** The rear brakes may moan or hum when released below 5 mph requiring replacement parking brake cables and brake pad retainers. (1996-99)

• **Trunk latch.** The trunk lid opens by itself from either the striker being out of adjustment or the driver accidentally hitting the release switch. The striker may be adjusted, and there is a revised switch to minimize accidental actuation. (1996-99)

RECALL HISTORY

1998: Alternator diode may have been damaged when built, eventually resulting in failure and electric short that could melt plastic housing.

1997-99 INFINITI QX4

1998 Infiniti QX4

FOR Passenger and cargo room • Build quality

AGAINST Engine noise • Fuel economy • Rear-seat entry/exit • Rear-seat room

EVALUATION

See the 1996-00 Nissan Pathfinder.

VALUE

See the 1996-00 Nissan Pathfinder.

SPECIFICATIONS

	4-door wagon
Wheelbase, in.	106.3
Overall length, in.	178.3
Overall width, in.	68.7
Overall height, in.	67.1
Curb weight, lbs.	4275
Cargo volume, cu. ft.	85.0
Fuel capacity, gals.	21.1
Seating capacity	5
Front head room, in.	39.5
Max. front leg room, in.	41.7
Rear head room, in.	37.5
Min. rear leg room, in.	31.8

Powertrain layout: longitudinal front-engine/rear- or 4-wheel drive

ENGINES

	ohc V6
Size, liters/cu. in.	3.3/201
Horsepower	168
Torque (lbs./ft.)	196

EPA city/highway mpg

4-speed OD automatic	15/19

City/highway mpg (as tested)

4-speed OD automatic	12.5

Built in Japan

RETAIL PRICES

	GOOD	AVERAGE	POOR
1997 QX4	$15,000-16,500	$13,800-15,200	$9,700-10,500
1998 QX4	17,000-18,500	15,500-17,000	10,700-11,700
1999 QX4	19,500-21,000	18,000-19,500	13,000-14,000
2000 QX4	22,500-24,500	21,000-23,000	15,500-16,800

AVERAGE REPLACEMENT COSTS

See the 1996-00 Nissan Pathfinder.

TROUBLE SPOTS

See the 1996-00 Nissan Pathfinder.

1990-94 ISUZU AMIGO

1990 Isuzu Amigo XS

FOR 4WD traction • Driver seating • Antilock brakes

AGAINST Acceleration • Fuel economy • Rear visibility

EVALUATION Essentially a shortened Isuzu pickup (topped by a button-down canvas roof), the Amigo feels huskier and more stable than some mini 4x4s. Unfortunately, it's too heavy for even the 2.6-liter engine, so both acceleration and fuel economy are mediocre. Road manners are better than many rivals, much like those of a compact 4WD pickup. The ride is firm but comfortable, noise levels fairly reasonable, braking distances acceptable. Handling appears balanced and safely predictable, provided that you respect the Amigo's short wheelbase and high center of gravity. Engaging 4WD is somewhat of a chore, as you must stop and get out to lock the manual hubs. Passenger and cargo space beat most rivals, but the optional rear bench is narrow and hard, not for long-term adult travel. Reclining front seats slide forward to ease access to the back, but getting there still isn't easy. Wide side pillars impair over-the-shoulder visibility, while the tailgate-mounted spare tire tends to block the rearward view. The Amigo's dashboard and instruments are almost carlike, with the exception of a low-mounted radio. Though not easy to erect, the snap-on canvas top is less complex than some.

VALUE Neither the quickest nor the thriftiest small sport-utility on the market, Amigo has quite a few virtues. Like its competitors, though, an Amigo is not a good bet for everyday transportation.

SPECIFICATIONS

	2-door wagon
Wheelbase, in.	91.7
Overall length, in.	168.1
Overall width, in.	70.1
Overall height, in.	69.9
Curb weight, lbs.	3615
Cargo volume, cu. ft.	51.0
Fuel capacity, gals.	21.9
Seating capacity	4
Front head room, in.	38.0
Max. front leg room, in.	42.5
Rear head room, in.	32.0
Min. rear leg room, in.	19.5

Powertrain layout: longitudinal front-engine/rear- or 4-wheel drive

ENGINES

	ohc I4	ohc I4
Size, liters/cu. in.	2.3/138	2.6/156
Horsepower	120	120
Torque (lbs./ft.)	123	146-150

EPA city/highway mpg

5-speed OD manual	18/21	18/21
4-speed OD automatic	NA	16/20

City/highway mpg (as tested)

5-speed OD manual	14.4

Built in Japan

RETAIL PRICES

	GOOD	AVERAGE	POOR
1990 Amigo 2WD	$1,200-1,800	$600-1,200	$100-200
1990 Amigo 4WD	1,800-2,400	1,200-1,800	300-500
1991 Amigo 2WD	1,600-2,300	1,000-1,700	200-400
1991 Amigo 4WD	2,300-3,000	1,700-2,300	500-700
1992 Amigo 2WD	2,000-2,800	1,400-2,100	400-600
1992 Amigo 4WD	2,800-3,600	2,200-2,900	600-1,000
1993 Amigo 2WD	2,500-3,300	1,900-2,600	600-900
1993 Amigo 4WD	3,400-4,200	2,700-3,500	900-1,300
1994 Amigo 2WD	3,000-4,000	2,300-3,200	700-1,200
1994 Amigo 4WD	4,000-5,000	3,300-4,200	1,200-1,600

AVERAGE REPLACEMENT COSTS

A/C Compressor	$570	Clutch, Pressure Plate, Bearing	560
Alternator	305	Exhaust System	430
Automatic Transmission or Transaxle	845	Radiator	710
Brakes	280	Shocks and/or Struts	280
Timing Chain or Belt	100	Universal Joints	140

TROUBLE SPOTS

• **Steering noise.** A knocking noise when the steering wheel is turned requires a steering column repair kit. (1990-94) Lack of grease causes squawks in column. (1993-94)

• **Doors.** Ice can build up under the front fender and, when the door is opened, the door and fender are damaged. A new fender liner is available to prevent buildup. (1990-94)

• **Steering noise.** Knocking in the steering column is caused by a defective steering shaft joint that must be replaced. (1991-92)

• **Oil leak.** Oil leak from the distributor shaft on 2.3-liter engine. (1990-93)

• **Air conditioner.** The air conditioner gradually becomes warmer due to ice forming on the evaporator. The root problem is a dislocated thermostat. (1993)

• **Air conditioner.** The air conditioner stops working because the evaporator ices up, requiring replacement of the thermostat on the evaporator. (1990-93)

• **Keys.** The ignition key can be hard to remove because the lens over the shift lever interferes with the shift cable. (1992)

• **Engine mounts.** Vibration at idle (unless caused by engine problems) is corrected with revised motor mounts. (1990-91)

RECALL HISTORY

1994: Latch in seatbelt buckle could engage only partially, causing tongue to come out during collision or hard braking.

1998-01 ISUZU AMIGO/RODEO SPORT

2000 Isuzu Amigo 2-door wagon

FOR Acceleration (V6) • Cargo room

AGAINST Acceleration (4-cyl) • Ride • Noise • Entry/exit

EVALUATION Amigos cannot match the class-leading compact sport utility vehicles, but they do have a few pluses. True low-range gearing makes the 4-wheel-drive version capable of off-road excursions, like the Jeep Wrangler, which is beyond the capacity of a Honda CR-V or Toyota RAV4. Performance is clearly superior with the V6 engine, which delivers far more power than the 4-cylinder. A test V6 Amigo 4x4 with the 5-speed manual gearbox was able to accelerate to 60 mph in 8.5 seconds, and averaged 17.3 mpg—both good figures for a compact SUV. A V6 model with automatic fared almost as well in gas mileage, averaging 16.9 mpg. Ride and handling are passable, but not exceptional. Small bumps are easily absorbed by the Amigo's big tires, but a stiff suspension and short wheelbase translate to bouncing and bounding over wavy pavement, potholes, and frost heaves. Ironman editions with Intelligent Suspension Control improve the Amigo's ride control, without adding much additional harshness. Space in front is adequate, but passengers face a high step-up into the interior. In addition, the rear seat is tough to reach and not very spacious for adults. Putting the vinyl soft-top up or down is a tedious chore, too.

VALUE Though far from perfect, the Amigo is more substantial than some small SUVs and more refined than a Wrangler. Otherwise, a moderate price might be its biggest advantage.

SPECIFICATIONS

	2-door conv.	2-door wagon
Wheelbase, in.	96.9	96.9
Overall length, in.	170.3	170.3
Overall width, in.	71.4	71.4
Overall height, in.	67.1	67.1
Curb weight, lbs.	3523	3589
Cargo volume, cu. ft.	62.5	62.5
Fuel capacity, gals.	17.7	17.7
Seating capacity	5	5
Front head room, in.	38.9	38.9
Max. front leg room, in.	42.1	42.1
Rear head room, in.	37.3	37.3
Min. rear leg room, in.	33.3	33.3

Powertrain layout: longitudinal front-engine/rear- or 4-wheel drive

ENGINES

	dohc I4	dohc V6
Size, liters/cu. in.	2.2/134	3.2/193
Horsepower	130	205
Torque (lbs./ft.)	144	214

EPA city/highway mpg

5-speed OD manual	21/24	18/21
4-speed OD automatic	NA	17/21

City/highway mpg (as tested)	dohc I4	dohc V6
5-speed OD manual		17.3
4-speed OD automatic		16.9

Built in Japan

RETAIL PRICES

	GOOD	AVERAGE	POOR
1998 Amigo 2WD	$7,000-8,200	$6,200-7,200	$4,000-4,700
1998 Amigo 4WD	8,300-9,500	7,300-8,500	4,800-5,500
1999 Amigo 2WD	8,500-10,500	7,500-9,500	5,000-6,500
1999 Amigo 4WD	10,000-11,500	9,000-10,500	6,200-7,500
2000 Amigo 2WD	10,000-12,500	9,000-11,500	6,300-8,000
2000 Amigo 4WD	12,500-14,000	11,500-13,000	7,700-9,000
2001 Rodeo Sport 2WD	11,800-14,000	10,800-13,000	—
2001 Rodeo Sport 4WD	14,000-15,500	13,000-14,500	—

AVERAGE REPLACEMENT COSTS

A/C Compressor	$430	Clutch, Pressure Plate,	
Alternator	585	Bearing	430
Automatic Transmission or		Constant Velocity Joints	330
Transaxle	795	Exhaust System	170
Brakes	220	Radiator	355
Timing Chain or Belt	210		

TROUBLE SPOTS

• **Fuel gauge.** A faulty fuel level sending unit prevents the fuel gauge from reading full. It is recalled for replacement. (1998)

• **Steering noise.** A rubbing noise from the steering wheel is caused by the coil assembly for the air bag. It must be replaced. (1998)

• **Engine stalling.** Engine may stall or fail to start because of a poor electrical ground. Isuzu was recalling vehicles to replace the engine ground wire harness. (1998)

• **Brakes.** The antilock brake system may malfunction. Isuzu conducted a campaign to replace the ABS electronic control unit. (1998)

• **Wheels.** The rear wheels may vibrate because they are not properly centered on the hubs. A centering ring is available. (1998-2000)

• **Pedals.** The rubber pad on the accelerator pedal may fall off. A revised pad is available under warranty. (1998-99)

RECALL HISTORY

1998-99: On certain vehicles, paint was applied unevenly on rear axles; could result in loosening of nut and detachment of bolt, causing separation of lower link from rear axle. **2001:** Incorrect rubber material may have been used for outer layer of fuel return hoses, which could ultimately crack and cause fuel leakage.

1996-99 ISUZU OASIS

1998 Isuzu Oasis

FOR Ride • Steering/handling • Entry/exit • Build quality • Fuel economy

AGAINST Engine noise • Road noise

EVALUATION

See the 1996-98 Honda Odyssey.

VALUE

See the 1996-98 Honda Odyssey.

SPECIFICATIONS

	4-door van
Wheelbase, in.	111.4
Overall length, in.	187.2
Overall width, in.	70.6
Overall height, in.	64.6
Curb weight, lbs.	3473
Cargo volume, cu. ft.	102.5
Fuel capacity, gals.	17.2
Seating capacity	7[1]
Front head room, in.	40.1
Max. front leg room, in.	40.7
Rear head room, in.	39.3
Min. rear leg room, in.	40.2

1. 6 passengers w/optional second-row captain's chairs.

Powertrain layout: transverse front-engine/front-wheel drive

ENGINES

	ohc I4	dohc I4
Size, liters/cu. in.	2.2/132	2.3/137
Horsepower	140	150
Torque (lbs./ft.)	145	152
EPA city/highway mpg		
4-speed OD automatic	21/26	21/26
City/highway mpg (as tested)		
4-speed OD automatic	21.8	20.6

Built in Japan

RETAIL PRICES

	GOOD	AVERAGE	POOR
1996 Oasis	$8,000-9,200	$7,200-8,300	$4,100-4,800
1997 Oasis	9,500-11,000	8,500-10,000	4,900-5,800
1998 Oasis	11,500-13,000	10,500-11,800	6,500-7,300
1999 Oasis	13,500-15,500	12,000-14,000	7,800-9,000

AVERAGE REPLACEMENT COSTS

See the 1996-98 Honda Odyssey.

TROUBLE SPOTS

See the 1996-98 Honda Odyssey.

RECALL HISTORY

1997-98: Certain ball joints can wear out prematurely and, in worst case, would separate, causing front suspension to collapse.

1991-97 ISUZU RODEO

1992 Isuzu Rodeo

FOR 4WD traction • Ride • Antilock brakes (4-wheel opt. after '96) • Passenger and cargo room

AGAINST Entry/exit • No shift-on-the-fly (pre '96) • Road noise • Wind noise • Fuel economy

EVALUATION Acceleration is adequate but less than brisk with the early V6 and automatic. The 3.2-liter V6, made available in 1993, is an improvement in terms of smoothness and quietness. That V6 works well with automatic, which changes gears smoothly and downshifts promptly for passing. Gas mileage is nothing to boast about. One test Rodeo averaged just 13.9 mpg. Ride is firm yet surprisingly comfortable, as the absorbent suspension handily soaks up just about every flaw on paved roads. Braking distances are acceptable, though a 2WD Rodeo turned out to be prone to abrupt front-wheel lockup. Road noise is prominent at highway speeds. Occupants are treated well in a Rodeo. Rear leg room is ample, even with the front seats all the way back. Head clearance is good all around, and the driving position is comfortable for most people. Back doors are quite narrow at sill level, and open only about 70 degrees, so larger folks might feel squeezed when getting in and out. The full-size spare tire mounted inside many models cuts considerably into cargo space, but the back seat folds flat to create a wide cargo floor. Except for too many confusing buttons controlling lights and wipers, and a low-mounted radio, the dashboard is fine.

VALUE The need to stop the vehicle to engage 4WD, then stop and back up to disengage it, is an inconvenience. Otherwise, the competent and tightly constructed Rodeo deserves a serious look, as it just might be the best Isuzu model on the market.

SPECIFICATIONS

	4-door wagon
Wheelbase, in.	108.7
Overall length, in.	176.5
Overall width, in.	66.5
Overall height, in.	65.4
Curb weight, lbs.	3545
Cargo volume, cu. ft.	74.9
Fuel capacity, gals.	21.9
Seating capacity	6
Front head room, in.	38.2
Max. front leg room, in.	42.5
Rear head room, in.	37.8
Min. rear leg room, in.	36.1

Powertrain layout: longitudinal front-engine/front- or 4-wheel drive

ENGINES

	ohc I4	ohv V6	ohc V6
Size, liters/cu. in.	2.6/156	3.1/191	3.2/193
Horsepower	120	120	175-190
Torque (lbs./ft.)	146-150	165	188
EPA city/highway mpg			
5-speed OD manual	18/22	15/19	16/19
4-speed OD automatic		15/18	15/18
City/highway mpg (as tested)			
5-speed OD manual			18.2
4-speed OD automatic		17.9	16.1

Built in USA

RETAIL PRICES

	GOOD	AVERAGE	POOR
1991 Rodeo S	$2,000-3,200	$1,400-2,600	$400-800
1991 Rodeo XS, LS	2,700-4,000	2,000-3,200	600-1,200
1992 Rodeo S	2,400-3,700	1,800-3,000	600-1,100
1992 Rodeo XS, LS	3,100-4,800	2,400-4,000	800-1,700
1993 Rodeo S	3,100-4,200	2,400-3,500	800-1,500
1993 Rodeo LS	4,000-5,400	3,300-4,600	1,200-2,200
1994 Rodeo S	4,000-5,200	3,300-4,500	1,200-2,100
1994 Rodeo LS	5,000-6,300	4,300-5,500	2,000-2,800
1995 Rodeo S	5,000-6,500	4,200-5,700	1,900-2,900
1995 Rodeo LS	6,200-7,800	5,500-7,000	2,800-3,700
1996 Rodeo S	6,000-7,500	5,100-6,500	2,600-3,400
1996 Rodeo LS	7,200-8,800	6,300-7,800	3,300-4,200
1997 Rodeo S	7,200-9,000	6,200-8,000	3,300-4,400
1997 Rodeo LS	8,400-10,200	7,400-9,200	4,100-5,100

AVERAGE REPLACEMENT COSTS

A/C Compressor	$685	Clutch, Pressure Plate,	
Alternator	295	Bearing	595
Automatic Transmission or		Exhaust System	320
Transaxle	1,375	Radiator	660
Brakes	280	Shocks and/or Struts	200
Timing Chain or Belt	100	Universal Joints	120

TROUBLE SPOTS

• **Steering noise.** A knocking noise when the steering wheel is turned requires a steering column repair kit. (1991-94)

• **Steering noise.** Lack of grease causes squeaks in column. (1994)

• **Transmission noise.** Lack of lube on the clutch shift fork pivot ball causes noises and squeaks. (1991-94)

• **Air conditioner.** The air conditioner gradually becomes warmer due to ice forming on the evaporator. The root problem is a mispositioned thermostat. (1993)

• **Cruise control.** The cruise control may not let the transmission shift down out of overdrive on hills. (1991)

• **Keys.** The ignition key can be hard to remove because the lens over the shift lever interferes with the shift cable. (1992)

RECALL HISTORY

1991 w/V6: Incorrect transmission-fluid dipstick may have been installed. **1993-94:** Camshaft plug can become dislodged, allowing oil to leak; can cause engine damage and fire. **1994:** Latch in seat-belt buckle could engage only partially, causing tongue to come out during collision or hard braking.

1998-01 ISUZU RODEO

1999 Isuzu Rodeo

FOR Passenger and cargo room • Acceleration (V6) • Standard antilock braking

AGAINST Road noise • Engine noise • Fuel economy

EVALUATION Rodeo's suspension produces a stable ride without pitching or bouncing, though small bumps and imperfections produce unpleasant choppiness. Larger bumps and potholes are not absorbed nearly as well as they should be, as the ride becomes downright harsh. Lack of power with the 4-cylinder engine and manual shift isn't a big drawback. Rodeos with the V6 feel considerably livelier than before, promising brisk acceleration and good passing power. The automatic transmission shifts smoothly and downshifts promptly. An LS 4WD averaged 15.8 mpg in mixed driving—about on target for its class. Interior space is greater than before, with good passenger room all around, except for a shortage of rear toe space. Even though the seat is not height-adjustable and may not suit everyone, the driver enjoys a commanding position. The firmly padded seat earns high marks on its own. Controls for the climate and audio systems are recessed and demand a little too much of a stretch for no-distraction use by the driver. Stereo controls are too small, though the simple dashboard is otherwise pleasing. Step-in height is a little lower than the midsize-SUV norm, so getting in and out is no great chore. Rear doors permit passengers to slip through fairly easily, though we'd be more pleased if they opened a bit wider. Forward visibility is fine thanks to the low cowl and hood line. Looking rearward, however, the optional outside spare tire interferes with the driver's view. Operation of the new side-opening tailgate is a cumbersome, two-handed process.

VALUE With the V6, a Rodeo accelerates better than most Japanese rivals, leaning toward the "sport" side of sport-utility. Prices are not cheap, however, and Rodeo has no standout features that put it above the competition. That makes it an acceptable choice, but not a compelling one.

SPECIFICATIONS

	4-door wagon
Wheelbase, in.	106.4
Overall length, in.	183.7
Overall width, in.	70.4

	4-door wagon
Overall height, in.	68.8
Curb weight, lbs.	4124
Cargo volume, cu. ft.	81.1
Fuel capacity, gals.	21.1
Seating capacity	5
Front head room, in.	38.9
Max. front leg room, in.	42.1
Rear head room, in.	38.3
Min. rear leg room, in.	35.0

Powertrain layout: longitudinal front-engine/rear- or 4-wheel drive

ENGINES

	dohc I4	dohc V6
Size, liters/cu. in.	2.2/134	3.2/193
Horsepower	129-130	205
Torque (lbs./ft.)	144	214

EPA city/highway mpg

5-speed OD manual	21/24	16/20
4-speed OD automatic	17/22	18/20

City/highway mpg (as tested)

5-speed OD manual	17.4
4-speed OD automatic	16.2

Built in USA

RETAIL PRICES

	GOOD	AVERAGE	POOR
1998 Rodeo 2WD	$8,500-11,000	$7,500-10,000	$4,200-6,000
1998 Rodeo 4WD	10,000-12,000	9,000-11,000	5,300-6,700
1999 Rodeo 2WD	10,000-12,000	9,000-11,000	5,300-6,700
1999 Rodeo LSE 2WD	13,000-14,000	12,000-13,000	8,000-8,700
1999 Rodeo 4WD	11,500-13,500	10,300-12,000	6,200-7,500
1999 Rodeo LSE 4WD	14,500-15,500	13,200-14,000	9,100-9,600
2000 Rodeo 2WD	11,500-14,000	10,500-12,800	6,400-8,000
2000 Rodeo LSE 2WD	14,500-16,000	13,000-14,500	9,000-10,000
2000 Rodeo 4WD	13,000-15,000	11,800-13,500	7,800-8,800
2000 Rodeo LSE 4WD	16,000-17,500	14,500-16,000	9,800-10,700
2001 Rodeo 2WD	13,500-16,500	12,000-15,000	—
2001 Rodeo LSE 2WD	17,000-19,000	15,500-17,500	—
2001 Rodeo 4WD	15,000-18,000	13,500-16,500	—
2001 Rodeo LSE 4WD	18,500-20,500	17,000-19,000	—

AVERAGE REPLACEMENT COSTS

A/C Compressor	$685	Clutch, Pressure Plate,	
Alternator	295	Bearing	1,110
Automatic Transmission or		Exhaust System	320
Transaxle	620	Radiator	660
Brakes	280	Shocks and/or Struts	200
Timing Chain or Belt	100	Universal Joints	120

TROUBLE SPOTS

• **Transmission slippage.** Delayed transmission engagement, after sitting overnight, may occur due to torque converter drain-down. (1998-99)

• **Fuel gauge.** The gas gauge may indicate full after a fill-up then not move until the tank is half empty. (1998)

• **Steering problems.** The steering wheel may shimmy or vibrate unless a steering yoke spring kit is installed. (1998)

• **Doors.** Unless the front fender liners have been replaced, ice and snow can build up between the door and fender which caused door damage when it is opened. (1998)

RECALL HISTORY

1998: Ground terminal was not properly crimped in engine wiring harness, which will eventually cause stress fracture; could result in "no-start"or engine stalling. **1998 w/optional floormat:** Repeated movement of feet can result in shifting of mat, which could interfere with gas pedal. **1998-99:** Paint was applied unevenly on rear axles of certain vehicles; could cause loosening of nut at lower link bracket bolt. **1999:** Vehicles fail to comply with federal requirement for "Occupant Protection in Interior Impact." **1998-99:** The rear-axle lower link may become separated from the rear axle.

1992-01 ISUZU TROOPER

1995 Isuzu Trooper 4-door wagon

FOR 4WD traction • Passenger and cargo room • Antilock brakes

AGAINST Fuel economy • Entry/exit • Lack of shift-on-the-fly (pre '96)

EVALUATION All three V6 engines are silky and quiet, if not quite frisky. An early automatic LS wagon accelerated to 60 mph in a wholly adequate 11.7 seconds, but speed trails off fast on steep grades. Although the automatic transmission hunts busily between gears in urban driving, it's smooth and responsive. Gas mileage isn't great—we averaged just 15.8 mpg. The 4-door has a stable, pleasantly supple ride, dealing with most bumps in a manner comparable to a large station wagon. It fails to soak up big bumps well, though, and feels somewhat harsh on rough pavement. A Trooper easily tackles tough off-road terrain. Quick highway cornering induces mild body lean, but little of the typical tall-4WD queasiness. Tire roar is low, but wind noise high. Braking is above average for the sport-utility class. Troopers rank among the roomiest sport-utility vehicles, though getting inside can be a chore due to the tall step-up. Head room is bountiful, and the back seats three adults comfortably. Visibility is great. The driver's area is attractive and convenient. Isuzu's 70/30 rear cargo door opens onto a tall, long cargo area.

VALUE Rating high on our list of upscale 4x4s, early Troopers trail such rivals as the Ford Explorer and Jeep Grand Cherokee mainly in their omission of shift-on-the-fly 4WD (on 1992-95 models) and an airbag (1992-94 models).

SPECIFICATIONS

	2-door wagon	4-door wagon
Wheelbase, in.	91.7	108.7
Overall length, in.	166.5	183.5
Overall width, in.	68.7	68.7
Overall height, in.	72.8	72.8
Curb weight, lbs.	4060	4210
Cargo volume, cu. ft.	68.3	90.0
Fuel capacity, gals.	22.5	22.5
Seating capacity	5	5
Front head room, in.	39.8	39.8
Max. front leg room, in.	40.8	40.8
Rear head room, in.	39.8	39.8
Min. rear leg room, in.	32.2	39.1

Powertrain layout: longitudinal front-engine/rear- or 4-wheel drive

ENGINES

	ohc V6	dohc V6	dohc V6
Size, liters/cu. in.	3.2/193	3.2/193	3.5/213
Horsepower	175-190	190	215
Torque (lbs./ft.)	188	195	230

EPA city/highway mpg

5-speed OD manual	16/18	14/17	16/19
4-speed OD automatic	14/18	14/17	15/19

City/highway mpg (as tested)

4-speed OD automatic	14.9	15.8	16.4

Built in Japan

RETAIL PRICES

	GOOD	AVERAGE	POOR
1992 Trooper	$3,100-4,500	$2,500-3,800	$800-1,600
1993 Trooper	3,700-5,200	3,000-4,500	1,100-2,000

	GOOD	AVERAGE	POOR
1994 Trooper	$4,500-6,000	$3,800-5,300	$1,700-2,600
1995 Trooper	6,000-8,200	5,200-7,300	2,700-4,000
1996 Trooper	7,500-10,000	6,500-9,000	3,500-5,000
1997 Trooper	9,000-12,000	8,000-11,000	4,500-6,700
1998 Trooper	10,700-14,000	9,500-12,500	5,600-7,500
1999 Trooper	12,500-15,000	11,000-13,500	7,000-8,000
2000 Trooper	14,500-18,000	13,000-16,500	8,700-10,500
2001 Trooper	16,500-22,000	15,000-20,000	—

AVERAGE REPLACEMENT COSTS

A/C Compressor	$1,260	Clutch, Pressure Plate, Bearing	660
Alternator	295	Exhaust System	370
Automatic Transmission or Transaxle	1,465	Radiator	740
Brakes	340	Shocks and/or Struts	320
Timing Chain or Belt	100	Universal Joints	190

TROUBLE SPOTS

• **Suspension noise.** The differential may chatter in turns requiring the oil to be drained and refilled including a bottle of limited-slip additive. (1992-93)

• **Windows.** The fuse for the power windows, cruise control, and instrument panel may blow due to an intermittent short in the three-four gear switch for the transmission. (1994)

• **Keys.** The ignition key can be hard to remove because the lens over the shift lever interferes with the shift cable. (1992)

RECALL HISTORY

1992-94: Camshaft plug can become dislodged from cylinder head, allowing oil to leak; can cause engine damage and fire. **1996:** Certain vehicles have incorrect rear center seatbelt buckle; tongue cannot be inserted. **1996-97:** Left front brake line can be damaged, resulting in fluid leakage, reduced brake effectiveness, and longer stopping distance. **1998:** Improperly installed transfer gearbox nuts may loosen; propeller shaft can then separate, resulting in sudden loss of drive to wheels and possible damage to critical components. **2000-01 w/TOD:** In certain high-speed frontal crashes, movement of engine compartment components can cause the potential for fuel leakage.

1995-01 JAGUAR XJ-SEDAN

1995 Jaguar XJ6 Vanden Plas

FOR Antilock brakes • Ride • Acceleration • Steering/handling

AGAINST Fuel economy • Cargo room • Control layout

EVALUATION The base 6-cylinder engine is smoother and quieter than its predecessor, delivering brisk acceleration from a standing start as well as strong passing power. The V12 isn't sufficiently stronger to justify its considerably higher price. We averaged just 14.7 mpg in an XJ6 sedan, though much of the driving was rush-hour commuting. Each engine demands premium gasoline, and the V12 is notoriously nonfrugal. Picking an XJR with its supercharged 6-cylinder engine yields a big performance boost. The "blown" six responds quickly to the throttle and delivers a smooth, steady power increase. The XJR also has a huskier tone than other models, but is just as refined as its less-vigorous mates. All models offer precise, responsive steering and handle adeptly, with less body lean in turns than previous sedans. Ride comfort has risen, too, as the suspension easily soaks up bumps and provides a stable highway ride. Because interior dimensions did not change much, space is adequate for four, but five will be squeezed. Tall people sitting up front may have to recline their seatback more than usual to get adequate head room. In fact, they might even have to slouch to clear the roof—not the sort of behavior that's expected in what is ostensibly a full-size sedan. Tall occupants might also be short on leg room in the back seat—unless they're in one of the stretched sedans. Instead of crowded, uncomfortable conditions, backseat riders in an extended-length Jag have room to relax and stretch their legs. Rear doors are much wider on the extended models, too, but you still need to duck under the low roof when entering or exiting. The dashboard design could be better. Some controls are mysterious, awkward, or both. Cargo space isn't as large as it should be, either. The trunk has a wide, flat floor; but the cargo area ends at the bottom of the rear window. Therefore, you don't have enough space for a foursome's golf bags, much less an abundant load of luggage. The same lack of storage space characterized prior Jaguar sedans.

VALUE After buying Jaguar in 1990, Ford Motor Company spent millions of dollars to provide engineering and manufacturing expertise. At the same time, Jaguar was permitted to remain independent in terms of styling and packaging its new sedan along traditional lines. As a result of the change in management, we've been impressed by the cars' performance, ergonomics, and apparent improvements in overall quality. Jaguar definitely has moved up in the luxury sedan field, coming closer to the leaders. Although that goal hasn't quite been reached, there's no question that a Jaguar has more character than many rivals, such as the Lexus LS 400.

SPECIFICATIONS

	4-door sedan	4-door sedan
Wheelbase, in.	113.0	117.9
Overall length, in.	197.8	202.7
Overall width, in.	70.8	70.8
Overall height, in.	53.1	53.1
Curb weight, lbs.	4080	4130
Cargo volume, cu. ft.	11.1	11.1
Fuel capacity, gals.	21.4	21.4
Seating capacity	5	5
Front head room, in.	37.2	37.2
Max. front leg room, in.	41.2	41.2
Rear head room, in.	36.3	36.8
Min. rear leg room, in.	34.7	39.2

Powertrain layout: longitudinal front-engine/rear-wheel drive

ENGINES	dohc I6	Supercharged dohc I6	dohc V8	Supercharged dohc V8	ohc V12
Size, liters/cu. in.	4.0/243	4.0/243	4.0/244	4.0/244	6.0/365
Horsepower	245	322	290	370	313
Torque (lbs./ft.)	289	378	290	387	353
EPA city/highway mpg					
4-speed OD auto.	17/23	15/21			12/16
5-speed OD auto.			15.8	16/21	
City/highway mpg (as tested)					
4-speed OD auto.	18.5	15.7			
5-speed OD auto.					

Built in England

RETAIL PRICES	GOOD	AVERAGE	POOR
1995 XJ6	$13,000-14,500	$12,000-13,500	$8,000-9,000
1995 Vanden Plas	15,000-16,500	13,800-15,000	9,500-10,300
1995 XJR Supercharged	17,500-19,000	16,000-17,500	11,000-12,000
1995 XJ12	16,000-17,500	14,500-16,000	10,000-11,000
1996 XJ6	16,000-17,500	14,500-16,000	10,000-11,000
1996 Vanden Plas	19,000-20,500	17,500-19,000	12,500-13,500
1996 XJR Supercharged	21,000-23,000	19,500-21,000	14,400-15,500
1996 XJ12	19,500-21,500	18,000-19,500	13,000-14,000
1997 XJ6	19,000-21,000	17,500-19,500	12,500-14,000
1997 Vanden Plas	22,000-24,000	20,500-22,000	15,000-16,000
1997 XJR Supercharged	24,000-26,000	22,000-24,000	16,500-17,800
1998 XJ8	25,000-27,000	23,500-25,000	18,000-19,000
1998 Vanden Plas	29,000-31,000	27,000-29,000	21,000-22,300
1998 XJR Supercharged	32,000-34,000	30,000-32,000	24,000-25,200
1999 XJ8	30,000-32,000	28,500-30,000	22,500-23,500
1999 Vanden Plas	35,000-37,500	33,000-35,000	26,000-27,300
1999 XJR Supercharged	37,500-40,000	35,000-37,500	28,000-29,500
2000 XJ8	36,000-38,500	34,000-36,500	27,000-28,500
2000 Vanden Plas	41,000-43,000	39,000-41,000	31,500-33,500
2000 XJR Supercharged	43,500-46,000	41,500-43,500	33,000-34,300
2000 Super. Vanden Plas	50,000-53,000	47,500-50,000	38,000-39,500

	GOOD	AVERAGE	POOR
2001 XJ8	$43,000-46,000	$41,000-44,000	—
2001 Vanden Plas	49,000-52,000	46,500-49,000	—
2001 XJR Supercharged	51,000-54,000	48,000-51,000	—
2001 Super. Vanden Plas	62,000-66,000	59,000-63,000	—

AVERAGE REPLACEMENT COSTS

A/C Compressor	$1,005	Exhaust System	925
Alternator	475	Radiator	730
Automatic Transmission or		Shocks and/or Struts	1,000
Transaxle	1,060	Timing Chain or Belt	705
Brakes	240	Universal Joints	215

TROUBLE SPOTS

• **Dashboard lights.** A check engine light may be caused by a faulty air injection check valve. (1995)

• **Hard starting.** Hard restarting when the engine has warmed up due to a problem with the fuel pressure control valve. (1995-96)

• **Dashboard lights.** Oil pressure gauge reads low when energy-saving motor oils are used. (1995)

• **Automatic transmission.** The company is replacing the 5-speed automatic transmissions whenever they are in the shop for other service due to an uspecified problem that could lead to a failure. (1999)

• **Power seat.** The power seat fuse repeatedly blows so Jaguar suggests replacing the original fuse with one having a 20-amp rating. (1995)

RECALL HISTORY

1995: On a few cars, steering assembly was fitted with incorrect nuts; can result in loss of steering control. **1998-99:** On small number of cars, fine cracks in gear teeth of geartrain inside transmission can result in breakage of teeth; can cause transmission to "lock up" below 15 mph.

1990-96 JEEP CHEROKEE

1991 Jeep Cherokee Sport 2-door wagon

FOR Wet-weather traction (4WD) • Acceleration (6-cylinder) • Passenger and cargo room

AGAINST Fuel economy • Acceleration (4-cylinder) • Noise

EVALUATION The base 4-cylinder Cherokee's engine is adequate with manual shift, weak under a heavy load, and downright feeble and unresponsive if hooked to an automatic transmission. With either transmission, the robust 6-cylinder engine lets you sprint away from stoplights and quickly pass other vehicles. Expect about 17 mpg with a manual-shift six, or 15 mpg with automatic. All models have higher-than-average wind, road, and engine noise. These vehicles are spacious inside for their modest exterior dimensions—though not quite comparable to the Grand Cherokee or a Ford Explorer. Four sit in comfort. Head room is generous all around, and with a little squeezing, back seats accommodate three adults. Folding that rear seatback produces great luggage space, with a long and flat floor, and volume is acceptable with the seatback up. The long steering column puts the wheel too close to the driver's chest.

VALUE Cherokees offer a lot of temptations, serving as an excellent alternative for those who cannot afford a Grand Cherokee or Explorer. Next to something like the latest Chevrolet Blazer, though, they do seem a step behind in civility.

SPECIFICATIONS

	2-door wagon	4-door wagon
Wheelbase, in.	101.4	101.4
Overall length, in.	166.9	166.9
Overall width, in.	67.7	67.7
Overall height, in.	63.8	63.8
Curb weight, lbs.	2905	2955

	2-door wagon	4-door wagon
Cargo volume, cu. ft.	71.8	71.8
Fuel capacity, gals.	20.2	20.2
Seating capacity	5	5
Front head room, in.	38.3	38.3
Max. front leg room, in.	41.4	41.4
Rear head room, in.	38.5	38.5
Min. rear leg room, in.	34.9	34.9

Powertrain layout: longitudinal front-engine/rear- or 4-wheel drive

ENGINES

	ohv I4	ohv I6
Size, liters/cu. in.	2.5/151	4.0/242
Horsepower	121-130	177-190
Torque (lbs./ft.)	141-150	224-225
EPA city/highway mpg		
5-speed OD manual	19/22	17/22
4-speed OD automatic		15/19
City/highway mpg (as tested)		
5-speed OD manual		17.0
4-speed OD automatic		15.0

Built in USA

RETAIL PRICES

	GOOD	AVERAGE	POOR
1990 Cherokee 2WD	$1,400-2,800	$800-2,200	$100-400
1990 Cherokee 4WD	2,100-4,000	1,400-3,300	400-1,100
1991 Cherokee 2WD	1,700-3,500	1,100-2,800	300-900
1991 Cherokee 4WD	2,500-4,500	1,800-3,800	500-1,500
1992 Cherokee 2WD	2,200-4,400	1,600-3,700	500-1,400
1992 Cherokee 4WD	3,200-5,500	2,500-4,700	800-2,200
1993 Cherokee 2WD	2,700-4,500	2,100-3,800	700-1,500
1993 Cherokee 4WD	3,700-5,700	3,000-49,00	1,100-2,300
1994 Cherokee 2WD	3,200-5,300	2,500-4,500	800-2,000
1994 Cherokee 4WD	4,200-6,300	3,500-5,500	1,400-2,700
1995 Cherokee 2WD	3,800-6,300	3,000-5,500	1,100-2,700
1995 Cherokee 4WD	4,800-7,500	4,000-6,700	1,800-3,500
1996 Cherokee 2WD	4,500-7,200	3,700-6,300	1,600-3,400
1996 Cherokee 4WD	5,700-8,300	4,900-7,300	2,500-4,000

AVERAGE REPLACEMENT COSTS

A/C Compressor	$390	Clutch, Pressure Plate,	
Alternator	355	Bearing	495
Automatic Transmission or		Exhaust System	270
Transaxle	680	Radiator	380
Brakes	265	Shocks and/or Struts	190
Timing Chain or Belt	185	Universal Joints	145

TROUBLE SPOTS

• **Transmission leak.** Automatic transmission fluid leaks from the speed sensor in the transmission. (1993-94)

• **Air conditioner.** If the air conditioner gradually stops cooling, the computer (PCM) may not be sending a signal to the compressor clutch relay to cycle off, which causes the AC evaporator to freeze up. (1991-95)

• **Automatic transmission.** If the transmission will not engage when first started, chances are the torque converter is draining down. A check valve in the fluid line leading to the transmission cooler should fix the problem. (1993) If the transmission won't upshift for about the first quarter mile in cool weather, it is probably due to defective cast iron seal rings in the governor drive. (1993-94)

• **Oil leak.** The rear main seals on 2.5- and 4.0-liter engines are prone to leakage if the vehicle is operated in dirty conditions. (1991-96)

RECALL HISTORY

1990 w/ABS: Hydraulic fluid may be contaminated. **1990 w/4.0-liter engine and automatic:** Could have intermittent high idle speed. **1990-91 w/ABS:** Improper insertion/crimping of hose fittings can result in loss of ABS function. **1990-91 w/ABS:** Hydraulic control unit for antilock braking system can experience excessive brake actuator piston seal wear, which could lead to loss of antilock function and reduced power assist. **1990-95 in 15 states and Washington, D.C.:** Front disc brake rotors can experience severe corrosion if operated for extensive period in "salt belt"; can eventually compromise structural integrity, allowing wear surface to separate from hub. **1991:** Jounce bumper could contact and collapse left rear brake tube. **1991 w/ABS:** Brake fluid tube may contact steering shaft and result in leakage. **1993:** Retainer clip that secures master cylinder rod to brake pedal was not installed properly. **1993-96:** High steering loads can cause steering-gear bolts to break or frame to crack. **1994:** Rear seatbelt bolts may not support passengers in sudden stop. **1995:** Certain airbags might not deploy in an accident. **1995:** Parking brake handle release button can separate, so parking brake may not hold and vehicle could roll inadvertently. **1996:** Fasteners that secure alternator fuse could have improper clamp load; arcing could cause fire in engine compartment. **1996:** Front disc brake rotors could corrode severely if operated for extensive period in certain "salt belt" states.

1997-01 JEEP CHEROKEE

1997 Jeep Cherokee

FOR Acceleration (6-cylinder) • Passenger room • Cargo room • Optional antilock brakes

AGAINST Acceleration (4-cylinder) • Fuel economy

EVALUATION Chrysler Corporation (now DaimlerChrysler) has done an admirable job of keeping a basically solid design fresh enough for today's tougher market. Most models that date back to 1984, as the Cherokee does, would have faded away long before. Cherokee's 4-cylinder engine provides only adequate acceleration with the 5-speed manual transmission, and is overmatched with automatic in anything other than gentle cruising. Of course, most Cherokees on the market are 6-cylinder. That engine is strong throughout the speed range, and delivers fuel economy typical of a midsize SUV: about 15 mpg with automatic and 17 mpg with manual shift. Cherokee suffers powertrain and road resonances that are absent in most competitive sport-utility vehicles. Wind noise at speed is prominent, too. Good balance and tidy dimensions make the Cherokee quite maneuverable in most situations. The firm base suspension provides a solid ride that absorbs all but the worst bumps, without jarring. An "Up Country" option, if installed, makes for a rough ride. Optional antilock braking feels strong and natural. A Cherokee really shows its age in interior accommodations. Less roomy than a Grand Cherokee or a Ford Explorer, it does carry four adults in comfort. However, the low-roof passenger compartment has no surplus of front shoulder room, a shortage of rear knee clearance, and fairly lofty step-in. Rear entry/exit is tight, too, thanks to narrow lower doorways. On the plus side, the dashboard is modern and convenient. Outward vision is good, though larger door mirrors would help when lane changing. Mounting the spare tire inside eats up cargo room, but there's still decent space with the rear seat in use, and a long load floor with that seat folded. An outside spare was available at Jeep dealerships, so look for one of that kind if cargo space is a major concern. Some Cherokees we tested when new had occasional interior rattles, as well as wider-than-usual panel gaps around the hood and tailgate.

VALUE Convenient 4-wheel-drive systems, commendable off-road capability, and civilized on road manners—for less than a Grand Cherokee or an Explorer—make the Cherokee an above average value. Despite an aging design and strong competition, Cherokees sold well in the late '90s and are not too expensive today unless you go for a fully-equipped model. Still, Cherokee is behind the times in room, ride, and refinement.

SPECIFICATIONS

	2-door wagon	4-door wagon
Wheelbase, in.	101.4	101.4
Overall length, in.	167.5	167.5
Overall width, in.	69.4	69.4
Overall height, in.	63.9	64
Curb weight, lbs.	3180	3224
Cargo volume, cu. ft.	69	69
Fuel capacity, gals.	20	20
Seating capacity	5	5
Front head room, in.	37.8	37.8
Max. front leg room, in.	41.4	41.4
Rear head room, in.	38	38
Min. rear leg room, in.	35	35

Powertrain layout: longitudinal front-engine/rear- or 4-wheel drive

ENGINES

	ohv I4	ohv I6
Size, liters/cu. in.	2.5/150	4.0/242
Horsepower	125	190
Torque (lbs./ft.)	150	225
EPA city/highway mpg		
5-speed OD manual	21/25	18/22
3-speed automatic	19/22	
4-speed OD automatic		16/21
City/highway mpg (as tested)		
5-speed OD manual		17.0
4-speed OD automatic		15.0

Built in USA

RETAIL PRICES

	GOOD	AVERAGE	POOR
1997 Cherokee 2WD	$5,800-8,200	$5,000-7,400	$2,600-4,000
1997 Cherokee 4WD	6,800-9,500	5,900-8,500	3,100-4,800
1998 Cherokee 2WD	6,700-9,500	5,900-8,600	3,100-4,900
1998 Cherokee 4WD	7,700-10,800	6,700-9,800	3,600-5,400
1999 Cherokee 2WD	8,000-11,000	7,000-10,000	4,000-5,700
1999 Cherokee 4WD	9,000-12,000	8,000-11,000	4,500-6,400
2000 Cherokee 2WD	9,400-12,500	8,400-11,500	4,800-6,700
2000 Cherokee 4WD	10,500-13,500	9,500-12,500	5,600-7,500
2001 Cherokee 2WD	11,000-14,500	10,000-13,200	—
2001 Cherokee 4WD	12,000-15,500	11,000-14,200	—

AVERAGE REPLACEMENT COSTS

A/C Compressor	$470	Clutch, Pressure Plate, Bearing	380
Alternator	350	Exhaust System	395
Automatic Transmission or Transaxle	1,215	Radiator	350
Brakes	375	Shocks and/or Struts	410
Timing Chain or Belt	240	Universal Joints	270

TROUBLE SPOTS

• **Windshield washer.** Because of a bad check valve, windshield washer fluid drips from the nozzle for the rear window and can cause paint staining. (1997)

• **Brake noise.** Grinding and scraping noises under hard braking are caused by the drive shaft hitting the floor pan and is fixed by replacing the front lower control arm. (1997)

• **Air conditioner.** The air conditioner gradually stops blowing cool air because the evaporator ices up. Replacing the low-pressure cycling switch usually fixes it. (1997-99)

• **Brakes.** The brake friction material transfers to the rotors (especially in warm, moist climates) causing brake pedal pulsation when stopping. New pads should correct it. (1997-99)

• **Fuel gauge.** The fuel gauge may show $\frac{1}{8}$ to $\frac{1}{4}$ full but the vehicle will run out of gas because of a defective sending unit that must be replaced. (1997)

• **Vehicle shake.** Vibration at speeds over 60 mph may be due to a misaligned or defective drive shaft. (1997-98)

RECALL HISTORY

1997: Accuracy of fuel tank-mounted fuel level sending unit can degrade over time, indicating significantly more fuel in reserve than is actually present. **1997-99 sold or registered in 15 states or Washington D.C.:** Front disc brake rotors can experience severe corrosion if operated for extensive period in the "salt belt." **1997-99:** Water and/or road salt in proximity of airbag control module could lead to corrosion and possible inadvertent deployment. **1998:** Power brake booster vacuum reservoir diaphragm can split or tear, causing increase in engine idle speed and loss of power assist during brake application. **1998:** Due to improperly-hardened front seatbelt shoulder turning loop anchors, front-seat occupant might not be properly restrained in a crash. **2001:** Some of the owner's manuals for these vehicles are missing instructions for properly attaching a child restraint system's tether strap to the tether anchorage.

1993-98 JEEP GRAND CHEROKEE

1993 Jeep Grand Cherokee Laredo

FOR Antilock brakes • Wet-weather traction (4WD) • Passenger and cargo room

AGAINST Fuel economy • Engine noise • Reliability (early models)

EVALUATION Base-engine power is adequate for most drivers, but the 5.2-liter V8 is much better, especially in low-speed acceleration. It delivers strong off-the-line pickup as well as brisk passing response. The 5.9-liter in the Limited model has even more power at low speeds. We averaged 16.5 mpg in a 6-cylinder Grand Cherokee, and a meager 13.3 mpg with a V8. All three engines can get noisy, though they're much quieter when cruising. Interior room is good, though the spare tire takes up space. Head and leg room are generous all around, and three adults fit in the rear seat. Entry/exit to the front requires only a slight step up. Rear doors are narrow at the bottom and don't open wide enough to allow large people to get in or out without bending a little. With the rear seatback up, luggage space isn't much greater than in a midsize car. Even with the child seat that became available during 1994, rear seatbacks can be folded down to create a long cargo floor.

VALUE We rate the Grand a step behind the Ford Explorer, but both lead the field in refinement, ability, and overall quality. An Explorer is more trucklike, a trait that some buyers like and others do not, but the Grand Cherokee offers impressive on- and off-road performance, plus a broad range of engine and 4WD choices. Early Grand Cherokees suffered some reliability problems, so a later model might be a better bet.

SPECIFICATIONS

	4-door wagon
Wheelbase, in.	105.9
Overall length, in.	179.0
Overall width, in.	70.9
Overall height, in.	64.7
Curb weight, lbs.	3614
Cargo volume, cu. ft.	79.3
Fuel capacity, gals.	23.0
Seating capacity	5
Front head room, in.	38.9
Max. front leg room, in.	40.9
Rear head room, in.	39.1
Min. rear leg room, in.	35.7

Powertrain layout: longitudinal front-engine/rear- or 4-wheel drive

ENGINES

	ohv I6	ohv V8	ohv V8
Size, liters/cu. in.	4.0/242	5.2/318	5.9/360
Horsepower	185-190	220	245
Torque (lbs./ft.)	200-225	285-300	345
EPA city/highway mpg			
5-speed OD manual	16/20		
4-speed OD automatic	15/20	14/18	13/17
City/highway mpg (as tested)			
4-speed OD automatic	16.5	13.3	14.6

Built in USA

RETAIL PRICES

	GOOD	AVERAGE	POOR
1993 Grand Cherokee 2WD	$3,800-4,500	$3,100-3,800	$1,200-1,600
1993 Grand Cherokee 4WD	4,700-6,000	4,000-5,200	1,800-2,500
1994 Grand Cherokee 2WD	4,800-5,700	4,100-4,900	1,900-2,400
1994 Grand Cherokee 4WD	6,000-7,500	5,200-6,600	2,700-3,500
1995 Grand Cherokee 2WD	6,000-7,500	5,200-6,500	2,700-3,400
1995 Grand Cherokee 4WD	7,300-9,000	6,500-8,100	3,500-4,500
1996 Grand Cherokee 2WD	7,500-9,500	6,700-8,500	3,600-4,800
1996 Grand Cherokee 4WD	8,800-11,000	7,800-10,000	4,400-5,800
1997 Grand Cherokee 2WD	$9,000-11,000	$8,000-10,000	$4,500-5,800
1997 Grand Cherokee 4WD	10,200-12,500	9,200-11,500	5,400-7,000
1998 Grand Cherokee 2WD	11,000-13,000	10,000-12,000	6,000-7,400
1998 Grand Cherokee 4WD	12,300-14,200	11,300-13,000	7,200-8,200

AVERAGE REPLACEMENT COSTS

A/C Compressor	$390	Clutch, Pressure Plate, Bearing	375
Alternator	360	Exhaust System	270
Automatic Transmission or Transaxle	700	Radiator	380
Brakes	300	Shocks and/or Struts	155
Timing Chain or Belt	195	Universal Joints	135

TROUBLE SPOTS

• **Oil leak.** A chronic oil leak at the filter on 5.2-liter engine is likely due to a warped adapter plate. (1995)

• **Transmission leak.** Automatic transmission fluid leaks from the speed sensor in the transmission. (1993-94)

• **Air conditioner.** If the air conditioner gradually stops cooling, the computer (PCM) may not be sending a signal to the compressor clutch relay to cycle off, which causes the A/C evaporator to freeze up. (1993-95)

• **Automatic transmission.** If transmission will not engage when first started, chances are the torque converter is draining down. A check valve in the fluid line leading to the transmission cooler should remedy the problem. (1993)

• **Oil consumption and engine knock.** Oil pump gear wear results in bucking and surging when the engine is warm and lack of lubrication when the engine is cold. (1993)

• **Engine misfire.** Rough idle and stalling can be traced to a defective idle air control motor. (1993-94)

• **Oil leak.** The rear main seals on 4.0-liter engines are prone to leakage if the vehicle is operated in dirty conditions. (1993-96)

• **Automatic transmission.** The transmission won't upshift for about the first quarter mile in cool weather due to defective cast iron seal rings in the governor drive. (1993-94)

RECALL HISTORY

1993: Molded plastic pin that connects upper and lower steering column shafts may be sheared; shafts could separate, causing total loss of steering control. **1993:** Eccentric cam adjuster bolts in both front lower suspension arm-to-front axle bracket attachments may fail, causing vehicle to pull to one side. **1993:** Retainer clip that secures master cylinder input rod to brake pedal could work loose, allowing separation, which may cause loss of braking. **1993-98 in 15 states and Washington, D.C.:** Front disc brake rotors can experience severe corrosion if operated for extensive period in "salt belt"; can eventually compromise structural integrity, allowing wear surface to separate from hub. **1995:** Parking brake release button can separate, so brake may not hold and vehicle could roll inadvertently. **1996:** Fasteners that secure alternator fuse could have improper clamp load; arcing could cause fire in engine compartment. **1996 w/Quadra-Trac, temporary spare tire, and 225/70R16 or 245/70R15 tires:** When temporary spare tire is in use, front axle can overheat; can force fluid out of seals, increasing risk of fire. **1996-98:** Front disc brake rotors could corrode severely if operated for extensive period in certain "salt belt" states. **1997:** Airbag could deploy inadvertently when ignition is shut off. **1997:** Fuel-level sending unit degrades over time, causing gauge to show significantlly more fuel in tank than is actually present. **1998:** Power brake booster vacuum reservoir diaphragm can split or tear; may cause increase in engine idle speed and loss of power brake assist.

1999-01 JEEP GRAND CHEROKEE

FOR Acceleration • Cargo room

AGAINST Fuel economy • Reliability (early models)

EVALUATION Handling and off-road ability are top Grand Cherokee strengths. Control in directional changes is good, despite a fair amount of body lean. Steering feels natural, though small corrections are needed at highway speeds. No midsize SUV rides more comfortably. The revised suspension handles all but the worst potholes with ease, but permits queasy fore-and-aft and side-to-side pitching motions through uneven pavement. Acceleration is adequate with the 6-cylinder engine, robust with the V8, and the new 4.7-liter is far smoother than the old 5.2-liter V8. The reworked 6-cylinder also is much quieter. A 6-cylinder 4WD Laredo averaged 16.1 mpg. Wind rush and tire roar may intrude at highway speeds,

2000 Jeep Grand Cherokee Laredo

but the quieter engines help lower overall interior noise levels. Transmissions shift with prompt smoothness. Braking is strong and smooth. Selec-Trac or Quadra-Trac furnish more than enough traction on even the most slippery streets, but Quadra-Drive offers the ultimate in 4WD grip. A Quadra-Drive Grand Cherokee can climb in and out of places that leave rivals spinning their tires, though gear whine is intrusive. Four adults get plenty of space. Grand Cherokees still aren't wide enough to seat three adults comfortably in back, and the rear seatback is too upright for best comfort, with little toe space ahead. Large outside mirrors are helpful, but roof pillars are too thick for full outward vision. Generously-sized bins and pockets provide plenty of storage space for small items. Relocating the spare tire opened up more luggage room, but it's still only adequate and rear seats are somewhat difficult to fold. Back-seat entry/exit is hampered by narrow door bottoms. Even the worst terrain elicits no squeaks or rattles from the stiffened body.

VALUE An even better dollar value than the old Grand Cherokee, this version offers good performance and overall design. Long-term mechanical reliability is still a question mark.

SPECIFICATIONS

	4-door wagon
Wheelbase, in.	105.9
Overall length, in.	181.5
Overall width, in.	72.3
Overall height, in.	69.4
Curb weight, lbs.	3916
Cargo volume, cu. ft.	72.3
Fuel capacity, gals.	20.5
Seating capacity	5
Front head room, in.	39.7
Max. front leg room, in.	41.4
Rear head room, in.	39.5
Min. rear leg room, in.	35.3

Powertrain layout: longitudinal front-engine/rear- or 4-wheel drive

ENGINES

	ohc I6	ohc V8
Size, liters/cu. in.	4.0/242	4.7/284
Horsepower	195	230-235
Torque (lbs./ft.)	230	295
EPA city/highway mpg		
4-speed OD automatic	16/21	15/20
5-speed OD automatic		15/20
City/highway mpg (as tested)		
4-speed OD automatic	15.7	16.1

Built in USA

RETAIL PRICES

	GOOD	AVERAGE	POOR
1999 Grand Cherokee Lar.	$15,000-17,000	$14,000-16,000	$10,000-11,500
1999 Grand Cherokee Ltd.	18,000-21,000	17,000-19,500	12,000-13,500
2000 Grand Cherokee Lar.	17,000-20,000	16,000-19,000	11,500-13,500
2000 Grand Cherokee Ltd.	20,500-24,000	19,300-22,500	14,300-16,300
2001 Grand Cherokee Lar.	19,200-22,500	18,200-21,200	—
2001 Grand Cherokee Ltd.	23,000-27,000	21,500-25,500	—

AVERAGE REPLACEMENT COSTS

A/C Compressor	$555	Brakes	490
Alternator	340	Constant Velocity Joints	1,405
Automatic Transmission or		Exhaust System	405
Transaxle	1,125	Radiator	620

TROUBLE SPOTS

• **Hard starting.** Engine may be hard to start due to an internal leak or bits of plastic wedged inside the fuel pump assembly. A new sealing ring or complete pump assembly could be required. (1999-2000)

• **Vehicle noise.** Popping/snapping noises are usually corrected by replacing the front driveshaft. In many cases, that unit probably has a dry universal joint. (1999)

• **Fuel odors.** The gas tank may fill slowly because of a problem with the filler pipe, which has been revised, and there is also a revised gas cap to replace binding ones. (1999)

• **Engine misfire.** The powertrain control module (engine computer) may have to be reprogrammed or replaced if the engine sags with the A/C on. (1999)

RECALL HISTORY

1999: Front seatbelt retractor on certain vehicles does not work properly. **1999:** Rear outboard seatbelt retractor spring can disengage from rewind mechanism, disabling retractor function and preventing belt from fitting snugly around occupant. **1999-00:** Inadequately manufactured seatbelt shoulder height adjustable turning loop top mounting bolt may not withstand sufficient force to function properly in certain impact situations. **2000:** Fuel tank on some vehicles may have suspect vent tube welds; separation of tube weld could result in fuel leakage. **2000:** Passenger airbag inflator assembly in small number of cars contains incorrect inflator charge amount, which could increase risk of passenger injury under certain crash conditions. **2000:** Improperly heat-treated end-of-travel stops in some steering gear units could result in sticking, binding, or seizing of the steering gear. **2001:** Some owner's manuals are missing full instructions for properly attaching a child restraint system's tether strap.

1990-95 JEEP WRANGLER

1991 Jeep Wrangler S

FOR Wet-weather traction • Acceleration (6-cylinder) • Maneuverability • Antilock brakes (optional with 6-cylinder)

AGAINST Ride/handling • Fuel economy • Entry/exit • Cargo room • Instruments/controls • Engine noise • Wind noise • Road noise

EVALUATION Acceleration and drivability are only adequate from the initial 6-cylinder engine; gas mileage mediocre. Meager is the word for acceleration from the 4-cylinder engine. Performance got a welcome boost from the fuel-injected six of 1991. Jeep claimed a 0-60-mph acceleration time of 9.7 seconds, versus 14.3 seconds for the old carbureted 6-cylinder engine. A stiff suspension makes for jarring travel over most surfaces. The Wrangler's narrow stance and short wheelbase promise good manueverability, but demand conservative cornering speeds. Climbing aboard isn't so easy, as it's a tall step over the doorsills. Once inside, you get a cramped rear seat and tiny cargo area (unless the rear seat is tilted out of the way). Tall people have ample head room all around to sit comfortably upright. Once aboard, you can expect to be assaulted by road noise and wind buffeting—whether the top is up or down. Gauges and controls are strung across the dashboard in a haphazard manner.

VALUE Seriously consider how you would use the vehicle, and if the compromises in on-road ride, handling, and fuel economy are worth it in the end. Also look at an Isuzu Amigo, which lacks the Jeep's classic image but feels just about as tough, as well as the Geo Tracker/Suzuki Sidekick, with their friendlier ergonomics. But none of those rivals have a muscular 6-cylinder engine like Wrangler's. We don't recommend any mini 4x4 as a daily driver, but plenty of people love them.

SPECIFICATIONS

	2-door conv.
Wheelbase, in.	93.4
Overall length, in.	153.0
Overall width, in.	66.0
Overall height, in.	69.6
Curb weight, lbs.	NA
Cargo volume, cu. ft.	43.2
Fuel capacity, gals.	15.0-20.0
Seating capacity	4
Front head room, in.	40.2
Max. front leg room, in.	39.4

	2-door conv.
Rear head room, in.	40.5
Min. rear leg room, in.	35.0

Powertrain layout: longitudinal front-engine/rear- or all-wheel drive

ENGINES

	ohv I4	ohv I6	ohv I6
Size, liters/cu. in.	2.5/150	4.0/242	4.2/256
Horsepower	117-123	180	112
Torque (lbs./ft.)	138-139	200	210

EPA city/highway mpg

5-speed OD manual	19/20	15/18	16/20
3-speed automatic	17/18	15/17	15/16

City/highway mpg (as tested)

5-speed OD manual	18.1		12.9
3-speed automatic		14.6	

Built in Canada

RETAIL PRICES

	GOOD	AVERAGE	POOR
1990 Wrangler S 4-cyl.	$1,800-2,500	$1,200-1,900	$300-600
1990 Wrangler 6-cyl.	2,500-3,700	1,800-3,000	500-1,000
1991 Wrangler S 4-cyl.	2,500-3,300	1,900-2,600	500-800
1991 Wrangler 6-cyl.	3,500-4,800	2,800-4,000	1,000-1,600
1992 Wrangler S 4-cyl.	3,200-4,000	2,500-3,300	800-1,200
1992 Wrangler 6-cyl.	4,500-5,900	3,800-5,000	1,700-2,400
1993 Wrangler S 4-cyl.	3,800-4,600	3,100-3,800	1,200-1,500
1993 Wrangler 6-cyl.	5,300-6,800	4,500-5,900	2,200-3,000
1994 Wrangler S 4-cyl.	4,500-5,400	3,800-4,500	1,700-2,100
1994 Wrangler 6-cyl.	6,200-7,700	5,400-6,800	2,800-3,600
1995 Wrangler S 4-cyl.	5,500-6,500	4,600-5,500	2,300-2,800
1995 Wrangler 6-cyl.	7,000-8,500	6,000-7,500	3,200-4,000

AVERAGE REPLACEMENT COSTS

A/C Compressor	$375	Clutch, Pressure Plate,	
Alternator	315	Bearing	690
Automatic Transmission or		Exhaust System	255
Transaxle	690	Radiator	355
Brakes	275	Shocks and/or Struts	180
Timing Chain or Belt	185	Universal Joints	130

TROUBLE SPOTS

• **Transmission leak.** Automatic transmission fluid leaks from the speed sensor in the transmission. (1992-94)

• **Automatic transmission.** If the transmission will not engage when first started, chances are the torque converter is draining down. A check valve in the fluid line leading to the transmission cooler should remedy the problem. (1993) If the transmission won't upshift for about the first quarter mile in cool weather, it is probably due to defective cast iron seal rings in the governor drive. (1992-94)

• **Oil leak.** The rear main seals on 2.5- and 4.0-liter engines are prone to leakage if the vehicle is operated in dirty conditions. (1991-96)

RECALL HISTORY

1990-91 in 15 states and Washington, D.C.: Front disc brake rotors can experience severe corrosion if operated for extensive period in "salt belt"; can eventually compromise structural integrity, allowing wear surface to separate from hub. **1990-92:** Front brake hoses can wear due to contact with splash shields. **1990-93:** Plastic fuel tank's sending unit gasket can crack, resulting in fuel and vapor leaks. **1991-93 w/manual shift:** Salt corrosion between starter solenoid wire and battery feed may short these connections.

1997-01 JEEP WRANGLER

FOR Optional antilock brakes • 4WD versatility • Maneuverability

AGAINST Fuel economy • Acceleration (4-cylinder) • Noise

EVALUATION Wranglers really are more carlike than before—far better in ride quality and ergonomics. Occupant comfort is vastly improved, though few would call the Wrangler experience comfortable. The new suspension is a lot more absorbent, true, but it still reacts abruptly to dips and bumps. Unless the pavement really gets nasty, though, the ride isn't jarring. A 4-cylinder Wrangler with manual shift has trouble merging or overtaking fast-moving freeway traffic. Performance in a 5-speed Wrangler with the 6-cylinder engine gets reasonably vigorous—though accompanied by considerable engine and gear noise. Fuel economy is tolerable, but no bonus. A 5-speed Sahara with the 6-cylin-

1997 Jeep Wrangler Sahara

der engine averaged 19.3 mpg. Wind noise is abundant where the roof meets the windshield frame. Doors seal poorly, too, with the canvas top in place. That canvas top also flutters, while the optional hardtop "drums" at highway speeds. Taking the top up and down is easier than before, but still a frustrating chore. Full instruments now are clustered in front of the driver, not spread out as in prior Wranglers. Two adults now fit in back without squeezing, but the cushion and backrest are hard and short. Interior storage is better than in earlier Wranglers. Space behind the back seat is modest.

VALUE True Wrangler fans don't fret about its flaws. For other potential owners, the great strides made in safety, ride quality, and refinement in this generation bring Wrangler closer than before to serving as an everyday vehicle.

SPECIFICATIONS

	2-door conv.
Wheelbase, in.	93.4
Overall length, in.	151.8
Overall width, in.	66.7
Overall height, in.	70.2
Curb weight, lbs.	3092
Cargo volume, cu. ft.	55.7
Fuel capacity, gals.	15.0-19.0
Seating capacity	4
Front head room, in.	42.3
Max. front leg room, in.	41.1
Rear head room, in.	40.6
Min. rear leg room, in.	34.9

Powertrain layout: longitudinal front-engine/rear- or 4-wheel drive

ENGINES

	ohv I4	ohv I6
Size, liters/cu. in.	2.5/151	4.0/242
Horsepower	120	181-190
Torque (lbs./ft.)	140	222-235

EPA city/highway mpg

5-speed OD manual	19/20	15/18
3-speed automatic	17/18	15/17

City/highway mpg (as tested)

5-speed OD manual		19.3
3-speed automatic		15.2

Built in USA

RETAIL PRICES

	GOOD	AVERAGE	POOR
1997 Wrangler SE 4-cyl.	$8,000-9,000	$7,200-8,100	$4,100-4,700
1997 Wrangler 6-cyl.	10,000-11,500	9,200-10,500	5,400-6,200
1998 Wrangler SE 4-cyl.	9,200-10,200	8,400-9,300	4,700-5,300
1998 Wrangler 6-cyl.	11,500-13,000	10,500-12,000	6,500-7,500
1999 Wrangler SE 4-cyl.	10,500-11,500	9,500-10,500	5,600-6,300
1999 Wrangler 6-cyl.	13,000-14,500	12,000-13,200	8,000-8,800
2000 Wrangler SE 4-cyl.	12,000-13,000	11,000-12,000	7,000-7,700
2000 Wrangler 6-cyl.	14,500-16,500	13,200-15,000	9,000-11,200
2001 Wrangler SE 4-cyl.	13,500-14,500	12,500-13,500	—
2001 Wrangler 6-cyl.	16,000-18,500	14,700-17,000	—

AVERAGE REPLACEMENT COSTS

A/C Compressor	$375	Clutch, Pressure Plate,	
Alternator	315	Bearing	2,165
Automatic Transmission or		Exhaust System	220
Transaxle	930	Radiator	300
Brakes	270	Shocks and/or Struts	190
Timing Chain or Belt	200	Universal Joints	220

TROUBLE SPOTS

- **Steering problems.** Fluid leaks from the power steering reservoir. (1997)
- **Doors.** The doors may not unlock with the key requiring replacement of the door latches. (1997)
- **Fuel gauge.** The gas gauge needle may not point to full, may show ⅛ to ¼ full when the tank is empty. (1997)
- **Fuel odors.** The gas tank may fill slowly or the pump nozzle will keep shutting off due to a problem with the fuel tank venting system. (1997)
- **Water leak.** Water may leak onto the passenger-side front floor due to leaks in the heater and air conditioner housing or from a problem with the evaporator drain tube. (1997)

RECALL HISTORY

1997: Airbag control module on some vehicles contains an error that can delay deployment in certain crash situations. **1997:** Airbag could deploy inadvertently when ignition is shut off. **1997 w/manual steering:** Driver's airbag wiring harness can break when steering wheel is turned to "full lock" position; in crash, airbag would not deploy. **1998:** Power brake booster vacuum reservoir diaphragm can split or tear; may cause increase in engine idle speed and loss of power brake assist. **1998:** Front seatbelt shoulder anchors were not properly heat treated and hardened; in a crash, occupant may not be properly restrained. **1999:** Instrument-panel ground attachment screws could loosen over time, possibly affecting gauges and/or defroster. **2001:** Some of the owner's manuals for these vehicles are missing instructions for properly attaching a child restraint system's tether strap to the tether anchorage.

1994-01 KIA SEPHIA

1997 Kia Sephia

FOR Fuel economy • Price • Optional antilock braking (certain later models)

AGAINST Noise • Stereo location • Build quality

EVALUATION Sephias broke no new technical ground, but offered competent—if unremarkable—performance. Even in its latest form, though, Sephia is a mediocre performer compared to most budget-range rivals. Acceleration is so-so, as are ride and handling. Even fuel economy has been unremarkable, as a recent test LS sedan with 5-speed averaged a nothing-special 22.7 mpg. An earlier GS model, in contrast, averaged almost 31 mpg, driving 40-percent of the time on the highway. Noise also has been a problem, and refinement lags way behind that of the class-leading Hondas and Toyotas. Engine noise is moderate, but road and wind noise are prominent. Ride quality isn't bad for a subcompact, though the suspension tends to "hammer" over bumps instead of absorbing them. Sephias boast more interior space than many subcompacts, especially in back. Trunk space is also good. Except for the stereo, which was mounted low and had small, hard-to-use buttons, the early dashboard was well laid out.

VALUE Prices have been attractive on the new-car market, and similarly tempting on used-car lots. Kia spokespersons claim their cars' resale value has been strong, but it's definitely not in the same league as a Toyota or Honda. That could be good news for used-car shoppers, but there's more to value than price—especially when reliability is a question mark. Refinement, too, lags well behind the class-leading Toyota Corolla and Honda Civic. On the whole, we've been underwhelmed by Sephia and Spectra. But as of 2001, Kias were covered by the industry's most comprehensive warranties, which adds to owner peace of mind. When that tempting price is factored into the equation, this South Korean subcompact might be a credible choice for the budget-conscious.

SPECIFICATIONS

	4-door hatchback	4-door sedan
Wheelbase, in.	100.8	100.8
Overall length, in.	176.2	174.4
Overall width, in.	66.9	66.9
Overall height, in.	55.5	55.5
Curb weight, lbs.	2560	2478
Cargo volume, cu. ft.	11.6	10.4
Fuel capacity, gals.	13.2	13.2
Seating capacity	5.0	5
Front head room, in.	39.6	39.6
Max. front leg room, in.	43.1	43.3
Rear head room, in.	36.6	37.9
Min. rear leg room, in.	34.4	34.4

The Spectra 4-door hatchback was added in 2000.

Powertrain layout: transverse front-engine/front-wheel drive

ENGINES

	ohc I4	dohc I4	dohc I4
Size, liters/cu. in.	1.6/98	1.6/98	1.8/109
Horsepower	88	105	122-125
Torque (lbs./ft.)	98	100	108-117

EPA city/highway mpg

5-speed OD manual	23/27	28/34	24/31
4-speed OD automatic	25/30	24/31	23/31

City/highway mpg (as tested)

5-speed OD manual		31.0	22.7

Built in South Korea

RETAIL PRICES

	GOOD	AVERAGE	POOR
1994 Sephia	$1,300-1,800	$800-1,200	$100-200
1995 Sephia	1,700-2,400	1,100-1,800	300-400
1996 Sephia	2,200-2,900	1,600-2,300	500-600
1997 Sephia	2,700-3,500	2,100-2,800	600-900
1998 Sephia	3,400-4,300	2,700-3,600	800-1,200
1999 Sephia	4,500-5,400	3,800-4,600	1,600-2,100
2000 Sephia	5,600-6,500	4,900-5,700	2,200-2,800
2001 Sephia	6,700-7,800	5,900-7,000	—

AVERAGE REPLACEMENT COSTS

A/C Compressor	$330	Clutch, Pressure Plate, Bearing	440
Alternator	290	Constant Velocity Joints	750
Automatic Transmission or Transaxle	660	Exhaust System	265
Brakes	270	Radiator	190
Shocks and/or Struts	200	Timing Chain or Belt	400

TROUBLE SPOTS

- **Fuel odors.** Gasoline burps back out of the filler pipe during refueling. (1998-99)

RECALL HISTORY

1994: Electronic speedometer sensor can seize, causing speedometer and cruise control (if equipped) to stop functioning. **1998-99:** Ball socket on windshield wiper link may be out of tolerance, resulting in disengagement from wiper motor drive under load; also, wiper arm retaining nut could be inadequately tightened, allowing wiper to slip and/or stop functioning. **1998-99:** If exposed to moisture, two connectors could corrode; over time, fuel pump will not receive enough current to operate, causing engine to stall. **1998-99:** If pin tension in fuel pump's ground connector is poor, or bolt securing connector to floor is not tightened sufficiently, poor connection as pump operates can create heat, which in turn increases resistance; eventually, pump may fail to operate, causing engine to stall. **1999:** Ball socket on windshield wiper link may be out of tolerance, resulting in link disengaging under load. Also, wiper arm retaining nut could be inadequately tightened. **1998-99:** A valve on the fuel-filler assembly could cause fuel shut-off before the tank reaches 95 percent capacity.

1995-01 KIA SPORTAGE

FOR Maneuverability • Visibility • Instruments/controls

AGAINST Acceleration (4-door) • Ride • Noise • Limited shift-on-the-fly 4WD • Interior materials

EVALUATION Handling with the Sportage wagon or convertible is a pleasant surprise, not unlike that of a good sporty small sedan. For its size, Sportage has a fairly wide track (width between wheels on the same axle), so stability in tight turns is good and body lean surprisingly modest. Springing is tight, though, so the ride is more "trucky" than car-like, with moderate bounce and pitch on patchy pavement. Even the

1997 Kia Sportage

manual-shift Sportage wagon feels sluggish in routine driving, especially when going up steep grades. Acceleration is even worse with the optional automatic transmission. Passing power ranks as adequate. Noise levels are fairly high from all sources, even in gentle highway cruising. The engine is exceptionally loud and gruff when worked even moderately hard. A new Sportage averaged 19 mpg in 4-wheel drive with a 5-speed, which was slightly less than a CR-V or RAV4 wagon. The wagon is shorter than most compact SUVs, yet provides adequate room for four adults. Head clearance is particularly good, even for 6-footers, though rear leg and knee space are limited. Easy entry/exit is another plus, thanks to rather large doors and relatively low step-in height. The convertible's back seat is best left to children. The driver enjoys a well-arranged dashboard with carlike instruments and controls, plus a clear view to all quarters—although the available outside spare tire gets in the way when looking directly aft. At least that outside spare frees up useful cargo room inside, and the wagon's rear seat easily folds to increase the space. Actually, getting decent cargo space in either body style requires folding of the back seat.

VALUE Looked at in terms of long-term value, a CR-V or RAV4 would be the better choice. Those two also are more pleasant to drive and better built. Worse yet, Kia has ranked near the bottom of the list in consumer surveys of reliability and customer satisfaction.

SPECIFICATIONS

	2-door conv.	4-door wagon
Wheelbase, in.	92.9	104.4
Overall length, in.	148.0-156.4	159.4-170.3
Overall width, in.	68.1	68.1
Overall height, in.	65.0	65.2
Curb weight, lbs.	3108	3280
Cargo volume, cu. ft.	39.4	55.4
Fuel capacity, gals.	14.0	15.8
Seating capacity	4	5
Front head room, in.	39.6	39.6
Max. front leg room, in.	44.5	44.5
Rear head room, in.	38.2	37.8
Min. rear leg room, in.	31.0	31.1

Powertrain layout: longitudinal front-engine/rear- or 4-wheel drive

ENGINES

	ohc I4	dohc I4
Size, liters/cu. in.	2.0/122	2.0/122
Horsepower	94	130
Torque (lbs./ft.)	114	127
EPA city/highway mpg		
5-speed OD manual	19/23	19/23
4-speed OD automatic		19/22
City/highway mpg (as tested)		
5-speed OD manual		19.0

Built in South Korea

RETAIL PRICES

	GOOD	AVERAGE	POOR
1995 Sportage 2WD wagon	$3,000-3,800	$2,300-3,100	$700-1,100
1995 Sportage 4WD wagon	4,000-4,800	3,200-4,000	1,200-1,700
1996 Sportage 2WD wagon	4,000-4,800	3,300-4,000	1,200-1,700
1996 Sportage 4WD wagon	5,000-5,800	4,200-5,000	1,800-2,300
1997 Sportage 2WD wagon	5,200-6,000	4,500-5,200	2,200-2,600
1997 Sportage 4WD wagon	6,200-7,100	5,400-6,300	2,700-3,300
1998 Sportage 2WD wagon	6,500-7,500	5,700-6,600	2,800-3,400
1998 Sportage 4WD wagon	7,500-8,500	6,600-7,500	3,500-4,100
1998 Sportage 2WD conv.	6,200-7,200	5,400-6,300	2,700-3,300
1998 Sportage 4WD conv.	7,000-8,000	6,200-7,100	3,200-3,800
1999 Sportage 2WD wagon	7,700-8,700	6,800-7,700	3,500-4,100
1999 Sportage 4WD wagon	8,600-9,600	7,600-8,600	4,100-4,800
1999 Sportage 2WD conv.	7,000-8,000	6,000-7,000	3,100-3,600
1999 Sportage 4WD conv.	$8,000-9,000	$7,000-8,000	$3,900-4,500
2000 Sportage 2WD wagon	9,000-10,000	8,000-9,000	4,400-5,000
2000 Sportage 4WD wagon	10,000-11,000	9,000-10,000	5,000-5,700
2000 Sportage 2WD conv.	8,000-9,000	7,000-8,000	3,800-4,500
2000 Sportage 4WD conv.	9,000-10,000	8,000-9,000	4,400-5,000
2001 Sportage 2WD wagon	10,500-11,800	9,500-10,500	—
2001 Sportage 4WD wagon	11,500-13,000	10,500-11,800	—
2001 Sportage 2WD conv.	9,000-10,000	8,000-9,000	—
2001 Sportage 4WD conv.	10,000-11,000	9,000-10,000	—

AVERAGE REPLACEMENT COSTS

A/C Compressor	$375	Clutch, Pressure Plate, Bearing	800
Alternator	315	Exhaust System	220
Automatic Transmission or Transaxle	600	Radiator	300
Brakes	270	Shocks and/or Struts	190
Timing Chain or Belt	200	Universal Joints	185

TROUBLE SPOTS

• **Transmission leak.** Some 1995 Sportage models with automatic transmissions may be experiencing fluid leaks from the automatic transmission cooler line. The fluid may be leaking through small cracks in the flared end of the cooler lines at the transmission which develops because of cooler line vibration (1995)

• **Dashboard lights.** The ABS and Brake warning lights are activated due to a faulty brake proportioning valve and may not set a trouble code. (1995)

• **Wipers.** The wiper blades come off the pivots on the arms. (1998)

RECALL HISTORY

1995: Nuts attaching rear axle bearing oil seal retainers and brake backing plates may be undertorqued, causing units to loosen or fall off; could cause oil leakage, rear brake damage, or separation of rear wheel/axleshaft from vehicle. **1996 EX:** Accelerator pedal assembly could bind or stick. **1996-97:** Rear hatch lock microswitch can malfunction, causing power door locks to unlock inadvertently. **1997-99:** Wires at C123 and C124 connectors can be put under tension by engine movement, loosening them, which can cause engine stalling. **1998-99 w/o antilock braking:** Steering intermediate shaft coupling can contact hydraulic brake pipe, causing fluid leakage.

1994-98 LAND ROVER DISCOVERY

1994 Land Rover Discovery

FOR Antilock brakes • Ride

AGAINST Fuel economy • Noise • Entry/exit • Price

EVALUATION Acceleration is fairly lively in a Discovery, but no quicker than the 6-cylinder Jeep Grand Cherokee or Ford Explorer. Gas mileage is nothing to brag about. We averaged just 13 mpg in a blend of expressway and suburban driving. Expect plenty of road noise and mechanical sounds, with constant gear whining. The Discovery's firm suspension manages to absorb most bumps smartly and does a good job of reducing body lean. Even so, it leans more in turns than a Grand Cherokee or Explorer, and the steering demands too much muscle at low speeds. Tall ground clearance is an advantage when off-road, but a hindrance to climbing aboard or exiting, and you tend to drive with your shoulder shoved against the door. Adults will feel comfortable in Discovery's first two rows of seats, but the jump seats are best left to children. Gauges are easy to see and well lit at night. Cargo space is abundant. As for assembly quality, our test vehicles have felt rock-solid.

VALUE Range Rover/Land Rover is perceived to be a luxury vehicle by some people, but that's definitely not the case with a Discovery. Interiors are surprisingly basic, unless the vehicle is fitted with leather upholstery. Before spending a wad of money on this vehicle, look at upscale versions of the Ford Explorer and Jeep Grand Cherokee.

SPECIFICATIONS

	4-door wagon
Wheelbase, in.	100.0
Overall length, in.	178.7
Overall width, in.	70.6
Overall height, in.	77.4
Curb weight, lbs.	4465
Cargo volume, cu. ft.	69.8
Fuel capacity, gals.	23.4
Seating capacity	7
Front head room, in.	37.4
Max. front leg room, in.	38.5
Rear head room, in.	39.2
Min. rear leg room, in.	36.3

Powertrain layout: longitudinal front-engine/4-wheel drive

ENGINES

	ohv V8
Size, liters/cu. in.	4.0/241
Horsepower	182
Torque (lbs./ft.)	233

EPA city/highway mpg

5-speed OD manual	12/16
4-speed OD automatic	12/16

City/highway mpg (as tested)

4-speed OD automatic	12.6

Built in England

RETAIL PRICES

	GOOD	AVERAGE	POOR
1994 Discovery	$7,500-8,500	$6,500-7,500	$3,500-4,200
1995 Discovery	9,000-11,000	8,000-10,000	4,500-5,800
1996 Discovery	11,000-13,000	10,000-12,000	6,000-7,400
1997 Discovery	13,500-15,500	12,000-14,000	8,000-9,500
1998 Discovery	17,000-19,000	15,500-17,500	11,000-12,500

AVERAGE REPLACEMENT COSTS

A/C Compressor	$1,390	Clutch, Pressure Plate, Bearing	1,210
Alternator	635	Constant Velocity Joints	235
Automatic Transmission or Transaxle	3,000	Exhaust System	440
Brakes	390	Radiator	820
Shocks and/or Struts	680	Timing Chain or Belt	840

TROUBLE SPOTS

• **Hard starting.** Starting difficulty in cold weather has been traced to oil that is too thick and a computer PROM with the wrong calibration. (1994-95)

• **Climate control.** The electrical connector for the rear defroster can short to the center high mount stop lamp (CHMSL) and blow a fuse. When this happens, the transmission cannot be shifted out of park. (All)

• **Transaxle leak.** The front axle stub seals and the rear axle hub seals tend to leak. (1994-96)

• **Doors.** The sound insulation pads in the doors can shift and plug the water drain holes which could lead to rust through. (All)

• **Sunroof/moonroof.** The sunroof may leak and water may drip from the latch or motor or front edge. (1994-96)

• **Vehicle shake.** The vehicle may vibrate when accelerating, especially between 30-40 mph due to a bad harmonic balancer or engine mount. (1994-95)

RECALL HISTORY

1994-98: Chafing of cruise-control wire against steering wheel coupler can cause insulation to fail; electrical grounding could then cause driver's airbag to deploy. **1995:** Wrong-sized driveshaft nuts on some vehicles can loosen, ultimately causing one or both driveshafts to disconnect. **1995-96:** Right front door may not latch fully, causing door to "bounce" back off seals; could open while vehicle is moving.

1990-96 LEXUS ES 250/300

FOR Acceleration • Antilock brakes • Ride/handling • Passenger and cargo room

AGAINST Road noise (ES 250) • Automatic transmission performance (ES 250) • Fuel economy • Rear visibility

1990 Lexus ES 250

EVALUATION The ES 250 has a comfortable ride, soaking up bumps with little notice. It also tends to display good control and stability at high speed, while the standard antilock brakes provide strong, safe stops with good control. Tire whine and road noise are intrusive, however. The ES 250 also provides a bright, airy interior with tall windows, which give the driver excellent visibility, though it's hard to see the trunk while backing up. Leg room is generous both front and back, but head room is about average. More distinctive styling and a 3.0-liter V6 gave the rebadged ES 300 both the extra size and power it needed. The 300 provides outstanding responsiveness and handling. The same smooth and quiet ride that has become a Lexus hallmark is quite evident in the ES 300. However, body roll is noticeable and the steering is on the light side. While not quite up to full European standards in the suspension or steering departments, the ride and handling should not be an issue with most buyers. Except in straight highway driving, we got under 20 mpg in an ES 300, which demands premium fuel. On the plus side, the ES 300 offers more passenger space than its compact external dimensions suggest. Leg room and head room are generous, even with the optional sunroof. Drivers enjoy a comfortably upright stance ahead of a tilt steering wheel and an attractive, well-arranged dashboard that mimics the panel design of the big LS 400. Some rear-seat space is sacrificed, however, for the sake of trunk room, which is more than adequate.

VALUE Much more than a glorified Camry, the ES 250/300 helped Lexus maintain a solid image in the luxury car market. Particularly in ES 300 form, this Lexus feels and behaves like the costlier, more luxurious automobile that it is.

SPECIFICATIONS

	4-door sedan	4-door sedan
Wheelbase, in.	102.4	103.1
Overall length, in.	183.1	187.8
Overall width, in.	66.9	70.0
Overall height, in.	53.1	53.9
Curb weight, lbs.	3164	3362
Cargo volume, cu. ft.	13.1	14.3
Fuel capacity, gals.	15.9	18.5
Seating capacity	5	5
Front head room, in.	37.8	37.8
Max. front leg room, in.	42.9	43.5
Rear head room, in.	36.6	36.6
Min. rear leg room, in.	32.3	33.1

Powertrain layout: transverse front-engine/front-wheel drive

ENGINES

	dohc V6	dohc V6	dohc V6
Size, liters/cu. in.	2.5/153	3.0/181	3.0/181
Horsepower	156	185	188
Torque (lbs./ft.)	160	195	203

EPA city/highway mpg

5-speed OD manual	19/26	18/24	
4-speed OD automatic	19/25	18/23	18/24

City/highway mpg (as tested)

5-speed OD manual	22.7		
4-speed OD automatic		19.5	19.3

Built in Japan

RETAIL PRICES

	GOOD	AVERAGE	POOR
1990 ES 250	$2,700-3,400	$2,100-2,700	$600-900
1991 ES 250	3,500-4,200	2,800-3,500	1,000-1,400
1992 ES 300	5,000-5,800	4,300-5,000	2,000-2,400
1993 ES 300	7,000-7,800	6,200-7,000	3,300-3,800
1994 ES 300	9,000-10,000	8,000-9,000	4,500-5,200
1995 ES 300	11,000-12,000	10,000-11,000	6,000-6,700

	GOOD	AVERAGE	POOR
1996 ES 300	$13,000-14,500	$11,800-13,000	$7,500-8,500

AVERAGE REPLACEMENT COSTS

A/C Compressor	$905	Clutch, Pressure Plate,	
Alternator	370	Bearing	670
Automatic Transmission or		Constant Velocity Joints	700
Transaxle	1,410	Exhaust System	435
Brakes	195	Shocks and/or Struts	870
Radiator	640	Timing Chain or Belt	190

TROUBLE SPOTS

• **Vehicle noise.** A new, self-lubricating stabilizer bar bushing will be installed if the original rear bushings squeak. (ES 300)

• **Transmission leak.** Automatic transmission fluid may leak from a casting knock hole or a bolt hole on the A51E transmission. (1994)

• **Climate control.** Because of an intermittent open condition in the temperature sensor circuit the ambient temperature display shows -22°F and the climate control misbehaves. The display will not change until the fuse for the air conditioning control unit is removed briefly. (1990-95)

• **Engine noise.** If a thumping noise comes from the engine during low speeds, it might require a larger main bearing on the No. 1 journal of the crankshaft. (1991)

• **Fuel gauge.** If the fuel gauge is inaccurate, a revised gauge will be installed to stabilize the indicator needle. (1990-92)

• **Water pump.** The water pump seals may leak. (1994-95)

RECALL HISTORY

1994-96 ES 300: Steering wheel set nut may not have been sufficiently tightened; could result in vibration and looseness in steering wheel, and ultimate separation.

1997-01 LEXUS ES 300

1997 Lexus ES 300

FOR Acceleration • Ride • Quietness • Passenger and cargo room • Build quality

AGAINST Rear visibility • Price

EVALUATION Acceleration is more than adequate. We timed an ES 300 at 7.6 seconds, accelerating from a standstill to 60 mph. Better yet, the engine is silent at idle speed, and almost silkily silent when rolling along under power. Quietness, in fact, might be this Lexus's single greatest asset. Wind rush is no more than a whisper at highway speeds, and road noise rarely amounts to more than a muted hum. This is one truly quiet sedan. Gas mileage isn't bad. Even hard city driving failed to push our overall figure below 20 mpg, though premium fuel is required. Steering is firmer than before, and quick, but lacks some road feel. In the same way, the Lexus suspension furnishes capable handling and offers more isolation from bumps and holes than a BMW 3-Series or Mercedes-Benz C-Class, yet the ES 300 is not as nimble as those competitors. Braking is swift and sure, except for marked nosedive in "panic" stops. The additional 1.3 inches of rear leg room is barely noticeable, but the Lexus interior is as inviting for four adults as any luxury automobile's. Six-footers can sit comfortably in tandem, although the back-seat occupants must ride with knees raised and have little toe room beneath the front seats. Visibility is fine all around, except that the high parcel shelf and narrow rear window eliminate any view of the trunk and rear corners while backing up. The driving position is excellent, with clear gauges, and handy switchgear. Cargo room shrunk by 1.3 cubic feet with the redesign, but the trunk still qualifies as roomy and usefully shaped. Workmanship is first-rate.

VALUE The ES 300 does just about everything a sedan of its class should, and does it very well. For shoppers who value comfort and elegance over sporty road manners, there's no better near-luxury sedan on the market.

SPECIFICATIONS

	4-door sedan
Wheelbase, in.	105.1
Overall length, in.	190.2
Overall width, in.	70.5
Overall height, in.	54.9
Curb weight, lbs.	3296
Cargo volume, cu. ft.	13.0
Fuel capacity, gals.	18.5
Seating capacity	5
Front head room, in.	38.0
Max. front leg room, in.	43.5
Rear head room, in.	36.2
Min. rear leg room, in.	34.4

Powertrain layout: transverse front-engine/front-wheel drive

ENGINES

	dohc V6
Size, liters/cu. in.	3.0/181
Horsepower	200-210
Torque (lbs./ft.)	214-220

EPA city/highway mpg

4-speed OD automatic	19/26

City/highway mpg (as tested)

4-speed OD automatic	20.5

Built in Japan

RETAIL PRICES	GOOD	AVERAGE	POOR
1997 ES 300	$16,000-17,000	$15,000-16,000	$10,500-11,200
1998 ES 300	18,000-19,500	16,800-18,000	11,800-12,700
1999 ES 300	20,500-22,000	19,000-20,500	14,000-15,000
2000 ES 300	23,000-25,000	21,500-23,500	16,000-17,500
2001 ES 300	25,500-27,500	24,000-26,000	—

AVERAGE REPLACEMENT COSTS

A/C Compressor	$990	Clutch, Pressure Plate,	
Alternator	410	Bearing	680
Automatic Transmission or		Constant Velocity Joints	710
Transaxle	1,410	Exhaust System	560
Brakes	205	Radiator	660
Shocks and/or Struts	890	Timing Chain or Belt	210

TROUBLE SPOTS

• **Dashboard lights.** A defective EVAP (evaporative emissions control) system charcoal canister causes the check engine light to glow. Both new car and emissions controls warranties apply. (1997-98)

• **Sunroof/moonroof.** Moonroof makes a throbbing noise when open unless revised deflector has been installed. (1997-98)

• **Steering noise.** Steering rack is noisy on early models. (1997)

• **Blower motor.** The blower motor fails when water from the windshield leaks past a seal and into the motor. (1997)

• **Electrical problem.** Using the wrong size cigar lighter or accessory plug causes the fuse to blow or damages the socket. (1997-98)

RECALL HISTORY

1997: In extreme cold, accumulated moisture can temporarily freeze in brake vacuum hose. **1997-98:** Steering wheel set nut may not have been sufficiently tightened; could result in vibration and looseness in steering wheel, and ultimate separation.

1999-01 LEXUS RX 300

FOR Ride • Passenger and cargo room • Build quality

AGAINST Audio and climate controls • Wind noise

EVALUATION Whether it has front-drive or all-wheel drive, an RX 300 delivers snappy off-the-line acceleration and has plenty of power throughout the speed range. The V6 is a model of refinement, augmented by flawless transmission behavior—though some early units exhibited uneven shifting until warmed up. An early 2WD model did 0-60 mph in 8.2 seconds and averaged 16.3 mpg—short of EPA estimates but better than most midsize SUVs. All-wheel drive doesn't slow it down much. An RX 300 feels like no other SUV—more like a luxury car or a minivan, unlike the posh but truck-flavored Mercedes M-Class. The ride is impressive, smothering large and small bumps with ease—better than

2000 Lexus RX 300

many cars and less bouncy than most SUVs on scalloped freeways. An RX 300 corners with fine stability and little body lean for an SUV, helped by responsive steering. Still, it's too big and heavy to be a truly sporty handler. Routine braking is good, though the pedal might be a trifle spongy. Some tire noise occurs on coarse pavement, but the RX 300 is pleasingly quiet overall—except with the sunroof open, when wind rushes past with a mighty roar. Entry/exit is a simple matter of stepping in and out. Five adults can ride without complaint and the center-rear position matches the comfort of the supportive outboard seats. The driver sits commandingly high, but roof pillars may be too thick for best outward vision. The tilt steering wheel does not adjust to suit everyone. Though it works well enough, the video-screen display for climate and audio settings is unorthodox and a little gimmicky. Other instruments and controls are attractively arranged, large, and functional. Conversion of the back seat is convenient, but the load floor isn't so long with seats up, and liftover is relatively high.

VALUE Essentially a "suburban utility vehicle" rather than a traditional SUV, the RX 300 is posh, refined, roomy, and pleasant to drive. Strong demand keeps prices high, but we recommend it highly.

SPECIFICATIONS

	4-door wagon
Wheelbase, in.	103.0
Overall length, in.	180.1
Overall width, in.	71.5
Overall height, in.	65.7
Curb weight, lbs.	3692
Cargo volume, cu. ft.	75.0
Fuel capacity, gals.	17.2
Seating capacity	5
Front head room, in.	39.5
Max. front leg room, in.	40.7
Rear head room, in.	39.2
Min. rear leg room, in.	36.4

Powertrain layout: transverse front-engine/front- or all-wheel drive

ENGINES

	dohc V6
Size, liters/cu. in.	3.0/183
Horsepower	220
Torque (lbs./ft.)	222

EPA city/highway mpg

4-speed OD automatic	19/24

City/highway mpg (as tested)

4-speed OD automatic	16.3

Built in Japan

RETAIL PRICES

	GOOD	AVERAGE	POOR
1999 RX 300	$24,500-27,000	$23,500-25,800	$19,500-20,500
2000 RX 300	27,000-29,500	25,800-28,300	21,500-23,000
2001 RX 300	30,000-33,000	28,500-31,500	—

AVERAGE REPLACEMENT COSTS

A/C Compressor	$555	Constant Velocity Joints	915
Alternator	310	Exhaust System	550
Automatic Transmission or Transaxle	955	Radiator	600
		Shocks and/or Struts	350
Brakes	380	Timing Chain or Belt	425

TROUBLE SPOTS

• **Exhaust system.** A booming noise from the exhaust system is corrected

by installing a damper weight. (1999)

• **Wind noise.** A throbbing wind noise from the moon roof is due to the location of the luggage rack cross bars. Repositioning them may reduce the sound. (1999)

• **Audio system.** Noises from the speakers (Nakamichi unit) can be corrected by exchanging the amplifiers under warranty. (1999)

RECALL HISTORY

1999: Headlights and taillights may not automatically illuminate in low ambient light, when headlight switch is placed in "Auto" position. **1999 w/optional traction control:** If one of the dual brake lines fails and driver applies brake, vehicle will feel unstable compared to vehicles with proper brake distribution.

1992-00 LEXUS SC 300/400

1998 Lexus SC 400

FOR Acceleration • Steering/handling • Antilock brakes • Build quality

AGAINST Fuel economy • Rear-seat room • Cargo room • Road noise

EVALUATION Lexus claimed a 1998-99 SC 400 would accelerate to 60 mph in 6.6 seconds, versus 7.9 for the SC 300. Both rank as quick in our book. Transmission response ranks as silken. Body roll in tight turns is barely evident. Overall, the SC 400 is far more agile than expected from a car of its weight. The ride is supple, the suspension is a lot firmer than the LS 400's, but never harsh. We averaged 17.2 mpg in an SC 400, versus 18 mpg in an SC 300. Both engines use premium fuel. Wind and engine noise are nearly muted, but road noise is a lot more noticeable. Lexus promoted these coupes as 2+2s. With 6-footers up front, seats will likely be pushed far enough back to nearly eliminate leg room in the rear. Head room is skimpy in back but surprisingly good up front, though an inch or two of that space is eaten up by the optional moonroof. The trunk is quite small for a car of this size. Visibility is clear even to the rear corners, despite the fact that the driver sits relatively low. A wide range of seat and steering-wheel adjustments helps each driver find the ideal position. Entry/exit is easier than in most coupes, because of special hinges that push the doors slightly forward. Long doors still are clumsy, though, and entering the back seat is a tight squeeze—especially on the driver's side.

VALUE Undeniably expensive even with many years of service behind them, these coupes nevertheless rank near the top of our list of luxury sport models.

SPECIFICATIONS

	2-door coupe
Wheelbase, in.	105.9
Overall length, in.	191.1
Overall width, in.	70.5
Overall height, in.	52.4
Curb weight, lbs.	3506
Cargo volume, cu. ft.	9.3
Fuel capacity, gals.	20.6
Seating capacity	4
Front head room, in.	38.3
Max. front leg room, in.	44.1
Rear head room, in.	36.1
Min. rear leg room, in.	27.2

Powertrain layout: longitudinal front-engine/rear-wheel drive

ENGINES

	dohc I6	dohc V8	dohc V8
Size, liters/cu. in.	3.0/183	4.0/242	4.0/242
Horsepower	225	250-260	290-300
Torque (lbs./ft.)	210-220	260-270	300-310

EPA city/highway mpg

5-speed OD manual	19/24		
4-speed OD automatic	18/24	18/23	

	dohc I6	dohc V8	dohc V8
5-speed OD automatic			18/25
City/highway mpg (as tested)			
5-speed OD manual	18.0		
4-speed OD automatic		17.2	

Built in Japan

RETAIL PRICES

	GOOD	AVERAGE	POOR
1992 SC 300	$6,500-7,500	$5,700-6,500	$3,000-3,700
1992 SC 400	7,400-8,400	6,500-7,400	3,500-4,200
1993 SC 300	8,500-10,000	7,500-9,000	4,200-5,200
1993 SC 400	9,400-10,500	8,400-9,500	4,800-5,600
1994 SC 300	11,000-12,500	9,800-11,000	5,800-6,700
1994 SC 400	12,000-13,500	10,800-12,000	6,700-7,500
1995 SC 300	13,000-14,500	11,700-13,000	7,600-8,500
1995 SC 400	14,300-15,500	13,000-14,000	8,800-9,500
1996 SC 300	16,000-17,500	14,500-16,000	10,000-11,000
1996 SC 400	17,500-19,000	16,000-17,500	11,000-12,000
1997 SC 300	19,500-21,000	18,000-19,500	13,000-14,000
1997 SC 400	21,500-23,500	20,000-22,000	14,800-16,000
1998 SC 300	23,000-25,000	21,500-23,500	16,000-17,500
1998 SC 400	25,500-27,500	23,500-26,000	18,000-19,500
1999 SC 300	27,000-29,000	25,000-27,000	19,300-20,500
1999 SC 400	30,000-32,000	28,000-30,000	22,000-23,500
2000 SC 300	31,000-33,000	29,000-31,000	23,000-24,500
2000 SC 400	35,000-37,000	33,000-35,000	26,500-28,000

AVERAGE REPLACEMENT COSTS

A/C Compressor...........	$1,160	Constant Velocity Joints	1,240
Alternator......................	730	Exhaust System	970
Automatic Transmission or		Radiator........................	680
Transaxle	1,410	Shocks and/or Struts....	1,310
Brakes	210	Timing Chain or Belt.....	290

TROUBLE SPOTS

• **Dashboard lights.** A defective EVAP (evaporative emissions control) system charcoal canister causes the check engine light to glow. Both new car and emissions controls warranties apply. (1997-98)

• **Audio system.** Because the radio antenna is not properly grounded, weak AM stations have static whenever another electrical device, such as wipers or turn signals, are used. (1992-94)

• **Doors.** Defective hinges cause a popping noise when the front doors are opened. Revised hinges are available. (1992-94)

• **Suspension noise.** Popping, clunking, or rattling noises from the rear are often due to a loose retaining nut on the support. (1992-94)

• **Automatic transmission.** The car may not upshift, downshift, or may start in the wrong gear on electronically shifted transmissions due to a faulty ground circuit. (1992)

• **Keyless entry.** The screw that holds the battery cover in place on the key transmitter falls out. (1992-95)

RECALL HISTORY

1996-97 SC 400: Improper assembly of terminal for starter motor switch can cause a short circuit.

1995-01 LINCOLN CONTINENTAL

1996 Lincoln Continental

FOR Acceleration • Passenger and cargo room • Instruments/controls • Antilock brakes

AGAINST Fuel economy • Noise • Electronic steering and suspension • Climate controls

EVALUATION Helped by its new V8 engine, this Continental is a lot quicker, a bit more agile—and loaded with electronic gadgetry. In acceleration, the newly energetic Continental can match a Cadillac Seville SLS. At 16.3 mpg, gas mileage has not improved and premium fuel is recommended. Despite its multiple adjustments, Lincoln's high-tech electronic suspension/steering fails to succeed fully. High mode makes the steering stiffer, without increasing feel; Low mode leaves the steering rather light and vague. The suspension also works best in Normal, as the other two modes have little effect on absorption of bumps. Interior space is great. Occupants have plenty of leg space front and rear, while head room is adequate for 6-footers, even with the optional moonroof. Storage space is fine. The Continental's trunk is wide, deep, and long. Reflecting off a mirror above the instrument cluster, the dramatic virtual image gauges are strikingly bright at night, but hard to read in bright sunlight. Controls are plentiful, and most are handy, but climate controls and seat heaters are recessed into the dashboard and hard to reach.

VALUE Lincoln evidently attempted to make the Continental both a sports sedan and a traditional luxury car. It's not quite either, but worth a look anyway. Because sales have been tepid, used-car prices may be appealing.

SPECIFICATIONS

	4-door sedan
Wheelbase, in.	109.0
Overall length, in.	206.3
Overall width, in.	73.3
Overall height, in.	55.9
Curb weight, lbs.	3911
Cargo volume, cu. ft.	18.1
Fuel capacity, gals.	18.0
Seating capacity	6
Front head room, in.	39.1
Max. front leg room, in.	41.8
Rear head room, in.	39.0
Min. rear leg room, in.	39.2

Powertrain layout: transverse front-engine/front-wheel drive

ENGINES

	dohc V8
Size, liters/cu. in.	4.6/281
Horsepower	260-275
Torque (lbs./ft.)	265-275

EPA city/highway mpg

4-speed OD automatic..	17/25

City/highway mpg (as tested)

4-speed OD automatic..	16.3

Built in USA

RETAIL PRICES

	GOOD	AVERAGE	POOR
1995 Continental	$6,000-7,000	$5,200-6,100	$2,700-3,300
1996 Continental	8,000-9,000	7,200-8,000	4,100-4,700
1997 Continental	10,500-11,500	9,500-10,500	5,600-6,300
1998 Continental	13,500-14,700	12,500-13,500	8,500-9,200
1999 Continental	17,000-18,500	15,500-17,000	11,000-12,000
2000 Continental	21,000-22,500	19,500-21,000	14,500-15,500
2001 Continental	25,000-27,000	23,000-25,000	—

AVERAGE REPLACEMENT COSTS

A/C Compressor...........	$435	Constant Velocity Joints	470
Alternator......................	510	Exhaust System	540
Automatic Transmission or		Radiator........................	290
Transaxle	870	Shocks and/or Struts....	1,165
Brakes	320	Timing Chain or Belt.....	795

TROUBLE SPOTS

• **Air conditioner.** Air conditioner output may be low or nonexistent because of a problem with the compressor clutch. (1995)

• **Suspension noise.** Clunking from the front end may be due to premature wear of the sway bar links. (1995-97)

• **Hard starting.** The engine may be hard to start or may stall after hot soak due to the idle air control valve sticking (1995-96) or a poor connection at the crank position sensor. (1995-97)

• **Steering noise.** The steering grunts or groans after making right hand turns, requiring replacement of the steering gear. (1995-97)

RECALL HISTORY

1995-96: "Autolamp" control module may fail. **1996:** Vehicle can move even though indicator shows Park. **1998:** Text and/or graphics for headlamp aiming instructions, provided in owner guides, are not sufficiently clear. **1999:** Fuel rail crossover hose was damaged during assembly, allowing fuel leakage. **2000:** Due to incorrectly formed pin shaft in seatbelt retractor, switching mechanism could become nonfunctional in some circumstances, preventing seatbelt webbing from being extracted. **2000-01:** A switch located in the plastic cover of the wiper motor gear case could malfunction and overheat, potentially resulting in loss of wiper function or fire.

2000-01 LINCOLN LS

2000 Lincoln LS

FOR Acceleration (V8) • Ride/handling • Seat comfort

AGAINST Automatic transmission performance • Climate controls

EVALUATION European in flavor, the LS is the dynamic equal of some costly import sedans. Low-speed steering feel could be firmer, but an LS turns crisply, cornering with grippy precision and modest body lean. Highway stability is impressive even in gusty crosswinds. The optional Sport Package controls body motions better than the base suspension, yet the ride remains pleasantly supple. Acceleration with the V8 feels strong. A test LS reached 60 mph in 7.3 seconds. An automatic-transmission V6 takes 9.3 seconds, according to Lincoln—not outstanding, yet the car feels adequately powered except on steep inclines or when real passing punch is required. Lincoln's automatic transmission can delay in responding to throttle inputs, though not as much as the S-Type's, and is slow to kick down for passing. Overall shift smoothness isn't the best, especially compared with BMW and Audi automatics. Lincoln's manual gearbox also lags, with notchy shift action and indistinct clutch movement. A V8 LS averaged 16.3 mpg using premium fuel, while a manual-shift V6 got 19.6 mpg. Engine sounds are muted, but tire noise intrudes on some coarse surfaces, which also yields some minor body drumming. Braking is swift and sure, despite indecisive pedal action. Although the interior feels less cramped than the S-Type's, the practical limit is four adults. Head clearance is so-so, but rear leg space is good even behind tall front occupants. An all-button climate system is not so easy to use. Large mirrors offset visibility lost to thickish rear roof pillars. Inside storage is limited, and only small suitcases stand upright in the trunk, which lacks depth and has bulky hinges.

VALUE Highly capable and mannerly on the road, an LS delivers a lot of features for the money. In addition, few near-luxury rivals are available with a V8 engine. Though not perfect, marred by rather ordinary interior furnishings, the LS can easily be compared with cars that cost a lot more.

SPECIFICATIONS

	4-door sedan
Wheelbase, in.	114.5
Overall length, in.	193.9
Overall width, in.	73.2
Overall height, in.	57.2
Curb weight, lbs.	3593
Cargo volume, cu. ft.	13.5
Fuel capacity, gals.	18.1
Seating capacity	5
Front head room, in.	40.4
Max. front leg room, in.	42.6
Rear head room, in.	37.5
Min. rear leg room, in.	37.7

Powertrain layout: longitudinal front-engine/rear-wheel drive

ENGINES

	dohc V6	dohc V8
Size, liters/cu. in.	3.0/181	3.9/235
	dohc V6	dohc V8
Horsepower	210	252
Torque (lbs./ft.)	205	267
EPA city/highway mpg		
5-speed OD manual	18/25	
4-speed OD automatic	18/25	17/23
City/highway mpg (as tested)		
5-speed OD manual	19.6	
4-speed OD automatic		16.3

Built in USA

RETAIL PRICES

	GOOD	AVERAGE	POOR
2000 LS V6	$21,200-23,500	$20,200-22,000	$16,200-17,500
2000 LS V8	23,500-25,500	22,000-24,000	18,000-19,500
2001 LS V6	24,500-26,500	23,000-25,000	—
2001 LS V8	27,500-29,000	26,000-27,500	—

AVERAGE REPLACEMENT COSTS

A/C Compressor	$410	Clutch, Pressure Plate, Bearing	615
Alternator	385	Constant Velocity Joints	900
Automatic Transmission or Transaxle	1,095	Exhaust System	465
Brakes	345	Radiator	450
Shocks and/or Struts	1,975	Timing Chain or Belt	610

TROUBLE SPOTS

• **Vehicle noise.** A droning noise at highway speeds while in 5th gear was being corrected by replacing the half-shafts. (2000)

• **Engine misfire.** Poor engine performance or a no-start condition may be the result of a loose fuel hose clamp causing an internal leak. (2000)

• **Steering problems.** Replacement steering wheels (on cars shipped with the wrong wheel) may have been installed without sufficiently tightening the locking nut. (2000)

• **Windows.** The rear window regulator cable may break, making it impossible to open or close the window. (2000-01)

RECALL HISTORY

2000-01: Front suspension lower ball joints on some vehicles were not tightened to specifications and could loosen and, ultimately, result in fracture of ball joint stud.

1993-98 LINCOLN MARK VIII

1996 Lincoln Mark VIII

FOR Acceleration • Steering/handling • Antilock brakes

AGAINST Rear visibility • Fuel economy • Rear-seat room • Wet-weather traction

EVALUATION With its new 280-horsepower V8 (290 with the LSC), the Mark VIII is quick off the line and once above 15 mph, really flies. The engine is silky smooth, has a sporty growl in hard acceleration, and delivers outstanding passing power at highway speeds. However, we averaged just 17.9 mpg, with our highest reading being 20.1 mpg. When we tested this car on snow and ice, we were disappointed with the performance of the optional traction control system. The rear wheels spun readily in snow, making takeoffs slow and laborious. The rear-drive Mark VIII is as agile as the front-drive Cadillac Eldorado, but has a more supple suspension. Steering and braking are top notch. As with many sport coupes, interior space is not one of the Mark's strong points. Tall passengers don't have much head room, even without the optional moonroof. Rear leg room is also limited. Taking a closer look at the interior, the gauges on the sweeping 2-tier dash are clearly marked and controls are intuitive. Directly astern visibility is mediocre.

VALUE Despite its excellent drivetrain and smooth suspension, Mark VIII has failed to impress us when compared with the less-expensive Buick Riviera or more-refined Lexus SC 300/400.

SPECIFICATIONS

	2-door coupe
Wheelbase, in.	113.0
Overall length, in.	207.3
Overall width, in.	74.8
Overall height, in.	53.6
Curb weight, lbs.	3768
Cargo volume, cu. ft.	14.4
Fuel capacity, gals.	18.0
Seating capacity	5
Front head room, in.	38.1
Max. front leg room, in.	42.6
Rear head room, in.	37.5
Min. rear leg room, in.	32.5

Powertrain layout: longitudinal front-engine/rear-wheel drive

ENGINES

	dohc V8	dohc V8
Size, liters/cu. in.	4.6/281	4.6/281
Horsepower	280	290
Torque (lbs./ft.)	285	290
EPA city/highway mpg		
4-speed OD automatic	18/26	18/26
City/highway mpg (as tested)		
4-speed OD automatic	17.9	

Built in USA

RETAIL PRICES

	GOOD	AVERAGE	POOR
1993 Mark VIII	$4,000-4,800	$3,000-4,000	$1,400-1,800
1994 Mark VIII	5,500-6,500	4,600-5,500	2,200-2,700
1995 Mark VIII	7,500-8,500	6,500-7,500	3,500-4,200
1996 Mark VIII	10,000-11,000	9,000-10,000	5,300-6,000
1997 Mark VIII	12,500-13,700	11,500-12,500	7,000-7,700
1998 Mark VIII	15,000-16,500	13,500-15,000	9,000-9,800

AVERAGE REPLACEMENT COSTS

A/C Compressor	$400	Exhaust System	485
Alternator	455	Radiator	465
Automatic Transmission or Transaxle	720	Shocks and/or Struts	1,060
		Timing Chain or Belt	445
Brakes	305	Universal Joints	160

TROUBLE SPOTS

• **Odometer.** Because of a software problem, the odometer may quit registering after 65,531 miles. (1995)

• **Hard starting.** If the engine does not want to start or cranks for a long time then stalls, the idle air control valve may be sticking. (1995-96)

• **Blower motor.** Squeaking or chirping blower motors are the result of defective brush holders. (1993-94)

• **Alternator belt.** The drive belt tensioner pulley or idler pulley bearings are apt to make a squealing noise when the engine is started in cold weather. (1993-96)

• **Engine stalling.** The in-tank fuel delivery module may cause low or no fuel pressure. (1995)

• **Automatic transmission.** The transmission may slip and the engine may flare when the transmission shifts into fourth gear, which can often be traced to a bad TR/MLP sensor. (1993-95)

• **Automatic transmission.** Transmission shudder or vibration under light acceleration or when shifting between third and fourth gear above 35 mph can be fixed by replacing the transmission fluid with Mercon® fluid. (1992-94)

RECALL HISTORY

1993-94: Headlights can flash intermittently as a result of a circuit-breaker opening.

1998-01 LINCOLN NAVIGATOR

FOR Passenger room • Cargo room • Instruments/controls • Standard antilock braking

AGAINST Fuel economy • Entry/exit • Maneuverability

2000 Lincoln Navigator

EVALUATION

See the 1998-01 Ford Expedition.

VALUE

See the 1998-01 Ford Expedition.

SPECIFICATIONS

	4-door wagon
Wheelbase, in.	119.1
Overall length, in.	204.8
Overall width, in.	79.9
Overall height, in.	76.7
Curb weight, lbs.	5667
Cargo volume, cu. ft.	116.4
Fuel capacity, gals.	30.0
Seating capacity	7/8
Front head room, in.	39.8
Max. front leg room, in.	41.0
Rear head room, in.	39.8
Min. rear leg room, in.	39.7

Powertrain layout: longitudinal front-engine/rear- or 4-wheel drive

ENGINES

	ohc V8	dohc V8
Size, liters/cu. in.	5.4/320	5.4/330
Horsepower	230-260	300
Torque (lbs./ft.)	325-345	355-360
EPA city/highway mpg		
4-speed OD automatic	13/17	13/18
City/highway mpg (as tested)		
4-speed OD automatic	12.0	12.5

Built in USA

RETAIL PRICES

	GOOD	AVERAGE	POOR
1998 Navigator 2WD	$20,000-21,500	$18,500-20,000	$13,500-14,500
1998 Navigator 4WD	21,500-23,000	20,000-21,500	14,800-15,800
1999 Navigator 2WD	23,000-24,500	21,500-23,000	16,000-17,000
1999 Navigator 4WD	25,000-26,500	23,500-25,000	18,000-19,000
2000 Navigator 2WD	26,500-28,000	25,000-26,500	19,300-20,500
2000 Navigator 4WD	28,500-30,000	27,000-28,500	21,000-22,000
2001 Navigator 2WD	31,000-33,000	29,500-31,000	—
2001 Navigator 4WD	33,000-35,000	31,000-33,000	—

AVERAGE REPLACEMENT COSTS

See the 1998-01 Ford Expedition.

TROUBLE SPOTS

See the 1998-01 Ford Expedition.

RECALL HISTORY

1998: Main battery cable can contact body panel in trunk, resulting in damage to cable insulation that could lead to short circuit, loss of electrical supply, or fire. **1998:** Certain off-lease vehicles, Canadian in origin but sold in the U.S., have daytime running lights that do not meet U.S. specifications. **1998:** Text and/or graphics for headlamp aiming instructions, provided in owner guides, are not sufficiently clear. **1998-00:** Bolts that attach trailer hitch assembly to frame could lose their clamp load; hitch could then separate from vehicle. **1999:** Retainer clip that holds master cylinder pushrod to brake pedal arm may be missing or partially installed, causing increased stopping distances. **1999:** Fuel line assemblies on some vehicles may have been damaged by supplier during manufacture, allowing leakage. **1999 w/4WD and 17-inch chrome steel wheels:** Clamp load can be lost on wheel lugs, due to insufficient wheel contact area with hub; in some cases, contact area can deform, resulting in loss of lug nut torque that can cause vibration or separation of wheel/tire from vehicle. **2000-01:** Some of the owner's manuals for these vehicles are missing instructions for properly attaching a child restraint system. **2000-01:** A switch located in the plastic cover of the wiper motor gear case could malfunction and overheat, potentially resulting in loss of wiper function or fire. **2001:** Driver's and/or outboard front passenger's seatbelt buckle may not fully latch. In the event of a crash, the restraint system may not provide adequate occupant protection.

1990-97 LINCOLN TOWN CAR

1996 Lincoln Town Car

FOR Antilock brakes (optional) • Passenger and cargo room

AGAINST Fuel economy • Maneuverability • Rear visibility

EVALUATION Despite its new V8 engine, Town Car can hardly be classified as a sprinter, given the fact it tips scales at over two tons, but once underway there's strong acceleration and passing power. One drawback to brisk acceleration seems to be the 4-speed automatic, which is slow to downshift at times. As for economy, we've averaged an unimpessive 17 mpg in city/expressway driving. New suspension and further upgrades designed to improve the car's handling arrive in the form of a Ride Control Package. The car retains much of its penchant for excessive body roll and the kind of pillowy ride characteristics preferred by domestic luxury car buyers. If you're not particular about handling, and need a spacious car, you've come to the right place. The Town Car is wide enough to accommodate six adults comfortably, while the large doors make entry and exit maneuvers effortless. For long trips, you can count on the spacious 22.3-cubic foot trunk to hold nearly all your worldly goods.Most controls are mounted high on the dashboard where they're easy to see and reach while driving. Though the power window, door lock, and mirror controls are grouped on the driver's door, they aren't backlit at night. Huge rear roof pillars hinder the view while backing up.

VALUE Big sedans like the Town Car and its main rival, the Cadillac Fleetwood, are plush, quiet, and comfortable. However, newer luxury models are now available that offer comparable luxury, more agility, and better overall economy.

SPECIFICATIONS

	4-door sedan
Wheelbase, in.	117.4
Overall length, in.	218.9
Overall width, in.	76.7
Overall height, in.	56.9
Curb weight, lbs.	4040
Cargo volume, cu. ft.	22.3
Fuel capacity, gals.	18.0
Seating capacity	6
Front head room, in.	39.1
Max. front leg room, in.	42.5
Rear head room, in.	38.0
Min. rear leg room, in.	41.1

Powertrain layout: longitudinal front-engine/rear-wheel drive

ENGINES

	ohv V8	ohc V8	ohc V8
Size, liters/cu. in.	5.0/302	4.6/281	4.6/281
Horsepower	150	190	210
Torque (lbs./ft.)	270	260-265	270-275
EPA city/highway mpg			
4-speed OD automatic	17/24	17/25	17/25

	ohv V8	ohc V8	ohc V8
City/highway mpg (as tested)			
4-speed OD automatic	16.6		17.0

Built in USA

RETAIL PRICES

	GOOD	AVERAGE	POOR
1990 Town Car	$2,300-2,900	$1,700-2,200	$300-600
1991 Town Car	2,800-3,500	2,200-2,800	600-900
1992 Town Car	3,500-4,200	2,800-3,500	900-1,200
1993 Town Car	4,200-5,000	3,500-4,200	1,400-1,800
1994 Town Car	5,000-6,000	4,200-5,100	1,800-2,200
1995 Town Car	7,000-8,300	6,200-7,300	3,000-3,700
1996 Town Car	9,000-11,000	8,000-10,000	4,300-5,300
1997 Town Car	11,500-13,000	10,200-11,500	6,000-6,800

AVERAGE REPLACEMENT COSTS

A/C Compressor	$390	Constant Velocity Joints	140
Alternator	375	Exhaust System	690
Automatic Transmission or Transaxle	700	Shocks and/or Struts	365
Brakes	265	Timing Chain or Belt	330

TROUBLE SPOTS

• **Vehicle noise.** A broken gusset or weld separation at the frame crossmember causes a rattle from the rear or the car. (1990-92)

• **Vehicle noise.** A chattering noise that can be felt coming from the rear during tight turns after highway driving is caused by a lack of friction modifier or over-shimming of the clutch packs in the Traction-Lok differential. (1990-96)

• **Air springs.** Air springs are prone to leaks caused by the bag rubbing against the axle or control arm. (Any so-equipped)

• **Hard starting.** If the engine does not want to start or cranks for a long time then stalls, the idle air control valve may be sticking. (1996)

• **Hard starting.** The connector at the starter solenoid tends to corrode resulting in a "no-crank" condition. (1991-94)

• **Alternator belt.** The drive belt tensioner pulley or idler pulley bearings are apt to make a squealing noise when the engine is started in cold weather. (1993-96)

• **Oil leak.** The oil filter balloons and leaks because the oil pump relief valve sticks. (1991-94)

• **Automatic transmission.** The transmission may slip and the engine may flare when the transmission shifts into fourth gear, which can often be traced to a bad TR/MLP sensor. (1992-95)

• **Automatic transmission.** Transmission shudder or vibration can be caused by improper transmission fluid. It requires that the transmission fluid (including fluid in the torque converter) be changed and that only Mercon® fluid be used. (1992-94)

RECALL HISTORY

1990-91 on cars in 25 states: corrosion of hood latch striker causes detachment, so hood can open unexpectedly. **1990-97 police/fleet/natural gas:** Bearing within lower ball joint can weaken slowly during use and eventually crack; could result in separation, allowing control arm to drop to the ground. **1991:** Distorted fuel lines may contact steering-column universal joint and be damaged. **1991-92:** Secondary hood latch may not engage; if primary latch releases when car is moving, hood could fly up. **1992-93:** Speed-control deactivation switch can develop short that could result in underhood fire, whether or not engine is running. **1994:** Brake pedal push rod retainer may be missing or improperly installed, which can cause disengagement and loss of braking. **1994:** Nuts and bolts that attach rear brake adapter to axle housing flange can loosen and separate, allowing damage to ABS sensor, hydraulic line, and parking brake cable. **1995:** Some passenger-side airbags may not inflate properly; also, igniter cap can separate, releasing hot gases. **1995:** Seal between fuel filler pipe and tank may not be fully cured, which could allow fuel to leak. **1995-96 fleet cars only:** Corrosion of inadequately lubricated Pitman arms can cause abnormal wear of joint, resulting in separation. **1995-97:** Passenger vehicles that have had the driver's airbag module replaced after April 5, 2000 may have modules with inflators that lack insufficient welds and may prevent proper inflation of the airbag. **1996:** Driver's door, when closed only to secondary latched position, may not sustain the specified 1000-pound transverse load. **1996:** Wrong parts may have been used to service seatbelts with switchable retractor for child restraints. **1996-97:** Replacement seatbelts made by TRW and sold by Ford may not restrain occupant in a collision. **1997:** Driver's airbag module could stay in position during deployment, but leave the steering wheel cavity afterward.

1998-01 LINCOLN TOWN CAR

1998 Lincoln Town Car

FOR Passenger room • Cargo room • Quietness • Standard side airbags (1999-up)

AGAINST Fuel economy • Rear visibility

EVALUATION With a tad more horsepower and a little less weight than before, the latest Town Car moves off the line in a fairly spirited manner. Even so, acceleration cannot match that of a Northstar-equipped Cadillac DeVille. A Cartier edition with the stronger engine took a somewhat leisurely 9.5 seconds to reach 60 mph. The reworked automatic transmission still upshifts seamlessly, but now it also downshifts more promptly for passing—though the latter task sometimes demands a hefty shove on the gas pedal. Ride quality remains smooth—velvety and absorbent, in fact—but the Town Car is now less floaty over pavement irregularities and more controlled than in the past, thanks to a revised suspension. Minor wheel pattering at speed can be expected, however, on some freeway surfaces. Handling also has improved, so the big sedan is no longer as wallowy and boatlike as Town Cars of the past. Less body roll in turns and sharper steering response help it tolerate spirited driving—if not exactly encourage such exuberant behavior. Accommodations always were spacious. Even though the latest Town Car is a bit trimmer, interior room has not suffered. Large doors make it easy to get in and out of both the front and rear seats. Head room is generous all around. Leg room is good but not great, and the car isn't really wide enough to fit six adults without real squeezing. Quietness is another long-standing Town Car tradition. If anything, the new model is even more serene inside than its predecessors, with almost no road or wind noise intruding, and no more than a muted roar from the engine. Gauges now are analog (needle-type) rather than digital, and very legible. User-friendly climate and audio controls are easy to see, reach, and use. Outward visibility is compromised by thick side and rear roof pillars and a tall rear deck. Trunk room is down about 10 percent. That still leaves a lot of luggage space, though much of the volume is again within a deep center well—which can be a strain when you need to load and remove heavy objects. Workmanship on our test Cartier sedan was flawless, though materials felt less-expensive than in some rivals.

VALUE Lincoln's Town Car is the last remaining American-brand, rear-drive, full-size luxury sedan. So, potential buyers aren't overloaded with alternatives. Fortunately, the refined Town Car continues to offer the traditional luxury-car values of spaciousness and splendid riding isolation, as well as a load of comforts and conveniences. Although we give higher marks to the latest front-drive Cadillac DeVille as a domestically built luxury automobile, the Town Car is worth considering—and priced far below imported competitors.

SPECIFICATIONS

	4-door sedan	4-door sedan
Wheelbase, in.	117.7	123.7
Overall length, in.	215.3	221.3
Overall width, in.	78.2	78.2
Overall height, in.	58.0	58.0
Curb weight, lbs.	4015	4215
Cargo volume, cu. ft.	20.6	20.6
Fuel capacity, gals.	19.0	19.0
Seating capacity	6	6
Front head room, in.	39.2	39.3
Max. front leg room, in.	42.6	42.6
Rear head room, in.	37.5	37.6
Min. rear leg room, in.	41.1	47.1

The Lincoln Town Car L joined the lineup in 2000.

Powertrain layout: longitudinal front-engine/rear-wheel drive

ENGINES

	ohc V8	ohc V8
Size, liters/cu. in.	4.6/281	4.6/281
Horsepower	200-225	220-240
Torque (lbs./ft.)	265-275	275-285
EPA city/highway mpg		
4-speed OD automatic	17/25	17/25
City/highway mpg (as tested)		
4-speed OD automatic	17.3	17.3

Built in USA

RETAIL PRICES

	GOOD	AVERAGE	POOR
1998 Town Car	$15,000-17,000	$13,800-15,500	$9,500-10,500
1999 Town Car	18,000-20,500	16,500-19,000	11,500-13,000
2000 Town Car	21,000-24,000	19,500-22,500	14,400-16,000
2001 Town Car	25,000-28,000	23,500-26,000	—

AVERAGE REPLACEMENT COSTS

A/C Compressor	$435	Exhaust System	525
Alternator	265	Radiator	460
Automatic Transmission or		Shocks and/or Struts	1,315
Transaxle	875	Timing Chain or Belt	415
Brakes	410	Universal Joints	195

TROUBLE SPOTS

• **Exhaust system.** The engine idles rough due to the exhaust system vibrating. Installing a damper on the right side of the Y-pipe corrects it. (1998-99)

• **Vehicle noise.** The heat shields come loose on the catalytic converter and muffler causing a rattling and buzzing noise. (1998-99)

• **Steering problems.** The steering wheel may vibrate and/or buzz. Power steering hose must be replaced. (1998)

• **Windshield.** Water may leak from the windshield area because of a gap in the sealer. (1998-99)

RECALL HISTORY

1998: Text and/or graphics for headlamp aiming instructions, provided in owner guides, are not sufficiently clear. **1998-00:** Jacking instructions are incorrect and, if followed, could result in vehicle dropping suddenly. **1998-99 limousine w/ball joint containing one-piece bearing:** Bearing within lower control arm ball joint can weaken slowly during use; eventually, crack could result in separation, allowing control arm to drop to ground. **2000-01:** A switch located in the plastic cover of the wiper motor gear case could malfunction and overheat, potentially resulting in loss of wiper function or fire. **2001:** A restraint control module (RCM) or a side or front crash sensor may have been assembled with one or more of the screws that mount the circuit board in the housing missing. **2001:** Driver's and/or outboard front passenger's seatbelt buckle may not fully latch. In the event of a crash, the restraint system may not provide adequate occupant protection.

1993-97 MAZDA 626

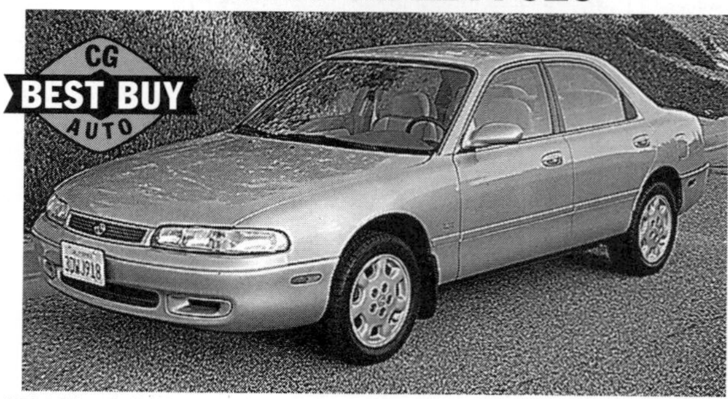

1994 Mazda 626

FOR Acceleration (V6) • Fuel economy • Steering/handling

AGAINST Automatic transmission performance • Road noise

EVALUATION A V6 and 5-speed deliver willing, capable performance and spirited acceleration. Both engines are smooth, free-revving, and fairly quiet, but neither has enough low-speed torque for pleasant, vigorous running with automatic. Automatics also are slow to downshift for passing. Worse yet, they suffer jerky full-throttle downshifts, especially with 4-cylinder power. A 4-cylinder achieved nearly 24 mpg, and a stick-shift V6 averaged 20.7 mpg. Ride quality is good, with the suspension filtering out most pavement imperfections. The sedan also handles better than you might expect. Body lean is moderate in turns, but the car feels secure and composed in spirited driving. "Panic" braking is swift and stable. Rear seating disappoints, and rear doors could be bigger. Head room is adequate for tall people, even with a power sunroof installed. Leg space is ample all around. Space also is adequate for rear passengers' feet under front seats. Split rear seatbacks fold down for additional cargo space. Wind noise is low on the highway, though the 4-cylinder gets a little loud at higher speeds.

VALUE All told, the solidly built 626 sedan is a strong contender against the Honda Accord and Toyota Camry, though the latter are quieter and more luxurious.

SPECIFICATIONS

	4-door sedan
Wheelbase, in.	102.8
Overall length, in.	184.4
Overall width, in.	68.9
Overall height, in.	51.6
Curb weight, lbs.	2804
Cargo volume, cu. ft.	13.8
Fuel capacity, gals.	15.9
Seating capacity	5
Front head room, in.	39.2
Max. front leg room, in.	43.5
Rear head room, in.	37.8
Min. rear leg room, in.	35.8

Powertrain layout: transverse front-engine/front-wheel drive

ENGINES

	dohc I4	dohc V6
Size, liters/cu. in.	2.0/122	2.5/153
Horsepower	114-118	160-164
Torque (lbs./ft.)	124-127	156-160
EPA city/highway mpg		
5-speed OD manual	26/34	21/26
4-speed OD automatic	23/31	20/26
City/highway mpg (as tested)		
5-speed OD manual	25.1	20.7
4-speed OD automatic	23.8	

Built in USA

RETAIL PRICES

	GOOD	AVERAGE	POOR
1993 626 DX, LX	$2,200-2,900	$1,600-2,200	$500-800
1993 626 ES	3,000-3,800	2,300-3,100	800-1,300
1994 626 DX, LX	2,700-3,500	2,100-2,800	700-1,100
1994 626 ES	3,800-4,600	3,100-3,800	1,100-1,500
1995 626 DX, LX	3,400-4,300	2,700-3,600	900-1,400
1995 626 ES	4,800-5,500	4,100-4,700	1,800-2,200
1996 626 DX, LX	4,500-5,700	3,800-4,900	1,500-2,300
1996 626 ES	6,200-7,000	5,400-6,200	2,800-3,200
1997 626 DX, LX	5,700-7,200	5,000-6,400	2,500-3,300
1997 626 ES	7,600-8,500	6,700-7,500	3,500-4,100

AVERAGE REPLACEMENT COSTS

A/C Compressor	$360	Clutch, Pressure Plate,	
Alternator	245	Bearing	625
Automatic Transmission or		Exhaust System	495
Transaxle	1,075	Radiator	410
Brakes	245	Shocks and/or Struts	670
Timing Chain or Belt	160		

TROUBLE SPOTS

• **Transaxle leak.** A damaged torque converter hub seal allows fluid to leak from the automatic transmission. (1994-96)

• **Engine noise.** A metallic tapping noise from the rear of the engine could be due to slippage between the exhaust camshaft driven gear and friction gear. (1993-95)

• **Engine knock.** Cars with a V6 engine built before March 1993 may have engine knock, especially when cold, due to carbon buildup in the combustion chamber. (1993-94)

• **Engine stalling.** If the engine stalls when the transmission is shifted into drive, the problem may be a cracked mass airflow snorkel tube. (1993-94)

• **Engine mounts.** Original motor mounts are prone to breakage. Mazda offers redesigned mounts as a replacement. (1993-94)

• **Air conditioner.** Poor A/C performance caused by defective relay will not let compressor cycle off on V6 models. (1993-95)

• **Power seats.** The insulation on the wires for the power seat can wear through causing a short circuit disabling the power seat. (1993-94)

• **Door handles.** The outer door handles may come loose and rattle. Replace the original retaining nuts with ones that won't come loose. (1993-95)

• **Wipers.** The welds holding the wiper arm support bracket break causing a creak or rattle when the wipers are running. (1993-95)

• **Vehicle shake.** Vibration in the steering wheel, shift lever, and floor is probably caused by mispositioned radiator dampers. (1993-95)

RECALL HISTORY

1994: Headlight wire that runs through turn-signal lever can fail where it is soldered to switch, causing loss of headlights. **1995:** Some passenger-side airbags may not inflate properly; also, igniter cap can separate, causing hot gases to be released. **1995-97 w/SAS sensor unit:** Airbag could deploy as a result of minor undercarriage impact. **1997:** Spring in timing belt tensioner can break and get caught, resulting in possible engine stalling.

2000 Mazda 626 LX

FOR Acceleration (V6) • Steering/handling • Build quality

AGAINST Road noise • Automatic transmission performance

EVALUATION Mazda wanted a quiet, refined compact for the next generation—and mostly succeeded in that quest. Engine and wind noise are well muffled, though tire roar is too audible over coarse pavement. Ride quality is firm, but absorbent. The longer wheelbase helps reduce pitch and hop on scalloped freeways, though high-speed dips induce some floatiness. Cornering is still decisive and sporty, with only mild body lean and stable front-drive responses. Quick, precise steering is helpful, but directional changes aren't really sport-sedan crisp. Braking is good, with little nosedive and steady tracking in hard stops. Four-cylinder performance is at least adequate with manual shift, but sluggish with automatic, whereas V6 models are lively either way. With either engine, though, the automatic can downshift with a jerk at times. A manual-shift model averaged a pleasing 22.5 mpg. Though a compact, the 626 rivals some midsize sedans, with space for 6-footers to sit in tandem without rear riders' knees digging into the front seats. Underseat foot room also is good. The cabin is still a bit narrow for uncrowded three-abreast grownup travel in back, but large doorways ease entry/exit. In terms of visibility, driving, seating, and dashboard layout; the 626 is competitive, but not terrific. Tall drivers might want a little more rearward seat travel to get further from the steering wheel. Interior decor has a tasteful, understated look. Small-items stowage is better than average, with roomy compartments in the dashboard and console, as well as map pockets. A 626 feels reassuring on rough roads.

VALUE A competent family 4-door, more mainstream than its predecessor, the 626 lost some of its sporting flair but still tops most rivals—especially with the V6 engine. LX versions offer the best combination of features and value in this competitive segment. Because it's often overlooked, prices are appealing.

SPECIFICATIONS

	4-door sedan
Wheelbase, in.	105.1
Overall length, in.	186.8
Overall width, in.	69.3
Overall height, in.	55.1
Curb weight, lbs.	2798
Cargo volume, cu. ft.	14.2
Fuel capacity, gals.	16.9
Seating capacity	5

	4-door sedan
Front head room, in.	39.2
Max. front leg room, in.	43.6
Rear head room, in.	37.0
Min. rear leg room, in.	34.6

Powertrain layout: transverse front-engine/front-wheel drive

ENGINES

	dohc I4	dohc V6
Size, liters/cu. in.	2.0/122	2.5/152
Horsepower	125-130	170
Torque (lbs./ft.)	127-130	163
EPA city/highway mpg		
5-speed OD manual	26/33	21/27
4-speed OD automatic	22/29	20/26
City/highway mpg (as tested)		
5-speed OD manual		22.5

Built in USA

RETAIL PRICES

	GOOD	AVERAGE	POOR
1998 626 4-cylinder	$7,700-9,000	$6,900-8,300	$4,500-5,400
1998 626 V6	9,200-10,500	8,200-9,500	5,500-6,300
1999 626 4-cylinder	9,200-10,500	8,300-9,500	5,700-6,600
1999 626 V6	10,600-12,100	9,600-11,100	6,800-7,900
2000 626 4-cylinder	10,800-12,000	9,800-11,000	6,800-7,800
2000 626 V6	12,200-14,000	11,200-13,000	8,000-9,000
2001 626 4-cylinder	12,800-14,000	11,800-13,000	—
2001 626 V6	14,300-16,000	13,300-15,000	—

AVERAGE REPLACEMENT COSTS

A/C Compressor	$405	Clutch, Pressure Plate, Bearing	470
Alternator	305		
Automatic Transmission or Transaxle	1,030	Constant Velocity Joints	670
		Exhaust System	270
Brakes	260	Radiator	505
Shocks and/or Struts	440	Timing Chain or Belt	280

TROUBLE SPOTS

• **Sunroof/moonroof.** A variety of sunroof problems may be due to broken or missing panel bumper clips, loose guides, or motor and cable problems. (1999)

• **Coolant leak.** Early production models with the 4-cylinder engine may leak coolant from the optional block heater. A redesigned heater, made of cast brass, can be retrofitted. (1998-99)

• **Vehicle noise.** The vapor emission control valve makes a clicking or tapping noise in the rear of the vehicle and can be quieted with a redesigned bracket. (1998-2000)

RECALL HISTORY

1999-00: Certain reservoir tank caps on brake master cylinder lack ventilation holes; as a result, pressure in tank can drop gradually as brake pad or shoe wears and ambient temperature drops. Also, pressure could reach a point where brake caliper and drum cylinder are pulled back by vacuum when vehicle is parked for a long time.

1994-97 MAZDA B-SERIES

1995 Mazda B-Series regular cab

FOR Acceleration (4.0-liter V6) • Antilock brakes • Payload capacity • Build quality

AGAINST Acceleration (4-cylinder) • Fuel economy • Passenger room (reg. cab)

EVALUATION

See the 1994-97 Ford Ranger.

VALUE

See the 1994-97 Ford Ranger.

SPECIFICATIONS

	ext. cab	reg. cab long bed	reg. cab short bed
Wheelbase, in.	125.2	113.9	107.9
Overall length, in.	202.7	197.5	184.5
Overall width, in.	69.4	69.4	69.4
Overall height, in.	64.1	64.0	64.0
Curb weight, lbs.	3197	2955	2927
Fuel capacity, gals.	20.5	17.0[1]	17.0
Seating capacity	5	3	3
Front head room, in.	39.4	39.1	39.1
Max. front leg room, in.	42.4	42.4	42.4
Rear head room, in.	35.6	—	—
Min. rear leg room, in.	41.2	—	—

1. 20.0 gals. optional.

Powertrain layout: longitudinal front-engine/rear- or 4-wheel drive

ENGINES

	ohc I4	ohv V6	ohv V6
Size, liters/cu. in.	2.3/140	3.0/182	4.0/245
Horsepower	98-112	140-147	160
Torque (lbs./ft.)	130-135	160-162	220-225
EPA city/highway mpg			
5-speed OD manual	22/27	19/25	18/23
4-speed OD automatic	20/25	18/24	17/23
5-speed OD automatic			16/22
City/highway mpg (as tested)			
5-speed OD manual			17.8
4-speed OD automatic			16.5

Built in USA

RETAIL PRICES

	GOOD	AVERAGE	POOR
1994 B2300	$2,500-4,000	$1,900-3,300	$500-1,300
1994 B3000 2WD	3,100-5,000	2,400-4,200	700-1,700
1994 B3000 4WD	4,500-5,800	3,800-5,000	1,600-2,200
1994 B4000 2WD	3,400-5,500	2,700-4,700	800-2,000
1994 B4000 4WD	5,000-6,500	4,300-5,700	1,900-2,700
1995 B2300 2WD	3,000-4,800	2,300-4,000	700-1,500
1995 B2300 4WD	4,500-5,500	3,800-4,700	1,700-2,100
1995 B3000 2WD	4,000-5,500	3,300-4,700	1,300-2,000
1995 B3000 4WD	5,500-6,500	4,700-5,600	2,300-2,700
1995 B4000 2WD	4,700-5,700	4,000-4,900	1,800-2,300
1995 B4000 4WD	6,000-8,000	5,200-7,200	2,600-3,800
1996 B2300 2WD	3,600-5,600	2,900-4,800	1,000-2,200
1996 B2300 4WD	5,600-6,800	4,800-6,000	2,500-3,000
1996 B3000 2WD	5,000-6,500	4,200-5,700	1,800-2,700
1996 B3000 4WD	6,500-8,000	5,500-7,000	2,800-3,600
1996 B4000 2WD	5,800-7,000	5,000-6,000	2,500-3,000
1996 B4000 4WD	7,000-9,500	6,000-8,500	3,100-4,500
1997 B2300 2WD	4,200-6,500	3,500-5,700	1,400-2,700
1997 B2300 4WD	6,200-7,500	5,200-6,500	2,600-3,300
1997 B4000 2WD	6,800-8,000	5,800-7,000	3,000-3,600
1997 B4000 4WD	8,000-10,500	7,000-9,500	3,800-5,300

AVERAGE REPLACEMENT COSTS

See the 1994-97 Ford Ranger.

TROUBLE SPOTS

See the 1994-97 Ford Ranger.

RECALL HISTORY

1994 in Southern California: Studs that attach master cylinder to power brake booster can develop stress cracking after extended period. **1994 w/manual shift:** Parking brake might not hold. **1994 V6:** Flexible hose in front fuel line is susceptible to cracking.

1998-01 MAZDA B-SERIES

FOR Acceleration (B4000) • Build quality • Passenger room (regular-cab)

1998 Mazda B-Series

AGAINST Engine noise • Acceleration (B2500) • Rear-seat comfort (extended-cab)

EVALUATION
See the 1998-01 Ford Ranger.

VALUE
See the 1998-01 Ford Ranger.

SPECIFICATIONS

	ext. cab	reg. cab
Wheelbase, in.	125.7	111.6
Overall length, in.	202.9	187.5
Overall width, in.	69.4	69.4
Overall height, in.	64.7	64.9
Curb weight, lbs.	3497	3242
Cargo volume, cu. ft.	NA	NA
Fuel capacity, gals.	20.5	17.0
Seating capacity	5	3
Front head room, in.	39.2	39.2
Max. front leg room, in.	42.2	42.4
Rear head room, in.	35.6	—
Min. rear leg room, in.	40.3	—

Powertrain layout: longitudinal front-engine/rear- or 4-wheel drive

ENGINES

	ohc I4	ohv V6	ohv V6	ohc V6
Size, liters/cu. in.	2.5/152	3.0/182	4.0/245	4.0/245
Horsepower	119	150	160	207
Torque (lbs./ft.)	146	185	225	238
EPA city/highway mpg				
5-speed OD manual	22/27	17/23	17/21	18/22
4-speed OD automatic	20/25	17/22	—	
5-speed OD automatic				16/22
City/highway mpg (as tested)				
5-speed OD manual	20.1			
4-speed OD automatic		18.2		
5-speed OD automatic			16.4	

Built in USA

RETAIL PRICES

	GOOD	AVERAGE	POOR
1998 B2500	$5,000-7,000	$4,200-6,200	$1,800-3,000
1998 B3000 2WD	7,500-8,500	6,700-7,600	3,500-4,200
1998 B3000 4WD	7,000-9,000	6,100-8,000	3,200-4,400
1998 B4000 2WD	8,000-9,000	7,100-8,000	4,000-4,500
1998 B4000 4WD	10,000 -11,000	9,000-10,000	5,200-5,800
1999 B2500	6,000-9,000	5,200-8,000	2,600-4,400
1999 B3000 2WD	8,500-10,000	7,500-9,000	4,000-5,000
1999 B3000 4WD	9,000-11,500	8,000-10,500	4,300-6,000
1999 B4000 2WD	7,500-11,000	6,500-10,000	3,400-5,800
1999 B4000 4WD	11,500-13,000	10,500-12,000	6,000-7,000
2000 B2500	7,000-10,000	6,200-9,000	3,300-5,000
2000 B3000 2WD	7,500-11,000	6,500-10,000	3,500-5,800
2000 B3000 4WD	9,000-12,000	8,000-11,000	4,500-6,300
2000 B4000 2WD	9,500-11,500	8,500-10,500	4,900-6,000
2000 B4000 4WD	13,000-14,500	12,000-13,500	8,000-8,800
2001 B2500	8,500-11,000	7,500-10,000	—
2001 B3000 2WD	9,000-12,000	8,000-10,800	—
2001 B3000 4WD	11,000-13,500	10,000-12,300	—
2001 B4000 2WD	11,500-13,000	10,500-11,800	—
2001 B4000 4WD	14,500-16,000	13,200-14,500	—

AVERAGE REPLACEMENT COSTS
See the 1998-01 Ford Ranger.

TROUBLE SPOTS
See the 1998-01 Ford Ranger.

RECALL HISTORY
1998 B4000 w/two-wheel drive and 4.0-liter engine: Flexible section of fuel line is too close to exhaust manifold; could result in damage to fuel line, and possible leakage. **1998-99 w/cruise control:** Cable can interfere with speed-control servo pulley and not allow throttle to return to idle when disengaging cruise control.

1990-97 MAZDA MIATA

1996 Mazda Miata MX-5

FOR Acceleration (manual transmission) • Steering/handling • Antilock brakes (optional) • Fuel economy

AGAINST Cargo room • Road noise

EVALUATION The Miata is lively, agile, simple, and fun-to-drive. While off-the-line acceleration is not terrific (0-60 in about 8.3 seconds), it shows flashes of brilliance in 2nd and 3rd gear, and it gets great mileage, with 25-27 mpg possible on a regular basis. The Miata maneuvers beautifully, is easy to handle, and hugs the road snugly. The ride can be choppy at times, given the fact body flex is the bane of all convertibles. Extra bracing added for the 1994 model year seems to improve the situation, however. Though the prominent exhaust note isn't inappropriate given the Miata's mission, there are also above-average quantities of wind and road noise. The cozy cockpit has well-placed gauges and controls, plus enough space to give tall people adequate room, permitting full enjoyment of the car's attributes. This is true despite the lack of any steering-wheel adjustment. Leg room is not a problem, but head room is tight. One golf bag or a couple of gym bags and the tonneau cover are about all that will fit in the small trunk, which also holds the mini-spare. There's also usable storage behind the seats (perhaps as much as afforded by the trunk).

VALUE Though the Miata has been around for eleven years now, the first-generation version still looks and feels as good as it did when it arrived in 1989. If you're looking for an affordable, fun-to-drive sports car, there's little need to search further.

SPECIFICATIONS

	2-door conv.
Wheelbase, in.	89.2
Overall length, in.	155.4
Overall width, in.	65.9
Overall height, in.	48.2
Curb weight, lbs.	2293
Cargo volume, cu. ft.	3.6
Fuel capacity, gals.	11.9[1]
Seating capacity	2
Front head room, in.	37.1
Max. front leg room, in.	42.7
Rear head room, in.	—
Min. rear leg room, in.	—

1. 12.7 gals. after 1993.

Powertrain layout: longitudinal front-engine/rear-wheel drive

ENGINES

	dohc I4	dohc I4
Size, liters/cu. in.	1.6/97	1.8/112
Horsepower	105-116	128-133
Torque (lbs./ft.)	100	110-114
EPA city/highway mpg		
5-speed OD manual	24/30	23/29

	dohc I4	dohc I4
4-speed OD automatic	24/28	22/28
City/highway mpg (as tested)		
5-speed OD manual	26.7	21.9

Built in Japan

RETAIL PRICES

	GOOD	AVERAGE	POOR
1990 Miata	$2,500-3,100	$1,900-2,400	$600-900
1991 Miata	3,000-3,700	2,400-3,000	800-1,200
1992 Miata	3,500-4,200	2,800-3,500	1,000-1,400
1992 M-Edition	3,900-4,500	3,300-3,800	1,300-1,600
1993 Miata	4,000-4,800	3,300-4,000	1,300-1,700
1993 M-Edition	4,600-5,400	3,900-4,600	1,700-2,200
1994 Miata	4,700-5,500	4,000-4,700	1,800-2,300
1994 M-Edition	5,500-6,300	4,700-5,500	2,300-2,800
1995 Miata	5,500-6,500	4,700-5,500	2,300-2,800
1995 M-Edition	6,700-7,500	5,900-6,600	3,100-3,600
1996 Miata	6,500-7,500	5,600-6,500	3,000-3,500
1996 M-Edition	7,800-8,500	7,000-7,600	4,000-4,400
1997 Miata	8,000-9,000	7,000-8,000	4,000-4,700
1997 M-Edition	9,500-10,500	8,500-9,500	4,900-5,600
1998 Miata	9,800-11,200	8,800-10,200	5,000-6,000
1998 M-Edition	11,500-12,500	10,500-11,500	6,500-7,200

AVERAGE REPLACEMENT COSTS

A/C Compressor	$435	Clutch, Pressure Plate,	
Alternator	245	Bearing	455
Automatic Transmission or		Exhaust System	290
Transaxle	940	Radiator	500
Brakes	245	Shocks and/or Struts	645
Timing Chain or Belt	205	Universal Joints	380

TROUBLE SPOTS

• **Engine noise.** A ticking noise from the top of the engine is likely due to inadequate hydraulic lash adjusters for the valves. (1990-93)

• **Oil leak.** Early models often developed an oil leak at the plug in the drain pan unless the plug was tightened by hand with the gasket squarely in place before snugging with a wrench. (1990)

• **Audio system.** If tapes get stuck in the Panasonic radio/tape player, the unit must be removed and sent to a factory service center. (1990)

• **Windows.** The windows may not fully open because a cable comes loose blocking the window's travel. (1992-94)

• **Timing belt.** There is a revised, more robust timing belt tensioner pulley to replace the original. (1990-94)

RECALL HISTORY

1990-91: Rear turn signal lamps may have insufficient amount of reflecting paint on inner surface. **1990-93 w/optional hardtop:** Plastic buckles on optional hoist accessory kit can break, causing hardtop to fall. **1991 w/ABS:** Return fluid line of front brake system on some cars is misconnected to return; when antilock comes into use, all fluid from front brakes goes to rear system, which may lead to increased stopping distance. **1995 w/SAS sensor unit:** Airbag could deploy as a result of minor undercarriage impact.

1995-01 MAZDA MILLENIA

1996 Mazda Millenia

FOR Antilock brakes • Acceleration (S) • Steering/handling • Quietness

AGAINST Automatic transmission performance • Rear visibility

EVALUATION The sedan rides smoothly on the highway and rather nicely in the city. Braking is excellent. Handling is responsive and sure-footed, with little body lean and firm steering that has ample feedback. Tire noise is moderate, and engine sounds are barely noticed. The base Millenia provides adequate acceleration, capable of reaching 60 mph in 9.4 seconds. By contrast, an S model took just 7.8 seconds to 60 mph and felt much stronger, especially in midrange passing sprints. Although the automatic transmission in both models is generally smooth and responsive, flooring the throttle can result in harsh, abrupt downshifts. Both models have returned similar gas mileage: 21.8 mpg for the S and 21.4 for the base. Space is adequate for four adults, and the dashboard is convenient and attractive. Rearward visibility is not so good, because wide roof pillars block the over-the-shoulder view. Also, the sedan's high tail makes parallel parking something of a challenge. In addition to a huge trunk, you get closed storage boxes in front doors.

VALUE A base-model Millenia delivers plenty of luxury at a lower price than rivals, but cannot match their performance. The costlier Millenia S has that attribute in abundance, serving as an alternative to an ES 300.

SPECIFICATIONS

	4-door sedan
Wheelbase, in.	108.3
Overall length, in.	189.8
Overall width, in.	69.7
Overall height, in.	54.9
Curb weight, lbs.	3220
Cargo volume, cu. ft.	13.3
Fuel capacity, gals.	18.0
Seating capacity	5
Front head room, in.	39.3
Max. front leg room, in.	43.3
Rear head room, in.	37.0
Min. rear leg room, in.	34.1

Powertrain layout: transverse front-engine/front-wheel drive

ENGINES

	dohc V6	Supercharged dohc V6
Size, liters/cu. in.	2.5/152	2.3/138
Horsepower	170	210
Torque (lbs./ft.)	160	210
EPA city/highway mpg		
4-speed OD automatic	20/27	20/28
City/highway mpg (as tested)		
4-speed OD automatic	21.4	21.8

Built in Japan

RETAIL PRICES

	GOOD	AVERAGE	POOR
1995 Millenia	$6,000-7,000	$5,000-6,000	$2,600-3,300
1995 Millenia S	7,000-8,000	6,000-7,000	3,200-3,900
1996 Millenia	7,500-8,500	6,500-7,500	3,500-4,200
1996 Millenia S	8,700-9,700	7,700-8,700	4,300-5,000
1997 Millenia	9,500-10,700	8,500-9,500	4,800-5,500
1997 Millenia S	11,000-12,200	10,000-11,000	6,000-6,700
1998 Millenia	11,500-12,700	10,500-11,500	6,300-7,000
1998 Millenia S	13,000-14,500	11,800-13,000	7,700-8,500
1999 Millenia	14,000-15,500	12,800-14,000	8,600-9,400
1999 Millenia S	15,700-17,200	14,500-15,800	10,000-11,000
2000 Millenia	16,500-18,000	15,000-16,500	10,500-11,500
2000 Millenia S	18,500-20,000	17,000-18,500	12,000-13,000
2001 Millenia	19,500-21,000	18,000-19,500	—
2001 Millenia S	21,500-23,000	20,000-21,500	—

AVERAGE REPLACEMENT COSTS

A/C Compressor	$1,500	Constant Velocity Joints	1,560
Alternator	755	Exhaust System	730
Automatic Transmission or		Radiator	580
Transaxle	1,525	Shocks and/or Struts	820
Brakes	230	Timing Chain or Belt	250

TROUBLE SPOTS

• **Engine noise.** Some engines make a metallic tapping noise requiring a new friction gear spring on the camshaft. (1995)

• **Headlights.** The headlight drain hoses can get kinked by the aiming screws causing fogging. (1995-96)

• **Steering problems.** The steering wheel may be off center requiring adjustment of the tie rods. (1995)

1990-98 MAZDA MPV

1991 Mazda MPV 4WD

FOR Antilock brakes (optional) • Wet-weather traction (4WD)

AGAINST Acceleration • Fuel economy

EVALUATION Acceleration on the early models ranged from anemic with the 4-cylinder to adequate with the V6. Over the years though, MPV gained weight without gaining horsepower or torque to compensate. The result is that rear-drive versions now feel sluggish in hilly terrain while the 4WD version, though well-suited to Northern climates, is downright slow. The extra weight is also sure to have a negative impact on fuel economy, which probably won't reach 20, even in normal highway driving. The suspension is stable on smooth roads, but stiff and choppy on rough surfaces. The steering seems too light at times, requiring frequent corrections to stay on course. However, the MPV has only moderate body lean and offers good grip, handling more like a car in most situations than a van. The removable rear bench seat added for 1996 marks a big improvement in convenience for the MPV.

VALUE While recent improvements are welcome, the MPV still lags well behind such class leaders in the field, like the new Chrysler minivans and the Ford Windstar in overall roominess, performance, and value.

SPECIFICATIONS

	4-door wagon
Wheelbase, in.	110.4
Overall length, in.	183.5
Overall width, in.	71.9
Overall height, in.	68.1
Curb weight, lbs.	3970
Cargo volume, cu. ft.	37.5
Fuel capacity, gals.	19.6
Seating capacity	8
Front head room, in.	40.0
Max. front leg room, in.	40.4
Rear head room, in.	39.7
Min. rear leg room, in.	33.4

Powertrain layout: longitudinal front-engine/rear- or all-wheel drive

ENGINES

	ohc I4	ohc V6
Size, liters/cu. in.	2.6/159	3.0/180
Horsepower	121	150-155
Torque (lbs./ft.)	149	165-169

EPA city/highway mpg

5-speed OD manual	20/25	
4-speed OD automatic	18/24	16/22

City/highway mpg (as tested)

4-speed OD automatic	17.2

Built in Japan

RETAIL PRICES

	GOOD	AVERAGE	POOR
1990 MPV 2WD	$1,500-2,200	$1,000-1,600	$200-400
1990 MPV 4WD	1,700-2,400	1,200-1,800	300-500
1991 MPV 2WD	2,000-2,700	1,400-2,100	400-600
1991 MPV 4WD	2,400-3,100	1,700-2,400	500-700
1992 MPV 2WD	2,500-3,300	1,900-2,600	600-900
1992 MPV 4WD	3,100-3,800	2,400-3,100	700-1,100
1993 MPV 2WD	3,000-4,000	2,300-3,300	700-1,200
1993 MPV 4WD	3,800-4,500	3,100-3,800	1,100-1,500
1994 MPV 2WD	3,600-4,600	2,900-3,800	1,000-1,500
1994 MPV 4WD	4,600-5,400	3,900-4,600	1,700-2,100
1995 MPV 2WD	4,500-5,700	3,800-4,900	1,600-2,300
1995 MPV 4WD	5,700-7,000	5,000-6,200	2,500-3,200
1996 MPV 2WD	5,800-7,500	5,000-6,600	2,900-3,500
1996 MPV 4WD	$7,500-9,000	$6,600-8,000	$3,500-4,500
1997 MPV 2WD	8,000-9,500	7,200-8,500	4,000-5,000
1997 MPV 4WD	9,500-11,000	8,500-10,000	4,800-5,800
1998 MPV 2WD	10,000-12,000	9,000-11,000	5,200-6,500
1998 MPV 4WD	12,000-14,000	10,800-12,500	6,500-7,500

AVERAGE REPLACEMENT COSTS

A/C Compressor	$905	Clutch, Pressure Plate, Bearing	540
Alternator	230	Exhaust System	510
Automatic Transmission or Transaxle	870	Radiator	590
Brakes	280	Shocks and/or Struts	520
Universal Joints	680		

TROUBLE SPOTS

• **Vehicle noise.** A groaning or grinding noise from the front end is caused by the mounting rubber on the upper spring seat. (1990-92)

• **Door handles.** Loose outer door handles can be fixed by replacing the original retaining nuts with ones that won't come loose. (1990-94)

• **Air conditioner.** Refrigerant leaks from the A/C at the condenser block are often difficult to find using a detector. (1990-93)

• **Cold starting problems.** The engine may not restart after sitting 30 minutes in the winter when fuels are more volatile. (1992-94)

• **Rear wipers.** The hinge on the rear wiper rusts and gets stiff decreasing the pressure of the blade against the glass. (1990-92)

• **Automatic transmission.** Third gear starts and failure to upshift is likely due to the one special short bolt for the transmission oil pan not being installed in the correct hole. If a long one is installed in its place, it damages the inhibitor switch. (1990-94)

RECALL HISTORY

1990-91: Front seatbelt release button can break and pieces can fall inside.
1990-91: Rear brake linings can change over time, producing inconsistent performance.

1993-97 MAZDA MX-6

1995 Mazda MX-6

FOR Acceleration (V-6) • Steering/handling • Refinement • Antilock brakes (optional)

AGAINST Rear-seat room • Ride (LS) • Automatic transmission performance

EVALUATION

See the 1993-97 Ford Probe.

VALUE

See the 1993-97 Ford Probe.

SPECIFICATIONS

	2-door coupe
Wheelbase, in.	102.8
Overall length, in.	181.5
Overall width, in.	68.9
Overall height, in.	51.6
Curb weight, lbs.	2625
Cargo volume, cu. ft.	12.4
Fuel capacity, gals.	15.5
Seating capacity	4
Front head room, in.	38.1
Max. front leg room, in.	44.0
Rear head room, in.	34.7
Min. rear leg room, in.	27.7

Powertrain layout: transverse front-engine/front-wheel drive

ENGINES

	dohc I4	dohc V6
Size, liters/cu. in.	2.0/122	2.5/153
Horsepower	114-118	160-164
Torque (lbs./ft.)	124-127	156-160

EPA city/highway mpg

5-speed OD manual	26/34	21/26
4-speed OD automatic	23/31	20/26

City/highway mpg (as tested)

5-speed OD manual		23.0

Built in USA

RETAIL PRICES

	GOOD	AVERAGE	POOR
1993 MX-6	$2,800-3,500	$2,200-2,800	$600-900
1993 MX-6 LS	3,400-4,100	2,700-3,400	800-1,200
1994 MX-6	3,500-4,200	2,800-3,500	900-1,300
1994 MX-6 LS	4,300-5,000	3,600-4,200	1,400-1,800
1995 MX-6	4,200-4,900	3,500-4,200	1,300-1,800
1995 MX-6 LS	5,200-6,000	4,500-5,200	2,100-2,500
1996 MX-6	5,500-6,500	4,700-5,700	2,200-2,800
1996 MX-6 LS	6,700-8,000	6,000-7,200	3,000-3,700
1997 MX-6	7,200-8,200	6,300-7,200	3,100-3,700
1997 MX-6 LS	8,500-9,500	7,600-8,500	4,200-4,800

AVERAGE REPLACEMENT COSTS

See the 1993-97 Ford Probe.

TROUBLE SPOTS

See the 1993-97 Ford Probe.

RECALL HISTORY

1994: Headlight wire that runs through turn-signal lever can fail where it is soldered to switch, causing loss of headlights. **1995-96 w/SAS sensor unit:** Airbag could deploy as a result of minor undercarriage impact. **1997:** Spring in timing belt tensioner can break and get caught, resulting in possible engine stalling.

1995-98 MAZDA PROTEGE

1995 Mazda Protege ES

FOR Optional antilock brakes (LX, ES) • Passenger room • Fuel economy • Ride

AGAINST Handling • Acceleration (automatic) • Radio controls (1995-96) • Entry/exit

EVALUATION Mazda obviously tuned the Protege's suspension more toward ride comfort than handling finesse, though steering response is good and the car reacts well in urban driving. Bumps are easily absorbed, though they often produce a loud "thump." Hard cornering brings lots of body lean, and the narrow 13-inch tires on DX and LX models start squealing early. The 14-inch ES tires have noticeably better cornering grip. Space inside is ample for four adults, with abundant front head and rear leg room. However, rear doors are narrow at the bottom, making it awkward to climb in and out. You get a good-sized trunk and an average sized glovebox. The 1.5-liter engine in DX and LX models delivers adequate acceleration with a manual transmission, though it's sluggish with automatic. With a full load, the 1.5-liter 4-cylinder might be short on strength. Surprisingly, the 1.8-liter engine in the ES doesn't seem that much stronger, despite its 30-horsepower advantage. Highway passing and merging are notably easier, however. Both engines should return above-average fuel economy. A manual-shift LX averaged 30.2 mpg. The dashboard is well laid out, with clear gauges and stalk-mounted light and wiper controls. Until the 1997 model year, however, the radio sat too low. Small buttons require a long look away from the road to make any adjustments. The radio moved to the top of the dashboard in 1997. Visibility is fine in all directions.

VALUE Exceptionally easy to drive, Protege provides a rewarding mixture of maneuverability, economy, and quietness, coupled with solid assembly quality.

SPECIFICATIONS

	4-door sedan
Wheelbase, in.	102.6
Overall length, in.	174.8
Overall width, in.	67.3
Overall height, in.	55.9
Curb weight, lbs.	2385
Cargo volume, cu. ft.	13.1
Fuel capacity, gals.	14.5
Seating capacity	5
Front head room, in.	39.2
Max. front leg room, in.	42.2
Rear head room, in.	37.4
Min. rear leg room, in.	35.6

Powertrain layout: transverse front-engine/front-wheel drive

ENGINES

	dohc I4	dohc I4
Size, liters/cu. in.	1.5/91	1.8/110
Horsepower	92	122
Torque (lbs./ft.)	96	117

EPA city/highway mpg

5-speed OD manual	32/39	26/33
4-speed OD automatic	27/35	23/30

City/highway mpg (as tested)

5-speed OD manual	30.2	
4-speed OD automatic		24.8

Built in Japan

RETAIL PRICES

	GOOD	AVERAGE	POOR
1995 Protege	$2,800-3,800	$2,200-3,100	$500-1,000
1996 Protege	3,500-4,800	2,800-4,000	800-1,400
1997 Protege	4,300-5,700	3,600-4,900	1,200-1,900
1998 Protege	5,500-7,000	4,700-6,000	1,700-2,400

AVERAGE REPLACEMENT COSTS

A/C Compressor	$420	Constant Velocity Joints	840
Alternator	350	Exhaust System	555
Automatic Transmission or		Radiator	500
Transaxle	1,460	Shocks and/or Struts	600
Brakes	230	Timing Chain or Belt	190

TROUBLE SPOTS

• **Engine knock.** If engine knock occurs in hot weather, there is a revised engine control computer that will correct the problem. (1995-96)

• **Steering problems.** The steering wheel may be off center requiring adjustment of the alignment (tie rods). (1995)

• **Exhaust system.** There is a new tailpipe tip available to eliminate a hooting noise from the exhaust. (1995-96)

RECALL HISTORY

1995 w/1.5-liter engine: Valve springs can develop minute cracks and break; can cause engine chatter, piston damage, and stalling. **1995:** Headlight wire can fail, causing loss of headlights with or without prior warning.

1999-01 MAZDA PROTEGE

2000 Mazda Protege ES

FOR Fuel economy • Ride

AGAINST Acceleration (automatic transmission)

EVALUATION   With the Protege, Mazda favors handling ability over ride comfort, unlike the tamer, softer Honda Civic or Toyota Corolla. Offering sportier road manners than many rivals, Proteges give a generally favorable impression, though the tradeoff is a slightly stiffer ride and markedly higher level of engine, road, and wind noise. Still, DX and LX editions take most bumps with firm control and yield a supple ride, with adequate steering and agile handling. Although the ES sedan shares their suspension, its high-profile tires—which sharpen handling—don't smother small road imperfections as well. Tepid acceleration is the foremost flaw of these models. Both engines offered in that period are slow from a stop. Acceleration does improve at about 20 mph, but passing power is lacking. Performance is adequate with manual shift, and a 5-speed ES scoots through traffic well enough, but automatic is disappointing. The extra horsepower available in 2001 provides a modest but welcome improvement. Visibility is good all around. Bodies are solid, and paintwork and exterior trim equal Honda/Toyota quality. Protege is one of the most spacious subcompact sedans, with relatively abundant front head room and rear leg room. Wide back doors make it easy to slide feet in and out. Rotary climate knobs are just out of the driver's reach, but the dashboard is well laid out. Open and covered bins, two cupholders, front-door map pockets, and a large glovebox provide good storage room. Trunk space is about average, though all models have a 60/40 split-folding rear seatback.

VALUE   Proteges often are overlooked by subcompact buyers. Too bad, because their roominess and driving pleasure equal—and even exceed—a Civic, Corolla, or Chevrolet Prizm. DX sedans, in particular, are a cut above most base-model subcompacts, with rich-looking plastic surfaces and appealing fabrics inside.

SPECIFICATIONS

	4-door sedan
Wheelbase, in.	102.8
Overall length, in.	174.0
Overall width, in.	67.1
Overall height, in.	55.5
Curb weight, lbs.	2449
Cargo volume, cu. ft.	12.9
Fuel capacity, gals.	13.2
Seating capacity	5
Front head room, in.	39.3
Max. front leg room, in.	42.2
Rear head room, in.	37.4
Min. rear leg room, in.	35.4

Powertrain layout: transverse front-engine/front-wheel drive

ENGINES

	dohc I4	dohc I4	dohc I4	dohc I4
Size, liters/cu. in.	1.6/97	1.8/110	2.0/121	2.0/121
Horsepower	105	122	130	140
Torque (lbs./ft.)	107	120	135	142
EPA city/highway mpg				
5-speed OD manual	29/34	26/30	25/31	25/31
4-speed OD automatic	26/33	24/29	25/30	
City/highway mpg (as tested)				
5-speed OD manual	26.6		24.5	

Built in Japan

RETAIL PRICES

	GOOD	AVERAGE	POOR
1999 Protege DX LX	$7,000-8,000	$6,200-7,200	$4,200-5,000
1999 Protege ES	8,500-9,500	7,500-8,500	5,200-6,000
2000 Protege DX LX	8,200-9,500	7,300-8,500	5,000-6,000
2000 Protege ES	10,000-11,000	9,000-10,000	6,200-7,000
2001 Protege DX LX	9,500-11,000	8,500-10,000	—
2001 Protege ES	11,500-12,500	10,500-11,500	—
2001 Protege MP3	15,000-16,000	14,000-15,000	—

AVERAGE REPLACEMENT COSTS

A/C Compressor	$810	Clutch, Pressure Plate, Bearing	475
Alternator	295	Constant Velocity Joints	1,200
Automatic Transmission or Transaxle	925	Exhaust System	355
Brakes	220	Radiator	435
Shocks and/or Struts	1,300	Timing Chain or Belt	265

TROUBLE SPOTS

• **Exhaust system.** A booming noise from the exhaust system is corrected by installing a stiffener over the front muffler and a damper weight near the rear muffler. (1999-2000)

• **Automatic transmission.** The automatic transmission may not shift out of second or third gear due to a defective solenoid (the system stores the wrong trouble code often making diagnoses incorrect). The powertrain control module was being replaced under the standard warranty. (1999)

• **Battery.** The battery may go dead due to excessive current drains from memories in components (like the radio memory or engine control computer). (1999)

• **Keys.** The key may be hard to insert or turn in the door lock because the flap breaks off and falls into the lock cylinder. (1999)

• **Doors.** The power door locks may malfunction if contacts get wet or corrode. Countermeasure switches with rubber seals are available and were being installed under the normal warranty. (1999)

RECALL HISTORY

2000-01: Brake fluid leakage could occur on certain vehicles, causing brake performance to be degraded.

1990-95 MERCEDES-BENZ 300/E-CLASS

1990 Mercedes-Benz 300CE 2-door coupe

FOR   Antilock brakes • Steering/handling • Ride

AGAINST   Fuel economy • Automatic transmission performance • Price

EVALUATION   Acceleration with 6-cylinder engines ranges from tepid to adequate. Gathering passing power at 40-60 mph requires flooring the throttle at times, and then you endure a long pause before the transmission reacts. An early 300E 4Matic averaged 18.7 mpg. Adding a V8 engine was just what was needed to make the Mercedes-Benz sedans match the acceleration of the Japanese-built Lexus LS 400 and Infiniti Q45. Throttle response at midrange speeds is noticeably stronger than in 6-cylinder models, though the automatic transmission sometimes shifts with an unseemly jerk. E-Class sedans are not very space-efficient, considering their 110.2-inch wheelbase. Front leg room is generous, but in the back it's only adequate. Because of rear-wheel-drive, with its intrusive drive shaft tunnel and a rather narrow interior, three adults will find a tight fit in the back seat. Trunk space is adequate, however. You can expect a stable, well-controlled highway ride, as well as precise steering and capable handling. With 4Matic 4-wheel-drive (available until 1994), it's virtually impossible to break the wheels loose. Even when you try to do so on wet pavement, this car sticks like glue. For drivers who don't need that much traction, ASD and ASR provide additional grip when it's needed, helping to maintain steering control.

VALUE   Service and maintenance can be expensive, but the assurances of longevity compensate in the long run. Strong resale value keeps prices high on the secondhand market.

SPECIFICATIONS

	2-door conv.	2-door coupe	4-door sedan	4-door wagon
Wheelbase, in.	106.9	106.9	110.2	110.2
Overall length, in.	183.9	183.9	187.2	188.2
Overall width, in.	68.5	68.5	68.5	68.5
Overall height, in.	54.8	54.9	56.3	59.8
Curb weight, lbs.	4025	3525	3525	3750
Cargo volume, cu. ft.	10.5	14.4	14.6	76.7
Fuel capacity, gals.	18.5	18.5	18.5	19.0
Seating capacity	4	4	5	5
Front head room, in.	37.6	36.0	36.9	37.4
Max. front leg room, in.	41.9	41.9	41.7	41.7
Rear head room, in.	35.5	36.8	36.9	36.8
Min. rear leg room, in.	24.8	28.6	33.5	33.9

Powertrain layout: longitudinal front-engine/rear-wheel drive

ENGINES

	Turbodiesel ohc I6	ohc I6	ohc I6	ohc I6	dohc I6
Size, liters/cu. in.	2.5/152	2.6/159	2.8/173	3.0/181	3.0/181
Horsepower	121	158	194	177	217
Torque (lbs./ft.)	165	162	199	188	195-201
EPA city/highway mpg					
4-speed OD auto.	26/31	19/24	NA	18/23	17/32
City/highway mpg (as tested)					
4-speed OD auto.	26.3			17.2	

ENGINES

	dohc I6	Diesel dohc I6	dohc V8	dohc V8
Size, liters/cu. in.	3.2/195	3.0/181	4.2/256	5.0/303
Horsepower	217	134	268-275	315-322
Torque (lbs./ft.)	229	155	295	347
EPA city/highway mpg				
4-speed OD automatic	20/26	26/32	18/24	16/19
City/highway mpg (as tested)				
4-speed OD automatic	20.8	25.1	15.5	

Built in Germany

RETAIL PRICES

	GOOD	AVERAGE	POOR
1990 260E/300E sedan	$4,000-6,000	$3,300-5,200	$1,300-2,500
1990 300TE wagon	6,000-7,000	5,200-6,200	2,700-3,400
1990 300CE coupe	6,500-7,500	5,700-6,500	3,000-3,600
1991 300D/E sedan	5,500-8,000	4,600-7,000	2,300-4,000
1991 300TE wagon	8,000-9,000	7,000-8,000	4,000-4,700
1991 300CE coupe	9,000-10,500	8,000-9,500	4,500-5,500
1992 300D/E sedan	7,000-10,000	6,000-9,000	3,200-4,000
1992 400E sedan	10,000-11,000	9,000-10,000	5,300-6,000
1992 500E sedan	14,000-16,000	12,500-14,500	8,500-10,000
1992 300TE wagon	10,000-12,000	9,000-11,000	5,300-6,700
1992 300CE coupe	11,000-12,500	10,000-11,500	6,000-7,000
1993 300D/E sedan	9,500-12,000	8,000-11,000	4,500-6,500
1993 400E sedan	12,000-13,500	11,000-12,000	7,000-7,700
1993 500E sedan	19,000-21,000	17,500-19,000	12,500-13,500
1993 300TE wagon	11,500-13,000	10,500-12,000	6,500-7,500
1993 300CE coupe	12,500-14,000	11,300-12,500	7,200-8,000
1993 300CE convertible	23,000-25,000	21,500-23,500	16,000-17,500
1994 E320	12,500-15,000	11,500-14,000	7,500-9,200
1994 E420	15,000-16,500	13,500-15,000	9,300-10,500
1994 E500	24,000-26,000	22,500-24,500	17,000-18,500
1994 E320 convertible	27,000-29,000	25,500-27,000	19,500-20,500
1995 E300D/320	14,500-19,000	13,000-17,500	9,000-12,000
1995 E420	17,500-19,000	16,000-17,500	11,000-12,000
1995 E320 convertible	31,000-33,500	29,000-31,500	23,000-24,700

AVERAGE REPLACEMENT COSTS

A/C Compressor	$925	Exhaust System	870
Alternator	440	Radiator	400
Automatic Transmission or Transaxle	1,060	Shocks and/or Struts	1,440
		Timing Chain or Belt	645
Brakes	190	Universal Joints	685

TROUBLE SPOTS

• **Brakes.** Brake squeal at low speeds (under 10 mph) may activate the antilock brake system. (1990-93)

• **Automatic transmission.** Harsh and erratic shifts are often due to a damaged dust cover on the vacuum modulator for the transmission. (1990-94)

• **Oil leak.** Oil enters the air filter. There are revised valve covers with improved oil separators available for the 3.0-liter engine. (1990)

• **Exhaust system.** Possible exhaust leak at the oxygen sensor caused by damaged catalytic converter. (1990-91 diesel)

• **Convertible top.** The locking tabs for the convertible top tend to wear and should be checked every 15,000 miles. (1990)

• **Automatic transmission.** The transmission may delay shifting into Drive or Reverse and may be corrected by installing reformulated Mercedes-Benz transmission fluid. (1990)

RECALL HISTORY

1990 300: Bolt used for brake strut support do not meet specification and may break, resulting in deterioration of steering and braking. **1990 300E/CE/TE/D/E4M/TE4M:** Under certain operating conditions, plastic cover of preresistor for auxiliary fan may melt, which could result in underhood fire. **1991-92 400E:** If car is restarted soon after shutoff and charcoal canister is saturated with fuel, fuel vapor may be expelled onto electric auxiliary radiator fan preresistor; under certain conditions, that preresistor could become hot enough to ignite the fuel. **1992 w/"ASR" automatic slip control:** Plastic brake hydraulic hose was misrouted too close to preresistor for auxiliary cooling fan, which becomes hot under certain conditions; could cause hose to melt and leak brake fluid onto hot preresistor, resulting in possible fire. **1992-95 E Class 124:** Front passenger metal footrest can, over time, abrade through wiring harness, causing short circuit; wires might then overheat, engine may stall, or airbag could inadvertently deploy.

1994-00 MERCEDES-BENZ C-CLASS

1995 Mercedes-Benz C-Class 4-door

FOR Antilock brakes • Steering/handling • Acceleration (C280, C36)

AGAINST Road noise • Rear-seat room • Wet-weather traction

EVALUATION Both the 4- and 6-cylinder engines are quiet and refined, even when pushed hard, but suffer rather leisurely acceleration from a standing start. Both of the 2001 V6 engines are quite smooth. The older engines do gather steam quickly and deliver strong passing power—especially the C280. A C280 sedan accelerated to 60 mph in a brief 8.3 seconds. The C320, introduced in 2001, did 0-60 in just 7.2 sec. The automatic transmission downshifts promptly to deliver passing power when it's needed, though upshifts can feel sloppy during hard acceleration. Steering response is excellent, and handling is balanced with fine grip through turns. You'll feel most of the bumps in either of these cars, even though the firm suspension absorbs the worst of the impacts. Road noise intrudes on the pleasure, too—especially emanating from the rear tires. Controls are laid out in a user-friendly manner, and you get a comfortable driving position. Though more spacious than its 190 predecessor, the C-Class isn't exactly roomy. Tall drivers might lack sufficient head or leg room, even with the seat position considerably rearward. Moving the driver's seat all the way back drastically cuts into rear leg space, which is only adequate even under the best conditions. Cargo space is good in a usefully square trunk, and an optional folding rear seatback provides extra space.

VALUE All told, we've been impressed with the C-Class. This sedan is well worth a look if you're shopping in the luxury end of the compact-car league.

SPECIFICATIONS

	4-door sedan
Wheelbase, in.	105.9
Overall length, in.	177.4
Overall width, in.	67.7
Overall height, in.	56.1
Curb weight, lbs.	3173
Cargo volume, cu. ft.	13.7
Fuel capacity, gals.	16.4
Seating capacity	5
Front head room, in.	37.2
Max. front leg room, in.	41.5
Rear head room, in.	37.0
Min. rear leg room, in.	32.8

Powertrain layout: longitudinal front-engine/rear-wheel drive

ENGINES

	dohc I4	dohc I4	Supercharged dohc I4
Size, liters/cu. in.	2.2/132	2.3/140	2.3/140
Horsepower	147	148	185
Torque (lbs./ft.)	155	162	200
EPA city/highway mpg			
4-speed OD automatic	23/29		
5-speed OD automatic		23/30	22/29

ENGINES

	dohc I-6	dohc I6	ohc V8
Size, liters/cu. in.	2.8/173	3.6/220	4.3/260
Horsepower	194	268-276	302
Torque (lbs./ft.)	199	284	302
EPA city/highway mpg			
4-speed OD automatic........	19/26	18/22	
5-speed OD automatic........	20/27	18/24	18/23
City/highway mpg (as tested)			
4-speed OD automatic........	19.2	19.7	

Built in Germany

RETAIL PRICES

	GOOD	AVERAGE	POOR
1994 C220	$10,000-11,000	$9,000-10,000	$5,300-6,000
1994 C280	11,500-12,500	10,500-11,500	6,500-7,200
1995 C220	12,000-13,000	11,000-12,000	7,000-7,700
1995 C280	14,000-15,000	13,000-14,000	9,000-9,700
1995 C36	19,000-21,000	17,500-19,500	12,500-14,000
1996 C220	14,000-15,000	13,000-14,000	9,000-9,700
1996 C280	16,000-17,500	14,800-16,200	10,300-11,400
1996 C36	22,000-24,000	20,500-22,500	15,000-16,000
1997 C230	16,000-17,500	15,000-16,200	10,500-11,500
1997 C280	18,500-20,000	17,000-18,500	12,000-13,000
1997 C36	26,000-28,000	24,000-26,000	18,500-20,000
1998 C230	18,500-20,000	17,000-18,500	12,000-13,000
1998 C280	21,500-23,000	20,000-21,500	14,800-16,000
1998 C43	30,000-32,500	27,500-30,000	21,500-24,000
1999 C230	21,000-22,500	19,500-21,000	14,400-15,500
1999 C280	24,000-25,500	22,500-24,000	17,000-18,000
1999 C43	34,000-36,000	31,500-33,500	25,000-26,300
2000 C230	24,000-25,500	22,500-24,000	17,000-18,000
2000 C280	27,000-29,000	25,500-27,500	19,500-21,000
2000 C43	39,000-42,000	36,500-39,500	29,500-31,500

AVERAGE REPLACEMENT COSTS

A/C Compressor...........	$865	Exhaust System	650
Alternator......................	330	Radiator.........................	445
Automatic Transmission or		Shocks and/or Struts....	1,200
Transaxle	1,035	Timing Chain or Belt.....	305
Brakes	200	Universal Joints............	545

TROUBLE SPOTS

• **Brake noise.** Brake squeal at low speeds (under 10 mph) may activate the antilock brake system. (1994-97)

• **Fuel gauge.** Erroneous fuel gauge readings are often due to a bad potentiometer on the fuel level sensor. (1994-96)

• **Clock.** The clock on the C220 may reset itself when starting the engine due to a faulty instrument cluster voltage regulator. (1994)

• **Dashboard lights.** The EC warning light may come on indicating loss of A/C refrigerant caused by a faulty refrigerant pressure sensor. (1997)

• **Hard starting.** The starter may corrode due to the windshield water draining onto it. (1994-96)

RECALL HISTORY

1994 C220: Cruise control linkage may be inadequately lubricated, subject to binding, so throttle will not return to closed position when pedal is released. **1994-95 C220/C280, C36:** In minor frontal impact, hood latch hook may not function properly as secondary safety catch. **1996 C280:** Drive belt pulley of a few 6-cylinder engines can develop fatigue cracks and break; car would then lack engine cooling, battery charging, and/or power steering.

1998-01 MERCEDES-BENZ CLK

FOR Steering/handling • Acceleration • Side airbags

AGAINST Rear-seat room • Cargo room • Rear-seat entry/exit

EVALUATION A CLK320 hit 60 mph in just 7 seconds, and yielded decent 21.6-mpg gas mileage—using the mandatory premium fuel. The CLK430 is slightly sleepy off the line but then rockets ahead, in keeping with Mercedes' claim of 6.1-second 0-60 time. That one averaged 20.2 mpg. We haven't timed a 430 or CLK55, but in test drives, both seem up to Mercedes' 0-60 claims of 6.1 and around 5 sec, respectively. Mercedes-Benz's 5-speed automatic transmission has a gear for just

1998 Mercedes-Benz CLK coupe

about every situation, and shifts with smooth authority. Braking is superb: swift and undramatic. Handling is responsive and stable, cornering response flat, though the CLK is not quite as agile as a BMW 3-Series. A firm but mostly comfortable ride lets you feel most bumps, but not really harsh impacts. That benefit is spoiled, however, by thumping over expansion joints and tire rumble on rough pavements. Road roar is noticeable, especially from the rear tires. Wind and mechanical ruckus are well checked. Both engines emit a pleasing, subdued snarl under hard throttle. Front occupants get decent room, but the feeling is snug rather than spacious. Expect skimpy back-seat leg room and tight rear-seat entry/exit, at least for adults, despite front seats that power forward after tilting their backrests. The rear seat is configured for two occupants only, and leg space vanishes with the front seat positioned fully aft. Front head room is just adequate for 6-footers, and head space in back is scant except for preteens. Cargo space isn't great either. The wheel only telescopes (no tilt), and several switches are poorly marked or placed. Over-the-shoulder views are not the best, but visibility is generally good. Controls are handy and user-friendly, once you've deciphered a few markings. Cabin decor is more clinical than cushy, not uncommon for Mercedes, though workmanship is generally fine inside and out. Mercedes-Benz took great pains to make its convertible solid, and succeeded admirably.

VALUE A comfortable and capable tourer, CLK offers Mercedes prestige and greater refinement, plus style and poise, for about the same money as Volvo's C70 coupe. High resale value has always been a "plus" for any Mercedes, though that makes secondhand prices high, too.

SPECIFICATIONS

	2-door conv.	2-door coupe
Wheelbase, in.	105.9	105.9
Overall length, in.	180.2	180.2
Overall width, in.	67.8	67.8
Overall height, in.	54.3	53.0
Curb weight, lbs.	3655	3240
Cargo volume, cu. ft.	9.9	11.0
Fuel capacity, gals.	16.4	16.4
Seating capacity	4	4
Front head room, in.	37.5	36.9
Max. front leg room, in.	41.9	41.9
Rear head room, in.	36.4	35.6
Min. rear leg room, in.	27.4	31.1

Powertrain layout: longitudinal front-engine/rear-wheel drive

ENGINES

	ohc V6	ohc V8	ohc V8
Size, liters/cu. in.	3.2/195	4.3/260	5.4/322
Horsepower	215	275	342
Torque (lbs./ft.)	229	295	376
EPA city/highway mpg			
5-speed OD automatic	21/29	18/25	17/24
City/highway mpg (as tested)			
5-speed OD automatic	21.6	20.2	14.9

Built in Germany

RETAIL PRICES

	GOOD	AVERAGE	POOR
1998 CLK320 coupe	$29,000-31,000	$27,500-29,500	$21,500-23,000
1999 CLK320 coupe	31,500-33,500	30,000-32,000	24,000-25,500
1999 CLK430 coupe	36,000-38,000	34,000-36,000	27,000-28,500
1999 CLK320 conv.	37,500-40,000	35,500-38,000	28,500-30,500
2000 CLK320 coupe	34,000-36,000	32,000-34,000	25,500-27,000

 Prices are accurate at time of publication.

	GOOD	AVERAGE	POOR
2000 CLK430 coupe	$40,000-42,500	$38,000-40,000	$31,000-32,500
2000 CLK320 conv.	41,000-43,500	39,000-41,500	320,00 -34,000
2000 CLK430 conv.	47,000-49,500	44,500-47,000	37,000-39,000
2001 CLK320 coupe	37,000-39,500	35,000-37,500	—
2001 CLK430 coupe	44,000-47,000	42,000-45,000	—
2001 CLK320 conv.	45,000-48,000	43,000-46,000	—
2001 CLK430 conv.	52,500-55,500	50,000-53,000	—
2001 CLK55 coupe	60,000-63,000	57,500-60,000	—

AVERAGE REPLACEMENT COSTS

A/C Compressor	$790	Clutch, Pressure Plate, Bearing	810
Alternator	475	Constant Velocity Joints	1,050
Automatic Transmission or Transaxle	1,105	Exhaust System	780
Brakes	755	Radiator	665
Shocks and/or Struts	1,595	Timing Chain or Belt	960

TROUBLE SPOTS

• **Dashboard lights.** The check engine light may come on due to a failure of the fuel tank pressure sensor or gasoline vapor purge control valve. (1998)

• **Starter.** The starter stops running before the engine is running due to lack of grease on the starter drive gear. (1998)

RECALL HISTORY

1999 CLK320: Due to defective weld, anchorages may not adequately secure front seatbelts in a crash.

1996-01 MERCEDES-BENZ E-CLASS

1998 Mercedes-Benz E320 4-door sedan

FOR Acceleration (gas engines) • Ride/handling • Build quality • Quietness

AGAINST Fuel economy (except diesel) • Instruments/controls • Price

EVALUATION All E-Class sedans are more athletic than most luxury 4-door models, if not so nimble as, say, a 5-Series BMW or Lexus GS. Steering is firm and precise, body lean modest in hard cornering. The taut suspension provides a comfortable highway ride and smothers most bumps and ruts around town. Silence is another virtue, so these sedans cruise quietly at highway speeds. Space is ample for four adults in any E-Class sedan, though a bulky transmission tunnel precludes true long-distance comfort for the person in the center rear position. All models offer good cargo capacity, flat load floors, large trunk openings, and low liftovers. The wagon's third seat easily folds flush with the cargo deck, but it's sized more for youngsters than grownups. The E-Class pilot gets good visibility from a comfortable, easily tailored driver's position. Gauges and controls are well designed and laid out, though markings on too many of the switches are not obvious. Acceleration is satisfying even in the Turbodiesel model, and brisk in the E320, which uses a smooth and responsive 6-cylinder gas engine. Moving up a notch, a recent E430 delivers stirring highway passing power. The automatic transmission downshifts promptly to deliver strong passing response. Fuel mileage is best with a diesel. An E320 sedan with the inline gas six got a so-so average of 21.1 mpg, with more than half the driving on highways. The V8 E420 amounts to a Teutonic muscle car, but it gets quite thirsty for fuel. Workmanship, as expected, is top-notch.

VALUE With its exceptional quality and strong performance, the E-Class deserves strong consideration among premium sedans. Best choice for value is the E320. With any model, high resale values translate to hefty prices on the used-car market.

SPECIFICATIONS

	4-door sedan	4-door wagon
Wheelbase, in.	111.5	111.5
Overall length, in.	189.4	190.4
Overall width, in.	70.8	70.8
Overall height, in.	56.7	59.3
Curb weight, lbs.	3460	3670
Cargo volume, cu. ft.	15.3	82.6
Fuel capacity, gals.	21.1	18.5
Seating capacity	5	7
Front head room, in.	37.6	38.6
Max. front leg room, in.	41.3	41.3
Rear head room, in.	37.2	37.0
Min. rear leg room, in.	36.1	36.1

Powertrain layout: longitudinal front-engine/rear- or all-wheel drive

ENGINES

	Diesel dohc I6	Turbodiesel ohc I6	dohc I6	ohc V6
Size, liters/cu. in.	3.0/183	3.0/183	3.2/195	3.2/195
Horsepower	134	174	217	221
Torque (lbs./ft.)	155	244	229	232
EPA city/highway mpg				
4-speed OD automatic	28/35		19/26	
5-speed OD automatic	26/33	26/34	20/27	21/29
City/highway mpg (as tested)				
4-speed OD automatic			18.3	
5-speed OD automatic		25.6		19.2

ENGINES

	dohc V8	dohc V8	dohc V8
Size, liters/cu. in.	4.2/256	4.3/260	5.4/322
Horsepower	275	275	349
Torque (lbs./ft.)	295	295	391
EPA city/highway mpg			
5-speed OD automatic	18/25	19/26	17/24
City/highway mpg (as tested)			
5-speed OD automatic	16.5		

Built in Germany

RETAIL PRICES

	GOOD	AVERAGE	POOR
1996 E300D	$18,500-20,000	$17,000-18,500	$12,000-13,000
1996 E320	21,000-23,000	19,500-21,500	14,400-16,000
1997 E300D	22,000-24,000	20,500-22,500	15,000-16,500
1997 E320	24,500-26,500	22,500-24,500	17,000-18,500
1997 E420	26,500-28,500	24,500-26,500	19,000-20,500
1998 E300TD	26,000-28,000	24,500-26,500	19,000-20,500
1998 E320	28,000-30,000	26,000-28,000	20,000-21,500
1998 E430	31,000-33,500	29,000-31,500	23,000-24,500
1999 E300TD	30,500-32,500	28,500-30,500	22,500-23,700
1999 E320	32,500-34,500	30,500-32,500	24,500-26,000
1999 E430	35,500-37,500	33,500-35,500	26,500-28,000
1999 E55	45,000-47,500	42,500-45,000	34,500-36,000
2000 E320	35,000-38,000	33,000-36,000	26,000-28,000
2000 E430	39,000-42,000	37,000-40,000	30,000-32,000
2000 E55	50,000-53,000	47,500-50,000	39,000-41,000
2001 E320	40,000-43,000	38,000-41,000	—
2001 E430	45,000-48,000	42,500-45,000	—
2001 E55	55,000-58,000	52,000-55,000	—

AVERAGE REPLACEMENT COSTS

A/C Compressor	$390	Constant Velocity Joints	845
Alternator	480	Exhaust System	845
Automatic Transmission or Transaxle	1,190	Radiator	440
Brakes	330	Shocks and/or Struts	1,630
		Timing Chain or Belt	710

TROUBLE SPOTS

• **Dashboard lights.** A malfunction in the fuel tank pressure sensor or the purge control valve (or both) will cause the check engine light to come on. (1997-98)

• **Headlights.** Headlight and parking light bulbs burn out prematurely on E 300 models and a kit with new sockets and bulbs is available. (1996-97)

RECALL HISTORY

1996 E320: Drive belt pulley on some cars can break. **1997:** Some passenger vehicles have experienced side airbag deployments in the absence of a crash.

1998-01 MERCEDES-BENZ M-CLASS

2000 Mercedes-Benz ML55

FOR Steering/handling • Build quality • Cargo room • Acceleration (ML430, ML55 AMG)

AGAINST Ride (ML430, ML55 AMG) • Fuel economy

EVALUATION Seeking to create an SUV that drives like a car, Mercedes-Benz took a clear lead. A Lexus RX 300 or BMW X5 feels more carlike, but few true SUVs are more pleasant to drive than an M-Class. Though an ML320 isn't that snappy moving from a stop, the smooth, responsive automatic transmission helps get the best out of its V6 engine. V8 models are noticeably quicker. Off-the-line-punch isn't great, but the ML430 gathers speed quickly and has good passing power. An ML320 accelerated to 60 mph in 9.1 seconds and averaged 13.9 to 15 mpg. An ML430 averaged 15.7 mpg, but the high-performance ML55 got only 12.9 mpg. Wind and road noise are low for an SUV, if higher than those of the RX300. Both V8 engines emit a throaty roar under hard throttle, but the V6 sounds coarse when pushed. Poised and stable in tight turns, the ML320 moves with far less body lean than most SUVs. Steering is precise and linear, though self-centering is weak. Braking is strong and stable. A smooth, supple, or-road ride is the rule in an ML320. Firmer suspensions and low-profile tires make other models stiff over bumps and broken pavement. Although the unique 4ETS system works transparently in light-duty, off-pavement driving, it's not as effective as traditional 4WD setups in heavy snow or on demanding off-road trails. Four adults have ample room, and three can almost fit comfortably in back. The rear seat slides forward about 3 inches for extra cargo space, but rear leg room then becomes tight. Step-in height is much lower than the SUV norm. Unusually wide doors provide easy entry/exit. Controls are easy to find and use, though some markings are not obvious. Outward vision is fine forward, but a bit cluttered by headrests directly astern. Load volume is ample and easy to use, with a low, flat floor. Sturdy construction is evident, despite occasional body shudder.

VALUE Mercedes leads the true-SUV pack for its blend of refinement, handling, overall competence, and carlike convenience. Strong resale values keep prices high.

SPECIFICATIONS

	4-door wagon
Wheelbase, in.	111.0
Overall length, in.	180.6
Overall width, in.	72.2
Overall height, in.	69.9
Curb weight, lbs.	4586
Cargo volume, cu. ft.	85.4
Fuel capacity, gals.	19.0
Seating capacity	5-7
Front head room, in.	39.8
Max. front leg room, in.	40.3
Rear head room, in.	39.7
Min. rear leg room, in.	38.0

Powertrain layout: longitudinal front-engine/4-wheel drive

ENGINES

	ohc V6	ohc V8	ohc V8
Size, liters/cu. in.	3.2/195	4.3/260	5.4/332
Horsepower	215	268	342
Torque (lbs./ft.)	233	288	376
EPA city/highway mpg			
5-speed OD automatic	16/20	15/19	14/18
City/highway mpg (as tested)			
5-speed OD automatic	13.9	15.7	12.9

Built in USA

RETAIL PRICES

	GOOD	AVERAGE	POOR
1998 ML320	$22,000-24,000	$21,000-23,000	$16,500-17,300
1999 ML320	25,000-27,000	23,500-25,500	18,500-19,500
1999 ML430	29,000-31,000	27,500-29,500	22,000-23,500
2000 ML320	28,000-30,000	26,000-28,000	20,500-22,000
2000 ML430	32,500-35,000	30,500-33,000	24,000-25,500
2000 ML55 AMG	49,000-52,000	46,000-49,000	39,000-40,500
2001 ML320	31,000-34,000	29,000-32,000	—
2001 ML430	36,000-39,000	34,000-37,000	—
2001 ML55 AMG	55,000-58,000	52,000-55,000	—

AVERAGE REPLACEMENT COSTS

A/C Compressor	$915	Constant Velocity Joints	1,750
Alternator	1,025	Exhaust System	775
Automatic Transmission or Transaxle	910	Radiator	810
		Shocks and/or Struts	990
Brakes	565	Timing Chain or Belt	515

TROUBLE SPOTS

• **Engine knock.** A knocking noise from the accessory drive belt or water pump is caused by the idler pulley not providing even tension. A countermeasure pulley with a smaller diameter will correct the problem. (1998)

• **Oil leak.** Engine oil may weep from the head gasket. Gaskets are being replaced under warranty. (1998)

• **Engine misfire.** Engine roughness, miss, or stalling may be due to a damaged mass airflow sensor (MAF). This dirt may be getting past the air cleaner due to a damaged gasket, loose cover or improperly installed air cleaner. (1998)

• **Fuel gauge.** The fuel gauge may not read full although the tank is full. The fuel sending unit was being replaced under warranty. (1998)

RECALL HISTORY

1998-99: Latching mechanism on seatbelt assembly was not assembled correctly. If plastic cover is loose during engagement of buckle tongue, the buckle could unlatch. **2000:** Seatbelt anchor in rear folding middle seating position may fail in a crash. **2001:** Faulty AAM II units could cause failure of high beam lights, instrument cluster, door locks, and wiper systems.

1990-97 MERCURY COUGAR

1991 Mercury Cougar XR7

FOR Acceleration (V8)

AGAINST Acceleration (V6) • Fuel economy • Visibility

EVALUATION

See the 1990-98 Ford Thunderbird.

VALUE

See the 1990-98 Ford Thunderbird.

SPECIFICATIONS

	2-door coupe
Wheelbase, in.	113.0
Overall length, in.	200.3
Overall width, in.	72.7
Overall height, in.	52.5
Curb weight, lbs.	3575
Cargo volume, cu. ft.	15.1
Fuel capacity, gals.	18.0
Seating capacity	5
Front head room, in.	38.1
Max. front leg room, in.	42.5
Rear head room, in.	37.5
Min. rear leg room, in.	35.8

Powertrain layout: longitudinal front-engine/rear-wheel drive

ENGINES

	ohv V6	Supercharged ohv V6	ohv V8	ohc V8
Size, liters/cu. in.	3.8/232	3.8/232	5.0/302	4.6/281
Horsepower	140-145	210	200	205
Torque (lbs./ft.)	215	315	275	280
EPA city/highway mpg				
5-speed OD manual..............		17/24		
4-speed OD automatic..........	19/27	17/23	17/24	17/25
City/highway mpg (as tested)				
4-speed OD automatic..........			15.5	18.2

Built in USA

RETAIL PRICES

	GOOD	AVERAGE	POOR
1990 Cougar	$1,500-2,200	$1,000-1,600	$200-400
1991 Cougar	2,000-2,700	1,400-2,000	400-700
1992 Cougar	2,500-3,200	1,900-2,500	600-900
1993 Cougar	3,100-3,800	2,400-3,100	800-1,300
1994 Cougar	3,600-4,300	2,900-3,500	1,000-1,500
1995 Cougar	4,400-5,200	3,700-4,400	1,500-1,900
1996 Cougar	5,600-6,500	4,900-5,700	2,100-2,700
1997 Cougar	7,000-8,000	6,100-7,000	2,700-3,300

AVERAGE REPLACEMENT COSTS

See the 1990-98 Ford Thunderbird.

TROUBLE SPOTS

See the 1990-98 Ford Thunderbird.

RECALL HISTORY

1990: Battery-to-starter cables on small number of cars with 3.8-liter engine are too long and could contact engine damper pulley. **1990-91:** Nuts that hold windshield wiper motor may loosen. **1990-93:** Ignition switch could suffer short circuit, which can cause overheating, smoke, and possibly fire in steering-column area. **1992-93 cars in specified states:** Movement of fuel lines can result in leakage. **1992-93 w/foglights:** Headlights may go out for various intervals as a result of circuit-breaker opening. **1996:** Driver's door, when closed only to secondary latched position, may not sustain the specified 1000-pound transverse load. **1996 w/semiautomatic temperature-control:** Under certain conditions, blower does not operate as intended.

1999-01 MERCURY COUGAR

2000 Mercury Cougar

FOR Exterior finish • Ride (base suspension)

AGAINST Rear visibility • Rear-seat room

EVALUATION Reasonably peppy with the base engine, a Cougar gains some low-end muscle if equipped with the V6, but passing power is unimpressive. So is acceleration, with almost 10 seconds needed to reach 60 mph in an automatic-transmission Cougar. The automatic shifts fluidly, but hunts annoyingly between gears in hilly terrain and lacks a provision to lock out overdrive fourth gear. Neither engine matches Japanese-brand rivals for refinement or high-revving fun. As for economy, we averaged 19.9 mpg with a five-speed V6, and 20.7 with automatic. Cougars handle well, gripping nicely in sweeping turns, but lack the twisty-road agility and poise offered by most import brands. A long wheelbase (for a coupe) hampers nimbleness, but helps the base suspension yield a relatively comfortable ride. The V6 Sport Group improves roadability, but at the expense of a thumpy, nervous ride. Brake-pedal feel has been inconsistent, ranging from mushy to touchy on new test models,

though stopping power is adequate. Road rumble and exhaust noise are intrusive. Front head and leg room are adequate in a rather claustrophobic interior. Bucket seats afford good lateral support, but aren't the most comfortable. The cramped rear seat is for preteens, with poorly shaped cushions. Split-folding rear seatbacks provide generous cargo space, but liftover is high. Lack of a redline on the tachometer, and low radio controls, mar an otherwise appealing dashboard. In addition, the cabin abounds with hard, cheap-looking plastic.

VALUE With their "new-edge" look, Cougars earn points for style and originality in the trendy sports-coupe segment, but score weaker in practical virtues and driving satisfaction. Most competitive threat is the Mitsubishi Eclipse, which was much improved for 2000 and handles better. A Dodge Avenger/Stratus coupe is roomier, and an Acura CL or Honda Prelude costs considerably more.

SPECIFICATIONS

	2-door coupe
Wheelbase, in.	106.4
Overall length, in.	185.0
Overall width, in.	69.6
Overall height, in.	52.2
Curb weight, lbs.	2892
Cargo volume, cu. ft.	14.5
Fuel capacity, gals.	15.5
Seating capacity	4
Front head room, in.	37.8
Max. front leg room, in.	42.5
Rear head room, in.	34.6
Min. rear leg room, in.	33.2

Powertrain layout: transverse front-engine/front-wheel drive

ENGINES

	dohc I4	dohc V6
Size, liters/cu. in.	2.0/121	2.5/155
Horsepower	125	170
Torque (lbs./ft.)	130	165
EPA city/highway mpg		
5-speed OD manual.................	24/34	19/28
4-speed OD automatic.............		20.29
City/highway mpg (as tested)		
5-speed OD manual.................		19.9
4-speed OD automatic.............		20.7

Built in USA

RETAIL PRICES

	GOOD	AVERAGE	POOR
1999 Cougar	$9,500-10,500	$8,500-9,500	$6,000-7,000
2000 Cougar	11,000-12,500	10,000-11,500	7,000-8,000
2001 Cougar	13,000-14,500	12,000-13,500	—

AVERAGE REPLACEMENT COSTS

A/C Compressor...........	$395	Clutch, Pressure Plate,	
Alternator.....................	535	Bearing	390
Automatic Transmission or		Constant Velocity Joints	850
Transaxle	790	Exhaust System	650
Brakes	455	Radiator........................	405
Shocks and/or Struts.....	1,300	Timing Chain or Belt.....	560

TROUBLE SPOTS

• **Automatic transmission.** Automatic transmission fluid may leak from the vent hose. A redesigned hose is available. (1999-2000)

• **Sunroof/moonroof.** If the sunroof rattles, there are revised guide shoes available. (1999)

• **Engine misfire.** The 2.5L and 3.0L engines were built with the timing marks for the camshafts in the wrong place and if replacement timing chains are installed using the marks, severe engine damage will result. (1999)

• **Climate control.** The blower may not work if the blower resistor goes bad. It is being replaced under warranty up to 6 years or 72,000 miles. (1999-2000)

• **Hard starting.** The engine may not start if the windshield wiper switch is in the low or intermittent position because the wiper wiring was installed too close to the antitheft control module. (1999-2000)

RECALL HISTORY

1999: In high humidity, door latch pawl on certain cars may stick in open or unlatched position, and door will not latch when closed. **1999:** Rough surface of heater-blower resistor's stainless steel blades can damage the copper surface of wiring harness connector, eventually resulting in increased resistance and an open circuit, leading to electrical arcing. **1999:** An open circuit in the wiring harness could lead to electrical arcing that could melt the connector housing material, increasing the potential for a fire. **1999:** Brake lamp switch terminals could overheat, potentially causing either loss of brake lamp function or continuously illuminated brake lamps. **1999-00 w/V6:** Battery cable may be misrouted and attachment to alternator cable under-torqued. If misrouted, cable could contact power steering line and insulation could wear, resulting in electrical short. **2000-01 w/adjustable pedals:** If grease from pedal assembly enters stoplamp switch, it can contaminate contacts leading to carbon buildup and, potentially, a short circuit.

1992-01 MERCURY GRAND MARQUIS

1992 Mercury Grand Marquis

FOR Acceleration • Passenger and cargo room • Antilock brakes (optional)

AGAINST Fuel economy • Steering feel • Climate controls • Radio controls (early models)

EVALUATION

See the 1992-01 Ford Crown Victoria.

VALUE

See the 1992-01 Ford Crown Victoria.

SPECIFICATIONS

	4-door sedan
Wheelbase, in.	114.4
Overall length, in.	212.0
Overall width, in.	77.8
Overall height, in.	56.8
Curb weight, lbs.	3776
Cargo volume, cu. ft.	6
Fuel capacity, gals.	18-20
Seating capacity	20.6
Front head room, in.	39.4
Max. front leg room, in.	42.5
Rear head room, in.	38.1
Min. rear leg room, in.	38.8

Powertrain layout: longitudinal front-engine/rear-wheel drive

ENGINES

	ohc V8
Size, liters/cu. in.	4.6/281
Horsepower	190-235
Torque (lbs./ft.)	265-275

EPA city/highway mpg
4-speed OD automatic ... 17/25

City/highway mpg (as tested)
4-speed OD automatic ... 16.0

Built in Canada

RETAIL PRICES

	GOOD	AVERAGE	POOR
1992 Grand Marquis	$2,600-3,300	$2,000-2,600	$400-800
1993 Grand Marquis	3,200-4,000	2,600-3,300	700-1,200
1994 Grand Marquis	3,800-4,500	3,100-3,800	1,100-1,500
1995 Grand Marquis	4,800-5,600	4,100-4,800	1,600-2,000
1996 Grand Marquis	6,300-7,300	5,500-6,500	2,300-2,800
1997 Grand Marquis	8,000-9,000	7,100-8,000	3,300-3,800
1998 Grand Marquis	9,800-11,000	8,800-10,000	4,500-5,200
1999 Grand Marquis	11,700-13,200	10,700-12,000	5,700-6,600
2000 Grand Marquis	13,700-15,200	12,500-14,000	7,100-8,500
2001 Grand Marquis	15,700-17,500	14,500-16,000	—

AVERAGE REPLACEMENT COSTS

See the 1990-98 Ford Crown Victoria.

TROUBLE SPOTS

See the 1990-98 Ford Crown Victoria.

RECALL HISTORY

1992-93: Speed-control deactivation switch can develop short that could potentially result in underhood fire. **1994:** Nuts and bolts that attach rear brake adapter to axle housing flange can loosen, allowing damage to ABS sensor, hydraulic line, or parking brake cable. **1995:** Seal between fuel filler pipe and fuel tank may not be fully cured, which could allow fuel to leak. **1995:** Some passenger-side airbags may not inflate properly; also, igniter end cap can separate, causing hot gases to be released. **1995:** Noncycling power window circuit breaker and cycling-type headlamp breaker were interchanged; in the event of short or overload in circuit, both headlamps can go out without warning. **1995:** Heads of rivets holding rear outboard seatbelt D-rings may fracture under load, reducing belt's restraining capability in an accident. **1996:** Driver's door, when closed only to secondary latched position, may not sustain the specified 1000-pound transverse load. **1996-00:** Replacement seatbelts made by TRW and sold by Ford may not restrain occupant in a collision. **1998-00:** Jacking instructions are incorrect and, if followed, could allow vehicle to drop suddenly. **2000:** During high-load conditions (ice, snow, or other debris), windshield wipers could become inoperative with no advance wiring. **2000:** Loose module could result in delayed airbag deployment. **2000:** Left rear seatbelt retractor attaching bolts may have been incorrectly tightened. **2001:** A restraint control module (RCM) or a side or front crash sensor may have been assembled with one or more of the screws that mount the circuit board in the housing missing. **2001:** Driver's and/or outboard front passenger's seatbelt buckle may not fully latch. In the event of a crash, the restraint system may not provide adequate occupant protection.

1997-01 MERCURY MOUNTAINEER

1998 Mercury Mountaineer

FOR Acceleration • Passenger and cargo room • Visibility • Antilock brakes

AGAINST Fuel economy • Ride

EVALUATION

See the 1990-98 Ford Explorer.

VALUE

See the 1990-98 Ford Explorer.

SPECIFICATIONS

	4-door wagon
Wheelbase, in.	111.5
Overall length, in.	188.5
Overall width, in.	70.2
Overall height, in.	67.6
Curb weight, lbs.	4139
Cargo volume, cu. ft.	81.6
Fuel capacity, gals.	21.0
Seating capacity	5
Front head room, in.	39.9
Max. front leg room, in.	42.4
Rear head room, in.	39.3
Min. rear leg room, in.	37.7

Powertrain layout: longitudinal front-engine/rear- or 4-wheel drive

ENGINES

	ohc V6	ohV V8
Size, liters/cu. in.	4.0/245	5.0/302
Horsepower	205-210	210-215
Torque (lbs./ft.)	240	288

EPA city/highway mpg
4-speed OD automatic ... 14/18

	ohc V6	ohV V8
5-speed OD automatic..	15/19	
City/highway mpg (as tested)		
4-speed OD automatic..		16.1

Built in USA

RETAIL PRICES

	GOOD	AVERAGE	POOR
1997 Mountaineer 2WD	$10,000-11,000	$9,000-10,000	$5,300-6,000
1997 Mountaineer 4WD	11,000-12,500	10,000-11,500	6,000-7,000
1998 Mountaineer 2WD	11,500-12,500	10,500-11,500	6,500-7,200
1998 Mountaineer 4WD	12,500-14,000	11,500-12,800	7,500-8,500
1999 Mountaineer 2WD	13,000-14,500	11,800-13,200	7,700-8,700
1999 Mountaineer 4WD	14,500-16,000	13,200-14,500	9,100-10,000
2000 Mountaineer 2WD	15,000-17,000	13,500-15,500	9,300-10,500
2000 Mountaineer 4WD/AWD	16,500-18,000	15,000-16,500	10,500-11,500
2001 Mountaineer 2WD	17,500-19,500	16,000-18,000	—
2001 Mountaineer 4WD/AWD	19,000-20,500	17,500-19,000	—

AVERAGE REPLACEMENT COSTS

See the 1990-98 Ford Explorer.

TROUBLE SPOTS

See the 1990-98 Ford Explorer.

RECALL HISTORY

1997: After operation at highway speeds, at below -20°(F), engine may not return to idle. **1997:** Gas-cylinder bracket may not properly support rear liftgate. **1997-98 w/SOHC 4.0-liter:** Fuel lines can be damaged and fire could result if vehicle is jump started and ground cable is attached to fuel line bracket near battery. **1997-98 w/4.0-liter engine:** A gap between the plate and bore of throttle body was too narrow, causing the throttle pedal to stick. **1998-99:** Speed control cable on certain vehicles can interfere with pulley, preventing throttle from returning to idle when disengaging the speed control. **1998-99:** Secondary hood latch on certain vehicles may corrode and stick in open position. **1999:** Right front brake line connection could separate, causing leakage when brake pedal is applied. **1999-00 w/4.0-liter engine and AWD:** Generic electronic module could "lock-up," so various functions (front wipers, interior lights, 4x4 system, etc.) could not be turned on or off. **2000 w/side airbags:** Side airbag could deploy if ignition key is in "run" position and seatbelt webbing is forcibly extracted from locked retractor with jerking motion.

1995-00 MERCURY MYSTIQUE

1996 Mercury Mystique

FOR Optional antilock brakes • Acceleration (V6) • Steering/handling

AGAINST Road noise • Rear-seat room • Stereo controls • Engine noise (4-cylinder)

EVALUATION

See the 1995-00 Ford Contour.

VALUE

See the 1995-00 Ford Contour.

SPECIFICATIONS

	4-door sedan
Wheelbase, in.	106.5
Overall length, in.	183.5
Overall width, in.	69.1
Overall height, in.	54.5
Curb weight, lbs.	2831

	4-door sedan
Cargo volume, cu. ft.	13.9
Fuel capacity, gals.	14.5
Seating capacity	5
Front head room, in.	39.0
Max. front leg room, in.	42.4
Rear head room, in.	36.7
Min. rear leg room, in.	34.3

Powertrain layout: transverse front-engine/front-wheel drive

ENGINES

	dohc I4	dohc V6
Size, liters/cu. in.	2.0/121	2.5/155
Horsepower	125	170
Torque (lbs./ft.)	130	165
EPA city/highway mpg		
5-speed OD manual..	24/34	21/31
4-speed OD automatic..	23/32	21/30
City/highway mpg (as tested)		
5-speed OD manual..		19.9
4-speed OD automatic..	20.7	19.5

Built in USA, Mexico

RETAIL PRICES

	GOOD	AVERAGE	POOR
1995 Mystique	$3,200-3,900	$2,600-3,200	$700-1,100
1996 Mystique	3,900-4,600	3,300-3,900	1,200-1,600
1997 Mystique	4,900-6,000	4,300-5,300	1,800-2,500
1998 Mystique	6,200-7,500	5,400-6,700	2,500-3,300
1999 Mystique	7,500-8,700	6,600-7,700	3,400-4,100

AVERAGE REPLACEMENT COSTS

See the 1995-00 Ford Contour.

TROUBLE SPOTS

See the 1995-00 Ford Contour.

RECALL HISTORY

1995: Some passenger-side airbags may not inflate properly; also, igniter end cap can separate, releasing hot gases. **1995:** Metal shield on plastic fuel filler pipe can develop static charge during refueling; could serve as ignition source for fuel vapors. **1995:** Fuel tank filler reinforcement can leak, resulting in fire. **1995:** Front seatbelt outboard anchor tabs may be cracked. **1995-96 w/traction control:** Throttle cables were damaged during assembly, leading to fraying or separation; could prevent engine from returning to idle. **1995-96 w/V6:** Tightening of the engine cooling fan motor bearings can result in increased motor torque and higher-than-normal motor current and accompanying high motor temperatures. **1995-98:** Automatic-transmission control can be damaged if subjected to certain interior cleaning products; gear indicator can deteriorate and incorrectly indicate actual gear position. **1996:** Fuel filler pipe vent hose may have less than intended level of ozone resistance, which could result in brittleness and cracking. **1996-98:** Terminals at headlight switch and wiring harness can experience heat damage as a result of overheating. **1996-98 w/o ABS:** Pressure-reducing valve in rear brakes may be subject to corrosion, which could result in malfunction when operated in areas that use salt compounds for de-icing or dust control. **1996-98:** An open circuit in the wiring harness could lead to electrical arcing that could melt the connector housing material, increasing the potential for a fire. **1998:** Text and/or graphics for headlamp aiming instructions, provided in owner guides, are not sufficiently clear. **1998:** Accelerator cable may have burr that could fray the core wire; cable could stick, bind, or cause high engine rpm. **1998:** Airbag sensor wiring insulation can become brittle and crack over time; could cause airbag warning light to illuminate and disable airbag system. **1998:** Front coil springs may fracture as a result of corrosion in high corrosion environments. **1999 w/automatic transmission:** Ignition key can be rotated to "Lock" position and removed, without shift lever being in "Park" position. **2000:** Improper label was installed on some cars, with incorrect instructions for activation of childproof safety locks.

1990-95 MERCURY SABLE

FOR Acceleration (3.8-liter V6) • Ride • Passenger and cargo room • Antilock brakes (optional)

AGAINST Fuel economy • Radio controls • Instruments/controls (electronic)

1992 Mercury Sable 4-door sedan

EVALUATION

See the 1990-95 Ford Taurus.

VALUE

See the 1990-95 Ford Taurus.

SPECIFICATIONS

	4-door sedan	4-door wagon
Wheelbase, in.	106.0	106.0
Overall length, in.	192.2	193.3
Overall width, in.	70.9	70.9
Overall height, in.	54.1	55.5
Curb weight, lbs.	3144	3292
Cargo volume, cu. ft.	18.0	83.1
Fuel capacity, gals.	16.0	16.0
Seating capacity	6	8
Front head room, in.	38.3	38.6
Max. front leg room, in.	41.7	41.7
Rear head room, in.	37.7	38.1
Min. rear leg room, in.	37.1	36.9

Powertrain layout: transverse front-engine/front-wheel drive

ENGINES

	ohv V6	ohv V6
Size, liters/cu. in.	3.0/182	3.8/232
Horsepower	140	140
Torque (lbs./ft.)	165	215
EPA city/highway mpg		
4-speed OD automatic	20/30	19/28
City/highway mpg (as tested)		
4-speed OD automatic		16.8

Built in USA

RETAIL PRICES

	GOOD	AVERAGE	POOR
1990 Sable	$1,300-1,900	$700-1,300	$100-200
1991 Sable	1,600-2,300	1,000-1,700	200-300
1992 Sable	2,000-2,700	1,400-2,000	300-400
1993 Sable	2,500-3,200	1,900-2,500	500-800
1994 Sable	3,000-3,900	2,400-3,200	800-1,200
1995 Sable	3,500-4,600	2,800-3,800	1,000-1,600

AVERAGE REPLACEMENT COSTS

See the 1990-95 Ford Taurus.

TROUBLE SPOTS

See the 1990-95 Ford Taurus.

RECALL HISTORY

1990-91: Front brake rotors on "salt belt" cars may suffer corrosion, resulting in reduced braking effectiveness, abnormal pedal effort, loud noise, and possible increase in stopping distance. **1990-95 sold or registered in 24 states or D.C.:** Rear lower subframe mount plate nut can experience corrosion cracking if subjected to long-term exposure to road salt; can result in fracture. **1991-95 w/3.8-liter engine, in 23 states:** Speed-control cable could freeze, causing throttle to stick and not return to idle. **1992 wagon:** Secondary portion of liftgate latch on some cars may not function, possibly allowing liftgate to open while car is in motion if latch is not in primary position. **1992-95 in AK, IA, MN, NE, ND, or SD:** During high winds, heavy drifting snow, and low temperatures, engine fan may become blocked or frozen and fail to rotate; can cause smoke/flame. **1993:** Controllers intended for use in rear-wheel-drive vehicles (instead of front drive) may have been installed on small number of cars with optional antilock braking, which could result in reduced braking ability. **1993 in 21 states:** Front coil springs can fracture as a result of corrosion combined with small cracks. **1993-94:** Headlights can flash intermittently as a result of a circuit-breaker opening. **1995:** On some cars, retainer clip that holds master-cylinder pushrod to brake pedal arm is missing or not fully installed; components can separate, resulting in loss of braking.

1996-99 MERCURY SABLE

1996 Mercury Sable 4-door sedan

FOR Optional antilock brakes • Acceleration (LS) • Steering/handling • Passenger and cargo room

AGAINST Automatic transmission performance (GS) • Rear visibility

EVALUATION

See the 1996-99 Ford Taurus.

VALUE

See the 1996-99 Ford Taurus.

SPECIFICATIONS

	4-door sedan	4-door wagon
Wheelbase, in.	108.5	108.5
Overall length, in.	199.7	199.1
Overall width, in.	73.0	73.0
Overall height, in.	55.4	57.6
Curb weight, lbs.	3388	3536
Cargo volume, cu. ft.	16.0	81.3
Fuel capacity, gals.	16.0	16.0
Seating capacity	6[1]	8
Front head room, in.	39.4	39.3
Max. front leg room, in.	42.6	42.6
Rear head room, in.	36.6	48.9
Min. rear leg room, in.	38.9	48.5

1. Five passengers with bucket seats.

Powertrain layout: transverse front-engine/front-wheel drive

ENGINES

	ohv V6	dohc V6
Size, liters/cu. in.	3.0/182	3.0/181
Horsepower	145	200
Torque (lbs./ft.)	170	200
EPA city/highway mpg		
4-speed OD automatic	20/29	20/29
City/highway mpg (as tested)		
4-speed OD automatic	15.7	18.9

Built in USA

RETAIL PRICES

	GOOD	AVERAGE	POOR
1996 Sable sedan	$4,500-5,700	$3,800-5,000	$1,600-2,400
1996 Sable wagon	5,100-6,100	4,400-5,300	2,000-2,700
1997 Sable sedan	6,000-7,200	5,300-6,500	2,700-3,500
1997 Sable wagon	6,700-7,700	5,900-6,900	3,100-3,800
1998 Sable sedan	7,500-8,500	6,700-7,500	3,500-4,200
1998 Sable wagon	8,500-9,500	7,500-8,500	4,000-4,700
1999 Sable sedan	9,000-10,000	8,000-9,000	4,500-5,300
1999 Sable wagon	10,000-11,000	9,000-10,000	5,100-6,000

AVERAGE REPLACEMENT COSTS

See the 1996-99 Ford Taurus.

TROUBLE SPOTS

See the 1996-99 Ford Taurus.

RECALL HISTORY

1996: Brake-fluid indicator can malfunction. **1996 w/AX4S automatic transaxle:** "Park" pawl shaft was improperly positioned during assembly; could result in park pawl occasionally not engaging when selector lever is placed in "Park" position, allowing vehicle to roll if parking brake has not been applied. **1996:** Small number of cars were inadvertently equipped with 18-

gallon fuel tank rather than 16-gallon as specified; displacement of tank's shipping plug could result in leakage. **1996:** "Park" pawl shaft may not be free to rotate; vehicle could roll as if in neutral, with shift lever in "Park" position. **1996-97:** "Park" pawl abutment bracket has sharp edge which can cause pawl to hang up and not engage gear. Vehicle can move even though indicator shows "Park." **1997:** Servo cover can separate, causing transmission fluid to leak and contact catalytic converter; could result in fire. **1997-98:** Headlamp aiming instructions in owner's manuals are not sufficiently clear. **1998-99:** Front seatbelt buckle attaching stud may have been improperly heat-treated, resulting in cracks. **1999:** Retainer clip can disengage from accelerator cable and fall into pedal arm pivot area; engine may not fully return to idle, and insulator could interfere with cable. **1999 w/"California" emissions pkg.:** Incorrect transmission oil cooler line was installed, which contacts ABS module bracket and, over time, can wear and develop a leak. **1999:** Seatbelt retractor may have incorrectly formed pin shaft that could, in some circumstances, prevent seatbelt webbing from being extracted.

RECALL HISTORY

2000: On certain vehicles, "vehicle capacity weight" and "designated seating capacity" information was not printed on the safety certification labels. **2000:** Headlamp switch knob on certain vehicles can fracture and separate, making it difficult to activate headlamps. **2000-01 w/adjustable pedals:** Grease from the adjustable-pedal assembly enters the stop lamp switch and can contaminate the contacts leading to carbon build up, and potentially, a short circuit. **2000-01:** A switch located in the plastic cover of the wiper motor gear case could malfunction and overheat, potentially resulting in loss of wiper function or fire. **2001:** Owner guides may not identify center rear seating position as having LATCH-compatible lower anchorages. **2001:** Child Safety Seat Anchor Latch (ISO-fix anchor) fasteners on certain vehicles do not have adequate residual torque; road vibrations could cause nut to loosen and separate from its stud.

2000-01 MERCURY SABLE

2000 Mercury Sable 4-door sedan

FOR Handling/roadholding • Rear-seat comfort • Cargo room

AGAINST Acceleration (ohv V6)

EVALUATION

See the 2000-2001 Ford Taurus.

VALUE

See the 2000-2001 Ford Taurus.

SPECIFICATIONS

	4-door sedan	4-door wagon
Wheelbase, in.	108.5	108.5
Overall length, in.	200.5	197.7
Overall width, in.	73.0	73.0
Overall height, in.	55.5	58.0
Curb weight, lbs.	3375	3540
Cargo volume, cu. ft.	16.0	81.3
Fuel capacity, gals.	16.0	16.0
Seating capacity	6	6
Front head room, in.	39.8	39.3
Max. front leg room, in.	42.2	42.2
Rear head room, in.	36.7	38.7
Min. rear leg room, in.	38.9	38.5

Powertrain layout: transverse front-engine/front-wheel drive

ENGINES

	ohv V6	dohc V6
Size, liters/cu. in.	3.0/182	3.0/181
Horsepower	153	200
Torque (lbs./ft.)	182	200
EPA city/highway mpg		
4-speed OD automatic	19/28	20/28
City/highway mpg (as tested)		
4-speed OD automatic		18.4

Built in USA

RETAIL PRICES

	GOOD	AVERAGE	POOR
2000 Sable GS	$11,300-12,300	$10,300-11,300	$7,000-7,800
2000 Sable LS	12,000-13,500	11,000-12,500	7,500-8,500
2001 Sable GS	12,800-14,000	11,800-13,000	—
2001 Sable LS	13,500-15,500	12,500-14,500	—

AVERAGE REPLACEMENT COSTS

See the 2000-2001 Ford Taurus.

TROUBLE SPOTS

See the 2000-2001 Ford Taurus.

1991-96 MERCURY TRACER

1993 Mercury Tracer 4-door sedan

FOR Fuel economy • Price

AGAINST Engine noise • Road noise • Rear-seat room • Control layout

EVALUATION

See the 1991-96 Ford Escort.

VALUE

See the 1991-96 Ford Escort.

SPECIFICATIONS

	4-door sedan	4-door wagon
Wheelbase, in.	98.4	98.4
Overall length, in.	170.9	171.3
Overall width, in.	66.7	66.7
Overall height, in.	52.7	53.6
Curb weight, lbs.	2409	2485
Cargo volume, cu. ft.	12.1	66.9
Fuel capacity, gals.	11.9	11.9
Seating capacity	5	5
Front head room, in.	38.4	38.4
Max. front leg room, in.	41.7	41.7
Rear head room, in.	37.4	38.5
Min. rear leg room, in.	34.6	34.6

Powertrain layout: transverse front-engine/front-wheel drive

ENGINES

	ohv I4	dohc I4
Size, liters/cu. in.	1.9/114	1.8/109
Horsepower	88	127
Torque (lbs./ft.)	108	114
EPA city/highway mpg		
5-speed OD manual	31/38	25/31
4-speed OD automatic	26/34	23/29
City/highway mpg (as tested)		
4-speed OD automatic	27.4	22.7

Built in USA, Mexico

RETAIL PRICES

	GOOD	AVERAGE	POOR
1991 Tracer	$1,100-1,600	$600-1,000	$100-200
1992 Tracer	1,400-1,900	800-1,300	100-300
1993 Tracer	1,700-2,300	1,100-1,700	200-400
1994 Tracer	2,000-2,700	1,400-2,100	400-600
1995 Tracer	2,500-3,200	1,900-2,500	600-800
1996 Tracer	3,200-4,000	2,500-3,300	800-1,200

AVERAGE REPLACEMENT COSTS

See the 1991-96 Ford Escort.

TROUBLE SPOTS

See the 1991-96 Ford Escort.

RECALL HISTORY

1991: Interference may occur between bolt that secures fuel line shield to lower dash and gas pedal, causing pedal to stick wide open. **1991:** On some cars, fatigue crack can develop in solder joint between fuel return tube and fuel pump sending unit. **1992:** Pins securing ignition lock in steering column housing can separate or move out of position, causing steering column to lock up. **1992:** Stoplamp switch could intermittently malfunction. **1993:** Driver's seat in some cars may not engage fully in its track; could move in event of crash. **1994-95:** A few driver-side airbags may have inadequately welded inflator canister, causing improper deployment and expelling hot gases. **1995 cars in certain states:** Cracks can develop in plastic fuel tank, resulting in leakage.

1997-99 MERCURY TRACER

1998 Mercury Tracer Trio 4-door sedan

FOR Fuel economy • Optional antilock brakes • Price

AGAINST Rear-seat room • Road noise

EVALUATION

See the 1997-99 Ford Escort/ZX2.

VALUE

See the 1997-99 Ford Escort/ZX2.

SPECIFICATIONS

	4-door sedan	4-door wagon
Wheelbase, in.	98.4	98.4
Overall length, in.	174.7	172.7
Overall width, in.	67.0	67.0
Overall height, in.	53.3	53.9
Curb weight, lbs.	2469	2532
Cargo volume, cu. ft.	12.8	63.4
Fuel capacity, gals.	12.8	12.8
Seating capacity	5	5
Front head room, in.	39.0	38.7
Max. front leg room, in.	42.5	42.5
Rear head room, in.	36.7	39.1
Min. rear leg room, in.	34.0	34.0

Powertrain layout: transverse front-engine/front-wheel drive

ENGINES

	ohc I4
Size, liters/cu. in.	2.0/121
Horsepower	110
Torque (lbs./ft.)	125
EPA city/highway mpg	
5-speed OD manual	28/37
4-speed OD automatic	26/34
City/highway mpg (as tested)	
5-speed OD manual	31.2

Built in USA, Mexico

RETAIL PRICES

	GOOD	AVERAGE	POOR
1997 Tracer sedan	$4,200-4,900	$3,500-4,200	$1,400-1,900
1997 Tracer wagon	4,700-5,400	4,000-4,700	1,800-2,200
1998 Tracer sedan	5,100-5,900	4,400-5,100	2,000-2,400
1998 Tracer wagon	5,700-6,400	5,000-5,600	2,400-2,800
1999 Tracer sedan	6,000-6,800	5,300-6,000	2,600-3,100
1999 Tracer wagon	6,600-7,500	5,800-6,700	3,000-3,500

AVERAGE REPLACEMENT COSTS

See the 1997-99 Ford Escort/ZX2.

TROUBLE SPOTS

• **Brake noise.** Clicking noises come from the brakes, especially after they are applied following a change in direction, due to excessive clearance in the caliper brackets. (1997-99)

• **Audio system.** Electrical noise caused by the electric fuel pump in the tank can cause a buzzing noise when the AM band of the radio is selected. (1997-98)

• **Cold starting problems.** The engine will not start or the cooling fan may not shut off (killing the battery) in cold weather due to moisture in the integrated relay control module. (1997-98)

• **Oil leak.** In cold weather, moisture can freeze in the PCV system and, when the engine is started, the dipstick pops out of its tube and oil leaks out. (1997-98)

• **Engine noise.** The blower motor may chirp or squeak at low speeds and is corrected with a replacement motor having better brushes. (1997)

• **Doors.** The dome light may come on while driving or fail to come on when the door is opened. (1997-98)

• **Fuel gauge.** The gas gauge may have an error of about ⅛ tank, may drop from full too fast, and the tank may take fuel slowly due to a problem with the fuel sending unit or slosh module. (1998)

• **Oil leak.** The PCV system can get clogged with ice in freezing temperatures causing crankcase pressure to build until oil blows out the dipstick tube and all over the engine. (1999)

• **Automatic transmission.** The transmission may not engage right away when shifting out of park after the car has been parked overnight because the torque converter drains down. (1997)

1993-98 MERCURY VILLAGER

1993 Mercury Villager Nautica

FOR Passenger room (front) • Steering/handling

AGAINST Control layout • Wind noise

EVALUATION

See the 1993-98 Nissan Quest.

VALUE

See the 1993-98 Nissan Quest.

SPECIFICATIONS

	3-door van
Wheelbase, in.	112.2
Overall length, in.	189.9
Overall width, in.	73.4
Overall height, in.	66.0
Curb weight, lbs.	3815
Cargo volume, cu. ft.	126.4
Fuel capacity, gals.	20.0
Seating capacity	7
Front head room, in.	39.4
Max. front leg room, in.	39.9
Rear head room, in.	39.7
Min. rear leg room, in.	34.8

Powertrain layout: transverse front-engine/front-wheel drive

ENGINES

	ohc V6
Size, liters/cu. in.	3.0/181
Horsepower	151
Torque (lbs./ft.)	174
EPA city/highway mpg	
4-speed OD automatic	17/23
City/highway mpg (as tested)	
4-speed OD automatic	19.7

Built in USA

RETAIL PRICES

	GOOD	AVERAGE	POOR
1993 Villager	$2,800-4,000	$2,100-3,300	$700-1,400

	GOOD	AVERAGE	POOR
1994 Villager	$3,800-6,000	$3,100-5,200	$1,200-2,700
1995 Villager	4,800-7,000	4,000-6,200	1,800-3,400
1996 Villager	6,000-8,200	5,100-7,200	2,500-4,000
1997 Villager	7,200-9,500	6,200-8,500	3,300-4,900
1998 Villager	9,000-12,000	8,000-11,000	4,500-6,500

AVERAGE REPLACEMENT COSTS

See the 1993-98 Nissan Quest.

TROUBLE SPOTS

See the 1993-98 Nissan Quest.

RECALL HISTORY

1993: Brake master cylinder on some vans was improperly assembled or could have been damaged during assembly, which can result in loss of braking at two wheels, causing increased pedal travel, higher pedal effort, and increased stopping distance. **1993:** One or both bolts securing automatic seatbelt restraint system tracks to B-pillars were not adequately tightened on some vans, increasing risk of injury in the event of a collision or sudden maneuver. **1993:** Fuel-filler hoses may have been cut prior to installation by knife used to open shipping box; fuel leakage could result, leading to fire if exposed to ignition source. **1993:** Leaves and other foreign matter can enter through cowl panel air intake during operation of front heater and/or air conditioner, resulting in buildup in the plenum that can lead to noise, odors, or even a vehicle fire. **1995 w/sliding third-row bench seats:** Cable that connects seat adjustment level to latch might be pinched in roller assembly, preventing latch on left side from fully engaging seat rail. **1995:** Rear lamp will not illuminate if the metal socket moves or separates from the plastic socket housing. This can result in failure of the stop or rear running lamps. **1996:** Power windows can be closed after ignition key is turned to "off" position and right front door is opened. **1997:** Fuel-line hoses could crack or split, resulting in leakage. **1997-98 w/battery supplied by GNB Technologies:** Defective negative battery post can cause acid leakage and related corrosion damage; could lead to engine fire or battery explosion. **1998:** Cracks have developed in the vent hose, allowing a fuel leak.

1999-01 MERCURY VILLAGER

2000 Mercury Villager

FOR Passenger and cargo room • Control layout

AGAINST Fuel economy • Interior materials

EVALUATION

See the 1999-01 Nissan Quest.

VALUE

See the 1999-01 Nissan Quest.

SPECIFICATIONS

	4-door van
Wheelbase, in.	112.2
Overall length, in.	194.7
Overall width, in.	74.9
Overall height, in.	70.1
Curb weight, lbs.	3944
Cargo volume, cu. ft.	135.6
Fuel capacity, gals.	20.0
Seating capacity	7
Front head room, in.	39.7
Max. front leg room, in.	39.9
Rear head room, in.	39.9
Min. rear leg room, in.	36.4

Powertrain layout: transverse front-engine/front-wheel drive

ENGINES

	ohc V6
Size, liters/cu. in.	3.3/200
Horsepower	170
Torque (lbs./ft.)	200

EPA city/highway mpg

4-speed OD automatic	17/24

City/highway mpg (as tested)

4-speed OD automatic	16.9

Built in USA

RETAIL PRICES

	GOOD	AVERAGE	POOR
1999 Villager	$11,800-12,800	$10,080-11,800	$7,300-8,300
1999 Sport Estate	13,300-14,300	12,300-13,300	8,500-9,500
2000 Villager	13,500-14,800	12,500-13,800	8,500-9,500
2000 Sport Estate	15,500-17,000	14,500-16,000	10,000-11,000
2001 Villager	15,500-17,000	14,500-16,000	—
2001 Sport Estate	17,500-19,500	16,500-18,500	—

AVERAGE REPLACEMENT COSTS

See the 1999-01 Nissan Quest.

TROUBLE SPOTS

See the 1999-01 Nissan Quest.

RECALL HISTORY

1999: Taillight socket's locking tab may have insufficient force to retain bulb. **1999:** Fuel tank retention strap (two per minivan) on some vehicles can break at spot welds, causing underbody rattle; if welds fail, there may be fuel leakage and/or separation of fuel tank from vehicle. **1999-00:** One or more of the five bolts that mount the rack-and-pinion steering gear may have been incorrectly tightened; could result in steering looseness and noise or vibration. Eventually, bolts could fracture or fall out. **2001:** Plastic trim cover around base of front seatbelt buckle may become trapped, eventually allowing bolt to loosen.

1997-01 MITSUBISHI DIAMANTE

1997 Mitsubishi Diamante

FOR Acceleration • Quietness • Ride

AGAINST Passenger and cargo room

EVALUATION Packing one of the biggest and "torquiest" engines in the near-luxury field, the Diamante delivers lively acceleration. A test model reached 60 mph in 8.1 seconds. Flooring the throttle produces a satisfying kick off the line and in passing maneuvers. Wind and road noise levels are generally low, though the engine can be a little coarse sounding at times and isn't as smooth as the near-luxury norm. As for economy, we averaged 19.7 mpg in a new Diamante, with a considerable amount of highway driving. The automatic transmission delivers clean, quick shifts, up and down the gears. Though billed as a sport sedan, Diamante is clearly biased toward comfort. It's not nearly as athletic as, say, a Mazda Millenia. A soft suspension absorbs most bumps easily, but detracts from handling prowess. This sedan floats a bit over pavement swells and fast humpbacks, and suffers marked body lean in tight turns. Tire roar is noticeable on pebbled pavement surfaces. Most buyers will like the choice of spring and shock absorber settings. With antilock braking, a Diamante fares well enough in panic stops, aside from an excess of queasy nosedive. Traction control is an advisable option to look for, because front tires can spin wildly on damp pavement. Passenger space did not really grow with the added length in this generation, although the back seat is roomier than before. Leg and foot room are abundant for four adults, though head space is scarce for 6-footers beneath the power sunroof (if installed). Storage space is below par, too, and pop-out cupholders are on the flimsy side. Interior materials look appealing and detail assembly is thorough, but the car does not feel quite as solid as some rivals. Door closure, for instance, has sounded a tad "tinny." And on rough roads, the Diamante simply doesn't feel as effectively screwed together as some competitors. Though simpler than the old one, the dashboard layout is rather "busy" and saddled with too-small radio buttons. Outward visibility is good, helped by a low dashboard top. The trunk is usefully spacious and easy to load, but hinges dip into the load-carrying area.

VALUE In this highly competitive class, although other near-luxury cars rate higher, Diamante's price on the used car market makes it worth considering. LS has been the "consumer" model, with the ES going largely to corporate fleets. Despite solid improvement in performance, room and refinement, some rivals—especially the Lexus ES 300—improved more and also promised greater prestige.

SPECIFICATIONS

	4-door sedan
Wheelbase, in.	107.1
Overall length, in.	194.1
Overall width, in.	70.3
Overall height, in.	53.9
Curb weight, lbs.	3494
Cargo volume, cu. ft.	14.2
Fuel capacity, gals.	19
Seating capacity	5
Front head room, in.	37.6
Max. front leg room, in.	43.6
Rear head room, in.	36.3
Min. rear leg room, in.	36.6

Powertrain layout: transverse front-engine/front-wheel drive

ENGINES

	ohc V6
Size, liters/cu. in.	3.5/213
Horsepower	205-210
Torque (lbs./ft.)	231

EPA city/highway mpg

4-speed OD automatic	18/24

City/highway mpg (as tested)

4-speed OD automatic	19.7

Built in Australia

RETAIL PRICES

	GOOD	AVERAGE	POOR
1997 Diamante ES	$9,500-11,000	$8,500-10,000	$4,900-5,800
1997 Diamante LS	11,000-12,000	10,000-11,000	6,000-6,700
1998 Diamante ES	11,000-12,500	10,000-11,000	6,000-6,700
1998 Diamante LS	12,500-14,000	11,500-12,800	7,500-8,300
1999 Diamante	13,000-14,500	11,800-13,000	9,000-9,800
2000 Diamante ES	15,000-16,700	13,800-15,200	9,600-10,500
2000 Diamante LS	16,500-18,000	15,000-16,500	10,400-11,400
2001 Diamante ES	17,500-19,500	16,000-18,000	—
2001 Diamante LS	19,000-21,000	17,500-19,500	—

AVERAGE REPLACEMENT COSTS

A/C Compressor	$560	Constant Velocity Joints	1,150
Alternator	690	Exhaust System	435
Automatic Transmission or		Radiator	400
Transaxle	970	Shocks and/or Struts	560
Brakes	340	Timing Chain or Belt	160

TROUBLE SPOTS

• **Engine noise.** Valve tap at start-up is common on DOHC models and usually goes away after a couple minutes, but replacement hydraulic valve adjusters are required if noise persists. (1997-2000)

RECALL HISTORY

1999-2000: Head of screw that holds retaining clip for parking brake shoe can become brittle and break off; could result in parking brake dragging and/or failure to hold vehicle properly.

1990-94 MITSUBISHI ECLIPSE

FOR Acceleration (except base, GS) • Wet-weather traction (AWD) • Handling/roadholding • Antilock brakes (optional)

AGAINST Rear-seat room • Cargo room • Engine noise • Road noise

EVALUATION Neither the base unit nor the GS equipped with the 92-horsepower 1.8-liter have enough low-speed muscle to be satisfying with the automatic transmission. However, when paired with the manual, these are fine for budget-minded sports car lovers. The DOHC version is much quicker in traffic and more responsive to the throttle. Both

1990 Mitsubishi Eclipse GS

the GS Turbo and GSX are faster still, but the front-drive GS Turbo suffers from very noticeable torque steer, which causes us to prefer the GSX, which spreads the abundant power evenly between all four wheels. The all-wheel-drive set-up gives the GSX outstanding grip, making it the best-handling sports car in its class. While we appreciate the antilock brakes provided on the GSX, we wish Mitsubishi could provide them as an option on all models. Ride quality varies, depending on model, ranging from compliant but occasionally choppy on base and GS version to taut and slightly choppy on those with firmer suspensions and larger tires. The low-slung fastback styling and compact dimensions provide only modest interior room. The tight cockpit up front and "for-pets-only" rear seat may not appeal to all tastes.

VALUE In our view, the first-generation Mitsubishi Eclipse ranks as one of the best values among small sports coupes. We rate the GS with the 135-horsepower DOHC 4-cylinder and the turbocharged all-wheel-drive GSX as the "picks of the litter."

SPECIFICATIONS

	2-door hatchback
Wheelbase, in.	97.2
Overall length, in.	172.8
Overall width, in.	66.7
Overall height, in.	51.5
Curb weight, lbs.	2542
Cargo volume, cu. ft.	10.2
Fuel capacity, gals.	15.9
Seating capacity	4
Front head room, in.	37.9
Max. front leg room, in.	43.9
Rear head room, in.	34.1
Min. rear leg room, in.	28.5

Powertrain layout: transverse front-engine/front- or all-wheel drive

ENGINES

	ohc I4	dohc I4	Turbocharged dohc I4
Size, liters/cu. in.	1.8/107	2.0/122	2.0/122
Horsepower	92	135	180-195
Torque (lbs./ft.)	105	125	203

EPA city/highway mpg

	ohc I4	dohc I4	Turbocharged dohc I4
5-speed OD manual	23/32	22/29	21/28
4-speed OD automatic	23/30	22/27	19/23

City/highway mpg (as tested)

5-speed OD manual		26.4	18.4

Built in USA

RETAIL PRICES

	GOOD	AVERAGE	POOR
1990 Eclipse	$1,100-1,700	$600-1,100	$100-200
1990 Eclipse Turbo	1,700-2,300	1,100-1,600	200-400
1991 Eclipse	1,400-2,100	800-1,500	100-300
1991 Eclipse Turbo	2,100-2,800	1,500-2,100	400-600
1992 Eclipse	1,800-2,600	1,200-1,900	300-500
1992 Eclipse Turbo	2,800-3,500	2,100-2,800	600-900
1993 Eclipse	2,200-3,200	1,600-2,500	500-800
1993 Eclipse Turbo	3,400-4,200	2,700-3,400	800-1,100
1994 Eclipse	2,600-3,800	1,900-3,100	600-900
1994 Eclipse Turbo	4,200-5,000	3,400-4,200	1,100-1,500

AVERAGE REPLACEMENT COSTS

A/C Compressor	$540	Clutch, Pressure Plate, Bearing	470
Alternator	320	Constant Velocity Joints	705
Automatic Transmission or		Exhaust System	680
Transaxle	770	Radiator	355
Brakes	215	Timing Chain or Belt	240
Shocks and/or Struts	465		

TROUBLE SPOTS

• **Steering problems.** Cars that drift or pull to the right may be cured by replacing the lower control arm with one having rear bushing with a built-in offset. (1994)

• **Oil pump.** Cars with the 2.0-liter engine have noisy oil pumps and a counter measure pump (with helical cut gears) is available and quieter. (1990-92)

• **Exhaust system.** Cars with turbo engines had an emissions recall to replace the oxygen sensor with one that could endure higher temperatures. (1991-92)

• **Vehicle shake.** Drivetrain vibrations may be eliminated by replacing the transmission mounting brackets. (1990-94)

• **Poor transmission shift.** Manual transmissions in which the shifter does not move smoothly between gears need a bottle of friction modifier added to the oil through the speedometer gear opening. (1990-92)

• **Brake noise.** Noise suppression shims were released to cure a squeaking problem with rear disc brakes. (1990-91)

• **Transaxle leak.** Transaxle end clutch oil seal could leak leading to a loss of overdrive (fourth gear). (1994)

• **Vehicle shake.** Vibration at idle is probably due to the upper radiator mounting posts not being centered in the mounting brackets. (1990-94)

RECALL HISTORY

1990: Operation of factory-installed sunroof in "non-standard" manner may cause hinge disengagement. **1990:** Diluted primer may have been used on windshield opening flanges on a small number of cars, which would not provide required retention of glass. **1990:** Headlamp wiring harness on some early models may break due to stress created by their pop-up devices. **1990-91:** Front seatbelt release button can break and pieces can fall inside. **1990-94 w/AWD:** Lockup of transfer case can occur, due to insufficient lubrication.

1995-99 MITSUBISHI ECLIPSE

1995 Mitsubishi Eclipse GS-T 2-door coupe

FOR   Optional antilock brakes • Acceleration (GS-T, GSX) • Steering/handling • All-wheel drive (GSX)

AGAINST   Acceleration (RS, GS w/automatic) • Rear-seat room • Cargo room • Road noise

EVALUATION   The base engine revs smoothly and quickly without excess noise, but it's no powerhouse. Therefore, acceleration with the automatic transmission is marginal for freeway on-ramps and in passing sprints. Progress is livelier with the slick-shifting 5-speed manual gearbox. Turbos are decidedly faster. Unfortunately, Eclipse still suffers from some "turbo lag." All Eclipse models offer nimble handling, good grip, and quick, accurate steering. On the downside, the ride turns choppy on freeways and rough roads, especially on turbocharged models. You also must endure plenty of road noise. All-wheel-drive models are capable of exhibiting race-carlike moves, of the sort matched only by big-buck coupes. Front occupants have adequate head room but may still feel crowded. The tiny back seat is strictly for preteens. The dashboard is well laid out, except for a center-mounted stereo unit that's too low. Cargo space is adequate, but with a tall liftover for loading and unloading. Spyder convertibles look sharp, and deliver fun-in-the-sun driving at a comparatively reasonable price. Unfortunately, several convertibles we've driven have suffered from serious shakiness, even when rolling down smooth roads.

VALUE   Though still one of the best sports coupes, the competition caught up with Eclipse during its second generation. Other than the all-wheel-drive model, this version of the Eclipse offers nothing you can't get for less money somewhere else.

SPECIFICATIONS

	2-door conv.	2-door hatchback
Wheelbase, in.	98.8	98.8
Overall length, in.	172.2	172.2
Overall width, in.	68.3	68.3
Overall height, in.	51.6	50.2
Curb weight, lbs.	2888	2767
Cargo volume, cu. ft.	5.1	16.6
Fuel capacity, gals.	16.9	16.9
Seating capacity	4	4
Front head room, in.	38.7	37.9
Max. front leg room, in.	43.3	43.3
Rear head room, in.	34.9	34.3
Min. rear leg room, in.	28.4	28.4

Powertrain layout: transverse front-engine/front- or all-wheel drive

ENGINES

	dohc I4	Turbocharged dohc I4	dohc I4
Size, liters/cu. in.	2.0/122	2.0/122	2.4/143
Horsepower	140	205-210	141
Torque (lbs./ft.)	130	214	148
EPA city/highway mpg			
5-speed OD manual	22/33	23/31	22/30
4-speed OD automatic	21/31	20/27	
City/highway mpg (as tested)			
5-speed OD manual	27.5	22.7	21.5
4-speed OD automatic		18.4	

Built in USA

RETAIL PRICES

	GOOD	AVERAGE	POOR
1995 Eclipse RS, GS	$4,000-5,200	$3,200-4,200	$1,200-1,800
1995 Eclipse GS-T, GSX	6,000-7,000	5,200-6,100	2,700-3,300
1996 Eclipse RS, GS	5,000-6,500	4,200-5,700	1,800-2,700
1996 Eclipse GS-T, GSX	7,500-8,700	6,500-7,700	3,500-4,200
1996 Spyder convertible	7,500-9,000	6,500-8,000	3,500-4,500
1997 Eclipse base, RS, GS	6,500-8,000	5,700-7,100	3,000-4,000
1997 Eclipse GS-T, GSX	8,800-10,000	7,800-9,000	4,300-5,200
1997 Spyder convertible	9,000-10,800	8,000-9,500	4,500-5,500
1998 Eclipse RS, GS	8,000-9,500	7,000-8,500	4,000-5,000
1998 Eclipse GS-T, GSX	10,000-11,500	9,000-10,500	5,300-6,300
1998 Spyder convertible	10,500-12,000	9,500-10,800	5,600-6,500
1999 Eclipse RS, GS	9,500-11,200	8,500-10,000	4,900-5,800
1999 Eclipse GS-T, GSX	11,500-13,000	10,500-12,000	6,500-7,500
1999 Spyder convertible	12,500-14,500	11,000-13,000	7,000-8,200

AVERAGE REPLACEMENT COSTS

A/C Compressor	$600	Clutch, Pressure Plate, Bearing	415
Alternator	360	Constant Velocity Joints	770
Automatic Transmission or Transaxle	975	Exhaust System	350
Brakes	310	Radiator	470
Shocks and/or Struts	520	Timing Chain or Belt	260

TROUBLE SPOTS

• **Engine misfire.** Misfiring is common due to carbon on the spark plugs and is corrected by replacing the plugs and plug wires. (1995)

• **Fuel pump.** Noisy fuel pump may be result of a bad fuel pressure regulator. (1995)

• **Rear axle noise.** Squeaking, rubbing, knocking, or tapping noises from the rear are eliminated by replacing the trailing arm bushings (1995-97) or the shock absorber insulator assembly. (1997-98)

• **Air springs.** The front springs make creaking, popping, or squeaking noises when going over bumps requiring insulators to be installed on the upper coils. (1995-99)

• **Fuel pump.** The vehicle is sensitive to fuel starvation caused by a clogged in-tank filter. (1995-97)

RECALL HISTORY

1995-96: Rubber boots on lower ball joint can become damaged, allowing dirt and water intrusion, which can cause excessive wear and possible separation. **1995-96:** Incorrectly installed gaskets for fuel pump and/or gauge unit could allow fuel or fumes to escape. **1995-98 w/AWD:** Lockup of transfer case can occur, due to insufficient lubrication. **1997:** On a few cars, improperly welded passenger head restraint support bracket on passenger side can break. **1998:** Dash panel pad can shift, interfering with throttle cable control. **1999:** The battery-cable wiring harness can become heat damaged, leading to malfunctions in the turn signals and oil-pressure lamp. **1999:** The steering-column multifunction switch levers can become loose or break.

2000-01 MITSUBISHI ECLIPSE

2000 Mitsubishi Eclipse GS

FOR Acceleration (V6) • Front seat comfort • Handling/roadholding

AGAINST Road noise • Rear-seat room • Rear visibility • Rear-seat entry/exit

EVALUATION More mature and refined than their rough-and-tumble predecessors, Eclipses deliver a pliant, comfortable, sporty-coupe ride. Handling is alert and responsive with little cornering lean and grippy front-drive predictability, though maneuvers are hampered by a large turning circle. Wheel patter still turns up on washboard surfaces, but it's not bothersome. Engines are much improved. Whereas the old 2.0-liter fours were throbby and loud, the new 2.4-liter is generally smooth and quiet. It packs respectable punch, at least with manual shift—which is a pleasure to use. The V6-powered GT doesn't rocket away like the old turbocharged models, but it's plenty quick—and naturally, suffers no turbo lag. A GT with automatic reached 60 mph in 8.3 seconds and averaged 21.8 mpg. Surprisingly, the V6 is hardly quieter than the 4-cylinder. Furthermore, the body transmits noticeable tire noise except on glassy pavement. Wind rush is nicely tamed, even with the frameless door glass. Despite a more spacious cabin feel, Eclipses remain cozy 2+2 models with a teeny back seat and wiggle-in entry/exit. Front buckets hug one's torso, and should be comfortable on long rides. Driving positions are low-slung, and visibility remains difficult directly aft and over the shoulder. Taller drivers might wish the tilt steering wheel moved higher. Gauges and controls are clear and handy, but air conditioner buttons are hard to see in daylight. Luggage space is generous in coupes with the back seat folded, limited in Spyders, but the load lip is lofty and the hatch lid heavy. Bulky doors may close with a tinny clang. Cowl shake occurs over bumps with a Spyder, but structural stiffness is acceptable and its soft top seals tightly.

VALUE Though not quite as inspiring as a Honda Prelude, Eclipses compare well against most anything in their class. A GT might be the best choice, but few will feel penalized in one of the less expensive 4-cylinder models. Spyders have no direct rivals in their price league.

SPECIFICATIONS

	2-door conv.	2-door coupe
Wheelbase, in.	100.8	100.8
Overall length, in.	175.4	175.4
Overall width, in.	68.9	68.9
Overall height, in.	52.8	51.6
Curb weight, lbs.	3042	2822
Cargo volume, cu. ft.	7.2	16.9
Fuel capacity, gals.	16.4	16.4
Seating capacity	4	4
Front head room, in.	39.4	37.9
Max. front leg room, in.	42.3	42.3
Rear head room, in.	34.5	34.9
Min. rear leg room, in.	29.4	30.0

Powertrain layout: transverse front-engine/front-wheel drive

ENGINES

	ohc I4	ohc V6
Size, liters/cu. in.	2.4/149	3.0/181
Horsepower	145-154	200-205
Torque (lbs./ft.)	163	205

EPA city/highway mpg

5-speed OD manual	23/31	20/28
4-speed OD automatic	20/28	20/27

City/highway mpg (as tested)	ohc I4	ohc V6
5-speed OD manual	23.3	
4-speed OD automatic		21.8

Built in USA

RETAIL PRICES	GOOD	AVERAGE	POOR
2000 Eclipse RS GS coupe	$11,800-13,500	$10,800-12,500	$7,300-8,500
2000 Eclipse GT coupe	14,200-15,500	13,200-14,500	9,200-10,500
2001 Eclipse RS GS coupe	13,800-15,700	12,800-14,700	—
2001 Eclipse GT coupe	16,500-18,000	15,300-16,500	—
2001 Spyder convertible	17,500-19,000	16,300-17,700	—
2001 Spyder GT conv.	20,000-22,000	18,500-20,500	—

AVERAGE REPLACEMENT COSTS

A/C Compressor	$585	Clutch, Pressure Plate, Bearing	460
Alternator	620	Constant Velocity Joints	1,220
Automatic Transmission or Transaxle	1,025	Exhaust System	370
Brakes	350	Radiator	495
Shocks and/or Struts	1,010	Timing Chain or Belt	340

TROUBLE SPOTS

• **Audio system.** A short causes popping noises from the speakers when the power seat is operated. A jumper harness with a filter has been released for installation under the seat. (1999-2001)

• **Vehicle noise.** Banging, creaking, and popping noises from the front end are usually due to dry stabilizer bar bushings. Revised bushings are available as replacements. (1999-2000)

• **Automatic transmission.** The automatic transmission may shudder, surge, or vibrate due to thermal breakdown of the original transmission fluid (SPII). The system must be flushed and refilled with revised fluid (SPIII). (1999-2001)

• **Hard starting.** The starter may not run due to a faulty theft-alarm relay (automatic transmission) or a faulty starter relay (manual transmission). Revised relays are available to fix the problem (2000)

• **Sunroof/moonroof.** The sunroof may skip/stick during operation requiring a countermeasure drive cable assembly. (2000-01)

RECALL HISTORY

2000 V6: Power steering pipe could wear through, allowing fluid leakage. Can result in a fire and continued loss of fluid will result in a loss of power assist, increasing the risk of a crash. **2001:** Bulge in fuel tank caused by manufacturing process on small number of vehicles resulted in thinning of material, increasing risk of fuel leakage.

1994-98 MITSUBISHI GALANT

1995 Mitsubishi Galant LS V-6

FOR Antilock brakes • Passenger and cargo room • Ride

AGAINST Rear visibility • Engine noise • Fuel economy

EVALUATION The Galant's 141-horsepower 4-cylinder has more than adequate acceleration and passing power with the automatic transmission. It shifts smoothly and downshifts without argument when it comes time to pass. The 160-horsepower unit found on 1994 GS models feels stronger still. Engine noise is abundant during hard acceleration. Galant's suspension absorbs bumps easily, while providing a stable, competent ride at highway speeds. The car handles corners with ease and the precise steering feel gives drivers a sense of confidence. Firm, supportive seats and a generous front cabin area are Galant strong points. However, rear-seat passengers have only adequate head room, and an inch less leg room than the previous model. The dashboard has an attractive four-dial gauge cluster, and climate controls are stacked atop the center stereo controls in the center console. In a welcome departure for Mitsubishi, the stereo is mounted high enough for easy operation, even when driving. The trunk provides ample space plus a wide flat floor and low liftover. Visibility is good, but wide rear roof pillars force the driver into neck-stretching during lane changes.

VALUE This generation of the Galant has several good qualities, and we consider it a solid buy. Nevertheless, it lacks a single distinguishing feature to help it stand out in the crowded field of midsize domestic and imported sedans, particularly given the absence of a V6 option.

SPECIFICATIONS

	4-door sedan
Wheelbase, in.	103.7
Overall length, in.	187.0
Overall width, in.	68.1
Overall height, in.	53.1
Curb weight, lbs.	2755
Cargo volume, cu. ft.	12.5
Fuel capacity, gals.	16.9
Seating capacity	5
Front head room, in.	39.4
Max. front leg room, in.	43.3
Rear head room, in.	37.5
Min. rear leg room, in.	35.0

Powertrain layout: transverse front-engine/front-wheel drive

ENGINES

	ohc I4	dohc I4
Size, liters/cu. in.	2.4/144	2.4/144
Horsepower	141-143	160
Torque (lbs./ft.)	148	160
EPA city/highway mpg		
5-speed OD manual	23/30	22/28
4-speed OD automatic	22/28	20/26
City/highway mpg (as tested)		
4-speed OD automatic	20.2	

Built in USA

RETAIL PRICES

	GOOD	AVERAGE	POOR
1994 Galant	$2,700-3,400	$2,100-2,700	$600-900
1994 Galant LS, GS	3,200-4,000	2,600-3,300	800-1,100
1995 Galant	3,300-4,000	2,600-3,300	800-1,100
1995 Galant LS	4,000-4,800	3,300-4,000	1,200-1,600
1996 Galant	4,300-5,100	3,600-4,300	1,400-1,800
1996 Galant LS	5,500-6,200	4,700-5,400	2,200-2,600
1997 Galant	5,500-6,400	4,800-5,600	2,300-2,700
1997 Galant LS	7,000-8,000	6,100-7,000	3,200-3,800
1998 Galant	7,000-7,800	6,200-6,900	3,300-3,700
1998 Galant LS	8,500-9,500	7,500-8,500	4,200-4,800

AVERAGE REPLACEMENT COSTS

A/C Compressor	$610	Clutch, Pressure Plate, Bearing	560
Alternator	335	Constant Velocity Joints	725
Automatic Transmission or Transaxle	865	Exhaust System	500
Brakes	220	Radiator	595
Shocks and/or Struts	460	Timing Chain or Belt	290

TROUBLE SPOTS

• **Exhaust system.** A revised Vehicle Emission Control Information (VECI) label was mailed to all owners who were to place it over the old one that contained incorrect information. (1994)

• **Steering problems.** Cars that drift or pull to the right may be cured by replacing the lower control arm with one having rear bushing with a built-in offset. (1994-95)

• **Dashboard lights.** The headlights and dash lights may dim during deceleration because the computer switches on the electric cooling fan. (1994-95)

• **Transaxle leak.** Transaxle end clutch oil seals could leak leading to a loss of overdrive (fourth gear). (1994)

• **Vehicle shake.** Vibrations on automatic transmission models are probably due to the upper radiator mounting posts not being centered in the mounting brackets. (1994)

RECALL HISTORY

1994-95: Grease was inadvertently applied to contact of stoplamp switch, causing it to heat up and allowing internal elements to melt; switch will stick on or off, causing ABS warning to disappear. **1995-96:** Rubber boots on lower ball joint can become damaged, allowing dirt and water intrusion, which can cause excessive wear and possible separation.

1999-01 MITSUBISHI GALANT

2000 Mitsubishi Galant GTZ

FOR Ride (base) • Steering/handling

AGAINST Rear seat entry/exit • Ride (GTZ)

EVALUATION Surprisingly entertaining on the road, especially with V6 power, the Galant delivers a solid driving feel. Both engines are smooth performers. The 4-cylinder delivers brisk takeoffs and cruises without strain at highway speeds, becoming vocal only at higher rpm. As expected, the V6 is somewhat smoother, quieter, and punchier, but commands premium fuel. A 4-cylinder model accelerated to 60 mph in 10.3 seconds, while a GTZ V6 did it 2 seconds quicker. The V6 works well with the transmission to deliver throttle response as good as any in its class. Wind rush is muted, but tire roar is noticeable on coarse pavement. Handling is front-drive balanced and predictable, while the Galant's ride is calm, controlled and absorbent—apart from minor tail hop over sharp lateral ridges. The GTZ model telegraphs small bumps more clearly than less-sporty Galants, but exhibits more precise steering and slightly less body lean in tight corners. Steering feel on lesser models is a bit numb. Simulated "panic" stops are short, true, and level, even without antilock braking. Interior space is sufficient, but with only average room for four adults on a longer ride. Adults in back lack leg space to avoid knees-up riding. Rear-seat entry/exit could be better, but front seats are long-haul supportive. Gauges and controls are well-positioned and obvious. Visibility is hindered only to the rear by the Galant's high-tail styling. With a flat floor and low liftover, the trunk is spacious enough but its lid feels flimsy. All models except the base DE have split-folding rear seatbacks. On the whole, interior decor is pleasant but on the bland side.

VALUE Though not quite a standout, the Galant is a pleasant, agreeably competent family 4-door that should be on the tentative shopping list of anyone considering an Accord or Camry. Packed with features for the money, the Galant mimics much of the driving satisfaction, if not the top-notch engineering, of Honda and Toyota models.

SPECIFICATIONS

	4-door sedan
Wheelbase, in.	103.7
Overall length, in.	187.8
Overall width, in.	68.5
Overall height, in.	55.7
Curb weight, lbs.	2835
Cargo volume, cu. ft.	14.0
Fuel capacity, gals.	16.3
Seating capacity	5
Front head room, in.	39.9
Max. front leg room, in.	43.5
Rear head room, in.	37.7
Min. rear leg room, in.	36.3

Powertrain layout: transverse front-engine/front-wheel drive

ENGINES

	ohc I4	ohc V6
Size, liters/cu. in.	2.4/143	3.0/181
Horsepower	145	195
Torque (lbs./ft.)	155	205
EPA city/highway mpg		
4-speed OD automatic	21/28	20/27
City/highway mpg (as tested)		
4-speed OD automatic	24.0	22.2

Built in USA

RETAIL PRICES

	GOOD	AVERAGE	POOR
1999 Galant	$9,200-11,000	$8,300-10,000	$5,800-6,800
1999 Galant LS GTZ	12,500-13,500	11,500-12,500	8,000-9,000

	GOOD	AVERAGE	POOR
2000 Galant	$10,800-13,000	$9,800-12,000	$6,800-8,500
2000 Galant LS GTZ	14,500-16,000	13,500-15,000	9,500-10,500
2001 Galant	12,500-15,000	11,500-14,000	—
2001 Galant LS GTZ	16,700-18,500	15,500-17,200	—

AVERAGE REPLACEMENT COSTS

A/C Compressor	$695	Constant Velocity Joints	1,430
Alternator	290	Exhaust System	280
Automatic Transmission or		Radiator	380
Transaxle	810	Shocks and/or Struts	860
Brakes	250	Timing Chain or Belt	465

TROUBLE SPOTS

• **Audio system.** A short causes popping noises from the speakers when the power seat is operated. A jumper harness with a filter has been released for installation under the seat. (1999-2001)

• **Vehicle noise.** Banging, creaking, and popping noises from the front end are usually due to dry stabilizer bar bushings. Revised bushings are available as replacements. (1999-2000)

• **Automatic transmission.** The automatic transmission may shudder, surge, or vibrate due to thermal breakdown of the original transmission fluid (SPII). The system must be flushed and refilled with revised fluid (SPIII). (1999-2001)

RECALL HISTORY

1999-00: Steering column multifunction switch levers can become loose or break over time; loosening or cracking can cause directional lamps that do not self-cancel or operate, headlamps that do not turn off, windshield washers that operate continuously, and/or windshield wipers that do not operate. **1999-00 w/V6:** On certain cars, battery cable wiring harness can become heat-damaged by front exhaust manifold, which could cause grounded circuits. This failure could cause any of the following to occur: (1) engine will not start because main fuse will blow if power lead is grounded; (2) low oil pressure warning lamp will illuminate if signal wire is grounded; (3) air conditioner will become inoperative if lead to magnetic clutch is grounded; and (4) turn signal/hazard lamps will become inoperative if voltage monitor lead is grounded. **2000:** Power steering pipe could wear through, allowing fluid leakage. Can result in a fire and continued loss of fluid will result in a loss of power assist, increasing the risk of a crash. **2001:** Bulge in fuel tank on small number of vehicles resulted in thinning of material, increasing risk of fuel leakage.

1993-96 MITSUBISHI MIRAGE

1993 Mitsubishi Mirage LS 2-door coupe

FOR Fuel economy • Maneuverability

AGAINST Noise • Acceleration (automatic) • Rear-seat room

EVALUATION Acceleration is lackluster with the basic 1.5-liter engine and either transmission. On the other hand, a Mirage with the 1.8-liter engine and 5-speed manual moves more than adequately—though it cannot be called snappy. An automatic transmission saps a lot of the verve from that engine, too. Fuel economy is good with any powertrain setup. We averaged 31.4 mpg in a mix of city and highway driving with a 1.8-liter Mirage. Interior design is pleasant, but seating arrangements clearly favor front-seat occupants. The backseat is too crowded for adults to be comfortable. Still, Mirages have an impressive list of plus points, starting with a good ride on most surfaces, and simple instruments and controls. You also get nimble and predictable handling, but

only if the car has power steering. Manual steering demands too much muscle for easy parking. The large trunk has a bumper-level opening for easy loading.

VALUE In short, Mirage ranks as a good small car, but hardly a great one. An ES or LS 4-door with the bigger engine does a good job, but it's not appreciably better than most rivals.

SPECIFICATIONS

	2-door coupe	4-door sedan
Wheelbase, in.	96.1	98.4
Overall length, in.	171.1	172.2
Overall width, in.	66.5	66.5
Overall height, in.	51.6	52.2
Curb weight, lbs.	2085	2195
Cargo volume, cu. ft.	10.7	10.5
Fuel capacity, gals.	13.2	13.2
Seating capacity	5	5
Front head room, in.	38.6	39.2
Max. front leg room, in.	42.9	42.9
Rear head room, in.	36.4	37.2
Min. rear leg room, in.	31.1	33.5

Powertrain layout: transverse front-engine/front-wheel drive

ENGINES

	ohc I4	ohc I4
Size, liters/cu. in.	1.5/90	1.8/112
Horsepower	92	113
Torque (lbs./ft.)	93	116
EPA city/highway mpg		
5-speed OD manual	32/39	26/33
3-speed automatic	28/32	
4-speed OD automatic		26/33
City/highway mpg (as tested)		
5-speed OD manual		33.1
4-speed OD automatic		24.3

Built in Japan

RETAIL PRICES

	GOOD	AVERAGE	POOR
1993 Mirage coupe	$1,200-1,800	$700-1,200	$100-200
1993 Mirage sedan	1,400-2,000	800-1,400	100-300
1994 Mirage coupe	1,500-2,200	900-1,600	200-400
1994 Mirage sedan	1,800-2,500	1,200-1,800	300-500
1995 Mirage coupe	2,000-2,700	1,400-2,000	400-600
1995 Mirage sedan	2,400-3,000	1,800-2,300	500-700
1996 Mirage coupe	2,500-3,300	1,800-2,600	500-800
1996 Mirage sedan	3,000-3,700	2,300-3,000	700-1,000

AVERAGE REPLACEMENT COSTS

A/C Compressor	$845	Clutch, Pressure Plate,	
Alternator	300	Bearing	435
Automatic Transmission or		Constant Velocity Joints	1,120
Transaxle	975	Exhaust System	215
Brakes	310	Radiator	455
Shocks and/or Struts	680	Timing Chain or Belt	180

TROUBLE SPOTS

• **Engine misfire.** Automatic transmission models may vibrate at idle due to the radiator being installed incorrectly. (1993-94)

• **Climate control.** Interior temperature control knob rotates but does not change the temperature due to a defective heater control lever. (1995)

• **Vehicle noise.** Popping or squeaking from the front is caused by the springs vibrating in their seats. (1993-94)

• **Hard starting.** The engine may not start when the transmission is in park or neutral or may start when in drive due to the park/neutral switch being out of adjustment. (1993-94)

• **Horn.** The horn(s) may be too high- or low-pitched or not sound at all. (1993)

• **Fuel pump.** The vehicle is sensitive to fuel starvation caused by a clogged in-tank filter. (1993-95)

RECALL HISTORY

1993: Automatic seatbelt system may fail to operate correctly during crash. **1993:** Due to cable abrasion, shoulder belt may become stuck. **1993 sold in Caribbean:** Shoulder-belt anchorage could remain at A-pillar when door was closed.

1997-01 MITSUBISHI MIRAGE

1998 Mitsubishi Mirage LS 4-door sedan

FOR Fuel economy • Price • Visibility

AGAINST Acceleration (DE) • Rear-seat room (coupes)

EVALUATION Unusually easy to drive, the latest Mirage scores well in a number of areas. Bonuses include a comfortable driving position, no-nonsense dashboard and sensibly placed controls, commanding visibility all around, and competitive passenger and cargo space. The only exception is the coupe's back seat, which is too small for adults to occupy comfortably. Ride, handling, and braking all rank as acceptable, but not outstanding. A Mirage corners nimbly and predictably, with front-drive security. Ride comfort is good, and quite nice indeed on the highway. But the experience can begin to get choppy when rolling through broken surfaces and freeway expansion joints. On coarse pavement, too, tire noise gets to be a problem. Wind rush is not excessive at highway speeds. On the negative side, engine noise remains relatively strong. Acceleration isn't so lively, except with the bigger engine and manual transmission. The new automatic transmission is a lot smoother in operation and more responsive than the old one, but because models with the smaller engine lack sufficient power, we'd avoid automatic. In fact, we'd avoid the smaller engine entirely, due to its minimal gusto. An LS coupe with the bigger engine averaged 30.9 mpg in mostly highway driving. An LS sedan with automatic achieved 26 mpg in a mix of city and highway operation. As expected, it's considerably easier to get into a 4-door than a 2-door, and the sedan offers more usable rear passenger space. Even so, leg and foot room out back are necessarily tight when sitting behind a tall front-seater. All models have a reasonably sized trunk with a flat floor. The LS coupe adds the extra versatility of a split-folding backseat (which was available as an option package for sedans).

VALUE Mirage is definitely worth a test drive if you're shopping in the Civic/Corolla neighborhood and wouldn't mind saving a few dollars.

SPECIFICATIONS

	2-door coupe	4-door sedan
Wheelbase, in.	95.1	98.4
Overall length, in.	168.1	173.6
Overall width, in.	66.5	66.5
Overall height, in.	51.4	52.6
Curb weight, lbs.	2127	2227
Cargo volume, cu. ft.	11.5	11.5
Fuel capacity, gals.	13.2	13.2
Seating capacity	5	5
Front head room, in.	38.6	39.8
Max. front leg room, in.	43.0	43.0
Rear head room, in.	35.8	37.4
Min. rear leg room, in.	31.1	33.5

Powertrain layout: transverse front-engine/front-wheel drive

ENGINES

	ohc I4	ohc I4
Size, liters/cu. in.	1.5/90	1.8/112
Horsepower	92	113
Torque (lbs./ft.)	93	116
EPA city/highway mpg		
5-speed OD manual	33/40	28/37
4-speed OD automatic	29/36	26/33
City/highway mpg (as tested)		
5-speed OD manual	34.1	30.9
4-speed OD automatic		26.0

Built in Japan

RETAIL PRICES

	GOOD	AVERAGE	POOR
1997 Mirage DE	$3,600-4,300	$3,000-3,600	$1,100-1,400
1997 Mirage LS	4,500-5,200	3,800-4,500	1,700-2,100
1998 Mirage DE	$4,500-5,200	$3,800-4,500	$1,700-2,100
1998 Mirage LS	5,400-6,100	4,700-5,300	2,300-2,700
1999 Mirage DE	5,500-6,300	4,800-5,500	2,400-2,800
1999 Mirage LS	6,400-7,100	5,600-6,300	2,900-3,300
2000 Mirage DE	7,000-7,800	6,200-7,000	3,300-3,800
2000 Mirage LS	8,000-8,800	7,100-7,800	4,000-4,400
2001 Mirage DE, ES	8,500-9,500	7,600-8,500	—
2001 Mirage LS	9,700-10,500	8,700-9,500	—

AVERAGE REPLACEMENT COSTS

A/C Compressor	$560	Clutch, Pressure Plate, Bearing	440
Alternator	430	Constant Velocity Joints	1,230
Automatic Transmission or Transaxle	1,020	Exhaust System	230
Brakes	330	Radiator	360
Shocks and/or Struts	715	Timing Chain or Belt	210

TROUBLE SPOTS

• **Spark plugs.** Spark plugs tend to foul if the vehicle is driven only short distances in cold weather. (1997-98)

RECALL HISTORY

1998: Poorly manufactured vacuum check valve in hose between intake manifold and brake vacuum booster.

1992-00 MITSUBISHI MONTERO

1992 Mitsubishi Montero LS

FOR 4WD traction • Passenger and cargo room • Acceleration (215-horsepower engine) • Quietness • Ride

AGAINST Fuel economy • Entry/exit • Acceleration (151-horsepower engine)

EVALUATION The 3.0-liter V6 is smooth and quiet, but could use a bit more muscle. Acceleration with the base engine, even in 177-horsepower form, is adequate rather than spirited. Passing power also ranks as adequate. With automatic, steep grades cause noticeable slowing and a lot of busy shifting. Fuel economy is on the dismal side: we averaged 16.5 mpg in city/highway driving. An SR with the 215-horsepower engine accelerated to 60 mph in a brisk 10.0 seconds. Economy sagged to a gloomy 13.8 mpg. Mitsubishi's Active-Trac 4WD system is convenient and easy to use. Montero is still one of the better-riding 4x4s, even more stable in corners than earlier versions, thanks to a slightly wider-stance. A Montero doesn't feel as agile as a Jeep Grand Cherokee, however, showing more body lean in turns and even a slight tipsy sensation. Wavy surfaces produce little bouncing, but the firm suspension does not absorb bumps well. The dashboard made everything easy to see, reach, and use, but the Multi Meter is little more than a gimmick. Passenger and cargo space are abundant, but the Montero sits high off the ground, so it's difficult to get in and out. Montero has more than enough cargo space for several grocery bags.

VALUE Despite some appealing features, Montero has not been at the top of our sport-utility list, when compared with such domestic rivals as the Ford Explorer, Jeep Grand Cherokee, and Chevrolet Blazer.

SPECIFICATIONS

	4-door wagon
Wheelbase, in.	107.3
Overall length, in.	188.9
Overall width, in.	66.7-73.9
Overall height, in.	73.4
Curb weight, lbs.	4265
Cargo volume, cu. ft.	72.7
Fuel capacity, gals.	24.3
Seating capacity	7
Front head room, in.	40.9
Max. front leg room, in.	40.3
Rear head room, in.	40.0
Min. rear leg room, in.	37.6

Powertrain layout: longitudinal front-engine/4-wheel drive

ENGINES

	ohc V6	ohc V6	ohc V6	dohc V6
Size, liters/cu. in.	3.0/181	3.0/181	3.5/213	3.5/213
Horsepower	151	177	200	215
Torque (lbs./ft.)	174	188	228-235	228
EPA city/highway mpg				
5-speed OD manual	15/18	15/18		
4-speed OD automatic	15/18	15/18	16/19	14/18
City/highway mpg (as tested)				
4-speed OD automatic	15.6	16.5	15.5	13.8

Built in Japan

RETAIL PRICES

	GOOD	AVERAGE	POOR
1992 Montero	$4,000-5,500	$3,300-4,700	$1,400-2,200
1993 Montero	5,000-7,000	4,200-6,200	1,800-3,000
1994 Montero	6,500-8,500	5,600-7,500	2,900-4,100
1995 Montero	8,200-9,800	7,200-8,800	4,100-5,100
1996 Montero	10,000-12,000	9,000-11,000	5,300-6,500
1997 Montero	12,000-14,000	10,800-12,700	6,800-8,000
1998 Montero	14,000-16,000	12,500-14,500	8,500-9,800
1999 Montero	16,000-18,000	14,500-16,500	10,000-11,300
2000 Montero	18,500-20,500	16,800-18,700	11,800-13,000

AVERAGE REPLACEMENT COSTS

A/C Compressor	$825	Clutch, Pressure Plate, Bearing	645
Alternator	410	Exhaust System	370
Automatic Transmission or Transaxle	930	Radiator	665
Brakes	330	Shocks and/or Struts	300
Timing Chain or Belt	405	Universal Joints	1,180

TROUBLE SPOTS

• **Manual transmission.** Hard shifting, gear clash, may come from the manual transmission due to a failure of the first-second gear synchronizers, while screeching noises are due to failed second-third synchros. (1992-95)

• **Paint/body.** Paint on the roof rack fades and peels. (1992-93)

• **Steering problems.** Shudder while cornering may be minimized by adding Mitsubishi Limited Slip Differential Additive to the rear differential. (1997)

• **Dashboard lights.** The check engine light may come on when the vehicle is driven at wide-open throttle. (1997)

RECALL HISTORY

1992-93: During conditions of full-lock steering and full-suspension travel, front brake hose can crack, resulting in leakage. **1992-94 sold in Puerto Rico:** Front brake hose can crack during full-lock steering and full suspension travel, resulting in fluid leakage. **1994-98:** Accessory cargo mats interfere with latching integrity of the folding third seats. **1997-98:** Front brake lines can develop pinholes due to chafing; brake fluid can leak, resulting in deteriorated performance and illumination of indicator lamp. **1999 w/4WD and automatic:** Transmission fluid could be vented onto hot exhaust system as a result of unanticipated heat generation.

1997-00 MITSUBISHI MONTERO SPORT

FOR Instruments/controls • Build quality

AGAINST Fuel economy • Entry/exit • Ride • Noise

EVALUATION A 4-cylinder engine isn't sufficient for a vehicle of this

1998 Mitsubishi Montero Sport LS

size and weight. With the 3.0-liter V6, acceleration from a standstill is only a little less sluggish, even with a light load aboard. Modest upgrades slow progress considerably, which can present a problem even when merging onto certain expressways. The 3.5-liter V6 in the '99 Limited yields more satisfying performance. We managed about 17 mpg in city/highway driving with one Sport, but another example—driven somewhat harder—couldn't beat 15 mpg. Use of the big Montero's chassis gives the Sport a stiff and lively ride on the highway. Overly light power steering is on the vague side. Although a Sport is far more stable than the bigger Montero in cornering, thanks to its lower stance, body lean is definitely noticeable in tight turns. Noise levels reach beyond the SUV norm. Large door mirrors generate plenty of turbulence on the highway, and the engine fan whines loudly at higher speeds. Tire noise is prominent, too. Ample ground clearance can be helpful for off-road operation, but the Sport's tall step-in makes getting in and out a chore, especially into the backseat. Four adults can ride without feeling claustrophobic, even when accompanied by a sizable load of luggage. Still, a low roofline limits head room for 6-footers, and rear leg space is no more than adequate. On some models, the spare tire mounts under the load deck so it doesn't cut into cargo space. Although the driver gets a commanding view, thick rear roof pillars hinder parking and lane-changes. Instruments are large and legible. Most minor controls are within easy reach.

VALUE All told, the Montero Sport is too slow, noisy, and stiff-riding to satisfy the driver who spends time on suburban roads than rural trails.

SPECIFICATIONS

	4-door wagon
Wheelbase, in.	107.3
Overall length, in.	178.3
Overall width, in.	66.7
Overall height, in.	65.6
Curb weight, lbs.	3980
Cargo volume, cu. ft.	79.3
Fuel capacity, gals.	19.5
Seating capacity	5
Front head room, in.	38.9
Max. front leg room, in.	42.8
Rear head room, in.	37.3
Min. rear leg room, in.	33.5

Powertrain layout: longitudinal front-engine/rear- or 4-wheel drive

ENGINES

	ohc I4	ohc V6	ohc V6
Size, liters/cu. in.	2.4/143	3.0/181	3.5/213
Horsepower	132	165-173	197-200
Torque (lbs./ft.)	148	186-188	223-228
EPA city/highway mpg			
5-speed OD manual	22/25	17/20	
4-speed OD automatic		19/22	16/20
City/highway mpg (as tested)			
4-speed OD automatic		17.3	16.8

Built in Japan

RETAIL PRICES

	GOOD	AVERAGE	POOR
1997 Montero Sport ES, LS	$7,800-10,500	$6,800-9,500	$3,800-5,700
1997 Montero Sport XLS	11,200-12,500	10,000-11,000	6,000-6,700
1998 Montero Sport ES, LS	9,000-12,000	8,000-11,000	4,500-6,500
1998 Montero Sport XLS	12,500-14,500	11,300-13,000	7,200-8,500
1999 Montero Sport ES, LS	10,500-13,500	9,500-12,300	5,600-7,500
1999 Montero Sport XLS	13,000-15,000	11,500-13,500	7,500-8,800
1999 Montero Sport Ltd.	14,500-16,200	13,000-14,700	9,000-10,200
2000 Montero Sport ES, LS	12,500-15,500	11,200-14,000	7,000-9,000
2000 Montero Sport XLS	15,500-17,500	14,000-16,000	9,500-10,800
2000 Montero Sport Ltd.	17,000-19,000	15,000-17,000	10,300-11,500

AVERAGE REPLACEMENT COSTS

A/C Compressor	$825	Clutch, Pressure Plate,	
Alternator	410	Bearing	645
Automatic Transmission or		Exhaust System	350
Transaxle	930	Radiator	650
Brakes	330	Shocks and/or Struts	800
Timing Chain or Belt	405	Universal Joints	560

TROUBLE SPOTS

• **Engine knock.** Models sold in California may have engine knock indicating possible welding flash entering the cylinders. (1997-98)

• **Vehicle shake.** The vehicle may shudder when making low speed turns and the condition may be corrected by adding a limited-slip differential additive. (1997)

• **Engine noise.** Valve tap for a couple minutes after startup is considered normal. (1997-98)

RECALL HISTORY

1999 w/4WD and automatic: Automatic transmission fluid could be vented onto hot exhaust system. **1999-2001 w/3.5-liter engine:** Brake vacuum hoses may fail causing a loss of power assist to the brakes and increase stopping distances.

1993-97 NISSAN ALTIMA

1994 Nissan Altima GLE

FOR Antilock brakes (optional) • Steering/handling • Instruments/controls • Fuel economy

AGAINST Engine noise • Road noise • Wind noise • Automatic transmission performance

EVALUATION Performance and fuel economy from the standard 150-horsepower 2.4-liter 4-cylinder engine are more than adequate. Even with the automatic transmission, passing response is fine. But when called upon to pass quickly or make a merging maneuver, aggressive use of the accelerator is required to coax the automatic to make its one- or two-gear downshift. Benefiting from its wide standard tires (205/60R-15s), the Altima is more athletic and nimble than all but the Accord. Ride quality is comfortable, if firm, and braking is strong and progressive. Also contributing to the car's handling prowess is its crisp steering response. The only potential drawback is a cabin that could use a bit more sound insulation. The interior provides adequate head room for all passengers and enough space for two adults in the rear seat. The trunk has a wide, flat floor, giving the Altima good cargo room for its size.

VALUE Overall, we rate Nissan's compact sedan highly and encourage buyers to give it a close look before buying anything in its league.

SPECIFICATIONS

	4-door sedan
Wheelbase, in.	103.1
Overall length, in.	180.5
Overall width, in.	67.1
Overall height, in.	55.9
Curb weight, lbs.	2853
Cargo volume, cu. ft.	14.0
Fuel capacity, gals.	15.9
Seating capacity	5
Front head room, in.	39.3
Max. front leg room, in.	42.6
Rear head room, in.	37.6
Min. rear leg room, in.	34.7

Powertrain layout: transverse front-engine/front-wheel drive

ENGINES

	dohc I4
Size, liters/cu. in.	2.4/146

	dohc I4
Horsepower	150
Torque (lbs./ft.)	154

EPA city/highway mpg

5-speed OD manual	24/30
4-speed OD automatic	21/29

City/highway mpg (as tested)

4-speed OD automatic	20.2

Built in USA

RETAIL PRICES

	GOOD	AVERAGE	POOR
1993 Altima	$2,500-3,200	$1,900-2,500	$600-800
1993 Altima SE, GLE	3,000-3,700	2,400-3,000	800-1,100
1994 Altima	3,000-3,700	2,300-3,000	700-1,000
1994 Altima SE, GLE	3,800-4,500	3,100-3,800	1,200-1,600
1995 Altima	3,800-4,500	3,100-3,700	1,200-1,500
1995 Altima SE, GLE	4,600-5,400	3,800-4,600	1,700-2,100
1996 Altima	4,800-5,500	4,000-4,700	1,800-2,200
1996 Altima SE, GLE	5,600-6,300	4,800-5,500	2,500-2,900
1997 Altima	6,000-6,800	5,200-6,000	2,700-3,200
1997 Altima SE, GLE	7,200-8,000	6,400-7,100	3,400-4,000

AVERAGE REPLACEMENT COSTS

A/C Compressor	$510	Clutch, Pressure Plate,	
Alternator	275	Bearing	440
Automatic Transmission or		Constant Velocity Joints	385
Transaxle	900	Exhaust System	475
Brakes	200	Radiator	280
Shocks and/or Struts	540	Timing Chain or Belt	755

TROUBLE SPOTS

• **Automatic transmission.** Burnt transmission fluid or no reverse gear signal a defective rear control valve and low/reverse brake. (1993-94)

• **Automatic transmission.** If the gauges quit working, the check engine light comes on, or the transmission shifts harshly, then a wiring harness may be chafing on the top of the transmission under the battery tray or the instrument wiring harness is chafing on the airbag harness support bracket. (1995)

• **Automatic transmission.** If the transmission does not shift properly until warmed up, make sure it is filled only with Nissanmatic "C" transmission fluid. (All)

• **Brakes.** Inspect the right rear brake hose for chafing on the rear suspension, which could lead to a leak and brake failure. (1995)

• **Oil leak.** Oil leaking from the front of the engine could be caused by a bad O-ring between the timing cover and the engine block. (1993-95)

• **Air conditioner.** Poor air conditioner performance may be caused by a refrigerant leak at the compressor joint connector and is fixed by replacing the O-ring. (1993-95)

RECALL HISTORY

1993-94: Engine movement can cause throttle-cable housing to pull out of its guide; engine may then not return to idle when gas pedal is released. **1995 w/automatic:** Shift lever lock plate can be broken; movement of lever without driver's knowledge can result in unexpected vehicle movement. **1995:** On a few cars, right rear brake hose may contact suspension component, causing abrasion and eventual leakage. **1997:** Seatbelts might not restrain occupant during a collision.

1998-01 NISSAN ALTIMA

1998 Nissan Altima GLE

FOR Quietness • Ride • Passenger room

AGAINST Automatic transmission performance

EVALUATION Acceleration is little-changed from the prior generation—in short, nothing to shout about. Our test GLE ran 0-60 mph in a so-so 10 seconds with automatic transmission. The 2000 models should be a bit swifter. There's also little change in the transmission's reluctance to downshift promptly, or in its abruptness when it does. Our test GXE returned a somewhat disappointing 20.3 mpg, while our GLE averaged 23.4 mpg, despite hard city driving and performance testing. Expect a smooth, absorbent ride except on washboard surfaces, where minor wheel pattering disturbs the calm. Alas, the ride exacts a tradeoff in mediocre body control over big humps and dips, plus more body lean in tight turns than we prefer. Even so, Altima handling is competently agile, aided by quick steering with good feedback. Braking with ABS proved to be safe and undramatic, if unexceptional by today's standards. Unlike previous Altimas, the current generation allows 6-footers to sit comfortably in tandem. The cabin still is not wide enough for three adults in back, but leg, knee, and foot space are all good, as is overall head room even with a power moonroof installed. Front bucket seats in the 2000 models are more supportive and better bolstered. The dashboard is nicely laid out, with clean gauges and convenient, guess-free controls that complement a comfortable driver's post. Commuters should welcome the new console-mount dual cupholders—much more useful than the rickety pull-out contraption of old. Visibility is good except over-the-shoulder, due to high tail styling and wide rear roof posts. Trunk space is good, but not great. A wide rear bumper shelf makes for some back-straining reaches, and the lid hinges intrude into the cargo area. The cabin has plenty of places for bric-a-brac, though not accessible to rear-seaters.

VALUE Acceptably solid and well-finished, Altima remains a must-see for value-minded buyers, due largely to its low noise levels and soft ride. Trunk lids have felt tinny, however. Though unexceptional, Altima ranks as a nice family compact—less bland after the 2000 revamp.

SPECIFICATIONS

	4-door sedan
Wheelbase, in.	103.1
Overall length, in.	183.5
Overall width, in.	69.1
Overall height, in.	55.9
Curb weight, lbs.	2859
Cargo volume, cu. ft.	13.8
Fuel capacity, gals.	15.9
Seating capacity	5
Front head room, in.	39.4
Max. front leg room, in.	42.0
Rear head room, in.	37.7
Min. rear leg room, in.	33.9

Powertrain layout: transverse front-engine/front-wheel drive

ENGINES

	dohc I4
Size, liters/cu. in.	2.4/146
Horsepower	150-155
Torque (lbs./ft.)	154-156

EPA city/highway mpg

5-speed OD manual	24/31
4-speed OD automatic	22/30

City/highway mpg (as tested)

5-speed OD manual	23.4
4-speed OD automatic	20.3

Built in USA

RETAIL PRICES

RETAIL PRICES	GOOD	AVERAGE	POOR
1998 Altima XE, GXE	$8,500-9,300	$7,700-8,400	$4,300-4,700
1998 Altima SE, GLE	9,500-10,300	8,600-9,300	5,000-4,400
1999 Altima XE, GXE	9,500-10,500	8,500-9,500	4,900-5,600
1999 Altima SE, GLE	10,500-11,500	9,500-10,500	5,600-6,300
2000 Altima XE, GXE	10,500-11,500	9,500-10,500	5,600-6,300
2000 Altima SE, GLE	11,800-13,000	10,800-11,800	7,700-8,300
2001 Altima XE, GXE	11,700-13,000	10,500-11,700	—
2001 Altima SE, GLE	13,000-14,500	11,500-13,000	—

AVERAGE REPLACEMENT COSTS

A/C Compressor	$610	Clutch, Pressure Plate, Bearing	430
Alternator	320	Constant Velocity Joints	1,235
Automatic Transmission or Transaxle	745	Exhaust System	180
Brakes	205	Radiator	330
Shocks and/or Struts	525	Timing Chain or Belt	775

TROUBLE SPOTS

• **Vehicle noise.** A broken BTV valve bracket causes a rattle under the hood. (1999-2000)

• **Keyless entry.** The remote keyless entry system is difficult to program. (1998)

1998-00 NISSAN FRONTIER

1999 Nissan Frontier King Cab SE 4WD

FOR Standard 4-wheel antilock brakes (selected models) • Control layout • Ride/handling

AGAINST Acceleration (4-cylinder) • Rear-seat comfort • Rear-only ABS on 2WD models

EVALUATION Nissan's coarse 2.4-liter twin cam four cylinder engine does not have enough get-up-and-go for even base model 2WD regular cabs. However, manual-transmission clutch and shift actions are light and smooth and the automatic shifts crisply and kicks down quickly for more passing power. The new V6 engine made available for 1999 brought a welcome power boost for 4x4s, but was needed almost as much in 4x2 models. Though stronger than a 4-cylinder, however, the V6 engine still is less robust than most rivals. The Supercharged V6 introduced in 2001 gives Frontier a needed shot in the arm even though it feels little faster than the top V6s in most rival compact pickups. A 4x4 King Cab V6 with manual shift took a leisurely 11.2 seconds to hit 60 mph, while the Supercharged V6 with automatic did 0-60 mph in an estimated 9.2 sec. Ride and handling are strong points, both ranking with the best small pickups. Bumps are taken in stride, and there's only moderate body lean in corners. Stopping power is only adequate with rear-only antilock braking, but swift and stable with the all-wheel system. Beware of the optional Off-Road Package, which makes the going a lot bouncier. Frontier has a fresh, carlike interior. That's pleasing, but the old-fashioned pull-out, umbrella-style hand brake is not. In addition, the automatic transmission's column-shift lever interferes with wiper stalk and climate controls. Climate and radio controls are mounted high, and within easy reach. All told, the interior design is far more modern than that of Nissan's previous pickup. Front head and leg room are generous for even 6-footers. As in every other extended-cab compact pickup, the King Cab's jump seats are child-size. Crew Cabs, added for 2000, maneuver just as easily as King Cab models. The Crew Cab's aft entryways are quite narrow, and there's little leg room ahead of the hard back bench unless a front seat is shoved far forward. Entry/exit is good to the front, and 4WD Frontiers do not have as high a step-in as some competing 4x4 models. Interiors use plenty of hard plastic. All but the base 2WD model have front-door map pockets. Cloth trim on seats and door panels is more upscale than in the typical compact pickup.

VALUE Neither the brawniest nor the most refined compact truck of them all, Frontier is still worth a close look. If the truck you find fits your needs, Frontier rates among the better small pickups.

SPECIFICATIONS

	crew cab	ext. cab	reg. cab
Wheelbase, in.	116.1	116.1	104.3
Overall length, in.	193.1	196.1	184.3
Overall width, in.	71.9	71.9	66.5
Overall height, in.	65.9	65.9	62.8
Curb weight, lbs.	3742	3685	2911
Fuel capacity, gals.	19.4	15.9	15.9
Seating capacity	5	5	3
Front head room, in.	39.3	39.3	39.3
Max. front leg room, in.	41.1	41.4	40.9
Rear head room, in.	37.8	—	—
Min. rear leg room, in.	30.7	—	—

Powertrain layout: longitudinal front-engine/rear- or 4-wheel drive

ENGINES

	dohc I4	ohc V6	Supercharged ohc V6
Size, liters/cu. in.	2.4/146	3.3/201	3.3/201
Horsepower	143	170	210
Torque (lbs./ft.)	154	200	246

EPA city/highway mpg		dohc I4	ohc V6	Supercharged ohc V6
5-speed OD manual		22/26	16/19	15/18
4-speed OD automatic		20/24	15/19	15/18
City/highway mpg (as tested)				
5-speed OD manual			14.0	
4-speed OD automatic		18.5		15.1

Built in USA

RETAIL PRICES	GOOD	AVERAGE	POOR
1998 Frontier 2WD	$5,000-8,500	$4,200-7,600	$1,900-4,000
1998 Frontier 4WD	7,500-9,800	6,500-8,800	3,500-5,000
1999 Frontier 2WD	6,000-9,500	5,100-8,500	2,600-4,700
1999 Frontier 4WD	8,500-11,500	7,500-10,500	4,200-6,200
2000 Frontier 2WD	7,500-12,500	6,500-11,500	3,500-6,800
2000 Frontier 4WD	11,000-14,500	10,000-13,000	6,000-8,000

AVERAGE REPLACEMENT COSTS

A/C Compressor	$725	Clutch, Pressure Plate,	
Alternator	410	Bearing	570
Automatic Transmission or		Exhaust System	260
Transaxle	850	Radiator	285
Brakes	355	Shocks and/or Struts	470
Timing Chain or Belt	180	Universal Joints	330

TROUBLE SPOTS

• **Engine noise.** Engine rattle at startup is corrected by installing new camshaft bolts and a timing chain tensioner. (1998-99)

RECALL HISTORY

1998 w/automatic transmission: Securing pin inside transmission control assembly of some trucks can loosen, allowing shift lever to be inadvertently moved out of the "Park" position with key in ignition. **1998 w/bucket seats:** In frontal crash, front seatbelt can slip between seat and seatback recliner handle, where it can be cut by sharp edge of lever. **1999-2000:** Taillight socket may have been improperly molded, resulting in locking tab having insufficient force to retain bulb.

1995-99 NISSAN MAXIMA

1995 Nissan Maxima SE

FOR Optional antilock brakes • Acceleration • Steering/handling • Ride

AGAINST Rear-seat comfort • Fuel economy

EVALUATION Performance leads off the car's strong points, ranking as little short of stunning. We timed a GXE with the automatic transmission at 7.9 seconds to 60 mph. Tromp the gas pedal to the floor, and a Maxima nearly leaps ahead. Only modest engine roar is heard on such occasions, as the Maxima is otherwise quiet-running. Passing power also is impressive, but the automatic unit is slow to downshift for passing at times, and occasionally shifts harshly. As for fuel economy, we averaged 24.1 mpg with one GXE and 21.4 mpg with another. Maxima offers a comfortable and stable ride, precise steering, and crisp handling. Body lean is noticeable in high-speed lane changes and when cornering swiftly, but the Maxima maintains a tight grip on the road surface. Maxima feels really big inside—more so than its outside appearance suggests. With a little more head room and rear leg room than its predecessor, the latest Maxima is more accommodating for tall passengers. The wide trunk has a flat floor that provides plenty of cargo space. Instruments and controls are well-positioned and easy to see and use while driving. The low dashboard permits a great view of the road ahead. Stereo and climate controls are in a slanted panel that's easy to reach. Round analog gauges are large.

VALUE If you're searching for a midsize sedan that reaches above the run-of-the-mill offerings, a Maxima of any 1995-97 vintage is definitely worth a trial run.

SPECIFICATIONS

	4-door sedan
Wheelbase, in.	106.3
Overall length, in.	187.7
Overall width, in.	69.7
Overall height, in.	55.7
Curb weight, lbs.	3001
Cargo volume, cu. ft.	14.5
Fuel capacity, gals.	18.5
Seating capacity	5
Front head room, in.	40.1
Max. front leg room, in.	43.9
Rear head room, in.	37.4
Min. rear leg room, in.	34.3

Powertrain layout: transverse front-engine/front-wheel drive

ENGINES

	dohc V6
Size, liters/cu. in.	3.0/181
Horsepower	190
Torque (lbs./ft.)	205
EPA city/highway mpg	
5-speed OD manual	22/27
4-speed OD automatic	21/28
City/highway mpg (as tested)	
5-speed OD manual	24.1
4-speed OD automatic	21.4

Built in Japan

RETAIL PRICES	GOOD	AVERAGE	POOR
1995 Maxima	$5,500-7,000	$4,600-6,000	$2,200-3,000
1996 Maxima	7,000-8,500	6,000-7,500	3,200-4,100
1997 Maxima	9,000-11,000	8,000-10,000	4,500-5,700
1998 Maxima	11,000-13,000	10,000-12,000	6,000-7,200
1999 Maxima	12,800-15,500	11,500-14,000	7,200-8,700

AVERAGE REPLACEMENT COSTS

A/C Compressor	$625	Clutch, Pressure Plate,	
Alternator	450	Bearing	515
Automatic Transmission or		Constant Velocity Joints	1,145
Transaxle	1,080	Exhaust System	375
Brakes	210	Radiator	445
Shocks and/or Struts	1,530	Timing Chain or Belt	1,305

TROUBLE SPOTS

• **Brake noise.** Groaning from the rear brakes is caused by the parking brakes not fully releasing, requiring new brake cables and pads. (1995-99)

• **Hard starting.** Hard starting, stalling, or stumbling under load could be caused by corrosion of the coolant sensor. (1995-96)

• **Hard starting.** If the engine does not start on the first attempt, the engine may crank very slowly on the second attempt because of a problem with the engine control computer. (1995)

• **Engine noise.** Noise from the front of the engine may be caused by excessive play in the timing chain for which a new tensioner and chain guide are required. (1995-96)

• **Brake noise.** Rear brakes rattle on rough road. (1995)

• **Rough idle.** Several problems (no-start, no A/C, rough running, etc.) can be traced to broken wires in the engine compartment where the harness bends near the right strut tower. (1995-97)

• **Engine knock.** Spark knock or ping may result from a defective onboard computer. (1995-97)

• **Clutch.** The clutch may slip when accelerating hard in 4th or 5th gear due to a problem with the friction material. (1995)

• **Automatic transmission.** The original automatic transmission (model F04) shift solenoids allowed slipping and premature wear. (1997)

2000-01 NISSAN MAXIMA

FOR Acceleration • Steering/roadholding • Ride

AGAINST Manual shift action

EVALUATION Redesigning improved what was already a smooth, swift, and polished performer. A Maxima corners with grippy assurance and only mild body lean. The sporty SE is a tad crisper thanks to its sport suspension, but all Maximas are agile and the driver benefits from quick, informative steering. On the negative side, the SE's tauter suspension

2000 Nissan Maxima SE

results in a somewhat choppy ride over bumps that other models comfortably absorb. Braking is quick and consistent, with excellent control. A responsive powertrain yields 0-60 mph acceleration in 7.9 seconds. In fact, the V6 feels truly muscular, delivering fine punch off the line and strong passing power. Test Maximas have averaged 20-22.5 mpg, but premium fuel is recommended. Automatic transmissions are free of lurching in full-throttle downshifts—a malady suffered by earlier Maximas. Manual-transmission models suffer from imprecise clutch takeup and slightly stiff shift action. Unless the front wheels are perfectly straight, too, there's some annoying steering-wheel tub during hard takeoffs. Although the practical limit is four grownups inside, each has a bit more wiggle room than in the past. Taller adults get enough head clearance beneath the optional moonroof, and a more upright rear seatback improves comfort on long trips. Still, 6-footers need to ride knees-up in back if a taller person is occupying the front seat ahead. Visibility is good except directly to the rear. Gauges and controls are simple and inviting, though lookalike knobs for audio volume and temperature could confuse. Rearward seat travel is good; power seat controls easy to reach. The trunk has a wide, low opening.

VALUE Quiet and athletic, the Maxima offers an appealing blend of performance, handling, and ride comfort, with refinement and amenities approaching the near-luxury class. Nissan's top sedan fares well against such tough adversaries as the Honda Accord and Toyota Camry.

SPECIFICATIONS

	4-door sedan
Wheelbase, in.	108.3
Overall length, in.	190.5
Overall width, in.	70.3
Overall height, in.	56.5
Curb weight, lbs.	3186
Cargo volume, cu. ft.	15.1
Fuel capacity, gals.	18.5
Seating capacity	5
Front head room, in.	40.4
Max. front leg room, in.	44.8
Rear head room, in.	37.2
Min. rear leg room, in.	35.4

Powertrain layout: transverse front-engine/front-wheel drive

ENGINES

	ohc V6
Size, liters/cu. in.	3.0/183
Horsepower	222-227
Torque (lbs./ft.)	217

EPA city/highway mpg

5-speed OD manual	22/28
4-speed OD automatic	20/28

City/highway mpg (as tested)

5-speed OD manual	20.0
4-speed OD automatic	20.0

Built in Japan

RETAIL PRICES

	GOOD	AVERAGE	POOR
2000 Maxima GXE	$15,500-16,500	$14,500-15,500	$11,000-12,000
2000 Maxima SE GLE	17,500-19,000	16,500-18,000	12,500-13,500
2001 Maxima GXE	17,500-18,500	16,500-17,500	—
2001 Maxima SE GLE	19,700-22,000	18,700-20,800	—

AVERAGE REPLACEMENT COSTS

A/C Compressor	$705	Clutch, Pressure Plate, Bearing	635
Alternator	290		
Automatic Transmission or Transaxle	1,310	Constant Velocity Joints	740
		Exhaust System	480
Brakes	455	Radiator	380
Shocks and/or Struts	470	Timing Chain or Belt	460

TROUBLE SPOTS

• **Vehicle noise.** Noises from the right front strut require replacement of the rubber spring seat. (2000)

• **Audio system.** Popping and crackling noises in the audio system are often due to cell phones plugged into the cigarette lighter. Using a different power source or moving the phone often helps. (2000)

• **Cold starting problems.** The engine may idle to slowly or stall when first started (below 40°F). Reprogramming of the powertrain control module is required. (2000)

• **Sunroof/moonroof.** The headliner may sag near the sunroof because the Velcro does not hold sufficiently. Additional clips were being installed under warranty. (2000)

1990-95 NISSAN PATHFINDER

1992 Nissan Pathfinder SE

FOR Acceleration • Wet-weather traction (4WD) • Passenger and cargo room • Antilock brakes (optional)

AGAINST Fuel economy • Entry/exit

EVALUATION Early Nissan Pathfinder models seemed to ride smoothly, with less of the rough bounce customary on some of the new truck-based compact sport utility vehicles. Adequate power finally arrived in 1990 when the 3.0-liter engine switched to multipoint fuel injection, giving the Pathfinder 180 horsepower, but low-end torque still is not sufficient to help the Pathfinder keep pace with the Explorer or Cherokee when called upon to climb hills or haul heavy loads. Given that the Pathfinder was not significantly changed after 1990, the newer Ford Explorer and Jeep Cherokee have provided more popular carlike features and handling, making Nissan's older design feel dated, too stiff, and unsophisticated. Gas mileage is dismal as well. In our test we only achieved 14.7 mpg with the automatic. The Pathfinder's 4WD system is another drawback. Since it lacks full shift-on-the-fly capability, it's far less convenient than most competitive part-time systems used by an ever-growing number of rivals. The handling is safe and predictable. Narrow rear doors combined with a high step-up make entry and exit a chore.

VALUE To its credit, the Pathfinder provides precise steering and ample cargo room. It's also rugged and as durable as a Swiss Army knife. Unfortunately, the compact sport-utility market has stampeded forward toward more carlike vehicles, effectively leaving the Pathfinder in the dust.

SPECIFICATIONS

	4-door wagon
Wheelbase, in.	104.3
Overall length, in.	171.9
Overall width, in.	66.5
Overall height, in.	65.7
Curb weight, lbs.	3795
Cargo volume, cu. ft.	31.9
Fuel capacity, gals.	21.1
Seating capacity	5
Front head room, in.	39.3

	4-door wagon
Max. front leg room, in.	42.6
Rear head room, in.	36.8
Min. rear leg room, in.	33.1

Powertrain layout: longitudinal front-engine/rear- or 4-wheel drive

ENGINES

	ohc V6
Size, liters/cu. in.	3.0/181
Horsepower	153
Torque (lbs./ft.)	180

EPA city/highway mpg

5-speed OD manual	15/18
4-speed OD automatic	15/18

City/highway mpg (as tested)

4-speed OD automatic	14.7

Built in Japan

RETAIL PRICES

	GOOD	AVERAGE	POOR
1990 Pathfinder 2WD	$2,400-3,100	$1,800-2,400	$500-800
1990 Pathfinder 4WD	3,500-4,500	2,800-3,700	1,000-1,500
1991 Pathfinder 2WD	2,900-3,600	2,300-2,900	700-1,100
1991 Pathfinder 4WD	4,000-5,000	3,300-4,200	1,300-1,800
1992 Pathfinder 2WD	3,500-4,200	2,800-3,500	1,000-1,400
1992 Pathfinder 4WD	4,500-5,500	3,700-4,700	1,600-2,200
1993 Pathfinder 2WD	4,100-4,800	3,400-4,100	1,400-1,800
1993 Pathfinder 4WD	5,200-6,200	4,400-5,400	2,100-2,700
1994 Pathfinder 2WD	5,000-5,800	4,300-5,000	2,000-2,400
1994 Pathfinder 4WD	6,000-7,200	5,200-6,300	2,700-3,400
1995 Pathfinder 2WD	6,200-7,300	5,400-6,400	2,800-3,400
1995 Pathfinder 4WD	7,200-8,500	6,400-7,500	3,400-4,100

AVERAGE REPLACEMENT COSTS

A/C Compressor	$540	Clutch, Pressure Plate, Bearing	470
Alternator	250	Exhaust System	275
Automatic Transmission or Transaxle	830	Radiator	460
Brakes	225	Shocks and/or Struts	295
Timing Chain or Belt	375	Universal Joints	170

TROUBLE SPOTS

• **Poor drivability.** A check engine light accompanied by poor drivability could be caused by water in the wiring connector for the oxygen sensor. (1995)

• **Coolant leak.** Coolant may leak from the front of the cylinder head, which may appear to be a head gasket, but comes from a threaded plug in the front of the head. (1990-95)

• **Hard starting.** If the engine is hard to start at high altitudes, it is flooding from too much fuel and a revised water temperature sensor will cure the problem. (1990-95)

• **Automatic transmission.** If the transmission does not shift properly until warmed up, make sure it is filled only with Nissanmatic "C" transmission fluid. (1990-95)

• **Air conditioner.** Rattling or rumbling from the blower may be caused by leaves and other debris that are not stopped by the fresh air grille. (1993-95)

• **Oil leak.** There is a revised pinion seal to correct oil leaks at both front and rear differentials on 2WD and 4WD models. (1992)

RECALL HISTORY

1990-91: Front seatbelt release button can break and pieces can fall inside.
1994: Latch plate in seatbelt buckle could engage only partially, causing tongue to come out of buckle during collision or hard braking.

1996-01 NISSAN PATHFINDER

FOR Passenger and cargo room • Instruments/controls • Ride • Steering/handling

AGAINST Rear-seat entry/exit • Engine noise • Fuel economy • Rear leg room

EVALUATION Softer-riding than before, with additional rear seat and cargo room, the new Pathfinder also delivers better acceleration and has a more modern dashboard. Because of its relatively low ride height, getting in and out of the front seats is easy. Despite large rear doors, how-

1996 Nissan Pathfinder LE

ever, the back seat presents more of a challenge, partly because those doors do not open 90 degrees. There's little room to swing your feet and legs through the narrow opening. The V6 engine is smoother than in the previous model, though a heavy throttle foot yields a loud engine roar—too gruff and growly when worked hard. The 2001 V6 brought Pathfinder/QX4 up to par with the competition. '01 Nissans claimed 0-60 mph in 8.8 sec—2.1 sec faster than earlier models. Low-speed response is good, though a Pathfinder cannot beat its domestic rivals—with V8 engines—in all-out acceleration. Fuel economy is on the dismal side, like most SUVs. An SE 4x4 with automatic averaged a meager 14.1 mpg in a combination of city, suburban, and highway driving. Ride and handling rank among the most carlike in the sport-utility field. A tight suspension and linear steering contribute to a sense of control. Even so, you get a surprising amount of body lean and tire squeal during fast turns. Road and wind noise are low. The Pathfinder's dashboard is one of the most user-friendly you can find, with all controls easy to see and reach. Head room is good all around, if not exceptional, but the rear seat offers barely enough leg room for anyone taller than about 5-foot-10. Cargo space is good, but folding the rear seats requires tilting the cushion, then removing the head restraints so the backrests can lie flat. Thick side roof pillars might impair the driver's over-the-shoulder views.

VALUE Pathfinders are not cheap, but largely because of excellent road manners and truck-tough construction, they're worth a look before buying an SUV in this class.

SPECIFICATIONS

	4-door wagon
Wheelbase, in.	106.3
Overall length, in.	178.3
Overall width, in.	68.7
Overall height, in.	67.1
Curb weight, lbs.	3675
Cargo volume, cu. ft.	85.0
Fuel capacity, gals.	20.8
Seating capacity	5
Front head room, in.	39.5
Max. front leg room, in.	41.7
Rear head room, in.	37.5
Min. rear leg room, in.	31.8

Powertrain layout: longitudinal front-engine/rear- or 4-wheel drive

ENGINES

	ohc V6
Size, liters/cu. in.	3.3/201
Horsepower	168
Torque (lbs./ft.)	196

EPA city/highway mpg

5-speed OD manual	16/18
4-speed OD automatic	15/19

City/highway mpg (as tested)

4-speed OD automatic	14.1

Built in Japan

RETAIL PRICES

	GOOD	AVERAGE	POOR
1996 Pathfinder 2WD	$8,000-9,500	$7,200-8,500	$4,100-4,900
1996 Pathfinder 4WD	9,000-10,500	8,100-9,500	4,600-5,500
1997 Pathfinder 2WD	9,500-11,200	8,500-10,200	4,900-6,000
1997 Pathfinder 4WD	10,500-12,500	9,500-11,500	5,600-6,800
1998 Pathfinder 2WD	11,500-13,500	10,500-12,500	6,500-7,700
1998 Pathfinder 4WD	12,800-14,500	11,700-13,200	7,600-8,500
1999 Pathfinder 2WD	13,500-16,500	12,300-15,000	8,200-9,800
1999 Pathfinder 4WD	14,800-17,500	13,500-16,000	9,200-10,800
2000 Pathfinder 2WD	16,000-18,500	14,500-17,000	10,000-11,500
2000 Pathfinder 4WD	17,500-20,000	16,000-18,500	11,000-12,500
2001 Pathfinder 2WD	19,000-22,000	17,500-20,500	—
2001 Pathfinder 4WD	20,500-23,000	19,000-21,500	—

AVERAGE REPLACEMENT COSTS

A/C Compressor	$660	Clutch, Pressure Plate,	
Alternator	460	Bearing	610
Automatic Transmission or		Exhaust System	460
Transaxle	1,115	Radiator	610
Brakes	670	Shocks and/or Struts	490
Timing Chain or Belt	490	Universal Joints	310

TROUBLE SPOTS

• **Brake noise.** A high-pitched squeal or whistle from the area of the front brakes is eliminated by replacing the baffle plate on both sides. (1996-98)

• **Airbags.** Airbag indicator light may flash, indicating a failure. Dealer will replace the SRS (supplemental restraint system) sensor under warranty. (1996)

• **Wheels.** The black anodized lug nuts' surfaces corrode (looking light white dust spots). Nissan will replace them with chrome lug nuts. (1996)

• **Suspension noise.** The front suspension squeaks on rough roads due to a problem between the strut rod and rubber bumper. (1996)

• **Audio system.** The radio may loose its presets and the clock its time due to voltage spikes. A replacement radio, less susceptible to this problem, is available. (1996)

• **Vehicle shake.** Vibrations at 30-40 mph are often the result of the front driveshaft being installed out of phase. (1996-97)

RECALL HISTORY

1996: Due to type of lubricant used, steering wheel effort at low ambient temperatures could increase. **1996:** Carpet padding on some vehicles could be too thick, catching driver's right foot.

1993-98 NISSAN QUEST

1996 Nissan Quest XE

FOR Passenger room • Steering/handling • Antilock brakes (optional)

AGAINST Control layout • Wind noise • Acceleration (with load)

EVALUATION Quest is a carlike, luxury-oriented people mover that stresses comfort over hauling. As a result, the Quest has a low step-in height that allows easy entry and exit. It also provides a very comfortable driving position, good visibility, and an ample supply of cupholders and cubbies. Although the 3.0-liter engine is adequate, it can't quite match the muscle provided by the larger V6s in front-drive minivans from Ford, GM, and Chrysler. When loaded, maneuvers such as merging onto freeways or passing slower traffic cannot be accomplished with quite the same ease. But, compared with other minivans, body lean is quite modest. Actually, Quest handles with more poise than some regular passenger cars. Ride quality is commendable, too—absorbent, yet stable and comfortable at highway speeds. The suspension is firm enough to minimize bouncing on wavy roads, and it soaks up most bumps without breaking a sweat. On the negative side, wind and road noise are excessive at highway speeds. Front headroom and legroom are both quite good, but only adequate for the middle- and rear-seat passengers. Stereo and climate controls are low on the dashboard and a long reach, hampered by small buttons. With all seats in their normal positions, the rear cargo area is tight. Trying to improve the Quest's hauling capacity requires removing the truly cumbersome center seats.

VALUE Compared with other minivans, the Quest has less interior room. It also lacks many of the features found on its rivals. Nevertheless, it's a good choice if you need more than a midsize station wagon but don't need the interior space provided in one of the bigger minivans.

SPECIFICATIONS

	3-door van
Wheelbase, in.	112.2
Overall length, in.	189.9
Overall width, in.	73.4
Overall height, in.	66.0
Curb weight, lbs.	3815
Cargo volume, cu. ft.	126.4
Fuel capacity, gals.	20.0
Seating capacity	7
Front head room, in.	39.4
Max. front leg room, in.	39.9
Rear head room, in.	39.7
Min. rear leg room, in.	34.8

Powertrain layout: transverse front-engine/front-wheel drive

ENGINES

	ohc V6
Size, liters/cu. in.	3.0/181
Horsepower	151
Torque (lbs./ft.)	174

EPA city/highway mpg
4-speed OD automatic	17/23

City/highway mpg (as tested)
4-speed OD automatic	19.7

Built in USA

RETAIL PRICES

	GOOD	AVERAGE	POOR
1993 Quest	$3,500-4,500	$2,800-3,700	$1,000-1,600
1994 Quest	4,300-5,500	3,600-4,700	1,500-2,100
1995 Quest	5,400-6,500	4,700-5,700	2,300-2,900
1996 Quest	7,000-8,200	6,200-7,200	3,200-3,800
1997 Quest	9,000-10,800	8,000-9,800	4,500-5,700
1998 Quest	11,000-13,000	9,800-11,500	5,900-7,000

AVERAGE REPLACEMENT COSTS

A/C Compressor	$330	Constant Velocity Joints	615
Alternator	300	Exhaust System	250
Automatic Transmission or		Radiator	505
Transaxle	835	Shocks and/or Struts	380
Brakes	255	Timing Chain or Belt	190

TROUBLE SPOTS

• **Suspension noise.** A new stabilizer bar and bushings are needed if there is a crunching or scraping noise from the front end. (1993-95)

• **Doors.** A rattle in either of the front doors may be caused by the door guard beam spot welds breaking loose. (1993-94)

• **Automatic transmission.** Burnt transmission fluid and no reverse gear may signal a defective rear control valve and low/reverse brake. (1993-94)

• **Coolant leak.** Coolant may leak from the front of the cylinder head, which may appear to be a head gasket, but comes from a threaded plug in the front of the head. (1993-95)

• **Tail/brake lights.** If the tail/brake lights work intermittently, the socket may be loose from the plastic connector. (1993-95)

• **Automatic transmission.** If the transmission does not shift properly until warmed up, make sure it is filled only with Nissanmatic "C" transmission fluid. (All)

RECALL HISTORY

1993-98: Cracks have developed in the vent hose, allowing a fuel leak. **1993:** Master cylinder on some vans was improperly assembled or damaged during assembly, which can result in loss of braking at two wheels, causing increased pedal travel and effort and increased stopping distance. **1993:** One or both bolts securing automatic seatbelt tracks to B-pillars were not adequately tightened on some vans, increasing risk of injury in collision or sudden maneuver. **1993:** Fuel filler hoses may have been cut prior to installation by knife used to open shipping box; fuel leakage could result, leading to fire if exposed to ignition source. **1993:** Leaves and other foreign matter can enter through cowl panel air intake during operation of front heater and/or air conditioner, resulting in build-up in the plenum that can lead to noise, odors, or even a vehicle fire. **1995 with sliding third-row bench seats:** Cable that connects seat adjustment level to latch might be pinched in roller assembly, preventing latch on left side from fully engaging seat rail. **1995:** Rear lamp socket may not illuminate, resulting in malfunction or stoplamp or rear running lamps. **1996:** Power windows can be closed after ignition key is turned to "off" position and right front door is opened.

1999-01 NISSAN QUEST

2000 Nissan Quest

FOR Passenger and cargo room • Control layout

AGAINST Interior material

EVALUATION In performance and accommodations, Quests differ little from their Mercury Villager counterparts. Acceleration is reasonably peppy from a standstill, but unimpressive in the 35-55 mph range. In fact, highway passing response borders on inadequate with a full load and the air conditioner working. Engine roar under heavy throttle is notable, though wind and tire noise are on par for this class. So is fuel economy. A test Quest, when new, averaged a less-than-frugal 16.9 mpg. Relatively compact in size, the Quest (and Villager) offer above-average minivan maneuverability, helped by firm steering with ample feel. Cornering response is crispest with the SE edition, which rides 16-inch tires instead of the usual 15-inch. The Quest's suspension soaks up bumps decently, but overall ride quality does not match that of longer-wheelbase minivans like the Dodge Grand Caravan and Toyota Sienna. Relatively cozy, the Quest's interior has scant clearance between any of the seats. Front seatbacks are narrow, though supportive cushions improve overall comfort. Low step-in height is pleasing, but third-row entry/exit is rather tight due to a low roof and narrow passageways. Cargo room is slim with the third seat in its normal position, though the available, adjustable-height parcel shelf is handy. The third-row bench can slide forward to free up a large cargo hold, but its release handle is difficult to reach. Second-row seats remove easily. Interior storage includes a removable net between front seats, double door pockets, and numerous bins. Despite targeting upscale buyers, the Quest and Villager contain a lot of hard-surfaced interior plastic items inside, along with industrial-look switchgear and unfinished edges.

VALUE Smaller outside and inside than most rivals, Nissan's Quest and the equivalent Mercury Villager are more maneuverable. Both trail the competition in refinement and acceleration. Quests have held their value more strongly, thus cost more secondhand.

SPECIFICATIONS

	4-door van
Wheelbase, in.	112.2
Overall length, in.	194.8
Overall width, in.	74.9
Overall height, in.	64.2
Curb weight, lbs.	3830
Cargo volume, cu. ft.	135.6
Fuel capacity, gals.	20.0
Seating capacity	7
Front head room, in.	39.7
Max. front leg room, in.	39.9
Rear head room, in.	39.9
Min. rear leg room, in.	36.4

Powertrain layout: transverse front-engine/front-wheel drive

ENGINES

	ohc V6
Size, liters/cu. in.	3.3/201
Horsepower	170
Torque (lbs./ft.)	200

EPA city/highway mpg

4-speed OD automatic	17/24

City/highway mpg (as tested)

4-speed OD automatic	16.9

Built in USA

RETAIL PRICES

	GOOD	AVERAGE	POOR
1999 Quest	$13,800-15,800	$12,800-14,800	$9,300-10,800
2000 Quest	16,900-18,500	15,000-17,500	11,000-13,000
2001 Quest	18,500-21,500	17,500-20,500	—

AVERAGE REPLACEMENT COSTS

A/C Compressor	$500	Constant Velocity Joints	1,150
Alternator	350	Exhaust System	385
Automatic Transmission or Transaxle	1,320	Radiator	410
		Shocks and/or Struts	900
Brakes	370	Timing Chain or Belt	455

TROUBLE SPOTS

• **Engine misfire.** Poor idle quality or stiff accelerator action is often traced to a dirty throttle body. Can be caused by overfilling the oil in the crankcase. (1999-2000)

• **Vehicle noise.** Rattling or banging noises from the rear are due to the leaf spring supports hitting the mountings. Washers were being installed as shims under warranty. (1999)

• **Windows.** The second and/or third windows may pop open as doors are closed or may not latch properly due to maladjustment of the latches. (1999)

• **Wipers.** The wipers may operate on their own due to a faulty multifunction. (1999)

RECALL HISTORY

1999: Taillight socket's locking tab may have insufficient force to retain the bulb. **1999:** Fuel tank retention strap (two per minivan) can break at spot welds, causing underbody rattle; if welds fail, there may be fuel leakage and/or separation of fuel tank from vehicle. **1999:** Second-row captain's chair on right side of some minivans may have inadequate lubrication of easy-entry/exit latch system, and actuator spring could deform, causing latch to remain in unlatched position; seat would then slide freely on track, and springs would move seat to easy-entry position. **1999-00:** One or more of the five bolts that mount rack-and-pinion steering gear may have been incorrectly tightened; could result in steering looseness and noise or vibration. Eventually, bolts could fracture or fall out.

1995-99 NISSAN SENTRA

1995 Nissan Sentra GXE

FOR Fuel economy • Ride • Optional antilock brakes (GXE, GLE)

AGAINST Acceleration (automatic transmission) • Rear-seat room • Seat comfort • Rear-seat entry/exit

EVALUATION In terms of quietness and solidity, the 1995 redesign moved Sentra from the middle to near the front of the subcompact class. Even when driven over the roughest roads, Sentras act and feel far more substantial than most small cars, with a supple yet well-controlled ride and a notable absence of body drumming and road rumble. Although wind noise rises appreciably above 60 mph, the little engine doesn't thrash or boom at most speeds. You'll need to work the 1.6-liter engine hard when mated to the automatic transmission. But, when mated to the slick-shifting 5-speed manual, the Sentra feels frisky. The 140-horsepower engine in the SE has good acceleration with automatic and feels even more lively with the 5-speed. Despite a bigger interior than prior models, Sentra remains practical for only four adults. Three grownups simply cannot fit comfortably in the back seat for longer trips. A functional, attractive dashboard gives the Sentra driver a user-friendly environment, but seats are flat and hard. Cargo space isn't the greatest, but the trunk has a flat floor and low opening at bumper level.

VALUE Solid and refined, Sentra looks like a good value in the small-car hunt. We'd even place it on a par with the Toyota Corolla—today's standard of comparison in the subcompact league.

SPECIFICATIONS

	4-door sedan
Wheelbase, in.	99.8
Overall length, in.	170.1
Overall width, in.	66.6

	4-door sedan
Overall height, in.	54.5
Curb weight, lbs.	2315
Cargo volume, cu. ft.	10.7
Fuel capacity, gals.	13.2
Seating capacity	5
Front head room, in.	39.1
Max. front leg room, in.	42.3
Rear head room, in.	39.5
Min. rear leg room, in.	32.4

Powertrain layout: transverse front-engine/front-wheel drive

ENGINES

	dohc I4	dohc I4
Size, liters/cu. in.	1.6/97	2.0/122
Horsepower	115	140
Torque (lbs./ft.)	108	132
EPA city/highway mpg		
5-speed OD manual	30/40	23/31
4-speed OD automatic	28/37	23/30
City/highway mpg (as tested)		
5-speed OD manual	31.7	25.4
4-speed OD automatic	24.9	

Built in USA

RETAIL PRICES

	GOOD	AVERAGE	POOR
1995 Sentra	$2,600-4,000	$2,000-3,300	$600-1,220
1996 Sentra	3,200-4,800	2,500-4,100	800-1,700
1997 Sentra	4,000-5,800	3,300-5,000	1,300-2,300
1998 Sentra	5,200-7,500	4,400-6,600	2,100-3,200
1999 Sentra	6,500-8,500	5,600-7,500	2,900-4,000

AVERAGE REPLACEMENT COSTS

A/C Compressor	$610	Constant Velocity Joints	1,120
Alternator	310	Exhaust System	320
Brakes	290	Radiator	300
Clutch, Pressure Plate, Bearing	390	Shocks and/or Struts	460
		Timing Chain or Belt	620

TROUBLE SPOTS

• **Audio system.** Cellular phones can interfere and cause noise from the radio speakers if the phone is plugged into the cigarette lighter socket near the radio rather than another 12-volt accessory socket. (1995-99)

• **Air conditioner.** Poor air conditioning may be due to refrigerant leaking from the service fitting valves. (1996)

• **Hard starting.** Starting difficulty and/or flooding while starting in cold weather at higher altitudes may require a revised powertrain control module (PCM). (1997-99)

• **Dashboard lights.** The check engine light comes on due to a problem with the rear heated oxygen sensor. (1995-96)

• **Fuel gauge.** The gauge may not register full due to the pump wires interfering with the float arm. (1995)

• **Horn.** The horn may sound when the wheel is turned due a spring slipping out of place in the steering column. (1995-99)

• **Brake noise.** The rear drum brakes may squeal, grind, or groan due to being over-adjusted. (1995)

• **Sunroof/moonroof.** The sunroof may tilt up, but not slide back due to a problem with the lifter mechanism. (1995-96)

RECALL HISTORY

1995 w/antilock brakes: Hydraulic actuator was not properly purged of all air; bubbles can cause increased pedal travel and stopping distances. **1995-96:** Front coil springs may not have sufficient corrosion resistance in areas where significant amounts of de-icing salts are applied to roads. **1995-98:** Water can enter and displace grease in wiper arm linkage joint, resulting in gradual wear over a period of time that could lead to separation of wiper linkage assembly. **1996:** Does not meet illumination requirements for brake light. **1996-97:** Stop/taillamps do not meet illumination requirements of Federal Motor Vehicle Safety Standard (FMVSS) No. 108.

2000-01 NISSAN SENTRA

FOR Fuel economy

AGAINST Rear-seat entry/exit

2000 Nissan Sentra SE

EVALUATION Sentras don't exactly feel underpowered. Still, a test GXE with a manual transmission needed a relatively leisurely 9.9 seconds to reach 60 mph. Automatic adds at least a second to that pace. With its bigger engine, the SE is quicker—but not by all that much unless it has the 5-speed, which helps this small sedan feel quite spirited. Automatic transmissions are smooth and responsive enough, but some 5-speeds have suffered imprecise shift action and overly sharp clutch engagement, which makes smooth driving tricky. As for economy, a GXE averaged 24.9 mpg, while an SE managed 28.5 mpg. Both had manual shift. Sentra's base suspension delivers safe, predictable front-drive handling, but only modest cornering grip on its standard all-season tires. Some bounding at higher speeds is noticeable, as is marked wheel patter on washboard-surfaced freeway segments. Although the ride isn't really bad, the suspension is less absorbent than that of a Honda Civic, Volkswagen Jetta, or Toyota Echo. A firmer suspension gives the SE sportier handling, with a slight loss of ride comfort. No model is really quiet, with tire roar higher than the class norm. Even without ABS, a GXE stopped in reasonably short distances with little nosedive and easy pedal modulation, but some sudden wheel lockup. Interior space could be more generous. The lack is most noticeable in back, where 6-footers can sit upright but have little leg or foot space if the front seat is pushed all the way back. Front seats don't move far, either, so tall drivers might also feel cramped. Entry/exit is hindered by small rear door openings. Gauges and controls are simple and handy. The radio is high, but smallish buttons and markings make it a little hard to use. Interior storage is above average, but trunk space is not, aggravated by a moderate-size opening and scant height beneath the parcel shelf.

VALUE Not as refined as a Civic or as roomy as a Ford Focus, Nissan's "entry-level" sedan is solid enough—and priced right on the secondhand market.

SPECIFICATIONS

	4-door sedan
Wheelbase, in.	99.8
Overall length, in.	177.5
Overall width, in.	67.3
Overall height, in.	55.5
Curb weight, lbs.	2548
Cargo volume, cu. ft.	11.6
Fuel capacity, gals.	13.2
Seating capacity	5
Front head room, in.	39.9
Max. front leg room, in.	41.6
Rear head room, in.	37.0
Min. rear leg room, in.	33.7

Powertrain layout: transverse front-engine/front-wheel drive

ENGINES

	dohc I4	dohc I4
Size, liters/cu. in.	1.8/110	2.0/122
Horsepower	126	145
Torque (lbs./ft.)	129	136
EPA city/highway mpg		
5-speed OD manual	27/35	24/31
4-speed OD automatic	26/33	24/30
City/highway mpg (as tested)		
5-speed OD manual	24.9	28.5

Built in Mexico

RETAIL PRICES

	GOOD	AVERAGE	POOR
2000 Sentra XE GXE	$8,500-10,000	$7,700-9,000	$5,000-6,000
2000 Sentra SE	10,000-11,000	9,000-10,000	6,200-7,000
2001 Sentra XE GXE	10,000-11,500	9,000-10,500	—
2001 Sentra SE	12,000-13,000	11,000-12,000	—

AVERAGE REPLACEMENT COSTS

A/C Compressor	$610	Clutch, Pressure Plate,	
Alternator	320	Bearing	430
Automatic Transmission or		Constant Velocity Joints	1,230
Transaxle	740	Exhaust System	345
Brakes	200	Radiator	325
Shocks and/or Struts	520	Timing Chain or Belt	770

TROUBLE SPOTS

• **Air conditioner.** If the air conditioner does not cool, the thermocouple in the evaporator may be at fault. A new probe must be installed in a different location. (2000-01)

• **Audio system.** Popping and crackling noises in the audio system are often due to cell phones plugged into the cigarette lighter. Using a different power source or moving the phone often helps. (2000)

• **Steering noise.** Squeaks or rattles from the front end when turning are often due to misaligned, and damaged, strut bearing not fully seated in its recess. It was being replaced under warranty. (2000)

• **Water leak.** The driver's side floor gets wet because the air conditioner evaporator drain hose has a tendency to fall off the pipe at the evaporator case. A hose clamp may help. (2000)

RECALL HISTORY

2000-01: Steel wheels could fail and separate from the mounting hub without prior warning. **2001:** Bolts used to attach each front suspension lower control arm to the body on the left and right sides may not have been properly manufactured and could fracture, increasing the risk of a crash.

2000-01 NISSAN XTERRA

2000 Nissan Xterra XE 4WD

FOR Cargo room

AGAINST Ride/handling • Rear-seat entry/exit • Wind noise

EVALUATION Nissan intended the Xterra to be backpack-functional and contemporary cool, yet in some ways it's rather stodgy. Acceleration is plodding with the 4-cylinder, but adequate with the V6. The automatic transmission works well, as do the brakes. An automatic 2WD SE reached 60 mph in 9.6 seconds. Even in 2WD form, the suspension is stiff enough to cause notable jiggle on bumpy pavements, though it won't pummel a person's kidneys. Cornering grip is decent for a high, narrow SUV, but steering is vague on-center. Compared to the nimble Honda CR-V, an Xterra feels rather ponderous. Fuel economy is midsize-level, not compact-frugal. One new 2WD V6 averaged 17.2 mpg; another just 14.6 mpg in harder driving. While it doesn't match a CR-V or Toyota RAV4 in convenient all-surface 4WD, an Xterra—which has a Low range—is designed to lead those rivals in off-road capability. An Xterra eagerly tackles difficult mountain trails, but its V6 drones under hard throttle, and a nagging wind whistle from the roof rack adds to intrusive noise levels. Nissan's no-frills approach is evident in utilitarian cabin furnishings. Most interior trim panels are noticeably thin, as is the door glass, though seat fabrics look durable. The simple dashboard works well, though lanky drivers might crave more rearward seat travel and using the "umbrella handle" parking brake is an old-fashioned chore. Lowish front bucket seats promise good head room for tall occupants, but impel a slightly legs-out posture. Rear head room is terrific, because the kicked-up roofline allows the bench seat to stand higher. Sadly, three grownups won't fit easily in back. Rear leg room is minimal unless front seats are pushed forward, and the back bench is hard. Step-in is high, and rear door bottoms are so narrow that entry/exit is a real squeeze. Cargo space beats a CR-V or RAV4 with the rear seat up.

VALUE Though less pleasant for everyday driving than the CR-V and RAV4, an Xterra offers truck toughness and off-road ability, along with V6 power. A V6 Xterra costs less than one of those less roomy 4-cylinder competitors.

SPECIFICATIONS

	4-door wagon
Wheelbase, in.	104.3
Overall length, in.	178.0
Overall width, in.	70.4
Overall height, in.	69.4
Curb weight, lbs.	3668
Cargo volume, cu. ft.	65.6
Fuel capacity, gals.	19.4
Seating capacity	5
Front head room, in.	38.6
Max. front leg room, in.	41.4
Rear head room, in.	37.5
Min. rear leg room, in.	32.8

Powertrain layout: longitudinal front-engine/rear- or 4-wheel drive

ENGINES

	ohc I4	ohc V6
Size, liters/cu. in.	2.4/146	3.3/200
Horsepower	143	170
Torque (lbs./ft.)	154	200
EPA city/highway mpg		
5-speed OD manual	19/24	16/18
4-speed OD automatic		15/19
City/highway mpg (as tested)		
4-speed OD automatic		14.6

Built in USA

RETAIL PRICES

	GOOD	AVERAGE	POOR
2000 Xterra 2WD	$14,000-17,000	$13,000-16,000	$9,000-11,500
2000 Xterra 4WD	17,500-19,500	16,300-18,300	12,000-13,000
2001 Xterra 2WD	16,000-19,500	15,000-18,500	—
2001 Xterra 4WD	20,000-23,000	18,500-21,500	—

AVERAGE REPLACEMENT COSTS

A/C Compressor	$590	Clutch, Pressure Plate,	
Alternator	290	Bearing	450
Automatic Transmission or		Constant Velocity Joints	730
Transaxle	1,490	Exhaust System	300
Brakes	330	Radiator	670
Shocks and/or Struts	875	Timing Chain or Belt	400

TROUBLE SPOTS

• **Vehicle noise.** Clunking or hammering noise under the floor can be traced to a loose torsion bar anchor at the crossmember. Spacer washers were being installed under warranty. (2000)

• **Engine misfire.** Poor idle quality when coasting with the clutch depressed was being corrected by reprogramming the powertrain control module. (2000)

• **Audio system.** Popping and crackling noises in the audio system are often due to cell phones plugged into the cigarette lighter. Using a different power source or moving the phone often helps. (2000)

• **Dashboard lights.** The check engine light comes on due to a poor electrical ground between the intake manifold and cylinder head on V-6 engines. (2000)

RECALL HISTORY

2000 w/automatic: Shift cable lock plate may be too brittle and could break, so transmission would not shift out of "Park" position and gear indicated may differ from gear that is actually engaged.

1992-97 OLDSMOBILE ACHIEVA

FOR Acceleration • Steering/handling • Antilock brakes (optional)

AGAINST Ride • Entry/exit

EVALUATION

See the 1992-98 Pontiac Grand Am.

VALUE

See the 1992-98 Pontiac Grand Am.

SPECIFICATIONS

	2-door coupe	4-door sedan
Wheelbase, in.	103.4	103.4

1993 Oldsmobile Achieva 2-door couype

	2-door coupe	4-door sedan
Overall length, in.	187.9	187.9
Overall width, in.	67.5	67.5
Overall height, in.	53.4	53.4
Curb weight, lbs.	2738	2799
Cargo volume, cu. ft.	14.0	14.0
Fuel capacity, gals.	15.2	15.2
Seating capacity	5	5
Front head room, in.	37.8	37.8
Max. front leg room, in.	43.3	43.3
Rear head room, in.	36.5	37.0
Min. rear leg room, in.	30.9	35.0

Powertrain layout: transverse front-engine/front-wheel drive

ENGINES	ohc I4	dohc I4	dohc I4	ohv V6	ohv V6
Size, liters/cu. in.	2.3/138	2.3/138	2.4/146	3.1/191	3.3/204
Horsepower	115-120	150-190	150	155-160	150
Torque (lbs./ft.)	140	145-160	150	185	185
EPA city/highway mpg					
5-speed OD man.	23/35	21/30	23/33		
3-speed auto.	24/32	23/29			20/29
4-speed OD auto.	22/31	21/30	22/32	20/29	
City/highway mpg (as tested)					
5-speed OD man.		25.1			
4-speed OD auto.				23.6	

Built in USA

RETAIL PRICES	GOOD	AVERAGE	POOR
1992 Achieva	$1,600-2,200	$1,000-1,600	$200-400
1993 Achieva	2,100-2,800	1,500-2,200	400-700
1994 Achieva	2,600-3,300	2,000-2,600	600-900
1995 Achieva	3,200-4,000	2,600-3,300	800-1,200
1996 Achieva	3,800-4,500	3,100-3,800	1,100-1,500
1997 Achieva	4,500-5,300	3,800-4,500	1,600-2,000

AVERAGE REPLACEMENT COSTS

See the 1992-98 Pontiac Grand Am.

TROUBLE SPOTS

See the 1992-98 Pontiac Grand Am.

RECALL HISTORY

1994: Welds in rear assembly of fuel tank may be insufficient to prevent leakage in certain rear-impact collisions, increasing risk of fire. **1996:** Front and/or rear hazard warning lamps might not work. **1996:** During deployment of the passenger airbag, the airbag can snag on a reinforcement inside the instrument panel. This might cause the airbag to not deploy properly. **1996:** Interior lamps might come on unexpectedly while vehicle is being driven. **1997:** Omitted fuse cover could result in short circuit and possible fire.

1999-01 OLDSMOBILE ALERO

FOR Acceleration (V6) • Quietness • Control layout

AGAINST Engine noise (4-cylinder) • Rear visibility (coupe) • Rear-seat entry/exit (coupe)

EVALUATION

See the 1999-01 Pontiac Grand Am.

VALUE

See the 1999-01 Pontiac Grand Am.

SPECIFICATIONS	2-door coupe	4-door sedan
Wheelbase, in.	107.0	107.0

2000 Oldsmobile Alero 2-door coupe

	2-door coupe	4-door sedan
Overall length, in.	186.7	186.7
Overall width, in.	70.1	70.1
Overall height, in.	54.5	54.5
Curb weight, lbs.	3026	3077
Cargo volume, cu. ft.	14.6	14.6
Fuel capacity, gals.	14.3	15.0
Seating capacity	5	5
Front head room, in.	38.4	38.4
Max. front leg room, in.	42.2	42.2
Rear head room, in.	37.0	37.0
Min. rear leg room, in.	35.5	35.5

Powertrain layout: transverse front-engine/front-wheel drive

ENGINES	dohc I4	ohv V6
Size, liters/cu. in.	2.4/146	3.4/207
Horsepower	150	170
Torque (lbs./ft.)	155	200
EPA city/highway mpg		
5-speed OD manual	22/31	
4-speed OD automatic	22/30	20/32
City/highway mpg (as tested)		
4-speed OD automatic		21.6

Built in USA

RETAIL PRICES	GOOD	AVERAGE	POOR
1999 Alero	$8,500-10,000	$7,700-9,000	$5,300-6,200
1999 Alero GLS	10,500-11,500	9,500-10,500	6,500-7,500
2000 Alero	9,800-11,200	8,900-10,200	6,300-7,200
2000 Alero GLS	12,000-13,500	11,000-12,500	8,000-9,000
2001 Alero	11,500-13,000	10,500-12,000	—
2001 Alero GLS	14,000-15,500	13,000-14,300	—

AVERAGE REPLACEMENT COSTS

See the 1999-01 Pontiac Grand Am.

TROUBLE SPOTS

See the 1999-01 Pontiac Grand Am.

RECALL HISTORY

1999-00: Console cover may not stay closed in a crash.

1995-99 OLDSMOBILE AURORA

1995 Oldsmobile Aurora

FOR Antilock brakes • Acceleration • Steering/handling • Passenger room

AGAINST Fuel economy • Wind noise • Rear visibility (1995)

EVALUATION Although the engine will not snap anyone's head back at takeoff, it delivers brisk acceleration and ample passing power. A test Aurora accelerated to 60 mph in a swift 8.2 seconds. The transmission shifts so smoothly, you'll seldom notice anything happening. Gas mileage is slightly better than expected: We averaged 20.3 mpg, but premium gasoline is required. Road noise is noticeable, but not excessive. However, wind noise has been prominent around the side windows on Auroras that have been tested. Ride control is commendable at high speeds. Optional V-rated tires make the ride noticeably stiffer, however. With either tires, an Aurora offers sporty handling, displaying only minimal body roll in turns and excellent grip. The Aurora's roomy interior has ample space for four adults. Controls are easy to reach and clearly labeled; analog gauges large and easy to read in a well-designed dashboard. Luggage space is ample, with a long, flat trunk floor, though the opening is too small to load bulky objects.

VALUE Carrying Oldsmobile a big step forward, Aurora is competitive with Japanese and European sedans that cost thousands more when new. We recommend that you give it a trial run if you're shopping in the luxury-sedan league.

SPECIFICATIONS

	4-door sedan
Wheelbase, in.	113.8
Overall length, in.	205.4
Overall width, in.	74.4
Overall height, in.	55.4
Curb weight, lbs.	3967
Cargo volume, cu. ft.	16.1
Fuel capacity, gals.	20.0
Seating capacity	5
Front head room, in.	38.4
Max. front leg room, in.	42.6
Rear head room, in.	36.9
Min. rear leg room, in.	38.4

Powertrain layout: transverse front-engine/front-wheel drive

ENGINES

	dohc V8
Size, liters/cu. in.	4.0/244
Horsepower	250
Torque (lbs./ft.)	260

EPA city/highway mpg

4-speed OD automatic	17/26

City/highway mpg (as tested)

4-speed OD automatic	20.3

Built in USA

RETAIL PRICES

	GOOD	AVERAGE	POOR
1995 Aurora	$6,500-7,500	$5,700-6,600	$3,000-3,500
1996 Aurora	8,000-9,200	7,100-8,200	4,000-4,600
1997 Aurora	10,000-11,200	9,000-10,200	5,200-5,800
1998 Aurora	13,000-14,200	11,800-12,700	7,500-8,000
1999 Aurora	16,000-17,500	14,500-16,000	9,800-11,000

AVERAGE REPLACEMENT COSTS

A/C Compressor	$500	Constant Velocity Joints	905
Alternator	380	Exhaust System	295
Automatic Transmission or Transaxle	1,070	Radiator	385
		Shocks and/or Struts	500
Brakes	430	Timing Chain or Belt	505

TROUBLE SPOTS

• **Vehicle noise.** A problem with the power brake booster check valve causes a noise from the dashboard. (1995-97)

• **Mirrors.** The automatic parking-assist outside mirrors may point too high. (1997)

• **Brake noise.** The brakes make noises due to a problem with the rotors for which there are replacements. (1997)

• **Electrical problem.** The door locks may quit working and the instrument panel fuse may blow due to a short circuit caused by a bolt inside either front door chafing the wiring harness. (1995)

• **Battery.** The floor pan can rust through where the battery is located due to acid venting requiring a replacement section of floor pan and battery hold-down kit. (1995-99)

• **Battery.** The floor pan rusts due to the battery venting or an overflow of acid.

(1995-99)

• **Seat.** The front seat does not heat, requiring replacement of the heating element in the seat or back cushions. (1995-99)

• **Keyless entry.** The keyless remote has a rather short range and can be corrected with a new module. (1996-97)

• **Electrical problem.** The plugs on some aftermarket devices will short out the accessory outlet or cigarette lighter blowing the fuse. (1995-99)

• **Poor transmission shift.** The transmission cooler hose gets twisted near the radiator, preventing the transmission from shifting into forward or reverse. (1997-99)

RECALL HISTORY

1995: Rear shoulder belt(s) do not retract. **1996:** Damaged capacitor may cause failure of "Key in the Ignition" and driver seatbelt-unbuckled warnings, and other functions. **1999:** Incorrect brake caliper assembly, brake pads, and caliper mounting bracket might be installed. **1999:** Brake booster to pedal assembly nuts may be loose.

1996-01 OLDSMOBILE BRAVADA

1996 Oldsmobile Bravada

FOR Antilock brakes • Acceleration • Passenger and cargo room • Ride

AGAINST Fuel economy • Rear-seat comfort

EVALUATION

See the 1995-01 Chevrolet Blazer.

VALUE

See the 1995-01 Chevrolet Blazer.

SPECIFICATIONS

	4-door wagon
Wheelbase, in.	107.0
Overall length, in.	180.9
Overall width, in.	66.5
Overall height, in.	67.0
Curb weight, lbs.	4184
Cargo volume, cu. ft.	74.2
Fuel capacity, gals.	19.0
Seating capacity	5
Front head room, in.	39.7
Max. front leg room, in.	42.4
Rear head room, in.	38.6
Min. rear leg room, in.	36.1

Powertrain layout: longitudinal front-engine/rear- or 4-wheel drive

ENGINES

	ohv V6
Size, liters/cu. in.	4.3/262
Horsepower	190
Torque (lbs./ft.)	250

EPA city/highway mpg

4-speed OD automatic	16/21

City/highway mpg (as tested)

4-speed OD automatic	18.7

Built in USA

RETAIL PRICES

	GOOD	AVERAGE	POOR
1996 Bravada	$9,000-10,000	$8,000-9,000	$4,400-5,000
1997 Bravada	10,500-12,000	9,500-11,000	5,500-6,300
1998 Bravada	12,000-13,500	10,800-12,200	6,700-7,500
1999 Bravada	14,000-15,500	12,500-14,000	8,300-9,000
2000 Bravada	16,500-18,500	15,000-17,000	10,200-11,500
2001 Bravada	19,000-21,000	17,500-19,500	—

AVERAGE REPLACEMENT COSTS

See the 1995-01 Chevrolet Blazer.

TROUBLE SPOTS

See the 1995-01 Chevrolet Blazer.

RECALL HISTORY

1996 w/AWD or 4WD: During testing, prop shaft contacted fuel tank, rupturing the tank; fuel leakage was beyond permissible level. **1996:** Solder joints can crack, causing windshield wipers to work intermittently. **1996-97:** Failure of an upper and lower control arm ball joint assembly could occur due to corrosion, resulting in impaired steering or steering loss, or a partial or complete collapse of the front suspension. **1998:** Fatigue fracture of rear-axle brake pipe can occur, causing slow fluid leak and resulting in soft brake pedal; if pipe breaks, driver would face sudden loss of rear-brake performance. **1998 w/AWD or 4WD:** On a few vehicles, one or both attaching nuts for lower control arm were not properly torqued; can result in separation from frame and loss of control.

1997-99 OLDSMOBILE CUTLASS

1998 Oldsmobile Cutlass

FOR Passenger and cargo room • Acceleration • Standard antilock brakes

AGAINST Steering feel • Engine noise

EVALUATION

See the 1997-01 Buick Century.

VALUE

See the 1997-01 Buick Century.

SPECIFICATIONS

	4-door sedan
Wheelbase, in.	107.0
Overall length, in.	192.0
Overall width, in.	69.4
Overall height, in.	56.9
Curb weight, lbs.	3102
Cargo volume, cu. ft.	17.0
Fuel capacity, gals.	15.2
Seating capacity	5
Front head room, in.	39.4
Max. front leg room, in.	42.1
Rear head room, in.	37.6
Min. rear leg room, in.	38.0

Powertrain layout: transverse front-engine/front-wheel drive

ENGINES

	ohv V6
Size, liters/cu. in.	3.1/191
Horsepower	150-160
Torque (lbs./ft.)	180-185

EPA city/highway mpg

4-speed OD automatic	20/29

City/highway mpg (as tested)

4-speed OD automatic	22.8

Built in USA

RETAIL PRICES

	GOOD	AVERAGE	POOR
1997 Cutlass	$6,500-7,500	$5,700-6,600	$3,000-3,500
1998 Cutlass	7,500-8,700	6,500-7,700	3,500-4,200
1999 Cutlass	8,500-9,700	7,500-8,700	4,200-4,800

AVERAGE REPLACEMENT COSTS

See the 1997-01 Buick Century.

TROUBLE SPOTS

See the 1997-01 Buick Century.

RECALL HISTORY

1997-98: A build-up of snow or ice restricts the movement of the passenger side windshield wiper arm, the pivot housing can crack and the wipers will not operate.

1990-96 OLDSMOBILE CUTLASS CIERA

1995 Oldsmobile Cutlass Ciera 4-door sedan

FOR Acceleration (V6 engine) • Passenger and cargo room • Quietness

AGAINST Acceleration (4-cylinder) • Ride

EVALUATION

See the 1990-96 Buick Century.

VALUE

See the 1990-96 Buick Century.

SPECIFICATIONS

	4-door sedan	4-door wagon
Wheelbase, in.	104.9	104.9
Overall length, in.	190.3	194.4
Overall width, in.	69.5	69.5
Overall height, in.	54.1	54.5
Curb weight, lbs.	2833	3086
Cargo volume, cu. ft.	15.8	74.4
Fuel capacity, gals.	16.6	16.5
Seating capacity	6	8
Front head room, in.	38.6	38.6
Max. front leg room, in.	42.1	42.1
Rear head room, in.	38.3	38.9
Min. rear leg room, in.	35.8	34.7

Powertrain layout: transverse front-engine/front-wheel drive

ENGINES

	ohv I4	ohc I4	ohv V6	ohv V6
Size, liters/cu. in.	2.2/133	2.5/151	3.1/191	3.3/204
Horsepower	120	110	160	160
Torque (lbs./ft.)	130	135	185	185

EPA city/highway mpg

	ohv I4	ohc I4	ohv V6	ohv V6
3-speed automatic	25/31	23/30		20/27
4-speed OD automatic			19/29	20/29

City/highway mpg (as tested)

	ohv I4	ohc I4	ohv V6	ohv V6
3-speed automatic		21.8		
4-speed OD automatic			20.1	

Built in USA

RETAIL PRICES

	GOOD	AVERAGE	POOR
1990 Cutlass Ciera	$1,400-2,000	$800-1,400	$100-300
1991 Cutlass Ciera	1,800-2,500	1,200-1,800	300-500
1992 Cutlass Ciera	2,200-2,900	1,600-2,200	500-700
1993 Cutlass Ciera	2,700-3,400	2,100-2,700	600-800
1994 Cutlass Ciera	3,200-4,000	2,500-3,300	800-1,000
1995 Cutlass Ciera	3,700-4,400	3,000-3,700	1,100-1,400
1996 Cutlass Ciera	4,300-5,200	3,600-4,400	1,500-2,000

AVERAGE REPLACEMENT COSTS

See the 1990-96 Buick Century.

TROUBLE SPOTS

See the 1990-96 Buick Century.

RECALL HISTORY

1990 w/Kelsey-Hayes steel wheels: Cracks may develop in wheel mounting surface; if severe, wheel could separate from car. **1990-91 w/six-way power seats or power recliner:** Short circuit could set seats on fire. **1990-96:** Rear outboard seatbelt anchorages may not withstand required load; in collision, metal may tear and allow anchor to separate from body. **1992 wagon:** Remote entry module may have a fault that causes actuation of interior lamps, door locks, and/or release of tailgate. **1993:** Right front brake hose on some cars is improperly manufactured. **1994 w/3.1-liter V6:** If primary accelerator control spring fails, backup spring will not return throttle to closed position. **1994:** Improperly tightened spindle nut can cause premature wheel bearing failure. **1994:** Water can cause short circuit in power-lock assembly.

1990-97 OLDSMOBILE CUTLASS SUPREME

1994 Oldsmobile Cutlass Supreme SL 2-door coupe

FOR Passenger and cargo room

AGAINST Rear-seat comfort • Engine noise (4-cylinder)

EVALUATION Many of the early Quad 4 engines—while eager—produced little power at low speeds. But when revved for optimum power, they became much noisier than either the 3.1-liter or 3.4-liter V6. The 24-valve V6 runs smoothly and quietly, revving quickly to higher speeds—even with the automatic. And the 3.1-liter V6 was gradually improved, with power rising from 135 horsepower in 1990 to 160 in 1994. Cutlass Supreme has a firm sports-oriented base suspension. While it provides good handling and stability, its firmness generates noticeable harshness over rough roads. The FE3 suspension in the International Series models (1990-1994) is even stiffer. Braking with standard 4-wheel disc and antilock brakes is good. Improvement in build quality means that road noise and harshness are under control, and the car offers fairly good ride comfort. Interior leg and head room are adequate, but the rear-seat cushions are too low and soft on long-distance comfort. There's also a roomy trunk and a handy cargo net on later models. The dual airbag instrument panel on 1995 models is a big improvement, putting the Supreme on par with its competition.

VALUE Despite all the changes that occurred, the final generation of the Cutlass Supreme was never quite able to catch up with the competition, even within GM. Only if the price really is right does this one deserve preference over, say, a Ford Taurus or Honda Accord.

SPECIFICATIONS

	2-door conv.	2-door coupe	4-door sedan
Wheelbase, in.	107.5	107.5	107.5
Overall length, in.	193.9	193.9	193.7
Overall width, in.	71.0	71.0	71.0
Overall height, in.	54.3	53.3	54.8
Curb weight, lbs.	3651	3307	3405
Cargo volume, cu. ft.	12.1	15.5	15.5
Fuel capacity, gals.	16.5	16.5	16.5
Seating capacity	5	6	6
Front head room, in.	38.7	37.8	38.5
Max. front leg room, in.	42.3	42.3	42.4
Rear head room, in.	38.9	37.0	38.3
Min. rear leg room, in.	34.8	35.8	36.2

Powertrain layout: transverse front-engine/front-wheel drive

ENGINES

	dohc I4	dohc I4	ohv V6	dohc V6
Size, liters/cu. in.	2.3/138	2.3/138	3.1/191	3.4/207
Horsepower	160	180	135-160	210-215
Torque (lbs./ft.)	155	160	180-185	215-220
EPA city/highway mpg				
5-speed OD manual		22/31		
3-speed automatic	22/29		19/27	
4-speed OD automatic			19/29	17/26
City/highway mpg (as tested)				
3-speed automatic	22.3			
4-speed OD automatic			20.6	

Built in USA

RETAIL PRICES

	GOOD	AVERAGE	POOR
1990 Cutlass Supreme	$1,900-2,500	$1,300-1,900	$400-600
1990 Convertible	2,800-3,500	2,100-2,800	700-1,000
1991 Cutlass Supreme	2,300-3,000	1,700-2,300	600-800
1991 Convertible	3,600-4,400	2,900-3,600	1,000-1,400
1992 Cutlass Supreme	2,700-3,700	2,100-3,000	700-1,100
1992 Convertible	4,400-5,200	3,700-4,400	1,600-2,000
1993 Cutlass Supreme	3,200-4,200	2,500-3,500	900-1,500
1993 Convertible	5,200-6,000	4,400-5,200	2,100-2,600
1994 Cutlass Supreme	3,700-4,400	3,000-3,700	1,100-1,600
1994 Convertible	6,000-7,000	5,200-6,100	2,700-3,200
1995 Cutlass Supreme	4,500-5,200	3,800-4,400	1,500-1,900
1995 Convertible	7,000-8,000	6,000-7,000	3,200-3,800
1996 Cutlass Supreme	5,400-6,100	4,600-5,300	2,100-2,500
1997 Cutlass Supreme	6,500-7,200	5,700-6,300	2,700-3,100

AVERAGE REPLACEMENT COSTS

A/C Compressor	$555	Constant Velocity Joints	470
Alternator	215	Exhaust System	470
Automatic Transmission or Transaxle	1,070	Radiator	340
		Shocks and/or Struts	1,855
Brakes	200	Timing Chain or Belt	170

TROUBLE SPOTS

• **Automatic transmission.** 4T60E transmissions may drop out of drive while cruising, shift erratically, have no third or fourth gear, or no second and third gear because of a bad ground connection for the shift solenoids. (1991-94)

• **Engine noise.** A rattling noise from the engine that lasts less than a minute when the car is started after sitting is often caused by automatic transmission pump starvation or a sticking pressure regulator valve. According to GM, no damage occurs and it does not have a fix for the problem. (1991-95)

• **Cold starting problems.** A tick or rattle when the engine is started may be due to too much wrist-pin-to-piston clearance. (1993-95)

• **Automatic transmission.** Model TH-125 or 440-T4 automatic transmissions may shift late or not upshift at all. The problem is a stuck throttle valve inside the transmission. (1990-94)

• **Valve cover leaks.** The plastic valve covers on the 3.1-liter engine were prone to leaks and should be replaced with redesigned aluminum valve covers. (1993-95)

• **Transaxle leak.** The right front axle seal at the automatic transaxle is prone to leak and GM issued a revised seal to correct the problem. (1992-94)

• **Steering noise.** The upper bearing mount in the steering column can get loose and cause a clicking, requiring a new bearing spring and turn signal cancel cam. (1994-96)

RECALL HISTORY

1990: Front shoulder belt guide loop fastener may pull through door-mounted anchor plate. **1990:** Brake lights may not illuminate. **1990:** Front shoulder belt webbing may separate at upper guide loops. **1990-91:** Steering shaft could separate. **1990-91 in 15 states:** Due to corrosion of retainers for front engine cradle bolts, where road salt usage is heavy, steering shaft could separate. **1990-91 in 14 states:** Rear cradle bolts could pull through retainers, due to corrosion; if both bolts pull through, steering shaft could separate from steering gear. **1991-92:** Front safety belts may not meet standard. **1992:** Reverse servo pin of automatic transmission may bind. **1993:** Manual recliner mechanisms on some front seats will not latch under certain conditions, causing seatback to recline without prior warning. **1993-94:** Brake lines can contact transmission bracket and wear through. **1994-95:** Wiper/washer may not operate. **1995:** Seatbelt anchor can fracture during crash. **1995:** Center rear seatbelt anchor plate could fracture in a crash. **1995-96:** Due to corrosion over time, airbag deployment could occur during vehicle start-up, while parked or idling, or while in operation. **1995-96:** The driver's airbag could deploy inadvertently and injure the driver.

1992-99 OLDSMOBILE EIGHTY EIGHT/REGENCY

1994 Oldsmobile Eighty Eight Royale

FOR Antilock brakes (optional) • Acceleration • Automatic transmission performance • Passenger and cargo room

AGAINST Steering feel • Fuel economy

EVALUATION

See the 1992-99 Buick LeSabre.

VALUE

See the 1992-99 Buick LeSabre.

SPECIFICATIONS

	4-door sedan
Wheelbase, in.	110.8
Overall length, in.	201.6
Overall width, in.	74.7
Overall height, in.	55.7
Curb weight, lbs.	3455
Cargo volume, cu. ft.	17.5
Fuel capacity, gals.	18.0
Seating capacity	6
Front head room, in.	38.7
Max. front leg room, in.	42.5
Rear head room, in.	38.3
Min. rear leg room, in.	38.7

Powertrain layout: transverse front-engine/front-wheel drive

ENGINES

	ohv V6	ohv V6	Supercharged ohv V6
Size, liters/cu. in.	3.8/231	3.8/231	3.8/231
Horsepower	170	205	225-240
Torque (lbs./ft.)	200-225	230	275-280
EPA city/highway mpg			
4-speed OD automatic	18/28	19/29	17/27
City/highway mpg (as tested)			
4-speed OD automatic	21.7	17.2	

Built in USA

RETAIL PRICES

	GOOD	AVERAGE	POOR
1992 Eighty Eight	$2,600-3,300	$2,000-2,600	$600-900
1993 Eighty Eight	3,100-3,800	2,500-3,100	800-1,100
1994 Eighty Eight	3,700-4,400	3,000-3,700	1,100-1,500
1995 Eighty Eight	4,400-5,500	3,700-4,800	1,500-2,200
1995 Regency	9,500-10,500	8,500-9,500	4,800-5,400
1996 Eighty Eight	5,500-6,500	4,800-5,700	2,300-2,800
1996 LSS	8,000-9,000	7,000-8,000	4,000-4,600
1997 Eighty Eight	7,000-8,000	6,200-7,200	3,300-3,900
1997 LSS	9,000-10,000	8,000-9,000	4,500-5,100
1998 Eighty Eight	8,500-9,500	7,600-8,500	4,200-4,700
1998 LSS	10,500-11,500	9,500-10,500	5,600-6,200
1998 Regency	11,500-12,500	10,500-11,500	6,300-7,000
1999 Eighty Eight	10,000-11,000	9,000-10,000	5,200-5,800
1999 LSS	12,500-13,500	11,500-12,500	7,300-7,900

AVERAGE REPLACEMENT COSTS

See the 1992-99 Buick LeSabre.

TROUBLE SPOTS

See the 1992-99 Buick LeSabre.

RECALL HISTORY

1992-93: Transmission cooler line in cars with certain powertrains, sold in specified states, can separate at low temperature. **1994-95:** On some cars, spring in

headlight switch can fail and lights would not remain illuminated. **1996:** Damaged capacitor may cause failure of "Key in the Ignition" warning chime and driver seatbelt unbuckled warning chime and indicator lamp; other functions also may be impaired. **1996 w/3.8-liter V6:** Backfire during engine starting can cause breakage of upper intake manifold, resulting in nonstart condition and possible fire. **1999:** Clip that secures linkage of transmission detent lever can loosen and disconnect; indicated gear would then differ from actual state of the transmission.

1998-01 OLDSMOBILE INTRIGUE

2000 Oldsmobile Intrigue

FOR Acceleration • Passenger and cargo room • Ride • Steering/handling • Standard antilock brakes

AGAINST Climate controls • Engine noise (early models)

EVALUATION Intrigue comes as close as any domestic sedan to equaling the feeling and philosophy of formidable import designs, such as the Nissan Maxima and Toyota Camry. It's inviting to drive, with little body lean and stable handling along twisty stretches. You also get plenty of "pull" from the 3.8-liter V6. An early GL accelerated to 60 mph in 7.6 seconds, averaging 21.7 mpg on regular fuel. Later models with the 3.5-liter engine turned out to be less frugal: in the 17.7 to 19.5 mpg neighborhood. The responsive automatic transmission is smooth-shifting and well-behaved. A solid structure and taut suspension provide a stable ride and comfortable handling, with very good grip and balance in turns. Little floating or wallowing can be discerned over uneven pavement. Intrigue has better steering feel than the Camry, and a more controlled ride than either the Maxima or the Camry. Still, you can get tire and suspension thump over sharp bumps and ridges. The ride remains comfortably absorbent, even with the Autobahn Package—an option on the GL that included firmer tires and larger brakes. Tires in the Autobahn Package provide better grip and crisper cornering behavior. Stopping power is strong, though some drivers might consider brake-pedal feel to be numb. Front bucket seats, which are firm and supportive, have ample fore/aft travel, giving tall folks room to stretch. Some shorter drivers might find the lower cushion a bit long. Others could consider the lumbar support to be too prominent. The rear seat is less spacious, though there's more than adequate head and leg room for most adults and the doors are wide enough for easy entry/exit. Intrigue's driving position is comfortable, commanding, and should suit most people. A tilt steering wheel has been standard, and a power driver's seat might be installed. Lexus could have designed the dashboard, which puts everything within easy sight and reach in a modern, attractive design. One exception: The automatic-temperature control panel on GL/GLS models is too low to reach easily while driving. Even more serious, it has difficulty defogging windows in some chilly, damp conditions. Cargo space is more than competitive for its class. The trunk floor is flat and wide, and there are no bulky hinges to intrude into the cargo area.

VALUE Intrigue is more sophisticated than the brash Grand Prix, and more nimble and poised than a Ford Taurus or Toyota Camry V6. If you're looking for an impressive midsize car with a thoughtful blend of features and performance, don't decide until you've driven this pleasant and surprising Olds.

SPECIFICATIONS

	4-door sedan
Wheelbase, in.	109.0
Overall length, in.	195.9
Overall width, in.	73.6
Overall height, in.	56.6
Curb weight, lbs.	3434
Cargo volume, cu. ft.	16.4
Fuel capacity, gals.	18.0
Seating capacity	5

	4-door sedan
Front head room, in.	39.3
Max. front leg room, in.	42.4
Rear head room, in.	37.4
Min. rear leg room, in.	36.2

Powertrain layout: transverse front-engine/front-wheel drive

ENGINES

	ohv V6	dohc V6
Size, liters/cu. in.	3.8/231	3.5/211
Horsepower	195	215
Torque (lbs./ft.)	220	230

EPA city/highway mpg

4-speed OD automatic	19/30	19/27

City/highway mpg (as tested)

4-speed OD automatic	21.7	19.0

Built in USA

RETAIL PRICES

	GOOD	AVERAGE	POOR
1998 Intrigue	$8,500-9,500	$7,500-8,500	$4,400-5,000
1998 Intrigue GLS	9,700-10,700	8,700-9,700	5,000-5,600
1999 Intrigue	10,000-11,000	9,000-10,000	5,200-5,800
1999 Intrigue GLS	11,500-12,500	10,500-11,500	6,300-7,000
2000 Intrigue	11,500-12,700	10,500-11,500	6,300-7,000
2000 Intrigue GLS	13,000-14,500	11,700-13,000	7,300-8,100
2001 Intrigue	13,500-15,000	12,200-13,500	—
2001 Intrigue GLS	15,500-17,000	14,000-15,500	—

AVERAGE REPLACEMENT COSTS

A/C Compressor	$460	Constant Velocity Joints	795
Alternator	220	Exhaust System	425
Automatic Transmission or Transaxle	855	Radiator	215
		Shocks and/or Struts	910
Brakes	390	Timing Chain or Belt	220

TROUBLE SPOTS

• **Brake noise.** During moderate application, the rear brakes make a moaning sound. New pads are available to correct the problem. (1998-99)

• **Alarm system.** If the key reminder continues to sound after the key is removed from the ignition and the power door locks do not work, the lock cylinder must be replaced. (1998-99)

• **Engine misfire.** The engine develops an ignition miss because the grease in the spark plug boots causes them to crack. (1998)

• **Wipers.** The windshield wipers may not park at the bottom of the windshield because water gets into the motor assembly and freezes. (1998)

RECALL HISTORY

1998-99: Some cars were built with rear-seat shoulder belts that could twist, allowing webbing to jam in retractor. **2000:** Internal fluid leaks in brake control unit of some cars may prevent rear brake proportioning, ABS, traction control, or stability control from performing as designed. **2000:** Some seatbelt assemblies were not properly heat treated and do not pass the load bearing requirement.

1991-96 OLDSMOBILE NINETY EIGHT

1991 Oldsmobile Ninety Eight

FOR Acceleration • Passenger and cargo room • Antilock brakes (optional) • Automatic transmission performance

AGAINST Fuel economy • Visibility

EVALUATION

See the 1991-96 Buick Park Avenue.

VALUE

See the 1991-96 Buick Park Avenue.

SPECIFICATIONS

	4-door sedan
Wheelbase, in.	110.8
Overall length, in.	205.7
Overall width, in.	74.6
Overall height, in.	54.8
Curb weight, lbs.	3412
Cargo volume, cu. ft.	20.2
Fuel capacity, gals.	18.0
Seating capacity	6
Front head room, in.	38.7
Max. front leg room, in.	42.5
Rear head room, in.	37.7
Min. rear leg room, in.	40.7

Powertrain layout: transverse front-engine/front-wheel drive

ENGINES

	ohv V6	ohv V6	Supercharged ohv V6	Supercharged ohv V6
Size, liters/cu. in.	3.8/231	3.8/231	3.8/231	3.8/231
Horsepower	170	205	225	240
Torque (lbs./ft.)	220	230	275	280

EPA city/highway mpg

4-speed OD automatic	18/27	19/30	17/27	18/27

City/highway mpg (as tested)

4-speed OD automatic	20.6		16.5	

Built in USA

RETAIL PRICES

	GOOD	AVERAGE	POOR
1991 Ninety Eight	$3,000-3,700	$2,400-3,000	$700-1,000
1992 Ninety Eight	3,700-4,500	3,000-3,800	1,100-1,500
1993 Ninety Eight	4,400-5,500	3,700-4,700	1,500-2,100
1994 Ninety Eight	5,200-6,000	4,400-5,200	2,000-2,500
1995 Ninety Eight	6,500-7,500	5,700-6,600	3,000-3,500
1996 Ninety Eight	8,000-9,200	7,000-8,200	3,800-4,400

AVERAGE REPLACEMENT COSTS

See the 1991-96 Buick Park Avenue.

TROUBLE SPOTS

See the 1991-96 Buick Park Avenue.

RECALL HISTORY

1991: Parking brake lever assembly may release when applied; parking brake may then not hold the vehicle. **1991:** Console-mounted shift lever may disengage, causing loss of gearshift operation. **1992-93:** Transmission cooler line in cars with certain powertrains, sold in specified states, can separate at low temperature. **1994-95:** Headlight switch spring can fail and prevent latching of headlamp in "On" position. **1995 w/Twilight Sentinel:** Current leakage can cause loss of headlights and parking lights; or, lights may turn on while car is parked. **1996:** Damaged capacitor may cause failure of "Key in the Ignition" warning chime and driver seatbelt unbuckled warning chime and indicator lamp; other functions also may be impaired. **1996 w/3.8-liter V6:** Backfire during engine starting can cause breakage of upper intake manifold, and result in non-start condition and possible fire.

1990-96 OLDSMOBILE SILHOUETTE

1991 Oldsmobile Silhouette

FOR Antilock brakes (optional) • Passenger and cargo room • Acceleration (3.8-liter V6)

AGAINST Visibility • Climate controls

EVALUATION

See the 1990-96 Chevrolet Lumina/APV.

VALUE

See the 1990-96 Chevrolet Lumina/APV.

SPECIFICATIONS

	3-door van
Wheelbase, in.	109.8
Overall length, in.	194.7
Overall width, in.	73.9
Overall height, in.	65.7
Curb weight, lbs.	3704
Cargo volume, cu. ft.	112.6
Fuel capacity, gals.	20.0
Seating capacity	7
Front head room, in.	39.2
Max. front leg room, in.	40.0
Rear head room, in.	39.0
Min. rear leg room, in.	36.1

Powertrain layout: transverse front-engine/front-wheel drive

ENGINES

	ohv V6	ohv V6	ohv V6
Size, liters/cu. in.	3.1/191	3.4/207	3.8/231
Horsepower	120	180	165-170
Torque (lbs./ft.)	175	205	200-225
EPA city/highway mpg			
3-speed automatic	19/23		17/24
4-speed OD automatic		19/26	17/25
City/highway mpg (as tested)			
4-speed OD automatic		18.5	17.2

Built in USA

RETAIL PRICES

	GOOD	AVERAGE	POOR
1990 Silhouette	$1,500-2,100	$900-1,500	$200-400
1991 Silhouette	2,000-2,700	1,400-2,000	400-600
1992 Silhouette	2,500-3,200	1,900-2,500	600-800
1993 Silhouette	3,100-3,800	2,400-3,100	800-1,000
1994 Silhouette	3,800-4,600	3,100-3,900	1,100-1,500
1995 Silhouette	4,800-5,600	4,000-4,800	1,700-2,200
1996 Silhouette	6,000-7,000	5,200-6,100	2,500-3,000

AVERAGE REPLACEMENT COSTS

See the 1990-96 Chevrolet Lumina/APV.

TROUBLE SPOTS

See the 1990-96 Chevrolet Lumina/APV.

RECALL HISTORY

1990: Rear modular seat frame hold-down hooks on some vans may not meet required pull force. **1990:** Right seat/shoulder belt retractor may have been installed in second-row left seat position. **1990-91:** Due to corrosion, shaft could separate from steering gear, resulting in crash. **1990-91 in 14 states:** Rear cradle bolts could pull through retainers, due to corrosion; if both bolts pull through, steering shaft could separate from steering gear. **1992-95:** Transmission cooler line in cars with certain powertrains, sold in specified states, can separate at low temperature. **1993-94 w/optional power sliding door:** Second-row, right-hand shoulder belt can become pinched between seat and door frame pillar trim. **1994:** Pawl spring may be missing from retractors for rear center lap belt. **1994:** Third-row seatbelt retractors may lock up when van is on a slope. **1995:** Brake pedal arm can fracture during braking, resulting in loss of brake operation.

1997-01 OLDSMOBILE SILHOUETTE

FOR Ride • Passenger and cargo room • Antilock brakes

AGAINST Fuel economy

EVALUATION

See the 1997-01 Chevrolet Venture.

VALUE

See the 1997-01 Chevrolet Venture.

SPECIFICATIONS

	3-door van	4-door van
Wheelbase, in.	112.0	120.0

1997 Oldsmoible Silhouette

	3-door van	4-door van
Overall length, in.	187.4	201.4
Overall width, in.	72.2	72.2
Overall height, in.	67.4	68.1
Curb weight, lbs.	3746	3942
Cargo volume, cu. ft.	133.0	155.9
Fuel capacity, gals.	20.0	25.0
Seating capacity	7[1]	7[1]
Front head room, in.	39.9	39.9
Max. front leg room, in.	39.9	39.9
Rear head room, in.	39.3	39.3
Min. rear leg room, in.	36.9	39.0

1. 8-passenger seating optional.

Powertrain layout: transverse front-engine/front-wheel drive

ENGINES

	ohv V6
Size, liters/cu. in.	3.4/207
Horsepower	180-185
Torque (lbs./ft.)	205-210
EPA city/highway mpg	
4-speed OD automatic	18/25
City/highway mpg (as tested)	
4-speed OD automatic	19.2

Built in USA

RETAIL PRICES

	GOOD	AVERAGE	POOR
1997 Silhouette regular	$8,000-9,000	$7,200-8,000	$4,000-4,500
1997 Silhouette extended	9,000-11,000	8,000-9,800	4,500-5,400
1998 Silhouette regular	10,000-11,000	9,000-10,000	5,300-5,900
1998 Silhouette extended	10,500-12,500	9,500-11,000	5,600-6,600
1999 Silhouette regular	12,000-13,500	11,000-12,300	6,800-7,700
1999 Silhouette extended	12,500-14,500	11,300-13,000	7,000-8,200
1999 Silhouette Premiere	15,000-17,000	13,500-15,500	9,200-10,500
2000 Silhouette extended	14,500-16,500	13,000-15,000	8,500-10,000
2000 Silhouette Premiere	18,000-20,000	16,500-18,500	11,000-12,500
2001 Silhouette extended	16,500-19,000	15,000-17,500	—
2001 Silhouette Premiere	21,000-23,000	19,500-21,500	—

AVERAGE REPLACEMENT COSTS

See the 1997-01 Chevrolet Venture.

TROUBLE SPOTS

See the 1997-01 Chevrolet Venture.

RECALL HISTORY

1997-98: Windshield wiper linkage arm can contact brake line connected to traction-control modulator valve; brake line can chafe, resulting in brake fluid leakage. **1997-98 w/bucket seats or split bench seat in second or third row:** Seat latch mechanism does not have protective covers; when activating release mechanism to roll a bucket seat forward, finger(s) could be severely injured, or severed, if they are not kept clear. **1997-2001 w/passenger-side sliding door:** Door closes but may not be latched. If this happens, the sliding door can open while the vehicle is in motion. **1998:** Broken shift cable fitting or loose shift linkage can occur; moving shift lever to "Park" position may not shift the transmission to "Park," and vehicle could roll. **1999:** Steering shaft on a few minivans could separate, as a result of collapsed sleeve. **2000 w/extended wheelbase:** Fuel tank rollover valve on small number of minivans is inoperative. **2000:** Some seatbelt assemblies were not properly heat treated and do not pass the load bearing requirement.

1990-95 PLYMOUTH ACCLAIM

1990 Plymouth Acclaim

FOR Acceleration (V6) • Antilock brakes (optional) • Passenger and cargo room

AGAINST Noise • Ride • Automatic transmission performance

EVALUATION

See the 1990-95 Dodge Spirit.

VALUE

See the 1990-95 Dodge Spirit.

SPECIFICATIONS

	4-door sedan
Wheelbase, in.	103.5
Overall length, in.	181.2
Overall width, in.	68.1
Overall height, in.	55.5
Curb weight, lbs.	2784
Cargo volume, cu. ft.	14.4
Fuel capacity, gals.	16.0
Seating capacity	6
Front head room, in.	38.4
Max. front leg room, in.	41.9
Rear head room, in.	37.9
Min. rear leg room, in.	38.3

Powertrain layout: transverse front-engine/front-wheel drive

ENGINES

	ohc I4	Turbocharged ohc I4	ohc V6
Size, liters/cu. in.	2.5/153	2.5/153	3.0/181
Horsepower	100	150	141-142
Torque (lbs./ft.)	135	180	171
EPA city/highway mpg			
5-speed OD manual	25/32	21/29	
3-speed automatic	23/27	19/23	20/27
4-speed automatic			21/29
City/highway mpg (as tested)			
5-speed OD manual	25.3		
3-speed automatic	22.9		
4-speed automatic			23.7

Built in USA

RETAIL PRICES

	GOOD	AVERAGE	POOR
1990 Acclaim	$1,000-1,500	$500-900	$100-200
1991 Acclaim	1,300-1,800	700-1,200	100-300
1992 Acclaim	1,600-2,100	1,000-1,500	200-300
1993 Acclaim	2,000-2,600	1,400-2,000	300-400
1994 Acclaim	2,400-3,100	1,800-2,400	400-600
1995 Acclaim	2,900-3,600	2,200-2,900	600-900

AVERAGE REPLACEMENT COSTS

See the 1990-95 Dodge Spirit.

TROUBLE SPOTS

•See the 1990-95 Dodge Spirit.

RECALL HISTORY

1990: Oil may leak from engine valve cover gasket. **1991:** Front outboard seatbelt may become difficult to latch; latch may open in sudden stop or accident. **1991:** Front disc brake caliper guide pin bolts may not be adequately tightened and could loosen. **1991:** Both airbag system front impact sensors may not be secured to mounting brackets, so airbag would not deploy. **1992:** Zinc plating of some upper steering column shaft coupling bolts caused hydrogen embrittlement and breakage of the bolt. **1994:** Seatbelt assembly on small number of cars may fail in accident, increasing risk of injury.

1996-00 PLYMOUTH BREEZE

1997 Plymouth Breeze

FOR Passenger and cargo room • Fuel economy

AGAINST Noise • Rear visibility • Acceleration (2.0-liter w/auto)

EVALUATION

See the 1995-00 Dodge Stratus.

VALUE

See the 1995-00 Dodge Stratus.

SPECIFICATIONS

	4-door sedan
Wheelbase, in.	108.0
Overall length, in.	186.7
Overall width, in.	71.7
Overall height, in.	51.9
Curb weight, lbs.	2929
Cargo volume, cu. ft.	15.7
Fuel capacity, gals.	16.0
Seating capacity	5
Front head room, in.	38.1
Max. front leg room, in.	42.3
Rear head room, in.	36.8
Min. rear leg room, in.	37.8

Powertrain layout: transverse front-engine/front-wheel drive

ENGINES

	ohc I4	dohc I4
Size, liters/cu. in.	2.0/122	2.4/148
Horsepower	132	150
Torque (lbs./ft.)	129	167
EPA city/highway mpg		
5-speed OD manual	26/27	
4-speed OD automatic	22/32	21/30
City/highway mpg (as tested)		
5-speed OD manual	30.2	
4-speed OD automatic	27.0	

Built in USA

RETAIL PRICES

	GOOD	AVERAGE	POOR
1996 Breeze	$4,000-4,700	$3,300-4,000	$1,200-1,600
1997 Breeze	5,000-5,800	4,200-5,000	1,900-2,400
1998 Breeze	6,200-7,000	5,400-6,200	2,700-3,200
1999 Breeze	7,500-8,300	6,700-7,400	3,500-4,000
2000 Breeze	8,800-9,800	7,800-8,800	4,300-4,800

AVERAGE REPLACEMENT COSTS

See the 1995-00 Dodge Stratus.

TROUBLE SPOTS

See the 1995-00 Dodge Stratus.

RECALL HISTORY

1996: Corrosion of ABS hydraulic control unit can cause solenoid valves to stick open; vehicle then tends to pull from a straight stop when brakes are applied. **1996-97:** Secondary hood latch spring can disengage if hood is slammed. **1996-97:** Lower ball joint can separate due to loss of lubrication; could cause loss of control. **1996-98 w/automatic:** Improperly adjusted cable could disable "ignition-park" interlock system. **1996-98 w/automatic:** If operator presses button to shift out of Park with key in locked position, pin can break; "ignition-park" interlock would then be nonfunctional. **1998-99:** Right rear brake tube can contact exhaust system clamp and wear a hole in it; tube could then leak, reducing braking effectiveness. **2000:** Incorrect child lock instruction label could cause confusion as to whether the childproof safety lock was activated. **2000:** A few cars were produced with unpainted fuel tank straps. **2000:** Inadequate weld on some vehicles could result in fatigue damage of right front brake tube. **2000:** Some of the owner's manuals for these vehicles are missing instructions for properly attaching a child restraint system's tether strap to the tether anchorage.

RECALL HISTORY

1995: Corrosion at fuel and rear-brake tubes may lead to brake fluid or fuel leakage. **1995:** Steering column coupler can become disconnected when vehicle sustains underbody impact. **1995-96 including "ACR competition" package:** Brake master cylinder can leak. **1996:** Wiring harness in Mexican-built cars could short-circuit; can cause various malfunctions, including stalling. **1997:** Airbag could deploy inadvertently when ignition is shut off. **1998:** Rear suspension crossmember on some cars may be missing spot welds; can result in structural cracks in body, and reduced rear-impact crash protection. **1999:** Front suspension lower control arms may have been inadequately welded and could separate.

1995-99 PLYMOUTH NEON

1995 Plymouth Neon 2-door coupe

FOR Optional antilock brakes • Ride • Passenger and cargo room • Fuel economy

AGAINST Noise • Automatic transmission performance

EVALUATION

See the 1995-99 Dodge Neon.

VALUE

See the 1995-99 Dodge Neon.

SPECIFICATIONS

	2-door coupe	4-door sedan
Wheelbase, in.	104.0	104.0
Overall length, in.	171.8	171.8
Overall width, in.	67.5	67.5
Overall height, in.	52.8	54.8
Curb weight, lbs.	2384	2416
Cargo volume, cu. ft.	11.8	11.8
Fuel capacity, gals.	11.2	11.2
Seating capacity	5	5
Front head room, in.	39.6	39.6
Max. front leg room, in.	42.5	42.5
Rear head room, in.	36.5	36.5
Min. rear leg room, in.	35.1	35.1

Powertrain layout: transverse front-engine/front-wheel drive

ENGINES

	ohc I4	dohc I4
Size, liters/cu. in.	2.0/122	2.0/122
Horsepower	132	150
Torque (lbs./ft.)	129	131
EPA city/highway mpg		
5-speed OD manual	28/38	28/38
3-speed automatic	25/33	25/33
City/highway mpg (as tested)		
5-speed OD manual	31.4	26.1

Built in USA, Mexico

RETAIL PRICES

	GOOD	AVERAGE	POOR
1995 Neon	$2,600-3,200	$2,000-2,600	$500-900
1996 Neon	3,200-3,900	2,500-3,200	800-1,200
1997 Neon	4,200-4,900	3,500-4,200	1,400-1,800
1998 Neon	5,200-6,000	4,500-5,200	2,000-2,500
1999 Neon	6,200-7,100	5,400-6,300	2,500-3,200

AVERAGE REPLACEMENT COSTS

See the 1995-99 Dodge Neon.

TROUBLE SPOTS

See the 1995-99 Dodge Neon.

1991-95 PLYMOUTH VOYAGER

1991 Plymouth Voyager

FOR Passenger and cargo room • Ride • Wet-weather traction (AWD) • Antilock brakes (later models)

AGAINST Acceleration (4-cylinder) • Fuel economy

EVALUATION

See the 1991-95 Dodge Caravan.

VALUE

See the 1991-95 Dodge Caravan.

SPECIFICATIONS

	3-door van	3-door van
Wheelbase, in.	112.3	119.3
Overall length, in.	178.1	192.8
Overall width, in.	72.0	72.0
Overall height, in.	66.0	66.7
Curb weight, lbs.	3305	3531
Cargo volume, cu. ft.	117.0	141.3
Fuel capacity, gals.	20.0	20.0
Seating capacity	7	7
Front head room, in.	39.1	39.1
Max. front leg room, in.	38.3	38.3
Rear head room, in.	36.6	38.5
Min. rear leg room, in.	37.6	37.7

Powertrain layout: transverse front-engine/front- or all-wheel drive

ENGINES

	ohc I4	ohc V6	ohv V6	ohv V6
Size, liters/cu. in.	2.5/153	3.0/181	3.3/201	3.8/204
Horsepower	100	142	150	162
Torque (lbs./ft.)	135	173	185	213
EPA city/highway mpg				
5-speed OD manual	20/28			
3-speed automatic	21/25	20/24		
4-speed OD automatic		19/25	18/23	17/23
City/highway mpg (as tested)				
3-speed automatic		17.0		
4-speed OD automatic			18.5	

Built in USA, Canada

RETAIL PRICES

	GOOD	AVERAGE	POOR
1991 Voyager	$1,400-2,000	$900-1,400	$200-400
1991 Voyager LE	1,700-2,300	1,100-1,600	300-500
1991 Grand Voyager	1,800-2,700	1,200-2,000	300-600
1991 Grand Voyager LE	2,400-3,000	1,800-2,300	500-800
1992 Voyager	1,700-2,400	1,100-1,700	300-600
1992 Voyager LE	2,300-3,000	1,600-2,300	500-800
1992 Grand Voyager	2,100-3,000	1,500-2,600	500-800
1992 Grand Voyager LE	2,800-3,500	2,100-2,800	800-1,200
1993 Voyager	2,000-2,800	1,400-2,100	400-800

	GOOD	AVERAGE	POOR
1993 Voyager LE	$2,800-3,500	$2,100-2,800	$800-1,100
1993 Grand Voyager	2,500-3,400	1,800-2,700	600-1,000
1993 Grand Voyager LE	3,400-4,100	2,700-3,300	1,100-1,500
1994 Voyager	2,400-3,200	1,700-2,500	500-900
1994 Voyager LE	3,300-4,000	2,600-3,300	1,000-1,400
1994 Grand Voyager	2,800-4,200	2,100-3,400	700-1,300
1994 Grand Voyager LE	4,000-5,000	3,200-4,200	1,400-1,800
1995 Voyager	3,000-4,200	2,300-3,500	800-1,400
1995 Voyager LE	4,000-4,800	3,300-4,000	1,300-1,700
1995 Grand Voyager	3,500-5,000	2,800-4,200	1,000-1,800
1995 Grand Voyager LE	4,900-6,000	4,200-5,200	1,800-2,500

AVERAGE REPLACEMENT COSTS

See the 1991-95 Dodge Caravan.

TROUBLE SPOTS

See the 1991-95 Dodge Caravan.

RECALL HISTORY

1991 w/ABS: High-pressure hose in antilock braking system may leak or detach, which increases likelihood of brake lockup. **1991 w/ABS:** High-pressure pump of antilock braking system may be porous, resulting in increased stopping distances. **1991, 93-94:** Liftgate support attaching bolts can break, resulting in liftgate falling unexpectedly. **1991-92:** Steering wheel mounting armature can develop cracks and separate from the center hub attachment to the steering column; can result in loss of vehicle control. **1991-93 w/ABS:** Piston seal in control unit can wear excessively; ABS could fail, and power assist might be reduced. **1991-93:** Seatbelt release button can stick inside cover, so buckle is only partially latched; also, center rear belt anchor clip can disconnect. **1991-93:** Due to improperly staked left windshield wiper pivot drive arm, wipers could cease to function. **1992:** Zinc plating of some upper steering column shaft coupling bolts caused hydrogen embrittlement and breakage. **1992:** Brake pedal pad attachment to pedal arm may not have adequate strength. **1992:** Fuel tank may drop, or lines may rupture near fuel tank, leading to possible fire. **1992:** Brake pedal pad attachment arm on small number of vehicles could break. **1992:** Bolts that attach gas strut to rear liftgate can accumulate fatigue damage, if loose; liftgate could fall suddenly. **1993-94:** Lug nuts on optional 15-inch stamped steel wheels may have been improperly installed, which could lead to wheel separation. **1993-95:** Wiring that initiates driver and/or passenger airbag could short immediately after turning ignition key to "on" position, causing airbag to deploy inadvertently.

1996-00 PLYMOUTH VOYAGER

1996 Plymouth Voyager Rallye

FOR Antilock brakes • Ride • Passenger and cargo room • Acceleration (3.3-, 3.8-liter)

AGAINST Fuel economy • Wind noise

EVALUATION

See the 1996-00 Dodge Caravan.

VALUE

See the 1996-00 Dodge Caravan.

SPECIFICATIONS

	3-door van	3-door van
Wheelbase, in.	113.3	119.3
Overall length, in.	186.3	199.6
Overall width, in.	75.6	75.6
Overall height, in.	68.5	68.4
Curb weight, lbs.	3528	3680
Cargo volume, cu. ft.	146.2	172.3

	3-door van	3-door van
Fuel capacity, gals.	20.0	20.0
Seating capacity	7	7
Front head room, in.	39.8	39.8
Max. front leg room, in.	41.2	41.2
Rear head room, in.	41.0	40.1
Min. rear leg room, in.	42.3	36.6

Powertrain layout: transverse front-engine/front-wheel drive

ENGINES

	dohc I4	ohc V6	ohv V6	ohv V6
Size, liters/cu. in.	2.4/148	3.0/181	3.3/201	3.8/231
Horsepower	150	150	158	180
Torque (lbs./ft.)	167	176	203	240

EPA city/highway mpg

3-speed automatic	20/25	19/24		
4-speed OD automatic	18/25		18/24	18/24

City/highway mpg (as tested)

4-speed OD automatic			16.7	

Built in USA, Canada

RETAIL PRICES

	GOOD	AVERAGE	POOR
1996 Voyager	$4,500-5,500	$3,700-4,700	$1,600-2,100
1996 Voyager SE	5,700-6,500	4,900-5,700	2,400-2,900
1996 Grand Voyager	5,600-6,400	4,800-5,600	2,300-2,800
1996 Grand SE, Expresso	6,500-7,500	5,500-6,500	2,800-3,400
1997 Voyager	5,500-6,500	4,700-5,600	2,200-2,800
1997 Voyager SE	6,800-7,500	5,900-6,500	3,000-3,400
1997 Grand Voyager	6,700-7,500	5,800-6,500	2,900-3,400
1997 Grand SE, Expresso	8,000-9,000	7,000-8,000	3,900-4,500
1998 Voyager	6,700-8,000	5,700-7,000	2,800-3,600
1998 Voyager SE, Expresso	8,800-9,800	7,800-8,800	4,400-5,000
1998 Grand Voyager	8,700-9,700	7,700-8,700	4,300-4,900
1998 Grand SE, Expresso	10,000-11,200	9,000-10,000	5,200-5,800
1999 Voyager	8,500-9,700	7,500-8,500	4,200-4,800
1999 Voyager SE, Expresso	10,500-11,500	9,500-10,500	5,500-6,100
1999 Grand Voyager	10,500-11,500	9,500-10,500	5,500-6,100
1999 Grand SE, Expresso	11,800-13,000	10,500-11,500	6,300-7,000
2000 Voyager	10,000-11,200	9,000-10,200	5,200-5,900
2000 Voyager SE	12,000-13,000	11,000-12,000	6,800-7,500
2000 Grand Voyager	12,000-13,500	10,800-12,000	6,600-7,500
2000 Grand SE	13,500-15,000	12,000-13,500	7,500-8,500

AVERAGE REPLACEMENT COSTS

See the 1996-00 Dodge Caravan.

TROUBLE SPOTS

See the 1996-00 Dodge Caravan.

RECALL HISTORY

1996 w/bench seats, from Windsor plant ("R" in 11th position of VIN): Rear-seat bolts can fracture; in accident, seat could break away. **1996:** Fuel can leak from tank at interface of fuel pump module attachment. **1996:** Tank rollover valve can allow fuel to enter vapor canister, resulting in potential leakage and fire. **1996:** Static charge could cause spark as tank is being filled; vapors could ignite. **1996:** On a few minivans, bolts holding integrated child seats can break. **1996-97 w/integrated child seats:** Shoulder harness restraint on child seat can be difficult to release when latch plate becomes contaminated. **1997:** Certain master cylinder seals will not seal adequately, allowing fluid to be drawn into power-assist reservoir. **1997:** A few wheels were damaged during mounting. **1997 w/P215/65R15 Goodyear Conquest tires on steel wheels:** Tires were damaged and may lose pressure suddenly. **1998 w/integrated child seats:** Shoulder harness webbing was incorrectly routed around reinforcement bar; can fail to restrain child properly.

1992-99 PONTIAC BONNEVILLE

FOR Acceleration • Automatic transmission performance • Passenger and cargo room

AGAINST Fuel economy • Ride (SSE, SSEi)

EVALUATION Even with the base engine, which currently delivers 205 horsepower, acceleration and passing response are brisk and sure. The supercharged version has all the feel of a burly V8, but requires the use of costlier premium unleaded. Expect real-world fuel economy of 17-

1992 Pontiac bonneville SE

18 in the city for the base engine, 25 on the highway. That drops to 15-16 city mileage for the supercharged version and 23-24 on the highway. Both engines team with an automatic that shifts promptly and smoothly. The CCR feature in the SSEi felt too loose and bouncy in Touring mode, and in Performance mode it failed to absorb bumps very well. Bonneville has the same spacious interior and trunk as its more sedate siblings at Buick and Oldsmobile. There's ample room for both passengers and cargo. The trunk is wide, has a flat floor that extends well forward, providing 18 cubic feet of storage. Inside, the seating is comfortable and the instrument panel is well-executed.

VALUE The Chrysler LH/LHS sedans are roomier and have more daring styling, but the Bonneville and its GM cousins are high-quality cars that can be tailored to suit a variety of tastes, from cushy luxury to sporty performance.

SPECIFICATIONS

	4-door sedan
Wheelbase, in.	110.8
Overall length, in.	200.6
Overall width, in.	74.5
Overall height, in.	55.7
Curb weight, lbs.	3446
Cargo volume, cu. ft.	18.0
Fuel capacity, gals.	18.0
Seating capacity	6
Front head room, in.	39.0
Max. front leg room, in.	43.0
Rear head room, in.	38.3
Min. rear leg room, in.	38.0

Powertrain layout: transverse front-engine/front-wheel drive

ENGINES

	ohv V6	ohv V6	Supercharged ohv V6
Size, liters/cu. in.	3.8/231	3.8/231	3.8/231
Horsepower	170	205	225-240
Torque (lbs./ft.)	200-225	230	275-280
EPA city/highway mpg			
4-speed OD automatic	18/28	19/29	17/27
City/highway mpg (as tested)			
4-speed OD automatic		17.0	16.5

Built in USA

RETAIL PRICES

	GOOD	AVERAGE	POOR
1992 Bonneville SE	$2,700-3,200	$2,100-2,500	$600-800
1992 SSE, SSEi	4,000-4,700	3,300-4,000	1,300-1,600
1993 Bonneville SE	3,300-4,000	2,600-3,300	800-1,100
1993 SSE, SSEi	4,500-5,200	3,800-4,400	1,600-2,100
1994 Bonneville SE	4,000-4,800	3,300-4,000	1,300-1,700
1994 SSE, SSEi	5,400-6,100	4,600-5,300	2,200-2,600
1995 Bonneville SE	4,800-5,600	4,000-4,800	1,700-2,200
1995 SSE, SSEi	6,400-7,200	5,500-6,200	2,800-3,300
1996 Bonneville SE	6,000-6,900	5,200-6,000	2,600-3,100
1996 SSE, SSEi	8,000-9,200	7,000-8,200	3,900-4,600
1997 Bonneville SE	7,500-8,500	6,500-7,500	3,300-3,900
1997 SSE, SSEi	10,000-11,500	9,000-10,300	5,200-6,000
1998 Bonneville SE	9,000-10,000	8,000-9,000	4,400-5,100
1998 SSE, SSEi	12,000-13,500	10,800-12,000	6,500-7,300
1999 Bonneville SE	11,000-12,500	10,000-11,300	5,800-6,700
1999 SSE, SSEi	14,000-16,000	12,500-14,500	8,200-9,500

AVERAGE REPLACEMENT COSTS

A/C Compressor	$460	Constant Velocity Joints	730
Alternator	190	Exhaust System	500
Automatic Transmission or		Radiator	360
Transaxle	970	Shocks and/or Struts	750
Brakes	230	Timing Chain or Belt	260

TROUBLE SPOTS

• **Oil consumption and engine knock.** 3.8-liter engines are prone to excessive oil consumption often accompanied by spark knock due to failure of the valve stem seals. (1993-95)

• **Automatic transmission.** 4T60E transmissions may drop out of drive while cruising; shift erratically; or have no second, third, or fourth gear because of a bad ground connection for the shift solenoids. (1992-94)

• **Engine noise.** A rattling noise from the engine when the car is started after sitting is often caused by automatic transmission pump starvation, or a sticking pressure regulator valve. (1992-95)

• **Engine noise.** Bearing knock was common on many 3.3- and 3.8-liter engines due to too much clearance on the number-one main bearing. (1992-94)

• **Cruise control.** If the cruise control doesn't stay engaged, or drops out of cruise, the brake switch can usually be adjusted. (1992-95)

• **Automatic transmission.** The 4T60E automatic transmission can suddenly go into neutral at highway speeds due to a problem with internal shift valves. (1995-97)

• **Transaxle leak.** The right front axle seal at the automatic transaxle is prone to leak and GM issued a revised seal to correct the problem. (1992-94)

• **Steering noise.** The upper bearing mount in the steering column can get loose and cause a clicking, requiring a new bearing spring and turn signal cancel cam. (1994-96)

RECALL HISTORY

1992: Parking brake lever may release one or more teeth when applied. **1992 w/console shift:** Control cable on some cars may disengage from bracket and falsely indicate gear position. **1992-93:** Transmission cooler line in cars with certain powertrains, sold in specified states, can separate at low temperature. **1995 w/Twilight Sentinel:** Excess current leakage can cause loss of headlights and parking lights. **1996:** Damaged capacitor may cause failure of "Key in the Ignition" warning chime and driver seatbelt unbuckled warning chime and indicator lamp; other functions may also be impaired. **1996 w/3.8-liter V6:** Backfire during engine starting can cause breakage of upper intake manifold, resulting in nonstart condition and possible fire. **1997:** Seat cover trim on a few cars does not meet flammability requirements. **1999:** Clip that secures linkage of transmission detent lever can loosen and disconnect; indicated gear would then differ from actual state of the transmission. **1999 w/chromed aluminum wheels:** Studs on some wheels could break, causing tire/wheel assembly to separate.

2000-01 PONTIAC BONNEVILLE

2001 Pontiac Bonneville SSEi

FOR Acceleration • Automatic transmission performance • Cargo room • Ride (SE)

AGAINST Fuel economy (SSEi) • Rear-seat comfort

EVALUATION Dynamically, at least, Bonneville matches the best front-drive full-size sedans. Despite a weight hike, acceleration is strong in SE and SLE sedans, with good throttle response. Performance is outstanding with the supercharged SSEi. With either engine, the transmission changes gears smoothly and downshifts come quickly for passing. An SE averaged 20.6 mpg, while the SSEi got just 15.7 mpg on premium gasoline. Engines are smooth, but wind rush and suspension/tire noises over coarse surfaces may appear. Softest-riding version is the

SE, which floats more over high-speed dips, but all are comfortable over bumps and nearly devoid of the front-end bobbing that some-times plagued previous Bonnevilles. A standard load-leveling rear suspension improves stability. Handling is impressive—balanced and composed—sharpest in the SLE and SSEi. Watch out for torque steer (pulling to one side in hard acceleration) in the SSEi. Though the SSEi's StabiliTrak can get confused during rapid sawing of the steering wheel, it should help the Bonneville stay on course in emergency maneuvers. Space is abundant for four adults, in an interior that has a more sporty flair than most full-size sedans. Still, the lost inch of rear headroom won't help taller passengers. A pro-truding center section in the rear seatback discourages 3-across seating, on a cushion that's soft and poorly shaped. Leather-covered buckets in the SSEi have 12 settings but aren't all that sup-portive. Instruments sit close to the driver, though the dashboard looks cluttered. Some plastic panels feel low-budget. Audio and climates controls are easy to reach and decipher.

VALUE Volume leader is the SE, which is a fine value. Supercharged power in the SSEi is satisfying, but at a far higher price—though Bonnevilles have not held their value especially well. Besides, a lot of cars on its level are more refined and promise more verve.

SPECIFICATIONS

	4-door sedan
Wheelbase, in.	112.2
Overall length, in.	202.6
Overall width, in.	74.2
Overall height, in.	56.6
Curb weight, lbs.	3590
Cargo volume, cu. ft.	18.0
Fuel capacity, gals.	18.5
Seating capacity	6
Front head room, in.	38.7
Max. front leg room, in.	42.6
Rear head room, in.	37.3
Min. rear leg room, in.	38.0

Powertrain layout: *transverse front-engine/front-wheel drive*

ENGINES

	ohv V6	Supercharged ohv V6
Size, liters/cu. in.	3.8/231	3.8/231
Horsepower	205	240
Torque (lbs./ft.)	230	280

EPA city/highway mpg

	ohv V6	Supercharged ohv V6
4-speed OD automatic	19/30	17/28

City/highway mpg (as tested)

	ohv V6	Supercharged ohv V6
4-speed OD automatic	20.6	15.7

Built in USA

RETAIL PRICES

	GOOD	AVERAGE	POOR
2000 Bonneville SE SLE	$14,500-17,000	$13,500-16,000	$10,000-12,000
2000 Bonneville SSEi	20,000-22,000	19,000-21,000	15,000-16,000
2001 Bonneville SE SLE	17,000-21,000	16,000-19,500	—
2001 Bonneville SSEi	23,000-25,000	21,500-23,500	—

AVERAGE REPLACEMENT COSTS

A/C Compressor	$525	Constant Velocity Joints	750
Alternator	275	Exhaust System	565
Automatic Transmission or Transaxle	895	Radiator	450
		Shocks and/or Struts	975
Brakes	485	Timing Chain or Belt	325

TROUBLE SPOTS

• **Steering noise.** A countermeasure high-pressure power steering hose will reduce vibrations, shudders or moans from the steering during slow-speed turns. (2000-01)

• **Horn.** If the horn becomes difficult to operate or sounds by itself in cold tem-peratures, the air bag module will have to be replaced. (2000)

• **Automatic transmission.** The column-mounted shift lever is hard to move out of park due to the interlock cable being too long. (2000)

• **Brake wear.** The original equipment rear brake pads cause a humming or moaning noise, especially when the brakes are hot or warm. (2000)

RECALL HISTORY

2000: Some cars have internal fluid leaks in brake hydraulic control unit;

when rear brake proportioning, antilock braking, traction control, or stability control feature is activated in some driving situations, feature may not per-form as designed.

1993-01 PONTIAC FIREBIRD

1996 Pontiac Firebird 2-door coupe

FOR Acceleration (V-8s) • Steering/handling • Antilock brakes

AGAINST Fuel economy (V-8s) • Ride • Noise • Rear-seat room • Entry/exit • Rear visibility

EVALUATION

See the 1993-01 Chevrolet Camaro.

VALUE

See the 1993-01 Chevrolet Camaro.

SPECIFICATIONS

	2-door conv.	2-door coupe
Wheelbase, in.	101.1	101.1
Overall length, in.	195.6	195.6
Overall width, in.	74.5	74.5
Overall height, in.	52.7	52.0
Curb weight, lbs.	3481	3311
Cargo volume, cu. ft.	12.9	33.7
Fuel capacity, gals.	15.5	15.5
Seating capacity	4	4
Front head room, in.	37.2	37.2
Max. front leg room, in.	43.0	43.0
Rear head room, in.	35.3	35.3
Min. rear leg room, in.	38.9	28.9

Powertrain layout: *longitudinal front-engine/rear-wheel drive*

ENGINES

	ohv V6	ohv V6	ohv V8	ohv V8
Size, liters/cu. in.	3.4/207	3.8/231	5.7/350	5.7/346
Horsepower	160	200	275-310	305-330
Torque (lbs./ft.)	200	225	325-340	335-350

EPA city/highway mpg

	ohv V6	ohv V6	ohv V8	ohv V8
5-speed OD manual	19/28	19/30		
6-speed OD manual			16/26	17/26
4-speed OD automatic	19/28	19/29	17/25	18/24

City/highway mpg (as tested)

	ohv V6	ohv V6	ohv V8	ohv V8
6-speed OD manual			16.0	15.5
4-speed OD automatic	18.8	18.8		

Built in Canada

RETAIL PRICES

	GOOD	AVERAGE	POOR
1993 Firebird	$3,600-4,300	$2,900-3,600	$1,000-1,400
1993 Formula, Trans Am	4,300-5,400	3,600-4,600	1,500-2,100
1994 Firebird coupe	4,200-4,900	3,500-4,200	1,400-1,800
1994 Formula, Trans Am	5,200-6,500	4,500-5,700	2,100-2,700
1994 Convertible	6,000-8,200	5,200-7,300	2,600-3,800
1995 Firebird coupe	5,200-5,900	4,500-5,100	2,100-2,400
1995 Formula, Trans Am	6,500-7,800	5,600-6,800	2,900-3,600
1995 Convertible	7,000-9,500	6,000-8,500	3,100-4,500
1996 Firebird coupe	6,500-7,200	5,800-6,400	3,000-3,300
1996 Formula, Trans Am	8,000-9,200	7,100-8,200	3,900-4,400
1996 Convertible	8,500-11,500	7,500-10,500	4,200-6,000
1997 Firebird coupe	8,000-8,800	7,100-7,900	3,900-4,400
1997 Formula, Trans Am	10,000-12,500	9,000-11,500	5,200-6,700
1997 Convertible	10,000-13,500	9,000-12,200	5,200-7,100
1998 Firebird coupe	9,800-10,800	8,800-9,800	5,100-5,600
1998 Formula, Trans Am	12,500-15,000	11,300-13,500	7,000-8,500
1998 Convertible	12,000-16,500	10,800-15,000	6,600-9,200

	GOOD	AVERAGE	POOR
1999 Firebird coupe	$11,800-13,000	$10,500-11,500	$6,400-7,000
1999 Formula, Trans Am	14,500-17,000	13,000-15,500	8,800-10,300
1999 Convertible	14,000-19,000	12,500-17,500	8,400-11,500
2000 Firebird coupe	13,800-15,000	12,500-13,500	8,400-8,900
2000 Formula, Trans Am	16,500-19,500	15,000-18,000	10,000-11,800
2000 Convertible	16,000-21,000	14,500-19,500	9,500-12,500
2001 Firebird coupe	15,800-17,200	14,500-15,700	—
2001 Formula, Trans Am	19,000-22,000	17,500-20,500	—
2001 Convertible	19,000-24,000	17,500-22,500	—

AVERAGE REPLACEMENT COSTS

See the 1993-01 Chevrolet Camaro.

TROUBLE SPOTS

See the 1993-01 Chevrolet Camaro.

RECALL HISTORY

1994: Misrouted V8 fuel line may contact "air" check valve; heat could damage line. **1995:** Lower coupling of steering intermediate shaft could loosen and rotate, resulting in loss of control. **1997:** Seatbelt retractors on some cars can lock-up on slopes. **1999 w/manual transmission:** Clutch master cylinder on a few cars may have incorrect retaining ring, preventing disengagement when clutch pedal is depressed.

1992-98 PONTIAC GRAND AM

1992 Pontiac Grand Am 4-door sedan

FOR Steering/handling • Acceleration (V6) • Antilock brakes (optional)

AGAINST Ride (GT) • Engine noise • Road noise • Rear-seat entry/exit

EVALUATION Acceleration with the base 115/120-horsepower Quad OHC is only adequate, and the engine becomes rough and raucous above 3000 rpm. Later 4-cylinders and V6s provide excellent acceleration and both V6s are smooth. All engines are fairly fuel efficient, but still have a ways to go before they catch the Honda Accord or Toyota Camry. The base suspension furnishes a fairly well-controlled ride, but allows lots of body lean in turns, and the base tires have only modest grip in the corners. The SE's optional handling suspension package and wider tires improve the Grand Am's road manners without adding undue ride harshness. The GT handles crisply during sudden changes in direction, but tends to jolt and thump more over bumps. The standard antilock brakes stop the Grand Am quickly and precisely. Though interior dimensions change only fractionally, the rear seat feels more spacious, partly due to new thin-line front seatbacks, more toe room under the front cushions, and a rear seatback that's not as vertical as before. Entry into the sedan is tight because doors are narrow at the bottom. With the new instrument panel, all gauges are larger and provide unobstructed views. Also, radio and climate-control systems are closer to the driver. Access to the trunk benefits from a new lid that opens at a 90-degree angle.

VALUE Grand Am has been far more successful than its cousins at Buick and Oldsmobile because Pontiac provides the right blend of image and price.

SPECIFICATIONS

	2-door coupe	4-door sedan
Wheelbase, in.	103.4	103.4
Overall length, in.	186.9	186.9
Overall width, in.	68.7	68.7
Overall height, in.	53.2	53.2
Curb weight, lbs.	2881	2954
Cargo volume, cu. ft.	13.2	13.2

	2-door coupe	4-door sedan
Fuel capacity, gals.	15.2	15.2
Seating capacity	5	5
Front head room, in.	37.8	37.8
Max. front leg room, in.	43.3	43.3
Rear head room, in.	36.5	37.0
Min. rear leg room, in.	33.9	34.9

Powertrain layout: transverse front-engine/front-wheel drive

ENGINES

	ohc I4	dohc I4	dohc I4	ohv V6	ohv V6
Size, liters/cu. in.	2.3/138	2.3/138	2.4/146	3.1/191	3.3/204
Horsepower	115-120	155-180	150	155	160
Torque (lbs./ft.)	140	150-160	160	185	185

EPA city/highway mpg

	ohc I4	dohc I4	dohc I4	ohv V6	ohv V6
5-speed OD man.	24/33	21/31	23/33		
3-speed auto.	24/31				19/29
4-speed OD auto.			22/32	21/29	

City/highway mpg (as tested)

	ohc I4	dohc I4	dohc I4	ohv V6	ohv V6
5-speed OD man.		21.7			
4-speed OD auto.			20.8	21.9	

Built in USA

RETAIL PRICES

	GOOD	AVERAGE	POOR
1992 Grand Am	$1,700-2,400	$1,100-1,700	$200-400
1992 Grand Am GT	2,200-2,800	1,500-2,100	300-600
1993 Grand Am	2,200-2,900	1,600-2,200	400-700
1993 Grand Am GT	2,800-3,500	2,100-2,800	700-1,000
1994 Grand Am	2,700-3,400	2,000-2,700	600-900
1994 Grand Am GT	3,400-4,000	2,700-3,300	800-1,100
1995 Grand Am	3,300-4,000	2,600-3,300	800-1,100
1995 Grand Am GT	4,100-4,800	3,400-4,000	1,300-1,700
1996 Grand Am	4,200-4,900	3,500-4,200	1,400-1,800
1996 Grand Am GT	5,100-6,000	4,300-5,200	1,900-2,500
1997 Grand Am	5,400-6,100	4,700-5,300	2,200-2,600
1997 Grand Am GT	6,500-7,300	5,700-6,400	2,800-3,200
1998 Grand Am	6,600-7,300	5,800-6,500	2,900-3,300
1998 Grand Am GT	7,900-8,600	7,100-7,700	3,800-4,200

AVERAGE REPLACEMENT COSTS

A/C Compressor	$540	Clutch, Pressure Plate, Bearing	555
Alternator	225	Constant Velocity Joints	565
Automatic Transmission or Transaxle	1,105	Exhaust System	380
Brakes	240	Shocks and/or Struts	540
Timing Chain or Belt	325		

TROUBLE SPOTS

• **Automatic transmission.** 4T60E transmissions may drop out of drive while cruising; shift erratically; or have no second, third, or fourth gear because of a bad ground connection for the shift solenoids. (1994)

• **Engine noise.** A rattling noise from the engine when the car is started after sitting is often caused by automatic transmission pump starvation or a sticking pressure regulator valve. (1994-95)

• **Engine noise.** A tick or rattle when the engine is started cold may be due to too much wrist-pin-to-piston clearance. (1994-95)

• **Engine noise.** Bearing knock was common on many 3.3-liter engines due to too much clearance on the number-one main bearing. (1992-93)

• **Radiator.** Some cars mysteriously lose coolant. The common problem is a bad seal on the pressure cap on the surge tank that is connected to the radiator. (1992-94)

• **Automatic transmission.** TH-125 automatic transmissions may shift late or not upshift at all. The problem is a stuck throttle valve inside the transmission. (1992-94)

• **Traction control indicator light.** The ETC warning light "ETC OFF" may glow and the cruise control stops working. If the computer failure memory is cleared, everything returns to normal. No current fix. (1996)

• **Ignition switch.** The ignition switch may not return from the start to the run position and the accessories such as the radio, wipers, cruise control, power windows, rear defroster, or heater may not work because the screws that hold the switch in place were overtightened. (1992-94)

• **Valve cover leaks.** The plastic valve covers on the 3.1-liter engine were prone to leaks and should be replaced with redesigned aluminum valve covers. (1994-95)

• **Transaxle leak.** The right front axle seal at the automatic transaxle is prone to leak. GM issued a revised seal to correct the problem. (1992-94)

RECALL HISTORY

1992: Bolts and nuts that attach bearing-hub assembly to rear axle are insufficiently tightened on some cars. **1992:** Small number of cars have incorrect upper spring seat at right rear. **1992 coupe:** Passenger-side easy-entry seat adjuster on some cars may fail to fully lock into position after seatback has been tilted and seat slid forward. **1994:** Welds in rear assembly of fuel tank may be insufficient to prevent leakage in certain rear-impact collisions, increasing risk of fire. **1996:** Steering-column lower pinch bolt was not properly tightened. This could cause loss of steering control. **1996:** Front and/or rear hazard warning lamps might not work. **1996:** Interior lamps might come on unexpectedly while vehicle is being driven. **1997:** Omitted fuse cover could result in short circuit and possible fire.

1999-01 PONTIAC GRAND AM

1999 Pontiac Grand Am GT 2-door coupe

FOR Acceleration (V6)

AGAINST Engine noise (4-cylinder) • Rear-seat entry/exit (coupe)

EVALUATION A Grand Am looks faster than it is in reality, though it's not really underpowered. The 4-cylinder engine provides enough zip for most driving, though it generates some idle shake and groans loudly under hard throttle. The V6 is quieter and smoother, swifter in around-town driving, and gets good mileage. Test V6 Grand Ams, when new, averaged 19.4 to 21.5 mpg. The well-behaved automatic transmission downshifts quickly and rarely "hunts" between gears. Manual shift adds a sporty tone, despite its somewhat notchy action. With either engine, the droning note of the sporty exhaust grows tiresome. Road and wind noise are reasonable, but tires roar intrusively and thump loudly over tar strips. Expect a choppy ride over sharp ridges and broken pavement, but the Grand Am is generally stable and resists wallowing. On smoother surfaces, the ride is firm but not harsh. Handling isn't Eurosedan-precise, of course, but turn-in is reasonably quick, with firm steering as well as good grip and balance in corners. Stopping power is adequate, with good pedal feel. Excess is the word for interior styling, with deeply recessed gauges and an overall cluttered look. Most controls are close at hand, though audio switches are small and poorly marked. Front leg room is generous and head room good, even with an optional sunroof. The supportive, comfortable driver's seat adjusts to most body types. Backseat space beats the compact average, but the coupe's rear seat is narrower, with less head room. Rear visibility is hampered by the rear spoiler (if installed). Although the trunk is spacious, its opening is small with an unusually high liftover that makes loading a chore.

VALUE "Expressive" styling and a sporty nature draw a lot of customers to Grand Ams, but the compact isn't as far ahead in basic engineering and construction. Though less refined than some rivals, it's competent in most respects and exhibits enjoyable road manners.

SPECIFICATIONS

	2-door coupe	4-door sedan
Wheelbase, in.	107.0	107.0
Overall length, in.	186.3	186.3
Overall width, in.	70.4	70.4
Overall height, in.	55.1	55.1
Curb weight, lbs.	3066	3116
Cargo volume, cu. ft.	14.6	14.6
Fuel capacity, gals.	14.3	14.3

	2-door coupe	4-door sedan
Seating capacity	5	5
Front head room, in.	38.3	38.3
Max. front leg room, in.	42.1	42.1
Rear head room, in.	37.2	37.6
Min. rear leg room, in.	35.5	35.5

Powertrain layout: transverse front-engine/front-wheel drive

ENGINES

	dohc I4	ohv V6	ohv V6
Size, liters/cu. in.	2.4/146	3.4/207	3.4/207
Horsepower	150	170	175
Torque (lbs./ft.)	155	195	205

EPA city/highway mpg

5-speed OD manual	22/31		
4-speed OD automatic	22/30	20/32	20/32

City/highway mpg (as tested)

4-speed OD automatic		19.4	

Built in USA

RETAIL PRICES

	GOOD	AVERAGE	POOR
1999 Grand Am	$8,800-9,800	$8,000-9,000	$5,700-6,400
1999 Grand Am GT	10,500-11,500	9,500-10,500	6,800-7,600
2000 Grand Am	10,200-11,500	9,200-10,500	6,600-7,600
2000 Grand Am GT	12,200-13,500	11,200-12,500	8,000-9,000
2001 Grand Am	12,000-13,500	11,000-12,500	—
2001 Grand Am GT	14,000-15,500	13,000-14,500	—

AVERAGE REPLACEMENT COSTS

A/C Compressor	$500	Constant Velocity Joints	905
Alternator	380	Exhaust System	455
Automatic Transmission or Transaxle	1,090	Radiator	450
		Shocks and/or Struts	535
Brakes	470	Timing Chain or Belt	505

TROUBLE SPOTS

• **Brakes.** Pulsation felt in the steering wheel and brake pedal is caused by faulty brake pads and discs. Revised parts are available. (1999-2000)

• **Paint/body.** The rear spoiler gets distorted in the hot sun. Also, water gets inside requiring drain holes to be drilled. (1999)

• **Water leak.** Water leaks under the door and onto the floor due to a bad door gasket. A countermeasure gasket is being installed under warranty. (1999-2000)

RECALL HISTORY

1999-00 : Console cover may not stay closed in a crash.

1990-96 PONTIAC GRAND PRIX

1993 Pontiac Grand Prix LE 4-door sedan

FOR Handling • Antilock brakes (optional)

AGAINST Ride (optional suspensions, tires) • Engine noise • Road noise • Rear-seat comfort

EVALUATION It's best to avoid models with the noisy 4-cylinder engine. However, the 3.1-liter V6 provides ample acceleration with much less noise and vibration. Turbo engines provide outstanding acceleration, but suffer from "turbo lag" and poor fuel economy. The best engine choice is the dohc 3.4-liter V6, which provides the acceleration of the turbo engine without the lag and ruckus. Inside, the cabin of the 1990-1993 Grand Prix with its backlit red gauge cluster works hard to emulate the continental flair of the BMW. However, Pontiac is not quite able to capture the European maturity or purposefulness. Revisions to the cabin in 1994 bring long overdue improvements. The new controls are both simpler to use and easier to reach. Large, soft-touch rotary dials replace the climate system's fussy, undersized switches and sliders. Select either the coupe or sedan and you should find the cabin capable of transporting four adults in relative pleasure—but the back seat is too low and uncomfortable. Pontiac's suspension tuning gives the Grand Prix somewhat more composed road manners than the Lumina, Regal, and Cutlass Supreme, especially over bumps and dips. Cornering ability is especially impressive on cars equipped with the Y99 rally suspension package, but drivers must endure a harsher ride.

VALUE We rate the Ford Taurus, Mercury Sable, and Honda Accord higher overall. But with the gradual improvements bestowed on the Grand Prix, it is a good choice as well.

SPECIFICATIONS

	2-door coupe	4-door sedan
Wheelbase, in.	107.5	107.5
Overall length, in.	194.8	194.9
Overall width, in.	71.9	71.9
Overall height, in.	52.8	52.8
Curb weight, lbs.	3243	3318
Cargo volume, cu. ft.	14.9	15.5
Fuel capacity, gals.	16.5	16.5
Seating capacity	6	6
Front head room, in.	37.8	38.6
Max. front leg room, in.	42.3	42.4
Rear head room, in.	36.6	37.7
Min. rear leg room, in.	34.8	36.2

Powertrain layout: transverse front-engine/front-wheel drive

ENGINES

	dohc I4	ohv V6	Turbocharged ohv V6	dohc V6
Size, liters/cu. in.	2.3/138	3.1/191	3.1/191	3.4/207
Horsepower	160	140-160	205	210-215
Torque (lbs./ft.)	155	180-185	220	200-215

EPA city/highway mpg

5-speed OD manual		19/28		17/27
3-speed automatic	21/29	19/27		
4-speed OD automatic		19/30	16/25	17/26

City/highway mpg (as tested)

4-speed OD automatic		20.1		18.7

Built in USA

RETAIL PRICES

	GOOD	AVERAGE	POOR
1990 Grand Prix	$1,500-2,100	$900-1,500	$100-300
1990 STE	2,100-2,700	1,500-2,000	400-700
1991 Grand Prix	1,800-2,500	1,200-1,900	300-700
1991 GT, STE	2,500-3,200	1,800-2,500	600-1,000
1992 Grand Prix	2,200-3,000	1,600-2,300	500-900
1992 GT, STE	3,000-3,800	2,300-3,000	800-1,200
1993 Grand Prix	2,700-3,500	2,000-2,800	600-1,100
1993 GT, STE	3,500-4,300	2,800-3,500	1,000-1,400
1994 Grand Prix	3,200-4,000	2,500-3,200	800-1,300
1995 Grand Prix	3,900-4,600	3,200-3,800	1,100-1,500
1996 Grand Prix	5,000-6,000	4,200-5,100	1,600-2,100

AVERAGE REPLACEMENT COSTS

A/C Compressor	$555	Clutch, Pressure Plate,	
Alternator	215	Bearing	385
Automatic Transmission or		Constant Velocity Joints	470
Transaxle	1,070	Exhaust System	470
Brakes	200	Radiator	340
Shocks and/or Struts	1,855	Timing Chain or Belt	170

TROUBLE SPOTS

• **Automatic transmission.** 4T60E transmissions may drop out of drive while cruising; shift erratically; or have no second, third, or fourth gear because of a bad ground connection for the shift solenoids. (1991-94)

• **Engine noise.** A rattling noise from the engine when the car is started after sitting is often caused by automatic transmission pump starvation or a sticking pressure regulator valve. (1991-95)

• **Engine noise.** A tick or rattle when the engine is started cold may be due to too much wrist-pin-to-piston clearance. (1994-95)

• **Automatic transmission.** TH-125 or 440-T4 automatic transmissions may

shift late or not upshift at all. The problem is a stuck throttle valve inside the transmission. (1990-94)

• **Valve cover leaks.** The plastic valve covers on the 3.1-liter engine were prone to leaks and should be replaced with redesigned aluminum valve covers. (1994-95)

• **Transaxle leak.** The right front axle seal at the automatic transaxle is prone to leak. GM issued a revised seal to correct the problem. (1992-94)

• **Steering noise.** The upper bearing mount in the steering column can get loose and cause a clicking, requiring a new bearing spring and turn signal cancel cam. (1994-96)

RECALL HISTORY

1990: Stoplamps may not illuminate. **1990 w/Kelsey-Hayes steel wheels:** Cracks may develop in wheel mounting surface. **1990-91:** Steering shaft could separate from steering gear. **1990-91 in 15 states:** Due to corrosion of front engine cradle bolts, where road salt usage is heavy, steering shaft could separate from steering gear. **1990-91 in 14 states:** Rear cradle bolts could pull through retainers, due to corrosion; if both bolts pull through, steering shaft could separate from steering gear. **1991:** Front door shoulder belt guide loops may be cracked. **1991 coupe:** Fog lamps, low-beam headlamps, and high-beam headlamp can be operated simultaneously on some cars, causing circuit breaker to overload and trip. **1992:** Reverse servo pin of 4-speed automatic transmission may bind. **1993:** Manual recliner mechanisms on some front seats will not latch under certain conditions, causing seatback to recline without prior warning. **1994-95:** Wiper/washer may operate intermittently, or not at all. **1995:** Seatbelt anchor can fracture in crash. **1995:** Center rear seatbelt anchor plate could fracture in a crash.

1997-01 PONTIAC GRAND PRIX

1997 Pontiac Grand Prix GTP

FOR Acceleration • Steering/handling • Passenger room • Cargo room

AGAINST Fuel economy (supercharged engine)

EVALUATION Acceleration from a standing start is adequate with the 3.1-liter V6, strong with the 3.8-liter, and almost ferocious with the supercharged engine—with no loss of refinement. The transmission changes gears with world-class smoothness, and downshifts quickly for passing. Our test 3.8-liter SE averaged 22.7 mpg in mostly highway driving—including a high of 27 on the highway and a low of 15 mpg in urban commuting. The GTP returned only 17-18 mpg—on the required premium gasoline—so its supercharged performance does not come cheap. Road noise is prominent on all models at highway speeds. Wind and engine noise are low, but tire thrum frequently intrudes. Braking is strong, but pedal modulation mediocre. Grand Prix feels agile and surefooted on winding roads. Steering is more precise than before. The SE and GT have a stable, comfortable ride with little bouncing over wavy surfaces. Their firm suspension absorbs most bumps well and provides capable handling with little body lean. The GTP's tauter suspension gives slightly sharper handling and it reacts more abruptly to potholes, yielding more tire thump, but the ride still does not rate as harsh. Head room is plentiful all around. There's ample room for four adults, and a fifth can squeeze into the rear seat. With front seats pushed all the way back, leg room is still adequate out back. The rear bench is low to the floor and provides little support. Doors open wide to allow easy entry/exit, though the rakish roofline provides a slight impediment. Overall, the dashboard looks busy and cluttered. Gauges and controls are well illuminated by Pontiac's traditional red lighting, and most switchgear is clearly labeled, easy to find and use. Uplevel stereos have small buttons that are haphazardly arranged, making it hard to pick out any particular one in a hurry. Visibility is good to the front and sides, but the high parcel shelf blocks the driver's view of the trunk when backing up. You get ample luggage space in a fairly deep trunk.

VALUE Pontiac's reworked midsize was a big hit from the start. Sales of the '97 model ran more than 50 percent of 1996 levels, though naturally its popularity tapered off later. Brashly styled with a confident stance, Grand Prix is a highly capable, sporty midsize car that challenges the class leaders in overall value.

SPECIFICATIONS

	2-door coupe	4-door sedan
Wheelbase, in.	110.5	110.5
Overall length, in.	196.5	196.5
Overall width, in.	72.7	72.7
Overall height, in.	54.7	54.7
Curb weight, lbs.	3396	3414
Cargo volume, cu. ft.	16.0	16.0
Fuel capacity, gals.	18.0	18.0
Seating capacity	5	6
Front head room, in.	38.3	38.3
Max. front leg room, in.	42.4	42.4
Rear head room, in.	36.5	36.7
Min. rear leg room, in.	36.1	35.8

Powertrain layout: transverse front-engine/front-wheel drive

ENGINES

	ohv V6	ohv V6	Supercharged ohv V6
Size, liters/cu. in.	3.1/191	3.8/231	3.8/231
Horsepower	160-175	195-200	240
Torque (lbs./ft.)	185-195	220-225	280
EPA city/highway mpg			
4-speed OD automatic	20/29	19/30	18/27
City/highway mpg (as tested)			
4-speed OD automatic		17.1	18.8

Built in USA

RETAIL PRICES

	GOOD	AVERAGE	POOR
1997 Grand Prix	$7,500-9,000	$6,600-8,000	$3,500-4,300
1998 Grand Prix	9,000-11,000	8,000-10,000	4,400-5,600
1999 Grand Prix SE	10,500-11,500	9,500-10,500	5,500-6,200
1999 Grand Prix GT, GTP	11,800-13,500	10,500-12,000	6,400-7,300
2000 Grand Prix SE	12,000-13,000	11,000-12,000	6,800-7,500
2000 Grand Prix GT, GTP	13,200-15,200	11,900-13,700	7,500-8,500
2001 Grand Prix SE	13,700-15,200	13,000-14,200	—
2001 Grand Prix GT, GTP	15,000-17,000	13,500-15,500	—

AVERAGE REPLACEMENT COSTS

A/C Compressor	$460	Constant Velocity Joints	795
Alternator	220	Exhaust System	425
Automatic Transmission or Transaxle	855	Radiator	215
		Shocks and/or Struts	910
Brakes	390	Timing Chain or Belt	220

TROUBLE SPOTS

• **Brake noise.** During moderate application, the rear brakes make a moaning sound. New pads are available to correct the problem. (1998-99)

• **Cruise control.** If the cruise control cancels when the wipers are running, the cruise control module and ground wires must be replaced. (1997-98)

• **Tail/brake lights.** If water leaks into the left tail light housing, it must be replaced with a counter-measure housing. (1997)

• **Door handles.** On white cars, the door handles turn yellow from the lock cylinder grease. The company will replace the cylinders under warranty and there is a colorless grease available. (1997-99)

• **Engine misfire.** The 3800 engine develops an ignition miss because the grease in the spark plug boots causes them to crack. (1997-98)

• **Doors.** The power door locks fail due to a rubber part breaking on the actuator arm inside the door. (1997)

• **Poor transmission shift.** The transmission may not shift out of third gear because the wires from the torque converter switch rub and short out on the air cleaner housing. (1998)

• **Wipers.** The windshield wipers may not park at the bottom of the windshield because water gets into the motor assembly and freezes. (1997-98)

RECALL HISTORY

1997: Windshield wipers may stop working, due to separation between drive pin and crescent in crank arm assembly. **1997-99:** When the hazard flasher switch is used to turn the hazard flashers on or off, the retained accessory power feature can be activated without a key in the ignition. **1999:** Driver's

airbag inflator modules could produce excessive internal pressure. In the event of a crash, the increased internal pressure can cause the inflator module to explode. **2000:** Front passenger airbag modules in a few cars have undersized inflator orifice; in a crash, this can cause inflator module to explode. **2000:** Some seatbelt assemblies were not properly heat treated and do not pass the load bearing requirement. **2001:** Passenger airbag inflator modules may have been built without the correct amount of explosive. Airbag explosion or failure could occur.

1995-01 PONTIAC SUNFIRE

1996 Pontiac Sunfire SE 2-door coupe

FOR Antilock brakes • Instruments/controls • Fuel economy

AGAINST Rear-seat comfort • Noise • Rear visibility

EVALUATION

See the 1995-01 Chevrolet Cavalier.

VALUE

See the 1995-01 Chevrolet Cavalier.

SPECIFICATIONS

	2-door conv.	2-door coupe	4-door sedan
Wheelbase, in.	104.1	104.1	104.1
Overall length, in.	182.4	181.9	181.7
Overall width, in.	68.4	67.4	67.3
Overall height, in.	51.9	53.2	54.8
Curb weight, lbs.	2835	2679	2723
Cargo volume, cu. ft.	9.9	12.4	13.1
Fuel capacity, gals.	15.2	15.2	15.2
Seating capacity	4	5	5
Front head room, in.	38.8	37.6	38.9
Max. front leg room, in.	42.4	42.4	42.4
Rear head room, in.	38.5	36.6	37.2
Min. rear leg room, in.	32.7	32.0	34.4

Powertrain layout: transverse front-engine/front-wheel drive

ENGINES

	ohc I4	dohc I4	dohc I4	ohv I4
Size, liters/cu. in.	2.2/133	2.3/138	2.4/146	2.2/133
Horsepower	120	150	150	115
Torque (lbs./ft.)	130	145	150	135
EPA city/highway mpg				
5-speed OD manual	25/37	22/32	22/33	22/32
3-speed automatic	24/31			23/29
4-speed OD automatic	25/34	21/31	22/32	
City/highway mpg (as tested)				
5-speed OD manual	25.2			
3-speed automatic	22.9			
4-speed OD automatic			21.0	

Built in USA

RETAIL PRICES

	GOOD	AVERAGE	POOR
1995 Sunfire	$3,300-4,000	$2,600-3,300	$800-1,200
1995 Sunfire GT	4,000-4,700	3,300-4,000	1,200-1,600
1995 Convertible	4,200-5,000	3,500-4,200	1,300-1,700
1996 Sunfire	4,000-4,700	3,300-4,000	1,200-1,600
1996 Sunfire GT	4,800-5,500	4,100-4,700	1,800-2,200
1996 Convertible	5,100-6,000	4,300-5,200	1,900-2,500
1997 Sunfire	5,000-5,800	4,300-5,000	1,900-2,300
1997 Sunfire GT	5,900-6,600	5,200-5,800	2,600-3,000
1997 Convertible	6,500-7,500	5,600-6,500	2,900-3,500
1998 Sunfire	6,000-6,700	5,200-5,900	2,600-3,000
1998 Sunfire GT	7,200-8,000	6,400-7,200	3,300-3,800
1998 Convertible	7,800-9,000	6,900-8,000	3,600-4,200

	GOOD	AVERAGE	POOR
1999 Sunfire	$7,000-7,800	$6,100-6,800	$3,200-3,600
1999 Sunfire GT	8,300-9,000	7,500-8,000	4,100-4,600
1999 Convertible	9,800-11,000	8,800-10,000	5,000-5,800
2000 Sunfire	8,200-9,000	7,300-8,000	4,000-4,500
2000 Sunfire GT	9,600-10,500	8,700-9,500	4,900-5,400
2000 Convertible	11,500-13,000	10,500-11,800	6,400-7,000
2001 Sunfire	10,000-11,000	9,000-10,000	—
2001 Sunfire GT	11,500-12,500	10,300-11,000	—

AVERAGE REPLACEMENT COSTS

See the 1995-01 Chevrolet Cavalier.

TROUBLE SPOTS

See the 1995-01 Chevrolet Cavalier.

RECALL HISTORY

1995: Welds were omitted from lower control arms; excessive loads can result in separation. **1995:** Automatic-transmission indicator may not reflect correct gear position. **1995-96:** Front or rear hazard warning lamps (four-way flashers), or both, do not flash when switch is activated. **1996:** Kinked accelerator cable in a few cars can result in unwanted acceleration. **1996:** Interior lamps might come on unexpectedly while vehicle is being driven. **1996-97:** Airbag could deploy inadvertently in a low-speed crash, or when an object strikes the floor pan. **1996-97:** Rear suspension trailing arm bolts can fatigue and break. **1997:** Spare tire on a few cars may have incorrect rim. **1998:** Wheel lug nuts on a few cars were not tightened securely, resulting in fracture of studs.

1990-96 PONTIAC TRANS SPORT

1996 Pontiac Trans Sport

FOR Acceleration (3.8-liter V6) • Passenger and cargo room

AGAINST Acceleration (3.1-liter V6) • Visibility

EVALUATION

See the 1990-96 Chevrolet Lumina/APV.

VALUE

See the 1990-96 Chevrolet Lumina/APV.

SPECIFICATIONS

	3-door van
Wheelbase, in.	109.8
Overall length, in.	194.5
Overall width, in.	74.6
Overall height, in.	65.7
Curb weight, lbs.	3598
Cargo volume, cu. ft.	112.6
Fuel capacity, gals.	20.0
Seating capacity	7
Front head room, in.	39.2
Max. front leg room, in.	40.1
Rear head room, in.	38.7
Min. rear leg room, in.	36.9

Powertrain layout: transverse front-engine/front-wheel drive

ENGINES

	ohv V6	ohv V6	ohv V6
Size, liters/cu. in.	3.1/191	3.4/207	3.8/231
Horsepower	120	180	165-170
Torque (lbs./ft.)	175	205	220-225
EPA city/highway mpg			
3-speed automatic	19/23		17/24
4-speed OD automatic		19/26	17/25

City/highway mpg (as tested)	ohv V6	ohv V6	ohv V6
4-speed OD automatic		17.1	17.2

Built in USA

RETAIL PRICES	GOOD	AVERAGE	POOR
1990 Trans Sport	$1,400-2,100	$800-1,500	$100-300
1991 Trans Sport	1,700-2,500	1,100-1,800	300-600
1992 Trans Sport	2,200-3,000	1,600-2,300	500-800
1993 Trans Sport	2,700-3,500	2,000-2,800	600-900
1994 Trans Sport	3,400-4,200	2,700-3,400	800-1,100
1995 Trans Sport	4,400-5,200	3,600-4,400	1,400-1,800
1996 Trans Sport	5,600-6,800	4,800-6,000	2,200-2,900

AVERAGE REPLACEMENT COSTS

See the 1990-96 Chevrolet Lumina/APV.

TROUBLE SPOTS

See the 1990-96 Chevrolet Lumina/APV.

RECALL HISTORY

1990: Rear modular seat frame hold-down hooks may not meet the required pull force. **1990:** Right seat/shoulder belt retractor may have been installed in second-row left seat position. **1990-91:** Steering shaft could separate from steering gear. **1990-91 in 14 states:** Rear cradle bolts could pull through retainers, due to corrosion; if both bolts pull through, steering shaft could separate from steering gear. **1992-95:** Transmission cooler line in cars with certain powertrains, sold in specified states, can separate at low temperature. **1993-94 w/optional power sliding door:** Shoulder belt can become pinched between seat and door frame pillar trim. **1994:** Pawl spring may be missing from retractors for rear center lap belts. **1994:** Third-row seatbelt retractors may lock up when van is on a slope. **1995:** On some cars, brake pedal arm can fracture during braking. **1995 w/3.1-liter engine:** Throttle cable support brackets could contact throttle-lever system and inhibit throttle return; engine speed would then decrease more slowly than anticipated.

1997-01 PONTIAC TRANS SPORT/MONTANA

1998 Pontiac Trans Sport Montana

FOR Ride • Passenger and cargo room • Antilock brakes

AGAINST Fuel economy • Rear-seat comfort

EVALUATION

See the 1997-01 Chevrolet Venture.

VALUE

See the 1997-01 Chevrolet Venture.

SPECIFICATIONS

	3-door van	4-door van
Wheelbase, in.	112.0	120.0
Overall length, in.	187.3	201.3
Overall width, in.	72.7	72.7
Overall height, in.	67.4	68.1
Curb weight, lbs.	3730	3942
Cargo volume, cu. ft.	126.6	155.9
Fuel capacity, gals.	20.0	25.0
Seating capacity	7[1]	7[1]
Front head room, in.	39.9	39.9
Max. front leg room, in.	39.9	39.9
Rear head room, in.	39.3	39.3
Min. rear leg room, in.	36.9	39.0

1. 8-passenger seating optional.

Powertrain layout: transverse front-engine/front-wheel drive

ENGINES

	ohv V6
Size, liters/cu. in.	3.4/207
Horsepower	180-185
Torque (lbs./ft.)	205-210

EPA city/highway mpg

4-speed OD automatic	18/25

City/highway mpg (as tested)

4-speed OD automatic	18.7

Built in USA

RETAIL PRICES

	GOOD	AVERAGE	POOR
1997 Trans Sport regular	$8,000-9,000	$7,200-8,100	$4,000-4,600
1997 Trans Sport extended	9,000-10,500	8,000-9,500	4,500-5,400
1998 Trans Sport regular	9,500-11,000	8,500-10,000	4,800-5,800
1998 Trans Sport extended	11,300-12,500	10,300-11,500	6,100-6,900
1999 Montana regular	11,000-12,500	10,000-11,300	5,900-6,700
1999 Montana extended	12,700-14,200	11,500-13,000	7,200-8,100
2000 Montana regular	13,000-14,500	11,800-13,200	7,400-8,200
2000 Montana extended	15,000-17,000	13,500-15,500	9,000-10,200
2001 Montana regular	15,500-17,500	14,000-16,000	—
2001 Montana extended	17,500-20,000	16,000-18,500	—

AVERAGE REPLACEMENT COSTS

See the 1997-01 Chevrolet Venture.

TROUBLE SPOTS

See the 1997-01 Chevrolet Venture.

RECALL HISTORY

1997-98: Windshield wiper linkage arm can contact brake line connected to traction-control modulator valve; brake line can chafe, resulting in brake fluid leakage. **1997-2001 w/passenger-side sliding door:** Door closes but may not be latched. If this happens, the sliding door can open while the vehicle is in motion. **1998:** Broken shift cable fitting or loose shift linkage can occur; moving shift lever to "Park" position may not shift the transmission to "Park," and vehicle could roll. **2000:** Some seatbelt assemblies were not properly heat treated and do not pass the load bearing requirement. **2001 Montana:** Passenger airbag inflator modules may have been built without the correct amount of explosive. Airbag explosion or failure could occur.

1994-98 SAAB 900

1996 Saab 900 SE Turbo 2-door convertible

FOR Acceleration (V6, turbo) • Steering/handling • Passenger and cargo room

AGAINST Ride • Wind noise • Road noise

EVALUATION This new Saab retained its upright stance and stuck to its hatchback design. As a result, it preserved such virtues as generous head and leg room, plus enormous cargo space from what is basically a very compact car. However, mainstream buyers may find the key position is too disorienting and the cabin too narrow. The dashboard is little changed, so most controls are close at hand. But the power-window buttons are mounted between the seats rather than on the door panels where they'd be more convenient to operate. The V6 feels strong and smooth, and works particularly well with the new 4-speed automatic. It shifts quickly and consistently with no hesitation. It downshifts smoothly, eagerly providing all the passing power you need. The 900's 2.3-liter 4-cylinder has adequate power with the manual, but feels underpowered when paired with the automatic. Body lean is evident when taking turns at speed, but these cars have a generally sporty feel, with precise steering and excellent grip. The taut suspension provides excellent control,

but combines with the modest wheelbase for a ride that's choppy enough over rough pavement to deter some buyers. Wind and road noise are disconcerting at highway speeds.

VALUE Mainstream shoppers interested in a near-luxury car still aren't likely to put the Saab 900 on their must-see list, but we credit Saab with making a better 900 for those who love and appreciate its quirky nature.

SPECIFICATIONS

	2-door conv.	2-door hatchback	4-door sedan
Wheelbase, in.	102.4	102.4	102.4
Overall length, in.	182.6	182.6	182.5
Overall width, in.	67.4	67.4	67.4
Overall height, in.	56.5	56.5	56.5
Curb weight, lbs.	3130	2940	2980
Cargo volume, cu. ft.	28.3	49.8	49.8
Fuel capacity, gals.	18.0	18.0	18.0
Seating capacity	4	5	5
Front head room, in.	39.3	39.3	39.3
Max. front leg room, in.	43.3	42.3	43.3
Rear head room, in.	37.9	37.8	37.8
Min. rear leg room, in.	36.0	36.2	36.2

Powertrain layout: transverse front-engine/front-wheel drive

ENGINES

	dohc I4	dohc I4	Turbocharged dohc I4	dohc V6
Size, liters/cu. in.	2.1/129	2.3/140	2.0/129	2.5/152
Horsepower	140	150	160-185	170
Torque (lbs./ft.)	133	155	188-194	167

EPA city/highway mpg

5-speed OD manual	20/26	20/29	21/28	18/25
3-speed automatic	18/21		19/23	
4-speed OD automatic		20/28		19/27

City/highway mpg (as tested)

5-speed OD manual		24.4		19.3

Built in Sweden

RETAIL PRICES

	GOOD	AVERAGE	POOR
1994 900	$4,200-6,000	$3,500-5,200	$1,400-2,400
1994 900 Turbo	5,800-6,800	5,000-6,000	2,500-3,100
1994 900 Convertible	5,500-7,500	4,600-6,500	2,200-3,400
1995 900	5,500-7,200	4,700-6,300	2,300-3,200
1995 900 Turbo	7,200-8,200	6,300-7,200	3,300-3,800
1995 900 Convertible	7,000-9,000	6,000-8,000	3,100-4,200
1996 900	7,000-9,000	6,100-8,000	3,200-4,200
1996 900 Turbo	8,500-10,000	7,500-9,000	4,000-4,800
1996 900 Convertible	9,500-11,500	8,500-10,500	4,800-6,000
1997 900	9,000-11,000	8,000-10,000	4,400-5,500
1997 900 Turbo	10,500-12,000	9,500-10,800	5,200-6,000
1997 900 Convertible	12,000-14,500	10,800-13,000	6,200-7,500
1998 900	11,000-13,000	9,800-11,800	5,500-6,800
1998 900 Turbo	12,500-14,000	11,500-12,700	7,000-7,700
1998 900 Convertible	14,500-17,000	13,000-15,500	8,000-9,500

AVERAGE REPLACEMENT COSTS

A/C Compressor...........	$665	Clutch, Pressure Plate, Bearing	655
Alternator.....................	455	Constant Velocity Joints	485
Automatic Transmission or Transaxle	1,250	Exhaust System	640
Brakes	265	Radiator........................	395
Shocks and/or Struts....	990	Timing Chain or Belt.....	630

TROUBLE SPOTS

• **Audio system.** Scratches or microscopic cracks in the rear window heater grid cause interference in the radio when the rear defroster is turned on. (All)

• **Poor drivability.** Stumble, stalling, or hesitation during the first minute after startup is corrected by replacing the engine control computer. (1994-95)

• **Engine fan.** The battery may go dead because the cooling fan relay, which allows the fan to run 10 minutes after the engine is turned off, keeps the fan on. (1994-96)

• **Transmission leak.** The gear selector shaft seal is prone to leak on manual transmissions. (1994-96)

• **Hard starting.** The turbo bypass valve is secured with plastic clamps that break, causing hard starting and poor drivability. (All)

RECALL HISTORY

1994: On some manual front seats, trigger springs at fore/aft lever do not properly lock the seat rails. **1994 hatchback:** Weld omitted from manual driver's seat rails. **1994:** Weld points for side-protection beam in rear door may be out of position. **1994-95:** Welds on recliner may be missing, allowing seatback to fall backward when under load. **1994-95 w/manual shift:** It is possible to move shift lever into reverse, remove key, and still be in neutral. **1994-97:** Corrosion can cause throttle lever to bind. **1994-98:** Instructions for properly aiming headlights were omitted. **1995 w/Bosch "Motronic 2.10.3":** Upon startup, engine speed may fluctuate for up to 30 seconds. **1995 convertible:** Steering-column shaft may be misaligned. **1996:** Seatbelt anchorage on some cars may not properly secure the occupant in an accident. **1997-98:** Airbag alert label on driver's sunvisor was omitted. **1998:** Static electricity can build up within the passenger-side airbag module and create enough of a charge to cause an inadvertent airbag deployment.

1999-01 SAAB 9-3

2000 Saab 9-3 SE 2-door convertible

FOR Acceleration • Brake performance • Cargo room (except convertible) • Rear-seat room/comfort (convertible)

AGAINST Turbo engine performance • Rear-seat entry/exit (except 4-dr) • Build quality (convertible) • Rear visibility

EVALUATION Compact Saabs deliver sporty driving in a space-efficient, if somewhat quirky, package. Overall acceleration is good. Base models are responsive but calm. A manual-transmission base car accelerated to 60 mph in 7.5 seconds, and averaged 19.4 mpg even in hard driving. High Output models are slightly faster. A 4-door averaged 21.3 mpg. Viggens react with serious spirit. On the downside, the turbocharger does not yield extra power until the engine reaches 3000 rpm or so, and "turbo lag" (delay after flooring the throttle) makes smooth driving difficult. Unruly steering-wheel tug occurs when pushed hard, too, unless front wheels are pointed dead-ahead. Handling is sporty, responsive, and predictable, with good cornering grip. SE models (and Viggens) ride quite stiffly. High-performance tires transmit a lot of irritating thump and jiggle on small, sharp bumps. Base models have softer tires and should be noticeably more compliant and comfortable on any road. Braking is swift and powerful. Relatively narrow and tall, hatchbacks have fairly ample space for five, plus cargo room that rivals a wagon. Convertibles seat only four, with very limited rear leg room. Rear visibility is so-so in hatchbacks and awful in top-up convertibles. Gauges and controls are well-located. The floor-mounted ignition switch is a long-time Saab hallmark. Sadly, so is the SE's obstinate automatic climate-control system. Detail finish is good and materials are classy. A test convertible suffered excessive body flex over bumps, but other Saabs have felt rigid and mostly rattle-free.

VALUE All models have their charms, but are compromised by turbo-engine performance. Saab loyalists are likely to love the quirky 9-3, but a Volvo S70 sedan or V70 wagon might be a more prudent choice for near-luxury motoring in the Swedish mode.

SPECIFICATIONS

	2-door conv.	2-door hatchback	4-door hatchback
Wheelbase, in.	102.6	102.6	102.6
Overall length, in.	182.2	182.2	182.2
Overall width, in.	67.4	67.4	67.4
Overall height, in.	56.0	56.2	56.2
Curb weight, lbs.	3140	2990	3040
Cargo volume, cu. ft.	28.3	46.0	46.0
Fuel capacity, gals.	16.9	16.9	16.9
Seating capacity	4	5	5
Front head room, in.	38.9	39.3	39.3
Max. front leg room, in.	42.3	42.3	42.3
Rear head room, in.	37.9	37.9	37.9
Min. rear leg room, in.	33.0	34.1	34.1

Powertrain layout: transverse front-engine/front-wheel drive

ENGINES

	Turbocharged dohc I4	Turbocharged dohc I4	Turbocharged dohc I4
Size, liters/cu. in.	2.0/121	2.0/121	2.3/140
Horsepower	185	200-205	225-230
Torque (lbs./ft.)	194	209	258
EPA city/highway mpg			
5-speed OD manual	19/27	20/27	20/31
4-speed OD automatic	19/25		
City/highway mpg (as tested)			
5-speed OD manual	19.4	21.3	

Built in Sweden

RETAIL PRICES

	GOOD	AVERAGE	POOR
1999 9-3	$13,500-14,500	$12,500-13,500	$9,000-10,000
1999 9-3 SE	16,000-17,000	15,000-16,000	11,000-12,000
1999 9-3 Convertible	20,000-22,000	18,500-20,500	14,500-16,000
1999 9-3 Viggen	23,000-25,000	21,500-23,500	17,000-18,000
2000 9-3	16,500-18,000	15,300-16,500	11,300-12,300
2000 9-3 SE	19,500-21,000	18,500-19,800	14,000-15,000
2000 9-3 Convertible	23,500-25,500	22,000-24,000	17,000-18,500
2000 9-3 Viggen	26,000-28,000	24,500-26,500	19,000-20,500
2000 Viggen Convertible	30,000-32,000	28,000-30,000	23,000-24,500
2001 9-3	20,000-22,000	18,500-20,500	—
2001 9-3 SE	24,000-26,000	22,500-24,500	—
2001 9-3 Convertible	27,000-29,000	25,500-27,000	—
2001 9-3 Viggen	30,000-32,000	28,000-30,000	—
2001 Viggen Convertible	35,000-37,500	33,000-35,500	—

AVERAGE REPLACEMENT COSTS

A/C Compressor	$775	Clutch, Pressure Plate, Bearing	830
Alternator	410	Constant Velocity Joints	1,290
Automatic Transmission or Transaxle	1,100	Exhaust System	775
Brakes	745	Radiator	700
Shocks and/or Struts	1,455	Timing Chain or Belt	655

TROUBLE SPOTS

• **Oil consumption.** A banjo bolt in the crankcase ventilation system should be replaced to prevent oil from possibly entering the combustion chamber (causing emissions) or starving the turbo bearing. (1999)

• **Automatic transmission.** A recall was issued to replace the shift lock solenoid that prevented the transmission from shifting out of park. (1999)

• **Brakes.** If the brake fluid reservoir cap is not installed properly, fluid can be sucked out of the reservoir through the cap's check valve. (1999-01)

• **Wipers.** The rear wiper may get loose or fall off unless thread-locking compound is applied to the hold-down nut. (1999)

• **Climate control.** There were several problems with the HVAC controls ranging from stiff controls to ticking motors to loose knobs and broken spindles. New parts were being installed under warranty. (1999)

RECALL HISTORY

1999 w/manual front seats, made March 4 - October 17, 1998: Failure of "Easy Entry" cable in front manual seats can cause seat fore/aft adjustable mechanism to be unlocked, reducing the restraint capability of the safety belts in a crash. **2001:** Airbag alert labels may not be permanently affixed.

1991-96 SATURN COUPE

FOR Antilock brakes (optional) • Fuel economy • Acceleration (SC2) • Instruments/controls

AGAINST Engine noise • Road noise • Acceleration (SC1) • Rear-seat room • Entry/exit

EVALUATION If possible, select a base model (1995-96) with the 100-horsepower base engine paired with the manual 5-speed. Acceleration is sluggish with the automatic. Also, the revised base engine performs better than the previous 85-horsepower unit. The more powerful twin-cam engine in the SC2 performs well with either transmission. We timed one with the automatic at 9.1 seconds to 60 mph. The

1995 Saturn SC2

same car averaged 25 mpg from mainly urban driving. The SC1 should prove even more economical. However, both engines are still too noisy at higher speeds. Like most other sports coupes, these two suffer from limited rear-seat room, though there's plenty of space in front for tall people. The gauges are clearly marked and well-lit at night, and the steering-column stalks for both lights and wipers are at the driver's fingertips. The early climate controls are too low in the center of the dashboard and require a long look away from the road to find the right switch.

VALUE Saturn coupes began to get lots of competition from rivals, but the used car certification program from Saturn dealerships could help ensure that buyers will get a good deal on a used Saturn. You also have the promise of higher-than-average customer service on repairs and warranty work after the purchase.

SPECIFICATIONS

	2-door coupe
Wheelbase, in.	99.2
Overall length, in.	173.2
Overall width, in.	67.5
Overall height, in.	50.6
Curb weight, lbs.	2284
Cargo volume, cu. ft.	10.9
Fuel capacity, gals.	12.8
Seating capacity	4
Front head room, in.	37.5
Max. front leg room, in.	42.6
Rear head room, in.	35.0
Min. rear leg room, in.	26.5

Powertrain layout: transverse front-engine/front-wheel drive

ENGINES

	ohc I4	ohc I4	dohc I4
Size, liters/cu. in.	1.9/116	1.9/116	1.9/116
Horsepower	85	100	124
Torque (lbs./ft.)	110	114	122
EPA city/highway mpg			
5-speed OD manual	27/37	29/40	25/35
4-speed OD automatic	26/35	27/37	24/34
City/highway mpg (as tested)			
5-speed OD manual	24.0	31.9	25.8

Built in USA

RETAIL PRICES

	GOOD	AVERAGE	POOR
1991 SC2	$1,800-2,400	$1,200-1,800	$200-500
1992 SC2	2,200-2,800	1,600-2,100	400-600
1993 SC1, SC2	2,600-3,300	1,900-2,600	500-800
1994 SC1, SC2	3,000-3,800	2,300-3,000	700-1,100
1995 SC1, SC2	3,600-4,400	2,900-3,700	900-1,300
1996 SC1, SC2	4,500-5,300	3,800-4,500	1,400-1,800

AVERAGE REPLACEMENT COSTS

A/C Compressor	$390	Clutch, Pressure Plate,	
Alternator	350	Bearing	530
Automatic Transmission or		Constant Velocity Joints	380
Transaxle	905	Exhaust System	298
Brakes	190	Radiator	350
Shocks and/or Struts	485	Timing Chain or Belt	295

TROUBLE SPOTS

• **Tail/brake lights.** A drop in fuel economy, brake noise, vehicle vibration and/or increased brake pedal travel could be caused by a misadjusted brake light switch that does not allow the pedal to return to full release. (1991-93)

• **Antenna.** A whistling wind noise may be coming from the radio antenna.

(1991-95)

• **Brake noise.** Brakes that growl or grind during low speed stops are repaired by replacing the front pads and machining the rotors. (1991-95)

• **Automatic transmission.** If the automatic transmission shifts harshly, erratically, or sticks in gear or neutral, iron sediment in the valve body may be the problem. (1993-94)

• **Cruise control.** If the cruise control fluctuates at speeds over 64 mph, a new control module assembly may be needed. (1991-95)

• **Doors.** If the doors will not open, the door latch assembly(s) will be replaced. (1991-93)

• **Trunk latch.** If the trunk can be opened without the key, Saturn will fix the release mechanism. (1991-93)

• **Engine noise.** Squealing from the front of the engine when the temperature is below 40°F will be fixed by replacing the drive belt idler pulley with one having a revised bearing. (1991-95)

RECALL HISTORY

1991-93: Generator wiring harness could suffer excessive current flow. **1992:** Automatic transaxle valve assemblies on some cars were improperly machined. **1993:** Brake booster housing on some cars could separate. **1993 SC2:** Battery cable terminal at solenoid may be formed incorrectly. **1994-95:** Some front seatback recliner gear teeth may wear excessively through repeated use; could cause seatback to slip partially rearward when force is applied. **1995 w/automatic:** Improperly adjusted cable makes it possible to shift from "Park" with key removed, or to remove key while lever is in position other than "Park." **1996:** Horn could become inoperable or activate without pressing button; under certain conditions, heat could build up, leading to underhood fire.

1997-00 SATURN COUPE

1998 Saturn SC2

FOR Fuel economy • Acceleration (SC2)

AGAINST Noise • Acceleration (SC1 w/auto) • Rear-seat room • Entry/exit

EVALUATION Acceleration with an SC1 is adequate with manual shift, but a little less satisfying with the 4-speed automatic transmission. When you need a quick burst of power, it might not be there. With either transmission, an SC2 coupe accelerates in a more lively manner. An SC2 with automatic takes off with some zest, though turning on the air conditioning takes a toll on performance. Highway passing power also is good with the SC2. Fuel economy is appealing with any coupe, but the frugality champ is an SC1 with the 5-speed gearbox. We've averaged a miserly 31.9 mpg in mixed city/highway driving, versus 26 mpg with an SC2 that was equipped with the 5-speed. Although noise levels are lower than before, both engines remain loud and rather coarse during hard acceleration. All Saturns corner with pleasing swiftness and control. Handling is surefooted and competent in both models, but the SC1's steering is lighter and less precise. Ride quality is good with either coupe, but the SC1's softer suspension makes it more livable on urban roads. You pay a penalty for the SC2's sportier handling, which promises less body lean in turns. Visibility is good to all directions, unlike most sports coupes, helped by thin roof pillars and large windows. Large, clear gauges inform the driver. Radio and climate controls are in a pod that protrudes from the dashboard, mounted too low for best access while driving. Power window and mirror controls are on the center console, unlit and difficult to find at night. Front seats offer plenty of room, but are rather low, surrounded by a high beltline and a vast dashboard top. Firm seats offer good lateral support. Leg room might have grown markedly in back, as measured with a ruler, but the rear seat cushion is so low that most adults have to sit with their knees nearly pointing at the ceiling.

Cargo space is adequate in a deep trunk.

VALUE All told, Saturns lack the refinement of most Japanese sports coupes. They're also noisier, but boast an impressive reliability record.

SPECIFICATIONS

	2-door coupe
Wheelbase, in.	102.4
Overall length, in.	180.0
Overall width, in.	67.3
Overall height, in.	52.4
Curb weight, lbs.	2308
Cargo volume, cu. ft.	11.4
Fuel capacity, gals.	12.1
Seating capacity	4
Front head room, in.	38.5
Max. front leg room, in.	42.6
Rear head room, in.	35.7
Min. rear leg room, in.	31.0

Powertrain layout: transverse front-engine/front-wheel drive

ENGINES

	ohc I4	dohc I4
Size, liters/cu. in.	1.9/116	1.9/116
Horsepower	100	124
Torque (lbs./ft.)	114	122
EPA city/highway mpg		
5-speed OD manual	28/39	26/36
4-speed OD automatic	27/37	24/34
City/highway mpg (as tested)		
5-speed OD manual	31.9	26.0

Built in USA

RETAIL PRICES

	GOOD	AVERAGE	POOR
1997 SC1	$6,000-6,700	$5,300-6,000	$2,600-3,000
1997 SC2	6,700-7,400	6,000-6,600	3,100-3,500
1998 SC1	7,000-7,800	6,300-7,000	3,300-3,700
1998 SC2	7,800-8,500	7,000-7,700	3,900-4,300
1999 SC1 3-door	8,000-8,800	7,200-8,000	4,100-4,600
1999 SC2 3-door	8,800-9,500	7,900-8,500	4,600-5,000
2000 SC1 3-door	9,000-10,000	8,000-9,000	4,700-5,300
2000 SC2 3-door	10,000-11,200	9,000-10,200	5,300-6,000

AVERAGE REPLACEMENT COSTS

A/C Compressor	$400	Clutch, Pressure Plate,	
Alternator	350	Bearing	530
Automatic Transmission or		Constant Velocity Joints	390
Transaxle	915	Exhaust System	310
Brakes	190	Radiator	350
Shocks and/or Struts	490	Timing Chain or Belt	300

TROUBLE SPOTS

• **Automatic transmission.** Cars with automatic transmissions may leak fluid from the upper, left-hand corner where the case was not manufactured properly. (1997-98)

• **Electrical problem.** Electrical accessories may quit working. The lock will have to be repaired. On some models, the key won't turn back to the lock position. (1997)

• **Hard starting.** If a car with a manual transmission won't start, the wiring harness is probably damaged from rubbing on the clutch pedal pivot causing a short circuit. (1997-98)

• **Air conditioner.** The air conditioning may stop working when the car is driven for extended times on the highway because the evaporator freezes up. (1997-98)

• **Engine misfire.** The engine may stall or quit running as if it has run out of gas even though the gauge shows ⅛-¼ tank; caused by a plugged evaporative emissions canister vent. (1997)

• **Windows.** The side windows may not go up or down, or they may rattle because the glass comes loose from the regulator. (1997-98)

RECALL HISTORY

1997: Belted occupant in front passenger seat could experience seat movement during a moderate frontal impact. **1997:** Lock-up feature of seatbelt may not work properly. **1997:** Ignition key can be removed while in "run" position. **1997:** Horn could become inoperable or activate without pressing button; leading to an underhood fire. **1999-00:** Some seatbelt shoulder guide anchor bolts were inadequately tightened at center pillar and could fall out.

2000: Armrest latch may open during a crash. **2000:** Some welds in instrument-panel carrier assembly were not strong enough; occupant, especially if unbelted, may have increased risk of injury in frontal crash. **2000:** Some brake-pipe-attachment nuts may not have been tightened properly, and leakage could occur. **2000:** Some rear bumper fasteners could be loose or missing; rear bumper may not absorb energy properly in a rear-end collision. **2000:** The fuel-tank Over Pressure Relief valve can become stuck open in a frontal collision, creating a fire hazard.

2000-01 SATURN L-SERIES

2000 Saturn LS2

FOR Acceleration (V6) • Cargo room (wagon) • Steering/handling

AGAINST Rear-seat comfort • Noise

EVALUATION A reasonably accomplished performer, the L-Series is distinguished by fine handling. Opel-derived suspension tuning pays off in impressive high-speed stability. These midsize Saturns corner with confidence and modest body lean. Steering is linear and communicative, though it may feel heavy at low speeds. Some 4-cylinder stick-shift models have felt too light at high speeds. Sedans and wagons handle nearly identically, though wagons ride marginally stiffer. Neither absorbs bumps as well as a Camry. Buyers get a firm, Eurostyle ride in exchange for sporty road manners. Stopping power and pedal feel are impressive. Saturn has claimed that the volume-leading LS1/L200 with automatic takes 9.8 seconds to reach 60 mph, while a V6/automatic LS2/L300 did it in 8.2. Some early V6 models showed poor throttle response at takeoff and slow downshifts when passing, but others felt spry even in hilly terrain. A test V6/automatic sedan averaged 19 mpg, while a 4-cylinder/automatic wagon got an impressive 26.6 mpg. L-Series models are as quiet as most competitors. Road, wind and engine noise are well-muffled. The 4-cylinder engine sounds richer under hard throttle than the V6. Four adults have as much room as in an Accord or Camry, even if the L-Series does not match their interior refinement. Cloth seats are more supportive than the optional leather. Rear leg space is ample, with head clearance for 6-footers, but the cushion is soft and low. Vision directly rearward is constricted by the high deck. Instruments are large and clear. Sedans have a large, accessible trunk. Interiors have a low-budget look. Door handles are uninviting plated plastic, and audio controls are small and plasticky.

VALUE Though not class leaders, L-Series models satisfy in most performance areas. Although cabins are roomy, they're furnished modestly. New-car prices undercut those of comparable Accord and Camry models, and Saturns are likely to remain lower than those competitors on the used-car market.

SPECIFICATIONS

	4-door sedan	4-door wagon
Wheelbase, in.	106.5	106.5
Overall length, in.	190.4	190.4
Overall width, in.	69.0	69.0
Overall height, in.	56.4	57.3
Curb weight, lbs.	2910	3075
Cargo volume, cu. ft.	17.5	71.3
Fuel capacity, gals.	13.1	13.1
Seating capacity	5	5
Front head room, in.	39.3	39.3
Max. front leg room, in.	42.2	42.3
Rear head room, in.	38.0	39.6
Min. rear leg room, in.	34.4	37.0

Powertrain layout: transverse front-engine/front-wheel drive

ENGINES

	dohc I4	dohc V6
Size, liters/cu. in.	2.2/134	3.0/183
Horsepower	135-137	182
Torque (lbs./ft.)	142-147	190
EPA city/highway mpg		
5-speed OD manual	24/32	
4-speed OD automatic	23/32	20/26
City/highway mpg (as tested)		
4-speed OD automatic	26.6	19.0

Built in USA

RETAIL PRICES

	GOOD	AVERAGE	POOR
2000 LS LS1 LW1	$10,500-12,000	$9,500-11,000	$7,000-8,000
2000 LS2 LW2	12,500-14,000	11,500-13,000	8,500-9,500
2001 L100 L200 LW200	12,500-14,500	11,500-13,500	—
2001 L300 LW300	15,000-17,000	14,000-16,000	—

AVERAGE REPLACEMENT COSTS

A/C Compressor	$475	Clutch, Pressure Plate,	
Alternator	260	Bearing	570
Automatic Transmission or		Constant Velocity Joints	770
Transaxle	1,110	Exhaust System	370
Brakes	360	Radiator	350
Shocks and/or Struts	490	Timing Chain or Belt	280

TROUBLE SPOTS

• **Hood/trunk.** A shorter release cable is available for the hood release. (2000)

• **Electrical problem.** Chafed wires for the cooling fan cause the #1 fuse to blow. The wires were being lengthened with splices. (2000)

• **Climate control.** The HVAC blower may only operate on high, requiring replacement of the resistor card. (2000)

• **Oil consumption.** The oil filter cap can be damaged if an open-end wrench or adjustable wrench is used to remove the cap. Only a socket wrench or cap-style oil filter tool are acceptable. (2000-01)

• **Seat.** The power seat may stop working because the wiring harness chafes the seat assembly. (2000-01)

RECALL HISTORY

2000 LS: Certain vehicles have inoperative valve within fuel tank assembly, which can result in fuel spillage in a rollover incident. **2000 LS:** Turn-signal lamps may not work, or work intermittently, when driver uses turn-signal lever or hazard warning switch. **2000 w/automatic:** Transaxle shift cable clip may be missing or improperly seated, allowing cable to slip out of bracket; driver may put lever into "Park," but transaxle may be in Reverse or Neutral. **2000:** Over Pressure Relief valve in fuel tank can become stuck open in a frontal collision; if vehicle rolls over, fuel spillage could occur. **2000 w/TRW seatbelt buckle assemblies:** Seatbelt buckle assemblies fail to conform to federal requirements, because buckle base was not properly heat treated. **2001:** Small number of vehicles may have passenger airbag inflator module with incorrect amount of generant.

1991-95 SATURN SEDAN/WAGON

1995 Saturn SL

FOR Antilock brakes (optional) • Fuel economy • Acceleration (SL2, SW2)

AGAINST Engine noise • Road noise • Acceleration (base) • Rear-

seat room

EVALUATION The single-cam engine in the SL1 and SW1 gives these cars adequate acceleration with the manual transmission, but with the automatic you often have to floor the throttle to keep up with traffic. The dual-cam engine provides lively acceleration and decent passing power with either transmission. Though some changes have been made over the years to decrease interior noise levels, engines still become loud and harsh at higher speeds. Both the sedans and wagons have ample head room in front for 6-footers to sit comfortably, though the front buckets don't go back far enough for tall people to stretch out. Passengers in the back have just as much head room but less leg room. The wagon's firm rear seat has an upright backrest that some may find uncomfortable. Entry/exit is easy to the front, but tight through the narrow rear doors. The import-inspired dash is easy to use, and outward visibility is unobstructed. Trunk space is good for the class and the split-rear seatbacks fold for more cargo room. Responsive handling and adept roadhandling are high points, particularly on the SL2 and SW2 models. And the addition of a softer suspension and tires for '93 on these level "2" models provide a noticeable improvement in ride quality.

VALUE Saturn sedans aren't the best choice in a subcompact, but overall they rank only slightly below the class-leading Honda Civic and Toyota Corolla.

SPECIFICATIONS

	4-door sedan	4-door wagon
Wheelbase, in.	102.4	102.4
Overall length, in.	176.3	176.3
Overall width, in.	67.6	67.6
Overall height, in.	55.5	53.7
Curb weight, lbs.	2325	2380
Cargo volume, cu. ft.	11.9	56.3
Fuel capacity, gals.	12.8	12.8
Seating capacity	5	5
Front head room, in.	38.5	38.8
Max. front leg room, in.	42.5	42.5
Rear head room, in.	36.3	37.4
Min. rear leg room, in.	32.6	32.6

Powertrain layout: transverse front-engine/front-wheel drive

ENGINES

	ohc I4	ohc I4	dohc I4
Size, liters/cu. in.	1.9/116	1.9/116	1.9/116
Horsepower	85	100	124
Torque (lbs./ft.)	110	114	122
EPA city/highway mpg			
5-speed OD manual	27/37	29/40	25/35
4-speed OD automatic	26/35	27/37	24/34
City/highway mpg (as tested)			
5-speed OD manual		31.9	
4-speed OD automatic			22.3

Built in USA

RETAIL PRICES

	GOOD	AVERAGE	POOR
1991 SL1, SL2	$1,200-2,000	$600-1,400	$100-300
1992 SL, SL1, SL2	1,500-2,500	900-1,900	200-500
1993 SL, SL1, SL2	1,800-2,900	1,200-2,200	300-800
1993 SW1, SW2 wagon	2,300-3,000	1,600-2,300	500-900
1994 SL, SL1, SL2	2,200-3,300	1,600-2,600	500-1,100
1994 SW1, SW2 wagon	2,800-3,500	2,100-2,800	700-1,200
1995 SL, SL1, SL2	2,700-4,000	2,000-3,200	600-1,400
1995 SW1, SW2 wagon	3,400-4,400	2,700-3,600	800-1,700

AVERAGE REPLACEMENT COSTS

A/C Compressor	$390	Clutch, Pressure Plate,	
Alternator	350	Bearing	530
Automatic Transmission or		Constant Velocity Joints	355
Transaxle	905	Exhaust System	300
Brakes	190	Radiator	295
Shocks and/or Struts	485	Timing Chain or Belt	295

TROUBLE SPOTS

• **Tail/brake lights.** A drop in fuel economy, brake noise, vehicle vibration, and/or increased brake pedal travel could be caused by a misadjusted brake light switch that does not allow the pedal to return to full release. (1991-93)

• **Antenna.** A whistling wind noise may be coming from the radio antenna. (1991-95)

- **Brake noise.** Brakes that growl or grind during low speed stops are repaired by replacing the front pads and machining, or replacing, the rotors. (1991-95)
- **Automatic transmission.** If the automatic transmission shifts harshly, erratically, or sticks in gear or neutral, iron sediment in the valve body may be the problem. (1993-94)
- **Cruise control.** If the cruise control fluctuates at speeds over 64 mph, a new control module assembly must be installed. (1991-95)
- **Engine stalling.** If the DOHC engine stalls and does not restart when coming to a stop, the oil may be the wrong viscosity. (1991-95)
- **Doors.** If the doors will not open, the door latch assembly(s) must be replaced. (1991-93)
- **Engine noise.** Squealing from the front of the engine when the temperature is below 40°F may be fixed by replacing the drive belt idler pulley with one having a revised bearing. (1991-95)

RECALL HISTORY

1991-93: Generator wiring harness could suffer excessive current flow. **1992:** Automatic transaxle valve assemblies on some cars were improperly machined. **1993:** Brake booster housing on some cars could separate. **1993 SL2/SW2:** Battery cable terminal at starter solenoid may be formed incorrectly. **1994-95:** Some front seatback recliner gear teeth may wear excessively through repeated use; could cause seatback to slip partially rearward when force is applied. **1995 SL w/manual steering:** Some pinion shafts could fracture, causing total loss of steering control. **1995 w/automatic:** Improperly adjusted cable makes it possible to shift from "Park" with key removed, or to remove key while lever is in position other than "Park."

1996-01 SATURN SEDAN/WAGON

1996 Saturn SL2

FOR Fuel economy • Optional antilock brakes and traction control • Acceleration (SL2/SW2)

AGAINST Noise • Acceleration (SL/SL1/SW1 w/auto) • Rear-seat comfort

EVALUATION Engine and road noise were reduced with the 1996 redesign, but these cars still failed to head the subcompact class in terms of refinement. Both engines sound coarse and unrefined in hard acceleration. Engines did quiet down somewhat in 1998, but road noise remains considerable at highway speeds. The '99 models appear quieter yet—markedly closer to the competition, finally. Automatic-transmission operation also had been imperfect. Shift quality improved in this generation, and the 4-speed automatic is less harsh than before. This automatic transmission generally changes gears smoothly and downshifts promptly for passing. Acceleration is lively with an SL2 sedan or SW2 wagon with either transmission. Other models rank as adequate with manual shift, and markedly more sluggish with automatic. We've averaged more than 30 mpg in an SL2 with the 5-speed. A 1998 SL1 with manual shift averaged 28.9 mpg. An SL2 with automatic averaged a bit above 25 mpg. Different tires gave the SL2/SW2 models a more comfortable ride, with less impact harshness and thumping on rough pavement. These sedans and wagons corner with pleasing swiftness and control. Body lean in turns is less in the SL2 and SW2, and their tires hold out longer before squealing in protest when you try an overly quick corner. On all models, the suspension absorbs minor bumps well, but rough roads can cause abrupt, even harsh reaction, which are felt by occupants. Front head and leg room is sufficient for taller folks, and firm seats provide good lateral support. Backseat room is adequate for people under 5-foot-10 or so, provided the front seats aren't pushed back too far. The back seat is not particularly comfortable, and getting in and out is awkward because the door opening is narrow at the bottom.

Dashboards flaunt large, clear gauges. Stereo and climate controls are mounted in a pod that protrudes from the dashboard, mounted too low for easiest access by the driver. Visibility is helped by the low dashboard and deep side windows, but the tail is too high to easily see straight rearward. Trunk space is adequate, and a low liftover eases the strain of loading/unloading luggage.

VALUE Despite some real improvements, these sedans and wagons still lag behind such rivals as the Civic and Corolla.

SPECIFICATIONS

	4-door sedan	4-door wagon
Wheelbase, in.	102.4	102.4
Overall length, in.	176.9	176.9
Overall width, in.	66.7	66.7
Overall height, in.	54.5	54.4
Curb weight, lbs.	2326	2392
Cargo volume, cu. ft.	12.1	24.9
Fuel capacity, gals.	12.1	12.1
Seating capacity	5	5
Front head room, in.	39.3	39.3
Max. front leg room, in.	42.5	42.5
Rear head room, in.	38.0	38.7
Min. rear leg room, in.	32.8	32.8

Powertrain layout: transverse front-engine/front-wheel drive

ENGINES

	ohc I4	dohc I4
Size, liters/cu. in.	1.9/116	1.9/116
Horsepower	100	124
Torque (lbs./ft.)	114	122
EPA city/highway mpg		
5-speed OD manual	29/40	25/35
4-speed OD automatic	27/36	24/34
City/highway mpg (as tested)		
5-speed OD manual	28.9	30.0
4-speed OD automatic		25.1

Built in USA

RETAIL PRICES

	GOOD	AVERAGE	POOR
1996 Saturn SL, SL1	$3,500-4,400	$2,800-3,700	$900-1,300
1996 Saturn SW1 wagon	4,300-5,000	3,600-4,200	1,400-1,700
1996 Saturn SL2	4,500-5,300	3,800-4,500	1,600-2,000
1996 Saturn SW2 wagon	4,700-5,500	4,000-4,700	1,700-2,100
1997 Saturn SL, SL1	4,500-5,600	3,800-4,900	1,600-2,300
1997 Saturn SW1 wagon	5,500-6,300	4,700-5,500	2,200-2,700
1997 Saturn SL2	5,700-6,500	4,900-5,700	2,400-2,800
1997 Saturn SW2 wagon	6,200-7,000	5,400-6,200	2,700-3,200
1998 Saturn SL, SL1	5,500-6,500	4,800-5,800	2,300-2,900
1998 Saturn SW1 wagon	6,700-7,500	5,900-6,700	3,000-3,500
1998 Saturn SL2	6,900-7,600	6,100-6,800	3,200-3,600
1998 Saturn SW2 wagon	7,500-8,400	6,700-7,600	3,500-4,000
1999 Saturn SL, SL1	6,500-7,500	5,700-6,700	3,000-3,600
1999 Saturn SW1 wagon	7,800-8,600	7,000-7,700	3,900-4,300
1999 Saturn SL2	7,800-8,600	7,000-7,700	3,900-4,300
1999 Saturn SW2 wagon	8,400-9,200	7,600-8,300	4,300-4,700
2000 Saturn SL, SL1	7,500-8,600	6,600-7,600	3,500-4,000
2000 Saturn SL2	8,800-9,800	7,800-8,800	4,400-5,000
2000 Saturn SW2 wagon	9,500-10,300	8,600-9,300	4,900-5,400
2001 Saturn SL, SL1	8,700-10,000	7,700-9,000	—
2001 Saturn SL2	10,000-11,000	9,000-10,000	—
2001 Saturn SW2 wagon	10,700-12,000	9,700-11,000	—

AVERAGE REPLACEMENT COSTS

A/C Compressor	$400	Clutch, Pressure Plate, Bearing	530
Alternator	350	Constant Velocity Joints	390
Automatic Transmission or Transaxle	915	Exhaust System	310
Brakes	190	Radiator	350
Shocks and/or Struts	490	Timing Chain or Belt	300

TROUBLE SPOTS

- **Automatic transmission.** Cars with automatic transmissions may leak fluid from the upper, left-hand corner where the case was not manufactured properly. (1997-98)
- **Electrical problem.** Electrical accessories may quit working. The lock will have to be repaired. On some models, the key won't turn back to the lock position. (1997)

• **Hard starting.** If a car with a manual transmission won't start, the wiring harness was probably damaged by rubbing on the clutch pedal pivot causing a short circuit. (1997-98)

• **Air conditioner.** The air conditioning may stop working when the car is driven for extended times on the highway because the evaporator freezes up. (1997-98)

• **Engine misfire.** The engine may stall or quit running as if it has run out of gas even though the gauge shows ⅛-¼ tank; caused by a plugged evaporative emissions canister vent. (1997)

• **Windows.** The side windows may not go up or down, or they may rattle because the glass comes loose from the regulator. (1997-98)

RECALL HISTORY

1996 SW1/SW2: Welds between roof and reinforcement panels do not meet specifications; flange sides could partially separate in a crash. **1996 SL w/manual steering:** Pinion gear could disengage from steering rack under high steering-system load conditions, such as parking or low-speed maneuvers. **1996-97:** Horn could become inoperable or activate without pressing button; heat could build up, leading to an underhood fire. **1996-97 SL w/manual steering:** Pinion bearing cage in steering gear can separate, disengaging and causing loss of control. **1997:** Ignition key can be removed while cylinder is in "run" position. **1999-00:** Some seatbelt shoulder guide anchor bolts were inadequately tightened at center pillar and could fall out. **2000:** Some brake pipe attachment nuts may have been improperly tightened; fluid leakage could occur. **2000:** Some welds in instrument-panel carrier assembly were not strong enough; occupant, especially if unbelted, may have increased risk of injury in frontal crash. **2000:** Some rear bumper fasteners could be loose or missing; rear bumper may not absorb energy as designed, in a rear-end collision. **2000:** The fuel-tank Over Pressure Relief valve can become stuck open in a frontal collision, creating a fire hazard. **2000:** Armrest latch may open during a crash.

1998-01 SUBARU FORESTER

1998 Subaru Forester

FOR Visibility • Maneuverability • Cargo room • Standard ABS (L, S) • Ride

AGAINST Acceleration (automatic transmission) • Instruments/controls • Engine vibrations • Rear-seat room

EVALUATION With all-wheel drive instead of 4-wheel drive, and built off a car rather than truck platform, Forester is not a true SUV. But any SUV owner who drives one will be immediately impressed by its blend of carlike manners and all-wheel-drive utility. Subaru's flat-4 has good low-rpm power and feels more lively with manual shift, but performs acceptably with the automatic transmission. That transmission shifts smoothly and kicks down promptly, but passing power that feels adequate with just a driver aboard feels subpar with a load of passengers and luggage. A Forester accelerated to 60 mph in 9.3 seconds—almost 2 seconds quicker than Honda's CR-V. Gas mileage is a bonus, compared to truck-type SUVs. We averaged 17 mpg in one automatic-transmission Forester, and 20.9 mpg in a long-term trial. Road and wind noise are constant highway companions, but to a lesser degree than in most other SUVs of any stripe. The engine is gruff when pushed hard, and the idle is lumpy with the air conditioning on. Handling isn't as nimble as a car's, but Forester is less ponderous than truck-based midsize SUVs and far more agile. Body lean is moderate in fast turns, and AWD provides reassuring grip. With a suspension tuned for the street and not the trail, Forester does not pitch or rock on uneven pavement, as do many true SUVs. Braking feels adequate, but pedal action is spongy. You can also expect a fair degree of nosedive in hard stops. Forester looks like a small sport-utility, but has the cabin space of a compact wagon. The driv-

ing position, while higher than in a traditional sedan, does not impart the "command-of-the-road" feeling of a true SUV. However, tall, thin roof pillars and a low cowl make for outstanding outward visibility to all directions. There's no step-up to speak of, and the doors open wide. So, entry and exit are inviting—though rear openings are quite narrow at the bottom. Head room is generous all around. Front leg room is good, but rear-seaters are squeezed for knee clearance and foot space. Forester's dashboard is well-designed, but some buttons hide behind the steering wheel and the radio controls are too small and low to operate easily while driving.

VALUE Forester is a worthy competitor for the better-publicized CR-V and RAV4. Hybrids are supposed to drive like cars, perform on-road like SUVs, and look like trucks. This one does.

SPECIFICATIONS

	4-door wagon
Wheelbase, in.	99.4
Overall length, in.	175.2
Overall width, in.	68.3
Overall height, in.	65.0
Curb weight, lbs.	3100
Cargo volume, cu. ft.	64.6
Fuel capacity, gals.	15.9
Seating capacity	5
Front head room, in.	40.6
Max. front leg room, in.	43.0
Rear head room, in.	39.6
Min. rear leg room, in.	33.4

Powertrain layout: transverse front-engine/all-wheel drive

ENGINES

	ohc H4
Size, liters/cu. in.	2.5/150
Horsepower	165
Torque (lbs./ft.)	162-166

EPA city/highway mpg
5-speed OD manual	21/27
4-speed OD automatic	21/26

City/highway mpg (as tested)
4-speed OD automatic	19.8

Built in Japan

RETAIL PRICES

	GOOD	AVERAGE	POOR
1998 Forester	$10,500-12,200	$9,500-11,200	$5,400-6,300
1999 Forester	12,000-14,000	11,000-13,000	6,800-8,000
2000 Forester	14,000-16,000	12,800-14,700	8,300-9,200
2001 Forester	16,000-18,200	14,500-16,700	—

AVERAGE REPLACEMENT COSTS

A/C Compressor	$725	Clutch, Pressure Plate, Bearing	565
Alternator	410	Constant Velocity Joints	730
Automatic Transmission or Transaxle	850	Exhaust System	260
Brakes	350	Radiator	285
Shocks and/or Struts	470	Timing Chain or Belt	180

TROUBLE SPOTS

• **Information stickers/paperwork.** Subaru warns that its vehicles should not be emissions tested on some dynamometers because of the potential for serious damage. (1998-00)

• **Windshield.** Windshield is easily chipped or scratched. (1998)

RECALL HISTORY

1998-99 w/antilock braking: In extremely cold weather, master cylinder seals could fail; brake pedal might then go to the floor, increasing stopping distance.

1993-01 SUBARU IMPREZA

FOR Airbags, dual (later models) • Optional antilock brakes • All-wheel drive (AWD models) • Instruments/controls

AGAINST Acceleration (early AWD models) • Rear-seat entry/exit • Rear-seat room • Cargo room

EVALUATION With the 2.2-liter engine, acceleration of an AWD model is more than adequate with a manual transmission and adequate with automatic. Simply put, a 1.8-liter model lacks sufficient snap when you need to merge into expressway traffic or pass other cars on the highway.

1993 Subaru Impreza 4-door sedan

	GOOD	AVERAGE	POOR
1999 Impreza RS, Outback	$10,200-11,500	$9,200-10,500	$5,200-6,000
2000 Impreza	10,000-11,500	9,000-10,500	5,100-6,000
2000 Impreza RS, Outback	12,500-13,700	11,500-12,500	7,000-7,700
2001 Impreza	12,000-13,500	11,000-12,500	—
2001 Impreza RS, Outback	14,500-16,000	13,000-14,500	—

AVERAGE REPLACEMENT COSTS

A/C Compressor	$725	Clutch, Pressure Plate, Bearing	565
Alternator	410	Constant Velocity Joints	730
Automatic Transmission or Transaxle	850	Exhaust System	260
Brakes	350	Radiator	285
Shocks and/or Struts	470	Timing Chain or Belt	180

The 2.5-liter on the RS is probably the best all-around engine, providing ample acceleration and good passing power. All engines sound gruff and feel rough with manual shift. Our 1993 test wagon with AWD and a 5-speed felt sluggish from startup, while an AWD sedan with automatic was downright slow. We averaged 24.8 mpg overall with the early AWD wagon—very nice for an AWD car. Interior space is comparable to that of a Honda Civic, Geo Prizm, or Toyota Corolla. That means sufficient space for four adults. But rear leg space is barely adequate if the front seats are pushed back. Tall drivers might want more seat travel to get farther from the steering wheel and pedals. Visibility is good to all directions. Cargo space isn't so great, even in the wagon. Rear entry/exit wins no prizes, either, as doors are quite narrow at the bottom and don't open very wide. Dashboards are logically laid out, with controls grouped around the gauge cluster—easy to find and operate. On the downside, using the pull-out cupholder blocks access to the stereo controls.

TROUBLE SPOTS

• **Engine misfire.** Bucking and jerking at slow speeds on all-wheel-drive cars is due to a defective transfer clutch. (1993-97)

• **Hard starting.** The engine may be hard to start after sitting in cold weather because ice forms on the fuel injectors. (1993-96)

• **Dashboard lights.** The hydraulic motor for the ABS system runs with the key turned off, which illuminates the ABS warning light on the dash. (1993-96)

• **Engine noise.** The knock sensors in the cylinder heads may fail, which can cause pinging under load. (1993-95)

RECALL HISTORY

1993 AWD: Fuel filler system does not comply with federal leakage requirements. **1994-95:** Inadvertent airbag deployment could occur after undercarriage contact of tow hooks with curbs, dips, speed bumps, etc.

VALUE With the exception of available AWD, the Impreza fails to stand apart. Later models might be more tempting—especially the Outback Sport wagon or the 2.5 RS coupe.

SPECIFICATIONS

	2-door coupe	4-door sedan	4-door wagon
Wheelbase, in.	99.2	99.2	99.2
Overall length, in.	172.2	172.2	172.2
Overall width, in.	67.1	67.1	67.1
Overall height, in.	55.5	55.5	55.5
Curb weight, lbs.	2400	2420	2750
Cargo volume, cu. ft.	11.1	11.1	62.1
Fuel capacity, gals.	13.2	13.2	13.2
Seating capacity	5	5	5
Front head room, in.	39.2	39.2	39.2
Max. front leg room, in.	43.1	43.1	43.1
Rear head room, in.	36.7	36.7	37.4
Min. rear leg room, in.	32.5	32.5	32.4

Powertrain layout: transverse front-engine/front- or all-wheel drive

ENGINES

	ohc F4	ohc F4	dohc F4
Size, liters/cu. in.	1.8/109	2.2/135	2.5/150
Horsepower	110-115	135-137	165
Torque (lbs./ft.)	110-120	140-145	162
EPA city/highway mpg			
5-speed OD manual	25/31	22/29	22/28
4-speed automatic			22/28
4-speed OD automatic	24/30	22/29	
City/highway mpg (as tested)			
5-speed OD manual		24.3	24.7
4-speed OD automatic		24.7	

Built in Japan

RETAIL PRICES

	GOOD	AVERAGE	POOR
1993 Impreza	$1,600-2,700	$1,000-2,100	$200-700
1993 Impreza AWD	2,300-3,100	1,600-2,400	500-900
1994 Impreza	2,100-3,500	1,500-2,800	400-1,000
1994 Impreza AWD	3,100-4,500	2,400-3,800	800-1,500
1995 Impreza	2,600-3,900	2,000-3,200	600-1,200
1995 Impreza AWD	3,600-5,200	2,800-4,400	900-1,800
1996 Impreza	3,400-5,000	2,700-4,300	800-1,700
1996 Impreza LX, Outback	4,800-6,000	4,000-5,200	1,600-2,200
1997 Impreza	4,500-6,500	3,800-5,700	1,500-2,600
1997 Impreza Outback	6,500-8,000	5,600-7,000	2,700-3,600
1998 Impreza	6,500-8,000	5,700-7,200	2,800-3,800
1998 Impreza RS, Outback	8,500-10,000	7,500-9,000	4,100-5,000
1999 Impreza	8,000-9,500	7,100-8,500	3,900-4,700

1990-94 SUBARU LEGACY

1990 Subaru Legacy LSi 4-door wagon

FOR Antilock brakes (optional) • Acceleration (turbo) • Wet-weather traction (AWD) • Handling/roadholding

AGAINST Fuel economy • Noise • Manual transmission linkage

EVALUATION The Legacy's 2.2-liter engine solves our chief complaint lodged against previous Subarus. Though some models have come across as rather rough and gruff, this newer 4-cylinder is smooth and comparatively quiet, delivering sprightly acceleration with either the 5-speed manual or 4-speed automatic. However, the 5-speed seemed a bit hesitant to engage during quick gear changes and was reluctant to go into reverse. The turbocharged engine is even more powerful, and virtually devoid of turbo lag. The downside is below-average fuel economy. We averaged only 17.4 mpg in our wagon in mostly urban driving. Head room and leg room are adequate for adults both front and rear, but the back door opening is a bit narrow at the bottom, making it difficult to swing your feet in and out. A comfortable driving position is aided by the standard tilt steering wheel and, on LS and higher models, an adjustable-height driver's seat. All controls are well-placed and easy to operate while driving. The spacious trunk is well-trimmed, with a bumper-level opening and low liftover height.

VALUE While the Legacy is not an outstanding value, the Subaru AWD models have few competitors, unless you step up to a sport-utility vehicle and risk losing your carlike amenities.

SPECIFICATIONS

	4-door sedan	4-door wagon
Wheelbase, in.	101.6	101.5
Overall length, in.	178.9	181.9

	4-door sedan	4-door wagon
Overall width, in.	66.5	66.5
Overall height, in.	53.5	54.7
Curb weight, lbs.	2740	2860
Cargo volume, cu. ft.	14.3	71.0
Fuel capacity, gals.	15.9	15.9
Seating capacity	5	5
Front head room, in.	38.0	38.4
Max. front leg room, in.	43.1	43.1
Rear head room, in.	36.0	37.8
Min. rear leg room, in.	34.8	35.0

Powertrain layout: transverse front-engine/front- or all-wheel drive

ENGINES

	ohc F4	Turbocharged ohc F4
Size, liters/cu. in.	2.2/135	2.2/135
Horsepower	130	160
Torque (lbs./ft.)	137	181
EPA city/highway mpg		
5-speed OD manual	23/31	19/25
4-speed OD automatic	22/29	18/23
City/highway mpg (as tested)		
5-speed OD manual	24.1	17.4
4-speed OD automatic	22.7	19.0

Built in USA, Japan

RETAIL PRICES

	GOOD	AVERAGE	POOR
1990 Legacy 2WD	$1,100-1,800	$600-1,200	$100-200
1990 Legacy AWD	1,300-2,000	700-1,400	100-300
1991 Legacy 2WD	1,500-2,300	900-1,700	200-400
1991 Legacy AWD	2,000-3,000	1,400-2,300	400-900
1992 Legacy 2WD	1,900-3,000	1,200-2,300	300-900
1992 Legacy AWD	2,500-3,300	1,800-2,600	600-1,000
1993 Legacy 2WD	2,300-3,500	1,600-2,800	500-1,100
1993 Legacy AWD	3,000-4,000	2,300-3,300	700-1,300
1994 Legacy 2WD	2,800-4,300	2,100-3,500	600-1,400
1994 Legacy AWD	3,500-5,500	2,800-4,700	900-1,900

AVERAGE REPLACEMENT COSTS

A/C Compressor	$430	Clutch, Pressure Plate, Bearing	480
Alternator	400	Constant Velocity Joints	460
Automatic Transmission or Transaxle	975	Exhaust System	340
Brakes	245	Radiator	360
Shocks and/or Struts	645	Timing Chain or Belt	195

TROUBLE SPOTS

• **Heater core.** A clicking noise caused by the heater mode door actuator can be fixed by installing a new resistor in the wiring harness. (1992-94)

• **Poor transmission shift.** Erratic shifting of the automatic transmission accompanied by a check engine light is often due to a corroded battery ground connection at the engine. (1990-94)

• **Hard starting.** Hard starting can be caused by silicone contaminating the ignition relay. (All)

• **Automatic transmission.** If it is difficult to shift out of park, the transmission's parking pawl must be replaced. (1990-91)

• **Automatic transmission.** If the transmission is slow to engage after being parked, the torque converter is draining down and a new cooler line with a check valve must be installed. (1990-91)

• **Seat.** Misaligned side rails prevent the seat from locking in place. Shims must be added to the outer rail to remedy the problem. (1990-94)

• **Vehicle noise.** Popping noises from the front end are usually due to loose stabilizer bar bushing clamps that must be rebent and reinstalled. (1990-92)

• **Brakes.** Some of the ABS (antilock brake system) hydraulic motors were faulty causing them to run intermittently even after the key is turned off. (1990-94)

• **Automatic transmission.** The automatic transmission dipstick may break requiring the broken bits to be removed. (1990+)

RECALL HISTORY

1990: Lever pin of defroster shutter door may become dislocated and allow the shutter to close, preventing defroster from functioning and affecting visibility. **1990-91:** Torque of latch screws on front doors may loosen over time, due to gap between latch base plate and inner door panel, so door could not be opened from inside the car. **1990-91:** Under certain conditions on cars with 4EAT electronically controlled automatic transmission, park gear may not disengage immediately when lever is moved from "Park" to "Reverse," which could result in abrupt vehicle movement and possible loss of control. **1990-93 all-wheel drive:** 5-speed manual gearbox may leak if driven continuously in extreme cold or high humidity; transmission could seize, bringing vehicle to sudden stop. **1992:** Top of fuel tank may have been punctured during assembly, which could cause fuel leakage that results in fire if leak occurs near an ignition source.

1995-99 SUBARU LEGACY

1995 Subaru Legacy Brighton 4-door wagon

FOR Antilock brakes (optional) • Wet-weather traction (traction control, AWD) • Passenger and cargo room • Visibility

AGAINST Engine noise • Fuel economy (AWD)

EVALUATION Legacy's 2.2-liter engine is adequate for most circumstances, but it throbs and feels strained in hard acceleration and in hilly country. It's also more gruff-sounding than most 4-cylinders. The dual-overhead-cam 2.5-liter engine is quieter and smoother, with both excellent acceleration and passing power. But note that fuel economy is unimpressive on the AWD models. Legacy's suspension strikes an admirable balance between ride and handling, with ride comfort taking precedence. Bumps are absorbed easily and all models feel stable. Body lean is noticeable in spirited cornering maneuvers, and the front end tends to plow when pushed hard—more so on front-drive versions than AWD models. A low dashboard and narrow roof pillars provide clear visibility in all directions. Front head and leg room are ample. In back, people under six feet tall should have adequate room, and both body styles provide outstanding cargo space.

VALUE With the addition of dual airbags, the new Legacy was a more competitive entry in the compact class. But its trump card remained the competent line of all-wheel-drive sedans and wagons, which Subaru finally stressed in its advertising.

SPECIFICATIONS

	4-door sedan	4-door wagon
Wheelbase, in.	103.5	103.5
Overall length, in.	180.9	183.9
Overall width, in.	67.5	67.5
Overall height, in.	55.3	57.1
Curb weight, lbs.	2570	2685
Cargo volume, cu. ft.	13.0	73.0
Fuel capacity, gals.	15.9	15.9
Seating capacity	5	5
Front head room, in.	38.9	39.5
Max. front leg room, in.	43.3	43.3
Rear head room, in.	36.7	38.8
Min. rear leg room, in.	34.6	34.8

Powertrain layout: longitudinal front-engine/front- or all-wheel drive

ENGINES

	ohc F4	ohc F4
Size, liters/cu. in.	2.2/135	2.5/150
Horsepower	135-137	155-165
Torque (lbs./ft.)	140-145	155-162
EPA city/highway mpg		
5-speed OD manual	23/30	21/27
4-speed OD automatic	23/30	20/26
City/highway mpg (as tested)		
5-speed OD manual	23.6	22.9

Built in USA, Japan

RETAIL PRICES

	GOOD	AVERAGE	POOR
1995 Legacy sedan	$3,700-6,500	$3,000-5,800	$1,000-2,500
1995 Legacy wagon	4,400-6,700	3,600-5,900	1,400-2,600
1996 Legacy	5,000-7,800	4,300-7,000	1,900-3,400
1996 LSi, 2.5GT, Outback	7,000-9,000	6,200-8,000	3,300-4,400
1997 Legacy	6,700-8,300	6,000-7,500	3,100-4,000
1997 Legacy GT, LSi	9,000-11,000	8,000-10,000	4,500-5,800
1997 Legacy Outback	10,500-11,500	9,500-10,500	5,300-6,000
1998 Legacy	8,500-10,500	7,600-9,500	4,300-5,500
1998 Legacy GT	10,500-11,800	9,500-10,800	5,500-6,300
1998 Legacy Outback	12,000-13,500	11,000-12,500	6,600-7,400
1999 Legacy	10,500-12,500	9,500-11,500	5,500-6,800
1999 Legacy GT, SUS	12,500-13,700	11,500-12,600	7,000-7,500
1999 Legacy Outback	13,500-14,500	12,500-13,500	7,700-8,300

AVERAGE REPLACEMENT COSTS

A/C Compressor	$560	Clutch, Pressure Plate, Bearing	515
Alternator	345	Constant Velocity Joints	460
Automatic Transmission or Transaxle	940	Exhaust System	565
Brakes	225	Radiator	360
Shocks and/or Struts	615	Timing Chain or Belt	195

TROUBLE SPOTS

• **Oil leak.** An oil leak between the oil pump and block is repaired by drilling out the oil return hole to 6mm diameter. (1995)

• **Poor transmission shift.** Hesitation or poor acceleration may be due to the powertrain control module (PCM) misinterpreting normal engine vibrations as knock, and retarding the ignition timing requiring a replacement PCM. (1999)

• **Dashboard lights.** If the check engine light comes on in cold weather it is likely due to ice forming in the vacuum line between the engine and transmission. (1995)

• **Automatic transmission.** Severely cracked secondary pulleys and pump drives cause the ECVT to slip. (1995)

• **Brakes.** Some of the ABS (antilock brake system) hydraulic motors were faulty causing them to run intermittently even after the key is turned off. (1995-98)

• **Automatic transmission.** The automatic transmission dipstick may break requiring the broken bits to be removed. (1995-97)

• **Alternator belt.** The company issued a (nonsafety) recall to replace the alternators. (1996 and some later)

• **Brake noise.** There may be a buzzing sound coming from the ABS (antilock brake system) hydraulic unit motor and/or an ABS warning light glowing, caused by a faulty ABS relay for which there is a revised part. (1995-97)

• **Rear axle noise.** Vibration and noise from the rear when traveling over 65 mph on vehicles with AWD requires countermeasure dampers on the rear crossmember. (1997-99)

RECALL HISTORY

1995: Front coil springs were produced with poor paint quality which, after continued exposure to corrosive salt, can result in breakage of the spring. **1995-96:** Inadvertent airbag deployment could occur after undercarriage contact of tow hooks with curbs, dips, speed bumps, etc. **1996-97:** Due to improper welding, fractures can occur on support bracket of front transverse link, resulting in separation and failure of front suspension. **1997:** Hazard warning switch can stick in intermediate position, so turn signals become inoperable. **1997:** Omitted bearing in throttle body assembly could eventually lead to incomplete return of throttle, resulting in fast idle. **1997-98 w/automatic transmission:** Due to poor welds, ignition key can stick, shift lever/linkages can break, and improper movement of shift lever can occur. **1998-99:** Purolator oil filter can fracture, causing vaporized oil spray and subsequent oil leak at hot exhaust system; could result in underhood fire. **1998-99 w/ABS:** In extremely cold weather, master cylinder seals could fail; brake pedal might then go to floor, increasing stopping distance.

1990-98 SUZUKI SIDEKICK

FOR 4WD traction • Maneuverability • Fuel economy

AGAINST Ride • Noise • Acceleration (automatic) • Rear-seat room

EVALUATION Acceleration with 80-horsepower engine is on the leisurely side, and the power boost in 1992 does not help much. The

1992 Suzuki Sidekick 2-door convertible

Sport model's larger engine finally offers acceptable performance. That 1.8-liter 4-cylinder works well with the 4-speed automatic transmission. A late-model wagon with manual shift averaged 25.3 mpg, though automatic dropped the figure to a so-so 21.4 mpg. However, even the latest Sidekick engines growl loudly under throttle. Wind and road noise are abundant at highway speeds, too. Reasonably stable in corners and on the highway, Sidekick suffers a somewhat stiff and jiggly ride on rough surfaces. Four-door models endure less choppiness, credited to their longer wheelbase, but they're not that much more comfortable overall. Tall and narrow, Sidekicks must be driven with care through turns. Sidekick's 4-wheel-drive system is not for use on dry pavement. Head room is plentiful up front, but the rear bench seat holds only two adults, for 4-passenger capacity. Worse yet, it's hard, with little leg space when the front seats are all the way aft—though space is adequate otherwise. In the Sidekick's narrow cabin, doors sit close to the seats, leaving little outside shoulder room. Cargo space is best in the 4-door, with its swing-open rear door and fold-down back seat.

VALUE Though better than the tiny old Samurai, this is still not a good choice for everyday driving, even in 4-door form.

SPECIFICATIONS

	2-door conv.	4-door wagon	4-door wagon
Wheelbase, in.	86.6	97.6	97.6
Overall length, in.	143.7	158.7	162.4
Overall width, in.	64.2	64.4	66.7
Overall height, in.	64.3	65.7	66.3
Curb weight, lbs.	2339	2632	2917
Cargo volume, cu. ft.	32.9	45.0	45.0
Fuel capacity, gals.	11.1	14.5	18.5
Seating capacity	4	4	4
Front head room, in.	39.5	40.6	40.6
Max. front leg room, in.	42.1	42.1	42.1
Rear head room, in.	39.0	40.0	38.6
Min. rear leg room, in.	31.7	32.7	32.7

Powertrain layout: longitudinal front-engine/rear- or 4-wheel drive

ENGINES

	ohc I4	dohc I4	dohc I4
Size, liters/cu. in.	1.6/97	1.6/97	1.8/112
Horsepower	80	95	120
Torque (lbs./ft.)	94	98	114
EPA city/highway mpg			
5-speed OD manual	25/27	23/26	23/25
3-speed automatic	23/24		
4-speed OD automatic		22/26	21/24
City/highway mpg (as tested)			
5-speed OD manual	25.3	24.8	
4-speed OD automatic		22.1	20.2

Built in Canada, Japan

RETAIL PRICES

	GOOD	AVERAGE	POOR
1990 Sidekick 2WD conv.	$1,000-1,600	$600-1,000	$100-200
1990 Sidekick 4WD conv.	1,500-2,000	900-1,400	200-300
1991 Sidekick 2WD conv.	1,300-1,900	700-1,300	100-300
1991 Sidekick 4WD conv.	1,800-2,400	1,200-1,800	200-400
1991 Sidekick 4-door	1,800-2,500	1,200-1,800	200-400
1992 Sidekick 2WD conv.	1,600-2,200	1,000-1,600	200-400
1992 Sidekick 4WD conv.	2,200-2,800	1,600-2,100	400-600
1992 Sidekick 2WD 4-door	1,900-2,500	1,300-1,800	300-400
1992 Sidekick 4WD 4-door	2,400-3,000	1,800-2,300	400-700
1993 Sidekick 2WD conv.	2,000-2,600	1,400-2,000	300-500
1993 Sidekick 4WD conv.	2,700-3,300	2,000-2,600	500-800
1993 Sidekick 2WD 4-door	2,400-3,000	1,700-2,300	400-700
1993 Sidekick 4WD 4-door	3,100-3,800	2,400-3,100	600-1,000

	GOOD	AVERAGE	POOR
1994 Sidekick 2WD conv.	$2,400-3,000	$1,800-2,300	$400-700
1994 Sidekick 4WD conv.	3,000-3,600	2,400-2,900	600-900
1994 Sidekick 2WD 4-door	2,800-3,400	2,100-2,700	500-800
1994 Sidekick 4WD 4-door	3,400-4,000	2,700-3,200	800-1,100
1995 Sidekick 2WD conv.	2,800-3,500	2,200-2,800	500-900
1995 Sidekick 4WD conv.	3,500-4,200	2,800-3,400	800-1,200
1995 Sidekick 2WD 4-door	3,100-3,800	2,400-3,100	600-1,000
1995 Sidekick 4WD 4-door	3,900-4,600	3,200-3,800	1,000-1,400
1996 Sidekick 2WD conv.	3,200-3,900	2,500-3,200	700-1,100
1996 Sidekick 4WD conv.	4,000-4,700	3,300-3,900	1,100-1,500
1996 Sidekick 2WD 4-door	3,500-4,200	2,800-3,400	800-1,200
1996 Sidekick 4WD 4-door	4,400-5,000	3,700-4,200	1,200-1,500
1997 Sidekick 2WD conv.	3,700-4,400	3,000-3,700	900-1,400
1997 Sidekick 4WD conv.	4,600-5,300	3,900-4,500	1,300-1,600
1997 Sidekick 2WD 4-door	4,000-4,800	3,300-4,000	1,000-1,400
1997 Sidekick 4WD 4-door	5,000-5,700	4,300-4,900	1,500-1,900
1998 Sidekick 2WD conv.	4,400-5,100	3,700-4,400	1,200-1,700
1998 Sidekick 4WD conv.	5,700-6,400	5,000-5,600	1,800-2,200
1998 Sidekick 2WD 4-door	4,800-5,500	4,100-4,700	1,400-1,800
1998 Sidekick 4WD 4-door	6,100-6,800	5,400-6,000	2,000-2,300

AVERAGE REPLACEMENT COSTS

A/C Compressor	$385	Clutch, Pressure Plate, Bearing	450
Alternator	420	Constant Velocity Joints	280
Automatic Transmission or Transaxle	515	Exhaust System	175
Brakes	250	Radiator	295
Shocks and/or Struts	650	Timing Chain or Belt	230

TROUBLE SPOTS

• **Hard starting.** Hard starting below freezing, especially at high altitudes, requires a Cold Start Harness Set. (1990)

• **Automatic transmission.** The automatic transmission may hunt between 40-45 mph. A time delay module kit for the torque converter clutch should correct the condition. (1990-95)

• **Automatic transmission.** The transfer case binds and can be damaged if driven on dry roads in 4WD mode. (1990-97)

• **Engine misfire.** Using premium fuel can trigger trouble codes and cause poor starting. (1996-97)

RECALL HISTORY

1990-91: Front seatbelt button can break and pieces can fall inside. **1996 4-doors:** Fuel tank can puncture during rear-end collision. **1996-97:** Mounting bolts that attach upper end of front struts to vehicle body could break, causing loss of control.

1990-95 TOYOTA 4RUNNER

1995 Toyota 4Runner SR5

FOR Passenger and cargo room • Ride (later models) • Antilock brakes (optional) • Wet-weather traction (4WD) • Reliability

AGAINST Fuel economy • Acceleration • Entry/exit • Noise • Handling

EVALUATION The 4Runner's chief attractions are tight, thorough assembly quality and a commendable reputation for quality. However, the 4Runner is much smaller inside than the top-selling Ford Explorer and Jeep Grand Cherokee, with barely adequate space for four adults. Exit/entry are hurt by a higher-than-usual stance—nearly two feet off the ground. Also, fuel economy is very mediocre. We averaged just 13.8 mpg with a V6 model in our last test. Acceleration is nothing special

either, even with the V6, which is hard-pressed to reach 60 mph in under 13 seconds. And you can forget the 4-cylinder, which is even slower. Plus points include the convenient 4WDemand system and 4-wheel antilock brakes. Some Japanese rivals still have not adopted either shift-on-the-fly 4WD or 4-wheel ABS. Unfortunately, ABS was optional instead of standard.

VALUE High prices remain one of the 4Runner's biggest problems. We prefer domestic rivals such as the Explorer, Grand Cherokee, Chevrolet Blazer, and GMC Jimmy, which have more room, a broader selection of features and models, plus better all-around performance for the money.

SPECIFICATIONS

	2-door wagon	4-door wagon
Wheelbase, in.	103.3	103.3
Overall length, in.	176.0	176.0
Overall width, in.	66.5	66.5
Overall height, in.	66.1	66.1
Curb weight, lbs.	3720	3760
Cargo volume, cu. ft.	78.3	78.3
Fuel capacity, gals.	17.2	17.2
Seating capacity	5	5
Front head room, in.	38.7	38.7
Max. front leg room, in.	41.5	41.5
Rear head room, in.	38.3	38.3
Min. rear leg room, in.	31.6	31.6

Powertrain layout: longitudinal front-engine/rear- or 4-wheel drive

ENGINES

	ohc I4	ohc V6
Size, liters/cu. in.	2.4/144	3.0/180
Horsepower	116	150
Torque (lbs./ft.)	140	180
EPA city/highway mpg		
5-speed OD manual	19/21	15/18
4-speed OD automatic		14/16
City/highway mpg (as tested)		
4-speed OD automatic		13.8

Built in Japan

RETAIL PRICES

	GOOD	AVERAGE	POOR
1990 4Runner	$3,200-4,500	$2,500-3,800	$700-1,300
1991 4Runner	4,000-5,500	3,200-4,700	1,100-2,000
1992 4Runner	5,000-6,500	4,300-5,700	1,800-2,600
1993 4Runner	6,000-7,500	5,200-6,600	2,500-3,300
1994 4Runner	7,000-8,500	6,200-7,500	3,200-3,900
1995 4Runner	8,000-10,000	7,100-9,000	3,800-4,800

AVERAGE REPLACEMENT COSTS

A/C Compressor	$1,155	Clutch, Pressure Plate, Bearing	500
Alternator	515	Constant Velocity Joints	155
Automatic Transmission or Transaxle	1,280	Exhaust System	261
Brakes	225	Radiator	515
Shocks and/or Struts	190	Timing Chain or Belt	615

TROUBLE SPOTS

• **Clutch.** A leaking or damaged direct clutch in the transfer case causes a slip or chatter on acceleration. (1990-92)

• **Clutch.** Because of clutch judder, the pressure plate and disc were enlarged (from 9.00 in. to 9.5 in. diameter) for 4x4 models. (1990-94)

• **Exhaust system.** In compliance with emission control regulations, the oxygen sensor should be replaced at 80,000 miles. (1993-94)

1996-01 TOYOTA 4RUNNER

FOR Optional antilock brakes • Ride • Quietness • Passenger and cargo room

AGAINST Entry/exit • Fuel economy • Price

EVALUATION Because this version weighs less and also comes with stronger engines, it can charge up hills that would have overtaxed the old 4Runner. On-the-road performance is therefore more relaxed, especially when towing a trailer or hauling a full load of people and cargo. Acceleration with the smooth V6 is indeed snappy in town, though highway passing is more ordinary. We recommend a V6, because the 4-cylinder engine, despite being enlarged, still lacks the torque to propel

1996 Toyota 4Runner SR5 V6

such a heavy vehicle. Later models with the dealer-installed super-charger accelerate with authority—moving to the head of the midsize sport-utility class—aren't overly noisy, and don't consume much more fuel. Solid-feeling on rough pavement, a 4Runner copes admirably when it encounters off-road terrain. Engine and tire noise are less noticeable than they used to be. The current suspension promises a comfortable ride on almost any surface. Steering is carlike and precise, delivering stable cornering. Running boards on the Limited are a virtual necessity when climbing aboard, due to the uncomfortably high step-in level. Once inside, space is ample for four adults, and not bad at all for a fifth. Cargo room is generous, even with the rear seat in use, helped by a spare tire that's mounted beneath the cargo floor. The 4Runner's power liftgate window is a convenience that's not offered by any other compact sport-utility.

VALUE Domestic rivals such as the Ford Explorer, Chevrolet Blazer, and Jeep Grand Cherokee might be better bargains, but a 4Runner includes Toyota's reputation for reliability.

SPECIFICATIONS

	4-door wagon
Wheelbase, in.	105.3
Overall length, in.	183.3
Overall width, in.	66.5
Overall height, in.	67.5
Curb weight, lbs.	3740
Cargo volume, cu. ft.	79.7
Fuel capacity, gals.	18.5
Seating capacity	5
Front head room, in.	39.2
Max. front leg room, in.	43.1
Rear head room, in.	38.7
Min. rear leg room, in.	34.9

Powertrain layout: longitudinal front-engine/rear- or 4-wheel drive

ENGINES

	dohc I4	dohc V6
Size, liters/cu. in.	2.7/164	3.4/207
Horsepower	150	183
Torque (lbs./ft.)	177	217
EPA city/highway mpg		
5-speed OD manual	16/21	16/19
4-speed OD automatic	18/22	16/19
City/highway mpg (as tested)		
5-speed OD manual		14.2
4-speed OD automatic		17.1

Built in Japan

RETAIL PRICES

	GOOD	AVERAGE	POOR
1996 4Runner 4-cyl.	$8,800-10,000	$7,900-9,000	$4,200-4,800
1996 4Runner V6	11,000-12,500	10,000-11,500	5,800-6,600
1996 4Runner Limited	13,500-15,000	12,000-13,500	7,800-8,600
1997 4Runner 4-cyl.	10,300-11,500	9,300-10,500	5,400-6,200
1997 4Runner V6	13,000-14,500	12,000-13,200	7,800-8,500
1997 4Runner Limited	14,500-16,000	13,000-14,500	8,700-9,500
1998 4Runner 4-cyl.	11,800-13,500	10,800-12,300	6,500-7,400
1998 4Runner V6	15,000-16,500	13,800-15,000	9,200-10,000
1998 4Runner Limited	17,200-19,000	15,700-17,500	10,700-11,700
1999 4Runner 4-cyl.	13,800-15,500	12,500-14,000	8,300-9,200
1999 4Runner V6	17,500-19,000	16,000-17,500	10,500-11,400
1999 4Runner Limited	20,000-21,800	18,500-20,300	13,000-14,000
2000 4Runner 4-cyl.	16,000-18,000	14,500-16,500	8,600-9,800
2000 4Runner V6	19,500-21,500	18,000-20,000	12,000-13,200
2000 4Runner Limited	22,500-25,000	21,000-23,500	14,000-15,500
2001 4Runner	$21,000-23,000	$19,500-21,500	—
2001 4Runner Limited	25,000-27,500	23,000-25,500	—

AVERAGE REPLACEMENT COSTS

A/C Compressor	$1,140	Clutch, Pressure Plate, Bearing	400
Alternator	485	Exhaust System	305
Automatic Transmission or Transaxle	940	Radiator	475
Brakes	220	Shocks and/or Struts	600
Timing Chain or Belt	610	Universal Joints	590

TROUBLE SPOTS

• **Oil leak.** Head gasket failures, particularly on higher mileage engines. In some cases the company has issued a service campaign or extended warranty. (1996)

RECALL HISTORY

1996 2WD: Sticker alerting driver to "particular handling and maneuvering characteristics of utility vehicles" was not affixed to driver's sunvisor. **1998-99:** Some wheel lug nuts are defective, causing loss of torque, fatigue fracture of wheel, and possible loss of wheel.

1995-99 TOYOTA AVALON

1995 Toyota Avalon XLS

FOR Optional antilock brakes • Passenger and cargo room • Quietness • Acceleration • Instruments/controls

AGAINST Fuel economy • Price

EVALUATION Except for more body lean and understeer on twisting roads, an Avalon drives much like the Toyota Camry. Although the Avalon's suspension is firmer, it still absorbs most bumps. Even on wavy roads, the sedan does not bounce or feel mushy. It also corners with good grip and moderate body lean. Because there's a negligible weight difference between Avalon and the V6 Camry, don't expect a discernible difference in acceleration or passing sprints. A test Avalon accelerated to 60 mph in 8.5 seconds—just about exactly as swift as a Camry. Toyota's V6 engine is just as silky smooth in the Avalon as in the Camry, and nearly silent. Better yet, it's complemented by a smooth, responsive automatic transmission. As for gas mileage, an early model averaged 19.4 mpg, driving mostly in rush-hour commutes. The V6 engine requires premium fuel. Space is ample for four adults, and six can tolerate shorter trips in models with the front bench seat. Leg space is generous in the backseat, and rear doors open wide for easy entry/exit. The trunk is wide and deep, with a long, flat floor. Low liftover height makes it easier to load and unload, too. Avalon's dashboard layout and materials are first-rate. Large round gauges are legible. Both the stereo and climate controls are high enough to easily see and reach while driving.

VALUE Roomy and competent, but markedly more costly than a Camry when new, Avalon might offer little excitement, but the sedan also suffers few faults. We've been impressed with the solid feel, good workmanship, and low noise levels.

SPECIFICATIONS

	4-door sedan
Wheelbase, in.	107.1
Overall length, in.	190.2
Overall width, in.	70.3
Overall height, in.	56.1
Curb weight, lbs.	3263
Cargo volume, cu. ft.	15.4
Fuel capacity, gals.	18.5

	4-door sedan
Seating capacity	5[1]
Front head room, in.	39.1
Max. front leg room, in.	44.1
Rear head room, in.	37.8
Min. rear leg room, in.	38.3

1. 6 passengers w/optional front bench seat.

Powertrain layout: transverse front-engine/front-wheel drive

ENGINES

	dohc V6
Size, liters/cu. in.	3.0/180
Horsepower	192-200
Torque (lbs./ft.)	210

EPA city/highway mpg
4-speed OD automatic	20/29

City/highway mpg (as tested)
4-speed OD automatic	21.1

Built in USA

RETAIL PRICES

	GOOD	AVERAGE	POOR
1995 Avalon	$7,500-8,500	$6,700-7,700	$3,500-4,200
1995 Avalon XLS	8,500-9,500	7,500-8,500	4,000-4,700
1996 Avalon	9,000-10,200	8,000-9,200	4,400-5,100
1996 Avalon XLS	10,200-11,500	9,200-10,500	5,200-6,000
1997 Avalon	11,000-12,200	10,000-11,000	5,900-6,500
1997 Avalon XLS	12,300-13,300	11,200-12,100	6,900-7,500
1998 Avalon	13,000-14,200	11,800-13,000	7,500-8,200
1998 Avalon XLS	14,500-15,500	13,300-14,200	8,500-9,100
1999 Avalon	15,000-16,500	13,700-15,000	9,000-9,800
1999 Avalon XLS	16,800-18,000	15,500-16,500	10,500-11,200

AVERAGE REPLACEMENT COSTS

A/C Compressor	$880	Shocks and/or Struts	850
Alternator	370	Constant Velocity Joints	1,100
Automatic Transmission or Transaxle	710	Exhaust System	365
		Radiator	465
Brakes	260	Timing Chain or Belt	190

TROUBLE SPOTS

• **Climate control.** The ambient temperature occasionally gets stuck on 22°F and the climate control system may not work properly. (1995-96)

• **Brake noise.** The front brakes make a groaning and grinding noise that is eliminated by replacing the brake rotors and installing special shims. (1997-99)

• **Brake noise.** The front or rear disc brakes may make a moaning noise that can be corrected with revised brake pads. (1995-97)

• **Suspension noise.** The front suspension is noisy when driving over speed bumps or washboard roads due to a bad rubber bushing in the upper strut mount. Countermeasure bushings have been released. (1997-99)

• **Antenna.** The radio may have poor reception or noise because of a poor antenna ground. (1997)

• **Vehicle noise.** There is a kit to eliminate wind noise from the A-pillars. (1995-96)

RECALL HISTORY

1997 in specified states: In extreme cold, accumulated moisture can temporarily freeze in brake vacuum hose.

2000-01 TOYOTA AVALON

FOR Acceleration • Automatic transmission performance • Quietness • Ride • Passenger room • Build quality

AGAINST Brake pedal feel • Handling

EVALUATION Toyota sought quieter running in the reworked Avalon, and handily achieved that goal. Except for mild tire rumble over very coarse pavement, this Avalon is a pleasantly hushed automobile. Even hard acceleration produces only a distant, rich engine sound. Acceleration is a tad better than before, thanks to little-changed weight and 10 extra horsepower—sufficient for nearly any situation. A test Avalon reached 60 mph in 8.3 seconds, and also averaged 21 mpg. The responsive automatic transmission is glassy smooth. Premium fuel is advised. Not only is the ride comfortable—close to plush, in fact—but drivers enjoy improved body control and firmer, more communicative steering. The new Avalon dashes through twisty roads with almost

2000 Toyota Avalon

sports-sedan poise—well ahead of domestic rivals. Only a couple of quibbles have come up, including a bit of body drumming over rough patches, and slightly unprogressive pedal action in routine braking. In the seriously spacious interior, 6-footers can ride in tandem, with plenty of leg-stretching room for both. Higher-set seats are matched by a raised roofline that provides fine all-around head room. Three adults fit adequately on front and back seats, though middle riders must straddle a hump and may lack foot room. Rear entry/exit is easy enough, and all seats are comfortably supportive. Though not as long as the old Avalon's trunk, the new one is taller with plenty of space. Climate and audio controls couldn't be better, but the steering-wheel rim can obscure the tops of gauges without some juggling of seat and wheel. Abundant space is provided for small-item stowage, including a massive glovebox. Visibility is good despite hard-to-see rear body corners, and mirrors are usefully large.

VALUE Spacious and posh, quiet and smooth-riding, the Avalon delivers Lexus-like attributes at a family-oriented price. Approaching the near-luxury league in features, comfort, and functional roadability, it could be the best full-size sedan on the market.

SPECIFICATIONS

	4-door sedan
Wheelbase, in.	107.1
Overall length, in.	191.9
Overall width, in.	71.7
Overall height, in.	57.7
Curb weight, lbs.	3330
Cargo volume, cu. ft.	15.9
Fuel capacity, gals.	18.5
Seating capacity	6
Front head room, in.	38.7
Max. front leg room, in.	41.7
Rear head room, in.	37.9
Min. rear leg room, in.	40.1

Powertrain layout: transverse front-engine/front-wheel drive

ENGINES

	dohc V6
Size, liters/cu. in.	3.0/181
Horsepower	210
Torque (lbs./ft.)	220

EPA city/highway mpg
4-speed OD automatic	21/29

City/highway mpg (as tested)
4-speed OD automatic	21.0

Built in USA

RETAIL PRICES

	GOOD	AVERAGE	POOR
2000 Avalon XL	$20,000-21,000	$19,000-20,000	$15,500-16,500
2000 Avalon XLS	22,000-23,500	20,800-22,000	16,800-17,800
2001 Avalon XL	22,500-24,000	21,300-22,500	—
2001 Avalon XLS	25,000-27,000	23,500-25,500	—

AVERAGE REPLACEMENT COSTS

A/C Compressor	$655	Constant Velocity Joints	950
A/C Compressor	510	Exhaust System	475
Automatic Transmission or Transaxle	1,330	Radiator	410
		Shocks and/or Struts	900
Brakes	450	Timing Chain or Belt	340

TROUBLE SPOTS

• **Sunroof/moonroof.** The moon roof may make noise because the silencer pads come loose and get wedged in the slider assembly. A revised pad was being installed under warranty. (2000)

• **Water leak.** Water leaks at the A-pillar (between windshield and front door) require sealing in the upper corner joint area. (2000)

RECALL HISTORY

2000: On certain cars, due to improper heat treatment, rear axle may not have adequate strength in some areas; shafts could fail or break after extended use. **2001:** Front sub frame assembly on small number of vehicles was not adequately welded and could fail.

1992-96 TOYOTA CAMRY

1992 Toyota Camry SE 4-door sedan

FOR Antilock brakes (optional) • Acceleration (V6) • Ride • Quietness • Passenger and cargo room

AGAINST Fuel economy (V6) • Rear-seat comfort

EVALUATION The 4-cylinder engine is smooth and responsive, giving the Camry sedan adequate acceleration and passing power, even with the automatic transmission. We averaged 10.9 seconds to 60 mph in our test and nearly 23 mpg. The V6 is much quicker, but uses more fuel (we averaged about 18 mpg in our test). However, the V6 is perhaps the most polished engine in this class and works in concert with a highly refined automatic to deliver virtually vibration-free performance. Camrys feature a soft, absorbent ride that soaks up most bumps and ruts quite easily. It also corners with good stability and has good traction on wet roads. While the Camry's 103.1-inch wheelbase put it in the compact class, it has more interior room than many mid-size models. Note, however, that the rear seatbacks tend to be stiff and too reclined, making them uncomfortable for some people. The trunk lid opens at bumper level to a wide, flat floor that reaches well forward. Split rear seatbacks fold down to add cargo space.

VALUE There's a lot of the Lexus ES 300 in the Camry, which we believe set the standard for refinement among midsize and compact family cars. It's smoother, quieter, and built with higher levels of quality than some luxury sedans costing thousands more. New Camrys generally sold for more than its compact rivals, so expect preowned models to also be priced a bit more, given Toyota's generally high resale value and strong reputation for reliability.

SPECIFICATIONS

	2-door coupe	4-door sedan	4-door wagon
Wheelbase, in.	103.1	103.1	103.1
Overall length, in.	187.8	187.8	189.4
Overall width, in.	69.7	69.7	69.7
Overall height, in.	54.9	55.1	56.3
Curb weight, lbs.	2910	2932	3263
Cargo volume, cu. ft.	14.9	14.9	74.8
Fuel capacity, gals.	18.5	18.5	18.5
Seating capacity	5	5	7
Front head room, in.	38.4	38.4	39.2
Max. front leg room, in.	43.5	43.5	43.5
Rear head room, in.	37.4	37.1	38.8
Min. rear leg room, in.	33.0	35.0	35.2

Powertrain layout: transverse front-engine/front-wheel drive

ENGINES

	dohc I4	dohc I4	dohc V6	dohc V6
Size, liters/cu. in.	2.2/132	2.2/132	3.0/180	3.0/180
Horsepower	130	125	185	188
Torque (lbs./ft.)	145	145	195	203
EPA city/highway mpg				
5-speed OD manual	22/30	23/31	18/24	
4-speed OD automatic	21/28	21/27	18/24	20/29

City/highway mpg (as tested)	dohc I4	dohc I4	dohc V6	dohc V6
4-speed OD automatic	22.9		18.5	17.5

Built in USA, Japan

RETAIL PRICES	GOOD	AVERAGE	POOR
1992 Camry sedan	$2,800-4,200	$2,100-3,500	$600-1,400
1992 Camry wagon	3,000-4,000	2,300-3,200	700-1,200
1993 Camry sedan	3,500-5,200	2,800-4,500	1,000-2,000
1993 Camry wagon	3,800-4,700	3,000-3,900	1,100-1,600
1994 Camry coupe, sedan	4,200-6,500	3,400-5,700	1,400-2,700
1994 Camry wagon	4,500-5,800	3,700-5,000	1,600-2,300
1995 Camry coupe, sedan	5,000-8,000	4,200-7,100	1,900-3,600
1995 Camry wagon	5,600-7,000	4,800-6,100	2,300-3,000
1996 Camry coupe, sedan	6,000-9,200	5,100-8,200	2,500-4,500
1996 Camry wagon	7,000-8,500	6,000-7,500	3,100-4,000

AVERAGE REPLACEMENT COSTS

A/C Compressor	$865	Clutch, Pressure Plate, Bearing	600
Alternator	375	Constant Velocity Joints	500
Automatic Transmission or Transaxle	1,067	Exhaust System	550
Brakes	145	Radiator	580
Shocks and/or Struts	800	Timing Chain or Belt	220

TROUBLE SPOTS

• **Air conditioner.** A problem with the expansion valve causes the air conditioner to gradually lose efficiency. (1992-93)

• **Automatic transmission.** A-40 series automatic transmissions may shift harshly because rubber check balls become smaller, blow through the plate, and get dislodged. (1992-96)

• **Suspension noise.** Front and rear sway bar bushings were redesigned using a self-lubricating material. (1992-95)

• **Hard starting.** Hard starting after cold soak is due to ignition coil voltage leaking to an inappropriate ground. (All)

• **Coolant leak.** Head gasket failures on 3.0-liter engines allows coolant to get into the cylinders. (All)

• **Trunk latch.** If the trunk won't stay open on sedans with a spoiler, the support torsion rod must be adjusted. (1992-96)

• **Water leak.** Water leaks on the passenger side come from two sources: the SRS wiring harness grommet and the fresh air intake plenum. (1992-93)

RECALL HISTORY

1994-96: Insufficiently tightened steering-wheel nut may cause steering vibration and looseness; nut could eventually come off, leading to separation from shaft. **1996:** On some cars, when taillight bulb is lit, its holder can deform.

1997-01 TOYOTA CAMRY/SOLARA

1998 Toyota Camry LE

FOR Acceleration (V6) • Ride • Quietness • Build quality

AGAINST Rear visibility • Steering feel

EVALUATION All models have less wind and road noise than average. Suspensions readily iron out the rough stuff, while providing a stable and comfortable highway ride. Cornering is marked by moderate body lean, with good grip and safe front-drive responses. Steering is quick and centers well after turns, but effort is too low and road feel is too numb for the best control. In addition, even the more firmly suspended Solara coupe tends to "float" over uneven surfaces. Smooth and quiet for a 4-cylinder, Camry's base engine provides adequate acceleration even with an automatic transmission. The V6 is far more impressive—smoother and quieter yet, yielding good pickup from low speeds as well as swift passing/merging action. An LE sedan with the V6 averaged a passable 20.4 mpg in hard city/freeway driving. A 4-cylinder model returned 22.5 mpg, despite more urban driving. Brakes work beautifully, capable of short, arrow-straight panic stops with little nosedive. Backseat space is greater than in the prior generation, but four adults will be more comfortable than five. Like most midsize cars, Camry does not have quite enough rear cabin width to permit uncrowded three-abreast travel. Head and leg room are ample, however, in both front and rear. Entry/exit isn't a problem, either, except into the backseat of the Solara coupe, due to low, narrow rear passageways and lack of a slide-forward driver's seat. Camry cargo space is competitive, and all models have a handy split-folding rear seatback. Solara's trunk opening is high, and space is not all that large. Dashboards are typical Toyota, conveniently organized and attractively styled. Most instruments and controls are easy to see and reach. One exception involves the climate panel, which is too low in the center for the easiest operation while driving.

VALUE Tight, careful assembly quality helps make the Camry a top-notch value, and a top choice in a midsize family sedan.

SPECIFICATIONS

	2-door conv.	2-door coupe	4-door sedan
Wheelbase, in.	105.1	105.2	105.2
Overall length, in.	190.0	190.0	188.5
Overall width, in.	71.1	71.1	70.1
Overall height, in.	55.5	55.1	55.4
Curb weight, lbs.	3437	3120	2998
Cargo volume, cu. ft.	8.8	13.8	14.1
Fuel capacity, gals.	18.5	18.5	18.5
Seating capacity	4	5	5
Front head room, in.	38.8	38.3	38.6
Max. front leg room, in.	43.3	43.3	43.5
Rear head room, in.	37.7	36.2	37.6
Min. rear leg room, in.	35.3	35.2	35.5

Powertrain layout: transverse front-engine/front-wheel drive

ENGINES

	dohc I4	dohc V6
Size, liters/cu. in.	2.2/132	3.0/183
Horsepower	133-138	194-200
Torque (lbs./ft.)	147	209-214
EPA city/highway mpg		
5-speed OD manual	23/31	20/28
4-speed OD automatic	23/30	19/26
City/highway mpg (as tested)		
4-speed OD automatic	22.5	20.4

Built in USA, Japan

RETAIL PRICES

	GOOD	AVERAGE	POOR
1997 Camry CE, LE	$8,000-9,500	$7,100-8,500	$4,000-4,800
1997 Camry XLE	10,000-11,500	9,000-10,500	5,200-6,000
1998 Camry CE, LE	9,500-11,000	8,500-10,000	4,800-5,600
1998 Camry XLE	11,500-12,800	10,500-11,800	6,200-7,000
1999 Camry CE, LE	11,000-13,000	10,000-11,800	5,900-7,000
1999 Camry XLE	13,000-14,500	11,800-13,200	7,500-8,000
1999 Camry Solara coupe	12,000-13,500	11,000-12,500	6,800-7,500
1999 Solara SLE coupe	14,500-16,500	13,200-14,500	8,900-9,700
2000 Camry CE, LE	12,500-14,500	11,500-13,200	7,300-8,000
2000 Camry XLE	14,500-16,000	13,200-14,500	8,900-9,700
2000 Camry Solara coupe	13,500-15,000	12,300-13,800	7,900-8,500
2000 Solara SLE coupe	16,500-18,000	15,000-16,500	10,000-11,000
2000 Camry Solara conv.	17,000-19,000	15,500-17,500	10,500-11,500
2000 Solara SLE conv.	21,000-23,000	19,500-21,500	13,500-15,000
2001 Camry CE, LE	14,000-16,500	12,700-15,000	—
2001 Camry XLE	16,500-18,500	15,000-17,000	—
2001 Camry Solara coupe	15,000-17,000	13,700-15,500	—
2001 Solara SLE coupe	19,000-21,000	17,500-19,500	—
2001 Camry Solara conv.	20,000-22,000	18,500-20,500	—
2001 Solara SLE conv.	24,000-26,000	22,500-24,500	—

AVERAGE REPLACEMENT COSTS

A/C Compressor	$890	Clutch, Pressure Plate,	
Alternator	380	Bearing	600
Automatic Transmission or		Constant Velocity Joints	510
Transaxle	1,105	Exhaust System	570
Brakes	160	Radiator	585
Shocks and/or Struts	840	Timing Chain or Belt	260

TROUBLE SPOTS

- **Suspension noise.** Noises from the front end when driving over dips in the road are a result of defective upper strut tower cushions. (1997-98)
- **Brake noise.** Original equipment brake pads are noisy causing groaning, grinding, squeaking, and vibration. A revised lining is available. (1997-98)
- **Audio system.** The CD player may not accept or eject CDs. (1997)
- **Power seats.** The front power seats may chatter requiring replacement of the seat adjuster assembly (1997-98) or manually operated seat cushion on driver's side moves. (1997)
- **Doors.** The fuel door does not open when the release is pulled due to weak spring. (1997-98)
- **Sunroof/moonroof.** The moonroof may rattle when it is opened about four inches, or the glass panel may get skewed and will not retract. (1997)

RECALL HISTORY

1997: Ignition key can be removed even when gearshift lever is not in "Park" position. **1997 in 19 states:** In extreme cold for an extended period, accumulated moisture can temporarily freeze in brake vacuum hose, resulting in elimination of power-brake assist. **1997:** Accumulated moisture can temporarily freeze in brake vacuum hose. **1997-98:** Insufficiently tightened steering-wheel nut may cause steering vibration and looseness; nut could eventually come off, leading to separation from shaft. **1998:** Some wheel lug nuts are defective, causing loss of torque, fatigue fracture of wheel, and possible loss of wheel. **1998:** Audiovox Securikey+ Security System can malfunction causing electrical failure; can cause engine to run poorly and stall, and electrical components can intermittently fail. **1998-2000 Camry made in KY:** Accelerator cable housing could be deformed at the cruise control actuator-to-throttle body connection. The accelerator inner-cable could wear away and eventually break, increasing the risk of a crash. **2000:** Due to improper heat treatment, certain rear axle shafts could fail or break after extended use. **2001 Camry:** Front subframe assembly was not adequately welded. This condition could cause failure of the assembly, increasing the risk of a crash.

1994-99 TOYOTA CELICA

1995 Toyota Celica 2-door convertible

FOR Optional antilock brakes • Acceleration (GT) • Steering/handling • Instruments/controls • Fuel economy

AGAINST Engine noise • Rear-seat room • Cargo room (exc. hatchback)

EVALUATION Handling is where Toyota's Celica excels: crisp, responsive, with fine grip in corners and minimal body lean. You get a surprisingly supple ride, too, even in a GT with the stiffly sprung Sports Package option. Sure, it's stiffer and choppier than other Celicas, but you get a little extra cornering precision with that Sport option. Braking is good, too, though it would be better if more models had antilocking. The 1.8-liter dual-cam 4-cylinder engine in an ST is smooth and lively with 5-speed manual shift, and economical, too. Optional 4-speed automatic saps its strength, because the engine lacks low-speed torque. The GT's 2.2-liter engine feels a lot stronger at all speeds, but makes plenty of noise doing it, roaring and throbbing in hard driving. As for economy, a GT hatchback with manual shift averaged 25.7 mpg. Tires aren't quiet, either—in any Celica. This is a typical 2+2 layout, with little rear space for adults, and six-footers face marginal head clearance if a Celica coupe is sunroof-equipped. Controls and gauges are well laid out on a modern-styled, convenient dashboard. Trunk space is passable in notchback models, but the hatchback offers more cargo volume. The convertible's top is power-operated, but blocks the rear view substantially and robs rear-seat room and cargo space.

VALUE Even though the price may be high, if you want two-passenger fun and reliability, a Celica is worth the extra bucks—partly due to Toyota's reputation for quality.

SPECIFICATIONS

	2-door conv.	2-door coupe	2-door hatchback
Wheelbase, in.	99.9	99.9	99.9
Overall length, in.	177.0	177.0	174.0
Overall width, in.	68.9	68.9	68.9
Overall height, in.	51.6	51.0	50.8
Curb weight, lbs.	2755	2395	2415
Cargo volume, cu. ft.	6.8	10.6	16.2
Fuel capacity, gals.	15.9	15.9	15.9
Seating capacity	4	4	4
Front head room, in.	38.7	34.3	34.3
Max. front leg room, in.	44.2	44.2	44.2
Rear head room, in.	34.1	29.2	29.2
Min. rear leg room, in.	18.9	26.6	26.6

Powertrain layout: transverse front-engine/front-wheel drive

ENGINES

	dohc I4	dohc I4
Size, liters/cu. in.	1.8/208	2.2/132
Horsepower	105-110	130-135
Torque (lbs./ft.)	115-117	145
EPA city/highway mpg		
5-speed OD manual	29/34	22/29
4-speed OD automatic	27/34	22/29
City/highway mpg (as tested)		
5-speed OD manual		25.7
4-speed OD automatic		17.6

Built in Japan

RETAIL PRICES

	GOOD	AVERAGE	POOR
1994 Celica	$3,800-5,300	$3,100-4,600	$1,100-1,800
1995 Celica	5,000-6,700	4,300-5,900	1,800-2,500
1995 Convertible	8,000-9,000	7,000-8,000	3,700-4,200
1996 Celica	6,500-8,000	5,800-7,200	2,900-3,700
1996 Convertible	9,500-10,700	8,500-9,700	4,600-5,300
1997 Celica	8,000-10,000	7,200-9,100	4,000-5,000
1997 Convertible	11,000-12,500	10,000-11,300	5,900-6,600
1998 Celica	10,500-12,000	9,500-11,000	5,500-6,300
1998 Convertible	12,500-14,000	11,000-12,800	6,800-7,700
1999 Celica	12,000-13,500	10,800-12,200	6,600-7,300
1999 Convertible	14,500-16,000	13,000-14,500	8,600-9,500

AVERAGE REPLACEMENT COSTS

A/C Compressor	$880	Clutch, Pressure Plate, Bearing	425
Alternator	340	Constant Velocity Joints	1,080
Automatic Transmission or Transaxle	710	Exhaust System	250
Brakes	210	Radiator	520
Shocks and/or Struts	970	Timing Chain or Belt	140

TROUBLE SPOTS

• **Automatic transmission.** Automatic transmissions may shift harshly due to rubber check balls in the valve body wearing out. (1994-99)

• **Convertible top.** Due to the balance rods rubbing, the convertible top wears at the sail panel near the rear window. (1995-97)

• **Wheels.** Proper wheel alignment may not be possible unless a special steering knuckle bolt is used. (1994-96)

• **Vehicle noise.** The fuel door release cable rattles. Installing foam pads inside the fender usually quiets it. (1994)

• **Audio system.** The Fujitsu 10-CD changer has a tendency to not accept or eject CDs. (1994-97)

• **Brake noise.** The original equipment brake pads make squeaking noise. (1994-96)

• **Climate control.** The rear defroster terminals tend to break on convertibles. (1995-97)

2000-01 TOYOTA CELICA

FOR Acceleration (GT-S 6-speed) • Handling/roadholding

AGAINST Acceleration (GT w/auto.) • Noise • Passenger room • Entry/exit

EVALUATION Agile handling and grippy cornering are the big Celica bonuses, augmented by sharp, responsive steering. The penalty is

2000 Toyota Celica GT-S

engines that must rev madly to achieve top performance. That requires a heavy throttle foot with automatic, or a lot of manual shifting—a pleasant task with the short-throw gearbox. Even so, only the 6-speed GT-S comes close to being lively when pushing on the gas pedal. A GT coupe with automatic is sluggish on long upgrades, if adequate otherwise. A manual-shift GT-S averaged 24.2 mpg, but demands premium fuel. High rpm translates to plenty of noise except in gentle cruising, and the sounds aren't that pleasing. Wind rush is noticeable, and tire roar occurs on many pavements. As in most sporty cars, the ride is firm and rather "busy" on most surfaces. Braking is excellent if the Celica is equipped with ABS. Race-car-type styling and shrinking of some exterior dimensions means the Celica's cabin is short on space. Even moderately tall occupants have limited head and leg room—enough to cramp some drivers. As expected, the back seat isn't really fit for people, and entry/exit is the crouch-and-crawl process typical in sporty coupes. Drivers sit low, race-car-style, and enjoy a good forward view as well as simple, handy controls and fine shifter/wheel/pedal spacing. Over-the-shoulder visibility is cluttered, due to the roofline, and the spoiler partly blocks traffic views at the rear. Gauges are legible, but the tachometer is not in the driver's direct line of sight, and warning lights are scattered. Interior stowage and cargo space are marginal.

VALUE Though capable and fun to drive, the Celica is noisy and lacks the low-end torque for decent acceleration with an automatic transmission. An Acura Integra offers similar high-rpm responses from a smoother 4-cylinder engine. Mitsubishi's Eclipse has a V6 option. Adventurous styling and Toyota's reputation for reliability help Celica appeal to the younger crowd, but prices are high.

SPECIFICATIONS

	2-door coupe
Wheelbase, in.	102.3
Overall length, in.	170.4
Overall width, in.	68.3
Overall height, in.	51.4
Curb weight, lbs.	2425
Cargo volume, cu. ft.	16.9
Fuel capacity, gals.	14.5
Seating capacity	4
Front head room, in.	38.4
Max. front leg room, in.	33.0
Rear head room, in.	35.0
Min. rear leg room, in.	17.1

Powertrain layout: transverse front-engine/front-wheel drive

ENGINES

	dohc I4	dohc I4
Size, liters/cu. in.	1.8/109	1.8/110
Horsepower	140	180
Torque (lbs./ft.)	125	133
EPA city/highway mpg		
5-speed OD manual	31/43	
6-speed OD manual		27/42
4-speed OD automatic	31/49	28/39
City/highway mpg (as tested)		
6-speed OD manual		24.2
4-speed OD automatic	30.3	

Built in Japan

RETAIL PRICES

	GOOD	AVERAGE	POOR
2000 Celica GT	$13,500-14,500	$12,500-13,500	$9,000-10,000
2000 Celica GT-S	15,500-17,000	14,300-15,800	10,500-11,500
2001 Celica GT	15,500-17,000	14,500-15,800	—
2001 Celica GT-S	18,500-20,000	17,000-18,500	—

AVERAGE REPLACEMENT COSTS

A/C Compressor	$405	Clutch, Pressure Plate,	
Alternator	535	Bearing	395
Automatic Transmission or		Constant Velocity Joints	910
Transaxle	690	Exhaust System	200
Brakes	220	Radiator	405
Shocks and/or Struts	1,010	Timing Chain or Belt	260

TROUBLE SPOTS

• **Seatbelts/safety.** The button that prevents the retractable portion of the seatbelt from going too far comes off. New buttons are available to fix this. (2000-01)

• **Climate control.** The knob for the heater flow control may be hard to turn. A revised mechanism improves the feel. (2000)

• **Wheels.** The wheel covers on early production models clicked or squeaked and were being replaced under warranty. (2000)

1990-92 TOYOTA COROLLA

1990 Toyota Corolla LE 4-door sedan

FOR Fuel economy • Ride (except GT-S) • Acceleration (GT-S) • All-wheel drive (All-Trac)

AGAINST Engine noise • Rear-seat room

EVALUATION Acceleration is far livelier in a GT-S than in any other Corolla. But that model came only with manual shift. Neither engine is quiet, but the GT-S is especially loud. If you like high-revving engines, however, you'll love the 4-cylinder in any Corolla. It's also smooth, responsive, and offers good acceleration and passing power with manual shift. With automatic, a Corolla moves off from a standing start readily enough, but the unit quickly shifts into higher gears. After pausing a moment or two, the transmission then downshifts abruptly. With its firmer suspension, a GT-S corners tenaciously, but suffers sharply in ride comfort. All Corollas handle nicely and hold the road well, but only the GT-S model offers anything resembling sports car moves. The easier-going suspension in a sedan or wagon soaks up rough roads with impressive resiliency, but the soft suspension permits ample body lean in corners. Sedans and wagons have roomier interiors than many rivals. Even so, adults sitting on the upright rear bench will need to have the front seats moved well forward to achieve sufficient leg room. Front bucket seats don't offer much rearward travel, so taller drivers might feel cramped. Head room is good all around; rear leg space even worse in coupes. The interior is well designed, and all controls are easily within the driver's reach.

VALUE This version of the well-built subcompact offers a more refined feel, smoother ride, and stronger performance than its 1980s predecessor, plus frugal gas mileage. We've ranked it among the subcompact leaders.

SPECIFICATIONS

	2-door coupe	4-door sedan	4-door wagon
Wheelbase, in.	95.7	95.7	95.7
Overall length, in.	172.2	170.3	171.5
Overall width, in.	65.6	65.2	65.2
Overall height, in.	49.6	52.4	54.5
Curb weight, lbs.	2414	2390	2436
Cargo volume, cu. ft.	11.7	12.7	64.5
Fuel capacity, gals.	13.2	13.2	13.2
Seating capacity	4	5	5
Front head room, in.	37.9	38.4	39.6
Max. front leg room, in.	42.9	40.9	40.9
Rear head room, in.	35.5	36.4	39.3

	2-door coupe	4-door sedan	4-door wagon
Min. rear leg room, in.	25.8	31.6	31.6

Powertrain layout: transverse front-engine/front- or all-wheel drive

ENGINES

	dohc I6	dohc I4
Size, liters/cu. in.	1.6/97	1.6/97
Horsepower	102	130
Torque (lbs./ft.)	101	105

EPA city/highway mpg

5-speed OD manual	28/33	25/31
3-speed automatic	26/29	
4-speed OD automatic	26/33	

City/highway mpg (as tested)

4-speed OD automatic	29.2

Built in Japan, Canada, USA

RETAIL PRICES

	GOOD	AVERAGE	POOR
1990 Corolla	$1,300-2,000	$700-1,400	$100-300
1990 Corolla GT-S	2,000-2,700	1,400-2,000	200-500
1991 Corolla	1,600-2,300	1,000-1,700	100-400
1991 Corolla GT-S	2,500-3,300	1,800-2,600	400-700
1992 Corolla	2,000-2,800	1,400-2,100	200-600

AVERAGE REPLACEMENT COSTS

A/C Compressor	$405	Clutch, Pressure Plate,	
Alternator	535	Bearing	395
Automatic Transmission or		Constant Velocity Joints	910
Transaxle	690	Exhaust System	200
Brakes	220	Radiator	405
Shocks and/or Struts	1,000	Timing Chain or Belt	160

TROUBLE SPOTS

• **Automatic transmission.** Poor first-to-second shift quality can be corrected with a redesigned clutch disc. (1990-92)

• **Sunroof/moonroof.** The vinyl headliner separates from the foam backing. (1992)

• **Windshield washer.** The windshield washer bottle tends to crack or break. (1990-92)

• **Audio system.** The wires for the front speakers get pinched by the glove box and the speakers quit. (1990-92) The cassette player may quit working in the fast forward, reverse, or play positions. (1992)

1993-97 TOYOTA COROLLA

1995 Toyota Corolla 4-door sedan

FOR Antilock brakes (optional) • Fuel economy • Ride

AGAINST Rear-seat room • Acceleration (automatic transmission)

EVALUATION The 1.8-liter gives the Corolla DX and LE (pre-1996) models quicker acceleration and stronger passing power than the base sedan's 1.6-liter unit. We timed a Corolla with the 1.8-liter at 10.9 seconds to 60 mph, which is slower than a Honda Civic, but quicker than most other rivals. Though the automatic transmission generally works well with the 1.8-liter engine, it's slow to downshift for passing, unless you floor the throttle. The optional 3-speed automatic provided with the 1.6-liter engine is not only slow to downshift, it can be harsh at times. However, fuel economy is good with either engine—generally averaging about 30 mpg. Corolla's suspension provides a stable highway ride and absorbs bumps better than some larger cars. Corolla is quieter than the similar Geo Prizm because Toyota includes more sound insulation in its cars. The car is roomier than most rivals, yet the rear seat is a tight fit for two adults, and more appropriate for children. Cargo space is adequate and can be expanded on DX models, thanks to the split-folding rear seatback.

VALUE Corollas generally sold for more than comparable subcompact rivals, so expect preowned models to also be priced a bit more, given Toyota's generally high resale value and strong reputation for reliability.

SPECIFICATIONS

	4-door sedan	4-door wagon
Wheelbase, in.	97.0	97.0
Overall length, in.	172.0	172.0
Overall width, in.	66.3	66.3
Overall height, in.	54.3	56.1
Curb weight, lbs.	2315	2403
Cargo volume, cu. ft.	12.7	64.8
Fuel capacity, gals.	13.2	13.2
Seating capacity	5	5
Front head room, in.	38.8	38.8
Max. front leg room, in.	42.4	42.4
Rear head room, in.	37.1	39.7
Min. rear leg room, in.	33.0	33.0

Powertrain layout: transverse front-engine/front-wheel drive

ENGINES

	dohc I4	dohc I4	dohc I4	dohc I4
Size, liters/cu. in.	1.6/97	1.6/97	1.8/110	1.8/110
Horsepower	100	105	105	115
Torque (lbs./ft.)	105	105	117	115
EPA city/highway mpg				
5-speed OD manual	31/35	27/34	29/34	27/33
3-speed automatic	26/30	26/29		
4-speed OD automatic			27/34	26/33
City/highway mpg (as tested)				
3-speed automatic	26.4			
4-speed OD automatic			30.1	30.5

Built in USA, Canada, Japan

RETAIL PRICES

	GOOD	AVERAGE	POOR
1993 Corolla	$2,400-3,500	$1,800-2,800	$500-900
1994 Corolla	3,000-4,000	2,300-3,300	700-1,200
1995 Corolla	3,700-4,900	3,000-4,200	1,000-1,700
1996 Corolla	4,500-5,700	3,800-4,900	1,600-2,200
1997 Corolla	5,500-6,500	4,800-5,700	2,400-3,000

AVERAGE REPLACEMENT COSTS

A/C Compressor	$925	Clutch, Pressure Plate, Bearing	515
Alternator	415	Constant Velocity Joints	805
Automatic Transmission or Transaxle	1,025	Exhaust System	550
Brakes	200	Radiator	440
Shocks and/or Struts	550	Timing Chain or Belt	155

TROUBLE SPOTS

• **Automatic transmission.** A-40 series automatic transmissions may eventually shift harshly because rubber check balls become smaller, blow through the plate, and get dislodged. (1993-96)

• **Water pump.** Water pumps leak due to a defective seal. (1993-94)

• **Windshield washer.** Windshield washer bottles frequently break. (1993-95)

RECALL HISTORY

1993-94: Snow or water can penetrate carpet and result in short and possible fire. **1993-95:** If liquid is spilled in console box area, airbag warning light can illuminate during normal driving conditions and cause airbag to malfunction, deploying inadvertently. **1994:** Anchor straps in certain seatbelt assemblies were improperly heat treated and can break. **1995:** Battery may have defective weld inside positive or negative terminal, which can result in a no-start condition or explosion. **1997:** If airbag computer experiences mechanical shock within very short time after engine is started, airbag can deploy inadvertently.

1998-01 TOYOTA COROLLA

FOR Fuel economy • Maneuverability

AGAINST Rear-seat room

1998 Toyota Corolla LE

EVALUATION Although the new car feels stronger at higher engine speeds, automatic-transmission models feel somewhat sluggish at first, failing to deliver a sharp jump off the line from a standstill. Acceleration, in fact, ranks about average for a subcompact. In addition, turning on the air conditioner deadens performance noticeably. The 4-speed automatic transmission provides smooth, timely upshifts and prompt downshifts for passing, but seems to cut engine power slightly during gear changes. Corolla suspensions are tuned to provide a comfortable ride, rather than sporty handling. Bumps are absorbed nicely, with good straight-line stability, but high-speed turns produce excessive body roll. This drawback is especially noticeable in the 1998 VE and CE, which lacked the LE model's front stabilizer bar. The front stabilizer went into all 1999 models, but body roll remains apparent—though the car is agile and predictable. All told, the ride is even quieter than before, with only moderate wind and road noise at highway speeds. Yes, the engine thrashes when worked hard, but it settles down nicely at cruising speeds. Braking with the optional ABS is swift and undramatic—just as it should be. Like previous Corollas, this latest version is short on backseat space, and not exactly bountiful up front, either. With average-sized folks seated up front, medium-sized adults can squeeze into the rear seats. Knee room will be snug, however. If front seats are moved more than halfway back, rear leg room becomes extremely tight. On the plus side, back doors are wide enough at the bottom so average-sized people slip easily through the openings. A low cowl and beltline help to give the driver a commanding position. Reaching the radio and climate controls is a bit of a stretch, but all are simple to use and clearly marked. Though useful in size, the trunk has hinges that dip down into the load space when the lid is closed.

VALUE Ranked as a Best Buy for new-car shoppers, Corolla is also appealing secondhand—but prices aren't the lowest by any means in the subcompact league.

SPECIFICATIONS

	4-door sedan
Wheelbase, in.	97.0
Overall length, in.	174.0
Overall width, in.	66.7
Overall height, in.	54.5
Curb weight, lbs.	2414
Cargo volume, cu. ft.	12.1
Fuel capacity, gals.	13.2
Seating capacity	5
Front head room, in.	39.3
Max. front leg room, in.	42.5
Rear head room, in.	36.9
Min. rear leg room, in.	33.2

Powertrain layout: transverse front-engine/front-wheel drive

ENGINES

	dohc I4
Size, liters/cu. in.	1.8/110
Horsepower	120-125
Torque (lbs./ft.)	122-126
EPA city/highway mpg	
5-speed OD manual	28/33
3-speed automatic	31/38
4-speed OD automatic	28/36
City/highway mpg (as tested)	
5-speed OD manual	27.5
4-speed OD automatic	30.1

Built in USA, Canada

RETAIL PRICES

	GOOD	AVERAGE	POOR
1998 Corolla VE	$7,000-7,800	$6,300-7,000	$3,200-3,600
1998 Corolla CE, LE	7,500-8,400	6,800-7,600	3,600-4,100

	GOOD	AVERAGE	POOR
1999 Corolla VE	$8,000-9,000	$7,200-8,100	$4,000-4,600
1999 Corolla CE, LE	8,500-9,500	7,700-8,600	4,400-5,000
2000 Corolla VE	9,000-10,000	8,100-9,000	4,700-5,300
2000 Corolla CE, LE	9,500-10,500	8,600-9,500	5,000-5,600
2001 Corolla CE, S	10,500-11,500	9,500-10,500	—
2001 Corolla LE	11,200-12,200	10,000-11,000	—

AVERAGE REPLACEMENT COSTS

A/C Compressor	$620	Clutch, Pressure Plate, Bearing	560
Alternator	490	Constant Velocity Joints	1,400
Automatic Transmission or Transaxle	785	Exhaust System	610
Brakes	440	Radiator	670
Shocks and/or Struts	1,080	Timing Chain or Belt	455

TROUBLE SPOTS

• **Airbags.** On cars with side impact protection, the company advises that replacement seat covers (leather or cloth) not be installed or the side airbags may not work properly. (1998)

• **Cruise control.** Some models may not shift into overdrive when the cruise control is on. A new cruise control computer is available. (1998)

• **Doors.** The dome light may not work when switched to "On," requiring replacement of the dome light assembly. (1998)

• **Water leak.** The rear quarter windows leak and a new molding strip will be installed under the normal warranty. (1998)

RECALL HISTORY

1998-99: Some lug nuts on cars distributed by Gulf States Toyota, Inc. are defective, causing loss of torque, fatigue fracture of wheel, and possible loss of wheel.

1990-97 TOYOTA LAND CRUISER

1992 Toyota Land Cruiser

FOR 4WD traction • Passenger and cargo room • Antilock brakes (later models)

AGAINST Fuel economy • Acceleration (4.0-liter) • Ride • Entry/exit • Price

EVALUATION Steering was vague and over-assisted in the early version, and the ride gets choppy, even on roads that look smooth. The 1991-97 version has a slightly wider stance, so it's a little less tipsy in corners. Still, don't expect to rush through fast curves or tight low-speed turns without plenty of body lean. Acceleration from early models is nothing to shout about, either: on the order of 15.4 seconds to reach 60 mph. The 4.5-liter engine gets its job done, bringing enough power and torque to move this big rig rather smartly. Heavy weight helps make fuel consumption horrid. An early Land Cruiser got only 10.5 mpg; another with the 4.0-liter engine managed just 13 mpg. The permanently engaged 4-wheel-drive system installed in 1991 is a bonus, giving the driver the advantage of 4WD but no duties to perform. Passenger space is ample all around. Seats are comfortable for long trips, and the cargo area is bountiful. A Land Cruiser stands tall, so step-up into the interior is high. Reaching the optional third seat is awkward because you have to clamber around the middle bench. It's kid-size, too, and leaves little cargo space at the rear. However, both the second and third seats pack up easily to expand cargo volume. Some controls in the pre-1991 model have a haphazard look, but full instrumentation was

standard. The interior got a lot more modern in 1991, with instruments and controls handier and better organized. Overall, the interior has a sturdy, high-grade look, and body construction is tight and solid.

VALUE Expensive and sold in modest numbers, Land Cruisers continue to attract a modest but eager following. Still, most buyers find a Ford Explorer or Jeep Cherokee to be a better value.

SPECIFICATIONS

	4-door wagon	4-door wagon
Wheelbase, in.	107.5[1]	112.2
Overall length, in.	184.0	189.8
Overall width, in.	70.9	76.0
Overall height, in.	68.9	73.2
Curb weight, lbs.	4480	4834
Cargo volume, cu. ft.	98.0	90.9
Fuel capacity, gals.	23.8	25.1
Seating capacity	5	8
Front head room, in.	40.0	40.3
Max. front leg room, in.	39.2	42.2
Rear head room, in.	40.4	40.0
Min. rear leg room, in.	34.6	33.6

1. 1990 model only.

Powertrain layout: longitudinal front-engine/4-wheel drive

ENGINES

	ohv I6	dohc I6
Size, liters/cu. in.	4.0/241	4.5/275
Horsepower	155	212
Torque (lbs./ft.)	220	275
EPA city/highway mpg		
4-speed OD automatic	12/14	13/15
City/highway mpg (as tested)		
4-speed OD automatic	13.0	12.6

Built in Japan

RETAIL PRICES

	GOOD	AVERAGE	POOR
1990 Land Cruiser	$6,200-7,200	$5,400-6,200	$2,600-3,100
1991 Land Cruiser	7,500-8,500	6,500-7,500	3,400-4,000
1992 Land Cruiser	9,000-10,000	8,000-9,000	4,400-5,000
1993 Land Cruiser	10,500-11,800	9,500-10,500	5,500-6,200
1994 Land Cruiser	12,500-14,000	11,500-12,700	7,400-8,100
1995 Land Cruiser	14,500-16,000	13,200-14,500	8,900-9,600
1996 Land Cruiser	17,500-19,500	16,000-18,000	10,800-12,000
1997 Land Cruiser	21,500-23,500	20,000-22,000	14,000-15,200

AVERAGE REPLACEMENT COSTS

A/C Compressor	$1,055	Clutch, Pressure Plate, Bearing	520
Alternator	375	Exhaust System	330
Automatic Transmission or Transaxle	1,010	Radiator	435
Brakes	230	Shocks and/or Struts	510
Timing Chain or Belt	885	Universal Joints	520

TROUBLE SPOTS

• **Automatic transmission.** Automatic transmissions have delayed engagement in reverse. (1990-96)

• **Audio system.** Static in the radio is caused by poor antenna ground. (1990-96)

• **Radiator.** The thermostat gasket had a tendency to leak in cold weather. (1990-95)

• **Vehicle noise.** The transfer case lever rattles and vibrates, and is corrected by installing a new boot and hardware. (1990-94)

RECALL HISTORY

1990: Heavy loads and high temperatures can create high pressure in fuel tank, resulting in cracks and leakage.

1998-01 TOYOTA LAND CRUISER

FOR Passenger room • Cargo room • Ride • Quietness • Build quality

AGAINST Fuel economy • Entry/exit

EVALUATION Though less "trucky" than in the past, both the Land Cruiser and the LX 470 are not really carlike, either. Even so, they're the most refined big SUVs to be found, more powerful than before and

1999 Toyota Land Cruiser

boasting additional sound insulation. Despite the Land Cruiser's still-hefty curb weight, its V8 engine is muscular enough to deliver brisk acceleration, helped by prompt, smooth shifts from the automatic transmission. A test model accelerated to 60 mph in a surprisingly swift 9 seconds. Wind and road noise in a Land Cruiser can be noticeable—mainly because the V8 is so well muted—whereas the LX 470 is quieter, in keeping with its luxury mission. We averaged 12.3 mpg in an early Land Cruiser, using the recommended premium fuel. A later edition returned 13.6 mpg. Ride comfort and control are good, both on-road and off. Though high-built, this wagon does not feel ponderous around town. It also handles confidently except in fast corners, where marked (though predictable) body lean is the rule, coupled with a slight tipsy sensation. Four-wheel-drive helps keeps the grip secure, while the Land Cruiser's independent front suspension yields a surprisingly absorbent ride. Helped by standard antilocking "panic" braking, distance and control are excellent for a vehicle of this type and weight. Head room and rear leg room are good, in contrast to prior models. There's also enough cabin width for three grownups in the middle bench seat. The available third-row seat is cramped and inaccessible for all but a preteen couple. Middle-row entry/exit isn't easy either, thanks to a tall step-up and narrow door bottoms. On the other hand, that high stance gives a commanding view of the road, though headrests impair vision out back. The user-friendly dashboard has simple new rotary climate controls, though a few other switches aren't so easy to see. Space behind the third seat is sufficient for grocery bags but not much more. That seat folds or removes fairly easily for generous maximum cargo room.

VALUE Though less expensive than its Lexus mate, Land Cruiser is not cheap and has less space than some less-costly rivals. Nevertheless, it's highly capable off-road, and as fast and comfortable as any competitor on-the-road. Built better than most, Land Cruiser delivers.

SPECIFICATIONS

	4-door wagon
Wheelbase, in.	112.2
Overall length, in.	192.5
Overall width, in.	76.4
Overall height, in.	73.2
Curb weight, lbs.	5115
Cargo volume, cu. ft.	97.5
Fuel capacity, gals	25.4
Seating capacity	5/8
Front head room, in.	40.6
Max. front leg room, in.	42.3
Rear head room, in.	39.8
Min. rear leg room, in.	34.3

Powertrain layout: longitudinal front-engine/all-wheel drive

ENGINES

	dohc V8
Size, liters/cu. in.	4.7/285
Horsepower	230
Torque (lbs./ft.)	320

EPA city/highway mpg

4-speed OD automatic	13/16

City/highway mpg (as tested)

4-speed OD automatic	12.0

Built in Japan

RETAIL PRICES

	GOOD	AVERAGE	POOR
1998 Land Cruiser	$30,000-32,500	$28,000-30,000	$21,500-23,000
1999 Land Cruiser	34,000-36,500	32,000-34,000	24,500-26,000
2000 Land Cruiser	38,000-41,000	36,000-38,500	28,000-29,500
2001 Land Cruiser	42,000-45,000	40,000-42,500	—

AVERAGE REPLACEMENT COSTS

A/C Compressor	$1,075	Clutch, Pressure Plate, Bearing	620
Alternator	390	Constant Velocity Joints	625
Automatic Transmission or Transaxle	1,100	Exhaust System	540
Brakes	395	Radiator	455
Shocks and/or Struts	605	Timing Chain or Belt	550

TROUBLE SPOTS

- **Vehicle noise.** Numerous squeaks and rattles from the glove box and center console. (1998)
- **Brake noise.** Rear brake squeaks are corrected with revised brake pads. (1998-99)
- **Air conditioner.** The air conditioner expansion valve makes a buzzing noise. The valve and an attached tube must be replaced to remedy the problem. (1998-99)
- **Hard starting.** The engine may fail to start if: the engine immobilizer system key's ring is over the top of the key; a Mobil-type transponder is on the key ring; or if another immobilizer key is on the same key ring. (1998-01)
- **Transmission noise.** The transmission makes a chattering noise when shifting from reverse to neutral or park. An additional check ball installed in the valve body will fix the problem. (1998)

1996-00 TOYOTA RAV4

1998 Toyota RAV4 4-door wagon

FOR Visibility • Maneuverability

AGAINST Noise • Rear-seat room

EVALUATION The RAV4 delivers a softer, more compliant ride as well as more responsive steering than truck-based SUVs. Unlike the Sidekick/Tracker, which often feels ready to lean over, the RAV4 feels stable and carlike while cornering swiftly, and robust when traversing rough roads. Its permanent 4-wheel-drive system is more convenient than the on-demand systems used by the early competition. Still, you can expect some choppiness on scalloped freeways and over patchy pavement, especially with the shorter-length 2-door model. Tire roar is always noticeable, and wind rush rises sharply as speed increases. The engine becomes quite boomy when worked hard, too. RAV4 also lags behind most small cars in terms of performance. A manual-shift 4WD 2-door accelerated to 60 mph in 10.5 seconds, but an automatic 4-door needed about 13 seconds—and that was without a load. We've averaged a disappointing 20.8 mpg from an automatic 4WD 4-door in city/highway driving. The lighter-weight front-drive models should be a little thriftier, and also quicker. Four adults fit comfortably inside a 4-door RAV, but backseaters don't get much leg or knee room. Rear entry/exit is a squeeze for larger folks, too. The 2-door is best enjoyed with two adults up front and two children in back, because its rear seat is even tighter than the 4-door's. Rear access also is more difficult, despite a slide-forward feature on the right-front seat. Cargo space is good in both body styles, considering their exterior dimensions. Though not as commanding as in some SUVs, the driving stance allows clear views all around, in either hardtop body style. In the recent convertible, however, the over-the-shoulder view is impaired when the rear roof is in place. On the plus side, the convertible's top fits well, though it takes a while to raise or lower. Most people are likely to be satisfied inside, though more rearward seat travel would be nice—especially for taller folks. The carlike dashboard is simple and convenient.

VALUE Despite the RAV4's pluses, Honda's CR-V is roomier, quieter, and more practical—a better compact wagon and mini SUV than Toyota's offering.

SPECIFICATIONS

	2-door conv.	2-door wagon	4-door wagon
Wheelbase, in.	86.6	86.6	94.9-98.0
Overall length, in.	147.6	147.6	163.8
Overall width, in.	66.7	66.7	66.7
Overall height, in.	65.0	65.2	65.4
Curb weight, lbs.	2723	2701	2789
Cargo volume, cu. ft.	35.3	34.7	57.9-68.3
Fuel capacity, gals.	15.3	15.3	15.3
Seating capacity	4	4	4-5
Front head room, in.	40.0	40.0	40.3
Max. front leg room, in.	39.5	39.5	39.5-42.4
Rear head room, in.	38.6	38.6	39.0
Min. rear leg room, in.	33.9	33.9	33.9

Powertrain layout: transverse front-engine/front- or 4-wheel drive

ENGINES

	dohc I4
Size, liters/cu. in.	2.0/122
Horsepower	120
Torque (lbs./ft.)	125

EPA city/highway mpg

5-speed OD manual	22/26
4-speed OD automatic	22/26

City/highway mpg (as tested)

4-speed OD automatic	20.8

Built in Japan

RETAIL PRICES

	GOOD	AVERAGE	POOR
1996 RAV4 2WD	$6,200-7,200	$5,500-6,400	$2,800-3,400
1996 RAV4 4WD	7,200-8,200	6,500-7,400	3,400-4,000
1997 RAV4 2WD	7,500-8,700	6,500-7,700	3,400-4,200
1997 RAV4 4WD	8,500-9,700	7,500-8,500	4,200-4,800
1998 RAV4 2WD	9,200-10,400	8,200-9,400	4,500-5,200
1998 RAV4 4WD	10,200-11,400	9,200-10,200	5,200-5,800
1999 RAV4 2WD	10,500-11,800	9,500-10,800	5,500-6,300
1999 RAV4 4WD	11,500-13,000	10,500-11,700	6,300-7,000
2000 RAV4 2WD	12,500-14,000	11,500-13,000	7,200-8,100
2000 RAV4 4WD	13,500-15,000	12,500-13,700	7,900-8,600

AVERAGE REPLACEMENT COSTS

A/C Compressor	$810	Clutch, Pressure Plate, Bearing	610
Alternator	475	Constant Velocity Joints	500
Automatic Transmission or Transaxle	1,080	Exhaust System	560
Brakes	160	Radiator	580
Shocks and/or Struts	800	Timing Chain or Belt	220

TROUBLE SPOTS

• **Audio system.** Static can be heard on the AM band when other electrical items such as wipers or turn signals are used due to a bad ground for the antenna. (1996)

• **Audio system.** The CDs get stuck and may not eject from the Fujitsu ten-CD player. (1997)

• **Brake noise.** The rear brakes make a whining noise because the backing plate is too thin. A thicker one is available. (1996)

RECALL HISTORY

1998: Audiovox Securikey+ Security Systems can malfunction causing electrical failure; can cause engine to run poorly and stall, and electrical components can intermittently fail.

1998-01 TOYOTA SIENNA

FOR Build quality • Standard antilock brakes • Side airbags (LE, XLE)

AGAINST Fuel economy • Radio placement

EVALUATION With several hundred pounds more weight to carry, the V6 that feels strong in a Camry feels merely adequate in a Sienna—and loses some of its snap with the air conditioning on. The transmission shifts smoothly and downshifts quickly for passing, so Sienna seldom feels underpowered. Acceleration time to 60 mph of 8.9 seconds affirms that opinion. Hard takeoffs induce mild steering-wheel tug that highlights the Sienna's lack of traction control. We averaged 15.9 mpg. A long-term Sienna returned 19.4 mpg, including a substantial amount of highway driving. Toyota recommends premium fuel. Suspension settings favor a

2000 Toyota Sienna XLE

smooth ride over sporty handling, but that's appropriate for this type of vehicle. Bumps are absorbed with little impact, and body lean in turns is moderate for a minivan. Overall road manners are composed and predictable, though Sienna can feel a little nose-heavy when entering freeway on-ramps. Braking is swift and stable. Road and wind noise are subdued, leaving the cabin serene at highway speeds. Sienna boasts a well-thought-out and pleasant cabin. The low floor makes it easy to climb in and out, yet the standard height-adjustable driver's seat affords a commanding view of the road. Front seats are spacious. Second-row passengers do not have an abundance of leg room if the front seats are pushed very far back, but knee clearance is generally good even in the rear row. Actually, adults can be comfortable anywhere if no seats are moved fully aft. Climate controls are easily accessed, but the radio is mounted low and recessed into the dashboard, requiring a long look away from the road to reach while driving. Numerous storage bins and drink holders of various sizes handle interior storage nicely. There's room for a double row of grocery bags in the back with all seats in place. The individual seats can be removed fairly easily, though they're heavy so it's a 2-person task. The tumble-folding rear seat makes it easy to expand the cargo area.

VALUE Toyota had fired a blank with its old Previa, but hit the bull's eye with Sienna. Priced to compete with similarly equipped domestic rivals and delivering better-than-expected power and economy, this highly refined new minivan is a formidable force and a must-consider on the used-minivan market.

SPECIFICATIONS

	4-door van
Wheelbase, in.	114.2
Overall length, in.	193.5
Overall width, in.	73.4
Overall height, in.	67.3
Curb weight, lbs.	3881
Cargo volume, cu. ft.	143.0
Fuel capacity, gals.	21.0
Seating capacity	7
Front head room, in.	40.6
Max. front leg room, in.	41.9
Rear head room, in.	40.7
Min. rear leg room, in.	36.5

Powertrain layout: transverse front-engine/front-wheel drive

ENGINES

	dohc V6
Size, liters/cu. in.	3.0/183
Horsepower	194-210
Torque (lbs./ft.)	209-220

EPA city/highway mpg

4-speed OD automatic	19/23

City/highway mpg (as tested)

4-speed OD automatic	19.4

Built in USA

RETAIL PRICES

	GOOD	AVERAGE	POOR
1998 Sienna	$13,000-15,500	$12,000-14,500	$7,800-9,300
1999 Sienna	15,000-18,500	14,000-17,500	9,000-10,500
2000 Sienna	17,000-21,500	15,800-20,000	10,300-12,500
2001 Sienna	19,500-24,000	18,000-22,500	—

AVERAGE REPLACEMENT COSTS

A/C Compressor	$1,140	Clutch, Pressure Plate, Bearing	410
Alternator	485	Constant Velocity Joints	890
Automatic Transmission or Transaxle	1,055	Exhaust System	315
Brakes	220	Radiator	475
Shocks and/or Struts	630	Timing Chain or Belt	610

TROUBLE SPOTS

• **Windows.** If the window switch on the passenger side quits working, an improved replacement switch may remedy the problem. (1998-99)

• **Brake noise.** Original brakes tend to groan and squeak. Replacement brake pads and rotors correct the problem. (1998)

• **Headlights.** The headlight aiming specifications are inadequate on dark roads, so they have been revised to allow aiming one-inch higher. (1998-99)

RECALL HISTORY

1998-99 w/lug nuts, Pt. No. 1207, supplied by Prime Wheel and distributed in TX, OK, LA, AR, and MS: Lug nuts are defective, causing loss of torque, fatigue fracture of wheel, and possible loss of wheel. **2001:** Front subframe assembly was not adequately welded. This condition could cause failure of the assembly, increasing the risk of a crash.

1993-98 TOYOTA SUPRA

1995 Toyota Supra Turbo

FOR Acceleration • Antilock brakes • Steering/handling

AGAINST Ride • Rear-seat room • Road noise • Rear visibility • Cargo room

EVALUATION The Turbo takes its time catching hold at low engine speeds; but when it does, the power surges into play dramatically. That can be annoying around town, actually—you get little power initially, but then an avalanche suddenly arrives as the twin turbos kick in. Handling is top-notch on all Supras, with little body lean through turns and tenacious grip from the low-profile tires. On normal roads—smooth and dry—you get a secure, planted feeling as the suspension soaks up bumps fairly well. On rough pavement, the Supra begins to lose its composure. Tires bang over every pavement flaw, transmitting every little ripple into the cockpit. Traction diminishes greatly on wet surfaces, too. The driver and passenger have ample head and leg room, but the back seat is basically for decoration. Cargo space also is limited, as the trunk is shallow and has a high liftover. Visibility is good to the front, fair to the sides, but poor to the rear, restricted by the narrow back window and tall tail. Gauges and controls are easy to see and reach, except for the radio, which is mounted too low.

VALUE Lofty performance and fine fit/finish make this Supra a worthy, if costly, contender—provided that you don't need to carry passengers out back.

SPECIFICATIONS

	2-door coupe
Wheelbase, in.	100.4
Overall length, in.	177.7
Overall width, in.	71.3
Overall height, in.	50.2
Curb weight, lbs.	3210
Cargo volume, cu. ft.	10.1
Fuel capacity, gals.	18.5
Seating capacity	4
Front head room, in.	37.5
Max. front leg room, in.	44.0
Rear head room, in.	32.9
Min. rear leg room, in.	23.8

Powertrain layout: longitudinal front-engine/rear-wheel drive

ENGINES

	dohc I6	Turbocharged dohc I6
Size, liters/cu. in.	3.0/183	3.0/183
Horsepower	220	320
Torque (lbs./ft.)	210	315
EPA city/highway mpg		
5-speed OD manual	18/23	
6-speed OD manual		17/24
4-speed OD automatic	18/24	18/24
City/highway mpg (as tested)		
5-speed OD manual	18.5	
4-speed OD automatic		18.7

Built in Japan

RETAIL PRICES

	GOOD	AVERAGE	POOR
1993 Supra	$9,000-10,000	$8,000-9,000	$4,400-5,000
1993 Supra Turbo	10,500-11,500	9,500-10,500	5,500-6,100
1994 Supra	10,500-12,000	9,500-11,000	5,500-6,300
1994 Supra Turbo	12,000-13,500	10,800-12,200	6,600-7,300
1995 Supra	12,000-13,500	11,000-12,500	6,800-7,700
1995 Supra Turbo	14,000-16,000	12,800-14,500	8,500-9,500
1996 Supra	14,000-15,500	13,000-14,500	8,700-9,500
1996 Supra Turbo	16,500-18,500	15,000-17,000	10,300-11,500
1997 Supra	16,500-18,500	15,200-17,000	10,500-11,500
1997 Supra Turbo	20,000-22,000	18,500-20,500	13,000-14,200
1998 Supra	19,000-21,000	17,500-19,500	12,200-13,500
1998 Supra Turbo	23,000-25,000	21,500-23,000	15,000-16,000

AVERAGE REPLACEMENT COSTS

A/C Compressor	$910	Clutch, Pressure Plate, Bearing	375
Alternator	395	Exhaust System	345
Automatic Transmission or Transaxle	1,025	Radiator	535
Brakes	230	Shocks and/or Struts	165

TROUBLE SPOTS

• **Water leak.** Water leaks from the removable roof lock strips. A replacement (which also sometimes leaks) is available. (1993-95)

1993-98 TOYOTA T100

1995 Toyota T100 regular cab

FOR Reliability

AGAINST Acceleration (4-cylinder, early V6) • Price

EVALUATION The 4-cylinder model delivers only modest performance and has been added to the line to serve primarily as a price leader. The 3.4-liter V6 provides adequate acceleration in 2WD models, but in the heavier Xtracab 4WD versions, the manual transmission is necessary in order to maintain lively acceleration for passing and climbing hills. With the automatic, the V6 gets off the line quickly and maintains strong acceleration if you keep the throttle wide open, but feels lethargic when a quick burst of power is needed in the 30-55 mph range. The 2WD models absorb most bumps easily, but there's too much bouncing on wavy roads with an empty cargo bed. However, it tends to be more stable than a lot of big pickups. Steering and handling are better, too. The stiffer suspension of the 4WD models produces a choppier ride, and the added ride height results in extra body lean when navigating turns. The T100's refinement is noticeable in the lack of cabin noise. The engines make themselves heard only during hard acceleration. Wind and road noise are both moderate. The big Toyota pickup earns high marks in most areas. It's wide enough for three adults to sit in front, but the middle passenger is required to rest their feet on the transmission tunnel and sit with knees only an inch or so from the stereo. The Xtracab's front passenger seat slides forward nicely, but it takes some twisting to climb into the rear seats. Once aboard, there's adequate leg and foot room for adults, and the slightly reclined backrest is a nice touch. But the rear-seat padding is quite thin and the lower cushion is uncomfortably flat. The T100's dashboard is modern and convenient, though when the dual cupholders near the top of the dash are being used, the climate controls are blocked.

VALUE The bottom line is this: If you want more than a compact pickup, don't need a V8 engine, and think getting added refinement is worth paying a little extra to get, the T100 is a great way to go.

SPECIFICATIONS

	ext. cab	reg. cab
Wheelbase, in.	121.8	121.8
Overall length, in.	209.1	209.1
Overall width, in.	75.2	75.2
Overall height, in.	68.2	67.2
Curb weight, lbs.	3550	3320
Fuel capacity, gals.	24.0	24.0
Seating capacity	6	3
Front head room, in.	39.6	39.6
Max. front leg room, in.	42.9	42.9
Rear head room, in.	37.8	NA
Min. rear leg room, in.	29.6	NA

Powertrain layout: longitudinal front-engine/rear- or 4-wheel drive

ENGINES

	dohc I4	ohc V6	dohc V6
Size, liters/cu. in.	2.7/163	3.0/181	3.4/181
Horsepower	150	150	190
Torque (lbs./ft.)	177	180	220
EPA city/highway mpg			
5-speed OD manual	20/24	16/21	17/21
4-speed OD automatic	19/22	16/20	17/20
City/highway mpg (as tested)			
5-speed OD manual	21.8		
4-speed OD automatic	18.7	15.7	

Built in Japan

RETAIL PRICES

	GOOD	AVERAGE	POOR
1993 T100 2WD	$3,500-4,800	$2,800-4,000	$800-1,300
1993 T100 4WD	5,000-6,500	4,300-5,700	1,800-2,600
1994 T100 2WD	4,300-6,000	3,600-5,200	1,400-2,300
1994 T100 4WD	6,200-8,000	5,500-7,200	2,700-3,500
1995 T100 2WD	5,100-8,000	4,400-7,200	1,900-3,500
1995 T100 4WD	7,500-10,000	6,700-9,100	3,400-4,800
1996 T100 2WD	6,000-9,500	5,200-8,700	2,500-4,500
1996 T100 4WD	9,000-11,000	8,100-10,000	4,400-5,500
1997 T100 2WD	7,100-11,000	6,200-10,000	3,100-5,500
1997 T100 4WD	10,500-12,000	9,500-11,000	5,200-6,200
1998 T100 2WD	8,200-12,200	7,300-11,200	3,900-6,300
1998 T100 4WD	12,500-14,000	11,300-12,500	6,500-7,200

AVERAGE REPLACEMENT COSTS

A/C Compressor	$1,310	Clutch, Pressure Plate, Bearing	940
Alternator	360	Exhaust System	260
Automatic Transmission or Transaxle	1,400	Radiator	575
Brakes	210	Shocks and/or Struts	190
Timing Chain or Belt	170	Universal Joints	205

TROUBLE SPOTS

• **Automatic transmission.** A-40 series automatic transmissions may shift harshly because rubber check balls become smaller, blow through the plate, and get dislodged. (1993-97)

• **Exhaust system.** In compliance with emission control regulations, the oxygen sensor will be replaced free at the 80,000-mile maintenance. (1993-95)

• **Water pump.** The water pump seal may leak. (1993-94)

1995-01 TOYOTA TACOMA

1995 Toyota Tacoma SR5 4WD Xrtacab extended cab

FOR Acceleration (V6) • Reliability

AGAINST Price • Engine noise • Ride • Step-in height (4WD)

EVALUATION Acceleration with the base engine feels brisk, particularly with the manual transmission. The 2.7-liter 4-cylinder in 4WD models has marginally more horsepower and torque, but feels more taxed in all driving situations. Tacomas with the 3.4-liter V6 have strong standing-start acceleration with either transmission. The 2001 test 2WD automatic V6 PreRunner Double Cab did 0-60 mph in a respectable 9.7 sec. And we averaged 16.1 mpg with 4WD and manual transmission, 19.4 with 2WD and automatic in our tests of V6 Xtracabs. Ride quality is poor. Tacoma pounds over bumps and bounds over dips in the pavement. Handling is nothing special either, but at least the brakes work well. Inside, the Tacoma feels rather spartan. There is enough room for two adults to stretch out in front, but the rear area, like in all compact pickups, is best left to cargo and not people. Controls are well-arranged, but are a bit on the small side—especially radio controls. Visibility is excellent and noise levels are only marginally higher than in comparable Ford or Chevy compact trucks. Tacoma's payload ratings are competitive with anything in this class, but even with the 3.4-liter V6, towing limits fall short of the Ranger and S-Series by about 1000 pounds. Note also that Tacoma has only a single 6.2-foot cargo bed length; while nearly all competitors offer a regular-cab model with a cargo bed of 7 or 7.5 feet.

VALUE The only advantage a Tacoma might have over domestic compacts would be in reliability. This is one case where we would shop the competition despite Toyota's reputation.

SPECIFICATIONS

	reg. cab	ext. cab	crew cab
Wheelbase, in.	103.3	121.9	121.9
Overall length, in.	184.5	203.1	202.3
Overall width, in.	66.5	66.5	70.1
Overall height, in.	61.8	62.0	67.5
Curb weight, lbs.	2560	2745	3430
Fuel capacity, gals.	15.1	15.1	18.5
Seating capacity	3	5	5
Front head room, in.	38.2	38.4	38.8
Max. front leg room, in.	41.7	42.8	42.8
Rear head room, in.	—	35.5	37.8
Min. rear leg room, in.	—	27.2	33.8

Powertrain layout: longitudinal front-engine/rear- or 4-wheel drive

ENGINES

	dohc I4	dohc I4	dohc V6
Size, liters/cu. in.	2.4/144	2.7/163	3.4/207
Horsepower	142	150	190
Torque (lbs./ft.)	160	177	220
EPA city/highway mpg			
5-speed OD manual	23/28	17/21	19/23
4-speed OD automatic	22/25	18/21	19/22
City/highway mpg (as tested)			
5-speed OD manual	20.1		19.2
4-speed OD automatic			16.7

Built in USA, Japan

RETAIL PRICES

	GOOD	AVERAGE	POOR
1995 Tacoma 2WD	$4,000-6,200	$3,300-5,400	$1,100-2,500
1995 Tacoma 4WD	6,000-9,000	5,200-8,100	2,500-4,300
1996 Tacoma 2WD	4,700-7,500	4,000-6,600	1,700-3,100

	GOOD	AVERAGE	POOR
1996 Tacoma 4WD	$7,200-10,500	$6,400-9,500	$3,200-4,900
1997 Tacoma 2WD	5,500-8,800	4,800-8,000	2,200-4,200
1997 Tacoma 4WD	8,000-12,500	7,200-11,500	3,900-6,000
1998 Tacoma 2WD	6,500-10,500	5,600-9,500	2,800-4,900
1998 Tacoma 4WD	9,500-14,000	8,500-13,000	4,800-7,500
1999 Tacoma 2WD	7,500-12,500	6,500-11,500	3,300-6,000
1999 Tacoma 4WD	10,500-15,500	9,500-14,200	5,500-8,400
2000 Tacoma 2WD	8,000-13,500	7,000-12,500	3,700-6,800
2000 Tacoma 4WD	11,000-17,000	10,000-15,700	5,900-9,500
2001 Tacoma 2WD	9,800-15,500	8,800-14,200	—
2001 Tacoma 4WD	13,000-20,000	11,800-18,500	—

AVERAGE REPLACEMENT COSTS

A/C Compressor	$1,315	Clutch, Pressure Plate, Bearing	915
Alternator	360	Exhaust System	242
Automatic Transmission or Transaxle	1,457	Radiator	520
Brakes	190	Shocks and/or Struts	210
Timing Chain or Belt	200	Universal Joints	200

TROUBLE SPOTS

• **Exhaust system.** In compliance with emission control regulations, the oxygen sensor will be replaced free at the 80,000-mile maintenance. (1995)

RECALL HISTORY

1995: Battery may have defective weld inside positive or negative terminal, which can result in a no-start condition or explosion. **1995-96:** Under certain conditions, front suspension support can crack. **1998-99:** Some wheel lug nuts are defective, causing loss of torque, fatigue fracture of wheel, and possible loss of wheel. **1999-2000:** Trailer towing wire harness may have deficient waterproofing and improper installation. An electrical short circuit will occur if water enters the converter housing.

1991-94 TOYOTA TERCEL

1991 Toyota Tercel 4-door sedan

FOR Antilock brakes (optional) • Fuel economy • Maneuverability

AGAINST Engine noise • Road noise • Wind noise • Rear-seat room

EVALUATION The tiny engine produces adequate acceleration, but is noisy and feels stressed at freeway speeds. Also the automatic transmissions are rather slow to downshift when asked to deliver extra passing power. Good fuel economy is a strong point, however. We averaged 26.3 mpg with a DX/automatic model. Once underway, we noticed the suspension allows lots of bouncing on wavy roads and the ride becomes choppy on rough surfaces. In addition, there is an above-average amount of annoying road noise. Maneuverability is small-car easy, but the car's handling prowess is hampered by the Tercel's tiny wheels and tires (155/80SR13s), which run out of grip early when asked to corner. Adults have ample room in front, but the rear seat is tight for anyone over 5-foot-10. On the plus side, the dashboard is simple, functional, and conveniently laid out.

VALUE Unfortunately for the Tercel, Toyota dictated that it be the low-price leader in the automaker's very full model lineup, and it shows. The car is simply outclassed by the plusher, more substantial subcompacts against which it must compete.

SPECIFICATIONS	2-door coupe	4-door sedan
Wheelbase, in.	93.7	93.7
Overall length, in.	161.8	161.9
Overall width, in.	64.8	64.8
Overall height, in.	53.2	53.2
Curb weight, lbs.	1950	2005
Cargo volume, cu. ft.	10.7	10.7
Fuel capacity, gals.	11.9	11.9
Seating capacity	5	5
Front head room, in.	38.7	38.7
Max. front leg room, in.	41.2	41.2
Rear head room, in.	36.7	36.1
Min. rear leg room, in.	31.9	31.9

Powertrain layout: transverse front-engine/front-wheel drive

ENGINES

	ohc I4
Size, liters/cu. in.	1.5/89
Horsepower	82
Torque (lbs./ft.)	90
EPA city/highway mpg	
5-speed OD manual	29/35
3-speed automatic	26/29
City/highway mpg (as tested)	
3-speed automatic	26.3

Built in Japan

RETAIL PRICES	GOOD	AVERAGE	POOR
1991 Tercel	$1,000-1,700	$500-1,100	$100-200
1992 Tercel	1,300-2,000	700-1,400	100-300
1993 Tercel	1,600-2,400	1,000-1,800	200-400
1994 Tercel	2,000-2,900	1,400-2,300	300-500

AVERAGE REPLACEMENT COSTS

A/C Compressor	$1,368	Clutch, Pressure Plate, Bearing	460
Alternator	355	Constant Velocity Joints	680
Automatic Transmission or Transaxle	1,010	Exhaust System	395
Brakes	190	Radiator	470
Shocks and/or Struts	635	Timing Chain or Belt	210

TROUBLE SPOTS

• **Air conditioner.** If the air conditioner does not cool, the compressor runs intermittently, or the A/C light flashes, the wiring harness must be rerouted and protected with a sleeve. (1991-94)

• **Windshield washer.** New windshield washer buttons were made available for servicing problems with the system. (1991-92)

• **Oil consumption.** Oil consumption due to worn valve stem seals may be eliminated by installing improved seals. (1991)

1995-98 TOYOTA TERCEL

1997 Toyota Tercel 4-door sedan

FOR Fuel economy • Maneuverability

AGAINST Noise • Rear-seat room

EVALUATION The latest engine is noisy, but its greater power shows up in quicker acceleration. Nevertheless, performance is still far from lively, even with a manual transmission. Automatic transmissions are rather slow to downshift to deliver suitable highway passing power. Fuel economy is exceptional: We averaged 30 mpg in a DX model with automatic. Though refreshingly frugal, long rides in a Tercel aren't all pleasure, by any means. The suspension allows a lot of bouncing on wavy roads, and the ride becomes choppy on rough surfaces. In addition, there's still plenty of road noise. Handling ability is hampered by narrow tires, which run out of grip early in hard cornering. Inside, the dashboard is simple, functional, and conveniently laid out, but the rear seat remains tight for anyone over 5-foot-10. Adults have ample room up front, but trunk space is on the skimpy side.

VALUE Far from exciting in concept or reality, Tercel's mission has been to be the least-expensive Toyota, and it shows against the plusher, more substantial Corolla and other subcompact leaders. On the other hand, Toyota's reputation for reliability makes the Tercel worth considering if you need basic transportation but are on a tight budget.

SPECIFICATIONS

	2-door coupe	4-door sedan
Wheelbase, in.	93.7	93.7
Overall length, in.	161.8	161.8
Overall width, in.	64.8	64.8
Overall height, in.	53.2	53.2
Curb weight, lbs.	1950	2005
Cargo volume, cu. ft.	9.3	9.3
Fuel capacity, gals.	11.9	11.9
Seating capacity	5	5
Front head room, in.	38.6	38.6
Max. front leg room, in.	41.2	41.2
Rear head room, in.	36.5	36.5
Min. rear leg room, in.	31.9	31.9

Powertrain layout: transverse front-engine/front-wheel drive

ENGINES

	dohc I4
Size, liters/cu. in.	1.5/89
Horsepower	93
Torque (lbs./ft.)	100

EPA city/highway mpg

5-speed OD manual	34/39[1]
3-speed automatic	31/35
4-speed OD automatic	30/39

City/highway mpg (as tested)

5-speed OD manual	32.5
4-speed OD automatic	30.0

1. 34/40 mpg w/4-speed manual.

Built in Japan

RETAIL PRICES

	GOOD	AVERAGE	POOR
1995 Tercel	$2,700-3,500	$2,100-2,800	$500-800
1996 Tercel	3,400-4,400	2,700-3,700	800-1,300
1997 Tercel	4,500-5,200	3,800-4,500	1,400-1,800
1998 Tercel	5,800-6,500	5,100-5,700	2,300-2,700

AVERAGE REPLACEMENT COSTS

A/C Compressor	$1,350	Clutch, Pressure Plate,	
Alternator	330	Bearing	370
Automatic Transmission or		Constant Velocity Joints	1,045
Transaxle	680	Exhaust System	355
Brakes	220	Radiator	305
Shocks and/or Struts	1,100	Timing Chain or Belt	190

TROUBLE SPOTS

• **Audio system.** A poor antenna ground causes static on the AM band of the radio. (1995-96)

• **Climate control.** Poor heater performance may be due to a defective thermostat. (1995-96)

• **Dashboard lights.** The check engine light may come on when the car is driven at altitudes above 5900 feet, which may require a new computer. (1995-96)

• **Windows.** The front windows may be hard to operate. (1995-96)

1995-01 VOLKSWAGEN CABRIO

FOR Antilock brakes • Steering/handling • Ride • Fuel economy

AGAINST Cargo room • Visibility

EVALUATION With either transmission, get-up-and-go is adequate from a stop, and passing power is decent on the highway. The engine produces a hearty growl under acceleration and cruises quietly. Gas mileage is a definite plus: Expect to average about 25 mpg. Road noise is moderate and top-up wind noise surprisingly low. The body feels more solid than most convertibles, and those Cabrios that

1995 Volkswagen Cabrio

we've driven when nearly new have been devoid of squeaks. A Cabrio is stable at highway speeds and its ride is firm, but absorbent enough to soak up most bumps. You enjoy sprightly handling and firm, precise steering, as well as good grip on wet roads. Front power-window switches are on armrests, while rear-window switches are mounted oddly at the dashboard center. Otherwise, the dashboard is conveniently laid out, with the climate controls and stereo mounted high enough to make them easy to see and operate. Space is ample for adults in front, and the rear seat holds two adequately. Front seats are firm and supportive, but not wide enough to be comfortable for stout people. A Cabrio's top folds flatter than the old Cabriolet's, so it interferes less with rear visibility. With the top raised, rear side glass and a large rear window provide generally good visibility for a convertible. No glovebox is included, and trunk capacity is meager—a mere 7.8 cubic feet.

VALUE If a sharp-looking, crisp-handling, solidly-built convertible is on your shopping list, Volkswagen might be the place to look. Prices aren't so cheap, however, and because sales never reached high levels, not too many are on the market.

SPECIFICATIONS

	2-door conv.
Wheelbase, in.	97.2
Overall length, in.	160.4
Overall width, in.	66.7
Overall height, in.	56.0
Curb weight, lbs.	2701
Cargo volume, cu. ft.	7.8
Fuel capacity, gals.	14.5
Seating capacity	4
Front head room, in.	38.7
Max. front leg room, in.	42.3
Rear head room, in.	36.6
Min. rear leg room, in.	31.1

Powertrain layout: transverse front-engine/front-wheel drive

ENGINES

	ohc I4
Size, liters/cu. in.	2.0/121
Horsepower	115
Torque (lbs./ft.)	122

EPA city/highway mpg

5-speed OD manual	23/30
4-speed OD automatic	22/28

City/highway mpg (as tested)

5-speed OD manual	27.5
4-speed OD automatic	25.1

Built in Germany, Mexico

RETAIL PRICES

	GOOD	AVERAGE	POOR
1995 Cabrio	$7,200-8,000	$6,500-7,200	$3,500-3,900
1996 Cabrio	8,000-9,000	7,200-8,000	4,000-4,500
1997 Cabrio	9,500-10,500	8,700-9,500	4,800-5,300
1998 Cabrio	11,000-12,500	10,000-11,500	5,800-6,700
1999 Cabrio	12,500-14,200	11,500-13,000	7,000-7,900
2000 Cabrio	14,000-16,000	12,800-14,500	8,000-9,000
2001 Cabrio	16,000-18,500	14,500-17,000	—

AVERAGE REPLACEMENT COSTS

A/C Compressor	$520	Clutch, Pressure Plate,	
Alternator	375	Bearing	370
Automatic Transmission or		Constant Velocity Joints	1,430
Transaxle	675	Exhaust System	380
Brakes	270	Radiator	380
Shocks and/or Struts	760	Timing Chain or Belt	110

TROUBLE SPOTS

- **Airbags.** Installing an aftermarket glove box could cause serious injury in the case of a deployment. (1995-96)
- **Doors.** The door locks tend to freeze in cold weather. New locks with drain holes are available. (1995-96)
- **Transmission noise.** The final drive ring-and-pinion gears get damaged from a chipped reverse gear in transmissions built before 01/04/97 when a strainer was added during production. (1995-97)
- **Dashboard lights.** The low coolant level light may come on due to a bad coolant sensor or improper antifreeze mixture. (1995-96)
- **Automatic transmission.** The transmission may shift late, may not upshift, or may downshift unnecessarily due to a bad transmission fluid temperature sensor. (1997)

1994-98 VOLKSWAGEN GOLF/JETTA

1996 Volkswagen Jetta GL

FOR Antilock brakes (optional) • Acceleration • Passenger and cargo room • Steering/handling • Maneuverability

AGAINST Engine noise • Road noise

EVALUATION The 4-cylinder models have adequate acceleration from a standing start and lively passing power with either transmission. The 4-speed automatic downshifts promptly, providing adequate power for passing, but lacks smoothness. Naturally, acceleration is a bit friskier and fuel economy is better with the standard 5-speed manual. We averaged 23.8 mpg with the automatic and 26.5 mpg with the 5-speed. The GTI VR6 and GLX Jetta models with their 2.8-liter V6 deliver very impressive acceleration, but be prepared to pay extra. Unlike their predecessors, the current models don't suffer the constant thumping from the suspension and tires. Road noise is still prominent at highway speeds and the exhaust is too loud when cruising at 60-65 mph. Like the previous models, these third-generation Golf and Jetta models have sporty handling for family cars. The steering is firm, and the tires grip well when taking turns at high speeds. The dashboard has a functional layout, with all controls mounted high for easy operation while driving. Since they ride on the same 97.4-inch wheelbase as the preceding models, interior space is about the same. All body styles have ample cargo space and the Jetta's trunk is huge when compared to the car's compact size.

VALUE Our only reservation with these delightful subcompacts is Volkswagen reliability and high prices. Otherwise they are an excellent choice that is a little out of the norm.

SPECIFICATIONS

	2-door hatchback	4-door hatchback	4-door sedan
Wheelbase, in.	97.4	97.4	97.4
Overall length, in.	160.5	160.5	173.4
Overall width, in.	66.7	66.7	66.7
Overall height, in.	56.2	56.2	56.1
Curb weight, lbs.	2511	2577	2647
Cargo volume, cu. ft.	17.5	16.9	15.0
Fuel capacity, gals.	14.5	14.5	14.5

	2-door hatchback	4-door hatchback	4-door sedan
Seating capacity	5	5	5
Front head room, in.	39.2	39.2	39.2
Max. front leg room, in.	42.3	42.3	42.3
Rear head room, in.	37.4	37.3	37.4
Min. rear leg room, in.	31.5	31.5	31.5

Powertrain layout: transverse front-engine/front-wheel drive

ENGINES

	ohc I4	ohc V6	Turbodiesel ohc I4
Size, liters/cu. in.	2.0/121	2.8/170	1.9/116
Horsepower	115	172	90
Torque (lbs./ft.)	122	173	149
EPA city/highway mpg			
5-speed OD manual	23/30	19/26	40/49
4-speed OD automatic	22/28	18/24	
City/highway mpg (as tested)			
5-speed OD manual	26.5	21.4	
4-speed OD automatic	23.8	20.3	

Built in Mexico

RETAIL PRICES

	GOOD	AVERAGE	POOR
1994 Golf	$3,200-4,000	$2,600-3,300	$800-1,200
1994 Jetta	3,500-4,500	2,800-3,800	900-1,500
1994 Jetta GLX	5,000-6,000	4,200-5,200	1,800-2,400
1995 Golf	4,000-5,200	3,300-4,500	1,100-1,800
1995 Golf GTI	5,500-6,500	4,700-5,700	2,200-2,800
1995 Jetta	4,500-5,500	3,800-4,800	1,500-2,100
1995 Jetta GLX	6,700-7,800	5,800-6,800	3,000-3,600
1996 Golf	5,000-6,200	4,300-5,400	1,800-2,400
1996 Golf GTI	6,500-7,500	5,700-6,600	2,900-3,500
1996 Jetta	5,700-6,700	5,000-5,900	2,400-3,000
1996 Jetta GLX	8,000-9,000	7,100-8,000	3,800-4,300
1997 Golf	6,300-7,500	5,600-6,700	2,800-3,400
1997 Golf GTI	8,000-10,000	7,000-9,000	3,900-4,500
1997 Jetta	7,000-8,000	6,300-7,200	3,300-3,800
1997 Jetta GLX	9,800-11,000	8,800-10,000	4,800-5,500
1998 Golf	7,800-9,000	6,900-8,000	3,600-4,200
1998 Golf GTI	9,500-11,500	8,500-10,500	4,500-5,700
1998 Jetta	8,500-9,800	7,600-8,800	4,000-4,700
1998 Jetta GLX	11,500-13,000	10,500-11,800	6,000-6,800

AVERAGE REPLACEMENT COSTS

A/C Compressor	$640	Clutch, Pressure Plate,	
Alternator	660	Bearing	530
Automatic Transmission or		Constant Velocity Joints	845
Transaxle	720	Exhaust System	485
Brakes	210	Radiator	585
Shocks and/or Struts	410	Timing Chain or Belt	110

TROUBLE SPOTS

- **Suspension noise.** A dull clunking noise from the front end may be due to too much free play in the upper MacPherson strut bearings. (1993-95)
- **Tire wear.** Cupping of the rear tires may be caused by too much positive rear toe, which is corrected by replacing the rear axle stub shafts. (1993-96)
- **Engine stalling.** If the engine occasionally loses power, stalls, or stumbles, the problem may be vibration of the mass airflow sensor. (1994)
- **Water leak.** Leaks at the bulkhead should have been corrected during predelivery inspection. (1994)
- **Poor drivability.** Magnetic interference can cause drivability problems if the shielding for the oxygen sensor wiring is damaged. (1994+)
- **Poor drivability.** Oil accumulating in the intake air system can eventually damage the mass airflow sensor causing drivability problems. (1994-95)

RECALL HISTORY

1994-95: Jack could collapse during use. **1994-95:** Misrouted rear brake line could be damaged by chafing, which may result in leakage and diminished braking in one circuit. **1994-95 w/V6 engine:** Improper material was used in manufacturing radiator fan motor shaft for VR6 engine, causing shaft to wear and become noisy; shaft could seize, rendering fan motor inoperative and eventually causing engine to overheat and stall.

1994-96: Bolts securing front hood latch can loosen over time, causing disengagement of hood striker from latch and possible unexpected opening of hood.

1999-01 VOLKSWAGEN GOLF/JETTA

2000 Volkswagen Jetta GLS

FOR Acceleration (V6) • Fuel economy (4-cyl, TDI) • Cargo room (Golf) • Quietness • ride/handling • Build quality

AGAINST Acceleration (4-cyl automatic) • Audio and climate controls • Rear-seat entry/exit (Golf) • Automatic transmission performance

EVALUATION Sporty road manners lead the list of merits. The ride is firm but comfortable, cornering stable, steering linear with fine on-center feel. GTI and V6 cars handle best with only a modest sacrifice in ride comfort, though they suffer more body lean than expected. Braking is terrific. With automatic, the 4-cylinder gas engine furnishes only modest acceleration for passing. A manual shift Jetta GL took 10.8 seconds to reach 60 mph. V6 models have authoritative acceleration and spirited passing response, though the automatic transmission is reluctant to downshift at moderate speeds. A 5-speed GTI GLX did 0-60 in 7.6 seconds and averaged 23.5 mpg. Jettas with V6/automatic returned 18.9 to 21.6 mpg, and a Golf GL 4-cylinder with 5-speed got a pleasing 25 mpg. Even with automatic, a turbo Jetta 1.8T accelerated 0-60 mph in 8.9 seconds and averaged 26.1 mpg. TDI models are surprisingly sprightly around town and get terrific mileage. A 5-speed TDI Golf averaged 41.5 mpg. Noise levels are among the lowest in the class. All engines are quiet, though the TDIs are somewhat noisier at high speeds. Interior materials and workmanship excel. Front head and leg room are exceptional. Rear seats are more subcompact-snug. Modest leg room shrinks quickly as front seats move back, though Golfs feel more spacious, thanks to their straight-back roofline. No body style is wide enough for three adults. All seats are comfortably firm. Height-adjustable front buckets are supportive on long trips. Gauges and switches are simple, logically arranged, and nicely backlit. Low audio and climate controls are tricky to adjust while driving. Rear access in 2-door Golfs far surpasses most coupes. Narrow doors make rear entry/exit a squeeze in Jettas and 4-door Golfs. Jettas have large trunks, and all have folding rear seatbacks.

VALUE Though priced at the top of the subcompact class when new, even base models had plenty of features as well as solid build quality. No competitor offers a V6, and few provide as much driving satisfaction.

SPECIFICATIONS

	2-door hatchback	4-door hatchback	4-door sedan	4-door wagon
Wheelbase, in.	98.9	98.9	98.9	99.0
Overall length, in.	163.3	163.3	172.3	173.6
Overall width, in.	68.3	68.3	68.3	68.3
Overall height, in.	56.7	56.7	56.9	58.5
Curb weight, lbs.	2723	2875	2853	3034
Cargo volume, cu. ft.	28.0	18.0	13.0	34.0
Fuel capacity, gals.	14.6	14.5	14.5	14.5
Seating capacity	5	5	5	5
Front head room, in.	38.5	38.5	38.7	38.6
Max. front leg room, in.	41.3	41.3	41.3	41.5
Rear head room, in.	37.7	37.7	37.2	38.3
Min. rear leg room, in.	33.3	33.3	33.3	33.5

Powertrain layout: transverse front-engine/front- or all-wheel drive

ENGINES

	ohc I4	Turbodiesel ohc I4	Turbo dohc I4	ohc V6
Size, liters/cu. in.	2.0/121	1.9/116	1.8/109	2.8/170
Horsepower	115	90	150	174
Torque (lbs./ft.)	122	155	155	181
EPA city/highway mpg				
5-speed OD manual	24/31	42/49	24/31	20/28
4-speed OD automatic	22/28	34/45	22/28	19/26
City/highway mpg (as tested)				
5-speed OD manual	25.0	41.5	26.1	23.5
4-speed OD automatic				21.6

Built in Mexico

RETAIL PRICES

	GOOD	AVERAGE	POOR
1999 Golf	$10,000-12,500	$9,000-11,500	$6,000-7,500
1999 Golf GTI	12,000-15,000	11,000-14,000	7,500-9,500
1999 Jetta	11,800-14,200	10,800-13,200	7,300-8,600
1999 Jetta GLX	15,000-16,000	14,000-15,000	10,000-11,000
2000 Golf	11,700-14,500	10,700-13,500	7,500-9,000
2000 Golf GTI	14,200-17,200	13,200-16,200	9,500-11,500
2000 Jetta	13,000-15,500	12,000-14,500	8,300-9,500
2000 Jetta GLX	17,000-18,000	16,000-17,000	11,500-12,500
2001 Golf	13,500-16,500	12,500-15,500	—
2001 Golf GTI	16,500-19,500	15,500-18,500	—
2001 Jetta	14,800-18,000	13,800-17,000	—
2001 Jetta GLX	20,000-22,000	19,000-20,500	—

AVERAGE REPLACEMENT COSTS

A/C Compressor	$495	Clutch, Pressure Plate, Bearing	470
Alternator	360	Constant Velocity Joints	1,370
Automatic Transmission or Transaxle	1,100	Exhaust System	370
Brakes	360	Radiator	405
Shocks and/or Struts	490	Timing Chain or Belt	280

TROUBLE SPOTS

• **Vehicle noise.** A humming noise when cornering may be coming from the differential. Draining the automatic transmission fluid and replacing it with synthetic gear may help. (1999)

• **Clutch.** Due to the return spring falling out of position, the clutch pedal may not fully return and the cruise may not disengage. (1999)

• **Engine noise.** Due to the throttle cable contacting the engine cover, the throttle pedal vibrates and there is a rapping noise under the hood. (1999-2000)

• **Audio system.** The door speakers may rattle due to loose rivets or wiring harness contacting the speakers. Requires new fasteners and rerouting wires. (1999)

RECALL HISTORY

1999: Sound-absorbing mat attached to inside of B-pillar side trim panel could ignite when exposed to exhaust gas of seatbelt pretensioner, if it's triggered during a crash. **1999 Jetta:** Some vehicles do not comply with head injury criterion requirements. **2000-01 Golf:** Front suspension control arm could gradually loosen and ultimate separate from its bracket, in normal driving.

1998-01 VOLKSWAGEN NEW BEETLE

1999 Volkswagen New Beetle

FOR Fuel economy • Acceleration (Turbo) • Standard antilock brakes • Side airbags • Build quality

AGAINST Rear-seat room • Visibility

EVALUATION The smooth-running base gas engine feels peppy with manual transmission, though it's short on power at speeds above 60 mph with either gearbox. VW's turbodiesel has no problem keeping up with traffic, but its passing power does not match that of the gas engine—and being a diesel, it suffers more vibration and noise. Although the turbocharged gasoline engine suffers a delay in power delivery below 3000 rpm, it accelerates strongly after that. The automatic transmission on one test car was slow to engage after being shifted from Park, but generally changed up and down smoothly and promptly. Our 2.0-liter test cars averaged 26.4 mpg with manual shift, 21.1 mpg with automatic. A GLS Turbo with automatic returned 22.7 mpg, while a stick-shift diesel got a super-frugal 42.1 mpg. Thanks in part to unusual-for-the-class 16-inch tires, the ride is comfortable but firm, soaking up most bumps with ease. Steering and handling are a notch above the class norm, but the slab-sided New Beetle gets jostled by crosswinds. Braking is strong and sure. Above 70 mph, passengers have to raise their voices to carry on a conversation, though automatic-transmission models are somewhat quieter on the highway, due to their gearing. Interiors brim with high-grade materials and expensive-looking touches, though it takes a few tries to become familiar with the unorthodox radio buttons. Power accessory switches mounted flat on the door panels are awkward to reach. Front seats are comfortable and supportive, and few cars of any size offer as much front head and leg room. In back, leg room is tight if the front seats are more than halfway back. More serious, passengers over 5-foot-6 will find their heads against the inner hatch lid. Front roof pillars are thick at their bases. Also, outside mirrors are mounted unusually high, cutting the driver's vision of some traffic. Interior storage space is skimpy. Luggage room under the rear hatch is modest, but the rear seats fold nearly flat to conveniently expand the cargo area. Paint quality and fit-and-finish have been excellent. Bodies have been solid and rattle-free on New Beetles tested.

VALUE As sport coupes go, this one is actually quite practical. The New Beetle's driving and emotional appeal are strong enough, too, to overcome its skimpy rear seat and visibility blind spots. New Beetles were in short supply and shockingly high demand at first, but that began to taper off somewhat, so more are likely to be available on used-car lots.

SPECIFICATIONS

	2-door hatchback
Wheelbase, in.	98.9
Overall length, in.	161.1
Overall width, in.	67.9
Overall height, in.	59.5
Curb weight, lbs.	2712
Cargo volume, cu. ft.	12.0-18.6
Fuel capacity, gals.	14.5
Seating capacity	4
Front head room, in.	41.3
Max. front leg room, in.	39.4
Rear head room, in.	34.6
Min. rear leg room, in.	33.0

Powertrain layout: transverse front-engine/front-wheel drive

ENGINES

	ohc I4	Turbodiesel ohc I4	Turbocharged dohc I4
Size, liters/cu. in.	2.0/121	1.9/116	1.8/109
Horsepower	115	90	150
Torque (lbs./ft.)	122	149-155	155
EPA city/highway mpg			
5-speed OD manual	23/29	41/48	25/31
4-speed OD automatic	22/27	34/44	23/27
City/highway mpg (as tested)			
5-speed OD manual	26.4	42.1	
4-speed OD automatic			22.7

Built in Mexico

RETAIL PRICES

	GOOD	AVERAGE	POOR
1998 New Beetle	$10,000-11,000	$9,100-10,000	$5,300-5,800
1999 New Beetle	11,500-12,800	10,500-11,800	6,400-7,200
1999 New Beetle GLX	13,000-14,500	12,000-13,200	7,800-8,500
2000 New Beetle	13,000-14,500	12,000-13,300	7,800-8,600
2000 New Beetle GLX	15,000-16,500	14,000-15,200	9,500-10,200
2001 New Beetle	$14,500-16,000	$13,200-14,700	—
2001 New Beetle GLX	16,500-18,500	15,000-17,000	—

AVERAGE REPLACEMENT COSTS

A/C Compressor	$630	Clutch, Pressure Plate, Bearing	570
Alternator	455	Constant Velocity Joints	535
Automatic Transmission or Transaxle	1,005	Exhaust System	590
Brakes	370	Radiator	335
Shocks and/or Struts	620	Timing Chain or Belt	160

TROUBLE SPOTS

- **Audio system.** Poor AM radio reception when switches (brake, lights, locks, etc.) are operated is usually due to the radio antenna cable being routed too close to the wiring harness. (1998-99)

- **Vehicle noise.** The dashboard may whistle at speeds over 45 mph because of poor sealing of the HVAC plenum. (1998-99)

- **Vehicle noise.** The speakers in the doors may rattle due to loose rivets. (1998-99)

- **Tire wear.** To reduce tire wear and improve handling, the rear wheel alignment specifications have been revised. (1998-2000)

1995-97 VOLKSWAGEN PASSAT

1995 Volkswagen Passat 4-door sedan

FOR Antilock brakes • Passenger and cargo room • Steering/handling • Fuel economy (TDI) • Traction control (GLX)

AGAINST No glove box • Ride (GLX)

EVALUATION Though not as strong or smooth as the engine in a Toyota Camry or Nissan Maxima, Passat's V6 delivers more than adequate power over a broad range of speeds. The manual shift's clutch and gearshift work smoothly. Passat's 4-speed automatic transmission does its job unobtrusively and downshifts promptly for passing. Naturally, the 4-cylinder GLS is slower in both standing-start acceleration and highway passing, but still adequate. For a real eye-opener, take a spin in the diesel-powered TDI edition. Our long-term test of a TDI revealed adequate power and a relatively high degree of refinement. You also get outstanding fuel economy. We've averaged 37.7 mpg, hitting 45 mpg during highway trips. A softened suspension and stiffened body structure in this generation yield improved ride quality. A Passat GLX still offers sporty handling, but absorbs bumps with less harshness. The TDI's suspension is softer yet, thus trading some handling prowess for greater composure over bumps. Controls for the radio and climate system are high in the center of the dashboard, easy to see and reach. The climate system is controlled by three clearly marked rotary knobs. Oddly, too, switches for front power windows are on door armrests, while those for rear windows are on the dashboard—a Volkswagen quirk. Because of the passenger airbag mounting position, no glovebox is installed. Interior storage is nevertheless adequate. Despite the Passat's compact 103.3-inch wheelbase, its interior is exceptionally roomy—especially in back, with ample leg room and enough head space for 6-footers. Both body styles have a split-folding rear seat. The sedan has a large trunk, with a flat floor and bumper-height opening for easy loading/unloading. Wagons have a flat, wide cargo area that provides generous luggage space.

VALUE Roomy, sporty, well-equipped: All told, this is an interesting and competent alternative to Japanese-brand sedans.

SPECIFICATIONS

	4-door sedan	4-door wagon
Wheelbase, in.	103.3	103.3
Overall length, in.	180.0	179.9
Overall width, in.	67.5	67.5
Overall height, in.	56.4	58.7
Curb weight, lbs.	3140	3197
Cargo volume, cu. ft.	14.4	68.9
Fuel capacity, gals.	18.5	18.5
Seating capacity	5	5
Front head room, in.	39.3	39.9
Max. front leg room, in.	41.5	41.5
Rear head room, in.	36.6	38.3
Min. rear leg room, in.	37.0	37.0

Powertrain layout: transverse front-engine/front-wheel drive

ENGINES

	Turbodiesel ohc I4	ohc I4	ohc V6
Size, liters/cu. in.	1.9/116	2.0/121	2.8/170
Horsepower	90	115	172
Torque (lbs./ft.)	149	122	177

EPA city/highway mpg

	Turbodiesel ohc I4	ohc I4	ohc V6
5-speed OD manual	38/47	21/29	19/26
4-speed OD automatic		20/27	18/25

City/highway mpg (as tested)

	Turbodiesel ohc I4	ohc I4	ohc V6
5-speed OD manual	37.7		
4-speed OD automatic			19.8

Built in Germany

RETAIL PRICES

	GOOD	AVERAGE	POOR
1995 Passat GLS	$5,000-6,000	$4,300-5,200	$1,800-2,500
1995 Passat GLX	6,000-7,000	5,300-6,200	2,500-3,100
1996 Passat GLS	6,200-7,500	5,400-6,600	2,600-3,400
1996 Passat TDI, GLX	7,800-9,000	6,800-8,000	3,500-4,300
1997 Passat	8,200-10,000	7,200-9,000	3,900-5,000

AVERAGE REPLACEMENT COSTS

A/C Compressor	$620	Clutch, Pressure Plate,	
Alternator	640	Bearing	585
Automatic Transmission or		Constant Velocity Joints	1,320
Transaxle	795	Exhaust System	440
Brakes	390	Radiator	485
Shocks and/or Struts	680	Timing Chain or Belt	360

TROUBLE SPOTS

• **Coolant leak.** A low coolant level malfunction can be the result of the wrong concentration of antifreeze or a bad coolant sensor. (1995-96)

• **Automatic transmission.** Automatic transmission may shift erratically due to an incorrect throttle angle setting. (1995-96)

• **Air conditioner.** Models equipped with a variable displacement A/C compressor may not cool properly due to restrictions in the system. (1995-96)

• **Manual transmission.** The manual transmission shift lever may knock or vibrate in forward gears requiring realignment of the selector shaft housing. (1995-96)

• **Wipers.** The windshield wipers may chatter because of misalignment of the wiper arms. (1996)

RECALL HISTORY

1995 w/VR6 engine: Radiator fan motor shaft could wear, become noisy and seize, rendering fan motor inoperative and eventually causing engine to overheat and stall.

1998-01 VOLKSWAGEN PASSAT

FOR Ride • Passenger room • Cargo room • Build quality • Side airbags • Standard antilock braking

AGAINST Acceleration (Turbo w/automatic) • Tire noise

EVALUATION Passat's suspension smothers all but the worst bumps and dips, and a tangibly solid structure only adds to the sense of comfort. Braking is swift and undramatic from most any speed. Wind noise is low. Turbo models are quiet enough and generally free of "turbo lag" hesitation, but with automatic transmission, it just does not have the brawn for quick getaways and easy high-gear climbing

1998 Volkswagen Passat GLS sedan

up long, steep grades. The Tiptronic's manual-shift capability helps somewhat, but the GLS Passat feels transformed with the standard 5-speed manual transmission, becoming lively, eager, and genuinely sporty. A Passat with Tiptronic averaged 22.2 mpg, but premium fuel is recommend. We'd recommend the V6 engine if you're not an ardent fan of manual transmissions. Passat's ace in the hole has always been generous interior room, and the new one continues that tradition. Expect spacious comfort for four adults (even five on short hops), plus an almost cavernous trunk and easy entry/exit. Six-footers have only about a half-inch of head clearance beneath the available moonroof, but leg room is plentiful all around. Combining readable gauges and simple controls, the dashboard also is Audi-like, except for simpler climate controls and different—but still very legible—gauges. Visibility is fine except to the rear, where the styling hides the car's corners. Like Audi's A4, Passat feels impressively stout, even on the worst roads. Overall fit and finish are equally satisfying, but interior decor looks a bit drab. Nothing feels low-budget, however, and the GLS V6 and GLX flaunt real wood trim. Materials and workmanship rival those of more costly automobiles.

VALUE Turbo-fours with automatic don't have much strength for a modern family 4-door. If possible, try the different engine/transmission combinations to see which one fits your needs. Otherwise, VW's largest car is suave, sporty, spacious, and solid. It's also strong on features per dollar and "European" personality. We'd give it a good long look.

SPECIFICATIONS

	4-door sedan	4-door wagon
Wheelbase, in.	106.4	106.4
Overall length, in.	184.1	183.8
Overall width, in.	68.5	68.5
Overall height, in.	57.4	59.0
Curb weight, lbs.	3120	3194
Cargo volume, cu. ft.	15.0	78.7
Fuel capacity, gals.	18.5	16.3
Seating capacity	5	5
Front head room, in.	39.7	39.7
Max. front leg room, in.	41.5	41.5
Rear head room, in.	37.8	39.7
Min. rear leg room, in.	35.3	35.3

Powertrain layout: transverse front-engine/front-wheel drive

ENGINES

	Turbocharged dohc I4	dohc V6
Size, liters/cu. in.	1.8/109	2.8/169
Horsepower	150-170	190-200
Torque (lbs./ft.)	155	206-207

EPA city/highway mpg

	Turbocharged dohc I4	dohc V6
5-speed OD manual	23/32	20/29
5-speed OD automatic	22.2	18/29

City/highway mpg (as tested)

	Turbocharged dohc I4	dohc V6
5-speed OD automatic	22.2	

Built in Germany

RETAIL PRICES

	GOOD	AVERAGE	POOR
1998 Passat 4-cylinder	$12,000-13,200	$11,000-12,200	$6,800-7,500
1998 Passat V6	13,000-14,000	12,000-13,000	7,500-8,200
1999 Passat 4-cylinder	14,000-15,200	13,000-14,000	8,200-8,800
1999 Passat V6	15,500-18,000	14,200-16,500	9,000-10,500
2000 Passat 4-cylinder	16,000-17,500	14,800-16,200	9,500-10,300
2000 Passat V6	18,000-21,000	16,500-19,500	10,800-12,000
2000 Passat V6 AWD	20,500-23,500	19,000-22,000	13,000-15,000
2001 Passat 4-cylinder	18,000-20,000	16,500-18,500	—
2001 Passat V6	20,000-24,000	18,500-22,500	—
2001 Passat V6 AWD	22,500-26,500	21,000-25,000	—

AVERAGE REPLACEMENT COSTS

A/C Compressor	$595	Clutch, Pressure Plate,	
Alternator	640	Bearing	585
Automatic Transmission or		Constant Velocity Joints	1,320
Transaxle	790	Exhaust System	595
Brakes	390	Radiator	560
Shocks and/or Struts	670	Timing Chain or Belt	430

TROUBLE SPOTS

• **Vehicle noise.** The speakers in the doors may rattle due to loose rivets. (1998-99)

• **Windows.** The windows suffer from stress cracks and distortion. (1999-2000)

RECALL HISTORY

1998: If engine backfires during cold-start, an air screen loosely seated in airflow meter can become damaged; screen pieces could enter intake system and prevent the throttle plate from returning to its full idle position. **1998-99 registered in AK, CO, CT, IL, IA, ME, MI, MT, MN, NB, NH, NY, ND, SD, VT, WI, and WY:** Control valve in vacuum hose connecting brake booster to intake manifold may not open or close fully at temperatures below -4 degrees (F) under certain driving conditions. **1998-99 w/automatic transmission:** Control valve may not open or close fully at temperatures below -4 degrees (F) under certain condition, causing insufficient vacuum for the brake booster. **1998-99:** Some tie rod seals may not seal properly; if moisture and/or dust particles enter the swivel bearing mechanism, the bearing could wear over time, diminishing steering control. **2000:** Sulfur in fuel could cause fuel gauge to read "full" when the tank is actually less than full.

1993-97 VOLVO 850

1994 Volvo 850 Turbo 4-door wagon

FOR Passenger and cargo room

AGAINST Acceleration (base) • Automatic transmission performance

EVALUATION These 850s drive much like Volvo's larger 960 models, but their trimmer size and superior suspension give them truly athletic cornering ability. The suspension is firm enough to provide a stable highway ride with little bouncing and absorbent enough to soak most bumps without braking stride. The standard engine lacks sufficient torque to provide good acceleration. But the turbocharged engine is an entirely different story. The 850 Turbo wagon can sprint from stop to 60 mph in an impressive 7.1 seconds. We do have a couple of disappointments to report, however. Turbocharged engines come only with a 4-speed automatic, which is often slow to downshift when climbing steep hills. Speaking of jolts, on the Turbo versions the ride is often a bit too stiff, with excessive tire thump on rough pavement. As you'd expect from Volvo, there's plenty of head and leg room for four adults, but the interior isn't quite wide enough for comfortable three-across seating in back. The sedan's spacious trunk has a low bumper-height opening, and the wagon has a long, flat cargo area when the rear seat is folded down.

VALUE Though we've not been overwhelmed by the 850, it represented a good job of breathing new life into what had become an outdated product line. With the side airbags and turbo engines, it also had more going for it than some rivals in the near-luxury market.

SPECIFICATIONS

	4-door sedan	4-door wagon
Wheelbase, in.	104.9	104.9
Overall length, in.	183.5	185.4
Overall width, in.	59.3	69.3
Overall height, in.	55.7	56.9
Curb weight, lbs.	3232	3342
Cargo volume, cu. ft.	14.7	67.0
Fuel capacity, gals.	19.3	19.3
Seating capacity	5	5
Front head room, in.	39.1	39.1
Max. front leg room, in.	41.4	41.4
Rear head room, in.	37.8	37.8
Min. rear leg room, in.	32.3	35.2

Powertrain layout: transverse front-engine/front-wheel drive

ENGINES

	dohc I5[1]	Turbocharged dohc I5
Size, liters/cu. in.	2.4/149	2.3/141
Horsepower	168-190	222-240
Torque (lbs./ft.)	162-191	221
EPA city/highway mpg		
5-speed OD manual	20/29	
4-speed OD automatic	20/29[1]	19/26
City/highway mpg (as tested)		
4-speed OD automatic	21.8	22.5

1. 1997 GLT models add a turbocharger to the 2.4-liter engine, which boosts the engine up to 190 horsepower. A slightly lower EPA highway rating of 27 mpg is the result.

Built in Sweden

RETAIL PRICES

	GOOD	AVERAGE	POOR
1993 850	$5,000-6,500	$4,200-5,600	$1,800-2,500
1994 850	6,000-8,000	5,100-7,000	2,300-3,500
1995 850	7,500-12,000	6,500-11,000	3,200-6,000
1996 850	9,000-14,500	8,000-13,200	4,400-7,500
1997 850	11,000-16,500	9,800-15,000	5,500-8,500

AVERAGE REPLACEMENT COSTS

A/C Compressor	$940	Clutch, Pressure Plate,	
A/C Compressor	395	Bearing	755
Alternator	425	Constant Velocity Joints	135
Automatic Transmission or		Exhaust System	330
Transaxle	1,305	Shocks and/or Struts	470
Brakes	170	Timing Chain or Belt	200

TROUBLE SPOTS

• **Cruise control.** If the cruise control will not engage, the plastic vacuum supply line may be damaged in the area of the left headlight. (1993-96)

• **Automatic transmission.** If the transmission is sometimes difficult to shift out of park, it is due to improper contact of the lockout microswitch. (1994-96)

• **Windshield washer.** If the windshield washer does not work well, the jet can be replaced with a larger one. (1993-94)

• **Engine noise.** Noise from the front of the engine at the drive belts may be caused by a defective belt tensioner and/or idler pulley. (1993-96)

• **Windshield washer.** Washer leaks at the rear window can be prevented by installing a pressure valve in the line near the upper hinge of the window. (1993-95)

RECALL HISTORY

1994: Ice can form on throttle linkage, resulting in uneven throttle return or loss of low-speed engine control. **1995 w/power seats:** Threaded insert that attaches safety belt catch was incorrectly manufactured and can reduce restraining capability. **1995:** Some jacks do not have the necessary load capacity. **1996-97:** Screws that attach throttle plate to the throttle shaft can loosen, possibly preventing throttle from returning to idle position. **1997:** Operation of headlight switch over extended period of time can result in inconsistent operation.

1991-98 VOLVO 940/960/S90/V90

FOR Acceleration (except base 940) • Antilock brakes • Ride/handling • Passenger and cargo room

AGAINST Acceleration (base 940) • Road noise • Wind noise

1996 Volvo 960 4-door sedab

EVALUATION These premium Volvo sedans provide very good passenger and cargo room, decent ride comfort, braking, and workmanship. But dropping the dual-overhead-cam engine from the powertrain lineup in '92 for the underpowered 114-horsepower engine used by the entry-level 240 dooms the base 940 to lackluster performance. Selecting the 940 Turbo is one alternative, but then you suffer with "turbo lag" waiting for the power to arrive. We prefer the smoother 6-cylinder. It gives the 960 brisk takeoffs and ensures spirited passing ability. The 6-cylinder produces sporty, aggressive tone in hard acceleration and cruises comfortably. We timed a 1995 sedan at a brisk 8.7 seconds, despite a reduction of 20 horsepower that year. Fuel economy is about average. We recorded 17.8 mpg with a 960 in mostly city and suburban commuting. On all cars, there is an excessive amount of wind noise at speed, and stiffer tires added in '95 produce additional unwanted noise and vibration over rough pavement. Suspension changes improve cornering for this large, boxy sedan, but the harsher ride makes the wagons more preferable.

VALUE Base models are decent values, but both the 940 and the 960 have trouble competing now against such refined benchmarks as the front-wheel-drive Lexus ES 300 and Acura Legend. We've rated the 960 highly in most areas, helped by Volvo's reputation for safety and durability, but rivals in its price class have similar features.

SPECIFICATIONS

	4-door sedan	4-door wagon
Wheelbase, in.	109.1	109.1
Overall length, in.	191.7	189.3
Overall width, in.	69.3	69.3
Overall height, in.	55.5	56.5
Curb weight, lbs.	3205	3280
Cargo volume, cu. ft.	16.8	74.9
Fuel capacity, gals.	19.8	19.8
Seating capacity	5	5
Front head room, in.	38.6	38.6
Max. front leg room, in.	41.0	41.0
Rear head room, in.	37.1	37.6
Min. rear leg room, in.	34.7	34.7

Powertrain layout: longitudinal front-engine/rear-wheel drive

ENGINES

	ohc I4	dohc I4	Turbocharged ohc I4	dohc I6
Size, liters/cu. in.	2.3/141	2.3/141	2.3/141	2.9/178
Horsepower	114	153	162	181-201
Torque (lbs./ft.)	136	150	195	199-197
EPA city/highway mpg				
4-speed OD automatic	20/28	18/23	19/22	17/26
City/highway mpg (as tested)				
4-speed OD automatic			17.6	17.8

Built in Sweden, Belgium, Canada

RETAIL PRICES

	GOOD	AVERAGE	POOR
1991 940	$3,000-5,000	$2,300-4,200	$600-1,500
1992 940	4,000-5,500	3,300-4,700	1,200-2,100
1992 960	4,500-5,500	3,800-4,700	1,500-2,100
1993 940	5,000-7,000	4,200-6,200	1,800-3,000
1993 960	5,800-6,800	5,000-6,000	2,400-3,000
1994 940	6,000-8,000	5,200-7,200	2,500-3,700
1994 960	6,800-8,500	6,000-7,600	3,000-4,000
1995 940	7,000-9,500	6,200-8,500	3,200-4,700
1995 960	8,200-9,500	7,400-8,500	4,200-4,800
1996 960	10,500-12,000	9,500-11,000	5,300-6,200
1997 960	13,000-14,500	12,000-13,200	7,500-8,200

	GOOD	AVERAGE	POOR
1998 S90, V90	$16,000-18,000	$14,800-16,500	$9,500-10,500

AVERAGE REPLACEMENT COSTS

A/C Compressor	$535	Constant Velocity Joints	165
Alternator	410	Exhaust System	340
Automatic Transmission or Transaxle	1,370	Radiator	380
Brakes	150	Shocks and/or Struts	1,075
		Timing Chain or Belt	145

TROUBLE SPOTS

• **Steering noise.** A springing sound from the steering wheel may be due to the retaining springs for the airbag. (1992-94)

• **Air conditioner.** If the idle speed drops when the A/C engages, a capacitor kit may be installed in the circuit for the fuel injection control module. (1992-94)

• **Automatic transmission.** If the transmission is sometimes difficult to shift out of park, it is due to improper contact of the lockout microswitch. (1994-96)

• **Brake noise.** Noisy, squealing brakes can be quieted by installing anti-noise shims between the brake pads and calipers. (1991-96)

• **Audio system.** Whining from the radio may be caused by a bolt on the side of the equalizer touching the cigar lighter socket. (1991) Whine while playing a tape is caused by interference from the cable harness under the dash. (1991-94)

RECALL HISTORY

All Accessory Child Car Seat: Predynamic test buckle release force is lower than required by federal standard and may not retain child in seat in event of a crash. **1991 944/945:** Chafed cable to seat heater, power seat, or seatbelt warning can develop low-resistance short circuit that could result in fire. **1991:** On cars with 80-liter fuel tank, seepage could occur from top of tank. **1991-93:** If car has been subjected to flood conditions, attempting to start the engine could cause airbag deployment. **1992-93:** Seatbelt webbing guide can break under heavy loads. **1993 944/945 Turbo:** Plastic hood insulation clip(s) on some cars could interfere with throttle operation. **1995:** Driver-side airbag may not deploy properly in a collision. **1996-97:** Screws that attach throttle plate to the throttle shaft can loosen, possibly preventing throttle from returning to idle position.

1998-01 VOLVO C70

2000 Volvo C70 convertible

FOR Acceleration • Steering/handling • Side airbags • Standard antilock brakes • Build quality

AGAINST Rear-seat room • Rear-seat entry/exit • Ride (17-inch wheel models)

EVALUATION As on the performance-oriented T5 versions of the S70/V70, the coupe has a firm and somewhat choppy but acceptably supple ride, without the prominent tire thumping that plagued performance-oriented 850 sedans. Even so, the available 17-inch tires elicit harsh reactions to bumps. A convertible or "base" coupe rides more softly on 16-inch rubber. Steering is numb on-center, but provides good feel otherwise. The sporty-handling C70 has ample grip and little body lean in turns. Acceleration is satisfying with the base model, and very strong if the 2.3-liter engine is installed. Standing-start movement is good with either engine, and passing power is excellent. Volvo claimed a 0-60 mph time of 6.9 seconds, but our test C70s have not felt quite that fleet. As for economy, a 2.3-liter model yielded 19.9 mpg. Neither inline 5-cylinder engine is as smooth as some of today's V6s and "turbo lag" (a moment's delay in power delivery) is still bothersome at low and midrange speeds. The back seat is tighter than in sedan models, and it's much harder to get into or out of. The convertible's narrower back seat is even less accommodating. Volvo tried to improve rear entry/exit with a power sliding feature for both front seats; but the seats move forward like snails. Leg room is ample in front and head room is good despite the standard power moonroof. The driver's seat is comfortable and supportive, and visibility is good to all directions—except in the convertible when its top is up. Driving position is easily tailored to fit. Trunk space is reasonable for a coupe, holding a weekend's worth of luggage for a couple, but less than the S70 sedan would offer.

VALUE Looks can be deceiving on the used-car market, as shoppers learn quickly. Volvo's 2-door companions are suave in shape, perform admirably, and offer excellent amenities, but Mercedes-Benz just might have the edge in quality and refinement for this league. Overall, all recent Volvo models have been solid and well-built. The coupe is no different. Volvo has aimed the C70 at young-thinking empty-nesters, ready for something with more style and sizzle than a minivan, sport-utility vehicle—or a Volvo sedan. Our experience suggests that the C70 is a worthy entry into that market and should be considered. Still, we'd pick the more refined Mercedes-Benz CLK320 coupe or convertible. Next to that example of excellence, Volvo's otherwise-able C70 comes across almost as crude.

SPECIFICATIONS

	2-door conv.	2-door coupe
Wheelbase, in.	104.9	104.9
Overall length, in.	185.6	185.7
Overall width, in.	71.5	71.5
Overall height, in.	56.0	55.7
Curb weight, lbs.	3630	3365
Cargo volume, cu. ft.	8.0	13.1
Fuel capacity, gals.	18.5	18.5
Seating capacity	4	4
Front head room, in.	37.4	37.4
Max. front leg room, in.	41.3	41.3
Rear head room, in.	36.6	36.6
Min. rear leg room, in.	34.6	34.6

Powertrain layout: transverse front-engine/front-wheel drive

ENGINES

	Turbocharged ohc I5	Turbocharged dohc I5
Size, liters/cu. in.	2.4/149	2.3/141
Horsepower	190	236
Torque (lbs./ft.)	199	243-244
EPA city/highway mpg		
5-speed OD manual		19/26
4-speed OD automatic	19/26	18/25
City/highway mpg (as tested)		
4-speed OD automatic		19.9

Built in Sweden

RETAIL PRICES

	GOOD	AVERAGE	POOR
1998 C70 coupe	$19,000-20,500	$17,800-19,000	$12,000-12,800
1998 C70 convertible	22,000-24,000	20,500-22,500	14,500-15,800
1999 C70 coupe	21,000-23,500	19,500-22,000	13,500-15,300
1999 C70 convertible	26,000-28,500	24,000-26,500	17,500-19,200
2000 C70 coupe	24,000-26,500	22,500-25,000	16,000-17,500
2000 C70 convertible	30,000-32,500	27,500-30,000	20,000-21,500
2001 C70 coupe	27,500-30,000	25,500-28,000	—
2001 C70 convertible	34,000-37,000	31,500-34,000	—

AVERAGE REPLACEMENT COSTS

A/C Compressor	$585	Clutch, Pressure Plate, Bearing	650
Alternator	410	Constant Velocity Joints	1,150
Automatic Transmission or Transaxle	920	Exhaust System	445
Brakes	310	Radiator	475
Shocks and/or Struts	1,435	Timing Chain or Belt	415

TROUBLE SPOTS

• **Vehicle noise.** A whining noise from the front of the car requiring dampers on both half-shafts. (1998-99)

• **Paint/body.** The drain holes in the rocker panels may be clogged with body sealer leading to premature rusting. (1998)

• **Convertible top.** The trim molding comes loose from the drip rail on convertibles. (1999)

• **Coolant leak.** Water may enter the passenger compartment between the firewall and engine compartment. Adding sealer between the two may fix the problem. (1998)

RECALL HISTORY

1998: Operation of headlight switch over extended period of time can result in inconsistent operation. **1998:** Frontal-passenger airbag may be overly sensitive to certain electrostatic discharges; could possibly cause inadvertent deployment. **2001 V70:** Rear outboard seatbelt anchorage bolts may have been incorrectly tightened. In the event of a crash, the seat occupant may not be properly restrained. **2001 V70:** Bolted joint attaching the bracket for the ISOFIX-type child restraint, may have been incorrectly tightened. In the event of a crash, the seat occupant may not be properly restrained, increasing the risk of injury.

1998-00 VOLVO S70/V70

1998 Volvo S70 4-door

FOR Acceleration (turbo models) • Steering/handling • Side airbags • Standard antilock brakes

AGAINST Road noise • Ride (T5, R models)

EVALUATION Acceleration with the base engine is adequate. However, things pick up considerably in the turbocharged models. Their passing punch is outstanding, but "turbo lag" (a momentary delay in power delivery) is evident at low speeds. The turbo engines are well suited to the automatic transmission, which shifts smoothly and downshifts promptly. Fuel economy has been better than expected. A T5 sedan returned 20.3 mpg, whereas an AWD wagon averaged 18.4 mpg. While those numbers aren't outstanding, they are very good for the near-luxury class. Wind noise is subdued, but the engines are vocal in hard acceleration and road noise can be prominent. All S/V70s handle well. Body lean is minimal, and the tires grip securely in turns. Ride quality varies greatly, depending on the model. Base and GLT models ride smoothly over broken pavement and skim over highway expansion joints. However, the T5 and R models have a stiffer suspension and tires, and thus ride harshly on rough pavement. The AWD provides terrific traction in all conditions, without requiring any special effort from the driver. Standard antilock brakes have good stopping power. Climate and radio controls are easier to use than in the past. Also, the switches for power windows and door locks are conveniently located on the door armrests instead of the center console. However, some other controls are hidden behind the steering wheel. Front and rear passenger room changed only slightly, compared to the 850, with the biggest additions coming in rear leg room. That translates into ample space for front-seat occupants, and adequate room for two passengers in back. At 15.1 cubic feet for the sedan, cargo space is more than adequate. The sedan also has a 60/40 split folding rear seat, which expands cargo capacity. Wagons have a generous cargo hold, made more versatile by standard folding rear seatbacks. Visibility is excellent to all directions, thanks to large side and rear windows.

VALUE S70/V70 models have been competitively priced against other near-luxury sedans, such as the Cadillac Catera and Infiniti I30. They offer a wagon and AWD choices that the others ignore. GLT versions, with their strong turbo engine, are the best all-around values in this line of younger-feeling Volvos.

SPECIFICATIONS

	4-door sedan	4-door wagon
Wheelbase, in.	104.9	108.5

	4-door sedan	4-door wagon
Overall length, in.	185.9	185.9
Overall width, in.	69.3	69.3-71.0
Overall height, in.	55.2	56.2-58.7
Curb weight, lbs.	3152	3259
Cargo volume, cu. ft.	15.1	77.2
Fuel capacity, gals.	18.5	18.5-21.1
Seating capacity	5	5
Front head room, in.	39.1	39.1
Max. front leg room, in.	41.4	41.4
Rear head room, in.	37.8	37.9
Min. rear leg room, in.	35.2	35.2

Powertrain layout: transverse front-engine/front- or all-wheel drive

ENGINES

	dohc I5	Turbocharged dohc I5	Turbocharged dohc I5
Size, liters/cu. in.	2.4/149	2.4/149	2.3/141
Horsepower	162-168	190-197	236-261
Torque (lbs./ft.)	162	199-210	243-258

EPA city/highway mpg

5-speed OD manual	20/29	—	19/25
4-speed OD automatic	20/28	19/27	18/25

City/highway mpg (as tested)

5-speed OD manual			20.3
4-speed OD automatic		19.7	

Built in Sweden, Belgium, Canada

RETAIL PRICES

	GOOD	AVERAGE	POOR
1998 S/V70 GLT	$13,000-17,000	$11,500-15,500	$7,000-9,500
1998 S/V 70 T5	16,000-18,000	14,500-16,500	9,500-10,500
1998 AWD, XC, R	18,000-20,500	16,500-19,000	11,000-12,000
1999 S/V70 GLT	$16,000-19,500	$14,500-18,000	$9,500-11,500
1999 S/V70 T5, AWD	19,500-22,000	18,000-20,000	12,500-13,800
1999 XC, R	22,000-25,000	20,500-23,000	14,200-15,800
2000 S/V70 GLT	19,000-23,000	17,500-21,500	12,000-14,500
2000 T5, AWD, XC, R	23,000-28,000	21,000-26,000	15,000-18,000

AVERAGE REPLACEMENT COSTS

A/C Compressor	$575	Clutch, Pressure Plate, Bearing	650
Alternator	410	Constant Velocity Joints	1,150
Automatic Transmission or Transaxle	920	Exhaust System	455
Brakes	310	Radiator	475
Shocks and/or Struts	1,400	Timing Chain or Belt	415

TROUBLE SPOTS

• **Fuel economy.** Due to contamination entering via the reference tub, oxygen sensors may fail prematurely. (1998)

• **Door handles.** Water gets into the door handle and freezes in cold weather. (1998)

RECALL HISTORY

1998: Operation of headlight switch over extended period of time can result in inconsistent operation. **1998:** Frontal-passenger airbag may be overly sensitive to certain electrostatic discharges; could possibly cause inadvertent deployment. **1998-99 V70 w/third seat:** Users of third seat can contact tailpipe when exiting the vehicle. **1999 S70:** Fuel-filter bracket configuration margins on some cars are insufficient; in the event of a crash, fuel leakage could occur.